STRUCTURED
COBOL
FUNDAMENTALS AND STYLE

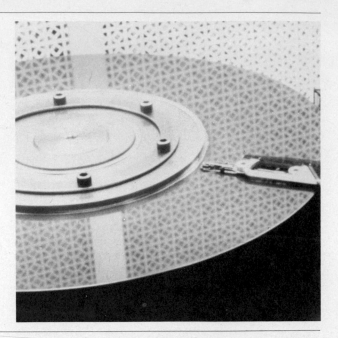

MAYFIELD PUBLISHING COMPANY

MITCHELL PUBLISHING, INC.

STRUCTURED
COBOL
FUNDAMENTALS AND STYLE

TYLER WELBURN

To my children,
Brent, Veronica, and Keith

COBOL is an industry language and is not the property of any company or group of organizations. No warranty, expressed or implied,
is made by any contributor or by the CODASYL Programming
Language Committee as to the accuracy and functioning of the programming system and language. Moreover, no responsibility is
assumed by any contributor, or by the committee, in connection
therewith.

The authors and copyright holders of the copyrighted material
used herein—FLOW-MATIC (trademark of Sperry Rand Corporation), Programming for the UNIVAC® I and II, Data Automation
Systems, copyrighted 1958, 1959, by Sperry Rand Corporation; IBM
Commercial Translator Form No. F 28-8013, copyrighted 1959 by
IBM; FACT, DSI 27A5260-2760, copyrighted 1960 by Minneapolis-
Honeywell—have specifically authorized the use of this material in
whole or in part, in the COBOL specifications. Such authorization
extends to the reproduction and use of COBOL specifications in
programming manuals or similar publications.

Library of Congress Catalog Card Number: 80-84013
International Standard Book Number: 0-87484-543-2

Manufactured in the United States of America
Mayfield Publishing Company
285 Hamilton Avenue, Palo Alto, California 94301
415-326-1640

Compositors: Acme Type Company and Frank's Type
Printer and binder: George Banta Company
Sponsoring editors: Chuck Murphy, Steve Mitchell
Manuscript editor: Nancy Palmer Jones
Text designer: Nancy Sears
Cover designer: Barbara Ravizza
Art designer and project coordinator: Lawrence Peterson
Technical artists: Al McCahan, Pat Rogondino, Lawrence Peterson
Production manager: Michelle Hogan

CONTENTS

APPENDICES

PREFACE

COBOL—like the English language—is a dynamic language that is continuously changing and evolving. Similarly, computers, information systems, and data processing are dynamic fields that are also undergoing continual change.

This text utilizes the most current COBOL program design and coding techniques together with contemporary business computer system concepts. It offers a solid foundation for beginning COBOL students to build upon as their knowledge and skills develop and grow along with the exciting field of computer technology.

Features of the Text

Structured COBOL: Fundamentals and Style is designed for teaching and learning, and it offers abundant features to aid both student and instructor.

Structured design and coding. Up-to-date structured design and coding principles are fully developed and are an integral part of the text.

American National Standard orientation. This text is designed for users of either 1968 or 1974 standards. Important differences between 1968 ANS and 1974 ANS are identified, and certain compatibility considerations for the next ANS are included as well. Although the text is not oriented to a specific vendor, commonly encountered IBM extensions are also identified and covered.

Systems concepts chapters. Five chapters (labeled A, B, C, D, and E) are included to teach business system concepts along with the coding. They contain no coverage of COBOL language per se but instead discuss background information on data concepts, record and report design, data validation, sorting and control breaks, and table handling.

Tandem presentation of programming concepts and coding on a program model-driven basis. Background concepts with which the COBOL programming student should be familiar; COBOL language organization, elements, and syntax; and COBOL application programming techniques are presented within the framework of commonly encountered business system programs. Concepts are developed step by step, proceeding from the simple to the more complex. Each program category builds upon and adds to the knowledge, techniques, and skills developed in the previous one. The programs presented in the text also serve as a ready reference for each application type and introduce the student to the fact that several traditional application program categories exist. This allows the student to analyze programming tasks in relation to program type and to use common approaches rather than "reinvent the wheel" for each program. Also, by this method of presentation, coding is never divorced from practical application. The specific integration of concepts, coding, and program models is presented in Figure P.1.

Programming style conventions. By trial and error, COBOL programmers have, over the years, developed programming style conventions. Establishment

Systems concept	Chapter	COBOL coding syntax	Program type	Program name
	1	Overview	Read-and-print	EMP-LIST
Data concepts	2	IDENTIFICATION DIVISION ENVIRONMENT DIVISION DATA DIVISION	Read-and-print	EMP-RPT
	3	PROCEDURE DIVISION OPEN PERFORM MOVE READ Non-numeric literals PERFORM/UNTIL CLOSE STOP Figurative constants WRITE ADVANCING integer	Read-and-print (continued)	EMP-RPT
	4	PICTURE BLANK WHEN ZERO SIGN MOVE Numeric literals JUSTIFIED RIGHT Data-name qualification		
Record and report design	5	ADD SUBTRACT MULTIPLY DIVIDE COMPUTE ROUNDED	Read-compute-and-print Read-compute-and-print with totals	CHGACCT TCHGACCT
	6	GO TO PERFORM/THRU		LABELS
	7	REDEFINES VALUE ACCEPT/FROM DATE ACCEPT/FROM DAY ACCEPT/FROM TIME READ/INTO ADVANCING identifier ADVANCING PAGE ADVANCING mnemonic-name WRITE/FROM	Read-compute-and-print with headings and totals	PAYROLL

Figure P.1. Text progression and integration

and use of such conventions significantly aids program readability and maintainability. In this text, applicable style considerations are presented, along with coding rules so that students can learn more quickly to approximate the coding of programmers with years of experience and will have a starting point regarding proper form. Because views differ as to what conventions are most appropriate to stress, whenever style conventions are introduced, they are

Systems concept	Chapter	COBOL coding syntax	Program type	Program name
	8	IF EXAMINE *(1968 ANS)* INSPECT		
Data validation	9	BLOCK CONTAINS	Data validation	DATA-VAL
Sorting and control breaks	10	USAGE	Control break (single-level) Control break (multiple level)	S-SLSRPT M-SLSRPT
	11	SORT MERGE	Sort	SRT-ONLY SRT-PRE SRT-P-P SRT-POST
Table handling	12	OCCURS Subscripts INDEXED BY SET PERFORM/VARYING SEARCH KEY	Table processing	STOCK
	App. A	REMARKS *(1968 ANS)* OCCURS/DEPENDING ON RENAMES ACCEPT DISPLAY ALTER GO TO/DEPENDING ON Case structure MOVE/CORRESPONDING ADD/CORRESPONDING SUBTRACT/CORRESPONDING ON SIZE ERROR NOTE *(1968 ANS)* PERFORM/TIMES STRING UNSTRING		
	App. B	COPY		
	App. C	Program interruptions		
	App. D	Language formats		

presented as recommendations rather than prescriptions. Conventions are summarized at the end of each chapter so that the instructor can review them with students and present alternative or additional style conventions.

Integration of program design material with each program type. Although modern structured design techniques are used throughout, this text begins swiftly without lengthy discussions of design techniques. Instead, design considerations are presented gradually throughout the text so that they can be easily learned and understood. In Chapter 6, after the student has had a chance to write a few programs and get familiar with COBOL coding, a number of design techniques and considerations are introduced.

Program design documentations. A structure chart is presented for each program coded in the text, and the logic of each program (except for the type of program presented in Chapter 11) is shown in both pseudocode and flowchart form. Structure charts are provided to show overall program organization and module definition. Pseudocode is used to present detailed processing logic. A very relaxed, English-like pseudocode is used to make comprehension easier for the beginning programming student. The logic is shown again in program flowchart form, again to aid the student, since many students are already familiar and feel comfortable with flowcharts.

Coding formats and examples. Whenever COBOL language entries are introduced in the text, they are accompanied by the language format (sometimes presented in simplified form). The language formats are presented in a shaded box for easy identification. When an example is first shown, it is hand coded on a coding sheet grid so that the student can easily visualize how the entry will look. (A convention used in the coding examples is that when an example does not apply to a program presented in the text, a data name is prefixed by XX, XY, or IN; a procedure name is prefixed by 999.)

Comprehensive programs. Thirteen comprehensive programs are included in the text. They are shown in reduced type to give the student an overview of the program as a whole. Portions of the programs are extracted and covered in more detail in the body of the text.

Combination tutorial/reference approach. Students very often react to COBOL textbooks in one of two ways: Either they feel that a book is a good reference manual but that it doesn't really explain how to write certain types of programs; or they feel that a book explains things well but that it is hard to use as a reference. This book blends both tutorial and reference features. Whenever a topic is presented, it is covered fully in one place; but to guard against information overload, topics are covered step by step and integrated with programming examples.

Summary material. In addition to a chapter summary, style summaries and ANS summaries are presented for each chapter where applicable.

Programming assignments. At the conclusion of most chapters, four programming assignments (lettered A, B, C, and D) are presented. These assignments relate directly to the material covered in the chapter. They are arranged in order of increasing complexity; assignment A is the easiest and quickest to code, and assignment D is the most involved.

Extensive end-of-chapter material. In addition to other learning aids, a list of key terms, questions, and, where appropriate, syntax exercises follow each chapter.

Numerous illustrations and examples. Over 500 figures illuminate the text.

Inside cover material. A mock-up of the IDENTIFICATION and ENVIRON-MENT divisions is presented on the inside front cover together with a checklist of other items which vary depending upon the computer systems being used. This page can be filled in at the beginning of the course and then used as a reminder for the coding of the first two divisions and as a reference when installation-dependent topics are mentioned in the text material. For easy reference, the COBOL reserved word list and the format notation legend is presented on the inside back covers.

Additional materials for instructors. An instructor manual is available for use with this text.

Acknowledgments
I really want to thank and express my appreciation to those who contributed to and improved this book (any errors which may remain are certainly my own). The original plan for this project was launched with the help and advice of Marilyn Bohl, IBM Corporation; Edward Rategan, College of San Mateo; and George Vlahakis, Evergreen Valley College. Barbara Comfort of J. Sargeant Reynolds Community College; Marjorie Leeson of Delta College; Anne M. McBride of California State University, Chico; and David Kroenke each reviewed portions of the manuscript and made a number of helpful comments and criticisms.

In addition, I received many good ideas from those instructors who attended my structured COBOL sessions at the National Computer Educator's Institute during the summers of 1979 and 1980. At the institutes, Susan Hinrichs of Missouri Western State College caused me to reexamine some of my views and made me keep digging for more projects and test data. Sandy Maceyka of the New York Board of Cooperative Educational Services at Fairport also contributed some excellent ideas and was always helpful and patient in answering my endless questions concerning a certain topic about which she is very knowledgeable.

Donald F. Nelson of Control Data Corporation and Chairman of the CODASYL COBOL Committee kept me abreast of language developments. I often tossed ideas around with Sondra Wallace of Hewlett-Packard Corporation; she always lovingly rejected the bad ones and cheerfully served back good ones.

Rosemary Amen devotedly aided in manuscript preparation; both in presence and absence. I must express special appreciation to all those associated with Mayfield Publishing who showed such dedication to this project. Michelle Hogan, production manager, contributed a very important idea, caught many of my inconsistencies, and furnished invaluable help. Nancy Sears, art director, provided sensitive attention and outstanding design assistance. Nancy Palmer Jones, copy editor, pared down my verbosity and weeded out most of my corny lines—but left enough to make me happy. Chuck Murphy, sponsoring editor, played an important role in bringing this text to press. Finally, I give special thanks to Lawrence Peterson, designer, who picked up all the pieces and whose untiring efforts and attention to quality contributed so much to this book.

I know that without the encouragement and assistance of Steve Mitchell, this text would never have made the transition from mind to paper. For his continuing support I am particularly grateful.

Tyler Welburn

CHAPTER 1

OVERVIEW OF A COBOL PROGRAM AND ITS DEVELOPMENT

This chapter provides an overview of a very simple COBOL program. You can use it to get a basic familiarity with the structure and elements of the COBOL language.

Before a programmer writes a program, the task the program is to accomplish must be identified. Thus, in the first part of this chapter, a data processing application is presented and we trace the program development process. Then we look at a COBOL program written to perform the task. The textual material skims through the program to identify key concepts and introduce terminology relating to the COBOL language.

Many find programming difficult—especially right at the start. So, if you are a beginning programming student, do not expect to understand fully the details of the sample program after reading this chapter. Nor should you expect to understand all the interrelationships of the COBOL language. The purpose of this chapter is to aquaint you with the basic concepts and terminology of program development, programming, and the COBOL language. The material presented in this overview chapter will be expanded upon in following chapters.

The Program Development Process

In most organizations, the program development process is handled by a group of systems analysts, programmers, and/or programmer/analysts. In this chapter, for simplicity, we assume that the entire program development process is handled by one programmer. This is in fact what happens in the business world when either the organization that the programmer works for is small or the scope of the program is limited.

Application Background

At Silicon Valley Manufacturing Company, a *name-and-address record* is prepared for each employee. Each record contains the following fields: *name, address, city-state-zip,* and *date-of-hire.* The complete file of name-and-address records is kept in alphabetical order according to name. Figure 1.1 depicts the name-and-address file, records, fields, and subfields.

The personnel manager for the company, Ms. Wanda Fast, needs an address list of the company's employees. After receiving management approval, she asks a programmer, Mr. Titus T. Code, to write a program to prepare an employee address list from the existing name-and-address file. The program development process that Titus follows consists of the following four phases: the specification phase, the design phase, the coding phase, and the testing phase.

Phase 1: The Specification Phase

After talking with Ms. Fast, Titus has a fairly good understanding of what the employee address list should look like, what data is available in the name-and-address records, and—because he is an experienced programmer—what steps the program must contain to produce the output report from the input file.

However, a fairly good understanding is not good enough to write an effective program. Precise documentation of the format of the output to be produced, the format of the input records to be used, and the processing steps that

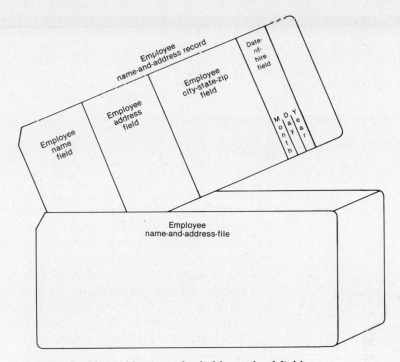

Figure 1.1 Name-and-address file, records, fields, and subfields

the program must perform is required. Thus, during the specification phase of the program development process, the programmer obtains or prepares the following specifications:

1. Illustrative layouts of the output and input records. These layouts include print charts, record layout forms, and display screen layouts (depending upon the media used for input and output).

2. Programming specifications. These specifications briefly describe the overall purpose of the program, identify the inputs and outputs, and list the major processing steps that are to occur.

3. Approval to proceed to the next step of the program development cycle. Depending upon the organization that the programmer works for, this approval may be required from the requestor (often called the user), the programmer's supervisor, or both.

The specifications that Titus uses are described below.

Illustrative layouts of the output and input records

Normally, the output record layouts are designed before the input record layouts. The requirements of the program (the results, or outputs) must be satisfied by the input records and program processing. So, to know exactly what the inputs must contain, the output records must be designed first.

Often, as in this case, the programmer plans how to produce a new report from existing records. Titus obtains a copy of the record layout of the name-and-address record from the company's data processing documentation library. This layout is shown in Figure 1.2.

The *record layout form*, modeled on the 80-column punched card, gives the column numbers or *positions* available to each field. This particular layout shows that the name field is located in positions 1-20, the address field in positions 21-44, the city-state-zip field in positions 45-68, and the date-of-hire field in positions 69–74.

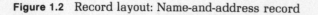

Figure 1.2 Record layout: Name-and-address record

With Ms. Fast's requirements in mind, Titus prepares a layout of the employee address list on a print chart. A *print chart* is a gridlike form used to define an output report to be produced by a computer printer. The programmer or analyst uses it to experiment with the order of data fields on a line, the amount of space between fields, and so forth. The completed print chart serves as a preview of how the computer-printed report will look. Later, it will be used as a reference when writing COBOL code for the employee address list. The print chart prepared by Titus is shown in Figure 1.3.

The numbers running horizontally across the top of the print chart denote the print positions available on the computer printer to be used. The numbers running vertically down the side of the chart represent the lines on one page of the report (in this case, the employee address list). The programmer places an X in each print position where data is to be printed. Figure 1.3 shows that the name field will be printed in positions 3-22, the address field will be printed in positions 27-50, and the city-state-zip field will be printed in positions 55-78.

The print chart shows two lines of X's: one at line 7 and another at line 9. By placing the first line of X's at line 7, Titus allows for a 6-line top-of-page margin. By placing the second line of X's at line 9, Titus indicates that the report lines are to be double-spaced. Programmers often show two horizontal lines for each line format to indicate whether the lines are to be single-, double-, or triple-spaced. Sometimes they merely note the vertical line-spacing requirements on the print chart.

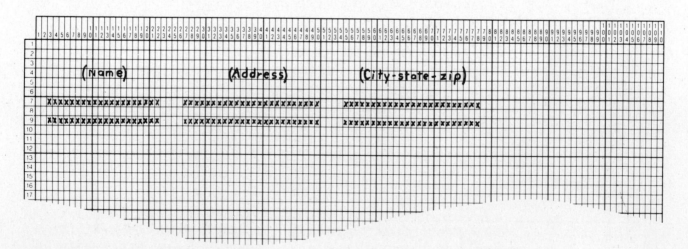

Figure 1.3 Print chart: Employee address list

Programming specifications

With a layout of the name-and-address record and a print chart for the proposed employee address list, Titus has graphic documentation of the input and output records that the program should process to produce the employee address list from the name-and-address file.

Before detailed design of a program begins, there should be a general description of the program, an identification of its inputs and outputs, and a list of its processing operations. Together, these documentation items constitute the *programming specifications*. They are generally written by a systems analyst or programmer after consultations with the user.

The programming specifications that Titus prepares for the program to produce the employee address list are shown in Figure 1.4. Titus also prepares a graphic depiction of the input, program, and output flow. This is called a *system flowchart* and is shown in Figure 1.5.

Approval to proceed to the design phase

Before the programmer starts designing the program, it is important that he or she review the record layouts and programming specifications with the person or department (the *user* or *user group*, respectively) who requested or will use the outputs produced by the program. This approval process helps to ensure that the programmer has correctly interpreted the application requirements. If there are errors or problem areas within the specifications, they are identified

---

PROGRAMMING SPECIFICATIONS

Program name: EMPLOYEE ADDRESS LIST   Program ID: EMP–LIST

```
Program description
    This program is to print an employee address list
    from input employee name–and–address records.

Input file(s)
    Employee name–and–address file

Output file(s)
    Employee address list

List of program operations
    1. Read each input employee name–and–address
       record.
    2. For each record, print the following fields on
       the employee address list in accordance with
       the format shown on the print chart:
            Employee name
            Employee address
            Employee city–state–zip
    3. Double–space each printed line.
```

Figure 1.4 Programming specifications: Employee address list program

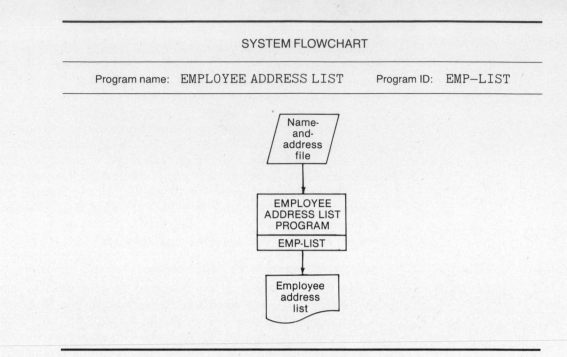

SYSTEM FLOWCHART

Program name: EMPLOYEE ADDRESS LIST   Program ID: EMP—LIST

Name-
and-
address
file

EMPLOYEE
ADDRESS LIST
PROGRAM

EMP-LIST

Employee
address
list

Figure 1.5 System flowchart: Employee address list program

and corrected before program design time and labor are invested in the project.

So, Titus reviews the print chart and the programming specifications for the employee address list program with Ms. Fast. She says the proposed employee address list is just exactly what she had in mind. (In many organizations, particularly larger ones, the approval may be formalized by signature—"signing off"—on the specifications or on a special form designed for this purpose.) Thus, armed with the approved input and output record layouts and the programming specifications, Mr. Titus T. Code has now completed the specification phase of the program development process and is ready to enter the design phase.

As a basis for designing the program, the programmer must have a basic understanding of fundamental program processing concepts. Figure 1.6 is an annotated illustration of the fundamental record-processing steps for a simple read-and-print program.

Phase 2:
The Design Phase

Consider the task of designing an automobile. Before an automobile designer designs a car, he is provided specifications regarding the vehicle's performance objectives. That is, he is told whether the proposed auto is to be a fuel-efficient economy car, a high-performance sports car, a full-size luxury car, or a high-cargo-area station wagon. Regardless of the type of car, the engine usually is placed up front, the passenger compartment somewhere near the middle, and the trunk at the rear. The designer works within this basic structure to meet the performance objectives by planning precisely the optimum form and location of the myriad assemblies and subassemblies that become part of the integrated machine.

The programmer's task is not unlike that of the automobile designer. The programmer is working with programming specifications to meet a data processing objective. There are certain tasks that must be accomplished within most business data processing programs: initializing fields, reading input

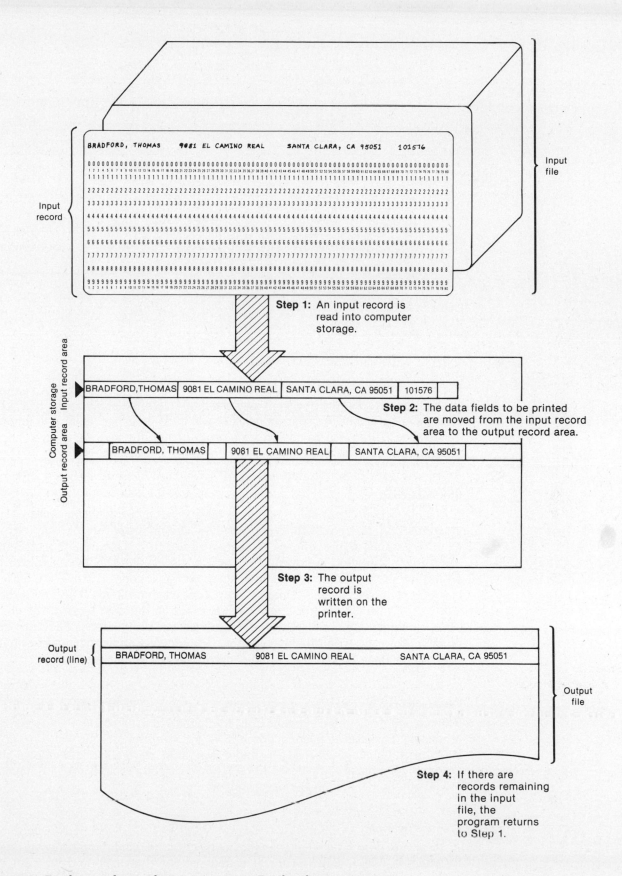

Figure 1.6 Fundamental record-processing steps: Read-and-print program

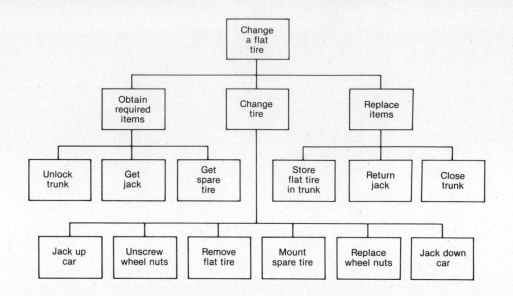

Figure 1.7 Hypothetical structure chart: Changing a flat tire

records, processing the input data, and writing output records. To perform each of these tasks, the program may use many detailed steps, or *instructions*. There are a number of program design tools used by programmers to identify these steps. Three will be used for the programs in this text: structure charts, pseudocode, and flowcharts.

Structure chart

A *structure chart* graphically depicts the hierarchy of program tasks. Since structure charts are tools of logic, they can also be prepared for nonprogramming tasks, such as the process of changing a flat tire. A hypothetical structure chart for this process is shown in Figure 1.7. Notice that the structure chart is an outline of the task to be accomplished; the most general steps are defined ("obtain required items," "change tire" and "replace items") and then these steps are broken down into their specific tasks on the next level of the chart. Thus structure charts display the overall program structure. They are supplemented by more detailed design aids. Pseudocode and program flowcharts are two common forms of detailed program design documentation.

Pseudocode

Pseudocode is a generic name for an English-like program documentation language. The use of pseudocode allows the programmer to write program logic in a language that (1) is understandable as English; (2) allows programming-language statements to be written directly from it; and (3) imposes few syntactical rules on the programmer.

Program flowchart

A *program flowchart* is a graphic method of documenting program logic. Flowcharts use specific symbols connected by flowlines to represent the various program operations.

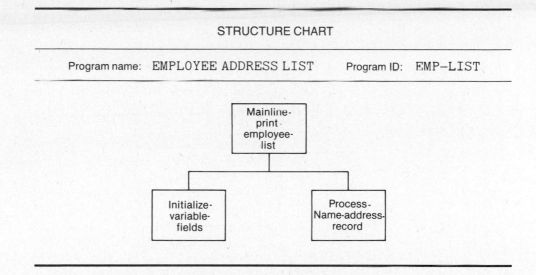

STRUCTURE CHART

Program name: EMPLOYEE ADDRESS LIST   Program ID: EMP—LIST

Figure 1.8 Structure chart: Employee address list program

Titus uses a structure chart to depict the overall program structure (Figure 1.8). From the structure chart, Titus writes the pseudocode shown in Figure 1.9. The same logic can be expressed in program flowchart form, as shown in Figure 1.10.

Structured walkthrough

After completing and checking the design documentation for accuracy, Titus asks one of his programmer colleagues, Mr. D. "Tex" Hols, to review his structure chart and pseudocode. Tex looks for possible errors, omissions, or weaknesses in the design and then tells Titus that the design documentation looks good to him.

This review of design documentation is termed a *structured walkthrough*. It is often performed at this point in the program development cycle to catch design problems before additional time and labor are expended in the coding phase. (Structured walkthroughs may also be performed in the coding phase.) They are valuable because it is often difficult for a programmer to spot errors he or she has made in design documentation. Explaining one's documentation to one or more colleagues as a doublecheck of the work often reveals design mistakes or questionable design logic. If such weaknesses are found, the programmer should make corrections or justify the techniques used. Once the programmer and the reviewing colleagues are satisfied that the documentation is correct, the programmer is ready to enter the coding phase.

Phase 3.
The Coding Phase

Using the documentation provided by the input record layout form, the output print chart, and the pseudocode or flowchart, the programmer writes (or *codes*) the program. Three steps take place during the coding phase:

Step 1: Write the source program on COBOL coding forms.
Step 2: Key the source program onto punched cards or onto a tape or disk storage medium.
Step 3: Compile the source program to obtain an object (machine-language) program.

A more detailed explanation of each of these steps follows.

PSEUDOCODE

Program name: EMPLOYEE ADDRESS LIST   Program ID: EMP—LIST

<u>Mainline-print-employee-list</u> module
1. Open the files.
2. Perform Initialize-variable-fields module.
3. Read the first employee name—and—address record.
4. Perform Process—name-address—record module until no more records.
5. Close the files.
6. Stop the run.

<u>Initialize-variable-fields</u> module
1. Set the end—of—file indicator to "No".

<u>Process—name-address-record</u> module
1. Clear the output line area.
2. Move the input Employee—name to the output line Employee—name.
3. Move the input Employee—address to the output line Employee-address.
4. Move the input Employee—city-state-zip to the output line Employee-city-state-zip.
5. Write the employee output line (double-spaced).
6. Read the next input record.

Figure 1.9 Pseudocode: Employee address list program

Write the source program

The programmer writes the source program on COBOL coding forms. An example, with the heading information filled in, is shown in Figure 1.11. Notice that there are places for the programmer to write the names of the system, the program, and his or her name.

In the area called "Punching Instructions," the programmer provides directions to the operator about how to key symbols that otherwise may be confused with one another or misunderstood. There are three pairs of symbols that commonly cause problems because of their close resemblance to each other:

- The numeral 0 and the letter O
- The numeral 1 and the letter I
- The numeral 2 and the letter Z

Observe that Titus identifies each of these symbols in the punching instructions area of the COBOL coding form. To differentiate the letters, he puts a slash through the numeral 0, serifs the 1, and slashes the Z. (There are probably as many programmers who slash the letter O as those who slash the zero

Program name: EMPLOYEE ADDRESS LIST   Program ID: EMP—LIST

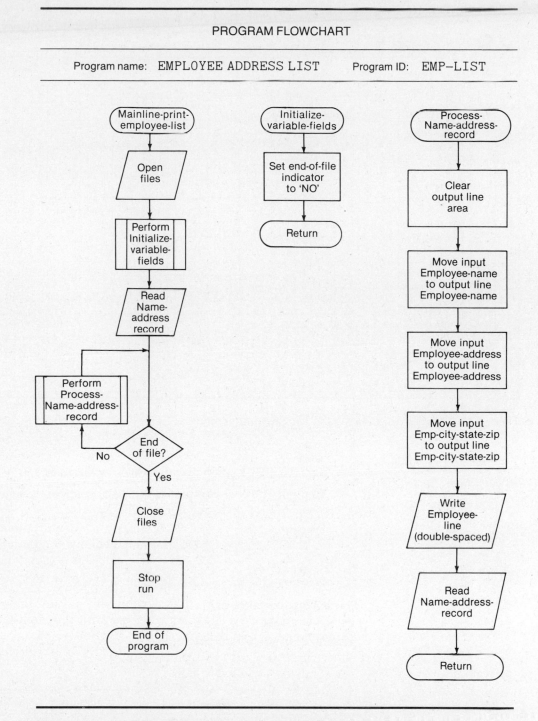

Figure 1.10   Program flowchart. Employee address list program

to differentiate the two symbols. However, the convention used in this text is to slash the zero.)

Look at the body of the COBOL coding form. Each line of COBOL coding is written so that it may be punched onto a card, keyed onto a tape or disk, or entered through a terminal. There are 80 positions in each line. They may contain any of the 51 symbols of the COBOL character set (see Figure 1.12).

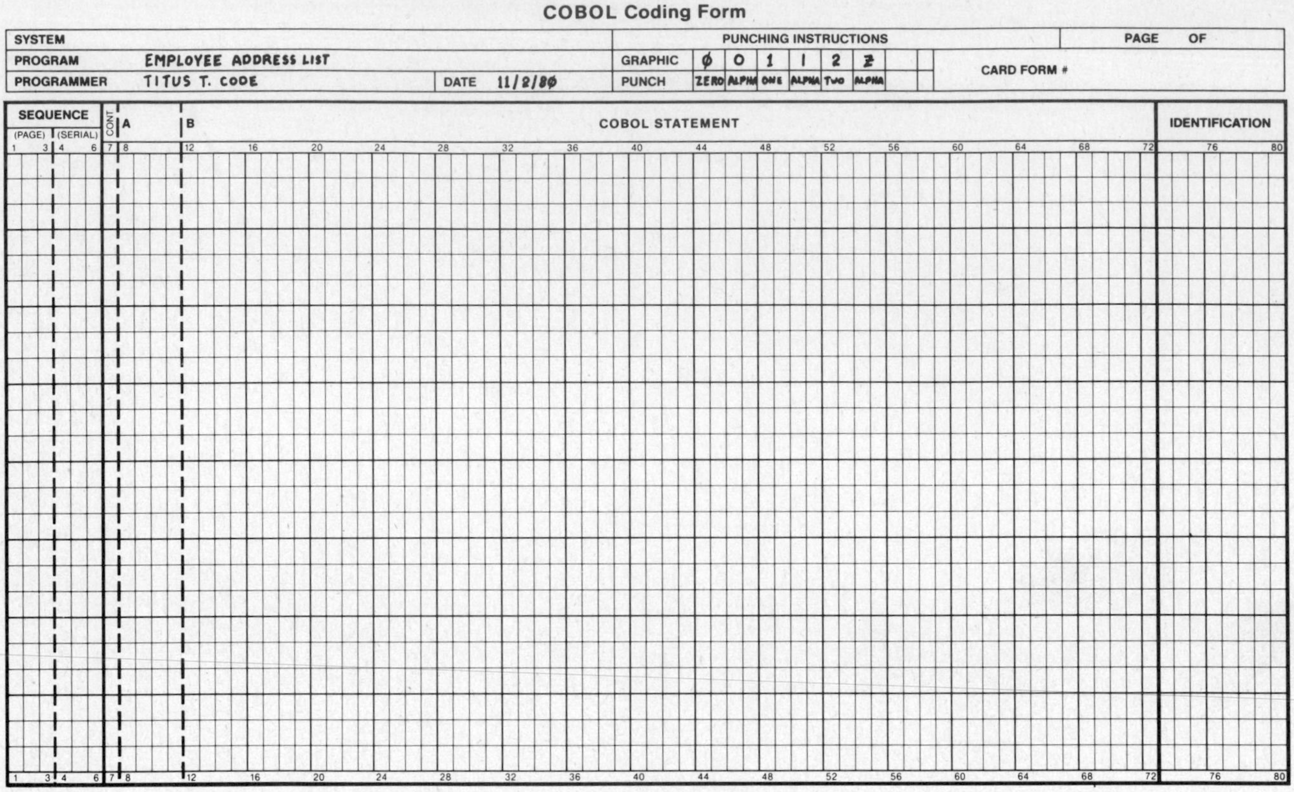

COBOL Coding Form

SYSTEM					PUNCHING INSTRUCTIONS							PAGE	OF
PROGRAM	EMPLOYEE ADDRESS LIST				GRAPHIC	Ø	O	1	I	2	Z		CARD FORM #
PROGRAMMER	TITUS T. CODE		DATE	11/2/8Ø	PUNCH	ZERO	ALPHA	ONE	ALPHA	TWO	ALPHA		

Figure 1.11   COBOL coding form with heading information

Each COBOL coding line has three main areas:

Positions 1–6:   Sequence—a page number in columns 1–3 and a line number in columns 4–6

Positions 7–72:   COBOL statement—a continuation indicator in column 7; an A area in columns 8–11; and a B area in columns 12–72

Positions 73–80:   Identification

Refer to Figure 1.13. It shows the first page of the employee address list program written by Titus. Let's discuss first the identification area, then the sequence area, and then the COBOL statement area.

Character	Meaning	Character	Meaning
0 through 9	Digit	,	Comma
A through Z	Letter	;	Semicolon
	Space (blank)	.	Period (decimal point)
+	Plus sign	"	Quotation mark
*	Asterisk	(	Left parenthesis
−	Minus sign	)	Right parenthesis
/	Stroke (virgule, slash)	>	Greater than symbol
=	Equal sign	<	Less than symbol
$	Currency sign		

Figure 1.12   COBOL character set

COBOL Coding Form

SYSTEM				PUNCHING INSTRUCTIONS					PAGE	OF
PROGRAM	EMPLOYEE ADDRESS LIST			GRAPHIC	Ø 0 1 1 2 Z					
PROGRAMMER	TITUS T. CODE	DATE 11/2/8Ø		PUNCH	ZERO ALPHA ONE ALPHA TWO ALPHA		CARD FORM #			

SEQUENCE (PAGE) (SERIAL)	CONT	A	B	COBOL STATEMENT	IDENTIFICATION
ØØ1Ø1Ø		IDENTIFICATION DIVISION.			EMP-LIST
ØØ1Ø2Ø		PROGRAM-ID.	EMP-LIST.		EMP-LIST
ØØ1Ø3Ø		AUTHOR.	TITUS T. CODE.		EMP-LIST
ØØ1Ø4Ø		INSTALLATION.	SILICON VALLEY MANUFACTURING COMPANY.		EMP-LIST
ØØ1Ø5Ø		DATE-WRITTEN.	NOV 2, 1980.		EMP-LIST
ØØ1Ø6Ø		DATE-COMPILED.			EMP-LIST
ØØ1Ø7Ø		SECURITY.	NONE.		EMP-LIST
ØØ1Ø8Ø		ENVIRONMENT DIVISION.			EMP-LIST
ØØ1Ø9Ø		CONFIGURATION SECTION.			EMP-LIST
ØØ11ØØ		SOURCE-COMPUTER.	IBM-37Ø.		EMP-LIST
ØØ111Ø		OBJECT-COMPUTER.	IBM-37Ø.		EMP-LIST
ØØ112Ø		INPUT-OUTPUT SECTION.			EMP-LIST
ØØ113Ø		FILE-CONTROL.			EMP-LIST
ØØ114Ø			SELECT NAME-ADDRESS-FILE-IN ASSIGN TO UT-S-INFILE.		EMP-LIST
ØØ115Ø			SELECT EMPLOYEE-LIST-OUT ASSIGN TO UT-S-PRTFILE.		EMP-LIST

Figure 1.13 Partial employee address list program on COBOL coding form

Identification

Titus writes the program identification EMP-LIST in this area of the COBOL coding form. Entries in this area are optional. They do not affect the COBOL program in any way. Most programmers do as Titus has done; they write the program name (or usually an abbreviation of it) in this area.

Sequence

Observe that Titus assigns sequence numbers to each program line. These sequence numbers are optional. That is, a program without sequence numbers may be compiled and executed successfully. But sequence numbers normally should be used by the COBOL programmer. The purpose of the sequence numbers is to identify the lines of the source program so that they can be maintained in the proper sequential order. The specific value of a number placed in the sequence area is not significant. What is important is that each program line be assigned a sequence number greater than that of the preceding line. Then, if a line of the program is positioned out of sequence, the COBOL compiler can identify the out-of-sequence condition. Figure 1.14 shows how one COBOL compiler identifies such an out-of-sequence condition.

Normally, the programmer assigns a 3-digit page number to each COBOL coding form and appends a zero (in position 6) to each preprinted 2-digit line number. Notice then, as with Titus's coding form in Figure 1.13, that the successive line numbers on a page differ by increments of 10 (from 010 to 020 to 030, and so on). By providing a span of 10 between each line originally written, the programmer facilitates the insertion of lines in sequential order.

Often, lines of coding must be added to programs. The need for additional lines may stem from programmer error, oversight, or new program require-

```
       001010  IDENTIFICATION DIVISION.
       001020  PROGRAM-ID.      EMP-LIST.
       001030  AUTHOR.          TITUS T. CODE.
       001050  DATE-WRITTEN.    NOV 2,1980.
  **001040  INSTALLATION.    SILICON VALLEY MANUFACTURING COMPANY.
   ↑ 001060  DATE-COMPILED. NOV 2,1980.
   │ 001070  SECURITY.        NONE.
   │ 001080  ENVIRONMENT DIVISION.
   │ 001090  CONFIGURATION SECTION.
   │ 001100  SOURCE-COMPUTER.  IBM-370.
   │ 001110  OBJECT-COMPUTER.  IBM-370.
   │ 001120  INPUT-OUTPUT SECTION.
   │ 001130  FILE-CONTROL.
   │ 001140      SELECT NAME-ADDRESS-FILE-IN ASSIGN TO UT-S-INFILE.
   └ 001150      SELECT EMPLOYEE-LIST-OUT ASSIGN TO UT-S-PRTFILE.
```

Double asterisk denotes a sequence number that is not greater in value than the preceding
sequence number. (Some COBOL compilers indicate out-of-sequence conditions
in a different way.)

Figure 1.14   Out-of-sequence condition

ments. When a line must be inserted, it can be written on an unnumbered line
and given a sequence number between the numbers of the lines where it is to
be sandwiched. Figure 1.15 shows how to add a line and indicate where it
belongs in the program sequence.

COBOL statement

The actual program entries are written in this part of the coding form. There
are two main areas: area A (positions 8–11) and area B (positions 12–72). Some
COBOL entries begin in area A, but most of them begin in area B. In the next
two chapters, we will cover which entries start in each area.

Preceding area A, there is a continuation indicator area (position 7). This
position has three uses: (1) to identify a line that is a continuation of what is
called a nonnumeric literal; (2) to specify a page-eject line; and (3) to indicate a
comment line. The former two uses are discussed later in the text. The last—to
indicate a comment line—is the most frequent use. A COBOL line with an
asterisk (*) in position 7 is not considered part of the actual program. Rather, it
is assumed to contain explanatory or documentary comments. Hence, a comment line has no effect on the program execution. The line added in Figure 1.15
is an example of a comment line.

We have covered some fundamental points about areas of the COBOL
coding form. We will take a closer look at Titus's EMP-LIST program later in
this chapter.

Key the source program

The handprinted program lines must be transferred to records on a computer-
readable storage medium. Depending upon the type of input equipment the programmer is working with, the program is keyed to punched cards, magnetic
tape, or magnetic disk, or is entered from some other type of terminal or
recording device.

Keying of a complete program is sometimes done by a data-entry operator
rather than by the programmer, just as a report written by an executive may
by typed by a typist or clerk. Where programmers have terminals and source
entry utilities (software aids that facilitate the keying of source programs) at
their disposal, however, they usually key the program themselves. Regardless of
who keys the original program, programmers commonly key the corrections or
modifications to an existing program.

Titus takes his completed coding forms to a data-entry operator, Ms. Kitty
Keyes. After she keys the program, it is ready for compilation.

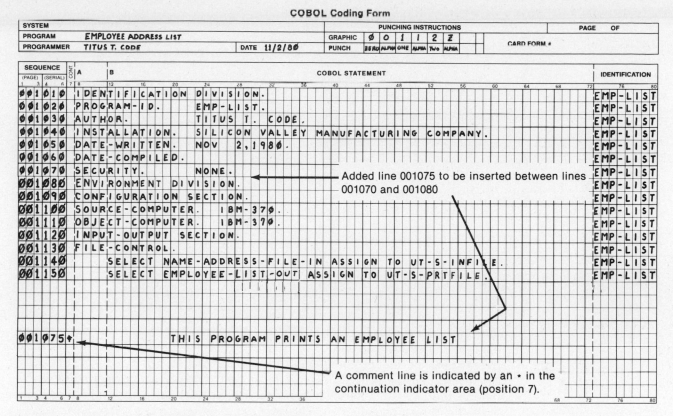

COBOL Coding Form

SYSTEM			PUNCHING INSTRUCTIONS						PAGE	OF
PROGRAM	EMPLOYEE ADDRESS LIST		GRAPHIC	Ø	O	I	I	2	Z	
PROGRAMMER	TITUS T. CODE	DATE 11/2/80	PUNCH	ZERO	ALPHA	ONE	ALPHA	TWO	ALPHA	CARD FORM #

```
001010  IDENTIFICATION DIVISION.                                    EMP-LIST
001020  PROGRAM-ID.     EMP-LIST.                                    EMP-LIST
001030  AUTHOR.         TITUS T. CODE.                               EMP-LIST
001040  INSTALLATION.   SILICON VALLEY MANUFACTURING COMPANY.        EMP-LIST
001050  DATE-WRITTEN.   NOV 2,1980.                                  EMP-LIST
001060  DATE-COMPILED.                                               EMP-LIST
001070  SECURITY.       NONE.                                        EMP-LIST
001080  ENVIRONMENT DIVISION.                                        EMP-LIST
001090  CONFIGURATION SECTION.                                       EMP-LIST
001100  SOURCE-COMPUTER.    IBM-370.                                 EMP-LIST
001110  OBJECT-COMPUTER.    IBM-370.                                 EMP-LIST
001120  INPUT-OUTPUT SECTION.                                        EMP-LIST
001130  FILE-CONTROL.                                                EMP-LIST
001140      SELECT NAME-ADDRESS-FILE-IN ASSIGN TO UT-S-INFILE.       EMP-LIST
001150      SELECT EMPLOYEE-LIST-OUT ASSIGN TO UT-S-PRTFILE.         EMP-LIST


001075*            THIS PROGRAM PRINTS AN EMPLOYEE LIST
```

Added line 001075 to be inserted between lines 001070 and 001080

A comment line is indicated by an * in the continuation indicator area (position 7).

Figure 1.15 Examples of added line and comment line

Compile the source program

The compilation process (see Figure 1.16) consists of submitting the source program as input to a COBOL compiler which produces an object program as output. The compiler also produces a listing of the source program. It indicates any errors or potential errors that it detects in the COBOL statements by printing out messages. Such messages are often referred to as *diagnostic messages*.

The errors that the compiler can detect are usually referred to as *syntactical errors*. Such errors occur when the language usage in the source program

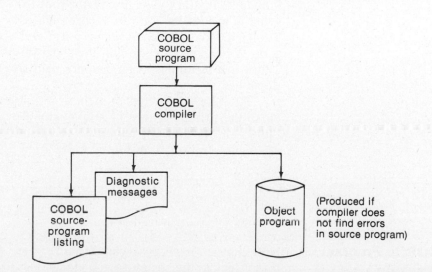

Figure 1.16 The compilation process

```
001010 IDENTIFICATION DIVISION.                                003050 01  EMPLOYEE-LINE-OUT.
001020 PROGRAM-ID.    EMP-LIST.                                 003060     02  VERTICAL-FORMS-CONTROL-OUT    PIC X(1).
001030 AUTHOR.        TITUS T..CODE.                            003070     02  EMPLOYEE-NAME-OUT             PIC X(20).
001040 INSTALLATION.  SILICON VALLEY MANUFACTURING COMPANY.     003080     02  FILLER                        PIC X(4).
001050 DATE-WRITTEN.  NOV 2,1980.                               003090     02  EMPLOYEE-ADDRESS-OUT          PIC X(24).
001060 DATE-COMPILED. NOV 2,1980.                               003100     02  FILLER                        PIC X(4).
001070 SECURITY.      NONE.                                     003110     02  EMPLOYEE-CITY-STATE-ZIP-OUT   PIC X(24).
001075*         THIS PROGRAM PRINTS AN EMPLOYEE ADDRESS LIST    003120     02  FILLER                        PIC X(56).
001080 ENVIRONMENT DIVISION.                                    004010 WORKING-STORAGE SECTION.
001090 CONFIGURATION SECTION.                                   004020 77  NAME-ADDRESS-FILE-END             PIC X(3).
001100 SOURCE-COMPUTER.  IBM-370.                               005010 PROCEDURE DIVISION.
001110 OBJECT-COMPUTER.  IBM-370.                               005020 MAINLINE-PRINT-EMPLOYEE-LIST.
001120 INPUT-OUTPUT SECTION.                                    005030     OPEN INPUT NAME-ADDRESS-FILE-IN
001130 FILE-CONTROL.                                            005040          OUTPUT EMPLOYEE-LIST-OUT.
001140     SELECT NAME-ADDRESS-FILE-IN ASSIGN TO UT-S-INFILE.   005050     PERFORM INITIALIZE-VARIABLE-FIELDS.
001150     SELECT EMPLOYEE-LIST-OUT ASSIGN TO UT-S-PRTFILE.     005060     READ NAME-ADDRESS-FILE-IN
002010 DATA DIVISION.                                           005070          AT END MOVE 'YES' TO NAME-ADDRESS-FILE-END.
002020 FILE SECTION.                                            005080     PERFORM PROCESS-NAME-ADDRESS-RECORD
002030 FD  NAME-ADDRESS-FILE-IN                                 005090          UNTIL NAME-ADDRESS-FILE-END IS EQUAL TO 'YES'.
002040     RECORD CONTAINS 80 CHARACTERS                        005100     CLOSE NAME-ADDRESS-FILE-IN
002050     LABEL RECORDS ARE OMITTED                            005110           EMPLOYEE-LIST-OUT.
002060     DATA RECORD IS NAME-ADDRESS-RECORD-IN.               005120     STOP RUN.
002070 01  NAME-ADDRESS-RECORD-IN.                              006010 INITIALIZE-VARIABLE-FIELDS.
002080     02  EMPLOYEE-NAME-IN            PIC X(20).            006020     MOVE 'NO ' TO NAME-ADDRESS-FILE-END.
002090     02  EMPLOYEE-ADDRESS-IN         PIC X(24).            007010 PROCESS-NAME-ADDRESS-RECORD.
002100     02  EMPLOYEE-CITY-STATE-ZIP-IN  PIC X(24).            007015     MOVE SPACES TO EMPLOYEE-LINE-OUT.
002110     02  EMPLOYEE-HIRE-DATE-IN.                           007020     MOVE EMPLOYEE-NAME-IN TO EMPLOYEE-NAME-OUT.
002120         03  EMPLOYEE-HIRE-MONTH-IN  PIC 9(2).            007030     MOVE EMPLOYEE-ADDRESS-IN TO EMPLOYEE-ADDRESS-OUT.
002130         03  EMPLOYEE-HIRE-DAY-IN    PIC 9(2).            007040     MOVE EMPLOYEE-CITY-STATE-ZIP-IN
002140         03  EMPLOYEE-HIRE-YEAR-IN   PIC 9(2).            007050          TO EMPLOYEE-CITY-STATE-ZIP-OUT.
002150     02  FILLER                      PIC X(6).            007060     WRITE EMPLOYEE-LINE-OUT
003010 FD  EMPLOYEE-LIST-OUT                                    007070          AFTER ADVANCING 2 LINES.
003020     RECORD CONTAINS 133 CHARACTERS                       007080     READ NAME-ADDRESS-FILE-IN
003030     LABEL RECORDS ARE OMITTED                            007090          AT END MOVE 'YES' TO NAME-ADDRESS-FILE-END.
003040     DATA RECORD IS EMPLOYEE-LINE-OUT.
```

Figure 1.17 Employee address list source-program listing

does not conform to the rules of the COBOL language. Either the programmer or the data-entry operator (or both) may be responsible for syntactical errors. Regardless of the origin, though, any detected errors must be corrected (rekeyed) and the source program must be compiled again. A compilation in which the compiler does not indicate any syntactical errors is customarily called a "clean compile."

Figure 1.17 shows the EMP-LIST source-program listing. Once a clean compile has been obtained, the testing phase can begin.

Phase 4:
The Testing Phase

There is a distinction between reviewing a novel for correct usage of English grammar and reviewing it for cohesiveness of the story. That is, a novel can be grammatically correct but still have a bad plot. Similarly, just because the programmer obtains a clean compile does not mean that the program will operate correctly. The COBOL compiler has no way of knowing what the programmer intended the program to do; it can only check that the programmer wrote the program in accordance with the syntactical requirements of the COBOL language. It is in the testing phase that the programmer ensures that the program is processing data in accordance with the programming specifications. Titus makes a test run of his program and obtains the output report in Figure 1.18. We can readily see that the program contains an error—a *program bug*. There are meaningless characters printed on each line of the employee address list.

Titus has neglected to include a statement instructing the computer to clear the print-line area of any meaningless extraneous data—often termed "junk" or "garbage"—before he constructed the print line. So, he writes the statement "MOVE SPACES TO EMPLOYEE-LINE-OUT", assigns it a sequence number of 007015 to place it at the correct point in the program, and keys this new line of code. Then Titus recompiles the program and tests it again. This time he obtains the proper output shown in Figure 1.19.

COBOL Program
Overview

Now that we have reviewed the full program development cycle, let's take a closer look at the structure and elements of the employee address list program that Titus has written.

```
BRADFORD, THOMAS        *X9081 EL CAMINO REAL      **SANTA CLARA CA 95051    8X&S$ **@/*T3

BRONSON. PATRICIA       /&1818 SANTA CRUZ AVENUE   /@LOS GATOS CA 95030

CARTWRIGHT, GILBERT     *X105 EAST CENTRAL AVENUE**CAMPBELL CA 95008         8X&S$ **@/*T3

COOK, KENNETH           /&496 REDWOOD AVENUE       /@SAN JOSE CA 95128

GARDNER, JOYCE          *X1014 STELLING ROAD       **CUPERTINO CA 95014      8X&S$ **@/*T3

JEFFERS. JOSEPH         /&1000 HYDE AVENUE         /@SAN JOSE CA 95129

KRISTENSEN, CARL        *X14199 SARATOGA AVENUE    **SARATOGA CA 95070       8X&S$ **@/*T3

LAWRENCE, KATHERINE     /&298 UNIVERSITY AVENUE    /@LOS GATOS CA 95030

LEE, SAMUEL             *X2140 JACKSON STREET      **SAN JOSE CA 95116       8X&S$ **@/*T3

LUCCHETTI, JOHN         /&13478 SOBEY ROAD         /@SARATOGA CA 95070
```

Figure 1.18   Employee address list test run with program bug

The textual material of a book is normally organized into chapters. Somewhat similarly, a COBOL program is organized into *divisions*. Although the author of a book usually chooses titles for chapters and determines their number and sequence as he or she sees fit, the COBOL programmer always works with four preassigned and prenamed divisions. The four divisions are always present, and they always appear in a predetermined order.

The order of the four divisions and their purposes (see Figure 1.20) are:

- IDENTIFICATION DIVISION—to identify and generally document the program
- ENVIRONMENT DIVISION—to define the computer and input-output devices used by the program
- DATA DIVISION—to describe the files, the records within the files, and the fields and subfields of the records used by the program
- PROCEDURE DIVISION—to express the actual instructions (the program logic) that the program is to perform

An annotated version of the program, which identifies structural components, is shown in Figure 1.21. You may wish to use it as a reference while reading the following material.

```
BRADFORD, THOMAS        9081 EL CAMINO REAL       SANTA CLARA CA 95051

BRONSON. PATRICIA       1818 SANTA CRUZ AVENUE    LOS GATOS CA 95030

CARTWRIGHT, GILBERT     105 EAST CENTRAL AVENUE   CAMPBELL CA 95008

COOK, KENNETH           496 REDWOOD AVENUE        SAN JOSE CA 95128

GARDNER, JOYCE          1014 STELLING ROAD        CUPERTINO CA 95014

JEFFERS. JOSEPH         1000 HYDE AVENUE          SAN JOSE CA 95129

KRISTENSEN, CARL        14199 SARATOGA AVENUE     SARATOGA CA 95070

LAWRENCE, KATHERINE     298 UNIVERSITY AVENUE     LOS GATOS CA 95030

LEE, SAMUEL             2140 JACKSON STREET       SAN JOSE CA 95116

LUCCHETTI, JOHN         13478 SOBEY ROAD          SARATOGA CA 95070
```

Figure 1.19   Employee address list test run with program bug corrected

IDENTIFICATION DIVISION

documents
the program

ENVIRONMENT DIVISION

defines computer and input-output devices

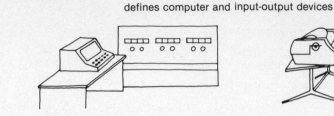

DATA DIVISION

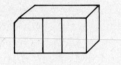

defines files, records,
fields, subfields, and
WORKING-STORAGE
fields

```
0 / 3 6
0 0 0 2
N O
```

PROCEDURE DIVISION

expresses program logic

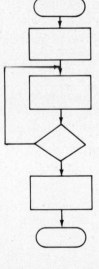

Figure 1.20 COBOL division structure

The IDENTIFICATION DIVISION: Documenting the Program

The IDENTIFICATION DIVISION (see Figure 1.22) comprises the first eight lines of the COBOL program. There is nothing complicated about this division; it simply contains information to document the program. Thus, although it serves an important function, it has no effect whatsoever upon the results the program provides.

The first line ("IDENTIFICATION DIVISION") is called a *division header*. The first word of each of the other lines of the IDENTIFICATION DIVISION is a *paragraph header*. There are six paragraph headers that may be used:

DIVISION: SECTION: Language elements:

```
001010  IDENTIFICATION DIVISION.
001020  PROGRAM-ID.      EMP-LIST.
001030  AUTHOR.          TITUS T. CODE.
001040  INSTALLATION.    SILICON VALLEY MANUFACTURING COMPANY.
001050  DATE-WRITTEN.    NOV 2.1980.
001060  DATE-COMPILED.   NOV 2.1980.
001070  SECURITY.        NONE.
001075*                  THIS PROGRAM PRINTS AN EMPLOYEE ADDRESS LIST
001080  ENVIRONMENT DIVISION.
001090  CONFIGURATION SECTION.
001100  SOURCE-COMPUTER.  IBM-370.
001110  OBJECT-COMPUTER.  IBM-370.
001120  INPUT-OUTPUT SECTION.
001130  FILE-CONTROL.
001140      SELECT NAME-ADDRESS-FILE-IN ASSIGN TO UT-S-INFILE.
001150      SELECT EMPLOYEE-LIST-OUT ASSIGN TO UT-S-PRTFILE.
002010  DATA DIVISION.
002020  FILE SECTION.
002030  FD NAME-ADDRESS-FILE-IN
002040      RECORD CONTAINS 80 CHARACTERS
002050      LABEL RECORDS ARE OMITTED
002060      DATA RECORD IS NAME-ADDRESS-RECORD-IN.
002070  01  NAME-ADDRESS-RECORD-IN.
002080      02  EMPLOYEE-NAME-IN               PIC X(20).
002090      02  EMPLOYEE-ADDRESS-IN            PIC X(24).
002100      02  EMPLOYEE-CITY-STATE-ZIP-IN     PIC X(24).
002110      02  EMPLOYEE-HIRE-DATE-IN.
002120          03  EMPLOYEE-HIRE-MONTH-IN     PIC 9(2).
002130          03  EMPLOYEE-HIRE-DAY-IN       PIC 9(2).
002140          03  EMPLOYEE-HIRE-YEAR-IN      PIC 9(2).
003010      02  FILLER                         PIC X(6).
003020  FD EMPLOYEE-LIST-OUT
003030      RECORD CONTAINS 133 CHARACTERS
003040      LABEL RECORDS ARE OMITTED
003050      DATA RECORD IS EMPLOYEE-LINE-OUT.
003050  01  EMPLOYEE-LINE-OUT.
003060      02  VERTICAL-FORMS-CONTROL-OUT     PIC X(1).
003070      02  FILLER                         PIC X(20).
003080      02  EMPLOYEE-NAME-OUT              PIC X(4).
003090      02  FILLER                         PIC X(24).
003100      02  EMPLOYEE-ADDRESS-OUT           PIC X(4).
003110      02  EMPLOYEE-CITY-STATE-ZIP-OUT    PIC X(24).
003120      02  FILLER                         PIC X(56).
004010  WORKING-STORAGE SECTION.
004020  77  NAME-ADDRESS-FILE-END              PIC X(3).
005010  PROCEDURE DIVISION.
005020  MAINLINE-PRINT-EMPLOYEE-LIST.
005030      OPEN INPUT NAME-ADDRESS-FILE-IN
005040           OUTPUT EMPLOYEE-LIST-OUT.
005050      PERFORM INITIALIZE-VARIABLE-FIELDS.
005060      READ NAME-ADDRESS-FILE-IN
005070          AT END MOVE 'YES' TO NAME-ADDRESS-FILE-END.
005080      PERFORM PROCESS-NAME-ADDRESS-RECORD
005090          UNTIL NAME-ADDRESS-FILE-END IS EQUAL TO 'YES'.
005100      CLOSE NAME-ADDRESS-FILE-IN
005110            EMPLOYEE-LIST-OUT.
005120      STOP RUN.
006010  INITIALIZE-VARIABLE-FIELDS.
006020      MOVE 'NO ' TO NAME-ADDRESS-FILE-END.
007010  PROCESS-NAME-ADDRESS-RECORD.
007015      MOVE SPACES TO EMPLOYEE-LINE-OUT.
007020      MOVE EMPLOYEE-NAME-IN TO EMPLOYEE-NAME-OUT.
007030      MOVE EMPLOYEE-ADDRESS-IN TO EMPLOYEE-ADDRESS-OUT.
007040      MOVE EMPLOYEE-CITY-STATE-ZIP-IN
007050          TO EMPLOYEE-CITY-STATE-ZIP-OUT.
007060      WRITE EMPLOYEE-LINE-OUT
007070          AFTER ADVANCING 2 LINES.
007080      READ NAME-ADDRESS-FILE-IN
007090          AT END MOVE 'YES' TO NAME-ADDRESS-FILE-END.
```

Annotations:

- IDENTIFICATION — Division header; Paragraph headers
- ENVIRONMENT — CONFIGURATION: Division header, Section header; INPUT-OUTPUT: Section header, Paragraph header, SELECT sentences
- DATA — Division header; Section header; FILE: File-description, Record-description (Record-description entry, Data-item-description entries); WORKING-STORAGE: Section header, Independent item
- PROCEDURE — Division header; Paragraph header; Statements; MAINLINE-PRINT-EMPLOYEE-LIST paragraph; INITIALIZE-VARIABLE-FIELDS paragraph; PROCESS-NAME-ADDRESS-RECORD paragraph

Figure 1.21 Annotated EMP-LIST program

```
001010 IDENTIFICATION DIVISION.
001020 PROGRAM-ID.    EMP-LIST.
001030 AUTHOR.        TITUS T. CODE.
001040 INSTALLATION.  SILICON VALLEY MANUFACTURING COMPANY.
001050 DATE-WRITTEN.  NOV 2,1980.
001060 DATE-COMPILED. NOV 2,1980.
001070 SECURITY.      NONE.
001075*            THIS PROGRAM PRINTS AN EMPLOYEE ADDRESS LIST
```

Figure 1.22 IDENTIFICATION DIVISION—EMP-LIST program

PROGRAM-ID, AUTHOR, INSTALLATION, DATE-WRITTEN, DATE-COMPILED, and SECURITY.

Each of the words used in the division and paragraph headers is a *reserved word*. Reserved words have special predefined meanings in the COBOL language.

Following the predefined paragraph headers are sentences that the programmer enters. For example, Titus gives this program a PROGRAM-ID (or name) of EMP-LIST. He also enters his name, the name of the data processing installation, the date the program was written, and so forth.

The ENVIRONMENT DIVISION: Defining the Computer and Input-Output Devices

The ENVIRONMENT DIVISION (see Figure 1.23) is the link from the predominantly hardware-independent COBOL program to the actual computers and physical data files used by the program.

The division is divided into two sections: the CONFIGURATION SECTION and the INPUT-OUTPUT SECTION. A *section header* line identifies each of these two sections.

CONFIGURATION SECTION

The computers to be used by the program are specified in this section. The SOURCE-COMPUTER paragraph tells the type of computer that will be used to compile the COBOL program. The computer that will execute the EMP-LIST program is identified in the OBJECT-COMPUTER paragraph. Usually, the source and object computers are the same but they may differ.

INPUT-OUTPUT SECTION

This section describes the data files used by the program. Each file is introduced and associated with an input-output device.

The EMP-LIST program uses two files—the input file containing name-and-address records and an output report file containing lines of employee data. There are two sentences—one for each file—in the FILE-CONTROL paragraph. Each of these two sentences contains two clauses: SELECT and ASSIGN.

The SELECT clause contains the word "SELECT" followed by a file name chosen by the programmer. The ASSIGN clause contains the word "ASSIGN" followed by the device name of the computer hardware on which the data file will reside. Applicable device names are specified by the company supplying the COBOL compiler (usually the computer manufacturer).

```
001080 ENVIRONMENT DIVISION.
001090 CONFIGURATION SECTION.
001100 SOURCE-COMPUTER.  IBM-370.
001110 OBJECT-COMPUTER.  IBM-370.
001120 INPUT-OUTPUT SECTION.
001130 FILE-CONTROL.
001140     SELECT NAME-ADDRESS-FILE-IN ASSIGN TO UT-S-INFILE.
001150     SELECT EMPLOYEE-LIST-OUT ASSIGN TO UT-S-PRTFILE.
```

Figure 1.23 ENVIRONMENT DIVISION—EMP-LIST program

```
002010 DATA DIVISION.
002020 FILE SECTION.
002030 FD   NAME-ADDRESS-FILE-IN
002040        RECORD CONTAINS 80 CHARACTERS
002050        LABEL RECORDS ARE OMITTED
002060        DATA RECORD IS NAME-ADDRESS-RECORD-IN.
002070 01   NAME-ADDRESS-RECORD-IN.
002080      02   EMPLOYEE-NAME-IN              PIC X(20).
002090      02   EMPLOYEE-ADDRESS-IN           PIC X(24).
002100      02   EMPLOYEE-CITY-STATE-ZIP-IN    PIC X(24).
002110      02   EMPLOYEE-HIRE-DATE-IN.
002120           03   EMPLOYEE-HIRE-MONTH-IN   PIC 9(2).
002130           03   EMPLOYEE-HIRE-DAY-IN     PIC 9(2).
002140           03   EMPLOYEE-HIRE-YEAR-IN    PIC 9(2).
002150      02   FILLER                        PIC X(6).
003010 FD   EMPLOYEE-LIST-OUT
003020        RECORD CONTAINS 133 CHARACTERS
003030        LABEL RECORDS ARE OMITTED
003040        DATA RECORD IS EMPLOYEE-LINE-OUT.
003050 01   EMPLOYEE-LINE-OUT.
003060      02   VERTICAL-FORMS-CONTROL-OUT    PIC X(1).
003070      02   FILLER                        PIC X(2).
003070      02   EMPLOYEE-NAME-OUT             PIC X(20).
003080      02   FILLER                        PIC X(4).
003090      02   EMPLOYEE-ADDRESS-OUT          PIC X(24).
003100      02   FILLER                        PIC X(4).
003110      02   EMPLOYEE-CITY-STATE-ZIP-OUT   PIC X(24).
003120      02   FILLER                        PIC X(54).
004010 WORKING-STORAGE SECTION.
004020 77   NAME-ADDRESS-FILE-END             PIC X(3).
```

Figure 1.24 DATA DIVISION—EMP-LIST program

In the FILE-CONTROL paragraph then, Titus names the input file of employee records NAME-ADDRESS-FILE-IN and links it to a device name of UT-S-INFILE. Similarly, he names the output employee address list file EMPLOYEE-LIST-OUT and links it to a device name of UT-S-PRTFILE.

A word chosen by the programmer (such as NAME-ADDRESS-FILE-IN or EMPLOYEE-LIST-OUT) is a *user-defined word*. A word specified by the compiler supplier is a *system name* (as are UT-S-INFILE and UT-S-PRTFILE).

The DATA DIVISION: Defining Files, Records, Fields, and Subfields

As the name of this division implies, the data to be processed by the program is defined here (see Figure 1.24). The DATA DIVISION of the EMP-LIST program has two sections: FILE and WORKING-STORAGE.

FILE SECTION

The data items (records, fields, and subfields) that appear in the input and output files are defined in the FILE SECTION. Each file selected in the ENVIRONMENT DIVISION must be described in this section. Thus, the FILE SECTION comprises file descriptions for all files used by the program. A *file-description* entry starts with the reserved word FD (*File Description*). This word is followed by the file name and by clauses that describe the file. Notice that the NAME-ADDRESS-FILE-IN clauses tell how many characters the records contain, whether the file contains label records, and the name used to refer to the data records.

After the FD entry for a file, the record formats within the file are described. The NAME-ADDRESS-FILE-IN has one record format; its description begins after the FD entry. The two-digit number 01 signifies that this line begins a *record-description* entry. The number 01 is a *level-number*. Following level-number 01 is the user-defined record name: NAME-ADDRESS-RECORD-IN.

A record is a collection of fields. Thus, after the record-description entry, there are descriptions of fields—termed *data-item* entries. The data-item description entries are identified by level numbers in the range from 02 through 49. Observe that when a level 02 item has subfields—as is the case with the EMPLOYEE-HIRE-DATE-IN field—a higher level number (03, in this case) is assigned to the subfields.

Each data-item description in the EMP-LIST program has three parts:

1. The two-digit level number (such as 02 or 03)
2. A user-defined name to identify and permit reference to the field
3. A PICTURE (or PIC, as it is usually abbreviated) clause, which defines the data class and length of the field (This clause is not present, however, when a field has subfields at the next level. The EMPLOYEE-HIRE-DATE-IN field is an example.)

A basic PICTURE clause is formed by the reserved word PIC, a space, and the number 9 or the letter X (depending upon whether the field is numeric or alphanumeric, respectively) followed by the length of the field enclosed in parentheses.

In summary, the FILE SECTION of the EMP-LIST program has two FD entries because it uses two files. After the FD entry for the input NAME-ADDRESS-FILE-IN, there is one 01 record-description entry because the file contains one record format. Similarly, the FD for the EMPLOYEE-LIST-OUT file has one 01 entry—EMPLOYEE-LINE-OUT—because there is one record format (or in this case, one line format) in the output report. After each 01 record-description entry, there are 02-level and 03-level data-item description entries as required to define the fields and subfields of each record.

WORKING-STORAGE SECTION

Other data fields that must be used in the program (in addition to those appearing in the input-output records) are defined in the WORKING-STORAGE SECTION. Fields used to accumulate totals or to indicate program conditions are examples. In this simple program, there is only one WORKING-STORAGE field: NAME-ADDRESS-FILE-END. It is preceded by the level-number 77, which indicates an independent data-item description entry. An *independent item* is a field that is not part of a record, is not a subfield of another field, and does not have subfields. The NAME-ADDRESS-FILE-END field is used to determine when the NAME-ADDRESS-FILE has reached an end-of-file condition.

Thus, the DATA DIVISION contains definitions of all data items—files, records, fields, and subfields—used by the COBOL program.

The PROCEDURE DIVISION: Coding the Program Logic

Figure 1.25 isolates the PROCEDURE DIVISION for the EMP-LIST program. Notice that, although paragraph names in the IDENTIFICATION and ENVIRONMENT DIVISIONS are reserved words, paragraph names in the PROCEDURE DIVISION are user-defined words. The paragraph names that Titus has chosen for this division are MAINLINE-PRINT-EMPLOYEE-LIST, INITIALIZE-VARIABLE-FIELDS, and PROCESS-NAME-ADDRESS-RECORD.

Within each of the paragraphs are a number of COBOL statements that specify actions to be taken. These statements can best be classified and discussed by reference to the verb that each contains. The EMP-LIST program contains the verbs OPEN, PERFORM, READ, CLOSE, STOP, MOVE, and WRITE.

Since COBOL was designed to be similar to English and somewhat self-documenting, even the beginning student can gain a general idea of what is happening in the PROCEDURE DIVISION by reading the statements. It is beyond the scope of this overview chapter to discuss each of the statements in detail, but a general narrative of the PROCEDURE DIVISION steps follows.

```
005010 PROCEDURE DIVISION.
005020 MAINLINE-PRINT-EMPLOYEE-LIST.
005030     OPEN INPUT NAME-ADDRESS-FILE-IN
005040         OUTPUT EMPLOYEE-LIST-OUT.
005050     PERFORM INITIALIZE-VARIABLE-FIELDS.
005060     READ NAME-ADDRESS-FILE-IN
005070         AT END MOVE 'YES' TO NAME-ADDRESS-FILE-END.
005080     PERFORM PROCESS-NAME-ADDRESS-RECORD
005090         UNTIL NAME-ADDRESS-FILE-END IS EQUAL TO 'YES'.
005100     CLOSE NAME-ADDRESS-FILE-IN
005110         EMPLOYEE-LIST-OUT.
005120     STOP RUN.
006010 INITIALIZE-VARIABLE-FIELDS.
006020     MOVE 'NO ' TO NAME-ADDRESS-FILE-END.
007010 PROCESS-NAME-ADDRESS-RECORD.
007015     MOVE SPACES TO EMPLOYEE-LINE-OUT.
007020     MOVE EMPLOYEE-NAME-IN TO EMPLOYEE-NAME-OUT.
007030     MOVE EMPLOYEE-ADDRESS-IN TO EMPLOYEE-ADDRESS-OUT.
007040     MOVE EMPLOYEE-CITY-STATE-ZIP-IN
007050         TO EMPLOYEE-CITY-STATE-ZIP-OUT.
007060     WRITE EMPLOYEE-LINE-OUT
007070         AFTER ADVANCING 2 LINES.
007080     READ NAME-ADDRESS-FILE-IN
007090         AT END MOVE 'YES' TO NAME-ADDRESS-FILE-END.
```

Figure 1.25 PROCEDURE DIVISION—EMP-LIST program

MAINLINE-PRINT-EMPLOYEE-LIST paragraph

This paragraph can be compared to the outline of a story. Programmers often refer to such a paragraph as *mainline* because it provides the main processing control structure for the program.

A simple read-and-print program usually needs two additional paragraphs: one to initialize the variable fields in the WORKING-STORAGE SECTION and one to process each input record. The paragraph to initialize the variable fields will be executed once whenever the program is run; the record-processing paragraph will be executed once for each input record processed. Figure 1.26 shows this paragraph flow: as long as NAME-ADDRESS-FILE-END is equal to "NO" the PERFORM statement will be executed.

The mainline paragraph, then, controls the sequence of when and how many times each paragraph is performed. The overall program flow for the EMP-LIST program as provided by the MAINLINE-PRINT-EMPLOYEE-LIST program is as follows:

1. The input and output files are opened (made available for access).
2. The INITIALIZE-VARIABLE-FIELDS paragraph is performed.
3. The first record is read from NAME-ADDRESS-FILE-IN.
4. The PROCESS-NAME-ADDRESS-RECORD paragraph is performed and repeated for each input record of NAME-ADDRESS-FILE-IN.
5. After all the input records have been read, the input and output files are closed (restricted from access).
6. The program run is stopped.

INITIALIZE-VARIABLE-FIELDS paragraph

A paragraph such as this is used to set the initial values of fields in WORKING-STORAGE that will contain variable values. In this program, there is only one such field; NAME-ADDRESS-FILE-END. It is set to "NO" to indicate that NAME-ADDRESS-FILE-IN has not yet reached an end-of-file condition.

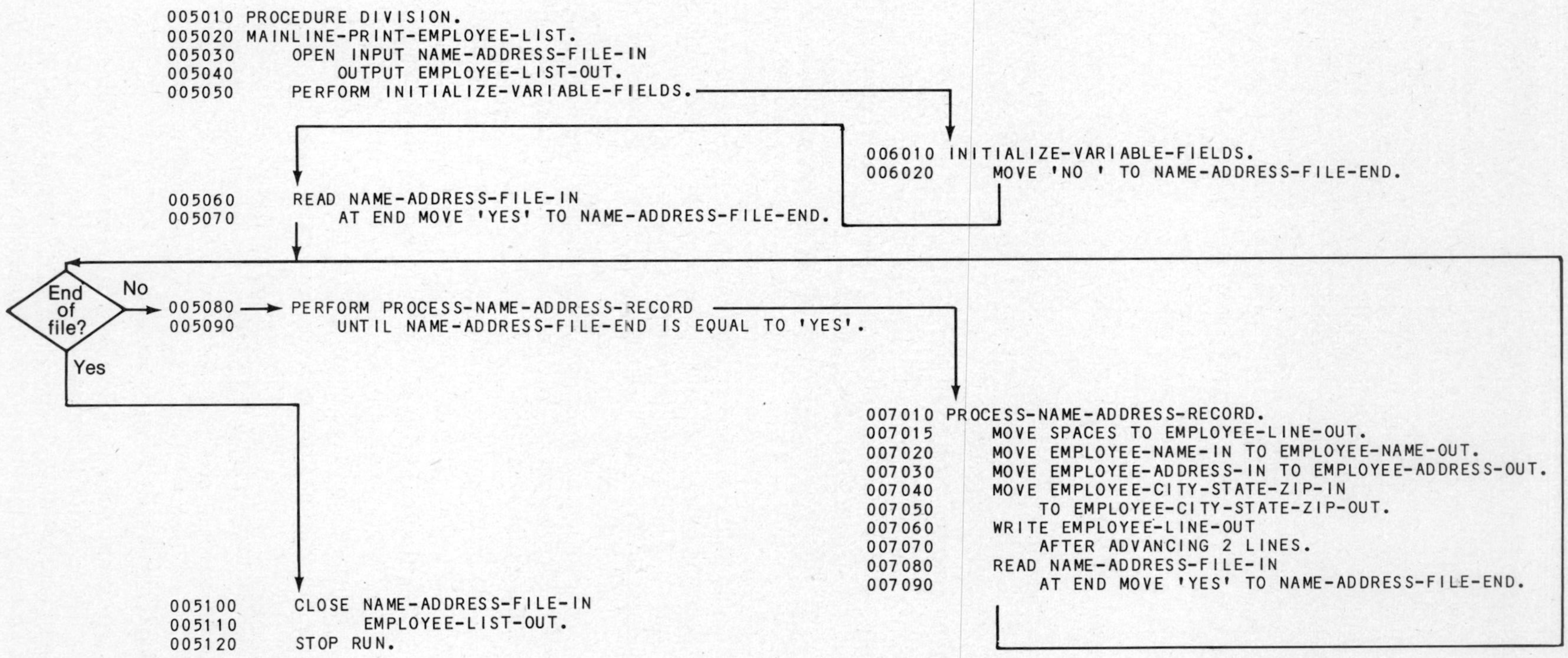

```
005010  PROCEDURE DIVISION.
005020  MAINLINE-PRINT-EMPLOYEE-LIST.
005030      OPEN INPUT NAME-ADDRESS-FILE-IN
005040           OUTPUT EMPLOYEE-LIST-OUT.
005050      PERFORM INITIALIZE-VARIABLE-FIELDS.


005060      READ NAME-ADDRESS-FILE-IN
005070          AT END MOVE 'YES' TO NAME-ADDRESS-FILE-END.

005080      PERFORM PROCESS-NAME-ADDRESS-RECORD
005090          UNTIL NAME-ADDRESS-FILE-END IS EQUAL TO 'YES'.




005100      CLOSE NAME-ADDRESS-FILE-IN
005110            EMPLOYEE-LIST-OUT.
005120      STOP RUN.
```

```
006010  INITIALIZE-VARIABLE-FIELDS.
006020      MOVE 'NO ' TO NAME-ADDRESS-FILE-END.
```

```
007010  PROCESS-NAME-ADDRESS-RECORD.
007015      MOVE SPACES TO EMPLOYEE-LINE-OUT.
007020      MOVE EMPLOYEE-NAME-IN TO EMPLOYEE-NAME-OUT.
007030      MOVE EMPLOYEE-ADDRESS-IN TO EMPLOYEE-ADDRESS-OUT.
007040      MOVE EMPLOYEE-CITY-STATE-ZIP-IN
007050          TO EMPLOYEE-CITY-STATE-ZIP-OUT.
007060      WRITE EMPLOYEE-LINE-OUT
007070          AFTER ADVANCING 2 LINES.
007080      READ NAME-ADDRESS-FILE-IN
007090          AT END MOVE 'YES' TO NAME-ADDRESS-FILE-END.
```

End of file?   No   Yes

Figure 1.26 Read-and-print program module flow

PROCESS-NAME-ADDRESS-RECORD paragraph

The following operations are executed for each record of NAME-ADDRESS-FILE-IN:

1. The EMPLOYEE-LINE-OUT area is cleared of extraneous data by moving a value of SPACES (blanks) to it.
2. Each of the data items to be printed on the EMPLOYEE-LINE-OUT is moved from the input record (NAME-ADDRESS-RECORD-IN) field to the output record (EMPLOYEE-LINE-OUT) field.
3. Once all the desired data has been placed on the EMPLOYEE-LINE-OUT, that line is written onto the printer.
4. The next record from NAME-ADDRESS-FILE-IN is read.

The PROCESS-NAME-ADDRESS-RECORD paragraph is repeated over and over, as long as there are records to be read. When the READ statement in this paragraph finds there are no more records to be read, the word "YES" is moved into the NAME-ADDRESS-FILE-END field in WORKING-STORAGE.

We have now looked briefly at a simple, but complete, COBOL program and its development. In Chapters 2 and 3, COBOL program entries will be explained to the level of detail necessary for you to write a COBOL program.

Summary

The program development process consists of four phases: the specification phase, the design phase, the coding phase, and the testing phase.

In the *specification phase*, the following documentation is obtained or prepared: (1) illustrative layouts of the output and input records; (2) programming specifications that briefly describe the overall purpose of the program, identify the inputs and outputs, and list the major processing steps that are to occur; and (3) approval to proceed to the next step of the program development cycle.

When in the *design phase*, the programmer may use a *structure chart* to depict program task relationships on a hierarchical basis. Each of these tasks may then be expressed in *pseudocode* (an English-like program documentation language), depicted graphically in a *program flowchart*, or represented by some other program design and documentation technique. The correctness of the program design may be verified by doing a *structured walkthrough* of the design documentation.

The *coding phase* steps are: (1) write the source program on COBOL coding forms, (2) key the program, and (3) compile the program. The coding forms are segmented to represent lines of COBOL entries. There are three areas on each line: sequence, COBOL statement, and identification.

In the *testing phase*, the programmer ensures that the program is processing data in accordance with the programming specifications.

Every COBOL program has four divisions. The IDENTIFICATION DIVISION identifies and generally documents the program. The computer and input-output devices used by the program are defined in the ENVIRONMENT DIVISION. The DATA DIVISION describes the files, the records within the files, and the fields and subfields of the records used in the program. The program logic instructions that tell the computer how to process the data are written in the PROCEDURE DIVISION.

Exercises

Terms for Definition

record layout form   system flowchart
print chart   user/user group
programming specifications   structure chart

pseudocode   diagnostic messages
program flowchart   syntactical errors
structured walkthrough   program bug
source program   "junk" or "garbage" data
compile   "clean" compile
compiler   mainline paragraph

Review Questions

1. Name the four phases of the program development process.

2. During which phase of the program development process are the following tasks generally performed?

   Draw program flowchart *Design*   *specification*
   Key program *code*   *Design*
   Write programming specifications *Specifer*   *Code*
   Write program *code*   *Test*
   Write pseudocode *Design*
   Debug program
   Prepare structure chart *pu*
   Test program
   Prepare print chart
   Compile program
   Prepare record layout
   Obtain "clean compile"
   Conduct structured walkthrough
   Draw system flowchart
   Correct diagnostic errors

3. Name, in correct sequence, the four COBOL Divisions and briefly describe the general purpose of each.
                                                       Identificat
4. Name the Division to which each of these Sections belongs: *Enviornment*
                                                       Data
   WORKING-STORAGE   *Procedural*
   EN INPUT-OUTPUT
   FILE
   CONFIGURATION

5. Name the Division and Section (if applicable) to which each of the following paragraphs belongs.

   ID PROGRAM-ID
   EN OBJECT-COMPUTER
   SECURITY
   ID AUTHOR
   FILE-CONTROL
   ID DATE-COMPILED
   INSTALLATION
   EN SOURCE-COMPUTER
   ID DATE-WRITTEN

6. What is FD an abbreviation for? *Feild Description*

7. Level-number 01 signifies a _____ -description entry.

8. Level-numbers 02 through 49 signify _____ -description entries.

9. Level-number 77 signifies an _____ -description entry.

10. Programmers often refer to the PROCEDURE DIVISION paragraph which provides overall program control as _____.

Programming Assignment 1-A

Key the EMP-LIST program and compile it. Correct any diagnostic errors and obtain a "clean" compile.

SYSTEMS CHAPTER A

DATA CONCEPTS

DATA CONCEPTS

Often, the organization of data within a data processing system is similar to that of a simple manual system. For instance, suppose data about a woman named Abigail Adams is stored in her friend's address and telephone number book. This book is an example of a manual information storage system. A sample page is depicted in Figure A.1.

There is space on the page to write letters, numbers, and other character symbols. The space in which each individual character symbol is recorded is analogous to a *character position* on a data processing storage medium. The page is ruled and labeled to record the following seven data elements about each person: name, address, city, state, zip code, telephone number, and area code. The area allocated for each of these data elements is referred to as a *field* in data processing terminology. Notice that the areas are of various sizes to accommodate the different number of character symbols that may be needed to express the data values. A field, therefore, may be defined as one or more contiguous character positions used to store a data element.

Together, the seven fields of each entry in the book hold the data recorded about one *data entity*. Such a collection of fields relating to the same data entity is referred to as a *logical record*.

The address-book page has room for five entries. An assemblage of logical records into a given physical area is termed a *physical record*. In this example, one page represents one physical record.

Books are often called "volumes," and the address book, which can hold a number of logical and physical records, is akin to a *volume* in data processing

Name ABIGAIL ADAMS		Telephone 999 - 9999
Address 407 OAK WAY		Area Code 415
City PALO ALTO	State CA	Zip 94304
Name CAROL ABBOTT		Telephone 999-7362
Address 2356 JUNIPER LANE		Area Code 415
City MENLO PARK	State CA	Zip 94026
Name JAN ARTHUR		Telephone 999-6623
Address 109 SPRUCE DRIVE		Area Code 408
City SARATOGA	State CA	Zip 95070
Name		Telephone
Address		Area Code
City	State	Zip
Name		Telephone
Address		Area Code
City	State	Zip

Figure A.1 Sample page from address book

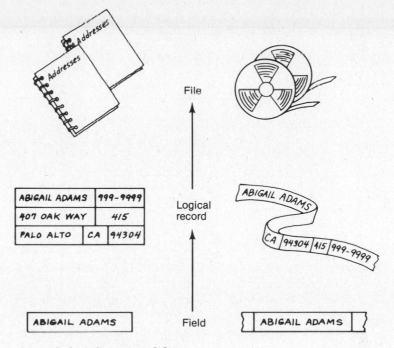

Figure A.2   Logical classifications of data

terminology. If Abigail's friend has only a few persons recorded in the address book, the volume is only partially used. If the friend records the addresses and telephone numbers of many acquaintances, more than one address book (or volume) may be required. A collection of logical (or physical) records—whether it consumes a portion of one volume, one volume, or multiple volumes—is called a *file*.

Six data processing terms have been introduced. Three of them—field, logical record and file—are logical collections of data. The remaining three—character position, physical record, and volume—can be considered physical assemblages. Figures A.2, A.3, and A.4 illustrate the conceptual hierarchy of these data storage classifications.

Logical Classifications of Data

Field

A field (or its subdivision, the subfield) is the smallest logical unit in a data processing system. Fields are composed of adjacent character positions on a data storage medium; these characters accommodate a logical unit of data.

In the determination of just what a logical unit of data is, there is often a degree of latitude. Look at the name field in the address-book example. Evidently, the designer of the address book considered one's full name a logical unit of data. There are situations, however, where it is desirable to consider the name as three separate logical units or fields: first name, middle initial, and last name. As another example, consider a six-digit date-of-birth field, as shown in Figure A.5. The month of birth, day of birth, and year of birth can be considered individual fields, but since they are normally used together to represent a specific date, it is probably more appropriate to consider them subfields of the date-of-birth field. Actually, there is little distinction between a subfield and a field. What *is* important is to identify and define the logical units of information to the level of detail required by the application.

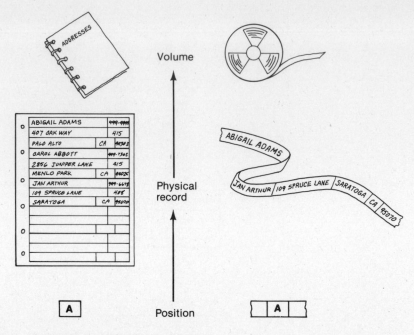

Figure A.3 Physical classifications of data

There are three primary characteristics of fields that the programmer must consider: data class, field length, and field type.

Data class

There are three basic classes of data: numeric, alphabetic, and alphanumeric. Figure A.6 gives examples of each.

Numeric fields contain the digits 0 through 9. Generally, fields to be operated on arithmetically must be of numeric data class. In addition to digits, numeric fields may contain the arithmetic signs plus (+) or minus (–).

Alphabetic fields contain the letters A through Z and blanks (which are often termed "spaces").

Alphanumeric (sometimes termed *alphameric*) fields may contain digits, letters, and other special characters ($, *, #, and so on). In actual practice, few fields are truly alphabetic (because of the use of special characters), so many programmers define all alphabetic fields as alphanumeric.

Field length

A field can range in length from a single digit or character to many characters. Fields are normally designed to be of fixed lengths, but variable-length fields are used in certain circumstances.

It is not difficult to specify the sizes of certain fields. Social security numbers, for example, require nine positions. Similarly, establishing field lengths for most other codes, dates, serial numbers, and the like is relatively straightforward. Quantity and dollar-amount fields, on the other hand, are not as easy to gauge. Often with arithmetic fields such as these, the highest value that may be recorded in the field is not known. Or, if it is known, that highest value may be a rare case or an exception condition.

Consider specifying the length of an inventory quantity field for a growing company manufacturing sophisticated electronic instruments. Most of its inventory items are high-priced components stocked in limited quantities, but the company does stock a multitude of a few things, like resistors and diodes. Thus,

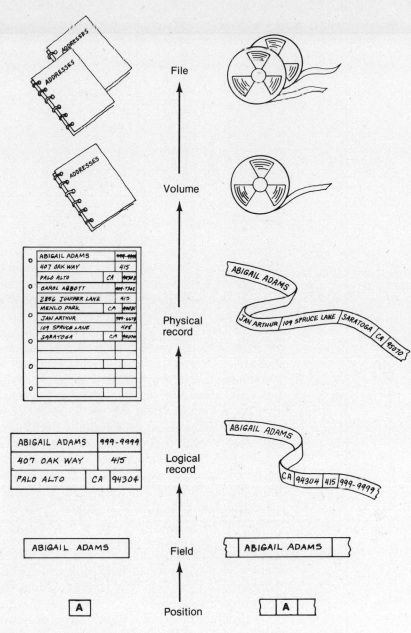

Figure A.4 Relationship of logical and physical classifications of data

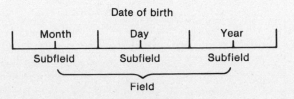

Figure A.5 The relationship of fields and subfields

Numeric	Alphabetic			Alphanumeric		
0	A	J	S	All numeric characters		
1	B	K	T	All alphabetic characters		
2	C	L	U	"	)	:
3	D	M	V	#	*	;
4	E	N	W	$	+	=
5	F	O	X	%	,	?
6	G	P	Y	&	-	@
7	H	Q	Z	'	.	[
8	I	R		(	/	]
9	Blank (space)					

Figure A.6 Classes of data

although most items will reflect only a modest quantity, certain items will dictate use of a field large enough to accommodate a much higher value.

Or, suppose that it is necessary to specify a balance-owed field as part of a customer accounts-receivable record. The amount owed is, of course, the sum of all purchases, other charges, and any finance charge, less payments. As such, the balance owed is the result of various arithmetic operations, the total of which is more difficult to predict than any of the detail entries. The best approach for the programmer/analyst is to provide a size ample for present conditions and reasonably consistent with expectations of future need.

For a numeric field that is the result of an arithmetic operation, the programmer/analyst must be especially careful to provide a field large enough for the largest result that can occur. When there are just two values involved in a calculation, the maximum size can be determined easily. In many situations, however, the total amount is the result of several successive operations (like the balance-owed field or the total of all items on an invoice). In such cases, the maximum size cannot be determined by means of a formula; it must instead be chosen by the programmer/analyst.

The size of certain alphanumeric fields can be as difficult to specify as the size of quantity and dollar-amount fields. Name, address, and city fields are examples of alphanumeric fields for which the programmer/analyst may have trouble specifying field lengths. Suggestions for making such specifications are presented in Figure A.7.

Although there was a day when programmers sought to use every digit position to its fullest, the decrease in electronic storage media costs has somewhat lessened the dearness of storage positions. At the same time, the in-

Field	This percentage of expected values . . .	. . . will be equal to or less than this many characters
Individual last name	98%	11
Individual full name	95%	18
Company name	95%	20
Street address	90%	18
City name	99%	17

Source: *Identification Techniques.* IBM Publication GC20-1707. *Form and Card Design.* IBM Publication GC20-8078.

Figure A.7 Expected character lengths of certain alphanumeric fields

creasing complexity and range of applications of most data processing systems have generally increased the amount of effort required to expand an inadequate field size. Thus, as a general rule, the programmer/analyst should select generous field sizes.

Field type

Fields can be classified according to the functions they serve as either *indicative* or *control* fields. Most fields are of the indicative type; they contain descriptive, reference, or quantitative data regarding an entity. Control fields perform identification functions. An important type of control field is a *key* field. The key field uniquely identifies a logical record and relates it to a data entity. For example, if a record contains information about a machine part, its key field is the part number; if the record describes an employee, its key field is an employee or social security number. The key field often (but not always) serves as the basis for organization of a file. In the address-book example, the name field uniquely identifies the data entity and hence can be considered the key field. Notice also that the address book is organized according to the first letter of the last name.

Logical Record

A logical record is a collection of fields related to the same data entity and arranged in a prescribed format. As has been mentioned, the collection of name, address, city, state, zip code, phone number, and area code fields about a particular person can be considered a logical record in the address-book example. A logical record must contain a key field that identifies it.

Logical records may be either fixed or variable in length. Refer to Figure A.8 for examples of fixed-length records. In a fixed-length record, all fields are fixed in length, and the position of each field within the logical record is the same in all records. Fixed-length fields and fixed-length records are much more commonly used than those of variable lengths, because they are simpler to process and control. However, in certain applications, the data does not efficiently conform to fixed-length record formats. For instance, consider a college student-records system in which it is necessary to store the following regarding each course a student has completed: course title, units earned, and letter grade (see Part B of Figure A.8). Suppose it takes a segment of eight characters to store such data for each course. A senior at the college may have completed 40 or more classes; an entering freshman may have completed none. If fixed-length records were used, space would be required in each record for as many class-completed segments as a finishing senior or graduate student might require; perhaps 75 eight-character segments (600 positions) would need to be allocated. Of these 600 positions, however, an entering freshman may need none; a sophomore may need only about one-fourth of the space; and so on. Clearly, the assignment of only as many class-completed segments as are necessary for each student—thus forming a variable-length record—is a more efficient approach. (Variable-length records are often handled more satisfactorily by data base management systems, which will be discussed later in this chapter.)

Another appropriate situation for a variable-length record is one in which, although the number of fields is uniform from one record to another, the lengths of certain fields are variable (see Part C of Figure A.8). In designing records for a library system, the programmer/analyst finds that the length of book titles varies greatly; the same is true of author names. Obviously, superfluous blank positions can be eliminated by using variable-length fields. Hence, a record is variable-length if (1) it contains a variable number of occurrences of fixed-length segments, or (2) it contains one or more variable-length fields.

Part A: Fixed-length records (Fixed number of fixed-length fields)

Name (20)	Address (20)	City (16)	State (2)	Zip code (5)	Area code (3)	Phone number (7)
CAROL ABBOTT	2356 JUNIPER LANE	MENLO PARK	CA	94025	415	9997362
ABIGAIL ADAMS	407 OAK WAY	PALO ALTO	CA	94304	415	9999999
JAN ARTHUR	109 SPRUCE DRIVE	SARATOGA	CA	95070	408	9986623

Part B: Variable-length records (Variable occurrences of fixed-length segments)

Student number (4) Student name (20) Courses completed (2) Course segment (8)

| 0007 | BOND J | 07 | CHEM1A 4 C | ENGL1A 3 C | HIST17 3 B | MATH5 4 A | MATH7 3 A | PE10 1 A | SPAN2 4 B |

| 1980 | WALLACE T | 03 | ENGL1A 3 A | HIST17 3 A | PHYS1A 4 A |

| 2555 | ADAMS A | 05 | ART21 2 B | BUS51 3 C | ENGLA 3 C | PE12 1 A | TYPG1 2 C |

Part C: Variable-length records (Variable-length fields)

Record length (2) Access number (6) Length (2) Author data (variable) Length (2) Title data (variable)

| 70 | 725630 | 12 | BOMBECK ERMA | 46 | I LOST EVERYTHING IN THE POST-NATAL DEPRESSION |

| 32 | 435786 | 14 | MICHENER JAMES | 06 | HAWAII |

| 63 | 834523 | 34 | BURDICK EUGENE & LEDERER WILLIAM J. | 17 | THE UGLY AMERICAN |

Figure A.8 Examples of fixed-length and variable-length records

File

A file is a defined collection of logical records. The address book is a collection of records about its owner's friends and associates. A company's accounts-receivable file is a collection of logical records on its account-holding customers. The *population* of a file (that is, the data entities included in it) and its *contents* (the data elements represented in its records) are dependent on the specific application; a magazine subscription file, for instance, requires subscriber records containing name, address, and subscription-expiration data while a student-records file is composed of records containing vital statistics, course enrollment, and scholastic performance data.

Physical Classifications of Data

Physical data characteristics are generally dependent on the specific type of data storage medium (cards, tape, disk, and so on) and the particular device (card reader, tape drive, disk unit) used by an application.

Character Position

A character position is the smallest addressable unit on a storage medium. For commercial data processing applications, one character position, or *byte*, is usually the addressable unit. However, certain equipment is oriented toward *words*. Each word holds a group of digits or characters.

Physical Record

A physical record is one or more logical records accessed as a group. In the address-book example, to find the address or telephone number of Abigail

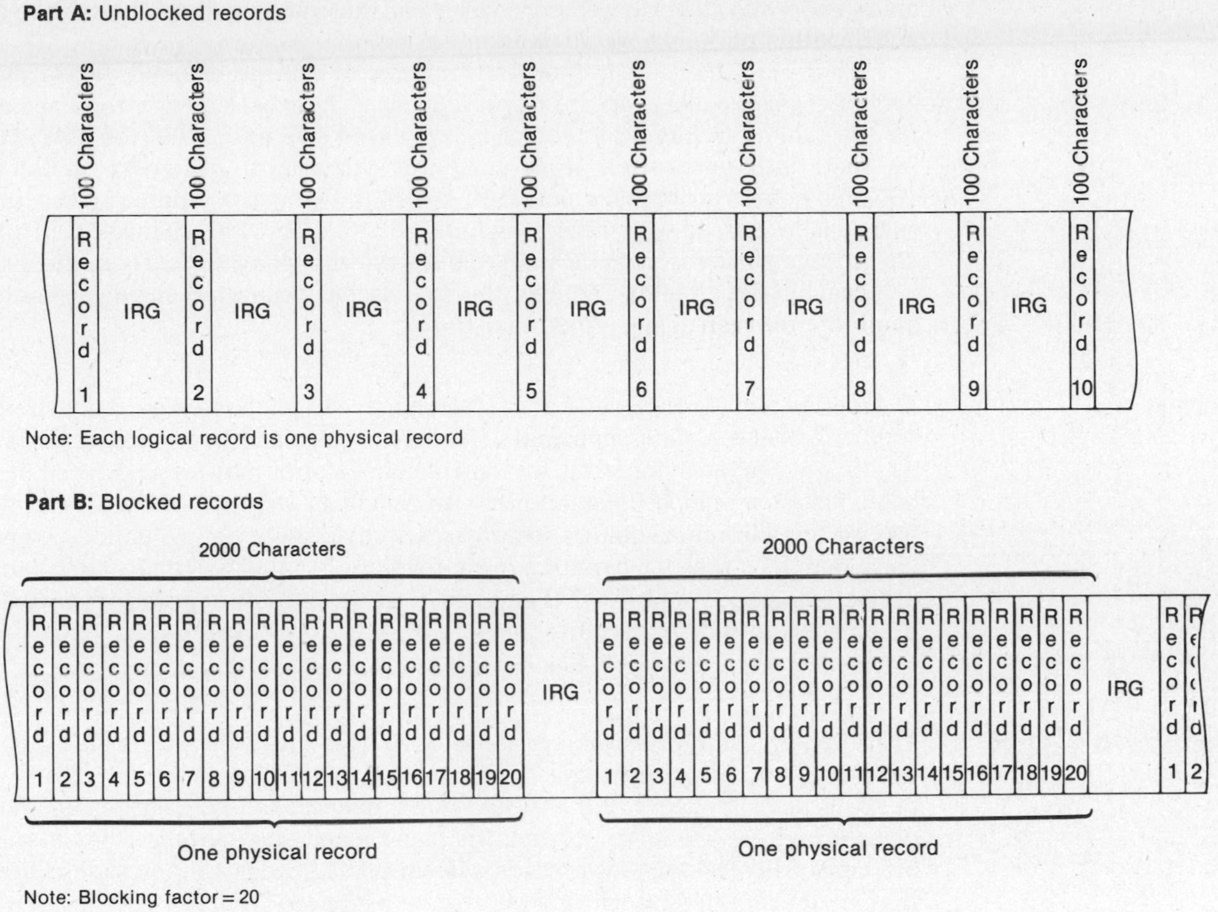

Part A: Unblocked records

Note: Each logical record is one physical record

Part B: Blocked records

Note: Blocking factor = 20

Figure A.9 Unblocked and blocked records

Adams, we must turn to the page on which data about her is listed. There, the logical records for up to five entities may be recorded. Just as a single page of the address book brings five logical records into view, a physical record on a data storage unit usually comprises several logical records. The page or physical record is the minimum amount of data that can be accessed.

A physical record is sometimes called a *record block,* or simply a *block.* The number of logical records present in one physical record, or block, is referred to as the *blocking factor.* If there are five logical records within a physical record (as in the address-book example), the blocking factor is five.

Generally, the larger the blocking factor used for a file, the more efficient the use of the data storage medium. This is because physical records are usually separated by unused space, often termed *inter-record gaps (IRGs)* or *inter-block gaps (IBGs)* on magnetic storage media. With fewer physical records, there is less unused space. Figure A.9 gives a general picture of unblocked and blocked records.

Another advantage of a large blocking factor is improved performance of the storage device. In the case of a tape drive, for example, the reading or writing of longer records means that the device can spend proportionately more time at maximum speed and less time accelerating or decelerating for a given read or write operation. An analogous situation exists in automobile performance. An automobile can move along optimally at cruising speed, but if many stops and starts are required over a given distance, the deceleration and acceleration periods consume additional time.

There is a tradeoff to these advantages of a large blocking factor, however. Larger blocking factors mean increased internal storage requirements for the computer. Since each block is processed as a unit, all of the block must be read into or written from computer storage at once. An unblocked 100-character record uses only 100 internal storage positions. If the same record is processed with a blocking factor of 20, then 2000 (20 times 100) internal storage positions must be available for the complete block. Thus, the use of a large blocking factor reduces the number of computer storage positions available for instructions and other data.

Volume

A lengthy piece of literature or reference material may be published in separate books; a voluminous data file may require multiple tapes or disks for its storage. On the other hand, a group of short stories may all be printed in one book, just as a number of small files can reside on one tape or disk. With data processing storage media, as with books, individual units are called *volumes*. For example, a reel of magnetic tape is considered a tape volume: a disk pack is a disk volume. Two reels of tape used to store one file may be identified as Volume 1 and Volume 2 of the file.

Data Base

Traditionally, data processing systems have been file-oriented. As an example, consider the data processing system of a typical college or university. To prepare payroll checks, the payroll system accesses the employee file. When class schedules are to be printed, the class-scheduling system uses the class-offerings file. The student-records system posts grades to the student file so that grade reports and transcripts can be prepared from it.

Each of these file-oriented systems may be effective in preparing the specific output for which it was designed (payroll checks, class schedules, grade reports, and transcripts). However, most businesses and organizations exist in a dynamic environment; as requirements change, new or modified outputs from data processing systems are needed.

Requests for outputs that require data from multiple file-oriented systems are usually difficult to fulfill. Suppose an administrative official of the college wants to know the average hourly cost of instruction offered to adults registered for night classes. This requires access to the files of three different systems: payroll, class scheduling, and student records. The programmer/ analyst who designs a program to access three files from three different systems may be confronted with incompatibility and complexity problems. For example, the systems may use different computer equipment or the files may be recorded in incompatible formats. As an added complexity, the records within one or more of the files may require rearranging, or sorting, into an appropriate sequence for processing. Efforts to overcome these incompatibility and complexity problems are often expensive or time-consuming.

These limitations of file-oriented systems have led to the development of *data base management systems*. A *data base* may be defined as a collection of data that is fundamental to an enterprise or organization. A data base management system allows an organization's data to be processed as an integrated whole; individual applications share the same data. Figure A.10 pictures the university data processing applications mentioned above as separate file-processing systems and as a data base management system.

ANS COBOL (1974) does not encompass data base processing. The Conference on Data Systems Languages (CODASYL—the group that developed

Part A: File-oriented systems

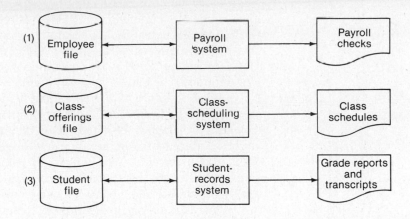

Part B: Data base management system

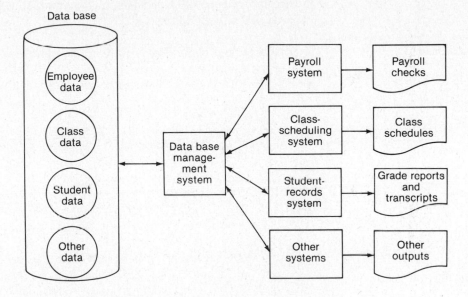

Figure A.10   File-oriented and data base management systems

COBOL) established a Data Base Task Group (DBTG) to define specifications for data base processing with the COBOL language. The specifications are currently in development.

Summary

Data processing storage media provide *character positions* for the storage of data. One or more continuous character positions used for the storage of a data element is termed a *field*. A collection of fields relating to one data entity is referred to as a *logical record*. An assemblage of logical records stored in a given physical area is called a *physical record*. Each storage module, such as a magnetic tape reel or magnetic disk pack, is known as a *volume*. A collection of logical records is a *file*. Fields, logical records, and files may be considered logical collections of data. Character positions, physical records, and volumes are physical assemblages.

Logical Classifications

Fields have the following attributes: data class, field length, and field type. *Data class* may be either numeric, alphabetic, or alphanumeric. *Field length* may range from a single character position to many. *Field type* may be either indicative or control. *Indicative* fields contain descriptive, reference, or quantitative data regarding an entity. *Control* fields perform identification functions. A control field that uniquely identifies a logical record and relates it to the data entity is known as a *key* field.

A *logical record* is a collection of fields related to the same data entity and arranged in a prescribed format. It must contain a key field to identify it. Logical records may be either *fixed* or *variable* in length. Fixed-length fields and records are predominantly used. However, where data does not conform to fixed-length formats, variable-length records may be designed. A record is variable in length if it (1) contains a variable number of occurrences of fixed-length segments, or (2) contains one or more variable-length fields.

A *file* is a defined collection of logical records.

Physical Classifications

A *character position* is the smallest addressable unit of data on a storage medium. A *physical record* is one or more logical records accessed as a unit. Individual units of data processing storage media that hold multiple physical records are called *volumes*.

Data Base

A *data base* is a collection of data fundamental to an enterprise or organization. A *data base management system* is a software aid that allows the data of an organization to be processed as an integrated whole.

CHAPTER 2

WRITING A COBOL PROGRAM: IDENTIFICATION, ENVIRONMENT, and DATA DIVISIONS

You should now have (1) a general understanding of the program development process, (2) knowledge of the basic structure of a COBOL program, and (3) familiarity with the COBOL coding form. Now, let's write a simple COBOL program.

In this and the next chapter, we will be concentrating on the coding phase of program development. We will consider again our Silicon Valley Manufacturing Company employee address list application.

Application background

Ms. Fast often used the employee address list produced periodically by the EMP-LIST program. After a few months, she decided it would be helpful to also have the employee's date-of-hire printed on each line. So she met with Titus to explain her new requirement.

Titus prepared a print chart for the revised report. He also modified the pseudocode to reflect the logic necessary to present the date-of-hire on the report. Titus was then ready to modify the COBOL program to produce the revised report.

From now on, you—rather than Titus—will be writing programs. This text will explain how to write them. Thus, the program to produce the revised employee address list is to be treated as a totally new program, which we will call the employee report—or EMP-RPT for short—to distinguish it from Titus' employee address list (EMP-LIST) program. Before starting to code, we should be certain that the programming specifications and design documentation are complete.

1. *Specification-phase documentation:*
   Programming specifications: The programming specifications for the employee report appear in Figure 2.1.

   System flowchart: The system flowchart is depicted in Figure 2.2.

   Print chart: The employee report print chart is shown in Figure 2.3.

   Input record layout: The format of the name-and-address records has not changed. It is depicted again for reference in Figure 2.4.

2. *Design-phase documentation:*
   Structure chart: The employee report structure chart is shown in Figure 2.5. Since the revision to the employee address list does not require any significant logic changes, this structure chart is the same (except for program name) as the employee address list structure chart shown in Chapter 1.

   Pseudocode and program flowchart: The employee report pseudocode is shown in Figure 2.6, the program flowchart in Figure 2.7.

COBOL format notation

In this and the following chapters, we look closely at the precise syntactical format of COBOL entries. A standard format notation has been developed to present the syntactical rules and requirements. The format notation is ex-

PROGRAMMING SPECIFICATIONS

Program name: EMPLOYEE REPORT   Program ID: EMP—RPT

Program description
   This program prints an employee address report
   from input employee name—and—address records.

Input file(s)
   Employee name—and—address file

Output file(s)
   Employee address report

List of program operations
   1. Read each input employee name—and—address
      record.
   2. For each record, print the following fields on
      the employee address list in accordance with
      the format shown on the print chart:
         Employee name
         Employee address
         Employee city—state—zip
         Employee date—of—hire
   3. Double—space each printed line.

Figure 2.1   Programming specifications: Employee report program

SYSTEM FLOWCHART

Program name: EMPLOYEE REPORT   Program ID: EMP—RPT

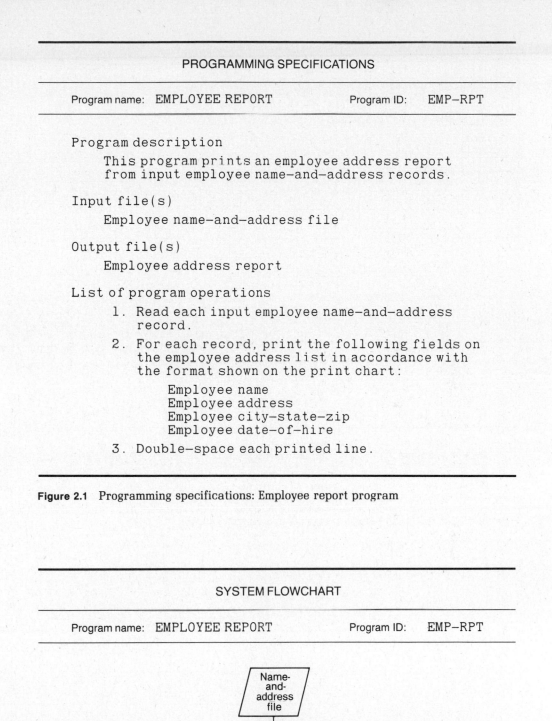

Figure 2.2   System flowchart: Employee report program

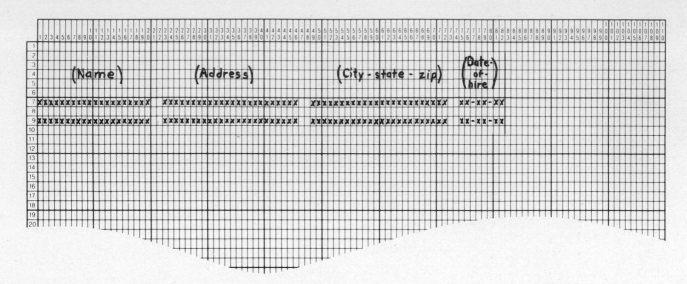

Figure 2.3 Print chart: Employee report program

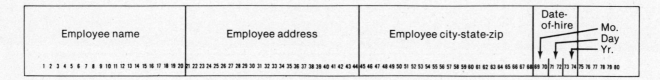

Figure 2.4 Record layout: Employee name-and-address record

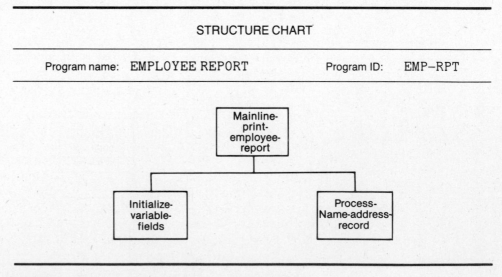

Figure 2.5 Structure chart: Employee report program

Program name: EMPLOYEE REPORT   Program ID: EMP–RPT

Mainline–print–employee–report module
    1. Open the files.
    2. Perform Initialize–variable–fields module.
    3. Read the first employee name–and–address
        record.   *parts Inventory record*
    4. Perform Process–name–address–record module
        until no more records. *part inventory record*
    5. Close the files.
    6. Stop the run.

Initialize–variable–fields module
    1. Set the end–of–file indicator to "No".

Process–name–address–record module
    1. Clear the output line area.
    2. Move the input Employee–name to the output line
        Employee–name.
    3. Move the input Employee–address to the output
        line Employee–address
    4. Move the input Employee–city–state–zip to the
        output line Employee–city–state–zip.
    5. Move the input Employee–date–of–hire to the
        output line Employee–date–of–hire.
    6. Write the employee output line (double–
        spaced).
    7. Read the next input record.

Figure 2.6 Pseudocode: Employee report program

plained in Figure 2.8. (It is also printed on the inside back cover of this text for quick reference.)

Using the Coding Form

First, the programmer fills in the COBOL coding form heading information as shown in Figure 2.9. Then we assign a page number of 001 to this first page of coding. Some programmers start with page 000; others start with page 005 or 010. Those who start with 005 or 010 usually increment each page number by a value of 5 or 10, so that the second page number is sequenced 010 or 020, respectively. This numbering approach provides a range of numbers between each assigned page number so that additional lines of coding can be inserted between existing lines if necessary. Remember though, the exact value of the page number doesn't really matter as long as each is greater in value than the preceding one.

We will use most or all of the 20 lines of page 001. We can indicate to the data-entry operator that the first three digits of the sequence numbers are

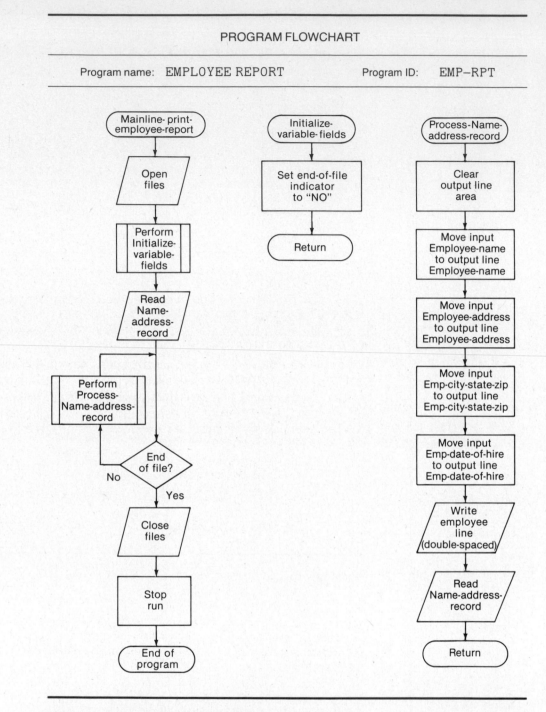

PROGRAM FLOWCHART

Program name: EMPLOYEE REPORT   Program ID: EMP–RPT

Mainline- print-employee-report
- Open files
- Perform Initialize-variable-fields
- Read Name-address-record
- Perform Process-Name-address-record
- End of file? — No (loop back) / Yes
- Close files
- Stop run
- End of program

Initialize-variable-fields
- Set end-of-file indicator to "NO"
- Return

Process-Name-address-record
- Clear output line area
- Move input Employee-name to output line Employee-name
- Move input Employee-address to output line Employee-address
- Move input Emp-city-state-zip to output line Emp-city-state-zip
- Move input Emp-date-of-hire to output line Emp-date-of-hire
- Write employee line (double-spaced)
- Read Name-address-record
- Return

Figure 2.7   Program flowchart: Employee report program

repeated on each line by drawing a "squiggly" line from the first entry of this data to the last. Drawing a squiggly line is like using ditto marks—but it's faster. It's a good idea to repeat the data at the end of the line to give the data-entry operator a chance to doublecheck the characters.

In position 6 (the rightmost digit of the sequence number), we'll place a zero and use a squiggly line to indicate that each of the numbered lines should end in zero. Position 6 could be left blank, but line numbers are easier to read when all three digits are always present.

Notation	Example	Meaning
Uppercase words underlined	<u>ADD</u>	Required reserved word
Uppercase words (not underlined)	IS	Optional reserved word
Lowercase words	identifier	Word or entry must be supplied by programmer
Brackets	[ROUNDED]	Optional feature
Braces	{ BEFORE / AFTER }	Alternatives
Ellipsis	. . .	Repetition may occur at user option
Punctuation		
Period	.	Required period
Comma	,	Optional punctuation
Semicolon	;	Optional punctuation

Figure 2.8 COBOL format notation

In the identification area, we'll write the abbreviation EMP-RPT. The squiggly line beneath it indicates that the identification should be repeated on each line of the program coding.

When programmers enter their programs using a source entry utility, they may be less concerned about line numbers and identification entries because the utility can automatically handle those functions. (Often in such cases, the identification area is used instead to record the date changed for lines of modified code.) Indeed, many experienced programmers using source entry

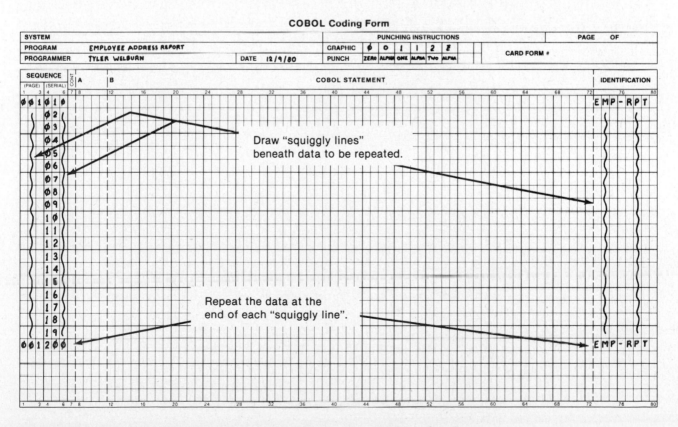

Figure 2.9 Heading, sequence, and identification entries on the COBOL coding form

utilities do not write the program on a coding form but instead key the program directly from their design documentation. For beginning COBOL programmers, however, it's usually helpful to fill out the coding form completely as we've described.

Now that the heading, sequence, and identification areas of the coding form are completed we can begin the actual program code. In this chapter, the IDENTIFICATION, ENVIRONMENT, and DATA DIVISION coding will be discussed. The next chapter will cover the PROCEDURE DIVISION.

Writing the IDENTIFICATION DIVISION

IDENTIFICATION DIVISION Header

The IDENTIFICATION DIVISION format is shown in Figure 2.10. We will explain each of the entries in detail.

Notice that the words IDENTIFICATION and DIVISION are underlined in the format notation. This means that they are required reserved words. A period follows the word DIVISION. If a period is shown in the format notation, it is required for the COBOL entry. Division headers are always area A entries, so they start in position 8 of the COBOL coding form.

When the IDENTIFICATION DIVISION header is written, it should appear exactly as shown in Figure 2.11. Observe that there is a blank space between the two words and a period immediately following the second word. All punctuation symbols—periods, hyphens, parentheses, and so on—occupy full character positions on the COBOL coding form.

PROGRAM-ID Paragraph

The first paragraph in the IDENTIFICATION DIVISION is the PROGRAM-ID paragraph. Like the division header, all paragraph headers are area A entries. All the words in the paragraph headers of the IDENTIFICATION DIVISION are reserved words. Each paragraph header is followed by a period. After the paragraph header, the programmer supplies the program-name. A name supplied by the programmer is called a user-defined word. We are naming this program EMP-RPT. Thus, the PROGRAM-ID paragraph is written as shown in

Format:

```
        IDENTIFICATION DIVISION.
        PROGRAM-ID. program-name.
       [ AUTHOR. [comment-entry] . . . ]
       [ INSTALLATION. [comment-entry] . . . ]
       [ DATE-WRITTEN. [comment-entry] . . . ]
       [ DATE-COMPILED. [comment-entry] . . . ]
       [ SECURITY. [comment-entry] . . . ]
```

Example:

```
001010 IDENTIFICATION DIVISION.
001020 PROGRAM-ID.      EMP-RPT.
001030 AUTHOR.          WELBURN.
001040 INSTALLATION.    SILICON VALLEY MANUFACTURING COMPANY.
001050 DATE-WRITTEN.    DEC  8,1980.
001060 DATE-COMPILED.   DEC  8,1980.
001070 SECURITY.        NONE.
001080*
001090*
001100*              THIS PROGRAM READS NAME-AND-ADDRESS RECORDS AND
001110*              PRINTS AN EMPLOYEE REPORT.
```

Figure 2.10 IDENTIFICATION DIVISION format

Format:

IDENTIFICATION DIVISION.

Example:

SEQUENCE		C O N T	A	B		COBOL STATEMENT															IDENTIFICATION	
(PAGE)	(SERIAL)																					
1	3	4	6	7	8	12	16	20	24	28	32	36	40	44	48	52	56	60	64	68	72	76	80

```
0 0 1 0 1 0   I D E N T I F I C A T I O N   D I V I S I O N .                    E M P - R P T
```

Figure 2.11 IDENTIFICATION DIVISION header example

Figure 2.12. Remember that the paragraph-name PROGRAM-ID contains a hyphen and must be followed by a period. Thus far, two types of COBOL words have been introduced: reserved words and user-defined words.

Reserved words

The words that have predefined meanings in the COBOL language are called *reserved words*. For example, when the COBOL compiler encounters the word PROGRAM-ID, it expects the next sentence to contain the program-name. Because reserved words have predefined meanings, they cannot be used as user-defined words. If the programmer tries to use a reserved word as a user-defined word the compiler still treats the word as reserved. That is, it misinterprets the programmer's intended meaning for the entry and issues a diagnostic message.

A complete list of the 308 COBOL reserved words is printed on the page facing the inside back cover of this text.

User-defined words

A *user-defined word* is created by the programmer in accordance with certain rules. Although there are seventeen categories of user-defined words, we need only be concerned with three types for the EMP-RPT program: program-names, data-names, and procedure-names. A *program-name*—such as EMP-RPT—is used to refer to the program as a whole. *Data-names* are used to refer to files, records, and data items (fields and subfields). *Procedure-names* are used to refer to sections or paragraphs within the PROCEDURE DIVISION.

A user-defined word must:

- Be composed only of alphabetic characters (A through Z), digits (0 through 9), and hyphens (-)

Format:

PROGRAM-ID. program-name.

Example:

SEQUENCE		C O N T	A	B		COBOL STATEMENT															IDENTIFICATION	
(PAGE)	(SERIAL)																					
1	3	4	6	7	8	12	16	20	24	28	32	36	40	44	48	52	56	60	64	68	72	76	80

```
0 0 1 0 2 0   P R O G R A M - I D .       E M P - R P T .                         E M P - R P T
```

Figure 2.12 PROGRAM-ID paragraph example

- Contain at least one letter. (Actually procedure-names may be composed entirely of digits. However, such a procedure name would be a poor choice, since it would be less meaningful than a name containing descriptive words. Also, the next revision of the ANS COBOL standard will probably require at least one letter in all user-defined words).
- Not exceed 30 characters
- Not begin or end with a hyphen
- Not contain any spaces within the word (that is, no embedded blanks are allowed)
- Not be the same as a reserved word

Figure 2.13 gives examples of valid and invalid user-defined words.

When creating a user-defined word, the programmer can let imagination run wild and use any sort of esoteric or nonsensical name, or cryptic abbreviations can be used to save handprinting and keying time. However, the programmer should strive to use a word that is meaningful and descriptive. That is, a field such as employee-pay-rate should be named PAY-RATE or RATE-OF-PAY rather than, say, ALPHA-DELTA, RTPY, or K3.

The hyphen serves a particular function in user-defined words and, for that matter, in certain reserved words. COBOL words are strings of characters delimited by one or more blanks. Often, two or more English words are used to form one COBOL word. If a space were left between the English words TELEPHONE NUMBER, the COBOL compiler would read the name as two words instead of one and would flag it as an invalid user-defined word. There are two errors in this example: (1) an embedded blank between the two English words and (2) an improper use of the reserved word NUMBER. If the words were written without the blank—TELEPHONENUMBER—a valid user-defined word would be formed, but it would be difficult to read and interpret. Writing the words with a hyphen—TELEPHONE-NUMBER—makes the name a single COBOL word and maintains readability.

The reserved word PROGRAM-ID is an example of a reserved word that contains a hyphen.

If we want to use meaningful and readable names as user-defined words, why didn't we name our program EMPLOYEE-REPORT instead of the abbreviated EMP-RPT? There is no doubt that the former name is more readable and understandable than the latter. We have just emphasized that meaningful and descriptive user-defined words should be used. The word EMPLOYEE-REPORT would fulfill all the user-defined word requirements: it is not a reserved word; it is composed of suitable characters; it contains at least one letter; it does not exceed 30 characters; it does not begin or end with a hyphen; and it does not

Valid user-defined words	Invalid user-defined words	Reason invalid
NUMBER-1-GRADE	#1-GRADE	# not allowed
GROSS-PAY	GROSS.PAY	. not allowed
GROSSPAY	GROSS PAY	Cannot contain embedded blank
GROSS-PAYROLL	-GROSS-PAYROLL	Cannot begin with hyphen
2ND-QUARTER-EARNINGS	2ND-QUARTER-EARNINGS-	Cannot end with hyphen
YTD-SOCIAL-SECURITY-TAX	YEAR-TO-DATE-SOCIAL-SECURITY-TAX	Cannot contain over 30 characters
X100	100 (as a data name)	Must contain at least one alphabetic character

Figure 2.13 Valid and invalid user-defined words

PROGRAM-ID	Truncated by the operating system
ACCOUNTS-PAYABLE	ACCOUNTS
ACCOUNTS-RECEIVABLE	ACCOUNTS
AC-PAYABLE	AC0PAYAB
AC-RECEIVABLE	AC0RECEI
EMP-LIST	EMP0LIST
PAYROLL-COMPUTATIONS	PAYROLL0
PAYROLL-REPORT	PAYROLL0
PAY-REPORT	PAY0REPO
PAY-COMPUTATIONS	PAY0COMP

Note: Many operating systems do not allow hyphens in program-names. The IBM OS Full ANS COBOL Compiler converts hyphens to zeros as shown.

Figure 2.14 Truncated program-names

contain embedded blanks. Then, why not name this program EMPLOYEE-REPORT?

An entry specified as a program-name is used not only as a COBOL user-defined word but also by the computer operating system to identify the program when it is stored in the computer's memory or on tape or disk. Since COBOL was designed to be English-like and to encourage good program documentation, the maximum length of a user-defined word was established at a rather generous value of 30 characters. However, most operating systems accommodate a much lower maximum number of characters (usually eight or so) in a program-name. If the COBOL programmer chooses a program-name that contains more characters than the operating system can handle, the program-name will usually be shortened, or truncated, when it is used by the operating system. Figure 2.14 shows some truncation examples.

If two program-names begin with the same sequence of characters, they may not be unique after truncation. Suppose that Silicon Valley Manufacturing has an operating system that allows up to eight characters in a program-name. If it had programs named EMPLOYEE-REPORT and EMPLOYEE-PAYROLL, after truncation the operating system would refer to both of them by the same eight-character name: EMPLOYEE. This could lead to confusion. So, even though COBOL allows program-names up to 30 characters in length, they should be limited to a length that is compatible with operating-system requirements.

AUTHOR Paragraph

Notice that the format in Figure 2.15 shows the AUTHOR paragraph enclosed in brackets. This means that it is an optional paragraph. If included, a comment-entry should be written after the paragraph header AUTHOR.

Although most words in a COBOL program are either reserved words or user-defined words, certain entries in the IDENTIFICATION DIVISION are classifed as *comment-entries*. Specifically, entries following the AUTHOR, INSTALLATION, DATE-WRITTEN, DATE-COMPILED, and SECURITY paragraph headers are comment-entries. A comment-entry may be any combination of characters acceptable to the computer. Thus, the rules for user-defined words need not be adhered to when forming comment-entries.

There is only one required paragraph in the IDENTIFICATION DIVISION: PROGRAM-ID. A minimum IDENTIFICATION DIVISION contains only the paragraph header and the PROGRAM-ID paragraph. However, the optional paragraphs provide useful documentation. They should normally be included.

Format:

[<u>AUTHOR</u>. [comment-entry] . . .]

Example:

SEQUENCE (PAGE) 1–3 (SERIAL) 4–6	CONT 7	A 8	B 12	COBOL STATEMENT	IDENTIFICATION 73–80

```
ØØ1Ø3Ø AUTHOR.       TYLER WELBURN.                                    EMP-RPT
```
or
```
ØØ1Ø3Ø AUTHOR.       TYLER KEITH WELBURN.
```
or
```
ØØ1Ø3Ø AUTHOR.       TYLER K. WELBURN.
```
or
```
ØØ1Ø3Ø AUTHOR.       TY WELBURN.
```
or
```
ØØ1Ø3Ø AUTHOR.       T. K. WELBURN.
```
or
```
ØØ1Ø3Ø AUTHOR.       WELBURN.
```

Figure 2.15 AUTHOR paragraph examples

INSTALLATION Paragraph

This optional paragraph is used to specify the organization or company data processing installation that will use the program. An example is shown in Figure 2.16.

DATE-WRITTEN Paragraph

The date when the COBOL program was written is recorded in this optional paragraph. The date may be expressed in numeric or word form, as shown in Figure 2.17. It often takes longer than one day to write a COBOL program. Some programmers record the day the program was started. Others just indicate the month and year.

DATE-COMPILED Paragraph

The date when the COBOL program was compiled is placed in this optional paragraph. Although the compilation date may be written by the programmer as a comment-entry, it usually is not. When the programmer writes the IDENTIFICATION DIVISION, he or she probably doesn't know exactly when the program will be compiled. The COBOL compiler will insert the DATE-COMPILED comment-entry if there is none. So, this paragraph is usually written without a comment-entry, as shown in Figure 2.18.

Format:

[<u>INSTALLATION</u>. [comment-entry] . . .]

Example:

SEQUENCE (PAGE) 1–3 (SERIAL) 4–6	CONT 7	A 8	B 12	COBOL STATEMENT	IDENTIFICATION 73–80

```
ØØ1Ø4Ø INSTALLATION. SILICON VALLEY MANUFACTURING COMPANY.              EMP-RPT
```
or
```
ØØ1Ø4Ø INSTALLATION. S.V. MFG. CO.                                      EMP-RPT
```

Figure 2.16 INSTALLATION paragraph examples

Format:

[DATE-WRITTEN. [comment-entry] . . .]

Example:

```
001050 DATE-WRITTEN.  DEC  8, 1980.                                EMP-RPT
                                  or
001050 DATE-WRITTEN.  DEC. 8, 1980.                                EMP-RPT
                                  or
001050 DATE-WRITTEN.  DECEMBER 8, 1980.                            EMP-RPT
                                  or
001050 DATE-WRITTEN.  12/08/80.                                    EMP-RPT
                                  or
001050 DATE-WRITTEN.  12-08-80.                                    EMP-RPT
                                  or
001050 DATE-WRITTEN.  DECEMBER, 1980.                              EMP-RPT
                                  or
001050 DATE-WRITTEN.  12/80.                                       EMP-RPT
```

Figure 2.17 DATE-WRITTEN paragraph examples

Of all optional paragraphs in this division, DATE-COMPILED is perhaps of greatest importance. When programmers are testing and debugging programs, they usually accumulate a collection of program listings. Inclusion of the DATE-COMPILED paragraph helps identify the most recent version. (Many operating systems also print the date of the compilation at the top of the first of every page of the program listing.)

SECURITY Paragraph

This optional paragraph is often omitted. It does have two occasional uses, though. One is to indicate a governmental security classification: UNCLASSIFIED, CLASSIFIED, SECRET, TOP SECRET, and so on. Another use is to provide copyright or trade-secret protection information. Figure 2.19 provides examples.

Recap of the IDENTIFICATION DIVISION

The IDENTIFICATION DIVISION has six paragraphs, only one of which—PROGRAM-ID—is required. Each paragraph header starts in area A of the COBOL coding form. The entries following the paragraph header are area B entries.

Format:

[DATE-COMPILED. [comment-entry] . . .]

Example:

```
001060 DATE-COMPILED.                                              EMP-RPT
```

Figure 2.18 DATE-COMPILED paragraph example

Format:

[<u>SECURITY</u>. [comment-entry] . . .]

Example:

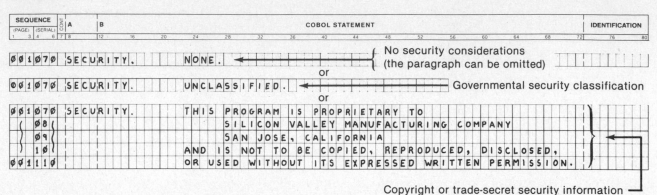

Figure 2.19 SECURITY paragraph examples

In addition to the paragraphs and their comment-entries, many COBOL programmers write other comment lines that provide brief descriptions of program functions. Such comments are usually placed after the PROGRAM-ID paragraph or at the end of the IDENTIFICATION DIVISION, as shown in Figure 2.20. (Comment lines must contain an asterisk in position 7 to inform the COBOL compiler that these are comments and not COBOL language entries.)

Spacing and Punctuation of COBOL Words

As mentioned before, all COBOL statement entries may be classified as either area A entries or area B entries. Area A entries must start in position 8. Area B entries cannot reside in area A (positions 8-11); they may begin anywhere in area B (positions 12-72), providing the following fundamental COBOL punctuation rules are adhered to:

- There must be at least one space between words. More than one space may be used when desired.

Figure 2.20 IDENTIFICATION DIVISION for EMP-RPT program

- When a period is shown in the COBOL format notation, it is required in the program.
- Whenever a period, comma, or semicolon is used, it must be followed by a space.

At least one blank space should follow the period that ends the paragraph header before an area B entry is coded. But, for neatness and readability, the programmer should vertically align the program-name and comment-entries of the IDENTIFICATION DIVISION. In the examples from the EMP-RPT program, all area B entries begin in position 23. COBOL programmers handle horizontal line spacing for the IDENTIFICATION DIVISION in various ways. Figure 2.21 shows some examples. The horizontal line spacing for statements in other divisions will be discussed when those statements are covered.

Although commas and semicolons may be used as punctuation in a COBOL program, the programmer should refrain from using them. If the program is written with proper organization and style, such punctuation will contribute little to its readability. On the other hand, when commas and semicolons are handprinted or printed on a computer printer with a worn ribbon, they may be

Part A: No horizontal line spacing style considerations (syntactically correct but somewhat difficult to read)

```
001010  IDENTIFICATION DIVISION.
  020  PROGRAM-ID. EMP-RPT.
  030  AUTHOR. WELBURN.
  040  INSTALLATION. SILICON VALLEY MFG CO.
  050  DATE-WRITTEN. DEC 8, 1980.
  060  DATE-COMPILED.
  070  SECURITY. NONE.
```

Part B: Separate line for each entry (probably a little easier to read but inconsistent since the compiler will place DATE-COMPILED on the paragraph-header line)

```
001010  IDENTIFICATION DIVISION.
  020  PROGRAM-ID.
  030      EMP-RPT.
  040  AUTHOR.
  050      WELBURN.
  060  INSTALLATION.
  070      SILICON VALLEY MFG CO.
  080  DATE-WRITTEN.
  090      DEC 8, 1980.
  100  DATE-COMPILED.
  110  SECURITY.
  120      NONE.
```

Part C: Vertically aligned program-name and comment-entries (easiest to read; this example is aligned to position 23 because the compiler to be used will start the DATE-COMPILED entry there)

```
001010  IDENTIFICATION DIVISION.
  020  PROGRAM-ID.      EMP-RPT.
  030  AUTHOR.          WELBURN.
  040  INSTALLATION.    SILICON VALLEY MFG CO.
  050  DATE-WRITTEN.    DEC 8, 1980.
  060  DATE-COMPILED.
  070  SECURITY.        NONE.
```

Figure 2.21 IDENTIFICATION DIVISION horizontal line spacing

Part A: Blank comment line (∗ in position 7)

SEQUENCE											

SEQUENCE (PAGE) (SERIAL)	CONT	A	B	COBOL STATEMENT	IDENTIFICATION
1 3 4 6	7	8	12 16 20 24 28 32 36 40 44 48 52 56 60 64 68	72 76 80

Ø Ø Ø Ø 1 Ø ∗ ... E M P - R P T

Part B: Blank statement line (blank in position 7, area A, and Area B)

Ø Ø Ø Ø 1 Ø ... E M P - R P T

Part C: Page-eject line (/ in position 7)

Ø Ø Ø Ø 1 Ø / ... E M P - R P T

Figure 2.22 Vertical line spacing on program listings

confused with periods. The comma and semicolon do not affect the COBOL program, but a period usually does. Thus, any gains in readability that the comma or semicolon might provide are outweighed by the risk of their misinterpretation by the programmer or data-entry operator.

Vertical Spacing of COBOL Lines

Vertically spacing COBOL lines to separate different parts of the program also enhances program neatness and readability. It is probably of lesser value than indentation, but it can add clarity by highlighting areas of coding.

Programmers handle vertical line spacing of COBOL programs by one of the following techniques (see Figure 2.22).

- Blank comment lines, in which an asterisk is placed in position 7 and the rest of area A and area B are left blank.

- Blank statement lines, which usually contain a line number but are blank in position 7, area A, and area B.

- Page-eject lines, which cause the COBOL program listing to be advanced to the next page—a page-eject line has a diagonal slash (/) in position 7.

Of these three methods, the blank comment line is recommended. Actually, the blank statement lines perhaps provide a "cleaner" look, but they don't always work as planned. Some COBOL compilers and source entry utilities have options to remove entirely blank lines. Due to programmer error or oversight, all the vertical spacing lines may thus be removed from the program. An advantage of the blank comment line is that it is more efficient for the COBOL compiler. (When the compiler encounters the asterisk in position 7 of a line, it knows that the line will not contain any COBOL code entries, and it can immediately proceed to the next line. Use of the wholly blank statement line, though, requires that the compiler scan the line, position by position, looking for COBOL code.) The page-eject technique can provide a generous expanse of white space, but it tends to cause a small portion of code to be placed on each printout page. This not only wastes paper and makes program listings bulky, but it also separates the material to such an extent that it's more difficult for the eye to scan the text. This, in turn, may make it more difficult to comprehend the program.

Regardless of the method used for vertical spacing, there are a multitude of ideas about where and how much "white space" should be left in a program. You can use your own discretion or follow the guidelines suggested in Figure 2.23, as we will do in this text.

	Number of blank comment lines	
Entry	Preceding	Following
Division headers	3 †	
Section headers	2	1
FD's	1	
01-level record descriptions	1	
PROCEDURE DIVISION paragraph headers	2	1

† Except IDENTIFICATION DIVISION

Figure 2.23 Guidelines for using blank comment lines

Writing the ENVIRONMENT DIVISION

Whereas most of a COBOL program is machine-independent, the coding of the ENVIRONMENT DIVISION is dependent upon the compiler, computer, and/or operating system being used. Each company supplying a COBOL compiler assigns words, called *system-names*, to specific computer models, input-output equipment, and other operating-environment features. The system-names chosen by one supplier usually differ from those chosen by another. This somewhat complicates discussion of the ENVIRONMENT DIVISION because many different vendors supply COBOL compilers.

In this text, we'll use the system-names for a COBOL compiler commonly encountered in large-scale data processing installations: the IBM OS/VS COBOL Compiler.

Regardless of the compiler used, the ENVIRONMENT DIVISION does have a standard format. The format shown in Figure 2.24 comprises two sections: CONFIGURATION and INPUT-OUTPUT.

ENVIRONMENT DIVISION Header

The ENVIRONMENT DIVISION header format is shown in Figure 2.25. The words ENVIRONMENT DIVISION are underlined in the format to indicate that this entry is required. It must start in area A and a period must follow the words.

CONFIGURATION SECTION Header

As shown in Figure 2.26 the CONFIGURATION SECTION header is another required entry that starts in area A and must be terminated by a period.

SOURCE-COMPUTER paragraph

This paragraph defines the computer that will be used to compile the COBOL program. Following the paragraph header is the system-name for the computer. A computer system-name is called a *computer-name*. Figure 2.27 shows the computer-name IBM-370. (If you are using a different computer, consult your computer's COBOL reference manual to obtain the appropriate computer-name.)

OBJECT-COMPUTER paragraph

The computer that will execute the compiled program is defined in this required paragraph. Usually, the same computer is used for compilation and execution. If so, the SOURCE-COMPUTER and OBJECT-COMPUTER computer-name entries are the same. This is true for the EMP-RPT program, so IBM-370 is repeated, as shown in Figure 2.28. (Again, refer to your computer's COBOL reference manual if you are using a different computer.)

Format:

ENVIRONMENT DIVISION.

CONFIGURATION SECTION.

SOURCE-COMPUTER. computer-name.

OBJECT-COMPUTER. computer-name.

[INPUT-OUTPUT SECTION.

FILE-CONTROL.

SELECT file-name

ASSIGN TO implementor-name.]

Example:

```
002010*
002020*
002030*
002040 ENVIRONMENT DIVISION.
002050*
002060*
002070 CONFIGURATION SECTION.
002080*
002090 SOURCE-COMPUTER.   IBM-370.
002100 OBJECT-COMPUTER.   IBM-370.
002110*
002120*
002130 INPUT-OUTPUT SECTION.
002140*
002150 FILE-CONTROL.
002160     SELECT NAME-ADDRESS-FILE-IN
002170         ASSIGN TO UT-S-INFILE.
002180     SELECT EMPLOYEE-REPORT-OUT
002190         ASSIGN TO UT-S-PRTFILE.
```

Figure 2.24 ENVIRONMENT DIVISION format

Format:

ENVIRONMENT DIVISION.

Example:

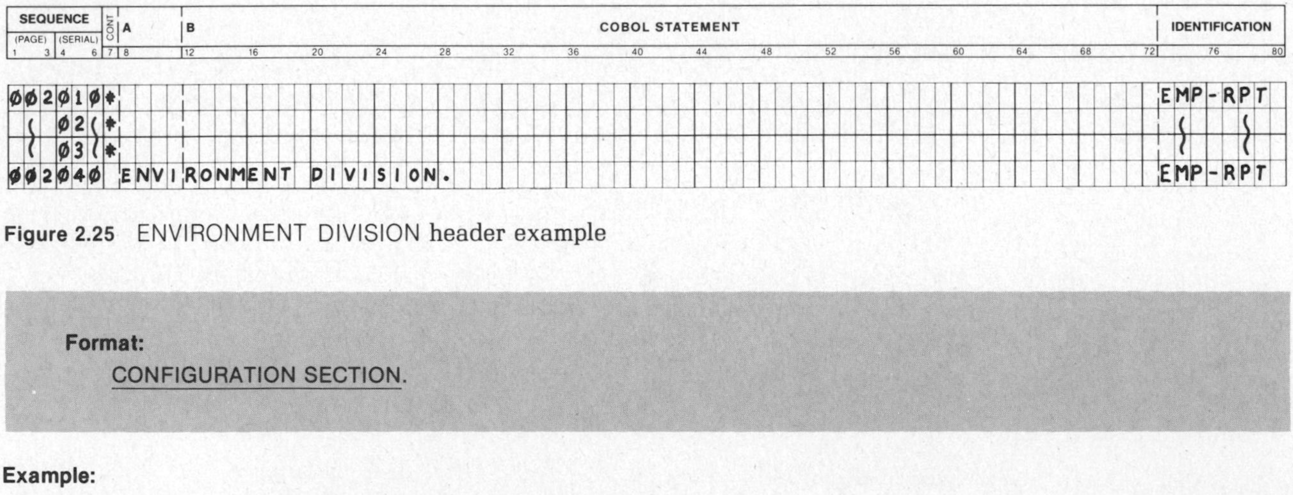

Figure 2.25 ENVIRONMENT DIVISION header example

Format:

CONFIGURATION SECTION.

Example:

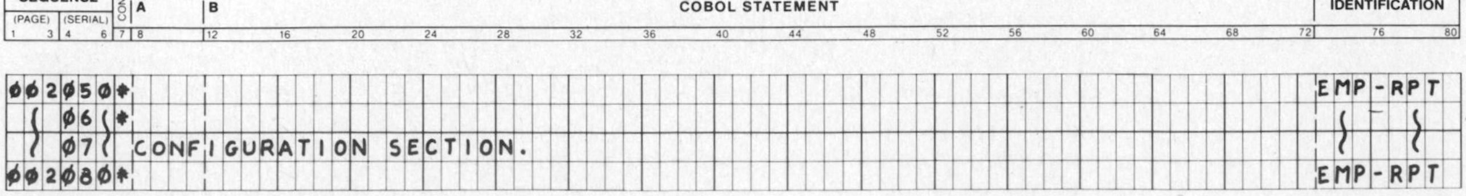

Figure 2.26 CONFIGURATION SECTION header example

Format:

SOURCE-COMPUTER. computer-name.

Example:

SEQUENCE		CONT	A	B	COBOL STATEMENT	IDENTIFICATION
(PAGE)	(SERIAL)					
1 3	4 6	7 8		12 16 20 24 28 32 36 40 44 48 52 56 60 64 68 72		76 80

```
002090  SOURCE-COMPUTER.  IBM-370.                              EMP-RPT
```

Figure 2.27 SOURCE-COMPUTER paragraph example

Format:

OBJECT-COMPUTER. computer-name.

Example:

SEQUENCE		CONT	A	B	COBOL STATEMENT	IDENTIFICATION
(PAGE)	(SERIAL)					
1 3	4 6	7 8		12 16 20 24 28 32 36 40 44 48 52 56 60 64 68 72		76 80

```
002100  OBJECT-COMPUTER.  IBM-370.                              EMP-RPT
```

Figure 2.28 OBJECT-COMPUTER paragraph example

INPUT-OUTPUT SECTION Header

The INPUT-OUTPUT SECTION defines the input and output files to be processed by the program. Although the format notation of Figure 2.29 shows this as an optional section, it is required if the program reads input files or writes output files. Since most COBOL programs process files, this section is practically always required.

FILE-CONTROL paragraph

The function of this paragraph is to associate each COBOL file with the type of input-output device to be used by the program. Figure 2.30 illustrates this relationship. For each file the program uses, a SELECT statement is required. We need only be concerned here with a minimal SELECT statement, as shown in Figure 2.31. It has two clauses: SELECT and ASSIGN. The SELECT clause contains the user-defined COBOL file-name. The ASSIGN clause specifies the particular input-output device used for the file. Our EMP-RPT program has two files, so we need two SELECT statements.

Notice that SELECT statements are area B entries. So, to write the SELECT statement for the input file, the word SELECT is written starting in position 12 and followed by a user-defined word for the file name. We have named the input file NAME-ADDRESS-FILE-IN. After the file-name, the reserved word ASSIGN is followed by what is called an *implementor-name*. The implementor-name is another type of system-name. We have specified the implementor-name UT-S-INFILE, which conforms to the implementor-name requirements for the compiler we are using.

Observe that the SELECT and ASSIGN clause have been written on separate lines. This is in keeping with a COBOL style consideration: place only one sentence, statement, clause, or phrase on each coding line. Following this convention makes programs easier to modify (since fewer words appear on

Format:

[<u>INPUT-OUTPUT SECTION</u>.]

Example:

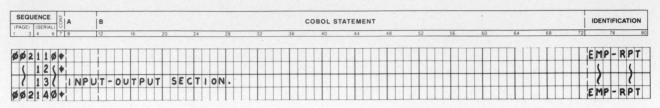

Figure 2.29 INPUT-OUTPUT SECTION header example

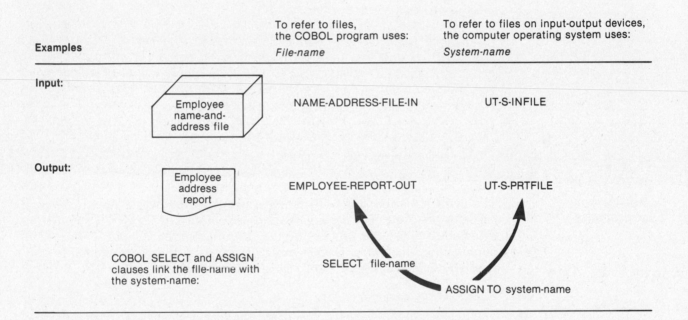

Figure 2.30 Relationship of SELECT and ASSIGN clauses

Format:

[<u>FILE-CONTROL</u>.

    <u>SELECT</u> file-name

        <u>ASSIGN</u> TO implementor-name .]

Example:

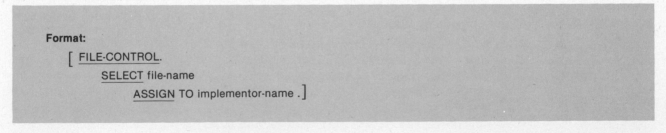

Figure 2.31 FILE-CONTROL paragraph example

each line). It thus reduces the possibility of making errors by minimizing the number of words that must be rekeyed when it is necessary to modify a line of code.

There is an associated style convention: when a sentence, statement, or clause extends over multiple lines, indent the second line and all additional lines. Although there are many alternate recommendations, indentations are usually made in four-space units. This is because the COBOL coding form has accentuated rulings after every fourth position (from position 8 to 72). It's easier to remember and use uniform 4-space indentations than any other indentation considerations.

It doesn't matter which file is selected first in the FILE-CONTROL paragraph. The only requirement is that each file used in the program be specified. However, it is logical to list the input file (or files) and then the output file (or files).

The user-defined word that we chose for the output printer file—the revised employee address list—is EMPLOYEE-REPORT-OUT. The file is assigned to UT-S-PRTFILE.

When choosing file-names, remember that they must conform to the rules for user-defined words and that each file-name must be unique. It is also a good idea to not refer to specific storage media in file-names. Because of technology and cost changes, the storage medium for which a file was originally designed may be replaced by another medium. For example, card files are often converted to tape or disk storage; printed outputs may be changed to a visual display terminal screen. File-names such as EMPLOYEE-CARDS or EMPLOYEE-PRINTOUT may become obsolete and lead to confusion later.

Recap of the ENVIRONMENT DIVISION

The complete ENVIRONMENT DIVISION for the EMP-RPT is shown in Figure 2.32. This division is relatively easy to write but difficult to discuss because it is dependent on the COBOL compiler being used. It contains two sections, CONFIGURATION and INPUT-OUTPUT. The former specifies the computer; the latter specifies input-output devices. In the FILE-CONTROL paragraph of the INPUT-OUTPUT SECTION, each file used by the program must be specified in a SELECT clause with its file-name and associated with an input-output device by an ASSIGN clause.

```
SEQUENCE        A   B                    COBOL STATEMENT                            IDENTIFICATION
(PAGE)(SERIAL)
002010*                                                                             EMP-RPT
   02*
   03*
   04 ENVIRONMENT DIVISION.
   05*
   06*
   07 CONFIGURATION SECTION.
   08*
   09 SOURCE-COMPUTER. IBM-370.
   10 OBJECT-COMPUTER. IBM-370.
   11*
   12*
   13 INPUT-OUTPUT SECTION.
   14*
   15 FILE-CONTROL.
   16     SELECT NAME-ADDRESS-FILE-IN
   17         ASSIGN TO UT-S-INFILE.
   18     SELECT EMPLOYEE-REPORT-OUT
002190        ASSIGN TO UT-S-PRTFILE.                                               EMP-RPT
```

Figure 2.32 ENVIRONMENT DIVISION for EMP-RPT program

Writing the DATA DIVISION

**DATA DIVISION
Header**

**FILE SECTION
Header**

The DATA DIVISION format is shown in Figure 2.33. We will study each entry. The words DATA DIVISION are underlined in the format to indicate that they are required. They must appear exactly as shown in Figure 2.34 and be followed by a period. The header must appear on a line that is free of any other coding in area B.

Like the FILE-CONTROL paragraph of the ENVIRONMENT DIVISION, the FILE SECTION is required if files are to be processed. It will be included in all programs in this text. The header should be written as shown in Figure 2.35. It must be followed by a period and appear on a separate line.

File-description (FD) entry

For each file selected in the ENVIRONMENT DIVISION, an FD (File-Description) level-indicator entry must be specified in the FILE SECTION of the DATA DIVISION. *Level-indicators* are two character alphabetic reserved words used to identify a specific type of file or a position in a hierarchy. Figure 2.36 shows an FD entry for our employee name-and-address file. Since the letters FD are an area A entry, they are written in positions 8 and 9. The file-name must be written in area B. Thus, there are always at least two blank spaces (positions 10 and 11) on the coding form between an FD indicator and the succeeding file-name. The file-name must be spelled exactly as it appears in the SELECT clause for the file.

Notice that there is no period after the file-name. That's because the FD entry contains additional clauses. All FD clauses are area B entries. For readability, the clauses are indented four spaces so that each begins in position 16.

There are three FD clauses in this example: RECORD CONTAINS, LABEL RECORDS, and DATA RECORD.

RECORD CONTAINS clause

The character length of the logical records within the file is specified in this clause. The format notation in Figure 2.37 shows this clause enclosed in brackets, which means it is an optional clause. It should be included, however

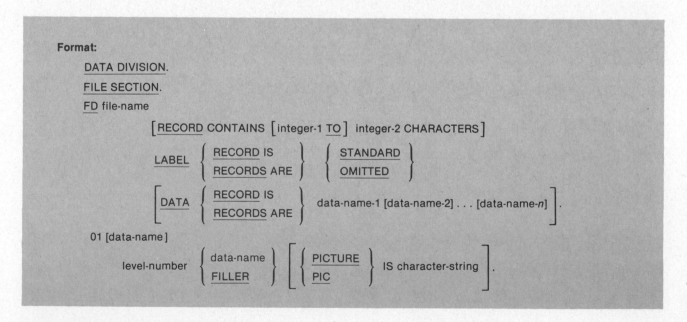

Figure 2.33 DATA DIVISION format

Format:

DATA DIVISION.

Example:

Figure 2.34 DATA-DIVISION header example

Format:

[FILE SECTION.]

Example:

Figure 2.35 FILE SECTION header example

Format:

FD file-name

    [RECORD CONTAINS [integer-1 TO] integer-2 CHARACTERS]

    LABEL $\begin{Bmatrix} \text{RECORD IS} \\ \text{RECORDS ARE} \end{Bmatrix}$ $\begin{Bmatrix} \text{STANDARD} \\ \text{OMITTED} \end{Bmatrix}$

    $\left[\text{DATA} \begin{Bmatrix} \text{RECORD IS} \\ \text{RECORDS ARE} \end{Bmatrix} \text{data-name-1 [data-name-2] . . . [data-name-}n] \right]$.

Example:

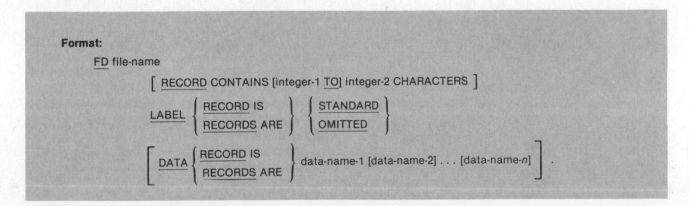

Figure 2.36 FD entry example

61

because (1) it provides useful documentation, and (2) it will be used by the compiler to check that the same number of positions have been correctly specified for the record. (This point is explained later in this chapter.)

If the records in the file are of variable length, the TO clause shown in the format notation can be used to specify minimum and maximum record lengths. Since this EMP-RPT program is to read fixed-length 80-character records, the clause RECORD CONTAINS 80 CHARACTERS suffices.

LABEL RECORDS clause

The LABEL RECORDS clause is used to indicate whether standard, nonstandard, or no labels are to be processed. A *label record* is written at the beginning of a file stored on magnetic tape, disk, or other electronic storage medium. It tells the name of the file, the date it was created, and so forth. Label records are not used for punched cards or printer files; they are optional for tape files; and they are required for disk files. We have specified LABEL RECORDS ARE OMITTED for the input file FD entry, as shown in Figure 2.38.

Notice that the format notation indicates this clause is required. LABEL RECORDS is the only required clause of the FD entry.

DATA RECORDS clause

The name of a record (or records) within the file is specified in this optional clause. In Figure 2.39, the user-defined record-name NA-NAME-ADDRESS-RECORD-IN has been specified for the employee name-and-address record. Although the clause has been specified in the EMP-LIST and EMP-RPT program, most programmers omit it because they feel it serves no purpose, except for documentation. Even the documentation it provides is of questionable value, because the record-names appear immediately after the FD entry anyway. It has been specified in these first two programs so that you recognize the clause, but it won't appear in the remaining programs in this text.

After the last clause written in the FD entry, a period must be written to end the sentence. (Although the FD clauses are usually written in the sequence shown here, they may appear in any order.)

Record-description entry

Immediately following the file-description entry, the logical records within the file must be specified. Records are described by first assigning a name to a record and then writing data-item (or field) descriptions showing the characteristics of fields within the record.

Defining the record

To define the record, the level-number 01 is written in area A and the name of the record (as defined in the DATA RECORDS clause of the FD entry, if used) is written in area B (see Figure 2.40). A record as a whole is always identified by level-number 01. Fields and subfields within the record are identified by level numbers in the range from 02 through 49. The level-number 01 always starts in area A; level-numbers 02 through 49 are area B entries.

Level numbers are assigned on a hierarchical basis. Each subfield has a level number that is higher than the field to which it is subordinate. Examples in the following material will illustrate the use of level numbers with fields and subfields.

About the choice of level numbers

Rather than use level numbers in straight numerical order (01, 02, 03, etc.), most programmers assign level numbers in increments of 5 or so (01, 05, 10, 15 and so on). This leaves numerical gaps so that fields or subfields can be further

Format:

[<u>RECORD</u> CONTAINS [integer-1 <u>TO</u>] integer-2 CHARACTERS]

Example:

SEQUENCE		C O N T	A	B	COBOL STATEMENT		IDENTIFICATION
(PAGE)	(SERIAL)						
1 3	4 6	7	8	12 16 20 24 28 32 36 40 44 48 52 56 60 64 68	72	76 80

```
003100            RECORD CONTAINS 80 CHARACTERS                          EMP-RPT
```

Figure 2.37 RECORD CONTAINS clause example

Format:

<u>LABEL</u> { <u>RECORD</u> IS / <u>RECORDS</u> ARE } { <u>STANDARD</u> / <u>OMITTED</u> }

Example:

SEQUENCE		C O N T	A	B	COBOL STATEMENT		IDENTIFICATION
(PAGE)	(SERIAL)						
1 3	4 6	7	8	12 16 20 24 28 32 36 40 44 48 52 56 60 64 68	72	76 80

```
003110            LABEL RECORDS ARE OMITTED                              EMP-RPT
```

Figure 2.38 LABEL RECORDS clause example

Format:

[<u>DATA</u> { <u>RECORD</u> IS / <u>RECORDS</u> ARE } data-name 1 [data-name-2] . . . [data-name-*n*]]

Example:

SEQUENCE		C O N T	A	B	COBOL STATEMENT		IDENTIFICATION
(PAGE)	(SERIAL)						
1 3	4 6	7	8	12 16 20 24 28 32 36 40 44 48 52 56 60 64 68	72	76 80

```
003120            DATA RECORD IS NA-NAME-ADDRESS-RECORD-IN.             EMP-RPT
```

Figure 2.39 DATA RECORDS clause example

Format:
01 [data-name-1]

Example:

SEQUENCE		C O N T	A	B	COBOL STATEMENT		IDENTIFICATION
(PAGE)	(SERIAL)						
0 1	6	7	8	12 16 20 24 28 32 36 40 44 48 52 56 60 64 68	72	76 80

```
003140 01  NA-NAME-ADDRESS-RECORD-IN.                                   EMP-RPT
```

Figure 2.40 Defining a record example

Part A: Numerical order assignment of level-numbers

SEQUENCE		CONT	A	B	COBOL STATEMENT	IDENTIFICATION
(PAGE)	(SERIAL)					

```
ØØØØ1Ø  Ø1  FIRST-LEVEL.
    2       Ø2  SECOND-LEVEL.
    3           Ø3  THIRD-LEVEL.
    4               Ø4  FOURTH-LEVEL.
    5                   Ø5  FIFTH-LEVEL.
ØØØØ6Ø                      Ø6  ETCETERA    PIC X.
```

Part B: Gap-level-number assignment

```
ØØØØ1Ø  Ø1  FIRST-LEVEL.
    2       Ø5  SECOND-LEVEL.
    3           1Ø  THIRD-LEVEL.
    4               15  FOURTH-LEVEL.
    5                   2Ø  FIFTH-LEVEL.
ØØØØ6Ø                      25  ETCETERA    PIC X.
```

Figure 2.41 Examples of level-number assignment methods

subdivided at a later time if necessary. Figure 2.41 shows an example of such "gap" level-number assignment.

Some programmers do not favor gap level-number assignment. They maintain that straight numerical order is easier to understand and follow than nonuniformly incremented numbers. Further, should other data-item subdivisions become necessary and if they are merely squeezed into gaps, the hierarchical indentations will be inconsistent. Since most subdivision changes should also cause indentation changes, the level numbers can be changed to retain straight numerical sequence at the same time that indentation changes are being made.

However, since most programmers do use gap level-number assignment, it will be used for this program and the remaining programs of this text.

Defining fields and subfields

Fields and subfields are defined by data-item description entries. Each data-item description begins in area B. It consists of a level number in the range from 02 through 49 followed by a data-name (a user-defined word for the field). If a field or subfield has no subordinate fields, the data-item description entry also contains a PICTURE clause. The PICTURE clause describes characteristics of the field or subfield.

Figure 2.42 shows the data-names chosen for the fields and subfields of the employee name-and-address record. To the left of the data-names are the level numbers.

A data item that has subordinate data items—like NA-NAME-ADDRESS-RECORD-IN and NA-EMPLOYEE-HIRE-DATE-IN—is termed a *group item.* Data items that are not subdivided are called *elementary items.* Notice that the group items do not have PICTURE clauses; the elementary items do. Thus, the length of a group item is the sum of its elementary item lengths.

There is an unused area at the end of each employee name-and-address record. Observe that the data-item description for that area has the name FILLER. Any area of a record that either does not contain data or is not used by that program may be named FILLER. The reserved word FILLER serves a function in record descriptions analogous to that of zeros in our Arabic numbering system: it is a placeholder. Even though we are not concerned with a particular

Format:

$$\text{level-number} \left\{ \begin{array}{l} \text{data-name} \\ \underline{\text{FILLER}} \end{array} \right\} \left[\left\{ \begin{array}{l} \underline{\text{PICTURE}} \\ \underline{\text{PIC}} \end{array} \right\} \text{IS character-string} \right]$$

Example:

SEQUENCE			CONT	A	B	COBOL STATEMENT		IDENTIFICATION
(PAGE) 1 3	(SERIAL) 4 6	7	8	12 16 20 24 28 32 36 40 44	48 52 56 60 64 68	72	76 80
0 0 3 1 3 0								E M P - R P T
	1 4			0 1	N A - N A M E - A D D R E S S - R E C O R D - I N .			
	1 5				0 5 N A - E M P L O Y E E - N A M E - I N	P I C X (2 0) .		
	1 6				0 5 N A - E M P L O Y E E - A D D R E S S - I N	P I C X (2 4) .		
	1 7				0 5 N A - E M P L O Y E E - C I T Y - S T A T E - Z I P - I N	P I C X (2 4) .		
	1 8				0 5 N A - E M P L O Y E E - H I R E - D A T E - I N .			
	1 9				1 0 N A - E M P L O Y E E - H I R E - M O N T H - I N	P I C 9 (2) .		
	2 0				1 0 N A - E M P L O Y E E - H I R E - D A Y - I N	P I C 9 (2) .		
	2 1				1 0 N A - E M P L O Y E E - H I R E - Y E A R - I N	P I C 9 (2) .		
0 0 3 2 2 0					0 5 F I L L E R	P I C X (6) .		E M P - R P T

Figure 2.42   Defining fields and subfields example

area of a record, if it is physically present it must be accounted for. The reserved word FILLER is generally used for such an area.

About indentation of level numbers

Since level-number 01 is an area A entry, it should be placed in positions 8 and 9. Level-numbers 02 through 49 cannot be written in area A, but they may begin in any area B positions from 12 through 72. It is a common practice to indent each data-item subdivision four spaces to the right of the level that precedes it. For example, level 01 starts in position 8, level 05 is indented to position 12, level 10 is indented to position 16, and so forth. However, if the record has many levels of subdivision, these four-space indentations may consume so much of the coding area that there is little room left to write the data-names and picture clauses. In such a case, indentations for two spaces are an acceptable alternative. Figure 2.43 shows examples of level indentations.

About choosing FILE SECTION data-names

Data-names must conform to the rules for user-defined words. They should be meaningful, descriptive, and readable. Another valuable programming practice is to relate the fields of a record to one another by data-name assignment. For example, all data-names of the name-and-address record description entry are prefixed with the characters NA, which stands for name-and-address record. When a common prefix is assigned to all fields within a record, the PROCEDURE DIVISION statements that refer to fields are more meaningful and the program logic is easier to follow than it would be otherwise. Figure 2.44 shows the relationship between the record layout and the file-description data-names.

Two-character prefixes are frequently used; large, complex systems may require the use of three- or four-character prefixes. Some programmers use the characters as a prefix; others prefer to use them as a suffix. Two-character prefixes will be used in this text. Also, for the first few programs, the data-names of the fields will be suffixed with IN or OUT to make the program logic easier for you to follow. (Actually, in a commercial data processing

Part A: Indentation of four spaces

SEQUENCE		CONT	A	B	COBOL STATEMENT	IDENTIFICATION

```
ØØØØ1Ø  Ø1  THE-UNIVERSE.
    Ø2      Ø5  MILKY-WAY-GALAXY.
    Ø3          1Ø  SOLAR-SYSTEM.
    Ø4              15  EARTH.
    Ø5                  2Ø  NORTH-AMERICAN-CONTINENT.
    Ø6                      25  UNITED-STATES-OF-AMERICA.
    Ø7                          3Ø  CALIFORNIA.
    Ø8                              35  LOS-ANGELES-COUNTY.
    Ø9                                  4Ø  CITY-OF-LOS-ANGELES.
    1Ø                                      45  HOLLYWOOD.
ØØØ11Ø                                          49  MOVING PICTURE X.
```

Part B: Indentation of two spaces (except where level 05 must start in area B)

```
ØØØØ1Ø  Ø1  THE-UNIVERSE.
    Ø2      Ø5  MILKY-WAY-GALAXY.
    Ø3        1Ø  SOLAR-SYSTEM.
    Ø4          15  EARTH.
    Ø5            2Ø  NORTH-AMERICAN-CONTINENT.
    Ø6              25  UNITED-STATES-OF-AMERICA.
    Ø7                3Ø  CALIFORNIA.
    Ø8                  35  LOS-ANGELES-COUNTY.
    Ø9                    4Ø  CITY-OF-LOS-ANGELES.
    1Ø                      45  HOLLYWOOD.
ØØØ11Ø                        49  MOVING PICTURE X.
```

Figure 2.43 Examples of level-number indentations

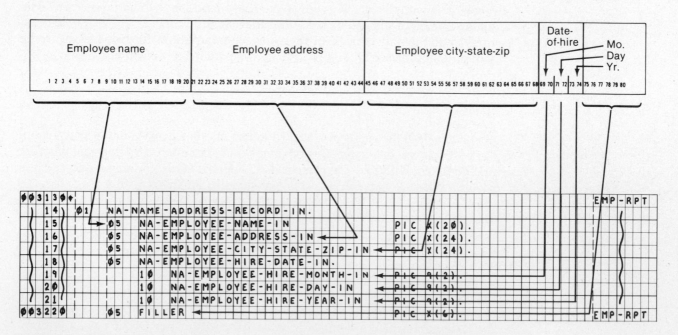

Figure 2.44 Relationship of employee name-and-address record to file-description data-names

installation, it is usually not a good idea to affix the words IN or OUT to data-names. This is because data-names within records are often standardized so that a particular record or field is always called by the same name. Sometimes a given record will be an input record at other times an output. The use of the indication IN or OUT interferes with consistent use of standard data-names.)

You may question why the NA prefix was not assigned to the FILLER area of the NA-NAME-ADDRESS-RECORD-IN. If this were done, a user-defined word would have been created. Either the reserved word FILLER or a user-defined word could be assigned to the unused area. But the reserved word FILLER is generally a better choice. All 01-level data-names (that is all record-names) and all data-names within a record-name that occur in the same hierarchical sequence must be unique. Often there is more than one unused area within a record. A user defined word like NA-FILLER could not be used more than once, whereas the reserved word FILLER could be used to name all unused areas.

PICTURE clauses

Each elementary data-item description must contain a PICTURE clause. This clause is used to specify the data class and the length attributes of the field being described. (It also serves certain other functions that will be covered in Chapter 4.) A basic PICTURE clause contains the reserved word PICTURE, or the abbreviation PIC, followed by a space and either an X or a 9, which is followed immediately by a number enclosed in parentheses that indicates the length of the field. The X and the 9 are *picture symbols*. The picture symbol X defines the field as alphanumeric; symbol 9 indicates a numeric field.

Figure 2.45 shows the PICTURE clause format and a PICTURE clause for the NA-EMPLOYEE-NAME-IN field. Notice that a blank space must follow the word PIC. Since the field is alphanumeric, the clause contains the picture symbol X. Immediately to the right of the X is the number 20 enclosed in parentheses. This indicates that the field is 20 character positions in length. The complete picture clause, then, is PIC X(20). The X(20) portion is called the picture *character-string*. There cannot be any blank spaces within a picture character-string.

Most programmers use the abbreviation PIC rather than the full word PICTURE. The abbreviation is just as understandable and it consumes fewer spaces on the coding line.

Notice that all the PICTURE clauses have uniformly started in position 48. It really doesn't matter where a picture clause starts, as long as it is in area B and there is one blank space following the data-name. However, PICTURE

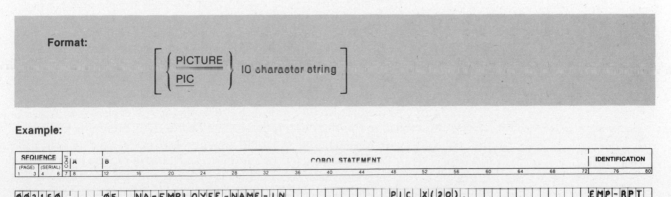

Figure 2.45 PICTURE clause example

Part A: Clauses not vertically aligned

```
000010      05  THIS-IS-PERFECTLY-LEGAL PIC X(15).
   02       05  BUT     PIC 9(3).
   03       05  IT-IS-DIFFICULT     PIC X(15).
            05  TO-READ-AND-REFERENCE PIC 9(2).
```

Part B: Clauses aligned near data-name

```
000010      05  THIS-IS               PIC X(1).
   02       05  EASY-ENOUGH           PIC 9(6).
   03       05  TO-READ               PIC X(24).
   04       05  BUT                   PIC 9(5).
   05       05  ONCE-IN-A-WHILE-A     PIC 9(8).
   06       05  LONG-NAME-WILL-WRECK-ALIGNMENT PIC X(4).
```

Part C: Clauses aligned far from data-name

```
000010      05  THIS-IS-OK-FOR-READING-TOO            PIC X.
   02       05  BUT-A-LONGER                          PIC 9(2).
   03       05  PICTURE-CHARACTER-STRING              PIC X(2).
   04       05  WILL-RUN-PAST-POSITION-72             PIC X(1).
```

Part D: Recommended alignment for FILE SECTION

```
001010      05  FOR-THE-FILE-SECTION      PIC X(5).
   02       05  POSITION-48               PIC 9(3).
   03       05  IS-JUST-ABOUT-RIGHT       PIC X(48).
```

Figure 2.46 Examples of PICTURE clause placement

clauses within a record description are easier to read if they are vertically aligned. In the FILE SECTION, position 48 is a good choice for this alignment; there the clauses will be far enough to the right so that most long or indented data-names can be accommodated and yet still leave room for the PICTURE clauses themselves. Figure 2.46 shows a few alignment alternatives.

Rather than use a number enclosed by parentheses to specify field length, as was done in the EMP-LIST programs, the picture symbol could be written a number of times equal to the length of the field being described. For example, PIC X (24) could be specified as PIC XXXXXXXXXXXXXXXXXXXXXXXX.

For picture character-strings containing only one type of picture symbol, the use of parentheses is superior to symbol repetition. It is easier to interpret a field length expressed as a number, especially for long fields. Also, it's often necessary to sum the values in a column of picture clauses to determine the length of a record. Adding numerically expressed values in parentheses is much easier than adding the repeated symbols.

We can now discuss further one of the reasons for specifying the RECORD CONTAINS clause in the file-description entry. The COBOL compiler computes the record length by summing the field lengths expressed in the PICTURE clauses. It does this whether or not the RECORD CONTAINS clause is specified. However, if the RECORD CONTAINS clause is present, the compiler checks the computed length with the RECORD CONTAINS length. If there is a discrepancy, the difference is identified and a diagnostic message is issued.

For example, suppose we had transposed the digits 24 of the NA-

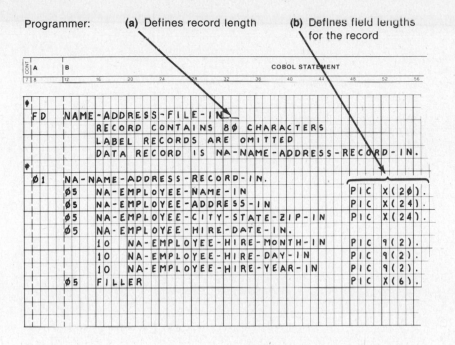

Programmer:
(a) Defines record length
(b) Defines field lengths for the record

COBOL compiler:

(a) Sums defined field lengths:

```
                      20
(incorrect entry)    +42
                     +24
                     + 2
                     + 2
                     + 2
                     + 6
                   = 98
```

(b) Compares sum of field lengths with record length in RECORD CONTAINS clause:

98 vs. 80

(c) If lengths are unequal, prints diagnostic message.

Figure 2.47 Relationship of the RECORD CONTAINS and PICTURE clause

EMPLOYEE-ADDRESS-IN length in the picture character-string (X(42)), or suppose we had written X(23) in error. Figure 2.47 shows that, for the first case, the compiler would detect that the sum of our field lengths was more than the 80 CHARACTERS specified in the RECORD CONTAINS clause. For the second case, the sum would be less. So, in addition to its documentation value, the RECORD CONTAINS clause helps the compiler identify certain record-description entry discrepancies.

We have now completed the file-description entry and record-description entry for the EMPLOYEE-FILE-IN. These entries must also be completed for the other file of the EMP-RPT program: EMPLOYEE-REPORT-OUT.

Defining the output file

Figure 2.48 shows the file-description and record-description entries for the output file EMPLOYEE-REPORT-OUT. As for the input file EMPLOYEE-FILE-IN, a file-description entry for the file and a record-description entry for the records in the file are required.

After recording FD and the user-defined file-name EMPLOYEE-REPORT-OUT, we specified RECORD CONTAINS 133 CHARACTERS. This record length is appropriate because the employee report will be printed on a standard line-printer. The width of a line for a standard line-printer is 132 characters.

Look again at the print chart in Figure 2.3. Notice that one employee line requires only 82 print positions. Thus, the defined record length could have been shorter. However, report requirements often change, so we have allowed for growth. It will be easier to modify the report format later, if necessary, with the entire 132 print positions already defined.

But why did we specify a record length of 133 rather than 132? In addition to the 132 print positions, a record being directed to a printer must contain one *forms-control character* at the beginning of the record. This character controls the vertical spacing of the record on the printed output page. The forms-control character is not printed. Instead it causes single-spacing, double-spacing, triple-spacing, and the like. Thus, the one forms-control character plus the 132

```
SEQUENCE        CONT  A   B                                        COBOL STATEMENT                          IDENTIFICATION
(PAGE)(SERIAL)
1  3 4  6  7 8    12    16    20    24    28    32    36    40    44    48    52    56    60    64    68  72    76    80

0040 10 *                                                                                                    EMP-RPT
    02     FD   EMPLOYEE-REPORT-OUT
    03            RECORD CONTAINS 133 CHARACTERS
    04            LABEL RECORDS ARE OMITTED
    05            DATA RECORD IS ER-EMPLOYEE-LINE-OUT.
    06 *
    07     01   ER-EMPLOYEE-LINE-OUT.
    08            05  ER-VERTICAL-FORMS-CONTROL-OUT      PIC X(1).
    09            05  ER-EMPLOYEE-NAME-OUT               PIC X(20).
    10            05  FILLER                             PIC X(2).
    11            05  ER-EMPLOYEE-ADDRESS-OUT            PIC X(24).
    12            05  FILLER                             PIC X(2).
    13            05  ER-EMPLOYEE-CITY-STATE-ZIP-OUT     PIC X(24).
    14            05  FILLER                             PIC X(2).
    15            05  ER-EMPLOYEE-HIRE-DATE-OUT.
    16               10  ER-EMPLOYEE-HIRE-MONTH-OUT      PIC 9(2).
    17               10  ER-DATE-HYPHEN-1-OUT            PIC X(1).
    18               10  ER-EMPLOYEE-HIRE-DAY-OUT        PIC 9(2).
    19               10  ER-DATE-HYPHEN-2-OUT            PIC X(1).
    20               10  ER-EMPLOYEE-HIRE-YEAR-OUT       PIC 9(2).
0042 10           05  FILLER                            PIC X(50).            EMP-RPT
```

Figure 2.48 File and record definition entries for the EMPLOYEE-REPORT-OUT file

print positions account for the record length of 133 characters. This need to include a forms-control character in the output record applies only to line-printer files. It does not pertain to card, tape, disk, or other output files.

As mentioned earlier, label records do not apply to printer files. So we have specified LABEL RECORDS ARE OMITTED. In the DATA RECORDS clause, we wrote the name ER-EMPLOYEE-LINE-OUT (for employee report detail line). A period must follow the FD entry.

In the record-description entry, we wrote the level-number 01 followed by the record-name ER-EMPLOYEE-LINE-OUT and a period. The first data-item description entry contains the data-name ER-VERTICAL-FORMS-CONTROL-OUT. This field will hold the forms-control character required to control vertical spacing on the output report. It will not be printed on the report. Figure 2.49 shows how the data-item description entries relate to the report. Notice that the reserved word FILLER is used to allow for the blank spaces between fields on the print line.

Recap of the FILE SECTION

Since this EMP-RPT program uses one input file and one output file, we have written two FD entries. Since each file has one record format, we have written one record-description entry after each file-description entry. We have thus completed the FILE SECTION of the program.

WORKING-STORAGE SECTION Header

The FILE SECTION of the DATA DIVISION is used to define the files, records, and fields to be read or written by the program. In addition to this input and output data, most programs process other data values for which storage is required. Records and fields required by the program but not defined within the input or output file-description entries are defined in the WORKING-STORAGE SECTION. The format of this section is shown in Figure 2.50. Figure 2.51 shows the WORKING-STORAGE SECTION header format and an example. A hyphen is required between the words WORKING and STORAGE.

SEQUENCE					COBOL STATEMENT	IDENTIFICATION

```
ØØ4Ø1Ø*                                                                    EMP-RPT
      Ø2) FD  EMPLOYEE-REPORT-OUT
      Ø3(         RECORD CONTAINS 133 CHARACTERS
      Ø4(         LABEL RECORDS ARE OMITTED
      Ø5(         DATA RECORD IS ER-EMPLOYEE-LINE-OUT.
      Ø6 *
      Ø7 Ø1  ER-EMPLOYEE-LINE-OUT.
      Ø8     Ø5  ER-VERTICAL-FORMS-CONTROL-OUT    PIC X(1).
      Ø9     Ø5  ER-EMPLOYEE-NAME-OUT             PIC X(2Ø).
      1Ø     Ø5  FILLER                           PIC X(2),
      11     Ø5  ER-EMPLOYEE-ADDRESS-OUT          PIC X(24).
      12     Ø5  FILLER                           PIC X(2).
      13     Ø5  ER-EMPLOYEE-CITY-STATE-ZIP-OUT   PIC X(24).
      14     Ø5  FILLER                           PIC X(2).
      15     Ø5  ER-EMPLOYEE-HIRE-DATE-OUT.
      16         1Ø  ER-EMPLOYEE-HIRE-MONTH-OUT   PIC 9(2).
      17         1Ø  ER-DATE-HYPHEN-1-OUT         PIC X(1).
      18         1Ø  ER-EMPLOYEE-HIRE-DAY-OUT     PIC 9(2).
      19         1Ø  ER-DATE-HYPHEN-2-OUT         PIC X(1).
      2Ø         1Ø  ER-EMPLOYEE-HIRE-YEAR-OUT    PIC 9(2).
ØØ421Ø     Ø5  FILLER                             PIC X(5Ø).        EMP-RPT
```

Name	Address	City State Zip	Hire Date
BRADFORD, THOMAS	9081 EL CAMINO REAL	SANTA CLARA CA 95051	09-01-78
BRONSON, PATRICIA	1818 SANTA CRUZ AVENUE	LOS GATOS CA 95030	05-01-72
CARTWRIGHT, GILBERT	105 EAST CENTRAL AVENUE	CAMPBELL CA 95008	01-15-79
COOK, KENNETH	496 REDWOOD AVENUE	SAN JOSE CA 95128	04-15-68
GARDNER, JOYCE	1014 STELLING ROAD	CUPERTINO CA 95014	07-31-74
JEFFERS, JOSEPH	1000 HYDE AVENUE	SAN JOSE CA 95129	08-01-74
KRISTENSEN, CARL	14199 SARATOGA AVENUE	SARATOGA CA 95070	11-15-71
LAWRENCE, KATHERINE	298 UNIVERSITY AVENUE	LOS GATOS CA 95030	04-01-70
LEE, SAMUEL	2140 JACKSON STREET	SAN JOSE CA 95116	02-15-72
LUCCHETTI, JOHN	13478 SOBEY ROAD	SARATOGA CA 95070	06-01-74
PAGE, PRENTISS	1991 GLEN BRAE DRIVE	SARATOGA CA 95070	02-01-79
PHILLIPS, SARAH	13631 TOYON DRIVE	CUPERTINO CA 95014	03-01-73
RODRIGUEZ, RAMON	1091 CAPRI DRIVE	CAMPBELL CA 95008	12-01-76
RUSSELL, DAVID	1315 MCCLELLAN ROAD	CUPERTINO CA 95014	03-01-73
SANCHEZ, SYLVIA	2124 MATHILDA AVENUE	SUNNYVALE CA 95010	08-15-78
SILVERMAN, NINA	701 POLLARD ROAD	LOS GATOS CA 95030	01-15-78
SMITH, JENNIFER	3281 BENTON ROAD	SANTA CLARA CA 95051	06-09-77
TANAKA, JAMES	1018 CURTNER AVENUE	SAN JOSE CA 95123	08-15-72
WALLACE, JANA	14291 JUNIPER LANE	SARATOGA CA 95070	10-15-78
WONG, WILLIAM	1314 EAST SANTA CLARA	SAN JOSE CA 95112	06-01-78

Figure 2.49 Relationship of data-item entries to employee-report line

Format:

[WORKING-STORAGE SECTION.]

[{77-level-description-entry | record-description-entry}] . . .

Figure 2.50 WORKING-STORAGE SECTION format

In the EMP-LIST program, a 77-level data-item was specified. Assignment of level-number 77 signifies that the data-item being described is an independent item—that is, it has no subordinate fields and is not a subfield of another field. A 77-level data-item is always an elementary item.

There is often a need for independent fields in a COBOL program. In a complex program, there may be many of them. Unfortunately, when a program contains many independent items, it is sometimes difficult to locate a specific field, since they tend to be listed randomly. Therefore we will not use level-number 77 in the remainder of this text.

A better approach is to segregate the WORKING-STORAGE fields required in a program into general categories just as topics are organized when building an outline. Then, instead of a haphazard list of independent fields, the fields can be organized within a record description. The level-numbers 01 through 49 discussed above can be used for this purpose. This makes WORKING-STORAGE SECTION fields easier to locate and thus contributes to program readability.

In this simple EMP-RPT program, only one WORKING-STORAGE field is required. It is used to indicate whether or not the end of NAME-ADDRESS-FILE-IN has been reached. That is, its data value will reveal whether or not there are any more employee name-and-address records to process.

You can think of this field as a two-state indicator. It must be capable of reflecting whether the end of the input file has been reached (a value of "YES") or not (a value of "NO"). Such indicators are often required for program control. The two-state devices used to turn on and turn off electric lights (or other electronic circuits) are called *switches.* Similarly, a field used as a two-state indicator is often called a *program switch,* or just a *switch.*

Format:

[WORKING-STORAGE SECTION.]

Example:

```
SEQUENCE   A   B                    COBOL STATEMENT                         IDENTIFICATION
004010                                                                      EMP-RPT
   020
   030     WORKING-STORAGE SECTION.
004040                                                                      EMP-RPT
```

Figure 2.51 WORKING-STORAGE SECTION header example

```
0 0 5 0 1 0 *                                                                                    E M P - R P T
      0 2 (*
      0 3 )  W O R K I N G - S T O R A G E   S E C T I O N .
      0 4 *
      0 5 (  0 1    W S - P R O G R A M - S W I T C H E S .
0 0 5 0 6 0    0 5    W S - E N D - O F - F I L E - S W I T C H              P I C   X ( 3 ) .              E M P - R P T
```

Figure 2.52 WORKING-STORAGE SECTION for EMP-RPT program

Figure 2.52 shows the 01-level record-description. The record-name is a user-defined data-name, WS-PROGRAM-SWITCHES. The prefix WS is assigned to indicate that this item is a WORKING-STORAGE SECTION field. Following the 01-level data-item is the definition of a 05-level data-item. It has the user-defined data name WS-END-OF-FILE-SWITCH. Its PICTURE clause is X(3). Thus, this field can hold the values "YES" or "NO".

Recap of the DATA DIVISION

Figure 2.53 shows the complete DATA DIVISION. The DATA DIVISION has two commonly used sections: FILE and WORKING-STORAGE. In the FILE SECTION, an FD entry must be specified for each file selected in the ENVIRONMENT DIVISION. Following the FD entry, a record-description entry must be written for each record format contained within the file. Each record description contains data-item descriptions. A data-item description contains a level number and user-defined data-name for the field. If an elementary item is being described, it also contains a PICTURE clause. Data-items required in the program but not defined in the FILE SECTION are described in the WORKING-STORAGE SECTION.

COBOL Language Element Summary

Reserved words are words that have predefined meanings in the COBOL language.

User-defined words are created by programmers in accordance with the following rules:

- Must be composed only of alphabetic characters (A through Z), digits (0 through 9), and hyphens (-)
- Must contain at least one letter
- Must not exceed 30 characters
- Must not begin or end with a hyphen
- Must not contain any spaces (embedded blanks)
- Must not be the same as a reserved word

Comment-entries are used in certain IDENTIFICATION DIVISION paragraphs. They may be any combination of characters acceptable to the computer being used.

System-names are words assigned by the company supplying the COBOL compiler. System names may be further classified as either *computer-names* or *implementor-names*.

Level-indicators are two-character alphabetic reserved words used to identify a specific type of file or a position in a hierarchy. The level-indicator FD identifies a file-description entry.

Level-numbers are two-digit numbers used to indicate the relationship of fields and subfields in the hierarchical structure of a logical record.

```
SEQUENCE  CONT A  B                    COBOL STATEMENT                          IDENTIFICATION
003010 *                                                                        EMP-RPT
   02  *
   03  *
   04     DATA DIVISION.
   05  *
   06  *
   07     FILE SECTION.
   08  *
   09     FD  EMPLOYEE-FILE-IN
   10         RECORD CONTAINS 80 CHARACTERS
   11         LABEL RECORDS ARE OMITTED
   12         DATA RECORD IS NA-NAME-ADDRESS-RECORD-IN.
   13  *
   14     01  NA-NAME-ADDRESS-RECORD-IN.
   15         05  NA-EMPLOYEE-NAME-IN              PIC X(20).
   16         05  NA-EMPLOYEE-ADDRESS-IN           PIC X(24).
   17         05  NA-EMPLOYEE-CITY-STATE-ZIP-IN    PIC X(24).
   18         05  NA-EMPLOYEE-HIRE-DATE-IN.
   19             10  NA-EMPLOYEE-HIRE-MONTH-IN    PIC 9(2).
   20             10  NA-EMPLOYEE-HIRE-DAY-IN      PIC 9(2).
   21             10  NA-EMPLOYEE-HIRE-YEAR-IN     PIC 9(2).
003220     05  FILLER                              PIC X(6).                    EMP-RPT


004010 *                                                                        EMP-RPT
   02     FD  EMPLOYEE-REPORT-OUT
   03         RECORD CONTAINS 133 CHARACTERS
   04         LABEL RECORDS ARE OMITTED
   05         DATA RECORD IS ER-EMPLOYEE-LINE-OUT.
   06  *
   07     01  ER-EMPLOYEE-LINE-OUT.
   08         05  ER-VERTICAL-FORMS-CONTROL-OUT    PIC X(1).
   09         05  ER-EMPLOYEE-NAME-OUT             PIC X(20).
   10         05  FILLER                           PIC X(2),
   11         05  ER-EMPLOYEE-ADDRESS-OUT          PIC X(24).
   12         05  FILLER                           PIC X(2).
   13         05  ER-EMPLOYEE-CITY-STATE-ZIP-OUT   PIC X(24).
   14         05  FILLER                           PIC X(2).
   15         05  ER-EMPLOYEE-HIRE-DATE-OUT.
   16             10  ER-EMPLOYEE-HIRE-MONTH-OUT   PIC 9(2).
   17             10  ER-DATE-HYPHEN-1-OUT         PIC X(1).
   18             10  ER-EMPLOYEE-HIRE-DAY-OUT     PIC 9(2).
   19             10  ER-DATE-HYPHEN-2-OUT         PIC X(1).
   20             10  ER-EMPLOYEE-HIRE-YEAR-OUT    PIC 9(2).
004210     05  FILLER                              PIC X(50).                   EMP-RPT


005010 *                                                                        EMP-RPT
   02  *
   03     WORKING-STORAGE SECTION.
   04  *
   05     01  WS-PROGRAM-SWITCHES.
005060     05  WS-END-OF-FILE-SWITCH               PIC X(3).                    EMP-RPT
```

Figure 2.53 DATA-DIVISION for EMP-RPT program

Level number	Indication
01	Record description
02 through 49	Data-item (field or subfield) description
77	Independent data-item

Picture symbols are used in a PICTURE clause to describe the data class, length, and certain other characteristics of a data-item.

Punctuation characters are used to comply with syntactical rules and to aid readability.

Punctuation character	Meaning
.	Period
'' or '	Quotation mark
(	Left parenthesis
)	Right parenthesis
	Blank space
,	Comma
;	Semicolon

Style Summary

General conventions:

- Make user-defined words meaningful and descriptive.
- Use hyphens in user-defined words to separate multiple English words and abbreviations.
- Do not use commas or semicolons as punctuation.
- Provide vertical spacing between divisions, sections, and certain paragraphs by inserting blank comment lines.
- Write only one COBOL sentence, statement, clause, or phrase per coding line.
- When a sentence, statement, or clause extends over multiple coding lines, indent each line after the first.
- When indentation is called for, indent in four-space units. Exceptions are cases where vertical alignment of entries is desired or where four-space indentations consume too much space on the coding line.

IDENTIFICATION DIVISION conventions:

- Limit the program-name to the maximum number of characters allowed by the operating system being used.
- Vertically align the program-name and comment-entries at position 23 (or where the compiler starts the DATE-COMPILED entry).

ENVIRONMENT DIVISION conventions:

- Write the SELECT statement so that the ASSIGN clause begins on a separate line. Indent the ASSIGN clause four spaces (to position 16).
- Sequence the SELECT statements so that the input files are listed first and then the output files.
- Do not choose file-names that refer to specific input-output devices (such as CARD-FILE, TAPE-FILE, or DISK-FILE).

DATA DIVISION conventions:

- Write each clause of the FD entry on a separate line. Indent each clause after the file-name to position 16.

- Use the optional RECORD CONTAINS clause of the FD.
- Omit the optional DATA RECORDS clause of the FD.
- Indent each data-item subdivision four spaces (level-number 05 at position 12, level-number 10 at position 16, and so forth). If four-space indentations consume too much room on the coding line, use two-space indentations.
- Use gap level-number assignment (01, 05, 10, 15, and so on).
- Prefix all data-names of a record with a two-, three-, or four-character abbreviation for that record. The prefix for each record of the program should be unique. Suffixes can also be used.
- To conserve space on the coding line, use the abbreviation PIC rather than the word PICTURE.
- Vertically align FILE SECTION PICTURE clauses at position 48.
- Express the field length in the picture character-string by a number enclosed in parentheses rather than by the repetition method.
- Do not use 77-level data-items. Instead, organize WORKING-STORAGE independent data-items into collections of logically related fields, using level-numbers 01 through 49.

Future ANS-COBOL Standard Compatibility Recommendations

- Place an asterisk in position 7 of each coding line of the following IDENTIFICATION DIVISION paragraphs:

  AUTHOR
  INSTALLATION
  DATE-WRITTEN
  DATE-COMPILED
  SECURITY

  These paragraph headers and comment-entries are scheduled to be removed from the next COBOL standard. By making them comment-lines, you may retain their documentation value.
- Do not use the DATA RECORDS clause of the FD. It is scheduled to be removed from the next COBOL standard.
- Do not use level-number 77. It is scheduled to be removed from the next COBOL standard.

Exercises

Terms for Definition

programming style
reserved word
user-defined word
program-name
data-name
procedure-name
comment-entry
comment-line
system-name
level-indicator

file-name
label record
record-description entry
data-item description entry
level-number
group data-item
elementary data-item
picture symbol
picture character-string
forms-control character

Review Questions

1. Name the one required paragraph of the IDENTIFICATION DIVISION.

2. Which of the following are reserved words?

ADVANCING	ALPHANUMERIC	ARE
ASSIGN	AUTHOR	CHARACTER
CHARACTERS	CLOSE	COBOL

CONSTANT	CONFIGURATION	CONTAIN
CONTAINS	DATA	DATE
DATE-COMPILED	DATE-WRITTEN	DATA-ITEM
DATA-NAME	DIVISION	ELEMENTARY
EMPLOYEE	ENVIRONMENT	FD
FILE	FILES	FILE-NAME
FILE-CONTROL	FILLER	GROUP
IDENTIFICATION	INPUT-OUTPUT	INSTALLATION
IS	LABEL	LINE
LINES	MOVE	NUMBER
NUMERIC	OBJECT-COMPUTER	OMITTED
OPEN	PIC	PICTURE
PROCEDURE	PROGRAM-ID	READ
RECORD	RECORDS	RUN
SECTION	SECURITY	SELECT
SOURCE-COMPUTER	SPACE	SPACES
STANDARD	STOP	THROUGH
THRU	TO	UNTIL
WORK-AREA	WORKING-STORAGE	WRITE

3. Some or all of the following are not valid user-defined words. Identify each one that is not and give the reason.

VALID-USER-DEFINED-WORD	ARE
VALIDUSERDEFINEDWORD	YTD-SOCIAL-SECURITY-TAX
INVALID-USER-DEFINED-WORD	MTD-S/S-TAX
A	25
AR-ACCOUNTS-RECEIVABLE-AMOUNT-IN	25-DOLLARS
AR-PAYMENTS	$25
AR PURCHASES	-25-DOLLARS
AR-CREDIT-LIMIT-	25DOLLARS50CENTS
AR-E20-20-CODE	25.50-DOLLARS-OWED
AR-E	

4. Why is a 132-character print-line record usually defined in the FD entry as RECORD CONTAINS 133 CHARACTERS?

5. How can a group data-item description entry be distinguished from an elementary data-item description entry?

6. What is the purpose of the CONFIGURATION SECTION of the ENVIRONMENT DIVISION?

7. What is the purpose of the FILE-CONTROL paragraph of the INPUT-OUTPUT SECTION of the ENVIRONMENT DIVISION?

8. If a program has one input file and two output files, _____ SELECT statements will be required in the _____ paragraph of the _____ SECTION of the _____ DIVISION.

9. If a program has two input files and one output file, _____ FD entries will be required in the _____ SECTION of the _____ DIVISION.

10. Identify two reasons why it is recommended that the RECORD CONTAINS clause be specified in the FD entry.

11. Identify the reserved words that may be specified in the LABEL RECORDS clause of the FD entry for the following input or output devices: card, printer, tape, disk.

12. Identify the level-numbers for the following types of description entries: record-description entry, data-item (field) description entry, independent item description entry.

13. What picture symbol is used for numeric digits; what picture symbol is used for alphanumeric characters?

14. Area A begins in what position; Area B begins in what position?

15. Identify the following areas of the COBOL coding form: positions 1–6, positions 7–72, position 7, positions 8–12, positions 12–72, positions 73–80.

16. A two-state indicator used for program control is commonly referred to by programmers as a program _____ .

Syntax/Debug Exercises

1. Some or all of the following IDENTIFICATION DIVISION entries are in error. For each entry containing one or more errors, rewrite it correctly in the fill-in area provided. If the entry is correct, place a check-mark (✔) in the fill-in area.

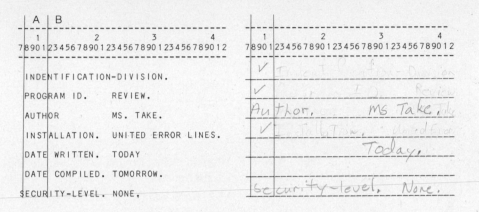

```
  A | B
-----|-------------------------------------
  1  |     2         3         4
7890 1 2345678901 2345678901 23456789012
-----|-------------------------------------
INDENTIFICATION-DIVISION.
PROGRAM ID.      REVIEW.
AUTHOR           MS. TAKE.
INSTALLATION.    UNITED ERROR LINES.
DATE WRITTEN.    TODAY
DATE COMPILED.   TOMORROW.
SECURITY-LEVEL.  NONE,
```

Fill-in (handwritten):
✔ The Identification Division
✔ Program ID. Review
Author.   MS Take, Id...
✔ Installation. United Error...
Today,
Security-level, None.

2. Some or all of the following ENVIRONMENT DIVISION entries are in error. For each entry containing one or more errors, rewrite it correctly in the fill-in area provided. If the entry is correct, place a check-mark (✔) in the fill-in area.

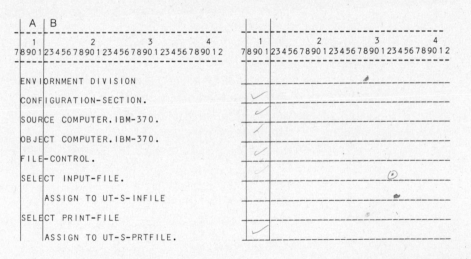

```
  A | B
-----|-------------------------------------
  1  |     2         3         4
7890 1 2345678901 2345678901 23456789012
-----|-------------------------------------
ENVIORNMENT DIVISION
CONFIGURATION-SECTION.
SOURCE COMPUTER.IBM-370.
OBJECT COMPUTER.IBM-370.
FILE-CONTROL.
SELECT INPUT-FILE.
      ASSIGN TO UT-S-INFILE
SELECT PRINT-FILE
      ASSIGN TO UT-S-PRTFILE.
```

3. Some or all of the following FD entries are in error. For each entry containing one or more errors, rewrite it correctly in the fill-in area provided. If the entry is correct, place a check-mark (✔) in the fill-in area.

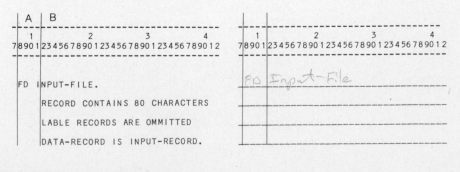

```
  A | B
-----|-------------------------------------
  1  |     2         3         4
7890 1 2345678901 2345678901 23456789012
-----|-------------------------------------
FD INPUT-FILE.
    RECORD CONTAINS 80 CHARACTERS
    LABLE RECORDS ARE OMMITTED
    DATA-RECORD IS INPUT-RECORD.
```

Fill-in (handwritten): FD Input-File

4. Some or all of the following record-description and data-item description entries are in error. For each entry containing one or more errors, rewrite it correctly in the fill-in area provided. If the entry is correct, place a check-mark (✓) in the fill-in area.

```
| A | B
  1        2        3        4
7 8 9 0 1 2 3 4 5 6 7 8 9 0 1 2 3 4 5 6 7 8 9 0 1 2

01  INPUT-RECORD

    05  IR-SS-NO        PIC 9(9).

    05  IR-NAME         PIC X(20)

    05  IR-ADDRESS      PICX(24).

    05  IR-CITY-STATE   PIC X(24).

    05  IR-ZIP-CODE     PIC 5(9).

    05  IR-DATE-BORN    PIC 9(6).

    10  IR-MO-BORN      PIC 99.

        10  IR-DA-BORN  PIC 9(2).

        10  IR-YR-BORN  PIC X(2).

    05  IR-SEX-CODE     PIC X (1).

    05  IR-PHONE-NO.    PIC 9(7).

    77  IR-CITY-BORN    PIC X(17).

    05  IR-STATE-BORN   PIC 2(X).

        05  IR-LIC-NO   PIC 9(X).

 05  FILLERS           PIC X(16)
```

Fill-in area:

```
  1        2        3        4
7 8 9 0 1 2 3 4 5 6 7 8 9 0 1 2 3 4 5 6 7 8 9 0 1 2

01  INPUT-RECORD

✓
```

Programming
Assignments

For each programming assignment, the following tasks are to be performed:

1. Draw a system flowchart
2. Prepare an input record layout
3. Prepare a print chart
4. Prepare a structure chart.
5. Prepare design documentation (pseudocode, program flowchart, etc.).
6. Code the first three divisions of the COBOL program (this may be done now after Chapter 2 has been covered).
7. Code the PROCEDURE DIVISION of the COBOL program (after Chapter 3 has been completed).

Programming
Assignment 2-A:
Parts List

Program description

A parts list is to be prepared from the parts file.

Input file

Parts file

Input record format

Parts record

Field location	Field name	Data class	Comments
1– 2	Record code	numeric	code "21"
3–12	Part number	alphanumeric	
20–45	Part description	alphanumeric	

Output file

Parts list

Output report line format

Print positions	Field name
10–19	Part number
25–50	Part description

Program operations

1. Read each input parts record.
2. Print an output parts report line as specified above for each parts record.
3. Single-space each report line.

Programming Assignment 2-B: Inventory List

An inventory list is to be prepared from the parts inventory file.

Input file

Parts inventory file

Input record format

Parts inventory record

Field location	Field name	Data class	Comments
1– 2	Record code	numeric	code "21"
3–12	Part number	alphanumeric	
20–45	Part description	alphanumeric	
46–50	Inventory balance	numeric	

Output file

Inventory list

Output report line format

Print positions	Field name
10–19	Part number
25–50	Part description
55–59	Inventory balance

Program operations:

1. Read each input parts inventory record.
2. Print an output parts inventory report line as specified above for each parts record.
3. Double-space each report line.

Programming Assignment 2-C: Customer List

Program description

A customer list is to be prepared from the customer account file.

Input file

Customer account file

Input record format: Customer account record

Field location	Field name	Data class	Comments
1– 2	Record code	numeric	code "23"
3– 7	Customer account number	numeric	
8–27	Customer name	alphanumeric	
28–49	Customer address	alphanumeric	
50–62	Customer city	alphanumeric	
63–64	Customer state	alphanumeric	
65–69	Customer zip code	numeric	

Output file
Customer list

Output report line format

Print positions	Field name
4–8	Customer account number
11–30	Customer name
34–55	Customer address
59–71	Customer city
74–75	Customer state
78–82	Customer zip code

Program operations

1. Read each input customer account record.
2. Print an output customer list report line as specified above for each customer accounts record.
3. Double-space each report line.

Programming Assignment 2-D: Employee Address/ Telephone List

Program description

An employee address/telephone list is to be prepared from the employee file.

Input file
Employee file

Input record format
Employee record

Field location	Field name	Data class	Comments
1– 2	Record code	numeric	code "24"
3–11	Employee social security number	numeric	
12–23	Employee last name	alphanumeric	
24–34	Employee first name	alphanumeric	
35	Employee middle initial	alphanumeric	
36–60	Employee address	alphanumeric	
61–73	Employee city	alphanumeric	
74–80	Employee telephone number	numeric	

Output file
Employee address telephone list

Output report line format

Print positions	Field name	Comments
1–12	Employee last name	
15–25	Employee first name	
27	Employee middle initial	
30–40	Employee social security number	Print hyphens sss-ss-ssss
43–67	Employee address	
70–82	Employee city	
85–92	Employee telephone number	Print hyphen †††-††††

Program operations
1. Read each input employee record.
2. Print an output employee address/telephone report line as specified above for each employee record. (Notice that hyphens are to be inserted in the social security and telephone number fields on the output report.)
3. Double-space each report line.

CHAPTER 3

WRITING A COBOL PROGRAM: THE PROCEDURE DIVISION

3

WRITING A COBOL PROGRAM:
THE PROCEDURE DIVISION

This chapter continues the discussion of the EMP-RPT program started in Chapter 2. Here we describe the PROCEDURE DIVISION and its elements.

PROCEDURE DIVISION Elements

The PROCEDURE DIVISION specifies the procedures that the computer is to perform to obtain the required results or outputs. Its format is shown in Figure 3.1. Each procedural step (input, arithmetic, data movement, decision, output, and so forth) is written as an English-like statement. These statements can be coded directly from the pseudocode or flowchart developed for the program. Figure 3.2 shows the pseudocode and PROCEDURE DIVISION statements for the EMP-RPT program. Let's first discuss the PROCEDURE DIVISION elements shown in Figure 3.3.

PROCEDURE DIVISION Header

Like other division headers, this is a required entry and must begin in area A. It must be spelled exactly as shown in Figure 3.4, must be followed by a period, and must appear on a line by itself.

PROCEDURE DIVISION Sections

Most programmers do not divide the PROCEDURE DIVISION into sections. Certain COBOL features, however, require the use of sections. It is generally considered good programming style to use sections only when necessary, as we will do in this text.

PROCEDURE DIVISION Paragraphs

The PROCEDURE DIVISION is formed by writing paragraphs. A paragraph within the PROCEDURE DIVISION is alternately called a *procedure*. Each paragraph starts with a procedure-name, beginning in position 8 of area A. It must be followed by a period. The procedure-name is a user-defined word.

PROCEDURE DIVISION Sentences and Statements

As in the English language, a paragraph in a COBOL program contains a series of sentences. Each *sentence* contains one or more statements. It is terminated by a period and followed by at least one blank space. A *statement* is a syntactically valid combination of words and symbols beginning with a verb. Figure 3.5 lists, by general category, the COBOL verbs that will be discussed in this text.

```
Format:
    PROCEDURE DIVISION.
   ⎧ section-name SECTION.
   ⎨
   ⎩ [Paragraph-name. [sentence] . . . ] . . . ⎬
```

Figure 3.1 PROCEDURE DIVISION format

PSEUDOCODE

Program name EMPLOYEE ADDRESS LIST   Program ID: EMP-RPT

Mainline-print-employee-report module
1. Open the files.
2. Perform Initialize-variable-fields module.
3. Read the first employee name-and-address record.
4. Perform Process-name-address-record module until no more records.
5. Close the files.
6. Stop the run.

Initialize-variable-fields module
1. Set the end-of-file indicator to "No".

Process-name-address-record module
1. Clear the output line area.
2. Move the input Employee-name to the output line Employee-name.
3. Move the input Employee-address to the output line Employee-address.
4. Move the input Employee-city-state-zip to the output line Employee-city-state-zip.
5. Move the input Employee-date-of-hire to the output line Employee-date-of-hire.
6. Write the employee output line (double-spaced).
7. Read the next input record.

```
006010*
006020*
006030*
006040 PROCEDURE DIVISION.

006050*
006060*
006070 MAINLINE-PRINT-EMPLOYEE-REPORT.
006080*
006090     OPEN INPUT NAME-ADDRESS-FILE-IN
006100          OUTPUT EMPLOYEE-REPORT-OUT.
006110     PERFORM INITIALIZE-VARIABLE-FIELDS.
006120     READ NAME-ADDRESS-FILE-IN
006130        AT END MOVE 'YES' TO WS-END-OF-FILE-SWITCH.
006140     PERFORM PROCESS-NAME-ADDRESS-RECORD
006150        UNTIL WS-END-OF-FILE-SWITCH IS EQUAL TO 'YES'.
006160     CLOSE NAME-ADDRESS-FILE-IN
006170           EMPLOYEE-REPORT-OUT.
006180     STOP RUN.

007010*
007020*
007030 INITIALIZE-VARIABLE-FIELDS.
007040*
007050     MOVE 'NO ' TO WS-END-OF-FILE-SWITCH.

008010*
008020*
008030 PROCESS-NAME-ADDRESS-RECORD.
008040*
008050     MOVE SPACES TO ER-EMPLOYEE-LINE-OUT.
008060     MOVE NA-EMPLOYEE-NAME-IN TO ER-EMPLOYEE-NAME-OUT.
008070     MOVE NA-EMPLOYEE-ADDRESS-IN TO ER-EMPLOYEE-ADDRESS-OUT.
008080     MOVE NA-EMPLOYEE-CITY-STATE-ZIP-IN
008090          TO ER-EMPLOYEE-CITY-STATE-ZIP-OUT.
008100     MOVE NA-EMPLOYEE-HIRE-MONTH-IN TO ER-EMPLOYEE-HIRE-MONTH-OUT.
008110     MOVE NA-EMPLOYEE-HIRE-DAY-IN TO ER-EMPLOYEE-HIRE-DAY-OUT.
008120     MOVE NA-EMPLOYEE-HIRE-YEAR-IN TO ER-EMPLOYEE-HIRE-YEAR-OUT.
008130     MOVE '-' TO ER-DATE-HYPHEN-1-OUT
008140              ER-DATE-HYPHEN-2-OUT.
008150     WRITE ER-EMPLOYEE-LINE-OUT
008160           AFTER ADVANCING 2 LINES.
008170     READ NAME-ADDRESS-FILE-IN
008180        AT END MOVE 'YES' TO WS-END-OF-FILE-SWITCH.
```

Figure 3.2 Relationship of pseudocode to PROCEDURE DIVISION of EMP-RPT

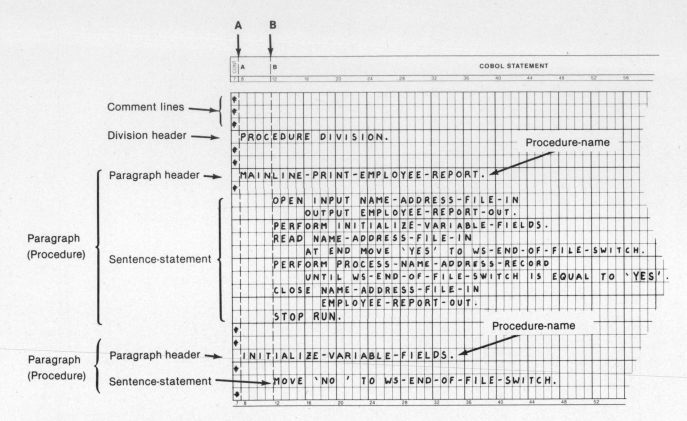

Figure 3.3 PROCEDURE DIVISION elements

Format:

<u>PROCEDURE DIVISION.</u>

Example:

SEQUENCE		CONT	A	B	COBOL STATEMENT	IDENTIFICATION
(PAGE)	(SERIAL)					

```
006010*                                              EMP-RPT
   02 *                                              {
   03 *                                              }
006040  PROCEDURE  DIVISION.                          EMP-RPT
```

Figure 3.4 PROCEDURE DIVISION header example

Arithmetic	Branching	Compiler-directing	Conditional	Data manipulation	Input/Output	Table-handling	Sort/Merge
ADD	GO TO	COPY	IF	INSPECT	ACCEPT	SEARCH	SORT
COMPUTE	PERFORM			(EXAMINE)	CLOSE	SET	MERGE
DIVIDE	STOP			MOVE	DISPLAY		
MULTIPLY				STRING	OPEN		
SUBTRACT				UNSTRING	READ		
					WRITE		

Figure 3.5 COBOL verbs discussed in this text

The end of a paragraph is signaled by the start of another paragraph (with a paragraph header in area A) or by the end of the program (no additional statements).

Although the PROCEDURE DIVISION is the last division of a COBOL program, the actual execution of the program really begins here. The first three divisions—IDENTIFICATION, ENVIRONMENT, and DATA—contain only declarative, or definition-type, specifications. The imperative instructions that the computer will execute are all contained in the PROCEDURE DIVISION.

This means that when the operating system gives control of required computer resources to the EMP-RPT program, the first instruction executed will be the first statement of the PROCEDURE DIVISION. The succeeding instructions will then be executed, one by one, in consecutive order, until a branching instruction—such as PERFORM or GO TO—is encountered. A *branching instruction* causes control to be transferred to a specific location in the program (rather than simply to the next consecutive instruction). When the STOP statement is executed, the computer resources allocated to the EMP-RPT program will be returned to the operating system.

MAINLINE-PRINT-EMPLOYEE-REPORT Paragraph

The MAINLINE-PRINT-EMPLOYEE-REPORT paragraph header is shown in Figure 3.6. MAINLINE-PRINT-EMPLOYEE-REPORT is a user-defined procedure-name. Like all procedure-names, it is written in area A, beginning in position 8. We could have formed any valid procedure-name for this paragraph. MAINLINE-PRINT-EMPLOYEE-REPORT is a good choice because this is the main program control module. The word *mainline* is often used by programmers to refer to such a module.

OPEN Statement

The first statement of the PROCEDURE DIVISION of the EMP-RPT program is an OPEN statement. Each file used by a COBOL program must be "opened" before any other input/output operations involving the file can be executed. The OPEN statement does not cause data records to be read from an input file or written to an output file. What it does do is initiate processing for a file. It makes available to the program an area into which an input record is to be read or into which an output record may be constructed. Also, if the use of label records was specified (LABEL RECORDS ARE STANDARD) in the file description for the file, the OPEN statement causes processing of the beginning label record. For an input file, the beginning label record is read and checked; for an output file, the beginning label record is written.

Figure 3.6 MAINLINE-PRINT-EMPLOYEE-REPORT paragraph

Format:

$$OPEN \begin{cases} \underline{INPUT} \text{ file-name-1 [file-name-2] ...} \\ \underline{OUTPUT} \text{ file-name-3 [file-name-4] ...} \\ \underline{I\text{-}O} \text{ file-name-5 [file-name-6] ...} \end{cases} ...$$

Example:

SEQUENCE		CONT	A	B	COBOL STATEMENT	IDENTIFICATION
(PAGE)	(SERIAL)					

```
006090        OPEN INPUT NAME-ADDRESS-FILE-IN              EMP-RPT
006100             OUTPUT EMPLOYEE-REPORT-OUT.              EMP-RPT
```

Figure 3.7 OPEN statement example

The OPEN statement format is shown in Figure 3.7. Notice that the reserved word INPUT must precede the name of the input file. Similarly, the reserved word OUTPUT must precede the name of the output file. The reserved word I-O is used to specify direct-access files upon which both input and output operations may be performed. If there are multiple files within a category, additional files are listed following the appropriate reserved word—INPUT, OUTPUT, or I-O—but the reserved word is not repeated.

Observe that the OPEN statement has been written on two lines in conformance with our general style conventions of one phrase per line and indentation of statement lines after the first. Thus, the file-names are vertically aligned. Figure 3.8 shows other examples of OPEN statements.

PERFORM Statement

After the files have been opened, the next instruction is a PERFORM statement. It is shown together with its format in Figure 3.9. PERFORM is a branching instruction. It transfers program control to the paragraph of the specified procedure-name. Thus, when this PERFORM statement is encountered, pro-

Part A: OPEN statements with repetition of the verb OPEN and the indication INPUT or OUTPUT for each file. Each OPEN indicates a separate statement that may or may not be a separate sentence.

SEQUENCE		CONT	A	B	COBOL STATEMENT	IDENTIFICATION
(PAGE)	(SERIAL)					

```
             OPEN INPUT  EMPLOYEE-FILE.
             OPEN INPUT  DEPARTMENTAL-FILE.
             OPEN OUTPUT EMPLOYEE-REPORT.
             OPEN OUTPUT DEPARTMENTAL-SUMMARY-FILE.
```

Part B: OPEN statement with verb OPEN and indication INPUT or OUTPUT specified just once for all files. (This approach is somewhat faster in execution but does consume more storage.) Since this is all one statement, the period may not appear before the statement has been completed.

```
             OPEN INPUT  EMPLOYEE-FILE
                         DEPARTMENTAL-FILE
                  OUTPUT EMPLOYEE-REPORT
                         DEPARTMENTAL-SUMMARY-FILE.
```

Figure 3.8 Other OPEN statement examples

PERFORM procedure-name

Example:

SEQUENCE		CONT	A	B	COBOL STATEMENT	IDENTIFICATION
(PAGE)	(SERIAL)					

`006110    PERFORM INITIALIZE-VARIABLE-FIELDS.                                    EMP-RPT`

Figure 3.9 PERFORM statement example

gram control will be transferred from this MAINLINE-PRINT-EMPLOYEE-REPORT paragraph to the start of the INITIALIZE-VARIABLE-FIELDS paragraph. The program continues processing the statements in this paragraph until the end of the performed procedure is reached. The end of the procedure is reached when another procedure-name (or the end of the program) is encountered.

Once the end of the performed procedure has been reached, the program returns to the next sequential statement after the PERFORM statement from which control was transferred. This PERFORM statement processing is shown in Figure 3.10.

INITIALIZE-VARIABLE-FIELDS Paragraph

This procedure contains a statement required to prepare for program processing. The INITIALIZE-VARIABLE-FIELDS paragraph header is shown in Figure 3.11. The user-defined procedure-name INITIALIZE-VARIABLE-FIELDS is writ-

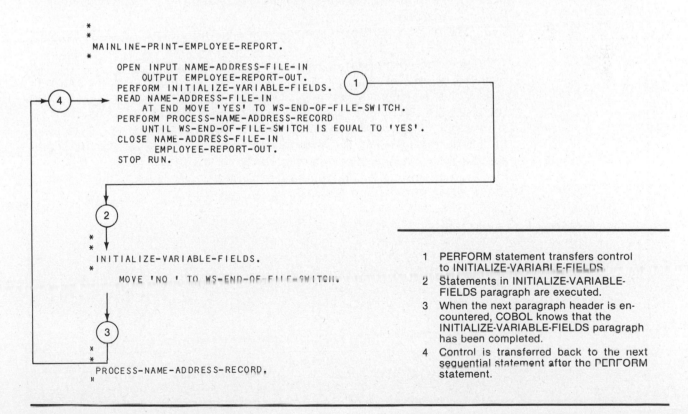

```
*
*
   MAINLINE-PRINT-EMPLOYEE-REPORT.
*
       OPEN INPUT NAME-ADDRESS-FILE-IN
            OUTPUT EMPLOYEE-REPORT-OUT.
       PERFORM INITIALIZE-VARIABLE-FIELDS.
       READ NAME-ADDRESS-FILE-IN
            AT END MOVE 'YES' TO WS-END-OF-FILE-SWITCH.
       PERFORM PROCESS-NAME-ADDRESS-RECORD
            UNTIL WS-END-OF-FILE-SWITCH IS EQUAL TO 'YES'.
       CLOSE NAME-ADDRESS-FILE-IN
             EMPLOYEE-REPORT-OUT.
       STOP RUN.


*
*
   INITIALIZE-VARIABLE-FIELDS.
*
       MOVE 'NO ' TO WS-END-OF-FILE-SWITCH.



*
*
   PROCESS-NAME-ADDRESS-RECORD.
*
```

1 PERFORM statement transfers control to INITIALIZE-VARIABLE-FIELDS.
2 Statements in INITIALIZE-VARIABLE-FIELDS paragraph are executed.
3 When the next paragraph header is encountered, COBOL knows that the INITIALIZE-VARIABLE-FIELDS paragraph has been completed.
4 Control is transferred back to the next sequential statement after the PERFORM statement.

Figure 3.10 PERFORM statement processing

SEQUENCE			A	B						COBOL STATEMENT								IDENTIFICATION	
(PAGE)	(SERIAL)	CONT																	
1 3	4 6	7 8		12 16 20 24 28 32 36 40 44 48 52 56 60 64 68													72	76 80	

```
007010*                                                    EMP-RPT
   02)*
   03( INITIALIZE-VARIABLE-FIELDS.
   04)*
007050    MOVE 'NO ' TO WS-END-OF-FILE-SWITCH.              EMP-RPT
```

Figure 3.11 INITIALIZE-VARIABLE-FIELDS paragraph

ten beginning in position 8 of area A. Again, any valid procedure-name could have been used, but the one chosen is descriptive of the function the procedure is to serve.

MOVE statement

To move data from one area of computer storage to another, the MOVE verb is used. The MOVE statement format together with the example from the INITIALIZE-VARIABLE-FIELDS procedure is shown in Figure 3.12.

The format for the MOVE statement shows that after the verb MOVE, either an identifier or a literal should be written. The word *identifier* indicates that a data-name (the name of a field in the DATA DIVISION) should be written. A *literal* is an actual value specified in the program. "Identifier-1" and "literal" are enclosed in brackets to show that the programmer can use either one of these elements. This first entry after the verb MOVE can be referred to as the *sending* field. It is the source of the data to be moved. The reserved word TO must follow the sending field.

After the word TO, another identifier is required. Here, the programmer must write a data-name for the *receiving* field. After the MOVE statement is executed, the receiving field will contain the data transmitted from the sending field. The MOVE statement does not alter the data contained in the sending field.

The format notation shows a third identifier enclosed in braces and followed by an ellipsis (three periods). The ellipsis indicates that additional data-names may be written. Thus, one MOVE statement may be used to transfer data from one sending field to one or more receiving fields.

When the program begins execution, fields defined in WORKING-STORAGE without a VALUE clause (which will be discussed in Chapter 7) will contain either (1) unpredictable data left from the previous program that used that area of storage, or (2) initialization values as provided by the operating

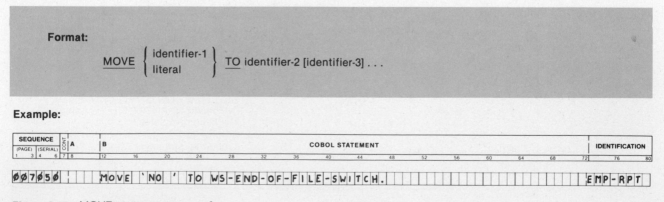

Format:

MOVE { identifier-1 / literal } TO identifier-2 [identifier-3] . . .

Example:

SEQUENCE			A	B						COBOL STATEMENT								IDENTIFICATION	
(PAGE)	(SERIAL)	CONT																	
1 3	4 6	7 8		12 16 20 24 28 32 36 40 44 48 52 56 60 64 68													72	76 80	

```
007050    MOVE 'NO ' TO WS-END-OF-FILE-SWITCH.              EMP-RPT
```

Figure 3.12 MOVE statement example

system. The COBOL programmer should initialize explicitly all fields that require a specific starting value.

So, to initialize the WS-END-OF-FILE-SWITCH, we use the statement MOVE 'NO ' TO WS-END-OF-FILE-SWITCH. Since program execution is just starting and no records have yet been read from the input NAME-ADDRESS-FILE-IN, the value of 'NO ' is a meaningful setting for the end-of-file switch. Clearly, the end of the input file has not been reached.

Remember that the sending field of a MOVE statement can be either a data-name identifier or a literal value. Here, a literal is being used as a sending field. The actual value to be moved—'NO '— was specified.

After the MOVE statement is executed, the WS-END-OF-FILE-SWITCH will contain the value specified: 'NO '.

Non-numeric literals

Two types of literals may be used in a COBOL program: numeric and non-numeric. The word 'NO ' is an example of a non-numeric literal. Numeric literals will be covered in Chapter 4.

Non-numeric literals must be enclosed by quotation marks (so that the COBOL compiler can distinguish them from data-names). Although the ANS COBOL standard calls for double quotes, many compilers use single quotation marks, as does this text. They can contain any characters (letters, digits, blank spaces, and special characters) that can be represented by the character set of the computer being used. Thus, the term "non-numeric" is somewhat misleading since a non-numeric literal may contain one or more numeric digits. (Indeed, it may contain only numeric digits). It is non-numeric in that such a value cannot be used in arithmetic calculations. A non-numeric literal can be up to 120 characters in length. The quotation marks that enclose the literal act as delimiters; they indicate the start and end of the literal value. They are not counted as part of the literal when determining its length.

Because the quotation marks act as delimiters, a quotation mark cannot appear singly as part of the literal itself (for it would be incorrectly interpreted as marking the end of the literal). If a quotation mark is part of a non-numeric literal, contiguous quotation marks must be used to express one quotation mark. The COBOL compiler will recognize the two contiguous marks as one quotation mark within the literal. It will not treat either mark of an adjacent pair as a delimiter. Figure 3.13 provides examples of valid and invalid non-numeric literals.

Looking at the MOVE statement in the INITIALIZE-VARIABLE-FIELDS paragraph, notice that the word NO is expressed as three characters: N, O, and a blank space. This is because the receiving field—WS-END-OF-FILE-SWITCH—is defined with a length of three characters. Although not required, it is efficient to make non-numeric literals the same length as the receiving field. Shorter non-numeric literals can be lengthened by providing blank spaces to the right of the literal data and to the left of the terminating quotation mark, as is done here. Figure 3.14 shows the effect of this MOVE statement.

Valid non-numeric literals	Invalid non-numeric literals	Reason invalid
'TOTAL AMOUNT'	TOTAL AMOUNT	Not enclosed by quotation marks
'6.05%'	'6.05%	Missing closing quotation mark
'COMPANY''S CONTRIBUTION'	'COMPANY'S CONTRIBUTION'	Single quotation mark not allowed in literal
'12345'	12345'	Missing beginning quotation mark

Figure 3.13 Valid and invalid non-numeric literals

Part A: Contents of WS-END-OF-FILE-SWITCH field when EMP-RPT program begins

X	*	3

Contents unpredictable: left from a previous program or initialized by operating system

Part B: Contents of WS-END-OF-FILE-SWITCH field after execution of MOVE statement

N	O	

Move 'NO ' to WS-END-OF-FILE-SWITCH.

Figure 3.14 Effect of MOVE statement upon WS-END-OF-FILE-SWITCH

READ Statement

The READ statement makes a logical record from an input file available to the program. The statement format is shown in Figure 3.15. Notice that, following the reserved word READ, the file-name—not the record name—is specified. Although the AT END phrase is shown in brackets and thus optional, it is required when accessing input files sequentially. That is, it is required when the program will read first the record physically located at the beginning of the file and then will read each succeeding record, one after another, until the end of the file is reached. As is the case with all card and tape and many disk files, NAME-ADDRESS-FILE-IN is to be accessed sequentially.

This READ statement within the MAINLINE-PRINT-EMPLOYEE-REPORT paragraph will cause the first record of the NAME-ADDRESS-FILE-IN to be read from the input file into the computer storage input area defined by the record-description entry for the file. Whatever was in the input area prior to execution of the READ statement will be overlaid by the data transmitted from the input device. The effect of the READ statement is shown in Figure 3.16. The data read into the input area stays there until the next READ is executed (or until the programmer explicitly moves other data into the input area).

AT END phrase

When writing a program, the programmer does not usually know exactly how many records will be contained in the input file (or files). Indeed, even if the precise number of records is known, that number should not be reflected in the program. For example, suppose a program is to be written to process a file containing 103 records. The programmer could write the program so that a READ statement would be executed exactly 103 times. This would not be wise, though, because record counts within a file are normally dynamic; they vary in

Format:

READ file-name

[AT END imperative-statement]

Example:

SEQUENCE					
(PAGE) (SERIAL)	CONT	A	B	COBOL STATEMENT	IDENTIFICATION
006120			READ NAME-ADDRESS-FILE-IN		EMP-RPT
006130			AT END MOVE 'YES' TO WS-END-OF-FILE-SWITCH.		EMP-RPT

Figure 3.15 READ statement example

Part A: Before READ statement is executed:

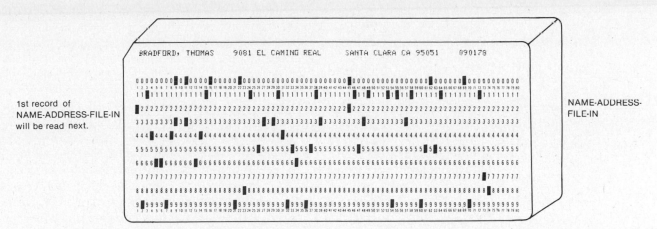

1st record of
NAME-ADDRESS-FILE-IN
will be read next.

NAME-ADDRESS-
FILE-IN

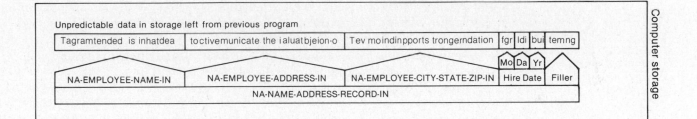

Computer storage

Part B: After READ statement has been executed:

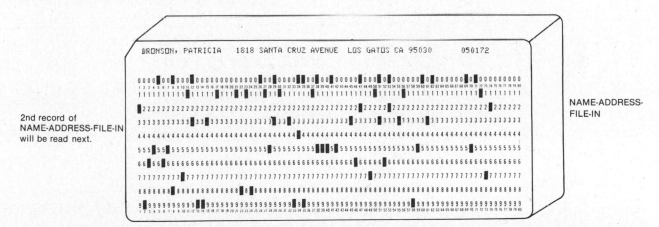

2nd record of
NAME-ADDRESS-FILE-IN
will be read next.

NAME-ADDRESS-
FILE-IN

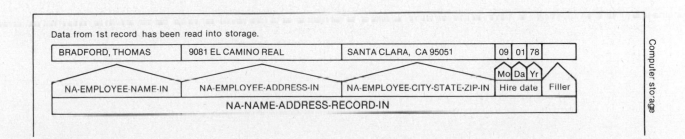

Computer storage

Figure 3.16 Effect of READ statement

size depending on file activity—which, in turn, is based upon business conditions and the like. Instead, the program should be written so that the READ statement will be executed until there are no more records to be read. Then, the READ statement should not be executed again. This technique of program control for sequential files is accomplished through use of the AT END phrase.

When the AT END phrase is specified, one or more statements must be written after the reserved words AT END. In the EMP-RPT program, we wrote the statement MOVE 'YES' TO WS-END-OF-FILE-SWITCH. The READ statement with the AT END phrase works as follows: If the READ statement successfully reads a record, the AT END phrase (which includes the statement or statements following the reserved words AT END and before the period) is ignored. However, if the READ statement detects that the end of the file has been reached—that there are no more remaining data records—the computer executes the statement or statements following the reserved words AT END. This logic is shown in Figure 3.17. There are two points to remember regarding the AT END phrase. First, the end-of-file condition is not detected when the last record is read. Rather it is detected when the next attempted READ (after the last record) occurs. Second, the period following the AT END statement or statements is very important. It determines which statements are ignored when a record has been read successfully.

Notice that the READ statement has been written following the style conventions of one phrase per line and an indented second line.

This READ statement within the MAINLINE-PRINT-EMPLOYEE-REPORT paragraph is used only to read the very first record of the input file. Actually, an end-of-file condition would not be expected on the very first READ, but it could happen, if, for instance, the file were empty.

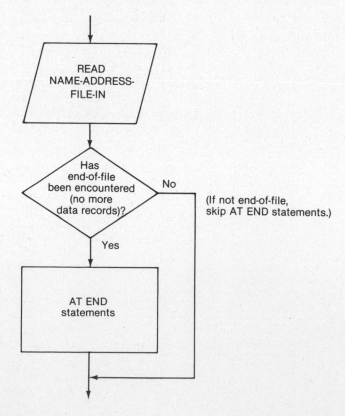

Figure 3.17 AT END phrase logic

Example:

SEQUENCE		C O N T	A	B	COBOL STATEMENT	IDENTIFICATION
(PAGE)	(SERIAL)					
1 3	4 6	7	8	12 16 20 24 28 32 36 40 44 48 52 56 60 64 68 72	76 80
006140				PERFORM PROCESS-NAME-ADDRESS-RECORD	EMP-RPT
006150				UNTIL WS-END-OF-FILE-SWITCH IS EQUAL TO 'YES'.	EMP-RPT

Figure 3.18 PERFORM/UNTIL statement example

PERFORM/UNTIL Statement

The format of the PERFORM/UNTIL statement is shown in Figure 3.18. It operates similar to the basic PERFORM statement already discussed; it transfers control to another procedure of the program and provides for return of control when that procedure has been completed. The PERFORM/UNTIL statement has one important distinction, however. It transfers control conditionally, depending upon the condition expressed following the reserved word UNTIL. If the condition is false, the named procedure is performed. It the condition is true, the procedure is not performed; instead, program execution continues with the next sequential instruction. Figure 3.19 illustrates this action of the PERFORM/UNTIL statement.

The effect of the PERFORM PROCESS-NAME-ADDRESS-RECORDS statement is conditional, depending upon whether WS-END-OF-FILE-SWITCH IS EQUAL TO 'YES'. As long as records are read successfully into the input area, the end-of-file indicator will be equal to 'NO '. This means that the condition WS-END-OF-FILE-SWITCH IS EQUAL TO 'YES' will be false. Therefore, the PROCESS-NAME-ADDRESS-RECORDS procedure will be performed.

Once the READ statement detects an end-of-file condition, (1) the value 'YES' will be placed in WS-END-OF-FILE-SWITCH; (2) the program will return to the PERFORM/UNTIL statement; (3) the PERFORM/UNTIL condition will be tested and determined to be true; and (4) program execution will continue at the next sequential statement following the PERFORM/UNTIL statement.

The PERFORM/UNTIL statement has been written to adhere to the style conventions of one phrase per line and an indented second line.

CLOSE Statement

The CLOSE statement is the next sequential statement and will be executed only after the end of the input file has been reached. After all input and/or output operations have been executed for a file and before the program execution ends, each file must be "closed." The CLOSE statement is used to terminate processing for a file. For files with label records, end-of-file labels are processed. For output files requiring end-of-file markings on the storage medium, such indication is written. The CLOSE statement format is shown in Figure 3.20.

The CLOSE statement contains the reserved word CLOSE followed by the file-name of each file to be closed. Unlike the OPEN statement, the reserved words INPUT, OUTPUT, and I-O are not specified; the COBOL compiler retains such knowledge from the OPEN statement. Again, the style consideration of one phrase per line is adhered to. The file names of the CLOSE statement are aligned vertically for easier reading. Figure 3.21 shows other ways of writing CLOSE statements.

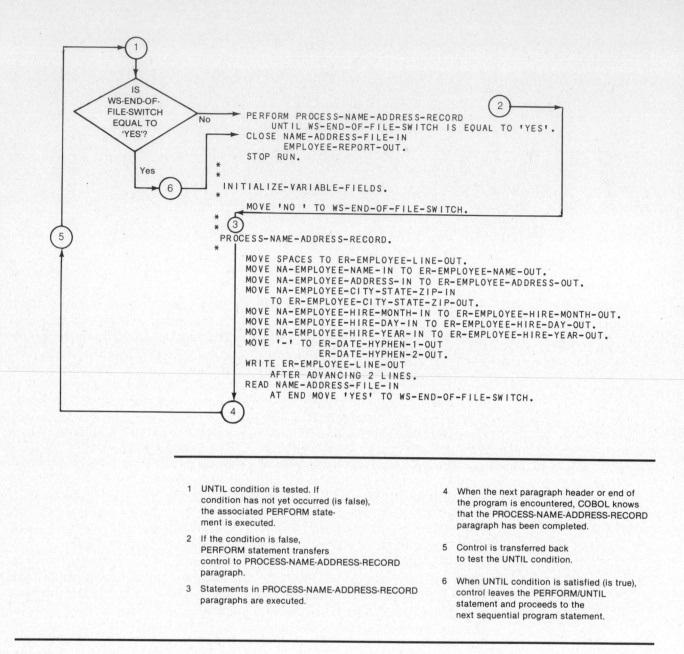

```
          ┌─────────────────┐
          │        1        │
          └─────────────────┘
                   │
          ╱───────────────╲
         ╱   IS            ╲
        ╱   WS-END-OF-      ╲
       ╱   FILE-SWITCH      ╲─── No ───►  PERFORM PROCESS-NAME-ADDRESS-RECORD        ┌───┐
        ╲   EQUAL TO        ╱                  UNTIL WS-END-OF-FILE-SWITCH IS EQUAL TO 'YES'. │ 2 │
         ╲   'YES'?        ╱             CLOSE NAME-ADDRESS-FILE-IN                    └───┘
          ╲───────────────╱                   EMPLOYEE-REPORT-OUT.
                   │                     STOP RUN.
                 Yes                  *
                   │                  *
                ┌───┐                 * INITIALIZE-VARIABLE-FIELDS.
                │ 6 │                 *
                └───┘                     MOVE 'NO ' TO WS-END-OF-FILE-SWITCH.
                                      *
                                      *  (3)
     ┌───┐                            * PROCESS-NAME-ADDRESS-RECORD.
     │ 5 │                            *
     └───┘                               MOVE SPACES TO ER-EMPLOYEE-LINE-OUT.
                                         MOVE NA-EMPLOYEE-NAME-IN TO ER-EMPLOYEE-NAME-OUT.
                                         MOVE NA-EMPLOYEE-ADDRESS-IN TO ER-EMPLOYEE-ADDRESS-OUT.
                                         MOVE NA-EMPLOYEE-CITY-STATE-ZIP-IN
                                             TO ER-EMPLOYEE-CITY-STATE-ZIP-OUT.
                                         MOVE NA-EMPLOYEE-HIRE-MONTH-IN TO ER-EMPLOYEE-HIRE-MONTH-OUT.
                                         MOVE NA-EMPLOYEE-HIRE-DAY-IN TO ER-EMPLOYEE-HIRE-DAY-OUT.
                                         MOVE NA-EMPLOYEE-HIRE-YEAR-IN TO ER-EMPLOYEE-HIRE-YEAR-OUT.
                                         MOVE '-' TO ER-DATE-HYPHEN-1-OUT
                                                    ER-DATE-HYPHEN-2-OUT.
                                         WRITE ER-EMPLOYEE-LINE-OUT
                                             AFTER ADVANCING 2 LINES.
                                         READ NAME-ADDRESS-FILE-IN
                ┌───┐                        AT END MOVE 'YES' TO WS-END-OF-FILE-SWITCH.
                │ 4 │
                └───┘
```

1 UNTIL condition is tested. If condition has not yet occurred (is false), the associated PERFORM statement is executed.

2 If the condition is false, PERFORM statement transfers control to PROCESS-NAME-ADDRESS-RECORD paragraph.

3 Statements in PROCESS-NAME-ADDRESS-RECORD paragraphs are executed.

4 When the next paragraph header or end of the program is encountered, COBOL knows that the PROCESS-NAME-ADDRESS-RECORD paragraph has been completed.

5 Control is transferred back to test the UNTIL condition.

6 When UNTIL condition is satisfied (is true), control leaves the PERFORM/UNTIL statement and proceeds to the next sequential program statement.

Figure 3.19 PERFORM/UNTIL statement logic

STOP Statement

When program execution is to be terminated, the STOP statement is used. It stops execution of the program and returns control to the operating system. The last statement to be executed in a COBOL program should normally be the STOP statement. Its format is shown in Figure 3.22.

Recap of the MAINLINE-PRINT-EMPLOYEE-REPORT Paragraph

The MAINLINE-PRINT-EMPLOYEE-REPORT paragraph is the main control procedure of the EMP-RPT program. It (1) opens the files; (2) causes the INITIALIZE-VARIABLE-FIELDS procedure to be performed once; (3) reads the first record from the input file; (4) causes the PROCESS-NAME-ADDRESS-RECORD procedure to be performed repeatedly until all records have been processed; then (5) closes the files; and (6) stops the program, thereby returning control to the operating system.

Format:

    CLOSE file-name-1 [file-name-2] . . .

Example:

SEQUENCE																				IDENTIFICATION	
(PAGE) (SERIAL)	CONT	A	B							COBOL STATEMENT											
1 3 4 6	7 8		12	16	20	24	28	32	36	40	44	48	52	56	60	64	68	72	76	80
Ø Ø 6 1 6 Ø			C L O S E N A M E - A D D R E S S - F I L E - I N																E M P - R P T	
Ø Ø 6 1 7 Ø			E M P L O Y E E - R E P O R T - O U T .																E M P - R P T	

Figure 3.20 CLOSE statement example

Part A: CLOSE statement with CLOSE verb specified once for each file. Notice that each CLOSE becomes a separate statement and may be a separate sentence.

SEQUENCE																				IDENTIFICATION	
(PAGE) (SERIAL)	CONT	A	B							COBOL STATEMENT											
1 3 4 6	7 8		12	16	20	24	28	32	36	40	44	48	52	56	60	64	68	72	76	80
			C L O S E E M P L O Y E E - F I L E .																	
			C L O S E D E P A R T M E N T A L - F I L E .																	
			C L O S E E M P L O Y E E - R E P O R T .																	
			C L O S E D E P A R T M E N T A L - S U M M A R Y - F I L E .																	

Part B: CLOSE statement with verb CLOSE specified just once for all files (this approach is faster in execution speed, although it consumes more storage).

			C L O S E E M P L O Y E E - F I L E																	
			D E P A R T M E N T A L - F I L E																	
			E M P L O Y E E - R E P O R T																	
			D E P A R T M E N T A L - S U M M A R Y - F I L E .																	

Figure 3.21 Other CLOSE statement examples

Format:

    STOP { RUN / literal }

Example:

SEQUENCE																				IDENTIFICATION	
(PAGE) (SERIAL)	CONT	A	B							COBOL STATEMENT											
1 3 4 6	7 8		12	16	20	24	28	32	36	40	44	48	52	56	60	64	68	72	76	80
Ø Ø 6 1 8 Ø			S T O P R U N .																E M P - R P T	

Figure 3.22 STOP statement example

Figure 3.23   PROCESS-NAME-ADDRESS-RECORD paragraph

The coding form contains:

```
 ØØ8Ø1Ø  *                                                                  EMP-RPT
    Ø2  *
    Ø3  PROCESS-NAME-ADDRESS-RECORD.
    Ø4  *
    Ø5      MOVE SPACES TO ER-EMPLOYEE-LINE-OUT.
    Ø6      MOVE NA-EMPLOYEE-NAME-IN TO ER-EMPLOYEE-NAME-OUT.
    Ø7      MOVE NA-EMPLOYEE-ADDRESS-IN TO ER-EMPLOYEE-ADDRESS-OUT.
    Ø8      MOVE NA-EMPLOYEE-CITY-STATE-ZIP-IN
    Ø9          TO ER-EMPLOYEE-CITY-STATE-ZIP-OUT.
    1Ø      MOVE NA-EMPLOYEE-HIRE-MONTH-IN TO ER-EMPLOYEE-HIRE-MONTH-OUT.
    11      MOVE NA-EMPLOYEE-HIRE-DAY-IN TO ER-EMPLOYEE-HIRE-DAY-OUT.
    12      MOVE NA-EMPLOYEE-HIRE-YEAR-IN TO ER-EMPLOYEE-HIRE-YEAR-OUT.
    13      MOVE '-' TO ER-DATE-HYPHEN-1-OUT
    14          ER-DATE-HYPHEN-2-OUT.
    15      WRITE ER-EMPLOYEE-LINE-OUT
    16          AFTER ADVANCING 2 LINES.
    17      READ NAME-ADDRESS-FILE-IN
 ØØ818Ø      AT END MOVE 'YES' TO WS-END-OF-FILE-SWITCH.            EMP-RPT
```

PROCESS-NAME-ADDRESS-RECORD Paragraph

This paragraph, shown in Figure 3.23, contains the statements to be executed repeatedly, as long as there are records in the input file. The user-defined procedure-name PROCESS-NAME-ADDRESS-RECORD is written beginning in area A (position 8) and followed by a period.

MOVE Statement

The first MOVE statement in this paragraph is used to clear the output area in which the line to be printed will be formed. When program execution begins, the record-description area for the ER-EMPLOYEE-LINE-OUT will contain data left from the last program that used this area of storage. Data will be moved from the NA-NAME-ADDRESS-RECORD-IN fields to certain fields within the ER-EMPLOYEE-LINE-OUT. The simplest way to clear all of the FILLER areas is to move blank spaces to the entire ER-EMPLOYEE-LINE-OUT. The statement MOVE SPACES TO ER-EMPLOYEE-LINE-OUT will set all 133 characters of the line to blank spaces. This is shown schematically in Figure 3.24.

Figurative constants

The word SPACES is a reserved word and a *figurative constant*. A figurative constant is similar to a literal in that it provides a way of introducing an actual value into a COBOL program. It differs from a literal in that the actual value is referenced—not by using the value—but rather by a reserved word such as SPACE or SPACES. Figurative constants are available for a few values commonly used in COBOL programs. The figurative constants SPACE and SPACES define blank-space data values. The words are equivalent; the singular and plural forms are provided to allow the COBOL program to be written like grammatically correct English. That is, we could write MOVE SPACE TO ER-EMPLOYEE-LINE-OUT or MOVE SPACES TO ER-EMPLOYEE-LINE-OUT. In both cases, the entire 133 characters of the line would be set to blank spaces. The figurative constants used in this text are shown in Figure 3.25.

The next six MOVE statements are examples of a MOVE statement with a data-name used to specify the sending field. Notice that each of the three subfields of the date-of-hire field—month, day, and year—were moved individually so that the separating hyphens could be inserted where they belong on the output line.

Part A: Before MOVE SPACES TO ER-EMPLOYEE-LINE-OUT (Unpredictable data occupies storage area)

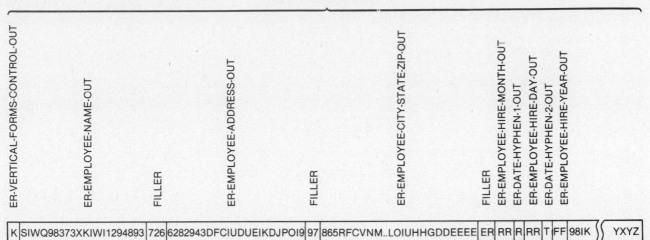

Part B: After MOVE SPACES TO ER-EMPLOYEE-LINE-OUT

Figure 3.24 Blanking the ER-EMPLOYEE-LINE-OUT

The statement MOVE '-' TO ER-DATE-HYPHEN-1-OUT ER-DATE-HYPHEN-2-OUT is an example of a MOVE statement with multiple (in this case, two) receiving fields.

WRITE Statement

Once the ER-EMPLOYEE-LINE-OUT has been fully developed, it can be written to the printer. The WRITE statement is used to cause a record to be transferred to an output device.

The WRITE statement format is shown in Figure 3.26. After the reserved word WRITE, the programmer specifies the record-name—not the file

Figurative constant †	Value that fills field
SPACE SPACES	Blank space
ZERO ZEROS ZEROES	Zero
QUOTE QUOTES	Quotation mark (This figurative constant is not often used. It is provided because quotation marks are used as the delimiters for non numeric literals and they are thus confusing to represent within the literal.)
HIGH-VALUE HIGH-VALUES	Highest possible value (Exact value varies depending upon the computer system being used.)
LOW-VALUE LOW-VALUES	Lowest possible value (Exact value varies depending upon the computer system being used.)
ALL [non-numeric literal]	Repeats the specified literal throughout the field

† Singular and plural forms are interchangeable

Figure 3.25 Figurative constants

Format:

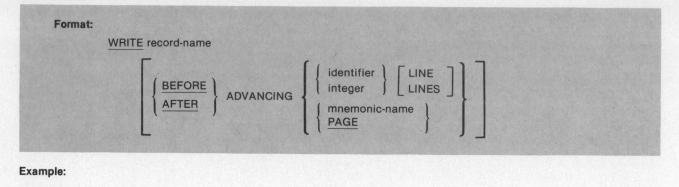

Example:

SEQUENCE		CONT	A	B	COBOL STATEMENT	IDENTIFICATION
(PAGE) (SERIAL)						

```
0 0 8 1 5 0       WRITE ER-EMPLOYEE-LINE-OUT                              EMP-RPT
0 0 8 1 6 0             AFTER ADVANCING 2 LINES.                          EMP-RPT
```

Figure 3.26 WRITE statement example

name—of the record to be written as output. The ADVANCING phrase applies to vertical forms spacing and is used only with output records directed to a printer device.

ADVANCING phrase

The ER-EMPLOYEE-LINE-OUT is directed to a printer file so the ADVANCING phrase is used. We could have specified either BEFORE ADVANCING or AFTER ADVANCING. The former option means that first the line will be written and then the paper form will be advanced (the line is written BEFORE ADVANCING the form). The latter option is used for the reverse situation: the form will be advanced and then the line will be written (the line is written AFTER ADVANCING the form). For most line-printers, it is more efficient mechanically to write the line after the form has been advanced. So the AFTER ADVANCING option is much more frequently used.

In the ADVANCING phrase, there are four alternate ways of expressing how many lines are to be advanced. The *integer* option is used in this EMP-RPT program. (The other options will be covered in Chapter 7.) With the integer option, the number of lines to be advanced is expressed as a number in the range from 0 to 99 (the range used by many COBOL compilers). Since the print chart for the output report calls for double-spacing, the integer 2 has been specified. After the indication of the number of lines, the optional reserved word LINE or LINES may be written. When using the integer option, this word makes the WRITE statement a bit more readable, so it's a good idea to include it.

Notice that the WRITE statement has been written one phrase per line and the second line is indented.

READ Statement

The READ statement in this paragraph is exactly the same as the one written in the MAINLINE-PRINT-EMPLOYEE-REPORT paragraph. Remember that the one in the mainline paragraph will be executed only once; it will attempt to read the first record of the input file. The READ statement in this PROCESS-NAME-ADDRESS-RECORD paragraph will be used to read all of the records after the first one. The PROCESS-NAME-ADDRESS-RECORD paragraph is the only procedure of the program that will be executed repeatedly, depending upon the status of the end-of-file indicator.

Ultimately, this READ statement will attempt to read a record but there will be none left to process. When this happens, the program will execute the statement following the reserved words AT END. At this time, the value 'YES' will be moved to WS-END-OF-FILE-SWITCH.

Recap of PROCESS-NAME-ADDRESS-RECORD Paragraph

This procedure (1) initializes the ER-EMPLOYEE-LINE-OUT to a value of SPACES; (2) moves the fields required for the report line from the NA-NAME-ADDRESS-RECORD-IN area to their proper locations on the ER-EMPLOYEE-LINE-OUT; (3) writes the line; and (4) reads the next name-and-address record.

READ Statement Placement

When a programmer first encounters a structured program, one topic invariably brings questions to mind: the placement and handling of READ statements. The READ statement is very important for sequential file processing because the AT END phrase is generally a prime determinant of overall program control.

Common questions about READ statement placement for the program just discussed may be something like this: "Why is a READ statement placed first in the MAINLINE-PRINT-EMPLOYEE-REPORT procedure and also at the end of the PROCESS-NAME-ADDRESS-RECORD procedure? Why not just put the READ statement at the beginning of the PROCESS-NAME-ADDRESS-RECORD procedure?" Figure 3.27 shows how such a program would look.

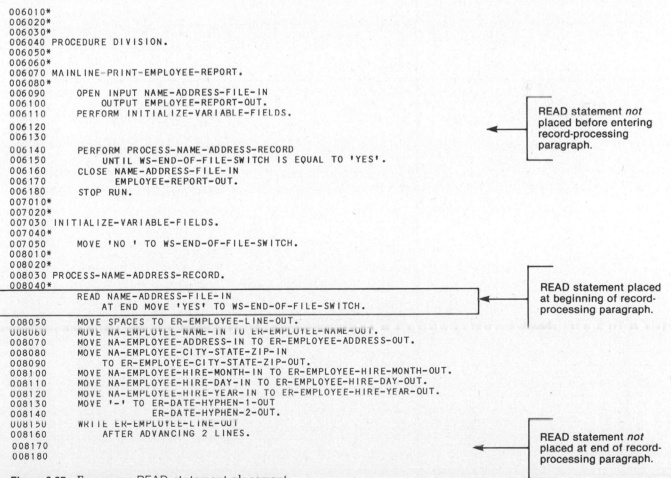

```
006010*
006020*
006030*
006040 PROCEDURE DIVISION.
006050*
006060*
006070 MAINLINE-PRINT-EMPLOYEE-REPORT.
006080*
006090     OPEN INPUT NAME-ADDRESS-FILE-IN
006100          OUTPUT EMPLOYEE-REPORT-OUT.
006110     PERFORM INITIALIZE-VARIABLE-FIELDS.         ◄── READ statement not placed before entering record-processing paragraph.
006120
006130
006140     PERFORM PROCESS-NAME-ADDRESS-RECORD
006150          UNTIL WS-END-OF-FILE-SWITCH IS EQUAL TO 'YES'.
006160     CLOSE NAME-ADDRESS-FILE-IN
006170           EMPLOYEE-REPORT-OUT.
006180     STOP RUN.
007010*
007020*
007030 INITIALIZE-VARIABLE-FIELDS.
007040*
007050     MOVE 'NO ' TO WS-END-OF-FILE-SWITCH.
008010*
008020*
008030 PROCESS-NAME-ADDRESS-RECORD.
008040*
       READ NAME-ADDRESS-FILE-IN
            AT END MOVE 'YES' TO WS-END-OF-FILE-SWITCH.    ◄── READ statement placed at beginning of record-processing paragraph.
008050     MOVE SPACES TO ER-EMPLOYEE-LINE-OUT.
008060     MOVE NA-EMPLOYEE-NAME-IN TO ER-EMPLOYEE-NAME-OUT.
008070     MOVE NA-EMPLOYEE-ADDRESS-IN TO ER-EMPLOYEE-ADDRESS-OUT.
008080     MOVE NA-EMPLOYEE-CITY-STATE-ZIP-IN
008090          TO ER-EMPLOYEE-CITY-STATE-ZIP-OUT.
008100     MOVE NA-EMPLOYEE-HIRE-MONTH-IN TO ER-EMPLOYEE-HIRE-MONTH-OUT.
008110     MOVE NA-EMPLOYEE-HIRE-DAY-IN TO ER-EMPLOYEE-HIRE-DAY-OUT.
008120     MOVE NA-EMPLOYEE-HIRE-YEAR-IN TO ER-EMPLOYEE-HIRE-YEAR-OUT.
008130     MOVE '-' TO ER-DATE-HYPHEN-1-OUT
008140                ER-DATE-HYPHEN-2-OUT.
008150     WRITE ER-EMPLOYEE-LINE-OUT
008160          AFTER ADVANCING 2 LINES.                   ◄── READ statement not placed at end of record-processing paragraph.
008170
008180
```

Figure 3.27 Erroneous READ statement placement

Here's the answer: A program so written would work just fine until the last record was read. Then, a duplicate or garbage line (depending upon operating system handling) would be printed at the end of the report. Figure 3.28 illustrates this improper processing.

The key principle is that the end-of-file indicator must be tested immediately after the READ statement. In the EMP-RPT program, the WS-END-OF-FILE-SWITCH is tested by the PERFORM/UNTIL statement. So, to make the end-of-file test occur immediately after the READ statement, the programmer must move the READ statement to the end of the PROCESS-NAME-ADDRESS-RECORD procedure. Of course, this means the record that is being read will not be processed (moved and written) until the *next* iteration of the PROCESS-NAME-ADDRESS-RECORD paragraph. Therefore, the first time the PROCESS-NAME-ADDRESS-RECORD procedure is executed, a record must already have been read. This initial READ was accomplished in the MAINLINE-PRINT-EMPLOYEE-REPORT procedure. This method of READ statement handling can be termed the *priming-read* method.

This is not the only way to handle READ statement placement, but it is straightforward and relatively easy to comprehend and use for simple COBOL programs. Thus, we will usually be employing this technique for programs of this text. In Chapter 10, however, an example of *conditional processing* READ statement placement will be provided.

BRADFORD, THOMAS	9081 EL CAMINO REAL	SANTA CLARA CA 95051
BRONSON. PATRICIA	1818 SANTA CRUZ AVENUE	LOS GATOS CA 95030
CARTWRIGHT, GILBERT	105 EAST CENTRAL AVENUE	CAMPBELL CA 95008
COOK, KENNETH	496 REDWOOD AVENUE	SAN JOSE CA 95128
GARDNER, JOYCE	1014 STELLING ROAD	CUPERTINO CA 95014
JEFFERS. JOSEPH	1000 HYDE AVENUE	SAN JOSE CA 95129
KRISTENSEN. CARL	14199 SARATOGA AVENUE	SARATOGA CA 95070
LAWRENCE, KATHERINE	298 UNIVERSITY AVENUE	LOS GATOS CA 95030
LEE, SAMUEL	2140 JACKSON STREET	SAN JOSE CA 95116
LUCCHETTI, JOHN	13478 SOBEY ROAD	SARATOGA CA 95070
PAGE, PRENTISS	1991 GLEN BRAE DRIVE	SARATOGA CA 95070
PHILLIPS, SARAH	13631 TOYON DRIVE	CUPERTINO CA 95014
RODRIGUEZ, RAMON	1091 CAPRI DRIVE	CAMPBELL CA 95008
RUSSELL. DAVID	1315 MCCLELLAN ROAD	CUPERTINO CA 95014
SANCHEZ, SYLVIA	2124 MATHILDA AVENUE	SUNNYVALE CA 95010
SILVERMAN, NINA	701 POLLARD ROAD	LOS GATOS CA 95030
SMITH. JENNIFER	3281 BENTON ROAD	SANTA CLARA CA 95051
TANAKA, JAMES	1018 CURTNER AVENUE	SAN JOSE CA 95123
WALLACE, JANA	14291 JUNIPER LANE	SARATOGA CA 95070
WONG, WILLIAM	1314 EAST SANTA CLARA	SAN JOSE CA 95112 ←— Last record
WONG, WILLIAM	1314 EAST SANTA CLARA	SAN JOSE CA 95112 ←— Erroneously printed a second time

Figure 3.28 Processing effect of erroneous READ statement placement

Common Errors of Beginning COBOL Programmers

There are certain errors that beginning COBOL programmers often experience. They are categorized here so that you can guard against them.

Figure 3.29 depicts some of the errors that will be discussed.

Syntactical Considerations

Omitted period

Whenever a period is shown in the COBOL format notation, it must be there. A period is always required to terminate a division header, section header, paragraph header, an FD entry (at the end of the complete entry), or a data-item description. A period is also required at the end of the sentence immediately preceding any of these entries.

Extra period

A period placed where it shouldn't be can cause problems. Beginning COBOL programmers sometimes mistakenly write a period between multiclause, multi-phrase, or multiline sentences such as the SELECT/ASSIGN, READ/AT END, and WRITE/AFTER ADVANCING entries. Sometimes, a period is erroneously placed after a data-name and before the picture clause of a data-item description.

Omitted hyphen

Remember that hyphens are often used in COBOL to join multiple English words into a single COBOL reserved or user-defined word. When a hyphen is called for, it must be used. Required hyphens are often omitted from the reserved words PROGRAM-ID, INPUT-OUTPUT, FILE-CONTROL, WORKING-STORAGE, and so forth. Similarly, each user-defined word must be a continuous string of characters. Hyphens must be used rather than blank spaces when forming a user-defined word from multiple English words or abbreviations.

Extra hyphens

Notice that, for division and section headers, a division or section name is separated from the reserved word DIVISION or SECTION by a blank space—not a hyphen. Because hyphens are used so frequently, there is sometimes a tendency to include them where they should not be present.

Omitted blank spaces

A blank space must be provided after a period. There is no converse error—using extra blank spaces—because whenever one blank space is required, any number of blank spaces may be provided.

Inadvertent blank spaces

Sometimes a blank space is erroneously placed in a picture character-string. (Of course, there should be a blank space between the reserved word PIC and the character-string.)

Area A/area B distinctions

All division, section, and paragraph names must start in area A. Also, the indicator FD and the level-number 01 must start in area A. Most other entries start in area B. Although an area A entry must start in position 8, an area B entry may begin in any area B position (12 through 72). Remember, when writing FD or 01 in positions 8 and 9, at least two blank spaces (positions 10 and 11) must be left before starting the file-name or record-name respectively. Otherwise, the name will begin in area A.

| Syntactical errors | Division | | | |
	IDENTIFICATION	ENVIRONMENT	DATA	PROCEDURE
Omitted period	IDENTIFICATION DIVISION. PROGRAM-ID. AUTHOR. INSTALLATION. DATE-WRITTEN. DATE-COMPILED. SECURITY.	ENVIRONMENT DIVISION. CONFIGURATION SECTION. SOURCE-COMPUTER. OBJECT-COMPUTER. INPUT-OUTPUT SECTION. FILE-CONTROL.	DATA DIVISION. FILE SECTION. WORKING-STORAGE SECTION. To terminate each FD sentence To terminate each data item description sentence	PROCEDURE DIVISION. To terminate each procedure-name To terminate each sentence
Extra period		SELECT file-name ASSIGN TO implementor-name	FD file-name RECORD CONTAINS integer CHARACTERS LABEL RECORDS ARE OMITTED DATA RECORD IS record-name. 02 data-name PIC X(5).	
Omitted hyphen	PROGRAM-ID DATE-WRITTEN DATE-COMPILED	SOURCE-COMPUTER OBJECT-COMPUTER INPUT-OUTPUT FILE-CONTROL	WORKING-STORAGE In data-names	In procedure-names
Extra hyphen	IDENTIFICATION DIVISION	ENVIRONMENT DIVISION CONFIGURATION SECTION INPUT-OUTPUT SECTION ASSIGN TO	RECORD CONTAINS LABEL RECORDS DATA RECORDS	PROCEDURE DIVISION AT END AFTER ADVANCING STOP RUN
Omitted blank space			PIC X(5)	
Inadvertent blank space			PIC X (5)	
Incorrect area A placement			FD FILE NAME	COBOL statements
Spelling	IDENTIFICATION	ENVIRONMENT	CHARACTER LABEL OMITTED	PROCEDURE PERFORM

Figure 3.29 Checklist of common syntactical errors

Spelling

When a reserved word is used, it must be spelled exactly as specified in the COBOL list of reserved words. Common misspellings are ENVIORNMENT instead of ENVIRONMENT (remember that there is "iron" in the word environment); LABLE rather than LABEL; OMITED or OMMITTED for OMITTED; PROCEEDURE instead of PROCEDURE; and PREFORM in place of PERFORM.

Consistent usage of user-defined words

When a user-defined word is chosen as (1) the file name for a file in the ENVIRONMENT DIVISION, (2) the data-name for a record or field in the DATA DIVISION, or (3) the procedure-name for a paragraph in the PROCEDURE DIVISION, its *exact* spelling must be used throughout the program. In everyday life, a guy named Gregory might well be called Greg, or a gal named Judy might decide to spell her name as Judi. No such latitude is allowed in COBOL. Once a user-defined word is chosen, all references to that name must be spelled in exact conformance with its original formation.

Logical Considerations

Data definition

The definitions of records and fields in the DATA DIVISION PICTURE clause must conform to the actual data as expressed in the programming specifications (which, of course, should define the actual data records and fields).

Program logic

The PROCEDURE DIVISION statements should be written to correspond to the logic expressed in the pseudocode or flowchart (which, of course, should express logic necessary to achieve the desired results).

COBOL Language Element Summary

Non-numeric literals are used to introduce actual values into a program. They:

- Must be enclosed by quotation marks
- May contain any characters acceptable to the computer being used
- Must not exceed 120 characters

Figurative constants are actual values to which reserved words have been assigned for coding convenience. SPACE and SPACES are equivalent figurative constants. They can be used to introduce blank spaces into a program.

Style Summary

PROCEDURE DIVISION:

- Don't use sections unless they are required by the COBOL syntax.
- Write the OPEN statement with each file name on a separate line and vertically aligned.
- Write the READ statement with the AT END phrase on a separate line and indented four spaces.
- Write the PERFORM/UNTIL statement with the UNTIL condition on a separate line and indented four spaces.
- When the MOVE statement will not fit on one coding line, write the reserved word TO and the receiving field on a separate line and indent them four spaces.
- If a MOVE statement has multiple receiving fields, write each receiving field (after the first one) aligned vertically on a separate line.
- Place the ADVANCING phrase of the WRITE statement on a separate line and indent it four spaces.

- Write the CLOSE statement with each file-name on a separate line and vertically aligned.

Exercises

Terms for Definition

procedure
procedure-name
sentence
statement

branching instruction
non-numeric literal
figurative constant

Review Questions

1. Sections are _____ in the PROCEDURE DIVISION.

2. A paragraph in the PROCEDURE DIVISION can be termed a _____ .

3. A procedure-name is a _____ word.

4. A PROCEDURE DIVISION paragraph contains a series of _____ .

5. A syntactically valid combination of words and symbols beginning with a verb is termed a _____ .

6. The following two COBOL verbs cause program control to be transferred to a specified location in the program (rather than the next consecutive statement): _____ and _____ .

7. Procedure-names begin in area _____ .

8. The _____ statement initiates processing for a file.

9. The _____ statement transfers data from one area of computer storage to another.

10. The _____ statement makes a logical record from an input file available to the program.

11. The _____ statement causes a record to be transferred to an output device.

12. The _____ statement terminates processing for a file.

13. The _____ statement terminates program execution.

Syntax/Debug Exercises

1. Some or all of the following PROCEDURE DIVISION statements are in error. For each entry containing one or more errors, rewrite it correctly in the fill-in area provided. If the entry is correct, place a check-mark (✔) in the fill-in area.

```
 A│B                                                  A│B
--│--------------------------------------------     --│--------------------------------------------
 1│    2        3         4                          1│    2        3         4
78│901234567890123456789012345678901 2              78│901234567890123456789012345678901 2
--│--------------------------------------------     --│--------------------------------------------
MAINLINE-PROCEDURE
   OPEN PAYROLL-FILE.                                  │_____
       OUTPUT PAYROLL-REPORT-FILE.                    │_____
   READ PAYROLL-FILE                                  │_____
       AT END MOVE 'YES' TO EOF-SW.                   │_____
   PERFORM PROCESS-PAYROLL-RECORD                     │_____
       UNTIL EOF-SW IS EQUAL TO 'YES'.                │_____
   CLOSE INPUT PAYROLL-FILE                           │_____
       OUTPUT PAYROLL-REPORT-FILE.                    │_____
   STOP-RUN.                                          │
```

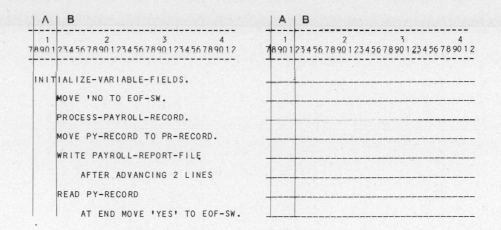

```
  A | B
    |
  1 |      2         3         4
7890 1 234 56 7890 1234567890 1234567890 12
INITIALIZE-VARIABLE-FIELDS.
    MOVE 'NO TO EOF-SW.
    PROCESS-PAYROLL-RECORD.
    MOVE PY-RECORD TO PR-RECORD.
    WRITE PAYROLL-REPORT-FILE
        AFTER ADVANCING 2 LINES
    READ PY-RECORD
        AT END MOVE 'YES' TO EOF-SW.
```

Programming Assignments

Complete the programming assignments in Chapter 2.

CHAPTER 4

PICTURE CLAUSES AND THE MOVE STATEMENT

4

4

PICTURE CLAUSES AND THE MOVE STATEMENT

We have discussed fundamentals of the PICTURE clause and the MOVE statement. PICTURE clauses are required for practically all elementary data-item descriptions in a COBOL program; the MOVE statement is the most frequently used verb in many COBOL programs. This chapter will cover each of these two important topics in more detail, and certain related topics will be covered. In the examples discussed in this chapter, we will sometimes express picture character-strings by the repetition method (rather than the parenthesis method) to aid learning and understanding. There will be additional PICTURE clause style considerations presented in this chapter.

PICTURE Clauses

PICTURE clauses describe the general characteristics and editing of an elementary data-item. They are used to specify:

1. The data class—numeric, alphabetic, alphanumeric, numeric edited, or alphanumeric edited—of the field
2. The size (or length) of the field
3. The location of an assumed decimal point (for numeric fields)
4. Whether or not a numeric field contains an arithmetic sign (positive or negative)
5. Any editing to be performed on the field

Thus far we have mentioned only two symbols that may be used in a picture character-string: 9 and X. There are many other picture symbols. We will discuss them in relation to the category of data-item that they describe: alphanumeric, alphabetic, numeric, numeric edited, and alphanumeric edited.

Describing Alphanumeric Data-Items

A field that contains letters, numbers, other characters, or any combination of these may be described as an alphanumeric data-item. We have already seen that the picture symbol X is used to define alphanumeric characters. Examples of alphanumeric fields are street-address, city-state-zip, and automobile license-number fields. Figure 4.1 shows alphanumeric PICTURE clause examples.

Describing Alphabetic Data-Items

A field that contains combinations of letters and blank spaces is considered an alphabetic field. An alphabetic field may be defined with the picture character A. Rarely do COBOL programmers use the symbol A in a picture character string, however, because there are few truly alphabetic fields. For example,

Field name	Data in storage	PICTURE clause
XX-STREET-ADDRESS	123bEASYbSTbbbbbbbbbbbbb	PIC X(24)
XX-CITY-STATE-ZIP	SLEEPYbHOLLOWbCAb99999bbb	PIC X(25)
XX-AUTO-LICENSE	401NAC	PIC X(6)

Note: b = blank space

Figure 4.1 Alphanumeric PICTURE clause examples

one might think that a name field would certainly be an example of an alphabetic field. But consider names such as O'Brien, D'angelo, or even Ann-Margret. The apostrophe and hyphen are not letters of the alphabet; hence, a field containing such data could not be considered purely alphabetic.

Since an alphanumeric description encompasses alphabetic fields, most programmers use the picture symbol X to define both fields that are alphanumeric and those that may contain only alphabetic characters. We will do likewise and not use the picture character A in this text.

Describing Numeric Data-Items

A field that contains numeric digits may be described as a numeric data-item. The picture symbol 9 is used to define numeric fields.

The reader may question why—since an alphanumeric description encompasses numeric fields—programmers don't just use the symbol X to represent numeric fields, too. Actually, COBOL programmers often do just that and will sometimes define numeric fields as alphanumeric data-items. There are certain instances however, when the alphanumeric definition is not appropriate for numeric fields.

First, COBOL arithmetic statements will only operate on fields defined as numeric. So if we defined a field used to store a quantity as alphanumeric, then we would not be able to add, subtract, multiply, divide, or otherwise compute with that field. Fields that will be used for arithmetic computations must be defined as numeric.

Another situation in which numeric definition should be used is when, to conserve storage, two numeric digits are packed into one position of computer storage. This is called packed decimal data representation and will be covered in a later chapter.

Numeric code-number or other integer (whole-number) numeric fields containing absolute (rather than algebraic) values could be defined as either alphanumeric (using X) or numeric (using 9). Examples are fields containing social security numbers, numeric dates, account numbers, and the like.

There are four numeric picture symbols: 9, V, S, and P. Examples of numeric PICTURE clauses are provided in Figure 4.2.

Symbol 9: To represent a numeric digit position, the programmer uses the picture symbol 9. Each numeric picture character-string must contain at least one 9. Up to eighteen digits may be described in the picture character-string for a numeric data-item.

Symbol V: The symbol V represents the location of an assumed decimal point. Recognize that the decimal point is *assumed* but not actually there.

In most commercial data processing systems, actual decimal points are not physically present in numeric fields. Instead, fields are assigned fixed lengths and the values are justified to the rightmost positions. By doing this, the alignment of the decimal point is uniform so that it need not be physically pre-

Field Name	Data in storage	PICTURE clause
XX-SOCIAL-SECURITY-NUMBER	566509224	PIC 9(9)
XX-DATE	120178	PIC 9(6)
XX-ACCOUNT-NUMBER	80256	PIC 9(5)
XX-MONTHLY-SALARY	0150000	PIC 9(5)V9(2)
XX-QUANTITY-SOLD	000(+) or 001( )	PIC S0(3)
XX-HOUSE-SELLING-PRICE	00799	PIC 9(5)P(2)
XX-RECYCLED-CAN-PRICE	8	PIC P(2)9(1)

Figure 4.2 Examples of numeric data-item PICTURE clauses

sent in the data but simply can be specified by the programmer. There are three reasons why decimal points are not actually represented in numeric fields. First, the decimal point would occupy a storage position and thus increase field storage requirements. Second, if data entry operators were required to key in decimal points, the resulting strokes would consume keying time. Third, every data entry operator stroke has a chance for error. The more strokes, the more chances for error. The more chances for error, the more errors.

So, rather than carrying actual decimal points in numeric fields, the assumed location is expressed by program specification. With COBOL, the picture symbol V is used to represent the location of an assumed decimal point.

Because the V signifies only the location and not an actual position of storage, it is not counted toward the size of the field being defined. For example, if a seven-position field were used to store monthly salary in dollars and cents, it could be defined as 99999V99. The picture character-string contains 8 characters, but the field length is correctly interpreted by COBOL to be seven positions. Figure 4.3 depicts the relationship between numeric field positions and the assumed decimal point.

Since a single numeric value may logically contain only one decimal point, only one V is allowed in each numeric picture character-string. If no V is present in the character-string, the decimal point is assumed to be after the rightmost digit of the field. Hence, a V written as the rightmost symbol of the character-string (e.g., 999V) is redundant.

Symbol S: Numeric fields may be considered either unsigned or signed. Fields with absolute values—telephone numbers, social security numbers, code numbers, and the like—are examples of fields that are considered unsigned. They are numeric fields that do not have positive or negative representations. Fields used for arithmetic, on the other hand, should normally be con-

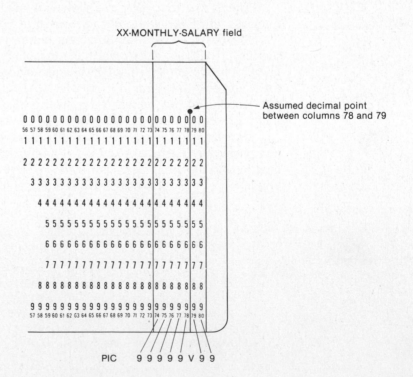

Figure 4.3 Relationship between numeric field positions and the assumed decimal point

sidered signed fields since computations can often produce either a positive or negative balance. For example, a field used to store each bank depositor's balance, although normally positive, must provide for representation of a negative balance if the account becomes overdrawn.

The numeric fields shown in Chapters 2 and 3 have all been unsigned fields. To specify a signed field, the picture symbol S is placed as the leftmost character of the picture character-string. Only one S may be used in a picture character-string and it must be the leftmost character.

Generally, you should specify a signed field for (1) all numeric fields defined in the WORKING-STORAGE SECTION that will be operated on arithmetically, and (2) for all FILE SECTION fields (that is, fields of the input and output records) that might possibly carry a sign.

Sign representation is another area that is dependent upon the vendor and model of computer being used. In this text, we will always use what can be referred to as *embedded*, or *overpunch*, sign representation. This is the most common method in use today. It means that positive or negative sign representation is embedded in the numeric field and does not occupy an additional storage position. Thus, although the symbol S occupies a position in the picture character-string, it is not counted toward the size of the field being defined. An example of this embedded sign representation with a punched card field is shown as Figure 4.4. The subject of signed fields will be covered further during discussion of the SIGN clause later in this chapter.

Symbol P: The symbol P is a numeric picture that is rarely used. We'll cover it here just in case you run into it in a COBOL program somewhere. The P indicates an assumed decimal scaling position. If a numeric value is to be represented in a field but the field does not physically contain all the digits, the symbol P is used as a placeholder to scale to the decimal point.

This concept can best be described by an example. Suppose we have a field that is used to express the selling price of a house. When the field was established, the programmer decided the following: "Well, we will need to provide for prices from a few thousand dollars (for some little shack) up to perhaps over a million dollars (for some mansion). That means 9 digits will be needed (9999999V99) to represent the selling price. But, the pennies, units of dollars, and tens of dollars are rarely specified for the sales price of a home. That is, someone may set a selling price of $79,900.00, but it would be odd to see a price of, say, $79,998.99." So, the selling price field was set up to hold only digits from the millions positions through the hundreds positions with a picture character string of 99999PP. A selling price of $79,900.00 would be stored in the field as 00799. So defined, the field consumes only five positions of storage. The P is used in the picture character-string as a placeholder to inform the COBOL compiler where the assumed decimal point is located. If the P symbols are on the right of the character-string, the decimal point is assumed to be to the right of the last P symbol.

The P symbol can also be used on the lefthand side of the character-string. Suppose we are buying used aluminum beverage cans for recycling. Although recyclers normally buy such scrap aluminum by the pound, let's hypothetically say that we want to express the average cost of a recycled 12-ounce beverage can as eight mils or $.008. Since this value has no dollar or penny values—only mils—a picture character string of PP9 can be formed. The field defined occupies only one position of storage. When the program does arithmetic with the field, however, COBOL considers the decimal point to be located to the left of the leftmost P.

A V placed as the rightmost or leftmost character of a picture character-string containing the symbol P is redundant because the decimal point is always assumed to be to the left of leftmost P symbols and to the right of

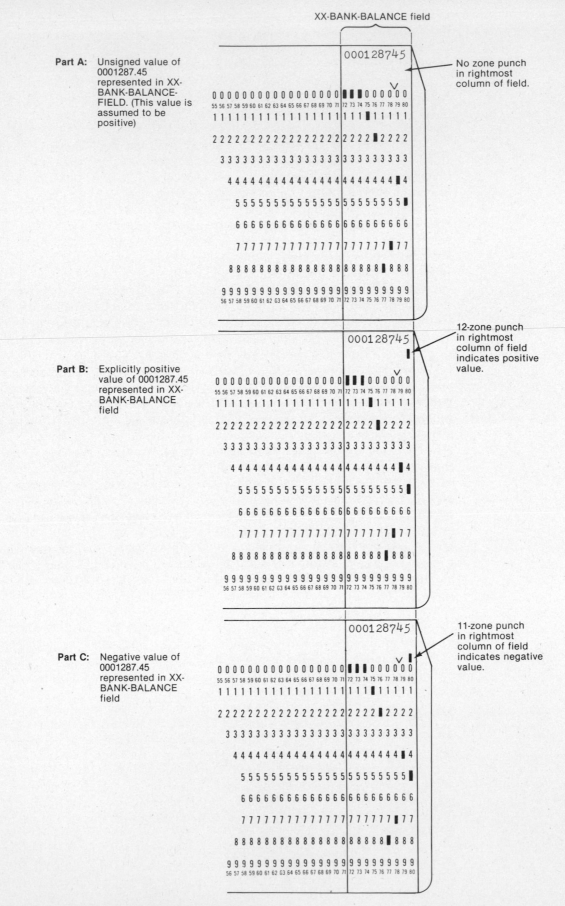

Figure 4.4 Example of embedded sign representation

rightmost P symbols. The P symbol is not counted towards the length of the data item.

P symbols are not generally used; their use is fraught with dangers and blessed with fewer and fewer benefits as data storage media and devices become less expensive. The dangers are evident from the examples discussed above. In the real estate selling price example—even though practically everybody rounds selling prices to at least even hundreds of dollars—the programmer should realize that some eccentric is going to demand that he receive every last penny of what he believes his property is worth. Similarly, the effects of inflation and the varying values of natural resources and other commodities are well known. Thus, the cost of a recycled aluminum container could easily leave the mil category and rise into the cent range.

If either of these situations occurred, programs with such definitions would require modification, or the integrity and straightforwardness of the system would be compromised. It is much safer to define all decimal digit positions rather than risk being "boxed in" by an insufficient field size. The only drawback is that a little more computer storage may be used. As the cost of memory decreases, scrimping on storage becomes less and less important. Figure 4.5 summarizes this section by showing some invalid and redundant numeric PICTURE clauses.

Describing Edited Data-Items

In COBOL, the term *edit* refers to the process of suppressing, inserting, or replacing certain characters within a field. Theoretically, all COBOL programs could be written without using any editing PICTURE clauses. In fact, usually the only place where editing PICTURE clauses are used is for output fields ultimately directed to a device whose output records will be read by humans (printers, screens, and so on). Also, any suppressing, inserting, or replacing of characters done through use of editing symbols could alternately be done through program logic.

COBOL programs frequently produce printed reports, however, and editing PICTURE clauses provide a convenient way of handling commonly-encountered character suppression, insertion, or replacement tasks. We will cover the editing symbols in detail.

There are two categories of edited data-items: numeric edited and alphanumeric edited. The former category is used far more frequently than the latter. Figure 4.6 lists all the picture symbols, including the editing symbols, by category.

Numeric edited data items

There are five classifications of numeric editing symbols: zero suppression and replacement, simple insertion, special insertion, fixed insertion, and floating insertion.

Zero suppression and replacement editing

There are two symbols in this classification: Z (zero suppression with blank space replacement) and * (zero suppression with asterisk replacement).

Symbol Z (zero suppression with blank space replacement): The symbol Z is probably the most frequently used editing symbol. In our everyday life, we usually suppress nonsignificant zeros. For example, if we record a quantity such as 803, we would write those three significant digits, even though the value 0803—written with a nonsignificant zero—is equivalent. We don't usually prefix number values with nonsignificant zeros because it takes extra effort to write them and because the extra zeros tend to make the value more difficult to read.

PICTURE clause	Reason invalid or redundant
PIC 999V	Redundant. Decimal point is assumed to be to the right of the rightmost 9 if no V in picture character-string.
PIC 99V99V9	Invalid. Only one decimal point is allowed in a numeric picture.
PIC 9(3)S	Invalid. S must be the leftmost symbol.
PIC 99S9	Invalid. S must be the leftmost symbol.
PIC 9PPV	Redundant. If P is the rightmost symbol, decimal point is assumed to be to the right of the rightmost P.
PIC VP9	Redundant. If P is the leftmost symbol, decimal point is assumed to be to the left of the leftmost P.

Figure 4.5 Examples of invalid and redundant numeric data-item PICTURE clauses

It takes extra effort to eliminate the nonsignificant zeros in computer programming, but it is usually done when preparing report outputs because it makes the data in the field easier to read. Remember that fixed-length fields are normally used because they are easier to process. The length selected for a numeric field is usually longer than, or at least as long as, the largest value that must be expressed in the field. When a value occupies less than the total number of digits of a numeric field, the leftmost positions will generally contain zeros. These are nonsignificant zeros because they do not affect the value of the data contained in the field.

Figure 4.7 shows an example of a quantity field defined in an input record as 99999 but which we want to print with nonsignificant zeros removed. Thus, the picture character-string for the print field should appear as ZZZZZ. If the input field contains all zeros, then the output field would appear as all blank spaces—nothing would be printed for that field.

Sometimes it may be desired to have some positions of a field zero-suppressed and others unconditionally printed. For example, suppose we wanted a single zero to be printed in the situation where the input field was all zeros. The picture character-string would then be specified as ZZZZ9. The 9 causes unconditional printing of that digit position, regardless of whether the zero is significant or nonsignificant.

Data category	Symbol	Meaning	Data category	Symbol	Meaning
Numeric	9	Numeric digit	Numeric edited (continued)		
	V	Assumed decimal point	Special insertion	.	Decimal point
	S	Arithmetic sign	Fixed insertion	–	Minus sign (fixed)
	P	Assumed decimal scaling position		+	Plus sign (fixed)
				CR	Credit symbol
Alphabetic	A	Alphabetic character		DB	Debit symbol
Alphanumeric	X	Alphanumeric character		$	Dollar sign (fixed)
Numeric edited			Floating insertion	–	Minus sign (floating)
Suppression and replacement	Z	Zero suppression with blank space replacement		+	Plus sign (floating)
				$	Dollar sign (floating)
	*	Zero suppression with asterisk replacement	Alphanumeric edited	/	Slash (stroke, diagonal, virgule)
Simple insertion	,	Comma		B	Blank space
	/	Slash (stroke, diagonal, virgule)		0	Zero
	B	Blank space			
	0	Zero			

Figure 4.6 Picture symbols by data category

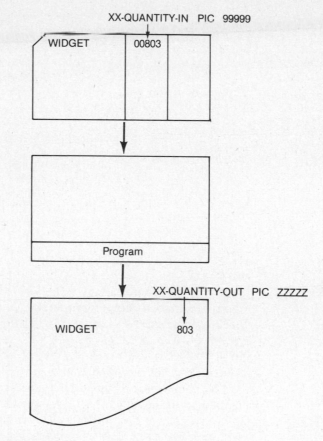

Figure 4.7 Editing example

For zero suppression, any combination of Z's and 9's may be specified, but the Z symbols must be the leftmost characters. That is, 9 may not precede Z in a picture character-string. Other examples of zero suppression with blank space replacement are shown in Figure 4.8.

*Symbol * (zero suppression with asterisk replacement):* The asterisk (*) may be used to replace zeros. When an asterisk is specified in the picture character-string, nonsignificant zeros are replaced by asterisks. Figure 4.9 shows examples. The asterisk is used far less frequently than the Z for zero suppression. Its main use is for printing a dollar amount on checks. Blank spaces before a dollar value on a check are not desirable; a dishonest individual could record more significant digits on the check and cash it for more

Data in storage	PICTURE clause of editing field	Edited result
00803	PIC ZZZZZ	803
10358	PIC ZZZZZ	10358
00002	PIC ZZZZZ	2
00000	PIC ZZZZZ	
00007	PIC ZZZZ9	7
00000	PIC ZZZZ9	0

Figure 4.8 Examples of zero suppression with blank space replacement

Data in storage	PICTURE clause of editing field	Edited result
0506	PIC ****	*506
1235	PIC ****	1235
0008	PIC ****	***8
0000	PIC ****	****
0001	PIC ***0	***1
0000	PIC ***9	***0

Figure 4.9 Examples of zero suppression with asterisk replacement

Data in storage	PICTURE clause of editing field	Edited result
01234	PIC ZZ,ZZ9	1,234
0056	PIC Z,ZZZ	56
5897	PIC ZZ,99	58,97
000000	PIC ZZZ,ZZZ	
00156	PIC 99,999	00,156

Figure 4.10 Examples of editing with the comma

Data in storage	PICTURE clause of editing field	Edited result
122580	PIC 99/99/99	12/25/80
030781	PIC 99/99/99	03/07/81
030781	PIC Z9/99/99	3/07/81
186	PIC 99/9	18/6
111139	PIC 99B99B99	11 11 39
566509224	PIC 999B99B9999	566 50 9224
0140	PIC 999900	014000
0140	PIC 999,900	014,000
0140	PIC ZZZ,900	14,000
0000	PIC ZZZ,900	000
0000	PIC ZZZ,Z00	00

Figure 4.11 Examples of editing with the slash, blank space, and zero

than its intended value. By replacing nonsignificant digits with the asterisk, the programmer makes it much more difficult to alter illegally the dollar amount.

Simple insertion editing

There are four simple insertion editing symbols: , (comma), / (slash), B (blank space), and 0 (zero). Figure 4.10 shows examples of editing with the comma; examples with the slash, blank space, and zero appear in Figure 4.11.

The comma: The comma is a frequently used insertion character. When we write integer numbers in everyday usage, a comma is placed to the left of each group of three integers so that longer strings of digits are easier to read. The picture symbol for comma is usually specified to obtain the same effect. Notice that, just as in everyday usage, if a location where a comma is specified does not have a preceding significant digit, the comma does not appear—it is replaced by a blank space.

The comma is not restricted to occuring every three integers. It may be placed anywhere in the character-string except as the rightmost symbol.

Insertion characters consume additional positions in the edited fields. That is, if a five-digit field in storage, defined as 9(5) is being edited with a PIC ZZ,ZZZ, it will require six positions in the output record (five digit positions plus one comma position).

The slash: The / symbol is commonly called a *slash* but is sometimes referred to as a *diagonal, stroke,* or *virgule.* We will call it a slash in this text.

The slash symbol is commonly used to separate the month, day, and year subfields of numeric dates. Suppose we have an input field containing a date expressed in six-digit month-month-day-day-year-year sequence. As we've mentioned, editing characters are not normally placed in input fields. However, we would not want to print dates on an output report without editing because they would be confusing and difficult to read. For instance, if the input date field contained the date of Christmas, 1981, without editing the date would appear as 122581. We are accustomed to reading a numeric date with slashes (or hyphens) placed between the month, day, and year, such as 12/25/81.

To specify such insertion of slashes, the programmer writes the picture character-string 99/99/99. If we wished to zero-suppress the first digit of the month so that a date of 030782 would be printed as 3/07/82, then we could write the picture character-string as Z9/99/99. We would never zero-suppress the first digit of the day, however, because a blank space within the date

(3/ 7/82) would fragment it and make it more confusing to read. Besides, this would require an illegal picture character-string, since a picture symbol 9 cannot precede the symbol Z.

Using the slash, of course, increases the length of the output field. The input date field is six digits in length; the output edited date consumes eight positions.

The blank space: The blank space insertion symbol does not have as many applications as the comma or slash, but there are certain instances where it comes in handy. If, for instance, we wanted blank spaces—rather than slashes—between the month, day, and year in the date-field example, we could construct the picture character-string as 99B99B99 or Z9B99B99. Or if we wanted a nine-digit social security number to be separated as we usually see it, a picture character-string of 999B99B9999 could be specified. Once again, observe that the nine-digit social security number field has been increased to eleven edited characters in the example above.

The symbol zero: The zero insertion character is used even less than the blank space. An example, however, can be drawn from the bean business. Beans and many other dry commodities are sold in bulk by hundred-pound units, termed hundredweights and abbreviated CWT (C is the Roman numeral for 100 and WT is a contraction for "weight"). If we record each bean sale in a field called XX-CWTS-SOLD and if we define the field as PIC 9(4), then the pounds of beans sold would always be a hundred times greater than the CWT value represented in the field. If we wanted to print the actual number of pounds sold, we could specify a picture character-string of 999900 or, better yet, 999,900, or, even better with regard to readability: ZZZ,Z00. These examples are illustrated in Figure 4.11.

Special insertion editing

There is just one special insertion character—the *decimal point.* It is classified as a special insertion character because it controls how data values are aligned in the field. We will be discussing this more in the latter part of this chapter; a few examples of decimal point insertion are shown here in Figure 4.12.

Whenever the decimal point is specified in a PICTURE clause, it will be printed unconditionally. Since it is mathematically impossible to have more than one decimal point in a decimal value, only one decimal point may be specified in each picture character-string.

Fixed insertion editing

There are five symbols used for fixed insertion editing: − (fixed minus sign), + (fixed plus sign), CR (credit symbol), DB (debit symbol), and $ (fixed dollar sign).

Data in storage	PICTURE clause of editing field	Edited result
000‸23	PIC ZZ9.99	0.23
000‸23	PIC ZZZ.99	.23
000‸08	PIC ZZZ.99	.08
000‸08	PIC ZZZ.ZZ	.08
000‸00	PIC ZZZ.ZZ	
1032‸56	PIC Z,ZZZ.99	1,032.56
0025‸00	PIC Z,ZZZ.99	25.00
103‸256	PIC ZZZ.999	103.256
25‸6	PIC ZZ.9	25.6

Note: ‸ = assumed decimal point

Figure 4.12 Examples of editing with the decimal point

Data in storage	Embedded sign	PICTURE clause of editing field	Edited result
00345	−	PIC ZZ,ZZ9 −	345 −
00345	+	PIC ZZ,ZZ9 −	345
00000		PIC ZZ,ZZ9 −	0
12836	−	PIC − ZZ,ZZ9	− 12,836
00087	−	PIC − ZZ,ZZ9	− 87
00087	+	PIC − ZZ,ZZ9	87

Figure 4.13 Examples of editing with the fixed minus sign

The fixed minus sign: The fixed minus sign symbol is a conditional picture symbol. That is, when specified in a picture character-string, the minus sign will only be printed if the data value placed in the edited data-item is negative. If the data value is positive or zero, a blank space will appear in the minus sign location. Examples of the use of the fixed minus sign are shown in Figure 4.13.

Only one fixed minus sign is allowed in the picture character-string. It must be specified as either the rightmost or leftmost symbol. Normally, a fixed minus sign will be specified as the rightmost symbol. It's usually easier to read a fixed minus sign printed to the right of the number because leftmost digits are often specified for zero suppression. Spaces between the minus sign and the numbers make the value difficult to read.

The fixed plus sign: The fixed plus sign is another conditional picture symbol. When specified, the plus sign will be printed if the data value placed in the edited data-item is positive or zero. If the data value is negative, a minus sign will be printed instead. Figure 4.14 provides examples.

As with the fixed minus sign, only one fixed plus sign may be specified and it must be either the rightmost or leftmost symbol of the picture character-string. Normally, it too is specified as the rightmost symbol.

The credit symbol: This is an editing symbol that occupies two character positions. It operates like the fixed minus sign: if the data value is negative, the letters CR will be printed; otherwise, the character positions will be left blank. See Figure 4.15 for examples.

Only one occurrence of the CR symbol is allowed in a picture character-string, and it must be the rightmost symbol.

The debit symbol: The debit symbol also occupies two character positions. Although the DB symbol is not used very often, there are two tricky things about it that should be mentioned.

First, most accountants use the abbreviation DR for debit, but the COBOL editing symbol is DB. Second, although the credit symbol operates like the fixed

Data in storage	Embedded sign	PICTURE clause of editing field	Edited result
0800ₐ56	−	PIC Z,ZZZ.99 +	800.56 −
0800ₐ56	+	PIC Z,ZZZ.99 +	800.56 +
0000ₐ00		PIC Z,ZZZ.99 +	.00 +
2000ₐ	+	PIC + 9999	+ 2000
2000ₐ	−	PIC + Z,ZZZ	− 2,000
0000ₐ		PIC + Z,ZZZ	+
0000ₐ		PIC Z,ZZZ +	+

Note: ₐ = assumed decimal point

Figure 4.14 Examples of editing with the fixed plus sign

Data in storage	Embedded sign	PICTURE clause of editing field	Edited result
25ᵥ00	!	PIC ZZ.99CR	25.00
25ᵥ00	−	PIC ZZ.99CR	25.00CR
00ᵥ00		PIC ZZ.99CR	.00
25ᵥ00	+	PIC ZZ.99BCR	25.00
25ᵥ00	−	PIC ZZ.99BCR	25.00 CR

Note: ᵥ = assumed decimal point

Figure 4.15 Examples of editing with the credit symbol

minus sign, the debit symbol does not operate like the fixed plus sign. The DB symbol works just like the CR symbol. That is, if the data value is negative, DB will be printed; if positive or zero, two blank spaces will appear. The debit symbol must also be the rightmost two characters of the picture character-string. Figure 4.16 gives examples of DB symbol usage.

When using symbols CR or DB, the person reading the report must know whether the symbol CR or the symbol DB is used to specify a negative or a reverse amount. That is, an accountant must know whether an account is an asset, liability, or a net worth account to interpret properly the meaning of debit or credit.

Data in storage	Embedded sign	PICTURE clause of editing field	Edited result
500	+	PIC ZZ9DB	500
500	−	PIC ZZ9DB	500DB
000		PIC ZZ9DB	0
500	+	PIC ZZ9BDB	500
500	−	PIC ZZ9BDB	500 DB

Figure 4.16 Examples of editing with the debit symbol

The CR and DB symbols would be more flexible for accounting applications if the programmer could cause DB to be printed for positive values and CR for negative values or have DB printed for negative values and CR for positive values. COBOL does not provide this flexibility, however. Where such handling is required, the programmer must write PROCEDURE DIVISION statements to accomplish it. After studying the IF statement in Chapter 8, you will know how this can be done. Figure 4.17 summarizes the handling of the four editing sign symbols.

Editing symbol in PICTURE character-string	Data-item result	
	Positive or zero	Negative
+	+	−
−	Space	−
CR	2 spaces	CR
DB	2 spaces	DB

Figure 4.17 Summary of the editing sign symbols

Data in storage	PICTURE clause of editing field	Edited result
010ᵥ00	PIC $ZZ9.99	$ 10.00
000ᵥ50	PIC $ZZ9.99	$ 0.50
050ᵥ00	PIC $999.99	$050.00

Note: ▴ = assumed decimal point.

Figure 4.18 Examples of editing with the fixed dollar sign

The fixed dollar sign: The fixed dollar sign is used to print a dollar sign preceding a number at a fixed location. It may only be specified once in a picture character-string, and it must be the leftmost symbol. Figure 4.18 provides examples of its use. The fixed dollar sign is commonly used on the first line and on total lines for dollar amounts listed in columns, as on a balance sheet or income statement. It is also used together with asterisk replacement of nonsignificant zeros for check amounts.

Floating insertion editing

Three of the fixed insertion symbols may also be specified as floating insertion symbols: − (floating minus sign), + (floating plus sign), and $ (floating dollar sign). Examples of floating insertion editing are shown in Figure 4.19.

The floating minus sign: The floating minus sign is used when it is desired to place the minus sign immediately to the left of a zero-suppressed value. The conditional action of the floating minus sign is exactly the same as that of the fixed minus sign. If the data value is negative, the minus sign is printed; if positive, a blank space will appear.

To specify a floating minus sign in a PICTURE clause, the programmer places the minus sign as the leftmost symbol of the picture character-string. Then, for every position that the minus sign is to float—that is, for each nonsignificant digit position to be zero-suppressed—the minus sign is repeated.

Remember that floating minus signs can only be placed to the left of the value. Since the symbol for a floating minus sign is the same as that used for a fixed minus sign, COBOL will only recognize the floating minus sign if there are multiple minus symbols in the PICTURE clause.

The floating plus sign: The floating plus sign is used in situations like those where the floating minus sign is used. The plus symbol is used where both plus

Data in storage	Embedded sign	PICTURE clause of editing field	Edited result
1086ᵥ59	−	PIC − −,− − −.99	− 1,086.59
0030ᵥ00	−	PIC − −,− − −.99	− 30.00
030ᵥ00	+	PIC − −,− − −.99	30.00
00000		PIC + + +,+ +9	+0
00208	−	PIC + + +,+ +9	− 208
23456	+	PIC + + +,+ +9	+ 23,456
2483ᵥ23		PIC $$,$$$.99	$2,483.23
0000ᵥ05		PIC $$,$$$.99	$.05
0450ᵥ99		PIC $$,$$$.99	$450.99

Note: ▴ = assumed decimal point

Figure 4.19 Examples of editing with the floating minus, plus, and dollar signs

Data in storage	PICTURE clause of editing field	Edited result
122580	PIC XX/XX/XX	12/25/80
030781	PIC XX/XX/XX	03/07/81
ABC	PIC XX/X	AB/C
122580	PIC XXBXXBXX	12 25 80
XYZ	PIC XBXX	X YZ
XYZ123	PIC XBXX/XXX	X YZ/123
A10	PIC XXX0	A100
12	PIC 0XX	012

Figure 4.20 Alphanumeric editing examples

and minus signs—rather than the minus sign and blank spaces—are desired to represent data value sign conditions. Picture character-strings using the floating plus sign are constructed like those for the floating minus sign (the plus sign is repeated in every position for which it will float).

The floating dollar sign: The floating dollar sign is used where the dollar sign is to be placed immediately to the left of a zero-suppressed amount rather than at a fixed location. The floating dollar sign is frequently used on check amounts (when asterisk replacement is not used) or on dollar amounts that are not listed in columns.

Alphanumeric edited data items

There is only one classification for alphanumeric editing symbols: simple insertion editing. There are three editing symbols: / (slash), B (blank space), and 0 (zero). They operate exactly like their respective numeric editing symbols except that they are used in conjunction with the alphanumeric picture symbol X rather than the numeric picture symbols. Examples are shown in Figure 4.20.

Recap of PICTURE Clauses

Forming PICTURE clauses

When forming a PICTURE clause, you will always want to choose symbols from the one appropriate category: alphanumeric, alphabetic, numeric, numeric edited, or alphanumeric edited. Do not mix symbols across category lines. For example, a picture character-string like XX,XXX is invalid because it uses both alphanumeric and numeric edited symbols. Figure 4.21 shows all the symbols by category.

Editing with hyphens

You may have noticed that there is not an editing symbol for the hyphen. That is because the hyphen symbol is the same as that used for the minus sign. You

Numeric	Numeric edited		Alphabetic	Alphanumeric	Alphanumeric edited
9	Z	.	A	X	/
S	*	—			0
V	,	+			B
P	/	CR			
	0	DB			
	B	$			

Figure 4.21 Picture symbol categories

might need to insert hyphens, for instance, in a social security number field. One way to do this is with MOVE statements, as was done in the EMP-RPT program of Chapter 3. Other methods will be used later in the text.

PICTURE clause style considerations

In the preceding chapter it was mentioned that the parentheses method for forming picture character strings usually offers better readability than the repetition method. That convention applies when the character-string is composed of the same symbol throughout. When the programmer forms editing picture character-strings, though, a clearer indication of the editing is usually provided by specifying each character rather than by using the parentheses method.

When a V appears in a numeric picture character-string, one convention that is often followed is to use the parentheses method before the V symbol and to use the repetition method after the V symbol. With a seven-digit signed dollars-and-cents field, for example, the picture character-string would take the form of S9(5)V99.

DATA DIVISION Clauses Related to PICTURE Clauses

There are two DATA DIVISION clauses that may be associated with data-item description entries and that are closely related to the PICTURE clause. These are the BLANK WHEN ZERO and the SIGN clause.

BLANK WHEN ZERO Clause

Often a numeric editing picture will be specified for a field but the editing is not desired when the value of the edited field is zero. As an example, suppose we have a date represented in an input field by a picture character-string of 9(6). For the output report, the editing picture character-string is 99/99/99. For certain records, however, the date will not be present in the input field. When the date is absent, the input date field will contain a value of zero. As a result, those records with a zero date would be printed as 00/00/00. There's nothing really wrong with such handling, but the appearance of the report would be improved by leaving the output date field blank for the zero date records.

The BLANK WHEN ZERO clause can be used to achieve the effect we want—that is, to print the edited value when the field contains a data value and omit the printing of that field altogether when the data value is zero. Figure 4.22 shows examples of the BLANK WHEN ZERO clause. Notice that it is

Format:

BLANK WHEN ZERO

Examples:

SEQUENCE		CONT	A	B	COBOL STATEMENT			IDENTIFICATION
(PAGE)	(SERIAL)							

```
05  XX-PRICE          PIC  ZZ,ZZZ.99    BLANK WHEN ZERO.
05  XX-CODE-NBR       PIC  99999        BLANK WHEN ZERO.
05  XX-DATE           PIC  99/99/99     BLANK WHEN ZERO.
```

Figure 4.22 BLANK WHEN ZERO example

specified in the data-item description entry. Observe also that, when another clause is added to the data-item description entry sentence, the period must not appear immediately after the picture character-string but rather after the last clause of the sentence. The BLANK WHEN ZERO clause is composed of three separate reserved words and thus contains no hyphens. This clause may be used only with numeric edited or numeric data-items.

There are some common applications of the blank-when-zero effect that may be handled either with the BLANK WHEN ZERO clause or without it. A simple case is where full zero suppression is specified. For example, using the BLANK WHEN ZERO clause with a PICTURE of ZZZZ is redundant. The same is true for PIC Z,ZZZ since a comma is suppressed whenever there are no significant digits preceding it. Usually, whenever a symbol 9 or an editing symbol other than Z, comma, minus, CR, or DB is specified, the BLANK WHEN ZERO clause must be included to obtain that result.

Use of the decimal point and zero-suppression symbols together in one picture character-string brings up several related points. There are only two ways of indicating zero suppression: (1) by specifying a Z in any or all of the leading numeric digit positions to the left of the decimal point (e.g., ZZ9, ZZ9.99, ZZZ, or ZZZ.99), or (2) by specifying a Z in all of the numeric digit positions (e.g., ZZZ.ZZ). Indicating zero suppression by specifying a Z in all numeric digit positions produces a blank-when-zero effect. That is, if there are Z's to the right of the decimal point, and if the data value is zero, then the digits *and the decimal point* are suppressed.

A combination of 9's and Z's to the right of the decimal point is not allowed. The logic behind this is that on the righthand side of the decimal point, nonsignificant zeros are the rightmost (rather than the leftmost) zeros. COBOL does not presently provide an editing symbol for terminal (rightmost nonsignificant) zero suppression of decimal values.

SIGN Clause

The SIGN clause is not used very often in COBOL programs. This is because each COBOL implementor defines its own arithmetic sign handling to the COBOL compiler and, as long as signs are represented for data in accordance with these rules defined by the implementor, there is no need for the SIGN clause.

There are two common arithmetic sign representation methods in use in commercial data processing today. We can refer to these as the *embedded* (or *overpunch*) and *separate character* representations.

The embedded method harks back to the days when analysts were concerned with squeezing every last morsel of usage out of the 80 columns of a punched card. The arithmetic sign of plus or minus is represented by a zone punch above the rightmost column of the field. This location was chosen because (1) the zone rows of a column are available when the field is of numeric data class, and (2) it doesn't consume an additional column for the sign. The embedded method has a disadvantage, though, because the representation for signed numbers and for letters overlap, which sometimes causes confusion and problems (For example, a + 1 is the same representation as the letter A; a − 4 is identical to the letter M, and so forth).

Disk, tape, and other forms of electronic storage media allow records of practically any desired length. This fact, coupled with the declining cost of storage, has made it more attractive to utilize a separate position for the sign and thus eliminate the possibility of confusion. Since many modern data-entry devices and computers, however, have been designed to replace and thus to be compatible with the older punched card equipment, sign representations for most commercial data processing applications are usually still handled by the embedded/overpunch method.

Format:

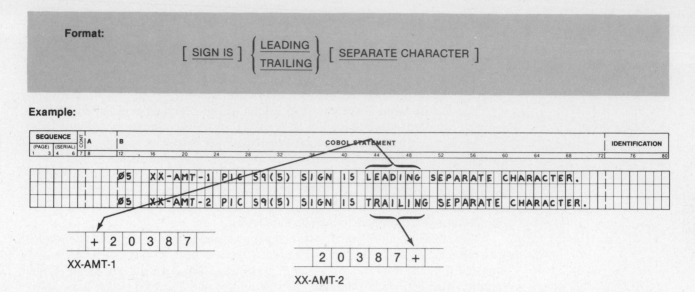

Example:

Figure 4.23 SIGN clause example

The SIGN clause is mentioned here because it applies directly to numeric PICTURE clauses. It is normally used only in those rare situations when the two sign methods—embedded/overpunch and separate character—are both used within a program. In this text, we will use the more common embedded/overpunch method of sign representation. For your information, then, the SIGN clause format is shown in Figure 4.23.

The MOVE Statement

If we always move data from sending fields to receiving fields of the exact same length, picture type, and decimal point location, then we have already covered (in Chapter 3) all you need to know about the MOVE statement. Often, however, it is necessary to move data from a shorter field to a longer field (or vice versa), from a numeric field to an alphanumeric field, from an elementary field to a group field, and so forth. Figure 4.24 summarizes MOVE statement categories and the results of each. Although there are many possible MOVE statement categories, we will cover the types most often encountered: (1) alphanumeric sending field to alphanumeric receiving field; (2) numeric sending field to numeric receiving field; (3) numeric sending field to numeric edited receiving field; (4) alphanumeric sending field to alphanumeric edited receiving field; and (5) group field moves. The other categories are mentioned at the end of this section.

Alphanumeric Sending Field to Alphanumeric Receiving Field

Whenever an alphanumeric field is moved to another field, the data in the field is normally aligned (or *justified*) to the leftmost position of the receiving field. That is, the data is moved from the leftmost position of the sending field to the leftmost position of the receiving field. Movement then continues from left to right.

If the sending and receiving fields are the same length (as were all the MOVE operations for the EMP-LIST program of Chapter 1 and the EMP-RPT program of Chapter 3), then the receiving field will contain exactly the same data as the sending field after completion of the MOVE. (Remember that the data in the sending field is not changed by the MOVE statement).

If, however, the sending and receiving fields are of different lengths, then the alphanumeric-to-alphanumeric MOVE handling will differ.

Sending field	Receiving field				
	Alphanumeric	Numeric	Alphanumeric edited	Numeric edited	Group
Alphanumeric	Left justification Receiving field shorter: truncation Receiving field longer: padding with spaces	ILLEGAL	Same as AN/AN Editing is performed	ILLEGAL	Same as AN/AN
Numeric *Integer*	Same as AN/AN	Decimal point alignment Receiving field shorter: truncation	Same as AN/AN Editing is performed	Same as N/N Editing is performed	Same as AN/AN
Noninteger	ILLEGAL	Receiving field longer: Padding with zeros	ILLEGAL		
Alphanumeric edited	Same as AN/AN	ILLEGAL	Same as AN/AN Editing is performed	ILLEGAL	Same as AN/AN
Numeric edited	Same as AN/AN	ILLEGAL	Same as AN/AN Editing is performed	ILLEGAL	Same as AN/AN
Group	Same as AN/AN	ILLEGAL	Same as AN/AN (No editing is performed)	ILLEGAL	Same as AN/AN

Note: Unshaded areas indicate most common MOVE categories

AN/AN = Alphanumeric to alphanumeric
N/N = Numeric to numeric

Figure 4.24 MOVE statement categories

Receiving field shorter than sending field

When the receiving field of an alphanumeric MOVE will not accommodate the entire sending field, the excess rightmost characters of the sending field are chopped off, or *truncated*. Only the leftmost characters of the sending field that will fit into the receiving field are thus moved. Figure 4.25 shows an example of this truncation.

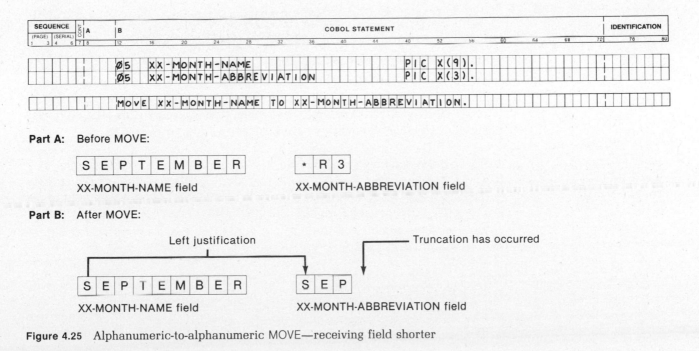

Part A: Before MOVE:

S E P T E M B E R — XX-MONTH-NAME field

* R 3 — XX-MONTH-ABBREVIATION field

Part B: After MOVE:

Left justification

S E P T E M B E R — XX-MONTH-NAME field

Truncation has occurred

S E P — XX-MONTH-ABBREVIATION field

Figure 4.25 Alphanumeric-to-alphanumeric MOVE—receiving field shorter

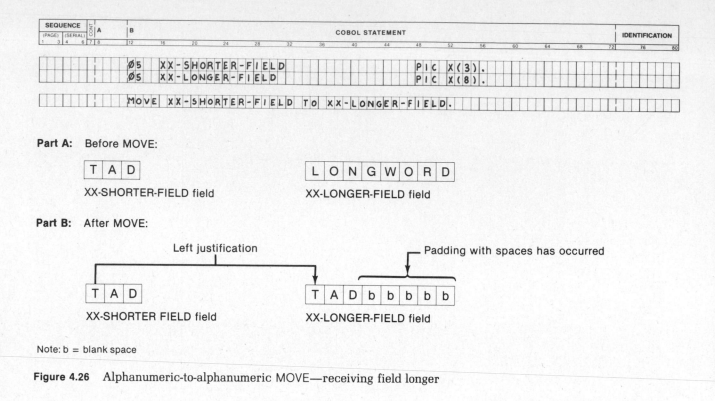

Part A: Before MOVE:

```
T A D
```
XX-SHORTER-FIELD field

```
L O N G W O R D
```
XX-LONGER-FIELD field

Part B: After MOVE:

Left justification

```
T A D
```
XX-SHORTER FIELD field

Padding with spaces has occurred

```
T A D b b b b b
```
XX-LONGER-FIELD field

Note: b = blank space

Figure 4.26   Alphanumeric-to-alphanumeric MOVE—receiving field longer

Receiving field longer than sending field

When the sending field is shorter than the receiving field of an alphanumeric move, the excess rightmost positions of the receiving field are filled, or *padded*, with blank spaces. This situation is shown in Figure 4.26. Notice that the padding with spaces has the effect of wiping out all other data that was in the field prior to the move.

Numeric Sending Field to Numeric Receiving Field

With numeric moves, the data values are decimal-point aligned in accordance with the PICTURE clauses.

Receiving field shorter than sending field

If either the integer or decimal portion of the receiving field is shorter than that portion of the sending field, truncation will occur. For the integer digits, excess leftmost digits are truncated; for the decimal digits, excess rightmost digits are truncated. Numeric truncation examples are shown in Figure 4.27.

Receiving field longer than sending field

If either the integer or decimal position portion of the receiving field is longer than that portion of the sending field, the excess positions of the receiving field are padded with zeros. For the integer digits, zeros will be inserted in the excess leftmost positions; for the decimal digits, the excess rightmost positions will be filled with zeros. Figure 4.28 provides examples.

Numeric Sending Field to Numeric Edited Receiving Field

When a "pure" numeric field (one containing 9, S, V, and/or P symbols in its PICTURE clause and without numeric editing symbols) is moved to a numeric edited field, the decimal point alignment, truncation, and zero-padding are handled just as they are for a numeric-to-numeric MOVE. In addition, the

SEQUENCE		CONT	A	B	COBOL STATEMENT	IDENTIFICATION

```
Ø5    XX-LONGER-AMOUNT                    PIC 9(5)V99.
Ø5    XX-SHORT-DECIMAL-POSNS              PIC 9(5)V9.
Ø5    XX-SHORT-INTEGER-POSNS             PIC 9(3)V99.
Ø5    XX-SHORT-AMOUNT                     PIC 9(2).
```

Part A: Receiving field contains fewer decimal positions

```
MOVE XX-LONGER-AMOUNT TO XX-SHORT-DECIMAL-POSNS.
```

Before MOVE:

| 2 | 0 | 3 | 6 | 8 | 5 | 4 |
XX-LONGER-AMOUNT field

| 8 | 5 | 4 | 0 | 2 | 6 |
XX-SHORT-DECIMAL-POSNS field

After MOVE:

Decimal point alignment   Truncation has occurred

| 2 | 0 | 3 | 6 | 8 | 5 | 4 |
XX-LONGER-AMOUNT field

| 2 | 0 | 3 | 6 | 8 | 5 |
XX-SHORT-DECIMAL-POSNS field

Part B: Receiving field contains fewer integer positions

```
MOVE XX-LONGER-AMOUNT TO XX-SHORT-INTEGER-POSNS.
```

Before MOVE:

| 2 | 0 | 3 | 6 | 8 | 5 | 4 |
XX-LONGER-AMOUNT field

| 0 | 8 | 5 | 0 | 0 |
XX-SHORT-INTEGER-POSNS field

After MOVE:

Decimal point alignment   Truncation has occurred

| 2 | 0 | 3 | 6 | 8 | 5 | 4 |
XX-LONGER-AMOUNT-field

| 3 | 6 | 8 | 5 | 4 |
XX-SHORT-INTEGER-POSNS field

Part C: Receiving field contains fewer integer and decimal positions

```
MOVE XX-LONGER-AMOUNT TO XX-SHORT-AMOUNT.
```

Before MOVE:

| 2 | 0 | 3 | 6 | 8 | 5 | 4 |
XX-LONGER-AMOUNT field

| ? | 0 |
XX-SHORT-AMOUNT field

After MOVE:

Decimal point alignment   Truncation has occurred

| 2 | 0 | 3 | 6 | 8 | 5 | 4 |
XX-LONGER-AMOUNT field

| 6 | 8 |
XX-SHORT-AMOUNT field

Note: ▲ indicates assumed decimal point

Figure 4.27 Numeric-to-numeric MOVE—receiving field shorter

SEQUENCE			A	B	COBOL STATEMENT		IDENTIFICATION

```
Ø5    XY-SHORTER-AMOUNT                    PIC 9(3)V99.
Ø5    XY-LONGER-DECIMAL-POSNS              PIC 9(3)V999.
Ø5    XY-LONGER-INTEGER-POSNS             PIC 9(5)V99.
Ø5    XY-LONGER-AMOUNT                     PIC 9(5)V999.
```

Part A: Receiving field contains more decimal positions

```
MOVE XY-SHORTER-AMOUNT TO XY-LONGER-DECIMAL-POSNS.
```

Before MOVE:

7 0 2 ▲ 1 5
XY-SHORTER-AMOUNT field

8 0 6 ▲ 5 4 3
XY-LONGER-DECIMAL-POSNS field

After MOVE:

Decimal point alignment

Excess positions are padded with zeros

7 0 2 ▲ 1 5
XY-SHORTER-AMOUNT field

7 0 2 ▲ 1 5 0
XY-LONGER-DECIMAL-POSNS field

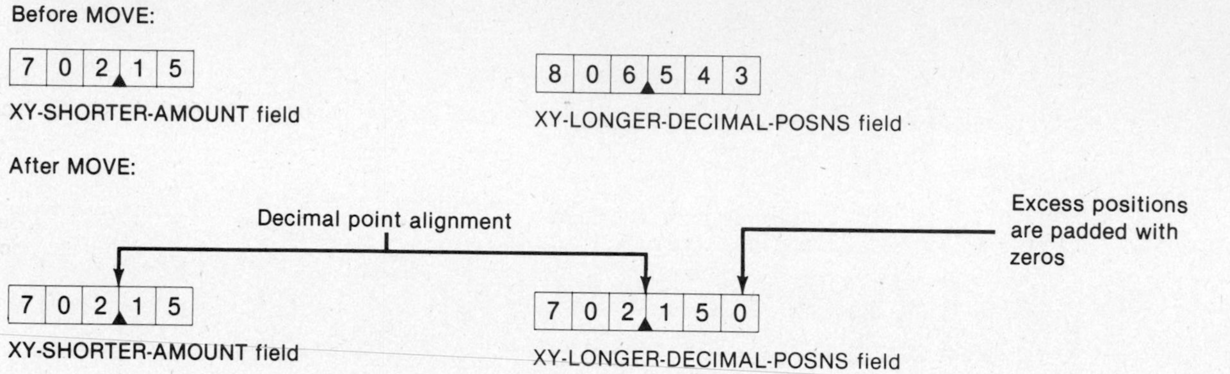

Part B: Receiving field contains more integer positions

```
MOVE XY-SHORTER-AMOUNT TO XY-LONGER-INTEGER-POSNS.
```

Before MOVE:

7 0 2 ▲ 1 5
XY-SHORTER-AMOUNT field

8 9 3 4 6 ▲ 5 5
XY-LONGER-INTEGER-POSNS field

After MOVE:

Decimal point alignment

7 0 2 ▲ 1 5
XY-SHORTER-AMOUNT field

0 0 7 0 2 ▲ 1 5
XY-LONGER-INTEGER-POSNS field

Excess positions are padded with zeros

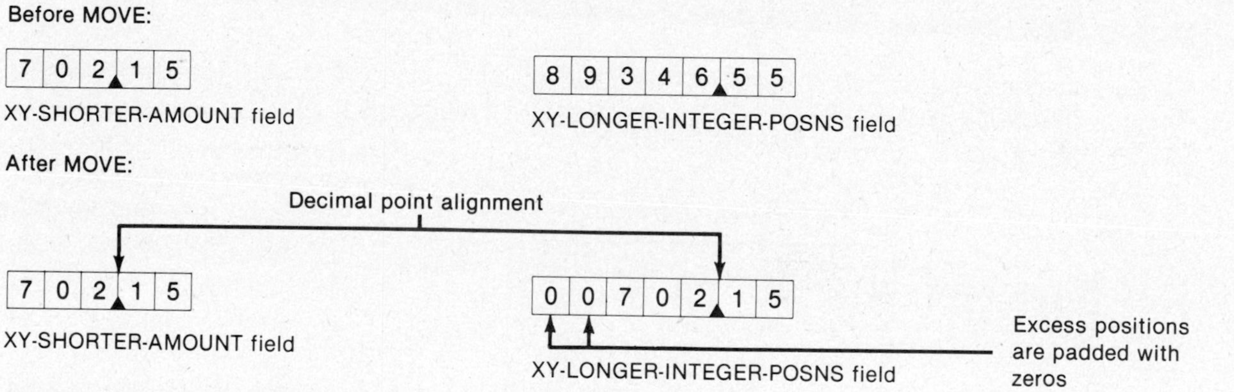

Part C: Receiving field contains more integer and decimal positions

```
MOVE XY-SHORTER-AMOUNT TO XY-LONGER-AMOUNT.
```

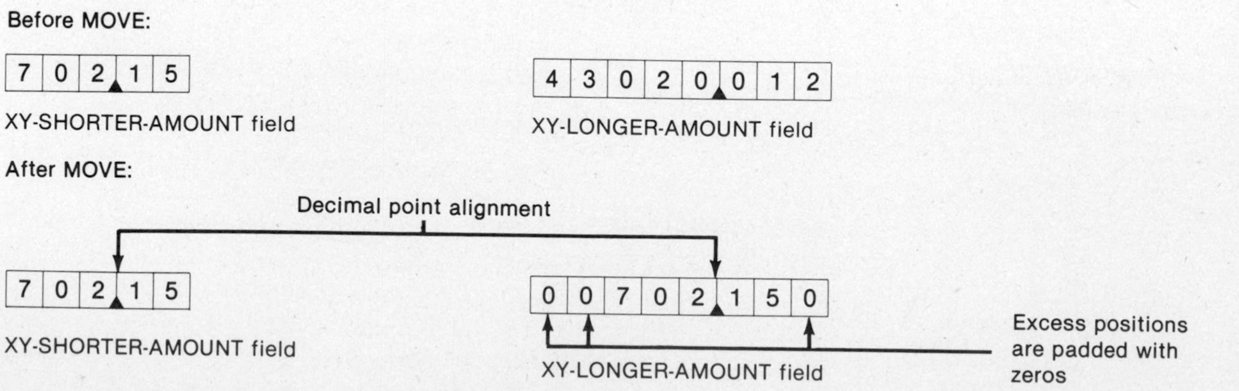

Before MOVE:

7 0 2 ▲ 1 5
XY-SHORTER-AMOUNT field

4 3 0 2 0 ▲ 0 1 2
XY-LONGER-AMOUNT field

After MOVE:

Decimal point alignment

7 0 2 ▲ 1 5
XY-SHORTER-AMOUNT field

0 0 7 0 2 ▲ 1 5 0
XY-LONGER-AMOUNT field

Excess positions are padded with zeros

Figure 4.28 Numeric-to-numeric MOVE—receiving field longer

Note: ▲ indicates assumed decimal point

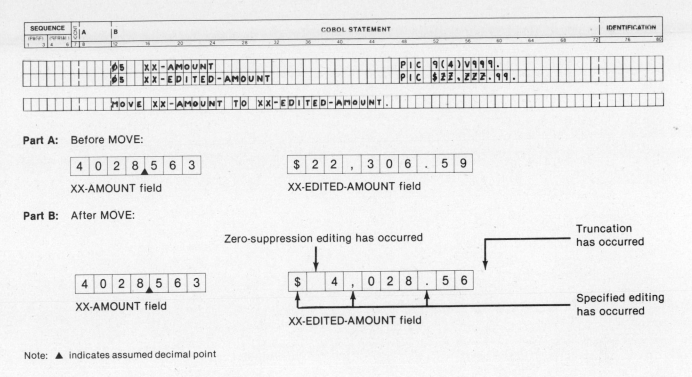

Part A: Before MOVE:

```
4 0 2 8 ▲ 5 6 3
```
XX-AMOUNT field

```
$ 2 2 , 3 0 6 . 5 9
```
XX-EDITED-AMOUNT field

Part B: After MOVE:

Zero-suppression editing has occurred

Truncation has occurred

```
4 0 2 8 ▲ 5 6 3
```
XX-AMOUNT field

```
$   4 , 0 2 8 . 5 6
```
XX-EDITED-AMOUNT field

Specified editing has occurred

Note: ▲ indicates assumed decimal point

Figure 4.29 Numeric-to-numeric-edited MOVE

editing specified for the receiving field is performed. An example is shown in Figure 4.29.

Alphanumeric Sending Field to Alphanumeric Edited Receiving Field

This particular MOVE statement category is not encountered as frequently as are the preceding three because there are only limited applications for the three alphanumeric editing characters. The alphanumeric-to-alphanumeric-edited MOVE operates exactly like an alphanumeric-to-alphanumeric MOVE with regard to truncation and blank-space padding. In addition, the specified editing (using the slash, the symbol B, or the zero) is performed.

Group Field Moves

Up to now, we have discussed moving of elementary fields. Group fields may also be moved. (Remember that an elementary field is the smallest subdivision of a data-item description. The elementary field is not further subdivided, and it contains the PICTURE clause. A group field is a collection of elementary and/or other group fields and does not have its own PICTURE clause.) Whenever a group field is specified as either the sending or receiving field of a MOVE statement, the rules for an alphanumeric-to-alphanumeric MOVE apply.

Other MOVE Statement Categories

Generally, the COBOL programmer should strive to have his or her MOVE statements fall into one of the five categories discussed above. However, there is one other category that may be encountered, and there are certain questionable or illegal MOVE statement categories that we will mention here.

Numeric integer sending field to alphanumeric receiving field

Sometimes it may be necessary to move the contents of a numeric integer field (one containing no decimal positions—that is, a whole number) to a field that is defined as alphanumeric. This is permissible and logical since numeric digits may appear in both numeric and alphanumeric fields. Such a MOVE operates

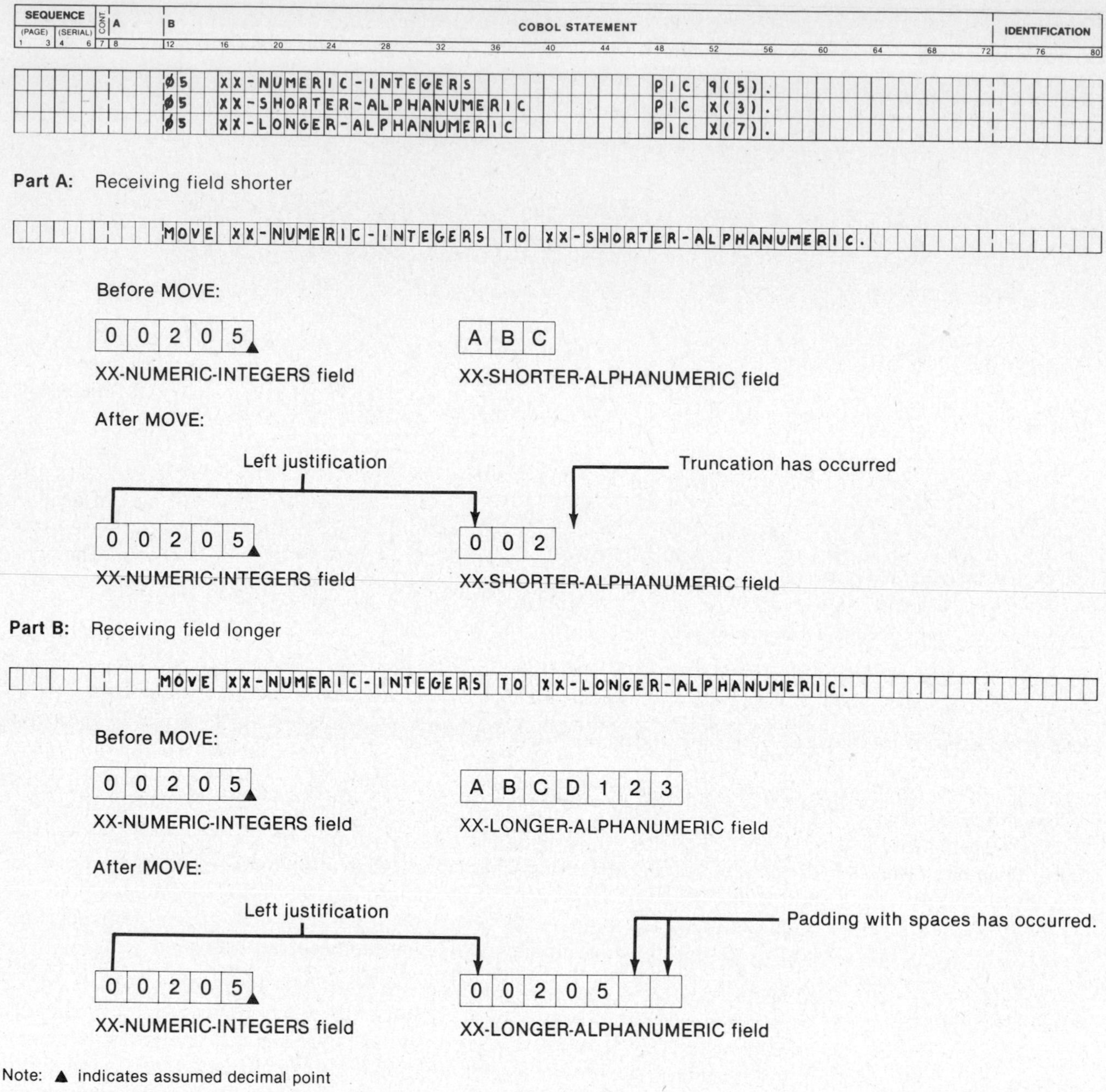

SEQUENCE		CONT	A	B	COBOL STATEMENT	IDENTIFICATION

```
Ø5    XX-NUMERIC-INTEGERS                    PIC  9(5).
Ø5    XX-SHORTER-ALPHANUMERIC                PIC  X(3).
Ø5    XX-LONGER-ALPHANUMERIC                 PIC  X(7).
```

Part A: Receiving field shorter

```
MOVE  XX-NUMERIC-INTEGERS  TO  XX-SHORTER-ALPHANUMERIC.
```

Before MOVE:

```
0  0  2  0  5▲                      A  B  C
```
XX-NUMERIC-INTEGERS field   XX-SHORTER-ALPHANUMERIC field

After MOVE:

Left justification   Truncation has occurred

```
0  0  2  0  5▲                      0  0  2
```
XX-NUMERIC-INTEGERS field   XX-SHORTER-ALPHANUMERIC field

Part B: Receiving field longer

```
MOVE  XX-NUMERIC-INTEGERS  TO  XX-LONGER-ALPHANUMERIC.
```

Before MOVE:

```
0  0  2  0  5▲                      A  B  C  D  1  2  3
```
XX-NUMERIC-INTEGERS field   XX-LONGER-ALPHANUMERIC field

After MOVE:

Left justification   Padding with spaces has occurred.

```
0  0  2  0  5▲                      0  0  2  0  5
```
XX-NUMERIC-INTEGERS field   XX-LONGER-ALPHANUMERIC field

Note: ▲ indicates assumed decimal point

Figure 4.30 Numeric-integer-to-alphanumeric MOVE

exactly the same as an alphanumeric-to-alphanumeric MOVE with regard to justification, truncation, and blank-space padding. An example is shown in Figure 4.30.

Although a numeric integer field may be moved to an alphanumeric field, it is *not* permissible to move a numeric field with decimal positions (one defined with the symbol V and decimal digits to the right) to an alphanumeric field.

Questionable or illegal MOVE statement categories

We have covered the normal and permissible MOVE statement categories. Other MOVE statement types will either yield questionable results or are illegal. Examples are shown in Figure 4.31.

1. It is *illegal* to:
   - MOVE alphanumeric-field TO numeric or numeric-edited field.
   - MOVE numeric-field-with-decimal-positions TO alphanumeric-field.
   - MOVE group-field TO numeric or numeric-edited field.
   - MOVE edited-field TO numeric or numeric-edited-field.

2. Editing will not be performed for the following statement:
   - MOVE group-field TO alphanumeric-edited-field.

Figure 4.31   Invalid MOVE statements

Concepts Related to MOVE Statements

There are a few concepts that are closely related to MOVE statement specifications. These are literals, the JUSTIFIED RIGHT clause, and the qualification of data-names.

Literals

As we mentioned in Chapter 3, a literal is an actual value specified in a COBOL program. One of the places it can be used is as the sending field of a MOVE statement. The sending field of a MOVE statement may thus specify either a data-name (as we have in the examples in this chapter) or a literal. There are two types of literals: non-numeric and numeric.

Non-numeric literals

Non-numeric literals and the rules for their formation were discussed in Chapter 3. With regard to the MOVE statement, a non-numeric literal (rather than a numeric literal) will normally be specified when moving actual values to an alphanumeric or group field. The term "non-numeric" is a bit misleading: even though termed non-numeric, such a literal may contain numbers. In fact, a non-numeric literal may be composed entirely of numbers. One of the main differentiations between a non-numeric and a numeric literal is that the former cannot be used for arithmetic operations. Arithmetic COBOL verbs will be discussed in the next chapter.

Numeric literals

When it is necessary to move a specified value to a numeric or numeric edited field, a numeric literal may be used as the sending field. When a numeric literal is used, the sending field is considered numeric and the MOVE category is determined by the receiving field.

To form a numeric literal, the programmer can use from one to eighteen numeric digits. In addition, a numeric literal may contain a plus or a minus sign and/or a decimal point.

Suppose that we wanted to move a value of 371 to a field with the data-name of XX-ANY-NUMERIC-FIELD. We could form the literal and write the MOVE statement as shown in Part A of Figure 4.32.

When forming a numeric literal, in addition to merely writing the numeric digits, the programmer must consider arithmetic sign handling. If the value were to be a negative 371, then the literal would, of course, be written with a minus sign, as shown in Part B of Figure 4.32. Whenever a plus or minus sign is included in a numeric literal, it must be written as the leftmost character of the literal.

When the value of the literal is positive, it may be written either without the plus sign—which indicates that the literal is assumed to be positive—or with the plus sign as shown in Part C of Figure 4.32. The best advice regarding when to use the plus sign is this: be consistent with the PICTURE of the receiv-

Part A: MOVE statement with an unsigned numeric literal (assumed positive):

SEQUENCE		CONT	A	B	COBOL STATEMENT	IDENTIFICATION
(PAGE)	(SERIAL)					

```
        MOVE 371 TO XX-ANY-NUMERIC-FIELD.
```

Part B: MOVE statement with a negative numeric literal:

```
        MOVE -371 TO XX-ANY-NUMERIC-FIELD.
```

Part C: MOVE statement with an explicitly positive numeric literal:

```
        MOVE +371 TO XX-ANY-NUMERIC-FIELD.
```

Figure 4.32 Examples of MOVE statements using numeric literals

ing field. That is, if the receiving field PICTURE contains an S (indicating that the field contains a sign representation), then it is consistent to use the plus sign. If, on the other hand, it does not contain an S (meaning that the field is unsigned), you should omit the plus sign.

When the literal contains decimal positions, a decimal point should be written to indicate where the decimal positions begin. Notice that, although a V is used to indicate an assumed decimal position in a picture character-string, a numeric literal cannot contain a V; it uses an actual decimal point to indicate the location. The decimal point may be written anywhere amongst the digits except as the rightmost character of the literal since COBOL might then confuse the decimal point and period (which are the same character symbol). This restriction causes little problem, though, for—just as in our everyday life—when no decimal point is written for a numeric value, the location of the decimal point is assumed to be to the right of the rightmost digit. Examples of valid and invalid numeric literals appear as Figure 4.33.

JUSTIFIED RIGHT Clause

Once in a while, a situation will occur where right justification of alphanumeric fields—rather than the left justification that COBOL normally provides—is required. For instance, consider a field that contains a six-digit date in month-month-day-day-year-year sequence. If we want to isolate the two rightmost year digits in a new two-digit year field, we can accomplish this through use of the JUSTIFIED RIGHT clause, as shown in Figure 4.34.

When the JUSTIFIED RIGHT clause is specified in the data-item description entry of an elementary alphanumeric field, data moved to that field will be justified to the right. Truncation or blank-space padding—depending upon

Valid numeric literals	Invalid numeric literals	Reason invalid
+ 238406	+ 238,406	Comma not allowed
− 1234567890.12345678	− 1234567890123456789	Over 18 digits
87.8	87V8	V not allowed
.0605	6.05%	% not allowed
+ 98.6	98.6 +	Plus sign must be leftmost
− 103	1 − 03	Minus sign must be leftmost
+ 100	+ − 100	Cannot have both plus and minus
+ 0	+	Must contain at least one digit

Figure 4.33 Valid and invalid numeric literals

Format:

$$\left\{ \begin{array}{l} \underline{\text{JUSTIFIED}} \\ \underline{\text{JUST}} \end{array} \right\} \text{ RIGHT}$$

Example:

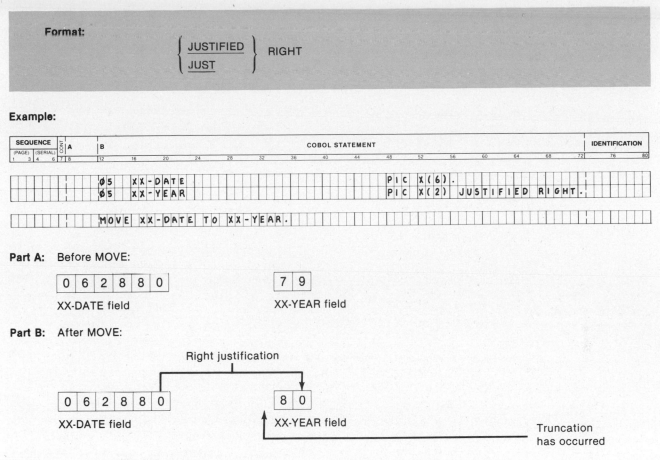

Part A: Before MOVE:

0	6	2	8	8	0

XX-DATE field

7	9

XX-YEAR field

Part B: After MOVE:

Right justification

0	6	2	8	8	0

XX-DATE field

8	0

XX-YEAR field

Truncation has occurred

Figure 4.34 JUSTIFIED RIGHT clause

whether the receiving field is shorter or longer than the sending field, respectively—will then be to the left.

One tricky thing about the JUSTIFIED RIGHT clause is that it applies only when the data-name containing the clause is used as the *receiving* field of a MOVE statement. When the JUSTIFIED RIGHT field is a sending field and the receiving field is not specified as JUSTIFIED RIGHT, right justification does not occur.

Qualification of Data-Names

When forming data-names for programs in this text, we have made each one unique. Use of data-name prefixes helps to make each data-name different. COBOL does not require that each field within a program have a unique data-name, though.

As shown in Figure 4.35, it is permissible to use the same data-name for different fields. However, whenever data-names are used for more than one field in the DATA DIVISION, there must be a unique data-name at a higher level (a lower level-number) that can be used to differentiate the fields with the same data-name. (By definition, then, each 01-level record-description data-name must be unique, since there can be no level number hierarchically above it).

When a field that has a non-unique data-name is referred to in the PROCEDURE DIVISION, it must be qualified by the data-name that differentiates it at a higher level. Otherwise, the COBOL compiler would not know which non-unique data-name was being referred to. To qualify a data-name, the programmer writes the reserved word IN (or OF) after the data-name and follows the reserved word with the differentiating data-name at the higher level.

DATA DIVISION:

SEQUENCE		CONT	A	B	COBOL STATEMENT		IDENTIFICATION

```
Ø1  RECORD-IN.
    Ø5  SOCIAL-SECURITY-NUMBER              PIC  9(9).
    Ø5  FULL-NAME.
        1Ø  LAST-NAME                       PIC  X(13).
        1Ø  FIRST-NAME                      PIC  X(11).
        1Ø  MIDDLE-INITIAL                  PIC  X(1).
```

```
Ø1  RECORD-OUT.
    Ø5  FULL-NAME.
        1Ø  FIRST-NAME                      PIC  X(11).
        1Ø  MIDDLE-INITIAL                  PIC  X(1).
        1Ø  LAST-NAME                       PIC  X(13).
    Ø5  SOCIAL-SECURITY-NUMBER              PIC  9(9).
```

PROCEDURE DIVISION:

```
MOVE SOCIAL-SECURITY-NUMBER IN RECORD-IN
    TO SOCIAL-SECURITY-NUMBER IN RECORD-OUT.
MOVE LAST-NAME IN FULL-NAME IN RECORD-IN
    TO LAST-NAME IN FULL-NAME IN RECORD-OUT.
MOVE FIRST-NAME IN FULL-NAME IN RECORD-IN
    TO FIRST-NAME IN FULL-NAME IN RECORD-OUT.
MOVE MIDDLE-INITIAL IN FULL-NAME IN RECORD-IN
    TO MIDDLE-INITIAL IN FULL-NAME IN RECORD-OUT.
```

Figure 4.35 Data-name qualification example

Even though COBOL provides for qualification of data-names, few programmers use qualifiers. There are two main reasons for this. First, it requires more writing in the PROCEDURE DIVISION and, with more writing, it introduces more places to make errors. Second, the use of data-name prefixes and/or suffixes is usually considered more readable and easier to work with. Use of unique data-name prefixes or suffixes minimizes situations where qualification can be used.

Summary

PICTURE clauses describe the following characteristics of fields: (1) data class (numeric, alphabetic, alphanumeric, numeric edited, or alphanumeric edited); (2) length; (3) assumed decimal point location; (4) arithmetic sign presence; and (5) editing. To form PICTURE clauses, the programmer may use the following picture symbols:

Numeric	Numeric edited		Alphabetic	Alphanumeric	Alphanumeric edited
9	Z	.	A	X	/
S	*	–			0
V	,	+			B
P	/	CR			
	0	DB			
	B	$			

Certain DATA DIVISION clauses are related to PICTURE clauses: The BLANK WHEN ZERO clause can be specified in the data-item description entry for a numeric or numeric edited field. Its use will cause blank spaces to appear—rather than the editing specified by the PICTURE clause—when the value of the data within the field is zero. For numeric fields with special or nonstandard arithmetic sign representation, the SIGN clause may be specified.

The MOVE statement: Depending upon the MOVE statement sending and receiving field types, right or left justification, truncation, padding, and/or decimal point alignment will occur:

Group 1. *Alphanumeric sending to alphanumeric receiving*
Numeric integer sending to alphanumeric receiving
Group sending or receiving
- Left justification in receiving field
- If receiving field is shorter, excess rightmost positions from sending field are truncated
- If receiving field is longer, excess rightmost positions in receiving field are padded with spaces

Group 2. *Alphanumeric sending to alphanumeric edited receiving*
- Same as Group 1
- Editing is performed for the receiving field in accordance with its PICTURE clause

Group 3. *Numeric sending to numeric receiving*
- Decimal point alignment
- If receiving field is shorter (on either side of the decimal point), excess sending field positions are truncated
- If receiving field is longer (on either side of the decimal point), excess receiving field positions are padded with zeros

Group 4. *Numeric sending to numeric edited receiving*
- Same as Group 3
- Editing is performed for the receiving field in accordance with its PICTURE clause

A *literal* is an actual value specified in a COBOL program. There are two types of literals: *numeric* and *non-numeric*. Non-numeric literals cannot be used in arithmetic operations and were covered in Chapter 3. A numeric literal must:

- Be composed only of digits (0 through 9); a sign character (plus or minus) and a decimal point
- Contain at least one digit but not more than 18 digits
- Contain not more than one sign character (plus or minus). When the sign character is used, it must be the leftmost character of the literal. (When the sign character is not used, the literal is considered of positive value.)
- Contain not more than one decimal point. When the decimal point is used, it may be located anywhere in the literal except in the rightmost position.

To provide for right justification of alphanumeric receiving fields, the programmer can specify the JUSTIFIED RIGHT clause in a data-item description.

When the same data-name is used to name more than one field in the DATA DIVISION, *qualification* of that data-name will be required in the PROCEDURE DIVISION.

Style Summary

PICTURE character-strings:

- Do not use the alphabetic symbol A. Instead use the symbol X for both alphabetic and alphanumeric fields.
- When the entire field is defined by the same symbol (or the same symbol plus an S), use the parentheses method. (For example, a seven-character alphanumeric field can be defined as PIC X(7); an eight-integer signed numeric field can be defined as PIC S9(8).)
- When the field contains editing characters, specify each symbol so that the editing PICTURE is more easily readable. (That is, write PIC $ZZ,ZZZ.99 — . not PIC $Z(2),Z(3).9(2) — .)
- When a V appears in a numeric picture character-string, use the parentheses method before the V and the repetition method after it (e.g., PIC 9(8)V99).

Qualification of data-names:

- Assign unique data-names so that qualification need not be used in the PROCEDURE DIVISION.

1968 ANS COBOL Restrictions

- The editing symbol slash is not available.
- The SIGN clause is not available.

Exercises

Terms for Definition

non-significant zeros
zero-suppression
assumed decimal point
embedded sign
edit
justified
truncated

padded
literal
numeric literal
non-numeric literal
alphanumeric literal
qualification

Review Questions

1. Name the five characteristics of fields that PICTURE clauses describe.
2. Name the five categories of PICTURE clauses.
3. Identify the picture symbol and category for each of the following:
   Numeric digit
   Signed field
   Assumed decimal point
   Decimal scaling position
   Alphabetic character
   Alphanumeric character
   Zero-suppression with blank space replacement
   Zero-suppression with asterisk replacement
   Comma insertion
   Slash insertion
   Zero insertion
   Blank space insertion
   Decimal point insertion
   Minus sign
   Plus sign
   Credit symbol
   Debit symbol
   Dollar sign

4. Write PICTURE character-strings for the following data-items:

    a. Five integer digit unsigned numeric field
    b. Seven integer digit signed numeric field
    c. Eight digit unsigned numeric field (six integers; two decimal places)
    d. Three digit signed numeric field (no integers; three decimal places)
    e. Two digit unsigned numeric field representing thousands and hundreds positions (tens and units positions are not stored for the value)
    f. One digit unsigned numeric field representing mils position of a cent amount (tens and hundreds decimal places are not stored for the value)
    g. Twenty-two position alphanumeric field
    h. Three integer digit numeric edited field with full zero suppression
    i. Four digit numeric edited dollars and cents field (two integers; two decimal places) with zero suppression of dollars positions and fixed dollar sign
    j. Five digit numeric edited dollars and cents field (three integers; two decimal places) with floating dollar sign
    k. Five integer digit numeric edited field with zero-suppression (on all but the units position) and with fixed minus sign as the rightmost position (provide standard comma insertion)
    l. Five integer digit numeric edited field with zero-suppression (on all but the units position) and with floating plus sign (provide standard comma insertion)
    m. Nine digit numeric edited dollars and cents field (seven integers; two decimal places) with fixed dollar sign and zero-suppression with asterisk replacement and credit symbol (provide standard comma insertion)
    n. Six digit date field with slash insertion

5. Identify the MOVE statement processing effects for the following (in the justification column enter "Left," "Right," or "Decimal point aligned"; in the appropriate excess positions column enter "Truncated," "Padded with SPACES," or "Padded with ZEROS"):

	Sending field PICTURE	Receiving field PICTURE	Justification	Excess sending field positions	Excess receiving field positions
a.	X(5)	X(5)			
b.	X(7)	X(3)			
c.	X(3)	X(5)			
d.	X(6)	X(5) JUSTIFIED RIGHT			
e.	X(7)	X(9) JUSTIFIED RIGHT			
f.	9(5)	X(5)			
g.	9(8)	X(6)			
h.	9(3)	X(2)			
i.	9(5)	9(5)			
j.	9(5)	9(4)			
k.	9(5)	9(7)			

6. To cause blank spaces to appear in a numeric or numeric edited field when the value of the data within the field is zero, the _____ clause is specified.

7. For numeric fields with special or non-standard arithmetic sign representation, the _____ clause is specified.

8. A numeric literal may be composed of
    a._____
    b._____
    c._____
    d._____

9. A numeric literal must contain at least _____ digit(s) but must not contain more than _____ digits.

10. When an arithmetic sign is specified in a numeric literal it must appear as the _____ character of the literal.

11. When a decimal point is specified in a numeric field it must not appear as the _____ character of the literal.

12. When the same data-name is specified for more than one field in the DATA DIVISION _____ of that data-name is required in the PROCEDURE DIVISION.

Syntax/Debug Exercises

1. Some or all of the following PICTURE character-strings are in error. Identify each erroneous character-string.

PIC 9(X)	PIC ZZ,ZZZ.ZZ
PIC 9(5)V	PIC 99,999.99
PIC S9(5)V99	PIC $*,***.99CR
PIC 999S	PIC $Z,ZZZ.99DR
PIC R(9)	PIC − − − −9.99
PIC 99PP	PIC − ZZZ.99 −
PIC PP99	PIC + ZZZ,ZZZ
PIC 9PP9	PIC ZZZ,ZZZ +
PIC 9(19)	PIC + + +,+ +9
PIC X(19)	PIC Z9/99/99
PIC X(3)V99	PIC Z9/Z9/99
PIC ZZ,ZZ,ZZ	PIC XX/XX/XX
PIC ZZ.ZZ.ZZ	PIC 999B99B9999
PIC ZZ,ZZZ.99	PIC XXXBXXBXXXX
PIC ZZ,Z99.99	PIC 99900
PIC ZZ,ZZ9.ZZ	PIC XXX00

2. Some or all of the following MOVE statements are not syntactically correct. Identify each incorrect statement.
DATA DIVISION entries:

```
01    MISC-FIELDS.

      05 ALPHANUM-FIELD          PIC X(7).
      05 NUM-INT-FIELD           PIC 9(7).
      05 NUM-DEC-FIELD           PIC S9(5)V99.
      05 NUM-EDIT-FIELD          PIC ZZ,ZZZ.99 − .
```

PROCEDURE DIVISION MOVE statements:

```
MOVE ALPHANUM-FIELD TO NUM-INT-FIELD.
MOVE NUM-INT-FIELD TO ALPHANUM-FIELD.
MOVE NUM-DEC-FIELD TO ALPHANUM-FIELD.
MOVE ALPHANUM-FIELD TO NUM-DEC-FIELD.
MOVE NUM-INT-FIELD TO NUM-EDIT-FIELD.
MOVE ALPHANUM-FIELD TO NUM-EDIT-FIELD.
MOVE NUM-EDIT-FIELD TO NUM-EDIT-FIELD.
MOVE NUM-DEC-FIELD TO MISC-FIELDS.
MOVE ALPHANUM-FIELD TO MISC-FIELDS.
```

Programming Assignment 4-A: Check Register

Program description
     A check register is to be printed from the check register file.
Input file
     Check register file

Input record format
Check register record

Field location	Field name	Data class	Comments
1- 2	Record code	numeric	code "41"
6-10	Check number	numeric	
11-29	Payee name	alphanumeric	
74-80	Check amount	numeric	assumed decimal point between positions 78 and 79

Output file

Check register

Output report line format

Print positions	Field name	Comments
10-14	Check number	
17-35	Payee name	
38-47	Check amount	Fixed dollar sign Zero-suppress non-significant dollar position zeros Insert comma and decimal point

Program operations

1. Read each input check register record.

2. Print an output check register report line as specified above for each check register record.

3. Double-space each report line.

Programming Assignment 4-B: Payroll Register

Program description

A payroll register is to be prepared from the payroll file.

Input file

Payroll file

Input record format
Payroll record

Field location	Field name	Data class	Comments
1- 2	Record code	numeric	code "42"
3-11	Employee social security number	numeric	
12-29	Employee name	alphanumeric	
41-45	Hours worked this period	numeric	assumed decimal point between positions 43 and 44
46-49	Hourly rate	numeric	assumed decimal point between positions 47 and 48
50-56	Gross pay	numeric	assumed decimal point between positions 54 and 55
65-70	Period-ending date	numeric	mmddyy format

Output file

Payroll register

Output report line format

Print positions	Field name	Comments
1–11	Employee social security number	Provide blanks: sss ss ssss
14–31	Employee name	
34–41	Period-ending date	Provide slashes: mm/dd/yy
43–48	Hours-worked this period	Zero-suppress non-significant integer positions Insert decimal point
51–56	Hourly rate	Fixed dollar sign Zero-suppress non-significant integer positions Insert decimal point
58–67	Gross pay	Floating dollar sign Zero-suppress non-significant integer positions Insert comma and decimal point

Program operations

1. Read each input payroll record.

2. Print an output payroll register report line as specified above for each payroll record.

3. Double-space each report line.

Programming Assignment 4-C: General Ledger Adjustment Report

Program description

A general ledger adjustment report is to be prepared from the account adjustment file.

Input file

Account adjustment file

Input record format

Account adjustment record:

Field location	Field name	Data class	Comments
1– 2	Record code	numeric	code "43"
3– 8	Account number	numeric	
9–28	Account name	alphanumeric	
31–40	Debit amount	numeric	assumed decimal point between positions 38 and 39; provide for negative values
41–50	Credit amount	numeric	assumed decimal point between positions 48 and 49 provide for negative values

Output file

General ledger adjustment report

Output report line format

Print positions	Field name	Comments
10–16	Account number	Zero-suppress non-significant digits in first four positions Insert period between 4th and 5th account digit
18–37	Account name	
41–55	Debit amount	Zero-suppress non-significant dollar digits Blank when zero Insert commas and decimal point Print CR if negative
61–75	Credit amount	Zero-suppress non-significant dollar digits Blank when zero Insert commas and decimal point Print DB if negative

Program operations

1. Read each input account adjustment record.

2. Print an output general ledger adjustment report line as specified above for each account adjustment record.

3. Single-space each report line.

Programming Assignment 4-D: Inventory Adjustment Report

Program description

An inventory adjustment report is to be prepared from the inventory adjustment file.

Input file

Inventory adjustment file

Input record format

Inventory adjustment record:

Field location	Field name	Data class	Comments
1– 2	Record code	numeric	code "21"
3–12	Part number	alphanumeric	
20–45	Part description	alphanumeric	
61–65	Inventory adjustment quantity	numeric	provide for negative amounts
66–74	Inventory adjustment amount	numeric	assumed decimal point between positions 72 and 73; provide for negative amounts
75–80	Inventory adjustment date	number	mmddyy format

Output file

Inventory adjustment report

Output report line format

Print positions	Field name	Comments
1–10	Part number	
12–37	Part description	

Print positions	Field name	Comments
39–46	Inventory adjustment date	Insert slashes mm/dd/yy
49–55	Inventory adjustment quantity	Zero-suppress non-significant digits Insert comma Print floating plus or minus sign
57–70	Inventory adjustment amount	Zero-suppress non-significant dollar digits Insert commas and decimal point Print CR if negative value

Program operations

1. Read each input inventory adjustment record.

2. Print an output inventory adjustment report line as specified above for each inventory adjustment record.

3. Double-space each report line.

SYSTEMS CHAPTER B

RECORD AND REPORT DESIGN CONCEPTS

RECORD AND REPORT DESIGN CONCEPTS

There are some basic concepts of record and report design with which the programmer/analyst should be familiar so that he or she can (1) interpret programming specifications correctly and (2) design records when called upon to do so.

Record Design

Records are usually designed and documented on some type of record layout worksheet. Figure B.1 shows examples of commonly used forms. When designing records, the programmer/analyst must consider logical record length, record identification, and field placement.

Logical Record Length

The length of punched card records is determined by the punched card equipment and media; it is normally either 80 or 96 characters of data per card. Magnetic tape, since it is a continuous medium, can accommodate records of practically any length. Although magnetic disk length may be limited to the character capacity of the recording track or sector, such lengths are usually large enough not to cause restraints in determining logical record length.

Part A: Record layout worksheet for 80-column punched card records.

Program _____ By _____ Date _____

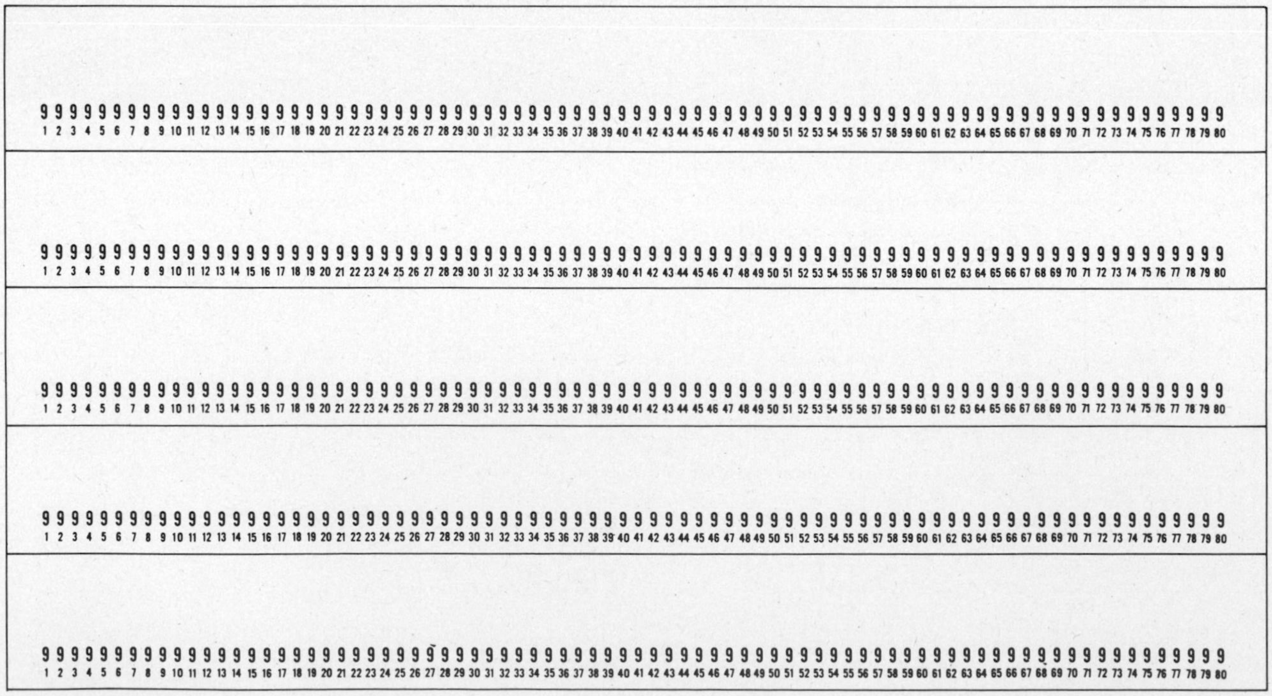

Figure B.1 Examples of record layout worksheets

Part B: General purpose record layout worksheets.

IBM RECORD FORMAT

INTERNATIONAL BUSINESS MACHINES CORPORATION

GX20-1702-1 UM/025 †
Printed in U.S.A.

APPLICATION . . . . RECORD NAME . . . . BY . . . . DATE . . . . PAGE . . . . OF . . . .

Field Name	
Characteristics*	
Position**	

**POSITION
Hexadecimal / Decimal
Numbering
from
00 to FF / 0 to 255

File Description _____
Recording Mode _____
Records per Block _____
Record Size _____
Label Records are _____
File Identification _____
File Serial Number _____
Retention Cycle _____
Organization Type _____

*CHARACTERISTICS
Check the box that corresponds to the characteristics used:

☐ System/360 Characteristic Codes

A - address value, full word
B - binary
C - character, 8-bit code
D - floating-point, double word
E - floating-point, full word
F - fixed-point, full word
H - fixed-point, halfword
P - packed decimal
S - address, base displacement
V - address, external symbol
X - hexadecimal, 4-bit code
Y - address value, halfword
Z - zoned decimal

☐ General Characteristics

A - alphabetic or blank
X - alphanumeric
9 - numeric
V - assumed decimal point

Examples of Signed Fields:
X9999   999X
X999V99 9999V9X

SORTING FIELDS (Major to Minor)

1		7	
2		8	
3		9	
4		10	
5		11	
6		12	

REMARKS _____

WHERE USED

| Input From | Output To |
| | |

| Date | Revisions By |
| | |

† The number of forms per pad may vary slightly.

IBM

INTERNATIONAL BUSINESS MACHINES CORPORATION

GX20-1702-1 UM/025 †
Printed in U.S.A.

PROPORTIONAL RECORD LAYOUT FORM

Application _____   Type of Records _____   By _____   Date _____   Page ___ of ___

RECORD NAME AND REMARK

*Two numbering arrangements, each in hexadecimal and decimal notation, are shown. Select the arrangement and notation used by checking the appropriate box to the left.
†The number of forms per pad may vary slightly.

Figure B.1 (continued)

147

Generally, the length of a logical record is determined by the number and length of the fields that it is to contain. To that aggregate length, the programmer should allocate an expansion area (that is, an unassigned FILLER area) to provide for the addition of new fields or an increase in the length of existing fields. If an expansion area is not provided, every field addition or length increase will lengthen the record itself. Normally, the FD and record-description in a COBOL program must be modified whenever the record length changes—even if the field being added or changed is not used by the program. When an expansion area is provided in the record, then perhaps only those programs using the new or changed field need be modified and recompiled. Thus, provision of an expansion area will help minimize program maintenance.

The amount of expansion area should be based upon the programmer/ analyst's evaluation of how long the system will be used and the plans for future development and enhancement of the system. Admittedly, such guesses are difficult to quantify. An expansion area of from 10 to 40 per cent of allocated record length is usually appropriate, however. (A higher percentage of expansion area must be assigned to shorter records to ensure that the area can be utilized effectively.)

The placement of expansion area is normally at the trailing end of the record. That is, currently required fields are defined adjacent to one another and the expansion area is the unused portion at the end of the record. On the other hand, if certain fields can be expected to increase in length, the expansion area should be provided adjacent to those fields. For example, if a customer number field is currently four digits in length but will require expansion to five digits, it would be wise to allow one or more digits of expansion area to the immediate left of the customer number field. Or, if a customer name field is currently 20 characters in length, and users feel that a 25-character field would be less restrictive, then an expansion area of five characters or more should be provided to the right of the customer name field. Normally, adjacent expansion areas should be specified to the left of numeric fields and to the right of alphanumeric fields. In this way the programmer minimizes data field realignment at the time of expansion.

Record Identification

Just as form numbers are usually assigned to paper documents, a record code should always be assigned to data processing records. By providing a record code, each processing program can then ensure that it is receiving the correct type of input records. For example, a payroll program should certainly not be reading accounts receivable records.

If a record code field is assigned to all logical records, then each different record type can be assigned a unique number. As an example, payroll name-and-address records could be assigned record code 21, payroll time records could be 23, accounts-payable vendor records could be code 30, and so forth.

The length of the record code field should be two, three, or four characters in length, depending upon the number of record types. A small organization will usually find a two-position code adequate; a very large corporation might allocate four or more places. Numeric record codes are usually easier to handle, but alphanumeric record coding systems are sometimes used.

It is a good practice to place the record code field in the same relative location for all record types. The best place for the record code field is at the beginning of each record.

Field Placement

Often it doesn't actually matter where fields are placed in a logical record; haphazard arrangement may present no processing difficulties. But there are a couple of field placement considerations that should be discussed.

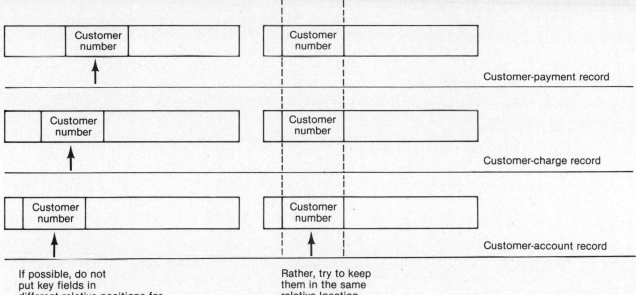

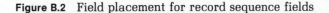

If possible, do not put key fields in different relative positions for different record types.

Rather, try to keep them in the same relative location.

Figure B.2 Field placement for record sequence fields

For card records that must be keypunched, field locations are normally specified in the order in which they are read from a source document. Such field placement facilitates the keypunching process. However, with the declining use of punched cards as a data entry medium, source document location of the data becomes less of a concern. Newer electronic data recording devices (terminals and key-to-disk devices, for instance) can place the fields at locations other than in the sequence keyed.

Another field placement consideration relates to record sorting requirements. Fields that determine the record sequence should be located in the same relative positions for all record types that will be sorted together. Figure B.2 illustrates this concept. Unfortunately, at the time a record is being designed, it is sometimes not possible to define or foretell all the future sorting requirements and alternate sorting provisions must sometimes be made.

Probably the best general recommendation for the placement of fields within a logical record is the following: (1) place the record code field first; (2) follow that by the key (or control) fields for that record (the field or group of fields that uniquely identify the data entity to which that record corresponds); (3) continue with indicative fields containing permanent or semipermanent data; (4) proceed with indicative fields containing temporary data; and (5) conclude the record with an expansion area. Figure B.3 provides an example of such field placement.

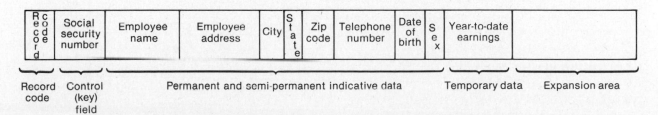

Figure B.3 Example of field placement in a logical record

Report Design

As we have illustrated in this text, reports are usually designed and documented on print charts. When designing a report, the programmer has three general data areas: the heading area, the body area, and the total area. Figure B.4 illustrates these report areas.

Report Areas

Heading area

The heading area of a report should contain data that will identify the report. Common examples of such data are report title, organization name, report date, and page number. Larger organizations often print a report code number on reports to uniquely identify each report and facilitate identification of which computer program printed the report. When dates are printed on reports, it is often appropriate to print two dates: (1) the date (or period-ending date) to which the report applies and (2) the date when the report was actually printed (or processed) by the computer. For example, consider an income statement for the month of October, 1981. The period-ending date of 10/31/81 should, of course, be printed at the top of each page of the report. But this income statement will probably not be processed until sometime in early November. Providing the run date on the report is very helpful in case the report is modified, corrected, or revised at a later date.

The bottom of the heading area usually gives column headings for the detail line fields printed below.

Report headings are usually repeated on each page of a report. Sometimes the headings are condensed or abbreviated for report pages after the first.

Body area

The body of a report usually contains detail lines, summary lines, and/or subtotal lines. A *detail line* is a line that is logically related to an input record, usually on a one-to-one basis. If one or more body lines are printed for each input record, such lines would be considered detail lines. A *summary line* is one where multiple input records are accumulated or otherwise summarized and printed as one line. A *subtotal line* presents an accumulation of previously printed detail or summary lines.

```
NATIONAL AEROSPACE CORP.                                                     PERIOD ENDING 07-18-80
LABOR DISTRIBUTION DETAIL                                                             PAGE   38
----------------------------------------------------------------------------------------------------
PERF  PERF     RES  P/R  EMPLOYEE                     CHARGE       REG    PRM    TOT    REG     PRM    SHIFT     TOTAL
POOL  DEPT SFT CODE CODE NO.    NAME      DATE        NUMBER       HRS    HRS    HRS   AMOUNT  AMOUNT  DIFRNTL   AMOUNT

 T    K5520  1 25510 F   24365  PATTON    07-16-80  905-500-017   8.00    .00    8.00   80.88   .00      .00     80.88
 T    K5520  1 25510 F   24365  PATTON    07-17-80  905-500-017   8.00    .00    8.00   80.88   .00      .00     80.88
     * TOTAL FOR EMPLOYEE 24365 PATTON                           40.00*   .00   40.00  404.40   .00      .00    404.40

 T    K5520  2 24010 R   24604  DAUGHERTY 07-14-80  506-950-400   8.00    .00    8.00   64.80   .00     8.08     72.88
 T    K5520  2 24010 R   24604  DAUGHERTY 07-15-80  506-950-400   8.00    .00    8.00   64.80   .00     8.08     72.88
 T    K5520  2 24010 R   24604  DAUGHERTY 07-16-80  506-950-500   8.00    .00    8.00   64.80   .00     8.08     72.88
 T    K5520  2 24010 R   24604  DAUGHERTY 07-17-80  506-950-400   8.00    .00    8.00   64.80   .00     8.08     72.88
 T    K5520  2 24010 R   24604  DAUGHERTY 07-18-80  506-950-410   6.00    .00    6.00   48.60   .00     6.06     54.66
     * TOTAL FOR EMPLOYEE 24604 DAUGHERTY                        38.00*   .00   38.00  307.80   .00    38.38    346.18

 T    K5520  2 24010 R   24615  HUBBELL   07-14-80  506-583-037   7.50    .00    7.50   72.00   .00      .00     72.00
 T    K5520  2 24010 R   24615  HUBBELL   07-15-80  506-583-037   8.00    .00    8.00   76.80   .00      .00     76.80
 T    K5520  2 24010 R   24615  HUBBELL   07-16-80  506-583-037   1.50    .00    1.50   14.40   .00      .00     14.40
 T    K5520  2 24010 R   24615  HUBBELL   07-16-80  506-583-040   7.00    .00    7.00   67.20   .00      .00     67.20
 T    K5520  2 24010 R   24615  HUBBELL   07-17-80  506-583-037   6.50    .00    6.50   62.40   .00      .00     62.40
 T    K5520  2 24010 R   24615  HUBBELL   07-18-80  506-583-037   5.00    .00    5.00   48.00   .00      .00     48.00
     * TOTAL FOR EMPLOYEE 24615 HUBBELL                          35.50*   .00   35.50  340.80   .00      .00    340.80

    ** TOTAL FOR DEPARTMENT K5520                              1283.85**        1400.50        1768.13          13210.11
                                                                     116.65           11233.68        208.30
```

Total area   Body area   Heading area

Figure B.4 Heading, body, and total report areas

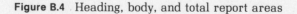

Total area

The total area is usually at the end of the report. Commonly printed in the total area are items such as record counts, final totals for columns, and the results of calculations (such as averages) made after all applicable input records have been processed. Descriptive words to identify the total figures are also commonly provided. Report lines containing such data are called *total lines*.

When page total or other data is printed at the bottom of each report page, the area in which they are printed is termed the *page footing* area.

Printer Specifications

Most line printers and many serial character printers provide a maximum of 132 print positions for each horizontal report line. Characters are usually printed on the print-line at 10 characters per inch. Hence, a 132-character line spans 13.2 inches.

Practically all printers print six lines to the vertical inch; a standard eleven-vertical-inch form will therefore contain a maximum of 66 lines of printing. (Usually, though, top and bottom margins consume some of the print-lines.) Many of the six-line-per-inch printers can also be operator-set to print eight lines to the inch, if desired. Voluminous reports may be printed at eight lines per inch to save paper. Examples of print-line spacing are shown in Figure B.5.

```
THESE  LINES  ARE  SINGLE  SPACED  8  TO  AN  INCH
THESE  LINES  ARE  SINGLE  SPACED  8  TO  AN  INCH
THESE  LINES  ARE  SINGLE  SPACED  8  TO  AN  INCH
```

```
THESE  LINES  ARE  SINGLE  SPACED  6  TO  AN  INCH
THESE  LINES  ARE  SINGLE  SPACED  6  TO  AN  INCH
THESE  LINES  ARE  SINGLE  SPACED  6  TO  AN  INCH
```

Figure B.5 Print line spacing

Tips on Report Design

Identify the report. Every output report should have a title or some other identifier. If the output is destined to be read or used by someone outside the company or division, the name of the issuing organization should appear on the report. The run date of the report should be specified; the period-ending date should also appear, when applicable. A report or program number that will uniquely identify the report should be assigned and noted on the output. For multipage reports, a page number should be provided.

Standardize the heading identification area. It is helpful to users and presents a uniform appearance to have the report identification items in standard locations from one report to the next within the organization. That is, try not to have the report title in the upper left-hand corner on one report and in the lower right-hand space of the heading area of another.

Label all output fields. Data fields should not be displayed on a report without descriptive text explaining what each field is. Such descriptions will usually take the form of column headings for detail line fields. For the total line and for other fields not contained in the regular lines, adjacent descriptive words on the same line may be required. Even though the programmer/analyst and the user may be very familiar with the report as it is being developed, data printed on reports without identification soon becomes confusing.

Position column headings properly. If a data field beneath a column heading contains a uniform number of characters to be printed on each line, it is probably most attractive to center the column heading. Usually, though, numeric fields will have blank positions to the left of the number (because of zero suppression) and alphanumeric fields will have blank positions to the right of the printed characters (because the length of the field is usually longer than the entry in the field).

So, column headings for numeric fields are more pleasing visually when offset or justified to the right boundary of the data column; column headings for alphanumeric fields are best positioned near the left limit of the data column.

Consider report width carefully. The maximum width of a printed report is usually 132 print positions. If the report can be accommodated easily in 85 print positions or less, it's a good idea to keep within that number; this allows the user to copy and file the report with 8½-inch-wide paper. Check to see if there are any special filing requirements that will dictate any other report widths. For example, if a report is to kept in a standard 3-ring binder, a left margin area must be provided for the binder holes.

Consider top and bottom margin requirements. If the report is to be bound on the horizontal edges—as many nylon-post binders do—a generous top and bottom margin must be provided. Otherwise, some of the report page will be obscured after it is bound.

Make the report visually attractive. Don't cram the data together in a bunch; space the fields across the chosen report width. Provide extra blank lines before and after subtotal and total lines; this "white space" will make them easier to locate and read.

Consider filing-code and identification-number placement. The upper right-hand corner of the page is usually the best place to print identification codes. For example, invoice numbers are usually printed at that location on an invoice form. If reports are to be filed in other than standard file drawers, however, another location may be preferable.

For numeric amounts, allow sufficient space for the largest possible value. For numeric amounts that are the result of an arithmetic operation, provide room for the largest possible amount that can occur. When just two values are involved in a calculation, the maximum size of the value can be determined easily. In many situations, however, the total amount will be the result of successive operations. When this is the case, the space required for the maximum value cannot be determined by formula but must be chosen by the programmer/analyst.

For numeric column amounts, allow space between columns on the detail lines large enough for the totals. When you are determining the number of horizontal print positions needed for numeric fields that contain column totals, it is the length of the *total* that must be provided for rather than the field length of the detail amounts. An alternate method, which conserves horizontal space on the detail line, is to offset the totals as shown in Figure B.6.

Be certain to leave room for and show a credit symbol or minus sign if a numeric amount could represent a negative value. Most numeric amount fields should provide for negative representations so that negative adjustments can be handled. It is usually adequate to use a minus sign to indicate negative amounts on internal reports. The minus sign is convenient to use because it occupies only one character position. However, it is generally preferable to use the CR symbol for formal accounting and other external reports. When indicating a credit balance on a customer's account, it's a good idea to print even further explanation—such as CREDIT BALANCE—DO NOT PAY—to ensure that the status of the account is understood.

Use appropriate editing. Suppress nonsignificant zeros of numeric amount fields, but numeric code numbers are usually easier to work with when their

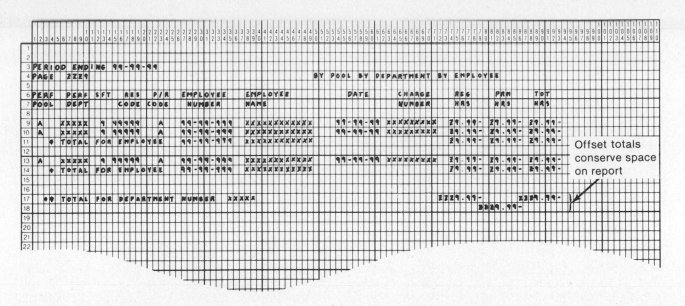

Figure B.6 Example of offset totals

leftmost zeros are *not* suppressed. Insert decimal points when decimal positions are to be printed for a number value. Providing there is sufficient space on the line, insert commas into amount fields with over three or four integers. Place slashes or hyphens in six-digit dates. Do not print dollar signs except on formal financial reports and checks; the column heading (plus the typical dollar-and-cents placement of the decimal point) should make it clear that it is a money figure.

Consider providing page totals for reports with numeric totals that will require manual reconciliation and/or modifications. When manual changes must be made to amounts on reports, a page total—that is, a column total of the amounts on that page—can make it easier for clerks to recompute correct report totals after changes have been made to detail amounts.

Use asterisks or some other legend to distinguish totals and subtotals from detail amounts. Accountants sometimes refer to these as "one-star," "two-star," and so forth, totals. An example is provided in Figure B.7.

Provide check protection for check amounts. The maximum amount of space allocated for check amounts on preprinted check forms will usually be larger than that required to handle the value of most checks. The unused space to the left could be altered fraudulently unless some protection method is employed.

One simple method of providing protection is to fill the area with nonsignificant zeros. For example, if spaces were provided for six dollar digits (not including punctuation commas) a value of $1,234.56 could be printed as $001,234.56. Such zero-filled amounts are usually difficult to read, however. A better approach would be to use asterisk protection. With this method, the nonsignificant zeros are printed as asterisks. Our example would then appear as the more readable $**1,234.56. An alternate method is to use a floating dollar sign, in which the dollar sign is printed immediately to the left of the leftmost significant digit. A further safeguard is to have a light background screen preprinted in the amount area. Any erasures or alterations will be more easily noticed, since they will be highlighted by disruption of the screen pattern. The various check protection methods are shown in Figure B.8.

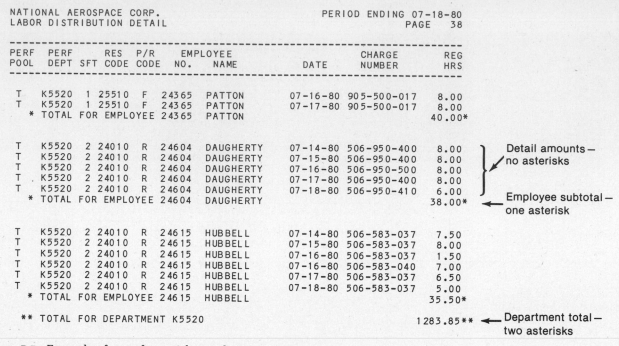

```
----------------------------------------------------------------------
PERF  PERF     RES  P/R   EMPLOYEE                  CHARGE         REG
POOL  DEPT SFT CODE CODE  NO.    NAME     DATE      NUMBER         HRS
----------------------------------------------------------------------

 T    K5520  1 25510  F  24365  PATTON    07-16-80 905-500-017    8.00
 T    K5520  1 25510  F  24365  PATTON    07-17-80 905-500-017    8.00
    * TOTAL FOR EMPLOYEE 24365  PATTON                           40.00*


 T    K5520  2 24010  R  24604  DAUGHERTY 07-14-80 506-950-400    8.00
 T    K5520  2 24010  R  24604  DAUGHERTY 07-15-80 506-950-400    8.00
 T    K5520  2 24010  R  24604  DAUGHERTY 07-16-80 506-950-500    8.00
 T    K5520  2 24010  R  24604  DAUGHERTY 07-17-80 506-950-400    8.00
 T    K5520  2 24010  R  24604  DAUGHERTY 07-18-80 506-950-410    6.00
    * TOTAL FOR EMPLOYEE 24604  DAUGHERTY                        38.00*


 T    K5520  2 24010  R  24615  HUBBELL   07-14-80 506-583-037    7.50
 T    K5520  2 24010  R  24615  HUBBELL   07-15-80 506-583-037    8.00
 T    K5520  2 24010  R  24615  HUBBELL   07-16-80 506-583-037    1.50
 T    K5520  2 24010  R  24615  HUBBELL   07-16-80 506-583-040    7.00
 T    K5520  2 24010  R  24615  HUBBELL   07-17-80 506-583-037    6.50
 T    K5520  2 24010  R  24615  HUBBELL   07-18-80 506-583-037    5.00
    * TOTAL FOR EMPLOYEE 24615  HUBBELL                          35.50*

   ** TOTAL FOR DEPARTMENT K5520                             1283.85**
```

Detail amounts—
no asterisks

Employee subtotal—
one asterisk

Department total—
two asterisks

Figure B.7 Example of use of asterisks to identify total levels

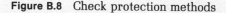

$001,234.56	Zero-filled
$**1,234.56	Asterisks
$1,234.56	Floating dollar sign
$ 1,234.56	Screening

Figure B.8 Check protection methods

Summary

When designing records, the programmer/analyst must consider logical record length, record identification, and field placement. The length of a logical record is usually determined by the aggregate total of its field lengths plus an expansion area. Each logical record type should contain a record code field to uniquely identify it. Field placement within records may depend upon data entry or sorting considerations.

There are three general data areas of a report: heading, body, and total. The *heading* area generally contains data such as organization name, report title, period-ending date, run date, page number, report number, and column headings. The *body* area contains detail lines, summary lines, and subtotal lines. The *total* area generally contains record counts, column totals, the results of calculations, and descriptive words. Such data printed at the bottom of each report page are termed *page footings*.

Most computers provide for 132 print positions per line at ten characters to the horizontal inch, and they print six or eight lines to the vertical inch.

The following are tips on report design:

- Identify the report.
- Standardize the heading identification area.
- Label all output fields.
- Position column headings properly.
- Consider report width carefully.

- Consider top and bottom margin requirements.
- Make the report visually attractive.
- Consider filing-code and identification-number placement.
- For numeric amounts, allow sufficient space for the largest possible value.
- For numeric column amounts, allow space between columns on the detail lines large enough for the totals.
- Be certain to leave room for and show a credit symbol or minus sign if a numeric amount could represent a negative value.
- Use appropriate editing.
- Consider providing page totals for reports with numeric totals that will require manual reconciliation and/or modifications.
- Use asterisks or some other legend to distinguish totals and subtotals from detail amounts.
- Provide check protection for check amounts.

CHAPTER 5

ARITHMETIC STATEMENTS AND REPORT TOTALS

157

ARITHMETIC STATEMENTS AND REPORT TOTALS

We will now make further use of the read-and-print logic that was defined in the first three chapters. This logic, together with the PICTURE clause and MOVE statement considerations explained in Chapter 4, will be used to develop programs that introduce arithmetic statements and the concept of developing report totals.

After a brief presentation of arithmetic field definition and arithmetic terminology, we will cover the five arithmetic verbs: ADD, SUBTRACT, MULTIPLY, DIVIDE, and COMPUTE. To conclude the chapter, program logic for a read-and-print program with report totals will be developed.

The Charge Account Report Program

To aid understanding of the arithmetic statements, we present here an example of a read-and-print program that also performs arithmetic calculations, the Charge Account Report (CHGACCT) program. In the latter part of the chapter, that program is expanded to produce a Charge Account Report with Totals (TCHGACCT) and is used to explain report total logic.

The Charge Account Report program is defined in the following figures:

Figure 5.1.   Record Layout: Charge Account Record
Figure 5.2.   Print Chart: Charge Account Report
Figure 5.3.   Programming Specifications: Charge Account Report Program
Figure 5.4.   System Flowchart: Charge Account Report Program
Figure 5.5.   Structure Chart: Charge Account Report Program
Figure 5.6.   Pseudocode: Charge Account Report Program
Figure 5.7.   Program Flowchart: Charge Account Report Program
Figure 5.8.   COBOL Coding: CHGACCT Program
Figure 5.9.   Output: Charge Account Report Program

The COBOL coding concepts for this read-compute-and-print CHGACCT program correspond to the coding for the read-and-print EMP-RPT program except that the CHGACCT program requires an extra WORKING-STORAGE SECTION field and introduces some arithmetic statements into the PROCEDURE DIVISION. The new concepts introduced in this CHGACCT program that were not present in the EMP-RPT program are identified on the program listing. They will be further discussed during our coverage of arithmetic field definition and arithmetic statements.

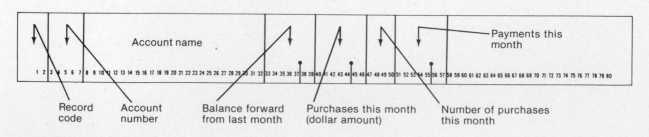

Figure 5.1   Record layout: Charge account record

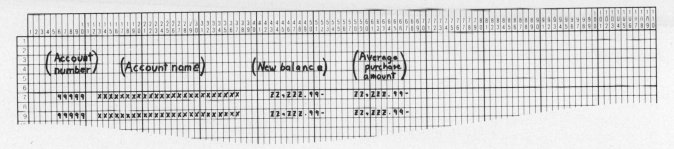

Figure 5.2 Print chart: Charge account report

PROGRAMMING SPECIFICATIONS

Program name: CHARGE ACCOUNT REPORT   Program ID: CHGACCT

Program description

　　This program is to print a charge account report from input charge account records.

Input file(s)

　　Charge account file

Output file(s)

　　Charge account report

List of program operations

A. Read each input charge account record.

B. For each record, the program should compute the new-balance and average-customer-purchase-amount.

　　1. New-balance is to be computed as follows:

　　　　a. Multiply the purchases-this-month by the sales tax rate of 6% to equal the sales-tax-amount.

　　　　b. Add the purchases-this-month and the sales-tax-amount to the balance-forward-from-last-month-amount to equal the new-balance.

　　2. Average-customer-purchase-amount is to be computed as follows:

　　　　a. Divide the purchases-this-month by the number-of-purchases-this-month. (Note: sales-tax-amount is not to be included in this average-customer-purchase-amount computation.)

C. For each record, print the following fields on the charge account report detail-line in accordance with the format shown on the print chart:

　　　　Account number
　　　　Account name
　　　　Account new-balance
　　　　Account average-purchase-amount

D. Double-space each detail-line.

Figure 5.3 Programming specifications: Charge account report program

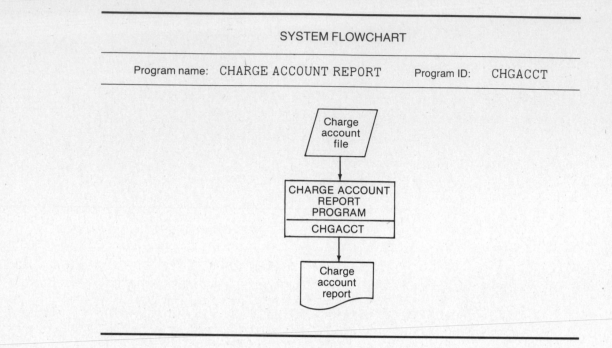

Figure 5.4 System flowchart: Charge account report program

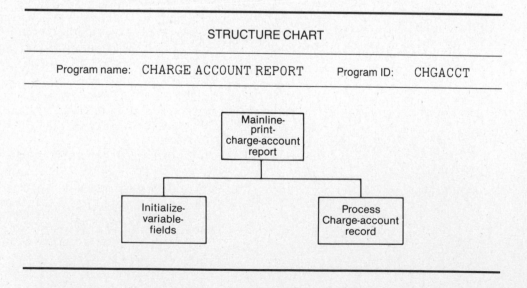

Figure 5.5 Structure chart: Charge account report program

Program name: CHARGE ACCOUNT REPORT   Program ID: CHGACCT

<u>Mainline-print-charge-account-report</u> paragraph
1. Open the files.
2. Perform Initialize-variable-fields paragraph.
3. Read the first charge account record.
4. Perform Process-charge-account-record paragraph until no more records.
5. Close the files.
6. Stop the run.

<u>Initialize-variable-fields</u> paragraph
1. Set the end-of-file indicator to "No".

<u>Process-charge-account-record</u> paragraph
1. Clear the output line area.
2. Move the input Account-number to the output detail-line Account-number.
3. Move the input Account-name to the output detail-line Account-name.
4. Multiply the Month-purchase-amount by .06 to equal the Month-sales-tax-amount.
5. Add the Month-sales-tax-amount, Month-purchase-amount, and Balance-forward less the Month-payments to equal the new-balance and move it to the output detail-line New-balance.
6. Divide the Number-of-month-purchases into the Month-purchase-amount to equal the Average-purchase-amount and move it to the output detail-line Average-purchase-amount.
7. Write the charge account detail-line (double-spaced).
8. Read the next input record.

Figure 5.6 Pseudocode: Charge account report program

Program name: CHARGE ACCOUNT REPORT   Program ID: CHGACCT

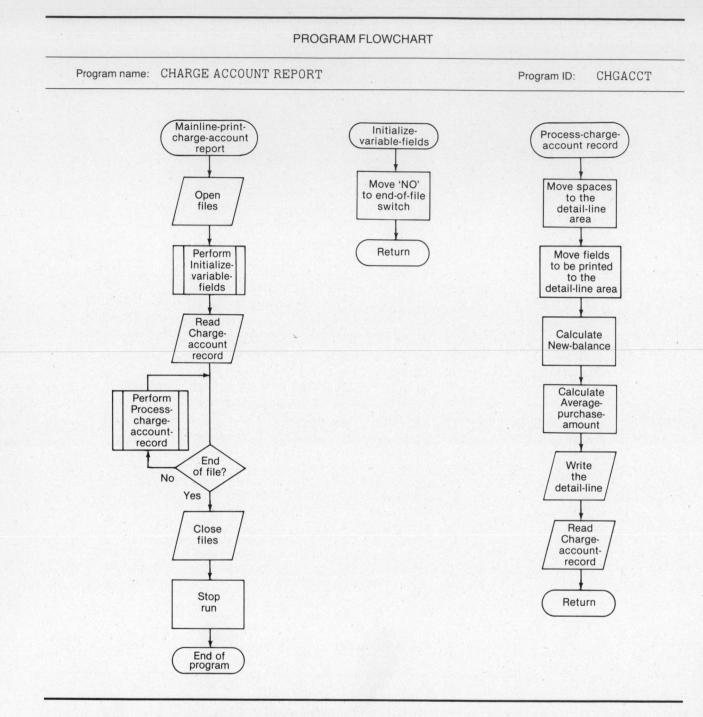

Figure 5.7 Program flowchart: Charge account report program

```
001010 IDENTIFICATION DIVISION.                           005020*
001020 PROGRAM-ID.    CHGACCT.                             005030 WORKING-STORAGE SECTION.
001030*AUTHOR.        WELDURN.                             005040*
001040*INSTALLATION.  SILICON VALLEY DISTRIBUTING COMPANY. 005050*
001050*DATE-WRITTEN.  JAN  5,1981.                         005060 01  WS-SWITCHES.
001060*DATE-COMPILED. JAN  6,1981.                         005070     05  WS-END-OF-FILE-SWITCH        PIC X(3).
001070*SECURITY.      NONE.                                005080*
001080*                                                    005090 01  WS-WORK-AREAS.
001090*                                                    005100     05  WS-BALANCE-WORK              PIC S9(5)V99.
001100*            THIS PROGRAM READS CHARGE ACCOUNT RECORDS, 006010*
001110*            COMPUTES THE NEW BALANCE AND AVERAGE PURCHASE 006020*
001120*            AMOUNT FOR THE ACCOUNT, AND PRINTS A CHARGE 006030*
001130*            ACCOUNT DETAIL LINE FOR EACH ACCOUNT.   006040 PROCEDURE DIVISION.
002010*                                                    006050*
002020*                                                    006060*
002030*                                                    006070 MAINLINE-PRINT-CHG-ACCT-REPORT.
002040 ENVIRONMENT DIVISION.                               006080*
002050*                                                    006090     OPEN INPUT  CHARGE-ACCOUNT-FILE-IN
002060*                                                    006100          OUTPUT CHARGE-ACCOUNT-REPORT-OUT.
002070 CONFIGURATION SECTION.                              006110     PERFORM INITIALIZE-VARIABLE-FIELDS.
002080*                                                    006120     READ CHARGE-ACCOUNT-FILE-IN
002090 SOURCE-COMPUTER.  IBM-370.                          006130          AT END MOVE 'YES' TO WS-END-OF-FILE-SWITCH.
002100 OBJECT-COMPUTER.  IBM-370.                          006140     PERFORM PROCESS-CHARGE-ACCOUNT-RECORD
002110*                                                    006150          UNTIL WS-END-OF-FILE-SWITCH IS EQUAL TO 'YES'.
002120*                                                    006160     CLOSE CHARGE-ACCOUNT-FILE-IN
002130 INPUT-OUTPUT SECTION.                               006170           CHARGE-ACCOUNT-REPORT-OUT.
002140*                                                    006180     STOP RUN.
002150 FILE-CONTROL.                                       007010*
002160     SELECT CHARGE-ACCOUNT-FILE-IN                   007020*
002170        ASSIGN TO UT-S-INFILE.                       007030 INITIALIZE-VARIABLE-FIELDS.
002180     SELECT CHARGE-ACCOUNT-REPORT-OUT                007040*
002190        ASSIGN TO UT-S-PRTFILE.                      007050     MOVE 'NO ' TO WS-END-OF-FILE-SWITCH.
003010*                                                    008010*
003020*                                                    008020*
003030*                                                    008030 PROCESS-CHARGE-ACCOUNT-RECORD.
003040 DATA DIVISION.                                      008040*
003050*                                                    008050     MOVE SPACES TO DL-DETAIL-LINE-OUT.
003060*                                                    008060     MOVE CA-ACCOUNT-NUMBER-IN TO DL-ACCOUNT-NUMBER-OUT.
003070 FILE SECTION.                                       008070     MOVE CA-ACCOUNT-NAME-IN TO DL-ACCOUNT-NAME-OUT.
003080*                                                    008080     MULTIPLY CA-MONTH-PURCHASE-AMT-IN BY .06
003090 FD  CHARGE-ACCOUNT-FILE-IN                          008090          GIVING WS-BALANCE-WORK.
003100     RECORD CONTAINS 80 CHARACTERS                   008100     ADD CA-BALANCE-FORWARD-IN TO WS-BALANCE-WORK.
003110     LABEL RECORDS ARE OMITTED.                      008110     ADD CA-MONTH-PURCHASE-AMT-IN TO WS-BALANCE-WORK.
003120*                                                    008120     SUBTRACT CA-MONTH-PAYMENTS-IN FROM WS-BALANCE-WORK.
003130 01  CHARGE-ACCOUNT-RECORD-IN.                       008130     MOVE WS-BALANCE-WORK TO DL-NEW-BALANCE-OUT.
003140     05  CA-RECORD-CODE        PIC X(2).             008140     DIVIDE CA-NBR-MONTH-PURCHASES-IN
003150     05  CA-ACCOUNT-NUMBER-IN  PIC X(5).             008150          INTO CA-MONTH-PURCHASE-AMT-IN
003160     05  CA-ACCOUNT-NAME-IN    PIC X(25).            008160          GIVING DL-AVG-PURCHASE-OUT.
003170     05  CA-BALANCE-FORWARD-IN PIC S9(5)V99.         008170     WRITE DL-DETAIL-LINE-OUT
003180     05  CA-MONTH-PURCHASE-AMT-IN PIC S9(5)V99.      008180          AFTER ADVANCING 2 LINES.
003190     05  CA-NBR-MONTH-PURCHASES-IN PIC S9(4).        008190     READ CHARGE-ACCOUNT-FILE-IN
003200     05  CA-MONTH-PAYMENTS-IN  PIC S9(5)V99.         008200          AT END MOVE 'YES' TO WS-END-OF-FILE-SWITCH.
003210     05  FILLER                PIC X(23).
004010*
004020 FD  CHARGE-ACCOUNT-REPORT-OUT
004030     RECORD CONTAINS 133 CHARACTERS
004040     LABEL RECORDS ARE OMITTED.
004050*
004060 01  DL-DETAIL-LINE-OUT.
004070     05  DL-VERTICAL-FORMS-CONTROL-OUT PIC X(1).
004080     05  FILLER                 PIC X(5).
004090     05  DL-ACCOUNT-NUMBER-OUT  PIC X(5).
004100     05  FILLER                 PIC X(5).
004110     05  DL-ACCOUNT-NAME-OUT    PIC X(25).
004120     05  FILLER                 PIC X(2).
004130     05  DL-NEW-BALANCE-OUT     PIC ZZ,ZZZ.99-.
004140     05  FILLER                 PIC X(5).
004150     05  DL-AVG-PURCHASE-OUT    PIC ZZ,ZZZ.99-.
004160     05  FILLER                 PIC X(65).
005010*
```

Figure 5.8 COBOL coding: CHGACCT program

00205	ALPHA MANUFACTURING	11.20	10.57
00495	CENTRAL BUILDING SUPPLY	221.49	52.24
01038	CITY BUSINESS SERVICES	85.17	40.17
08047	DOWNTOWN VARIETY	1,028.90	133.50
10080	GENERAL DISTRIBUTING	1,634.52	192.75
12143	HOLLYWOOD FASHIONS	103.05	51.55
15169	KINGS REST HOTEL	32.69-	10.00
18543	MOUNTAIN HARDWARE	4,589.42	206.17
20469	NORDIC SPORTING GOODS	27.13	25.60
42189	PLEASANT VIEW LANES	14.35	4.51
80565	STANDARD SUPPLY	215.65	20.34
92300	WALKER PHARMACY	10.60	10.00

Figure 5.9 Output: Charge account report program

Definition of Arithmetic Fields

Whenever there are fields to be operated upon arithmetically, the characteristics of each field must be specified properly in the picture character-string. Specifically, each field must be defined as numeric; and the field length, decimal point location, and arithmetic sign must be considered.

Notice in the COBOL code for the CHGACCT program that the four input fields used in computations (CA-BALANCE-FORWARD-IN, CA-MONTH-PURCHASE-AMT-IN, CA-NBR-MONTH-PURCHASES-IN, and CA-MONTH-PAYMENTS-IN) are all defined as numeric fields. The picture symbol 9 is used to define each decimal digit position of each field. For those three fields that contain decimal fraction positions, the picture symbol V is used to specify the location of the assumed decimal point. Because these three fields contain dollars-and-cents amounts, the assumed decimal point is indicated by specifying a V between the second and third positions from the right of each field. It's important to recall that the assumed decimal symbol V does not consume a storage position. It is specified only to inform the COBOL compiler how to align decimal points for arithmetic computations.

Each picture character-string begins with the symbol S which indicates that these are signed numeric fields. Remember that a signed field is one that can contain either positive or negative values. For example, the CA-BALANCE-FORWARD-IN field would normally contain a positive value indicating how much money each customer owed at the beginning of the monthly period. But, if a customer overpaid his or her account (or otherwise generated a credit balance due to returns, credits, and so on), the field would then contain a negative amount.

As discussed in Chapter 4, the symbol S will not cause a separate storage position to be assigned to the field.

Arithmetic Element Terminology

While discussing arithmetic COBOL statements, we will refer to arithmetic element terminology. Figure 5.10 defines such terminology through illustration.

The ADD Statement

The ADD statement may take one of two general forms called Format-1 and Format-2, respectively. One causes the sum to be stored in one of the fields being added; the other places the sum in a separate field—not one of the addends.

ADD (Format-1)

The format notation for a Format-1 ADD statement, together with an example from the CHGACCT program, is shown in Figure 5.11.

Adding two fields

In the example, identifier-1 is the CA-BALANCE-FORWARD-IN field. Identifier-m is the WS-BALANCE-WORK field. After the addition has taken place, the sum is stored in the WS-BALANCE-WORK field. Thus, the value of WS-BALANCE-WORK before execution of the ADD statement is no longer available.

Addition	Subtraction	Multiplication	Division	
512 Addend	236 Minuend	503 Multiplicand	Quotient	Remainder
+ 17 Addend	− 89 Subtrahend	× 8 Multiplier	51	1
529 Sum	147 Difference	4024 Product	5 ⌐256	
			Divisor Dividend	

Figure 5.10 Arithmetic element terminology

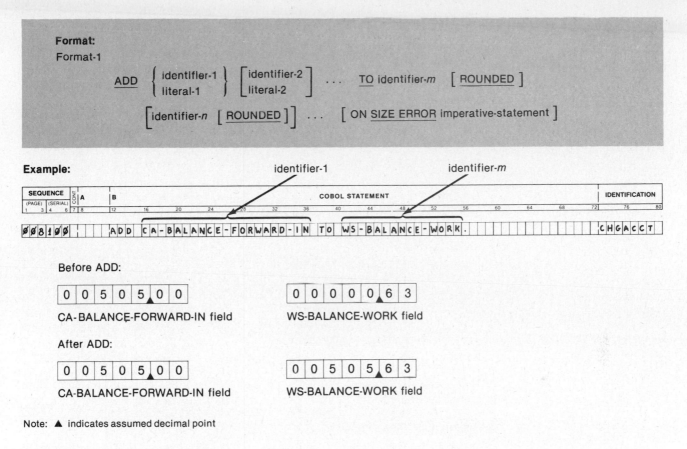

Format:
Format-1

ADD { identifier-1 / literal-1 } [identifier-2 / literal-2] ... TO identifier-*m* [ROUNDED]

[identifier-*n* [ROUNDED]] ... [ON SIZE ERROR imperative-statement]

Example:

identifier-1   identifier-*m*

| SEQUENCE | | CONT | A | B | COBOL STATEMENT | IDENTIFICATION |

Ø Ø 8 1 Ø Ø   ADD CA-BALANCE-FORWARD-IN TO WS-BALANCE-WORK.   CHGACCT

Before ADD:

| 0 | 0 | 5 | 0 | 5 | ▲ | 0 | 0 |

CA-BALANCE-FORWARD-IN field

| 0 | 0 | 0 | 0 | 0 | ▲ | 6 | 3 |

WS-BALANCE-WORK field

After ADD:

| 0 | 0 | 5 | 0 | 5 | ▲ | 0 | 0 |

CA-BALANCE-FORWARD-IN field

| 0 | 0 | 5 | 0 | 5 | ▲ | 6 | 3 |

WS-BALANCE-WORK field

Note: ▲ indicates assumed decimal point

Figure 5.11 Format-1 ADD statement

With the Format-1 ADD statement, all identifiers must be data-names of numeric fields, and all are addends to the addition. The sum (or sums) will always be placed in the field identifier (or identifiers) following the reserved word TO. This means that, for field identifiers written after the word TO, the original value is no longer available after the addition has been made. It is replaced by the sum. The value of field identifiers written before the word TO remain unchanged after the addition, however.

Adding more than two fields

More than two fields may be added together by one ADD statement if desired. Figure 5.12 provides an example that could have been used in the CHGACCT program. The fields CA-BALANCE-FORWARD-IN, CA-MONTH-PURCHASE-AMT-IN and WS-BALANCE-WORK are all addends. After the addition has been made, the sum will be stored in the WS-BALANCE-WORK field because it is specified after the reserved word TO. Any number of fields to be added together may be written before the word TO. (The format notation indicates this flexibility by using the ellipsis after identifier-2.)

Adding numeric literal values

Whenever brackets or braces are used in a COBOL statement format notation, it means that alternate specification types are provided for. Notice in the format notation that the addends before the word TO may be specified as either identifiers (that is, data-names of numeric fields) or as numeric literals (actual values). Figure 5.13 shows an example of a Format-1 ADD statement that uses a numeric literal. Recognize that a numeric literal cannot be written after the

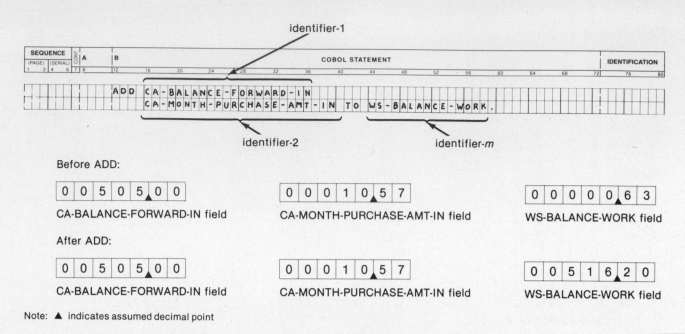

Figure 5.12 Format-1 ADD statement with more than two addends

word TO. That's because addends specified there must receive the sum. The sum must be stored in a field; it can't be stored in a literal.

Developing more than one sum

Although not a particularly common occurrence, more than one sum may be developed with the Format-1 ADD statement. A sample statement and its processing effect is shown in Figure 5.14.

Writing the Format-1 ADD statement

To write a Format-1 ADD statement, the programmer must write the reserved word ADD followed by at least one numeric field identifier (data-name) or numeric literal. The format notation reveals that the second identifier or literal is optional because it is enclosed in brackets. The word TO must be written and followed by one or more numeric field identifiers.

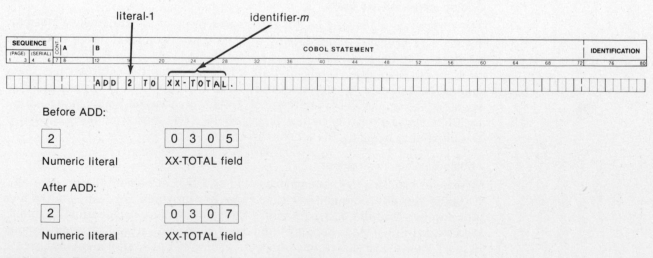

Figure 5.13 Format-1 ADD statement with a numeric literal

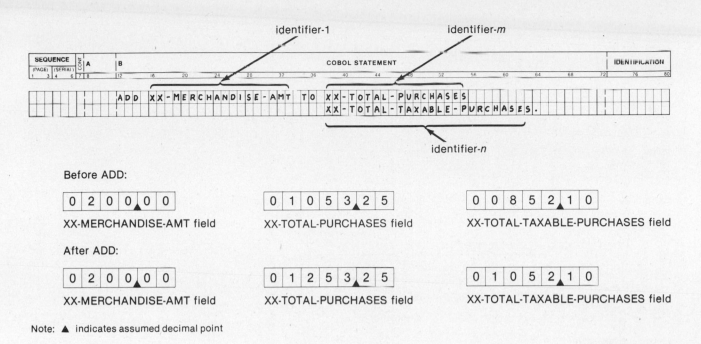

identifier-1   identifier-*m*

| SEQUENCE | | | A | B | COBOL STATEMENT | IDENTIFICATION |

```
ADD XX-MERCHANDISE-AMT TO XX-TOTAL-PURCHASES
                          XX-TOTAL-TAXABLE-PURCHASES.
```

identifier-*n*

Before ADD:

| 0 2 0 0 ▲ 0 0 |

XX-MERCHANDISE-AMT field

| 0 1 0 5 3 ▲ 2 5 |

XX-TOTAL-PURCHASES field

| 0 0 8 5 2 ▲ 1 0 |

XX-TOTAL-TAXABLE-PURCHASES field

After ADD:

| 0 2 0 0 ▲ 0 0 |

XX-MERCHANDISE-AMT field

| 0 1 2 5 3 ▲ 2 5 |

XX-TOTAL-PURCHASES field

| 0 1 0 5 2 ▲ 1 0 |

XX-TOTAL-TAXABLE-PURCHASES field

Note: ▲ indicates assumed decimal point

Figure 5.14   Format-1 ADD statement with more than one sum

Notice that there are two optional phrases provided with the Format-1 ADD statement: ROUNDED and ON SIZE ERROR. These two phrases may be used with all arithmetic statements. The ROUNDED option will be covered later in this chapter; ON SIZE ERROR is discussed in Appendix A.

ADD (Format-2)

The format notation for the Format-2 ADD statement is shown with an example in Figure 5.15.

Adding two or more values

With the Format-2 ADD statement, two or more addends are specified before the reserved word GIVING. Each addend may be specified as either a numeric field data-name identifier or as a numeric literal.

The sum of the addition is placed in the field written after the reserved word GIVING. The field (or fields) that will receive the sum may be either a numeric or numeric edited field. Usually, just one sum field is specified after GIVING. Sometimes, though, the sum value may be specified for other fields. In such cases, additional numeric or numeric edited data-names may be written as shown in Figure 5.16.

It is important to recognize that, with the Format-2 ADD statement, the sum field or fields (those specified after the word GIVING) are not included in the addition. Whatever value was present in such fields before execution of the ADD statement is not considered in the arithmetic and is eradicated when it is replaced by the sum value. Because the Format-2 ADD statement provides for a separate sum field, all addends retain their original value.

Writing the Format-2 ADD statement

When writing the Format-2 ADD statement, the programmer must write the reserved word ADD followed by (a) two or more numeric field data-name identifiers, or (b) one or more numeric field data-name identifiers and one or more numeric literals. The reserved word GIVING is then written and followed by one or more numeric or numeric edited field data-name identifiers.

Format:
Format-2

$$\text{\underline{ADD}} \left\{ \begin{array}{l} \text{identifier-1} \\ \text{literal-1} \end{array} \right\} \left\{ \begin{array}{l} \text{identifier-2} \\ \text{literal-2} \end{array} \right\} \left[\begin{array}{l} \text{identifier-3} \\ \text{literal-3} \end{array} \right] \dots$$

$$\text{\underline{GIVING} identifier-}m \ [\ \underline{\text{ROUNDED}}\ ] \ [\ \text{identifier-}n \ [\ \underline{\text{ROUNDED}}\ ]\ ] \dots$$

$$[\ \text{ON \underline{SIZE} \underline{ERROR} imperative-statement}\ ]$$

Example:

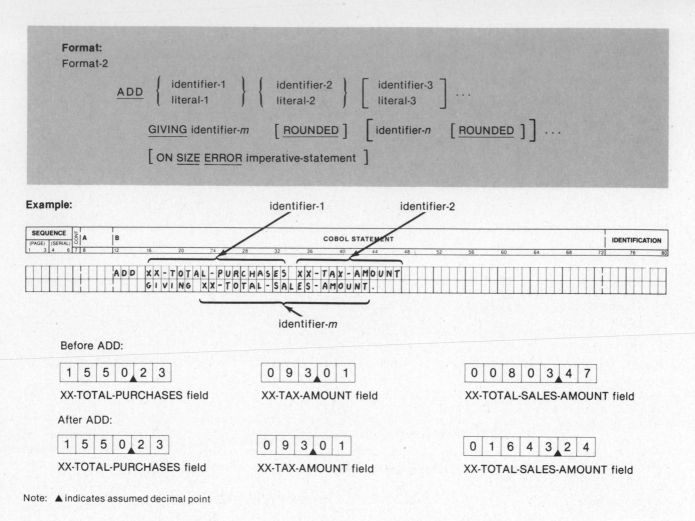

Note: ▲ indicates assumed decimal point

Figure 5.15 Format-2 ADD statement

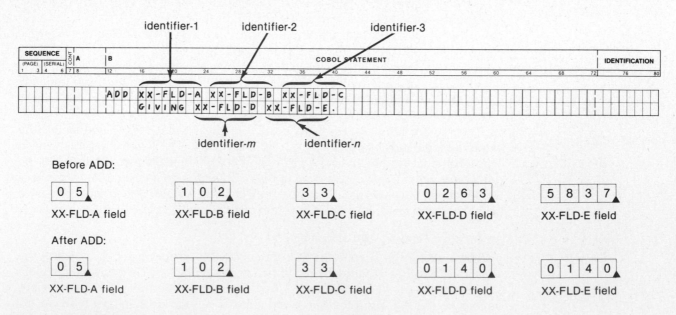

Note: ▲ indicates assumed decimal point

Figure 5.16 Format-2 ADD statement with more than two addends

One tricky point to keep in mind is that, although the reserved word TO is used in the Format-1 ADD statement, it is not to be specified with the Format-2 ADD statement. To do so causes a compiler diagnostic error message.

The SUBTRACT Statement

The SUBTRACT statement, just like the ADD statement, has two formats.

SUBTRACT (Format-1)

The format notation for the Format-1 SUBTRACT statement and an example from the CHGACCT program are shown in Figure 5.17.

Subtracting one value from another value

The Format-1 SUBTRACT statement adheres to many of the same syntactical considerations that apply to the Format-1 ADD statement. Namely, identifier-1 may be a numeric field data-name identifier or a numeric literal; identifier-*m* must be a numeric field data-name identifier. The difference will be stored in identifier-*m*. This means that the presubtraction value of identifier-*m* will not be available after execution of the subtraction operation.

Subtracting multiple values from another value

An example of a Format-1 SUBTRACT statement with multiple subtrahends is shown in Figure 5.18. Each subtrahend may be either a numeric field data-name identifier or a numeric literal and must be written before the reserved

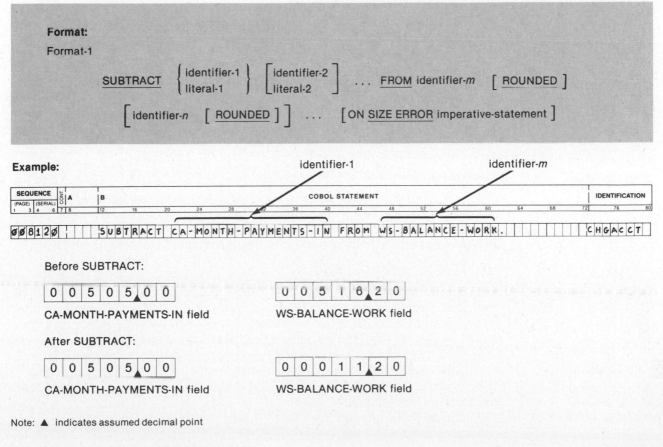

Figure 5.17 Format-1 SUBTRACT statement

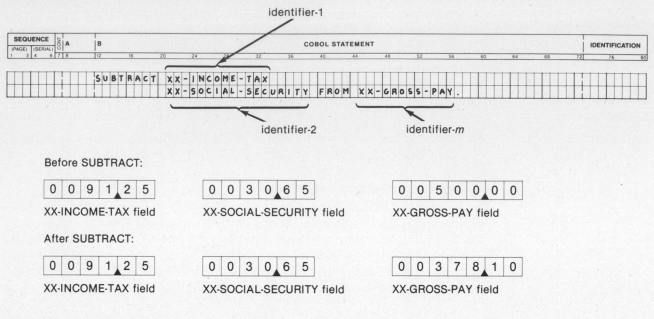

identifier-1

| SEQUENCE | | | A | B | | COBOL STATEMENT | | IDENTIFICATION |

SUBTRACT XX-INCOME-TAX
XX-SOCIAL-SECURITY FROM XX-GROSS-PAY.

identifier-2   identifier-*m*

Before SUBTRACT:

| 0 | 0 | 9 | 1 | 2 | 5 |

XX-INCOME-TAX field

| 0 | 0 | 3 | 0 | 6 | 5 |

XX-SOCIAL-SECURITY field

| 0 | 0 | 5 | 0 | 0 | 0 | 0 |

XX-GROSS-PAY field

After SUBTRACT:

| 0 | 0 | 9 | 1 | 2 | 5 |

XX-INCOME-TAX field

| 0 | 0 | 3 | 0 | 6 | 5 |

XX-SOCIAL-SECURITY field

| 0 | 0 | 3 | 7 | 8 | 1 | 0 |

XX-GROSS-PAY field

Note: ▲ indicates assumed decimal point

Figure 5.18 Format-1 SUBTRACT statement with multiple subtrahends

word FROM. When multiple subtrahends are written, COBOL first sums the subtrahends and then subtracts them from the minuend (or minuends) written after the word FROM.

Subtracting one or more values from more than one value

An example of a Format-1 SUBTRACT statement with multiple minuends is shown as Figure 5.19. Each minuend must be a numeric field data-name identifier. This statement causes the subtrahend to be subtracted from each minuend and each result is then stored in its minuend field.

Writing the Format-1 SUBTRACT statement

To write the Format-1 SUBTRACT statement, the programmer must write the reserved word SUBTRACT and follow it by one or more numeric field data-name identifiers or numeric literals. The reserved word FROM must then be written and followed by one or more numeric field data-name identifiers.

SUBTRACT (Format-2)

The Format-2 SUBTRACT statement format notation is shown in Figure 5.20 together with an example. With the format-2 SUBTRACT statement, one or more subtrahends are specified before the reserved word FROM. After the word FROM, the minuend is written. Each subtrahend and the minuend may be specified as either a numeric data-name field identifier or as a numeric literal.

One or more identifiers are written after the word GIVING to receive the value of the difference. The fields that receive the difference may be either numeric or numeric edited fields.

Observe that the reserved word FROM is used in both the Format-1 and Format-2 SUBTRACT statements. (This is not parallel to the ADD statement where the word TO is used with Format-1 but must be omitted from Format-2.)

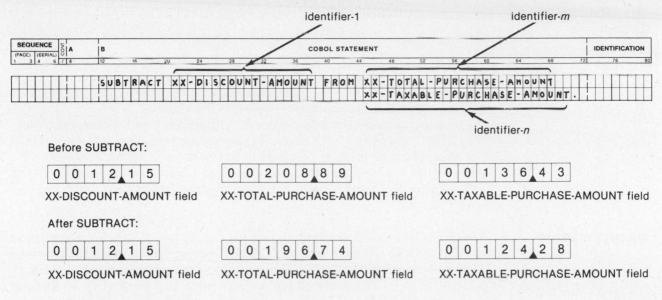

Figure 5.19 Format-1 SUBTRACT statement with multiple minuends

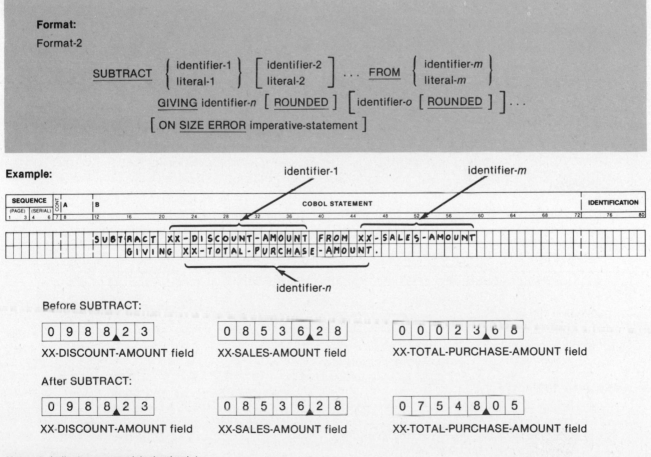

Figure 5.20 Format-2 SUBTRACT statement

The MULTIPLY Statement

As with the ADD and SUBTRACT statements, the MULTIPLY statement also has two formats.

MULTIPLY (Format-1)

An example of a Format-1 MULTIPLY statement together with the format notation is shown in Figure 5.21. Identifier-1 may be either a numeric field data-name identifier or a numeric literal and may be considered the multiplicand. Only one identifier may be specified before the reserved word BY. After BY, one or more numeric field data-name identifiers may be written. Each identifier after the word BY acts as a multiplier. After execution of the multiplication operation, the product is stored in the field (or fields) written after the word BY. This means that the premultiplication value of the field (or fields) written after the word BY will not be available after the multiplication has been executed.

MULTIPLY (Format-2)

Figure 5.22 shows the format notation for the Format-2 MULTIPLY statement together with an example from the CHGACCT program. Both the multiplicand (identifier-1) and the multiplier (identifier-2) may be either numeric fields or numeric literals. These identifiers written after the word GIVING must be fields of either numeric or numeric edited type.

The DIVIDE Statement

The DIVIDE statement has five formats.

DIVIDE (Format-1)

The Format-1 DIVIDE statement is shown in Figure 5.23 together with an example. Identifier-1 is the divisor and must be either a numeric field or a numeric

Format:

Format-1

$$\underline{\text{MULTIPLY}} \left\{ \begin{array}{l} \text{identifier-1} \\ \text{literal-1} \end{array} \right\} \quad \underline{\text{BY}} \text{ identifier-2} \quad [\ \underline{\text{ROUNDED}}\ ]$$

$$\left[\ \text{identifier-3}\ [\ \underline{\text{ROUNDED}}\ ]\ \right] \ldots [\ \text{ON}\ \underline{\text{SIZE ERROR}}\ \text{imperative-statement}\ ]$$

Example:

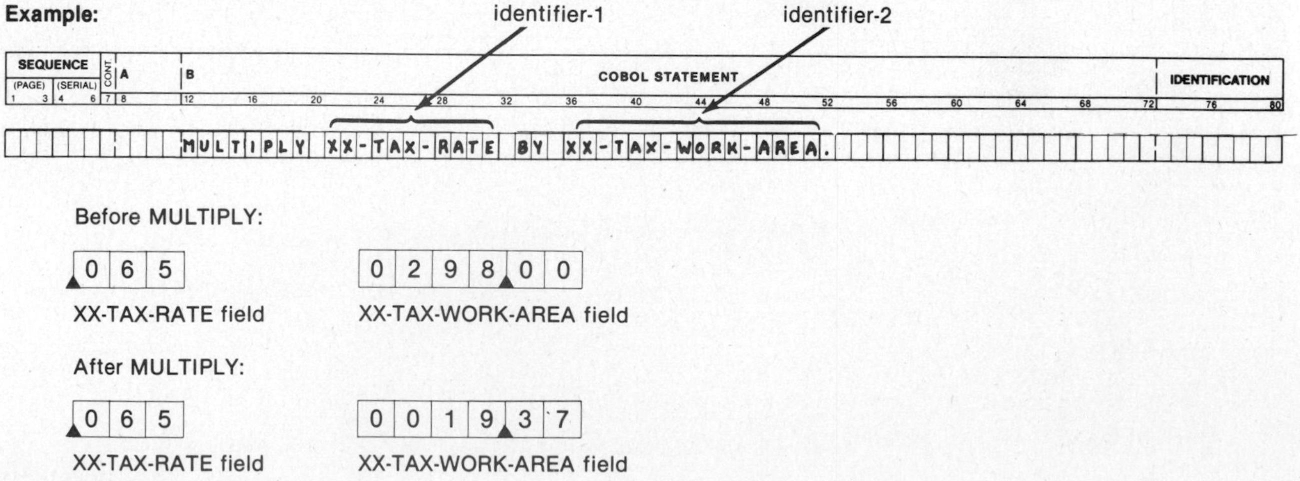

```
MULTIPLY XX-TAX-RATE BY XX-TAX-WORK-AREA.
```

Before MULTIPLY:

| 0 | 6 | 5 |

XX-TAX-RATE field

| 0 | 2 | 9 | 8 | 0 | 0 |

XX-TAX-WORK-AREA field

After MULTIPLY:

| 0 | 6 | 5 |

XX-TAX-RATE field

| 0 | 0 | 1 | 9 | 3 | 7 |

XX-TAX-WORK-AREA field

Note: ▲ indicates assumed decimal point

Figure 5.21 Format-1 MULTIPLY statement

Format:
Format-2

$$\text{MULTIPLY} \left\{ \begin{array}{l} \text{identifier-1} \\ \text{literal-1} \end{array} \right\} \underline{\text{BY}} \left\{ \begin{array}{l} \text{identifier-2} \\ \text{literal-2} \end{array} \right\}$$

$$\underline{\text{GIVING}} \text{ identifier-3 } [\underline{\text{ROUNDED}}] \; [\text{Identifier-4 } [\underline{\text{ROUNDED}}]] \; \dots$$

$$[\text{ON } \underline{\text{SIZE ERROR}} \text{ imperative-statement}]$$

Example:

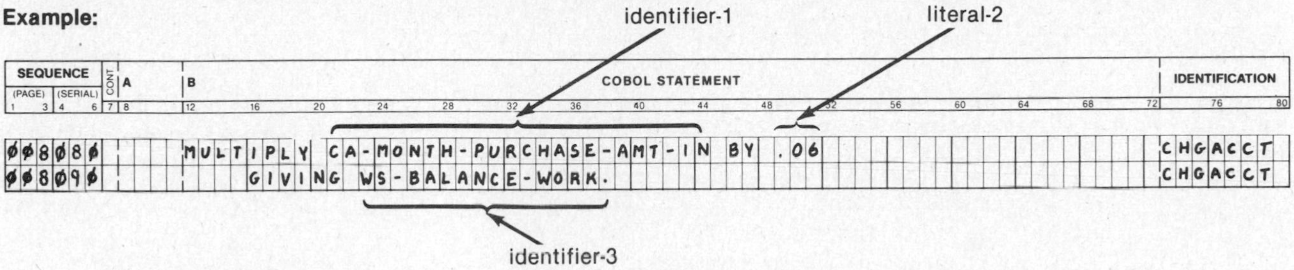

identifier-1   literal-2

SEQUENCE		CONT	A	B	COBOL STATEMENT	IDENTIFICATION

```
ØØ8Ø8Ø      MULTIPLY CA-MONTH-PURCHASE-AMT-IN BY .06        CHGACCT
ØØ8Ø9Ø          GIVING WS-BALANCE-WORK.                     CHGACCT
```

identifier-3

Before MULTIPLY:

0	0	0	1	0	5	7

CA-MONTH-PURCHASE-AMT-IN field

0	6

Numeric literal

5	0	8	3	6	4	7

WS-BALANCE-WORK field

After MULTIPLY:

0	0	0	1	0	5	7

CA-MONTH-PURCHASE-AMT-IN field

0	6

Numeric-literal

0	0	0	0	0	6	3

WS-BALANCE-WORK field

Note: ▲ indicates assumed decimal place

Figure 5.22 Format-2 MULTIPLY statement

Format:
Format-1

$$\underline{\text{DIVIDE}} \left\{ \begin{array}{l} \text{identifier-1} \\ \text{literal-1} \end{array} \right\} \underline{\text{INTO}} \text{ identifier-2 } [\underline{\text{ROUNDED}}]$$

$$[\text{identifier-3 } [\underline{\text{ROUNDED}}]] \; \dots \; [\text{ON } \underline{\text{SIZE ERROR}} \text{ imperative-statement}]$$

Example:

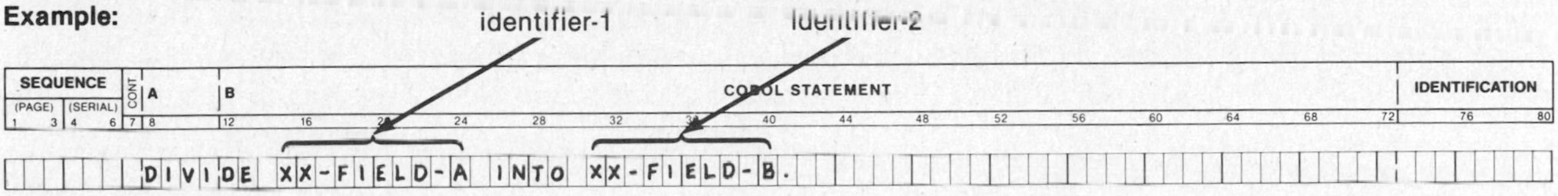

identifier-1   identifier-2

SEQUENCE		CONT	A	B	COBOL STATEMENT	IDENTIFICATION

```
        DIVIDE XX-FIELD-A INTO XX-FIELD-B.
```

Before DIVIDE:

0	1	0

XX-FIELD-A field

2	5	4	6	3	0

XX-FIELD-B field

After DIVIDE:

0	1	0

XX-FIELD-A field

0	2	5	4	6	3

XX-FIELD-B field

Note: ▲ indicates assumed decimal place

Figure 5.23 Format-1 DIVIDE statement

173

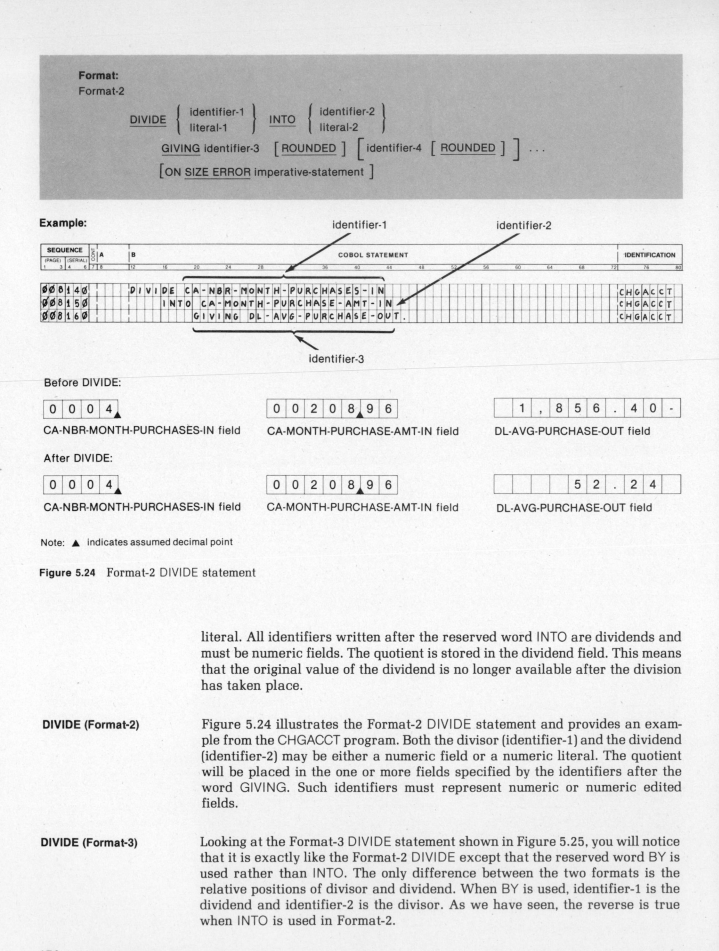

Format:
Format-2

$$\text{\underline{DIVIDE}} \begin{Bmatrix} \text{identifier-1} \\ \text{literal-1} \end{Bmatrix} \text{\underline{INTO}} \begin{Bmatrix} \text{identifier-2} \\ \text{literal-2} \end{Bmatrix}$$

$$\text{\underline{GIVING}} \text{ identifier-3 } [\text{ \underline{ROUNDED} }] [\text{ identifier-4 } [\text{ \underline{ROUNDED} }]] \dots$$

$$[\text{ON \underline{SIZE ERROR}} \text{ imperative-statement }]$$

Example:

identifier-1   identifier-2

SEQUENCE						COBOL STATEMENT													IDENTIFICATION	

```
ØØ8140     DIVIDE CA-NBR-MONTH-PURCHASES-IN                    CHGACCT
ØØ8150        INTO CA-MONTH-PURCHASE-AMT-IN                    CHGACCT
ØØ8160        GIVING DL-AVG-PURCHASE-OUT.                      CHGACCT
```

identifier-3

Before DIVIDE:

| 0 | 0 | 0 | 4 ▲ |

CA-NBR-MONTH-PURCHASES-IN field

| 0 | 0 | 2 | 0 | 8 ▲ | 9 | 6 |

CA-MONTH-PURCHASE-AMT-IN field

| 1 | , | 8 | 5 | 6 | . | 4 | 0 | - |

DL-AVG-PURCHASE-OUT field

After DIVIDE:

| 0 | 0 | 0 | 4 ▲ |

CA-NBR-MONTH-PURCHASES-IN field

| 0 | 0 | 2 | 0 | 8 ▲ | 9 | 6 |

CA-MONTH-PURCHASE-AMT-IN field

| | | | 5 | 2 | . | 2 | 4 |

DL-AVG-PURCHASE-OUT field

Note: ▲ indicates assumed decimal point

Figure 5.24 Format-2 DIVIDE statement

literal. All identifiers written after the reserved word INTO are dividends and must be numeric fields. The quotient is stored in the dividend field. This means that the original value of the dividend is no longer available after the division has taken place.

DIVIDE (Format-2) Figure 5.24 illustrates the Format-2 DIVIDE statement and provides an example from the CHGACCT program. Both the divisor (identifier-1) and the dividend (identifier-2) may be either a numeric field or a numeric literal. The quotient will be placed in the one or more fields specified by the identifiers after the word GIVING. Such identifiers must represent numeric or numeric edited fields.

DIVIDE (Format-3) Looking at the Format-3 DIVIDE statement shown in Figure 5.25, you will notice that it is exactly like the Format-2 DIVIDE except that the reserved word BY is used rather than INTO. The only difference between the two formats is the relative positions of divisor and dividend. When BY is used, identifier-1 is the dividend and identifier-2 is the divisor. As we have seen, the reverse is true when INTO is used in Format-2.

$$\underline{\text{DIVIDE}} \left\{ \begin{array}{l} \text{identifier-1} \\ \text{literal-1} \end{array} \right\} \underline{\text{BY}} \left\{ \begin{array}{l} \text{identifier-2} \\ \text{literal-2} \end{array} \right\}$$

$$\underline{\text{GIVING}}\ \text{identifier-3}\ \left[\ \underline{\text{ROUNDED}}\ \right]\ \left[\ \text{identifier-4}\ \left[\ \underline{\text{ROUNDED}}\ \right]\ \right]\ \dots$$

$$\left[\ \text{ON}\ \underline{\text{SIZE ERROR}}\ \text{imperative-statement}\ \right]$$

Example:

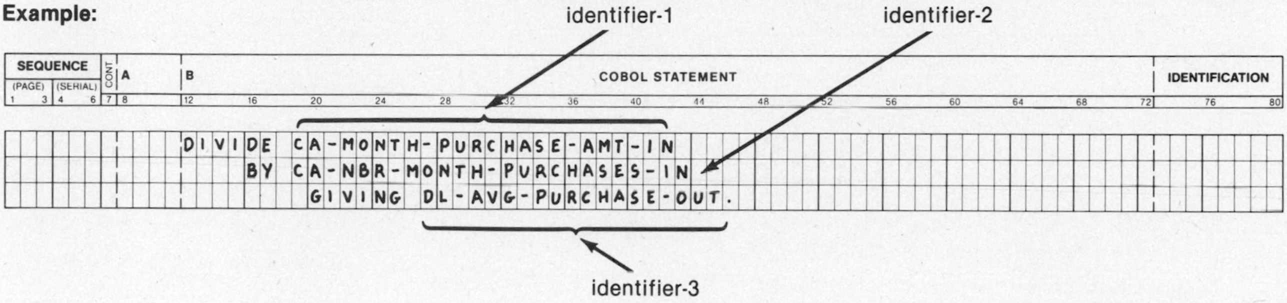

Before DIVIDE:

`0 0 2 0 8 ▲ 9 6`
CA-MONTH-PURCHASE-AMT-IN field

`0 0 0 4 ▲`
CA-NBR-MONTH-PURCHASES-IN field

`1 , 8 5 6 . 4 0 -`
DL-AVG-PURCHASE-OUT field

After DIVIDE:

`0 0 2 0 8 ▲ 9 6`
CA-MONTH-PURCHASE-AMT-IN field

`0 0 0 4 ▲`
CA-NBR-MONTH-PURCHASES-IN field

`5 2 . 2 4`
DL-AVG-PURCHASE-OUT field

Note: ▲ indicates assumed decimal point

Figure 5.25 Format-3 DIVIDE statement

DIVIDE (Format-4)

The Format-4 DIVIDE statement, shown together with an example in Figure 5.26, is also similar to the Format-2 statement. The Format-4 statement allows specification of a field (identifier-4) into which the remainder obtained from the division operation is stored. Following the reserved word REMAINDER, the data-name of an elementary numeric field is written to receive the remainder value. Notice that, in this format using REMAINDER, only one quotient field (identifier-3) may be specified. (This contrasts with the Format-2 DIVIDE statement, which allows more than one quotient field.)

DIVIDE (Format-5)

The Format-5 DIVIDE statement is equivalent to the Format-4 statement except that the word BY is used instead of the word INTO. The format notation and an example is shown in Figure 5.27. As in Format-3, the first identifier or literal represents the dividend and the second is the divisor.

The COMPUTE Statement

The COMPUTE statement is an alternative to the four basic arithmetic verbs just discussed. It allows the expression of arithmetic calculations in a manner

Format:
Format-4

$$\text{\underline{DIVIDE}} \left\{ \begin{array}{l} \text{identifier-1} \\ \text{literal-1} \end{array} \right\} \text{\underline{INTO}} \left\{ \begin{array}{l} \text{identifier-2} \\ \text{literal-2} \end{array} \right\}$$

$$\text{\underline{GIVING}} \quad \text{identifier-3} \left[\text{\underline{ROUNDED}} \right] \text{\underline{REMAINDER}} \quad \text{identifier-4}$$

$$\left[\text{ON \underline{SIZE ERROR}} \quad \text{imperative-statement} \right]$$

Example:

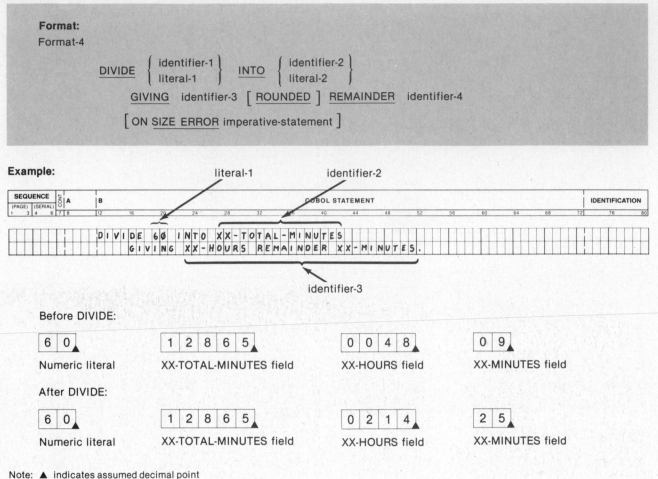

Before DIVIDE:

| 6 | 0 ▲ |

Numeric literal

| 1 | 2 | 8 | 6 | 5 ▲ |

XX-TOTAL-MINUTES field

| 0 | 0 | 4 | 8 ▲ |

XX-HOURS field

| 0 | 9 ▲ |

XX-MINUTES field

After DIVIDE:

| 6 | 0 ▲ |

Numeric literal

| 1 | 2 | 8 | 6 | 5 ▲ |

XX-TOTAL-MINUTES field

| 0 | 2 | 1 | 4 ▲ |

XX-HOURS field

| 2 | 5 ▲ |

XX-MINUTES field

Note: ▲ indicates assumed decimal point

Figure 5.26 Format-4 DIVIDE statement

similar to normal arithmetic notation. Figure 5.28 shows the format notation for the COMPUTE statement with an example. In the arithmetic-expression portion of the COMPUTE statement, there are five arithmetic operator symbols that may be used. These are shown in Figure 5.29.

When more than one calculation appears in the arithmetic expression of a COMPUTE statement, the operations will be executed in a specific order. This sequence adheres to the normal conventions for the hierarchy of arithmetic operations within an expression. The order is as follows: (1) exponentiation operations are done; (2) multiplication and division calculations are made; and (3) addition and subtraction operations are performed.

As an example, consider the statement: COMPUTE X = A + B / C. The first calculation executed would be B / C. The quotient from that division would then be added with the value of A to obtain the sum X.

Sometimes there will be multiple calculations from one of the three hierarchical categories listed above. When this occurs, the operations within each category are executed starting from left to right within the expression. To illustrate, consider this statement: COMPUTE X = A − B / C + D * E. The sequence in which the calculations will occur is as follows:

Format:
Format-5

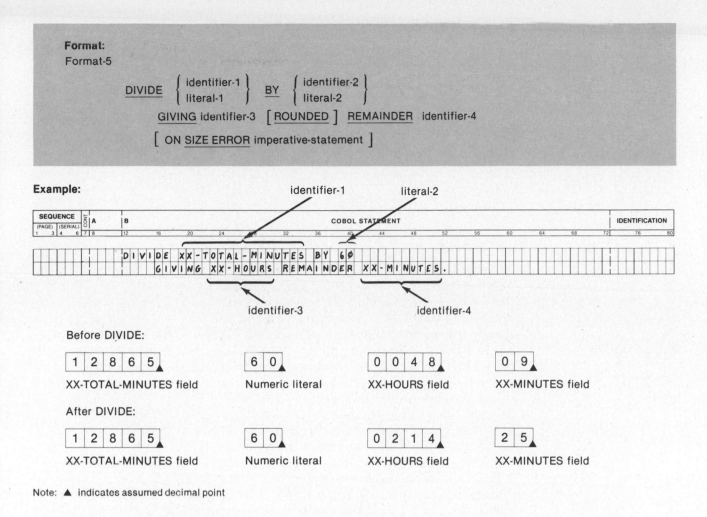

DIVIDE $\left\{\begin{array}{l}\text{identifier-1}\\ \text{literal-1}\end{array}\right\}$ <u>BY</u> $\left\{\begin{array}{l}\text{identifier-2}\\ \text{literal-2}\end{array}\right\}$

<u>GIVING</u> identifier-3 [<u>ROUNDED</u>] <u>REMAINDER</u> identifier-4

[ON <u>SIZE ERROR</u> imperative-statement]

Example:

identifier-1   literal-2

SEQUENCE		CONT	A	B	COBOL STATEMENT						IDENTIFICATION
(PAGE)	(SERIAL)										
1 3	4 6	7	8	12 16 20 24 28 32	36 40 44 48 52 56 60 64 68	72	76 80

```
DIVIDE XX-TOTAL-MINUTES BY 60
       GIVING XX-HOURS REMAINDER XX-MINUTES.
```

identifier-3   identifier-4

Before DIVIDE:

1 2 8 6 5 ▲	6 0 ▲	0 0 4 8 ▲	0 9 ▲
XX-TOTAL-MINUTES field	Numeric literal	XX-HOURS field	XX-MINUTES field

After DIVIDE:

1 2 8 6 5 ▲	6 0 ▲	0 2 1 4 ▲	2 5 ▲
XX-TOTAL-MINUTES field	Numeric literal	XX-HOURS field	XX-MINUTES field

Note: ▲ indicates assumed decimal point

Figure 5.27 Format-5 DIVIDE statement

Format:

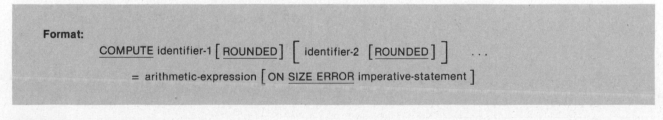

<u>COMPUTE</u> identifier-1 [<u>ROUNDED</u>] [identifier-2 [<u>ROUNDED</u>]] . . .

= arithmetic-expression [ON <u>SIZE ERROR</u> imperative-statement]

Example:

SEQUENCE		CONT	A	B	COBOL STATEMENT						IDENTIFICATION
(PAGE)	(SERIAL)										
1 3	4 6	7	8	12 16 20 24 28 32	36 40 44 48 52 56 60 64 68	72	76 80

```
COMPUTE XX-FLD-X = XX-FLD-A + XX-FLD-B - XX-FLD-C * XX-FLD-D
                 / XX-FLD-E ** XX-FLD-F
```

Figure 5.28 COMPUTE statement

Arithmetic operator symbol	Meaning
+	Addition
−	Subtraction
*	Multiplication
/	Division
**	Exponentiation

Figure 5.29 Arithmetic operator symbols for COMPUTE statement

1. B / C
2. D * E
3. A — (quotient from Step 1)
4. (difference from Step 3) + (product from step 2)

Suppose we wanted to add two fields (A and B) and then divide the sum by another field (C). If the statement were written as COMPUTE X = A + B / C, the wrong answer would result because the division of B by C would occur before A is added to B. To override the normal sequence of operations, parentheses are used. Parentheses are used in a COMPUTE statement just as they are in algebra. That is, operations within the innermost set of parentheses are evaluated first and then evaluation proceeds through the outermost set. Equal parentheses levels are evaluated on a left to right basis. Thus, by writing the above statement with parentheses—COMPUTE X = (A + B) / C—the desired computation will be obtained.

Most programmers use parentheses within a COMPUTE statement regardless of whether or not the parentheses are actually required to override the normal sequence of arithmetic operations. There are two reasons for this. First, with complex expressions, it is sometimes difficult to determine exactly when each operation will be performed by the compiler. It is simpler and less risky just to write the parentheses where appropriate to ensure the desired sequence. Second, it is easier to read and understand an arithmetic expression written with parentheses. An example of COMPUTE statements to handle the arithmetic of the CHGACCT program is shown in Figure 5.30.

The ROUNDED Phrase

It is common practice to "round off" the answer to arithmetic calculations. For example, when figuring six percent sales tax on a purchase of $49.30, the tax amount is $2.958. Dollars-and-cents amounts are usually expressed to the nearest penny. Thus, an actual tax amount of $2.958 should be rounded to $2.96.

The optional ROUNDED phrase can be used with all COBOL arithmetic statements. The specific location of the phrase within each statement has been shown in the format notations. To specify rounding of any calculation, the pro-

```
COMPUTE WS-BALANCE-WORK = CA-BALANCE-FORWARD-IN
               + CA-MONTH-PURCHASE-AMT-IN
               + (CA-MONTH-PURCHASE-AMT-IN * .06)
               - CA-MONTH-PAYMENTS-IN.
COMPUTE DL-AVG-PURCHASE-OUT = CA-MONTH-PURCHASE-AMT-IN
               / CA-NBR-MONTH-PURCHASES-IN.
```

Figure 5.30 COMPUTE statements for charge account report program

grammer simply writes the reserved word ROUNDED after the identifier that will receive the result.

When ROUNDED is specified, COBOL makes the calculation and carries it out to one more decimal position than actually specified in the PICTURE clause of the result field. Then, if that extra decimal position is 5 or greater, the answer is rounded up; if it is 4 or less, the answer is not changed. The extra decimal position is then no longer needed, so it is truncated.

In the CHGACCT program, we could—and really should—have specified the ROUNDED phrase with the MULTIPLY and DIVIDE statements. An example of how those two statements would appear with the ROUNDED phrase is shown in Figure 5.31.

Unless there is a specific reason for not rounding, the ROUNDED option generally should be used whenever the result of a calculation may contain more decimal positions than have been specified in the PICTURE clause for the result field.

Choosing the Arithmetic Statement to Use

After studying the arithmetic statements that COBOL provides, you may have some questions about which statement or particular format to use in certain instances. We will discuss here some areas where there may be questions.

Whether to Use the INTO or the BY Option of the DIVIDE Statement

The decision about whether to use the INTO (formats 1, 2, and 4) or the BY (formats 3 and 5) option of the DIVIDE statement is usually based on personal preference. The INTO form was the one provided in the original COBOL language. It was specified because, in this statement, the physical relationship between the divisor and the dividend is the same as when the divisor and dividend are written down for pencil-and-paper solution—that is, first the divisor is written and then the dividend is placed to the right. Some programmers suggested, however, that it might be more natural to write the DIVIDE statement with the dividend first and the divisor to the right, as it is normally done in an algebraic (or a COBOL COMPUTE) arithmetic expression. Thus, COBOL now provides the BY option.

Recognize that, whenever the BY operator is used, the GIVING clause must be specified. That is because, without the GIVING clause, COBOL follows the convention of placing the answer in the last field specified. If the BY form of the DIVIDE statement were allowed without the GIVING clause, the divisor would be the last identifier. Divisors often have fewer integer positions than dividends. So, to guard against inadvertent errors where the quotient value could not be contained within the divisor field, COBOL does not allow use of the BY form without the GIVING clause.

When to Use the REMAINDER Clause of the DIVIDE Statement

The REMAINDER clause is not specified very often in COBOL programs for the same reason that remainders are not referred to in everyday arithmetic: most people prefer to work with remainders expressed as decimal position values.

SEQUENCE															
(PAGE) (SERIAL)	CONT	A	B					COBOL STATEMENT							IDENTIFICATION

```
008080        MULTIPLY CA-MONTH-PURCHASE-AMT BY .06                    CHGACCT
008090            GIVING WS-BALANCE-WORK ROUNDED.                       CHGACCT

008140        DIVIDE CA-NBR-MONTH-PURCHASES-IN                         CHGACCT
008150            INTO CA-MONTH-PURCHASE-AMT-IN                         CHGACCT
008160            GIVING DL-AVG-PURCHASE-OUT ROUNDED.                   CHGACCT
```

Figure 5.31 ROUNDED phrase incorporated into charge account report program

The programmer, then, need only ensure that enough decimal positions are provided for the field that is to contain the quotient; these decimal positions will express the "remainder" of the division. (They may be ROUNDED or not, depending upon the programming specifications.)

The REMAINDER clause will usually be used, however, when expressing values that, by tradition, use a base other than ten. Time and length measurements are examples. Most of us are more comfortable reading a 192-minute period of time as 3 hours and 12 minutes rather than 3.2 hours. Similarly, a length of 28 inches is usually more understandable when expressed as 2 feet 4 inches rather than 2.33 feet. To produce the more easily understood results, the programmer should specify the hours and feet fields as integer quotient fields; the minutes and inches fields would be specified in the REMAINDER clause.

When to Use the GIVING Clause

Each of the four basic arithmetic verbs can be used with or without the GIVING clause. There are a few considerations that may be discussed regarding which format to use for a given arithmetic calculation.

First, the GIVING clause should be used when all factors in the calculation are needed for later calculations or other uses. For example, suppose we need the sum of A and B early in processing, but later in the program we will use the original values of both A and B again. If the ADD statement were written without the GIVING clause—ADD A TO B—the original value of B would be lost. In this instance, the statement should be written with the GIVING clause so that another field is specified to hold the sum of A and B. By writing such a statement—ADD A B GIVING C—we retain the original value of B.

Often, the results of a calculation are to be placed in a numeric edited field. Remember that a numeric edited field cannot be used as a factor in an arithmetic statement. It may, however, appear in the GIVING clause. This, then, is another example of when it may be convenient to use the GIVING clause.

The GIVING clause is not usually specified when running totals or accumulations into a WORKING-STORAGE field are being made. In such instances, Format-1 statements are more effective. For example, if we were totaling test scores from each input record (so that a class average could be computed later) an ADD statement without the GIVING clause, like ADD XX-TEST-SCORE-IN TO WS-TOTAL-TEST-SCORES-ACCUM, is appropriate.

Whether to Use the Basic Arithmetic Statements or the COMPUTE Statement

Practically any calculation can be made either with the four basic arithmetic verbs or with the COMPUTE statement. There are only two exceptions: (1) the REMAINDER clause can only be specified with the DIVIDE statement; it cannot be used with COMPUTE, and (2) exponentiation—raising a number to a power—can only be accomplished with the COMPUTE statement.

For the great majority of arithmetic operations, though, either the basic arithmetic verbs or the COMPUTE statement can be used. Which should be chosen? There are two schools of thought on this matter.

One view is to always (except for exponentiation, of course) use the four basic arithmetic verbs. Those who espouse this view maintain that the basic verbs are more understandable to most business-oriented programmers. Further, many have observed that the arithmetic expressions within a COMPUTE statement often become long and complicated. Use of the basic arithmetic verbs ensures that even complex expressions are broken down into relatively simple, step-by-step calculations. Another drawback to the COMPUTE statement is that, since the COBOL compiler handles the intermediate results of the arithmetic expressions, certain field size errors may creep into the COMPUTE statement unless the programmer is alert to this problem.

On the other hand, those who favor use of the COMPUTE statement contend that an algebraic expression is more understandable than a string of ADD, SUBTRACT, MULTIPLY, and/or DIVIDE statements. Further, the COMPUTE statement generally provides more efficient processing, especially for more complicated calculations, than does the use of individual arithmetic statements. This is because the compiler can keep track of work areas and can minimize the storage and conversion of intermediate calculations.

So, unless there is an organization standard mandating use of one or the other, programmers use either the arithmetic verbs, COMPUTE statements, or—depending upon the individual calculations—a combination of both within a COBOL program. Where the COMPUTE statement is used, it is a good idea to limit each expression to three or four factors. This keeps it from getting too complicated.

Accumulating and Printing Report Totals

Suppose, at the end of the Charge Account Report, that we want to print (1) the total number of charge account records that were processed; (2) the total of the account balances for all charge accounts processed; and (3) the average purchase amount for all accounts combined. Such would be an example of accumulating and printing report totals. These are common functions for a report program. Let us examine what we can add to our CHGACCT program to provide for the accumulation and printing of these totals. This modified program will be called TCHGACCT to indicate that it is the CHGACCT program with report Totals. The various changes required for the programming documentation and coding will be discussed. In the figures, changes and additions to the original program are shaded.

Documentation and Program Changes

Record layout changes

Since we are modifying only the output report, there are no changes to be made to the input charge account record layout.

Print chart changes

A new line format must be added to the Charge Account Report print chart to define the exact location of the totals. The revised print chart is shown in Figure 5.32.

In the CHGACCT program, the name DL-DETAIL-LINE-OUT was assigned to the detail line that contains the account number, name, balance, and average purchase amount from each input record. One DL-DETAIL-LINE-OUT was printed for each CHARGE-ACCOUNT-RECORD-IN that was read.

A line that is based on accumulations from detail lines is commonly termed a *total line*. Total lines often contain record counts, descriptive words, column totals, and the results of calculations completed after all input records have been processed. Our TCHGACCT program contains an example of each of these. The total number of accounts has been obtained by counting each record processed. The word ACCOUNTS is an example of a descriptive word printed to identify what the value printed to the left of it is. The total of the account balances is a column total. The average purchase amount is a computation that cannot be made until after all input records have been processed.

Programming specification changes

Specific definition of the totals to be computed and the vertical-form spacing requirements for the total line must be included in the programming specifications. The programming specifications for the TCHGACCT program are shown in Figure 5.33.

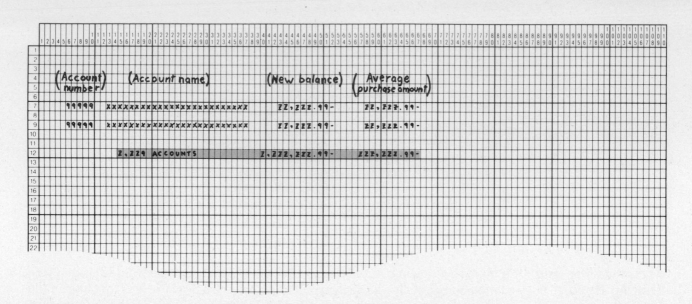

Figure 5.32 Print chart: Charge account report with totals program

---

PROGRAMMING SPECIFICATIONS

Program name: CHARGE ACCOUNT REPORT   Program ID: TCHGACCT
WITH TOTALS

Program description

  This program is to print a charge account report
  from input charge account records.

Input file(s)

  Charge account file

Output file(s)

  Charge account report

List of program operations

A. Read each input charge account record.

B. For each record, the program should compute the
    new-balance and average-customer-purchase-
    amount.

    1. New-balance is to be computed as follows:

        a. Multiply the purchases-this-month by the
            sales tax rate of 6% to equal the sales-tax-
            amount.

        b. Add the purchases-this-month and the
            sales-tax-amount to the balance-forward-
            from-last-month-amount to equal the new-
            balance.

Figure 5.33 Programming specifications: Charge account report with totals program

2. Average-customer-purchase-amount is to be computed as follows:

    a. Divide the purchases-this-month amount by the number-of-purchases-this-month. (Note: sales-tax-amount is not to be included in this average-customer-purchase-amount computation.)

C. For each record, print the following fields on the charge account report detail-line in accordance with the format shown on the print Account number chart:

    Account number
    Account name
    Account new-balance
    Account average-purchase-amount

D. Double-space each detail-line.

E. After all the input charge account records have been processed, the program should print the following total fields on the charge account report total-line in accordance with the format shown on the print chart:

    1. Total number of accounts (to be computed by counting 1 for each charge account record)

    2. Total accounts receivable (to be computed by summing account new-balances)

    3. Total average purchase amount (to be computed by summing the purchases-this-month amount for all charge account records and summing the number-of-purchases-this-month amount for all charge account records, and then dividing the first sum by the second sum)

F. Triple-space the total-line from the last detail-line.

Figure 5.33 (continued)

Structure chart changes

Another paragraph—to print report totals—must be added to the structure chart. The TCHGACCT structure chart is shown in Figure 5.34.

Pseudocode and flowchart changes

The pseudocode and flowchart must reflect requirements of the new programming specifications and structure chart. The revised pseudocode is shown in Figure 5.35 and the revised flowchart appears in Figure 5.36.

COBOL coding changes

The COBOL code must be modified in accordance with the revised pseudocode or flowchart. The COBOL code for the TCHGACCT program is shown in Figure 5.37.

Coding Considerations for the TCHGACCT Program

IDENTIFICATION DIVISION considerations

The PROGRAM-ID has been changed to show the new program name: TCHGACCT. Comment lines have been added to describe the additional program function—the printing of a total-line.

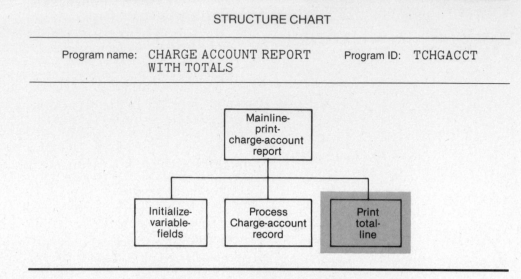

STRUCTURE CHART

Program name: CHARGE ACCOUNT REPORT WITH TOTALS   Program ID: TCHGACCT

Figure 5.34 Structure chart: Charge account report with totals program

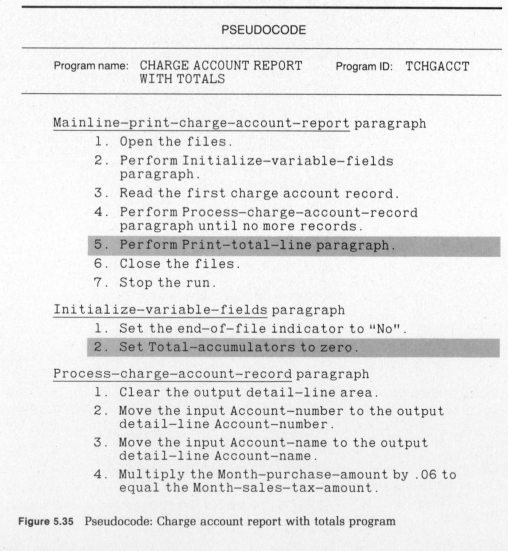

PSEUDOCODE

Program name: CHARGE ACCOUNT REPORT WITH TOTALS   Program ID: TCHGACCT

Mainline-print-charge-account-report paragraph
1. Open the files.
2. Perform Initialize-variable-fields paragraph.
3. Read the first charge account record.
4. Perform Process-charge-account-record paragraph until no more records.
5. Perform Print-total-line paragraph.
6. Close the files.
7. Stop the run.

Initialize-variable-fields paragraph
1. Set the end-of-file indicator to "No".
2. Set Total-accumulators to zero.

Process-charge-account-record paragraph
1. Clear the output detail-line area.
2. Move the input Account-number to the output detail-line Account-number.
3. Move the input Account-name to the output detail-line Account-name.
4. Multiply the Month-purchase-amount by .06 to equal the Month-sales-tax-amount.

Figure 5.35 Pseudocode: Charge account report with totals program

5. Add the Month-sales-tax-amount, Month-purchase-amount, and Balance-forward less the Month-payments to equal the new-balance and move it to the output detail-line New-balance.

6. Divide the Number-of-month-purchases into the Month-purchase-amount to equal the Average-purchase-amount and move it to the output detail-line Average-purchase-amount.

7. Write the charge account detail-line (double-spaced).

8. Add 1 to the Total-number-of-accounts.

9. Add the New-balance to the Total-accounts-receivable-amount.

10. Add the Month-purchase-amount to the Total-month-purchase-amount.

11. Add the Number-month-purchases to the Total-number-month-purchases.

12. Read the next input record.

Print-total-line paragraph

1. Clear the output total-line area.

2. Move the Total-number-of-accounts to the output total-line area.

3. Move the Total-accounts-receivable-amount to the output total-line area.

4. Divide the Total-number-month-purchases into the Total-month-purchase-amount and move the quotient to the Average-purchase-amount in the output total-line area.

5. Write the charge account total-line (triple-spaced).

Figure 5.35 (continued)

ENVIRONMENT DIVISION Considerations

There are no changes required to the ENVIRONMENT DIVISION. Some beginning COBOL programmers erroneously think that a SELECT statement should be added to provide for the total-line. This indicates a lack of understanding of the difference between a file and a record. In this TCHGACCT program, a new record—the charge account total-line—is being added to the program, not a new file. This new record is to be part of the same charge account report file that contains the charge account detail-line records.

DATA DIVISION Considerations

FILE SECTION considerations

A record-description entry for the charge account TL-TOTAL-LINE-OUT has been added. It contains data-item descriptions of fields in the report total-line as defined in the print chart. The prefix TL, for Total Line, has been assigned to each of the data fields.

WORKING-STORAGE SECTION considerations

Data-item descriptions of the fields necessary to accumulate the totals are specified under the WS-TOTAL-ACCUMULATORS record-description entry.

Program name: CHARGE ACCOUNT REPORT WITH TOTALS   Program ID: TCHGACCT

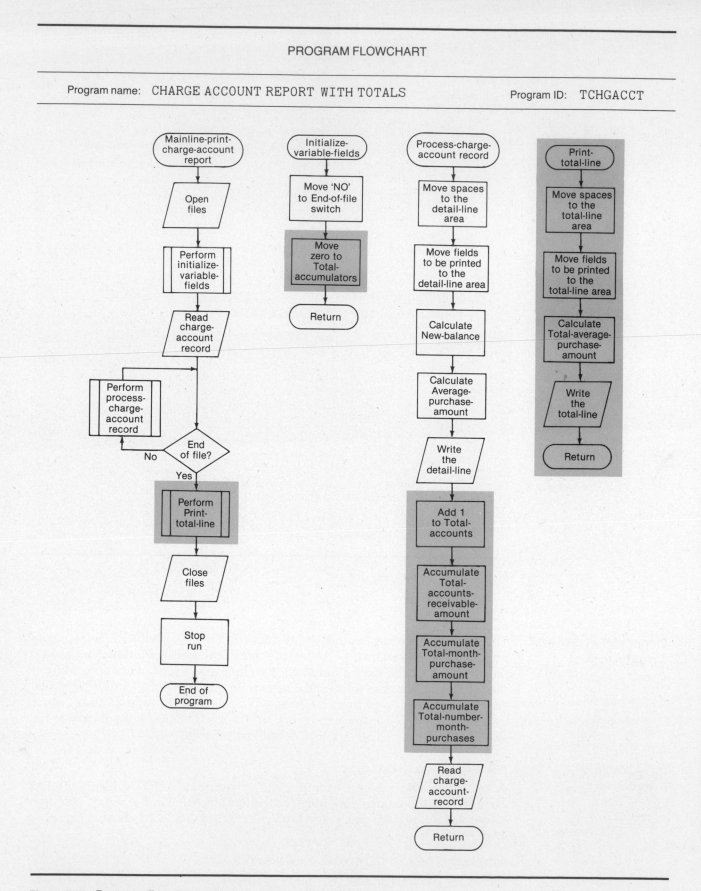

Figure 5.36 Program flowchart: Charge account report with totals program

```
001010 IDENTIFICATION DIVISION.                              005010*
001020 PROGRAM-ID.    TCHGACCT.                              005020*
001030*AUTHOR.        WELBURN.                               005030 WORKING-STORAGE SECTION.
001040*INSTALLATION.  SILICON VALLEY DISTRIBUTING COMPANY.   005040*
001050*DATE-WRITTEN.  JAN 12,1981.                           005050*
001060*DATE-COMPILED. JAN 13,1981.                           005060 01  WS-SWITCHES.
001070*SECURITY.      NONE.                                  005070     05  WS-END-OF-FILE-SWITCH         PIC X(3).
001080*                                                      005080*
001090*                                                      005090 01  WS-WORK-AREAS.
001100*          THIS PROGRAM READS CHARGE ACCOUNT RECORDS.  005100     05  WS-BALANCE-WORK               PIC S9(5)V99.
001110*          COMPUTES THE NEW BALANCE AND AVERAGE PURCHASE 005110*
001120*          AMOUNT FOR THE ACCOUNT, AND PRINTS A CHARGE 005120 01  WS-TOTAL-ACCUMULATORS.
001130*          ACCOUNT DETAIL LINE FOR EACH ACCOUNT.       005130     05  WS-TOTAL-NBR-ACCOUNTS-ACCUM   PIC S9(4).
001140*                                                      005140     05  WS-TOTAL-ACCTS-RCVBL-ACCUM    PIC S9(8)V99.
001150*          AFTER ALL INPUT CHARGE ACCOUNT RECORDS HAVE 005150     05  WS-TOTAL-MONTH-PURCH-AMT-ACCUM PIC S9(7)V99.
001160*          BEEN PROCESSED A REPORT TOTAL LINE WILL BE  005160     05  WS-TOTAL-NBR-MONTH-PURCH-ACCUM PIC S9(6).
001170*          PRINTED.                                    006010*
002010*                                                      006020*
002020*                                                      006030*
002030*                                                      006040 PROCEDURE DIVISION.
002040 ENVIRONMENT DIVISION.                                 006050*
002050*                                                      006060*
002060*                                                      006070 MAINLINE-PRINT-CHG-ACCT-REPORT.
002070 CONFIGURATION SECTION.                                006080*
002080*                                                      006090     OPEN INPUT  CHARGE-ACCOUNT-FILE-IN
002090 SOURCE-COMPUTER.  IBM-370.                            006100          OUTPUT CHARGE-ACCOUNT-REPORT-OUT.
002100 OBJECT-COMPUTER.  IBM-370.                            006110     PERFORM INITIALIZE-VARIABLE-FIELDS.
002110*                                                      006120     READ CHARGE-ACCOUNT-FILE-IN
002120*                                                      006130          AT END MOVE 'YES' TO WS-END-OF-FILE-SWITCH.
002130 INPUT-OUTPUT SECTION.                                 006140     PERFORM PROCESS-CHARGE-ACCOUNT-RECORD
002140*                                                      006150          UNTIL WS-END-OF-FILE-SWITCH IS EQUAL TO 'YES'.
002150 FILE-CONTROL.                                         006155     PERFORM PRINT-TOTAL-LINE.
002160     SELECT CHARGE-ACCOUNT-FILE-IN                     006160     CLOSE CHARGE-ACCOUNT-FILE-IN
002170          ASSIGN TO UT-S-INFILE.                       006170          CHARGE-ACCOUNT-REPORT-OUT.
002180     SELECT CHARGE-ACCOUNT-REPORT-OUT                  006180     STOP RUN.
002190          ASSIGN TO UT-S-PRTFILE.                      007010*
003010*                                                      007020*
003020*                                                      007030 INITIALIZE-VARIABLE-FIELDS.
003030*                                                      007040*
003040 DATA DIVISION.                                        007050     MOVE 'NO ' TO WS-END-OF-FILE-SWITCH.
003050*                                                      007060     MOVE ZEROS TO WS-TOTAL-ACCUMULATORS.
003060*                                                      008010*
003070 FILE SECTION.                                         008020*
003080*                                                      008030 PROCESS-CHARGE-ACCOUNT-RECORD.
003090 FD  CHARGE-ACCOUNT-FILE-IN                            008040*
003100     RECORD CONTAINS 80 CHARACTERS                     008050     MOVE SPACES TO DL-DETAIL-LINE-OUT.
003110     LABEL RECORDS ARE OMITTED.                        008060     MOVE CA-ACCOUNT-NUMBER-IN TO DL-ACCOUNT-NUMBER-OUT.
003120*                                                      008070     MOVE CA-ACCOUNT-NAME-IN TO DL-ACCOUNT-NAME-OUT.
003130 01  CHARGE-ACCOUNT-RECORD-IN.                         008080     MULTIPLY CA-MONTH-PURCHASE-AMT-IN BY .06
003140     05  CA-RECORD-CODE           PIC X(2).            008090          GIVING WS-BALANCE-WORK ROUNDED.
003150     05  CA-ACCOUNT-NUMBER-IN     PIC X(5).            008100     ADD CA-BALANCE-FORWARD-IN TO WS-BALANCE-WORK.
003160     05  CA-ACCOUNT-NAME-IN       PIC X(25).           008110     ADD CA-MONTH-PURCHASE-AMT-IN TO WS-BALANCE-WORK.
003170     05  CA-BALANCE-FORWARD-IN    PIC S9(5)V99.        008120     SUBTRACT CA-MONTH-PAYMENTS-IN FROM WS-BALANCE-WORK.
003180     05  CA-MONTH-PURCHASE-AMT-IN PIC S9(5)V99.        008130     MOVE WS-BALANCE-WORK TO DL-NEW-BALANCE-OUT.
003190     05  CA-NBR-MONTH-PURCHASES-IN PIC S9(4).          008140     DIVIDE CA-NBR-MONTH-PURCHASES-IN
003200     05  CA-MONTH-PAYMENTS-IN     PIC S9(5)V99.        008150          INTO CA-MONTH-PURCHASE-AMT-IN
003210     05  FILLER                   PIC X(23).           008160          GIVING DL-AVG-PURCHASE-OUT ROUNDED.
004010*                                                      008170     WRITE DL-DETAIL-LINE-OUT
004020 FD  CHARGE-ACCOUNT-REPORT-OUT                         008180          AFTER ADVANCING 2 LINES.
004030     RECORD CONTAINS 133 CHARACTERS                    008182     ADD 1 TO WS-TOTAL-NBR-ACCOUNTS-ACCUM.
004040     LABEL RECORDS ARE OMITTED.                        008184     ADD WS-BALANCE-WORK TO WS-TOTAL-ACCTS-RCVBL-ACCUM.
004050*                                                      008186     ADD CA-MONTH-PURCHASE-AMT-IN
004060 01  DL-DETAIL-LINE-OUT.                               008107          TO WS-TOTAL-MONTH-PURCH-AMT-ACCUM.
004070     05  DL-VERTICAL-FORMS-CONTROL-OUT PIC X(1).       008188     ADD CA-NBR-MONTH-PURCHASES-IN
004080     05  FILLER                   PIC X(5).            008189          TO WS-TOTAL-NBR-MONTH-PURCH-ACCUM.
004090     05  DL-ACCOUNT-NUMBER-OUT    PIC X(5).            008190     READ CHARGE-ACCOUNT-FILE-IN
004100     05  FILLER                   PIC X(5).            008200          AT END MOVE 'YES' TO WS-END-OF-FILE-SWITCH.
004110     05  DL-ACCOUNT-NAME-OUT      PIC X(25).           009010*
004120     05  FILLER                   PIC X(2).            009020*
004130     05  DL-NEW-BALANCE-OUT       PIC ZZ,ZZZ.99-.      009030 PRINT-TOTAL-LINE.
004140     05  FILLER                   PIC X(5).            009040*
004150     05  DL-AVG-PURCHASE-OUT      PIC ZZ,ZZZ.99-.      009050     MOVE SPACES TO TL-TOTAL-LINE-OUT.
004160     05  FILLER                   PIC X(65).           009060     MOVE WS-TOTAL-NBR-ACCOUNTS-ACCUM TO TL-TOTAL-NBR-ACCTS-OUT.
004170*                                                      009070     MOVE 'ACCOUNTS' TO TL-ACCOUNTS-WORD-AREA-OUT.
004180 01  TL-TOTAL-LINE-OUT.                                009080     MOVE WS-TOTAL-ACCTS-RCVBL-ACCUM TO TL-TOTAL-ACCTS-RCVBL-OUT.
004190     05  TL-VERTICAL-FORMS-CONTROL-OUT PIC X(1).       009090     DIVIDE WS-TOTAL-NBR-MONTH-PURCH-ACCUM
004200     05  FILLER                   PIC X(14).           009100          INTO WS-TOTAL-MONTH-PURCH-AMT-ACCUM
004210     05  TL-TOTAL-NBR-ACCTS-OUT   PIC Z,ZZ9.           009110          GIVING TL-AVG-PURCHASE-OUT ROUNDED.
004220     05  FILLER                   PIC X(1).            009120     WRITE TL-TOTAL-LINE-OUT
004230     05  TL-ACCOUNTS-WORD-AREA-OUT PIC X(8).           009130          AFTER ADVANCING 3 LINES.
004240     05  FILLER                   PIC X(10).
004250     05  TL-TOTAL-ACCTS-RCVBL-OUT PIC ZZ,ZZZ,ZZZ.99-.
004260     05  FILLER                   PIC X(5).
004270     05  TL-AVG-PURCHASE-OUT      PIC ZZ,ZZZ.99-.
004280     05  FILLER                   PIC X(65).
```

Figure 5.37 COBOL coding: TCHGACCT program

These fields will be incremented as each record is read. The WS-TOTAL-NBR-ACCOUNTS-ACCUM field will be used to total the number of accounts. An accumulation of all the account balances will be made in the WS-TOTAL-ACCTS-RCVBL-ACCUM field. The WS-TOTAL-MONTH-PURCH-AMT-ACCUM field will be used to develop the total of all the monthly purchases. The total number of purchases made during the month will be accumulated in the WS-TOTAL-NBR-MONTH-PURCH-ACCUM field.

Observe that each of the four total fields has been defined with a PICTURE clause whose length is consistent with the length of its respective field in the charge account TL-TOTAL-LINE-OUT. Notice also that each field has been given a numeric—not numeric edited—PICTURE. Remember that only a "pure" numeric field can be used as a factor in arithmetic statements.

MAINLINE-PRINT-CHG-ACCT-REPORT paragraph

Control must be transferred to the PRINT-TOTAL-LINE procedure. However, the PRINT-TOTAL-LINE procedure should not be invoked until after all input records have been processed, nor can it be executed after the output CHARGE-ACCOUNT-REPORT-OUT file has been closed. Hence, the statement PERFORM PRINT-TOTAL-LINE has been placed where it will be executed after all iterations of the PROCESS-CHARGE-ACCOUNT-RECORD have been completed and prior to closing of the files.

INITIALIZE-VARIABLE-FIELDS paragraph

When the program begins, each of the four WS-TOTAL-ACCUMULATORS fields may contain unpredictable values. For the accumulations of each field to be correct, each field should initially be set to a value of zero. This is accomplished by the statement: MOVE ZEROS TO WS-TOTAL-ACCUMULATORS. ZERO is a figurative constant. It may also be written as ZEROS or ZEROES. Regardless how it is written, the effect is the same: the receiving field is filled with zeros. Thus, by moving ZEROS to the group field WS-TOTAL-ACCUMULATORS, each of the four elementary fields within it is set to a value of zero.

PROCESS-CHARGE-ACCOUNT-RECORD paragraph

When processing each charge account record, this procedure must make the four accumulations required for the report total. The processing steps are as follows:

1. A numeric literal value of 1 is added to the WS-TOTAL-NBR-ACCOUNTS-ACCUM field to count each record as it is processed.

2. Since the current account balance has been computed in the WS-BALANCE-WORK field, that field is added to the WS-TOTAL-ACCTS-RCVBL-ACCUM field to accumulate the total of all account balances.

3. Determining the average monthly purchase amount for all accounts will require two accumulations: monthly purchases and number of purchases during the month. The monthly purchases for all accounts are accumulated by the statement ADD CA-MONTH-PURCHASE-AMT-IN TO WS-TOTAL-MONTH-PURCH-AMT-ACCUM.

4. The second average monthly purchase amount computation—total number of purchases during the month for all accounts—is handled by the statement ADD CA-NBR-MONTH-PURCHASES-IN TO WS-TOTAL-NBR-MONTH-PURCH-ACCUM.

Observe that these four accumulation statements have been placed after all the detail processing for each record has been completed (the WRITE statement is the last detail processing step). Actually, these accumulation statements could have been placed at various locations in the paragraph and the program would still produce the correct totals. It is more logical and it enhances program readability, however, to do the totals processing for a record after detail processing has been completed.

PRINT-TOTAL-LINE paragraph

This procedure formats and prints the total-line. The following program steps are provided for:

1. All 133 characters of the charge account TL-TOTAL-LINE-OUT are set to a value of SPACES. If this were not done, unwanted "garbage" characters might be printed in the FILLER areas of the total-line.

00205	ALPHA MANUFACTURING	11.20	10.57
00495	CENTRAL BUILDING SUPPLY	221.49	52.24
01038	CITY BUSINESS SERVICES	85.17	40.17
08047	DOWNTOWN VARIETY	1,028.90	133.50
10080	GENERAL DISTRIBUTING	1,634.52	192.75
12143	HOLLYWOOD FASHIONS	163.95	51.55
15169	KINGS REST HOTEL	32.69-	10.00
18543	MOUNTAIN HARDWARE	4,589.42	206.17
20469	NORDIC SPORTING GOODS	27.13	25.60
42189	PLEASANT VIEW LANES	14.35	4.51
80565	STANDARD SUPPLY	215.65	20.34
92300	WALKER PHARMACY	10.60	10.00
	12 ACCOUNTS	7,969.69	63.12

Figure 5.38 Output: Charge account report with totals program

2. The total number of accounts is moved from the WORKING-STORAGE field WS-TOTAL-NBR-ACCOUNTS-ACCUM to the total-line.
3. The non-numeric literal ACCOUNTS is moved to the total-line to identify what the leftmost number on the total-line is.
4. The total of all account balances is moved from the WORKING-STORAGE field WS-TOTAL-ACCTS-RCVBL-ACCUM to the total-line.
5. The average purchase amount for all accounts is computed (WS-TOTAL-NBR-MONTH-PURCH-ACCUM is divided into WS-TOTAL-MONTH PURCH-AMT-ACCUM) and placed in the total-line field.
6. The total-line is written, triple-spaced from the last detail-line.

The output format for TCHGACCT is shown in Figure 5.38.

A Discussion of Implicit Redefinition

When there are multiple 01-level record-descriptions established within one FD, all record-descriptions occupy the same area of storage. This reuse of the same storage area for multiple record-descriptions is termed *implicit redefinition*.

In the TCHGACCT program, the CHARGE-ACCOUNT-REPORT-OUT file has two 01-level record-descriptions: DL-DETAIL-LINE-OUT and TL-TOTAL-LINE-OUT. Both record-descriptions occupy the same 133 character positions of storage.

Notice, in the PROCESS-CHARGE-ACCOUNT-RECORD paragraph, there is a statement MOVE SPACES TO DL-DETAIL-LINE-OUT. In the PRINT-TOTAL-LINE paragraph, the statement MOVE SPACES TO TL-TOTAL-LINE-OUT is specified. Since both the DL-DETAIL-LINE-OUT and TL-TOTAL-LINE-OUT records occupy the same area of storage, it doesn't really matter which of the two record-names is used. That is, even though it would be confusing documentation, in the PRINT-TOTAL-LINE paragraph we could have specified MOVE SPACES TO DL-DETAIL-LINE-OUT and the correct result would have been obtained: the 133 character positions used for the DL-DETAIL-LINE-OUT and TL-TOTAL-LINE-OUT record area would be blanked.

It is important for the programmer to recognize that when multiple record-descriptions are defined in the FILE SECTION for a given FD, such implicit redefinition occurs. This means, of course, that the two different records could not be built or formatted simultaneously, for then one would overlay the other. Observe that in the TCHGACCT program, the TL-TOTAL-LINE-OUT record was not formatted until after all the DL-DETAIL-LINE-OUT records were processed. (If program specifications call for such handling, the different records could be formatted alternately—just not simultaneously.)

Often, programmers will describe records for a file in the WORKING-STORAGE SECTION rather than the FILE SECTION. Doing so usually eliminates the considerations of implicit redefinition. Such WORKING-STORAGE SECTION definition of input and output records will be discussed in Chapter 7.

A Discussion of Double-Buffering

In order to increase processing efficiency, many COBOL compilers establish two or more I/O areas for each file. The compiler then switches from one I/O area to the other. This allows better utilization of the channels that carry the input from input devices to the computer main storage and the output from main storage to the output devices. This multiple I/O area handling is often termed *double-buffering*. A diagram of its effect is shown in Figure 5.39.

Although double-buffering is handled automatically by the compiler, it does create one programming consideration: when to clear an output record area. Notice in the CHGACCT and TCHGACCT programs, the output print-line was cleared before each DL-DETAIL-LINE-OUT was constructed. It might appear that such clearing could be handled just once in the INITIALIZE-VARIABLE-FIELDS paragraph. However, with double-buffering, only the first of the two print-line areas would be cleared; "garbage" would probably be printed on the second, fourth, sixth, and so forth, print-lines. When "junk"

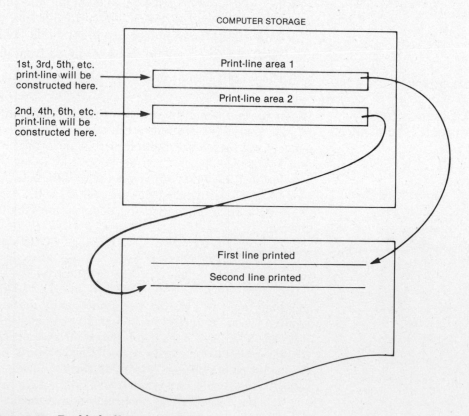

Figure 5.39 Double-buffering example

Format:

$$\left[\underline{RESERVE}\ \text{integer-1}\ \left[\begin{array}{c} \text{AREA} \\ \text{AREAS} \end{array} \right] \right]$$

Example:

Part A: Eliminating double-buffering

SEQUENCE				COBOL STATEMENT	IDENTIFICATION

```
SELECT XX-ANY-FILE
ASSIGN TO UT-S-DEVICE
RESERVE 1 AREA.
```

Part B: Explicitly specifying the number of I/O areas

```
SELECT XX-ANY-FILE
ASSIGN TO UT-S-DEVICE
RESERVE 2 AREAS.
```

Figure 5.40 RESERVE clause example

data appears on every other print-line, chances are a programming oversight regarding double buffering is present.

Occasionally, to conserve storage, only one I/O area may be requested for a file. This is specified by the RESERVE clause of the SELECT statement. Its format and an example are shown in Figure 5.40. Recognize that the number of I/O areas assigned to each file is dependent upon the particular COBOL compiler. Thus, the RESERVE clause may be used to increase or decrease the number of I/O areas provided by the compiler.

Summary

Whenever fields are to be operated upon arithmetically, each field must be defined as numeric, and the field length, decimal point location, and arithmetic sign must be considered. A summary of arithmetic statements is presented as Figure 5.41. The optional phrase ROUNDED may be specified for the answer field of any arithmetic statement that is to be rounded off.

When designing a report program that accumulates and prints report totals, the following report total considerations must be provided for:

DATA DIVISION:

1. A record-description for the total-line must be specified.
2. The input record fields to be operated on arithmetically must be defined as numeric.
3. Fields must be specified in WORKING-STORAGE to accumulate the totals.

PROCEDURE DIVISION:

1. The WORKING-STORAGE accumulator fields must be initialized to zero.
2. After detail processing for each input record has been completed, the total accumulations should be made.
3. A procedure to print the total-line must be performed after all input records have been processed and before the output report file has been closed.

Figure 5.41 Summary of arithmetic statements

Format	Verb	Operand 1	Connector	Operand 2	GIVING	Result	(ROUNDED)	REMAINDER	Remainder	(ON SIZE ERROR)
Format-1	ADD	Addend(s) Numeric identifier or Numeric literal	TO	Addend(s)/Sum(s) Numeric identifier			(ROUNDED)			(ON SIZE ERROR) Imperative statement
Format-2	ADD	Addend Numeric identifier or Numeric literal		Addend(s) Numeric identifier / Numeric literal	GIVING	Sum(s) Numeric identifier or Numeric edited identifier	(ROUNDED)			(ON SIZE ERROR) Imperative statement
Format-1	SUBTRACT	Subtrahend(s) Numeric identifier or Numeric literal	FROM	Minuend(s)/Difference(s) Numeric identifier			(ROUNDED)			(ON SIZE ERROR) Imperative statement
Format-2	SUBTRACT	Subtrahend(s) Numeric identifier or Numeric literal	FROM	Minuend Numeric identifier / Numeric literal	GIVING	Difference(s) Numeric identifier or Numeric edited identifier	(ROUNDED)			(ON SIZE ERROR) Imperative statement
Format-1	MULTIPLY	Multiplicand Numeric identifier or Numeric literal	BY	Multiplier(s)/Product(s) Numeric identifier			(ROUNDED)			(ON SIZE ERROR) Imperative statement
Format-2	MULTIPLY	Multiplicand Numeric identifier or Numeric literal	BY	Multiplier Numeric identifier / Numeric literal	GIVING	Product(s) Numeric identifier or Numeric edited identifier	(ROUNDED)			(ON SIZE ERROR) Imperative statement
Format-1	DIVIDE	Divisor Numeric identifier or Numeric literal	INTO	Dividend(s)/Quotient(s) Numeric identifier			(ROUNDED)			(ON SIZE ERROR) Imperative statement
Format-2	DIVIDE	Divisor Numeric identifier or Numeric literal	INTO	Dividend Numeric identifier / Numeric literal	GIVING	Quotient(s) Numeric identifier or Numeric-edited identifier	(ROUNDED)			(ON SIZE ERROR) Imperative statement
Format-3	DIVIDE	Dividend Numeric identifier or Numeric literal	BY	Divisor Numeric identifier / Numeric literal	GIVING	Quotient(s) Numeric identifier or Numeric-edited identifier	(ROUNDED)			(ON SIZE ERROR) Imperative statement
Format-4	DIVIDE	Divisor Numeric identifier or Numeric literal	INTO	Dividend Numeric identifier / Numeric literal	GIVING	Quotient Numeric identifier or Numeric-edited identifier	(ROUNDED)	REMAINDER	Remainder Numeric identifier	(ON SIZE ERROR) Imperative statement
Format-5	DIVIDE	Dividend Numeric identifier or Numeric literal	BY	Divisor Numeric identifier / Numeric literal	GIVING	Quotient Numeric identifier or Numeric-edited identifier	(ROUNDED)	REMAINDER	Remainder Numeric identifier	(ON SIZE ERROR) Imperative statement
	COMPUTE	Numeric identifier or Numeric edited identifier (ROUNDED)	=	Arithmetic expression						(ON SIZE ERROR) Imperative statement

Implicit redefinition refers to the situation where multiple 01-level record-descriptions within one FD occupy the same area of storage.

Double-buffering utilizes multiple I/O areas to increase processing speed. When it is required that the number of I/O areas be varied from the standard number provided by the compiler, the RESERVE clause may be specified in the SELECT statement.

Style Summary

- Use parentheses within COMPUTE statement arithmetic expressions to control the sequence of arithmetic operations rather than relying upon the normal sequence of operations. By doing so, you make the expression easier to read and understand, and you help ensure that the correct computation is made.

- Try to limit each COMPUTE statement arithmetic expression to three or four factors in order to prevent overly complicated logic.

1968 ANS COBOL Restrictions

- Multiple answer fields may not be specified for any arithmetic statement (ADD, SUBTRACT, MULTIPLY, DIVIDE, or COMPUTE).

Exercises

Terms for Definition

hierarchy of arithmetic operations
total line
implicit redefinition

double-buffering
I/O areas

Review Questions

1. What three characteristics must be considered when defining a numeric field to be used for arithmetic computations?

2. Numeric literals may be used in arithmetic statements providing they are not specified as _____.

3. An arithmetic statement may contain a numeric edited item only as _____ .

4. Two phrases that may be specified for any arithmetic statement are ____ and ____ .

5. An ADD statement may contain how many addends? *many*

6. Although the reserved word TO must be specified for the Format-1 ADD statement, it must be _____ when the Format-2 ADD statement (with the GIVING phrase) is written.

7. The reserved word FROM (must/must not) be specified for the Format-1 SUBTRACT statement; it (must/must not) be specified for the Format-2 SUBTRACT statement.

8. The reserved word ____*BY*____ is specified between the multiplier and multiplicand of the MULTIPLY statement.

9. When a DIVIDE statement is written with the reserved word ____*By*____ , the first identifier is the dividend; the second identifier is the divisor.

10. When a DIVIDE statement is written with the reserved word ____*into*____ , the first identifier is the divisor; the second identifier is the dividend.

11. Can you determine why COBOL syntax requires that a DIVIDE statement with the reserved word BY must contain a GIVING phrase?

12. List the hierarchy of arithmetic operations that apply to the COMPUTE statement.

13. Identify the value of X as a result of the following COMPUTE statements. (A = 4; B = 10; C = 2)

    X = A + B / C
    X = (A + B) / C
    X ROUNDED = A + (B / C)

14. Suppose it is necessary to divide a 7-position dollars-and-cents field (S99999V99) by 2 and place the answer, ROUNDED to the nearest penny, in a dollars-and-cents field called XX-WHOLESALE-AMOUNT. Which one of the following picture character-strings may be specified for the XX-WHOLESALE-AMOUNT to provide for the correct rounding, sign handling, and to ensure that a SIZE ERROR does not occur?

S99999V999	99999V999
S9999V99	9999V99
S99999V99	99999V99
S9999V999	9999V999

15. List four items that can appear in a total line.

16. Why must WORKING-STORAGE fields used for accumulations *not* contain editing symbols?

17. Why should WORKING-STORAGE fields used for arithmetic generally contain the PICTURE symbol S?

18. Implicit redefinition of record-descriptions occurs within the _____ SECTION but not in the _____ SECTION of the DATA DIVISION.

19. Although double-buffering is handled automatically by most COBOL compilers, what must the programmer remember prior to constructing each line in the FILE SECTION?

20. The number of I/O areas assigned to each file may be explicitly specified by the _____ clause of the SELECT sentence.

Syntax/Debug Exercises

1. Some or all of the following arithmetic statements contain syntax errors. Rewrite each erroneous statement correctly. (Consider each data-name to be a numeric data-item.)

    a. ADD XX-DEPOSIT XX-OLD-BALANCE. *TO*

    b. ADD XX-DEPOSIT TO XX-OLD-BALANCE.

    c. ADD XX-REG-HOURS TO XX-PREM-HOURS
        GIVING XX-TOTAL-HOURS.

    d. ADD XX-AMOUNT TO 10. *switch*

    e. ADD XX-AMOUNT 10 GIVING XX-ADJ-AMOUNT. *switch + TO*

    f. ADD XX-DAY-1 XX-DAY-2 XX-DAY-3
        XX-DAY-4 XX-DAY-5 XX-DAY-6
        XX-DAY-7 GIVING XX-WEEK.

    g. SUBTRACT XX-CHECK-AMOUNT
        FROM XX-BALANCE.

    h. SUBTRACT XX-CHECK-AMOUNT
        XX-SERVICE-CHARGE
            GIVING XX-BALANCE.

    i. MULTIPLY 60 TIMES XX-HOURS.

    j. MULTIPLY XX-HOURS BY 60.

    k. MULTIPLY XX-HOURS X 60 *BY*
        GIVING XX-MINUTES.

    l. DIVIDE XX-MINUTES BY 60
        GIVING XX-HOURS.

    m. DIVIDE XX-MINUTES INTO 60 *BY*
        GIVING XX-HOURS.

    n. DIVIDE XX-MINUTES BY 60.

    o. DIVIDE XX-TOTAL-SCORES
        BY XX-NBR-STUDENTS.

    p. DIVIDE XX-NBR-STUDENTS
        INTO XX-TOTAL-SCORES.

q. DIVIDE 60 INTO XX-MINUTES
       GIVING XX-HOURS
          REMAINDER XX-MINUTES.

r. DIVIDE XX-AMT BY 2
       GIVING XX-AMT ROUNDED
         XX-AMT-UNROUNDED.

s. COMPUTE XX-AVG ROUNDED
       = (XX-TOTAL / XX-NBR).

t. COMPUTE XX-A = XX-B X XX-C + XX-D.

u. COMPUTE XX-W = ((XX-R + XX-S) −
              (XX-Y / XX-Z).

*Programming
Assignment 5-A:
Order Report*

Program description

    An order report is to be printed from the order file. This report will contain detail lines and a total line.

Input file

    Order file

Input record format

    Order record

Field location	Field name	Data class	Comments
1– 2	Record code	numeric	code "51"
6–29	Customer name	alphanumeric	
30–49	Product description	alphanumeric	
55–60	Unit price	numeric	assumed decimal point between positions 58 and 59
65–67	Quantity ordered	numeric	provide for negative sign

Output file

    Order report

Output report line formats

Print positions	Field name	Comments
		Detail Line
5–28	Customer name	
31–50	Product description	
53–55	Quantity ordered	Zero-suppress non-significant zeros
58–64	Unit price	Zero-suppress non-significant dollar position zeros. Insert decimal point
68–81	Extension amount	Zero-suppress non-significant dollar position zeros. Insert commas and decimal point. Print CR if amount is negative
		Total Line
67–81	Total extension amount	Zero-suppress non-significant dollar position zeros. Insert commas and decimal point. Print CR if amount is negative
82		Print an asterisk

Program operations

1. Read each input order record.

2. Compute the extension amount by multiplying the unit price by the quantity ordered.

3. Print an output order report detail line as specified above for each order record.

4. Double-space each detail line.

5. After all input order records have been processed, print the output order report total line as specified above (triple-spaced from the last detail line).

Programming Assignment 5-B: Test Score Report

Program description

A test score report is to be printed from the test result file. This report will contain detail lines and a total line.

Input file

Test result file

Input record format

Test result record

Field location	Field name	Data class	Comments
1- 2	Record code	numeric	code "52"
6-25	Student name	alphanumeric	
28-30	Test score	numeric	

Output file

Test score report

Output report line formats

Print positions	Field name	Comments
	Detail Line	
15-34	Student name	
42-44	Test score	Zero-suppress non-significant zeros
	Total Line	
20-33		Print TOTAL STUDENTS
35-37	Total number of students	
39-44	Total test scores	Zero-suppress non-significant zeros Insert comma
45		Print an asterisk
48-60		Print AVERAGE SCORE
62-64	Average score	Zero-suppress non-significant zeros

Program operations

1. Read each input test result record.

2. For each input test result record, add 1 to an accumulator containing the total number of students and add the test score to a total test scores accumulator.

3. Print an output test score detail line as specified above for each test result record.

4. Double-space each detail line.

5. After all input test score records have been processed, print the output test score total line as specified above (triple-spaced from the last detail line).

Program description
A sales report is to be printed from the order file. This report will contain detail lines and two total lines.

Input file
Order file

Input record format
Order record

Field location	Field name	Data class	Comments
1- 2	Record code	numeric	code "51"
6-29	Customer name	alphanumeric	
72-80	Purchase amount	numeric	assumed decimal point between positions 78 and 79

Output file
Order report

Output report line formats

Print positions	Field name	Comments

Detail Line

Print positions	Field name	Comments
3-26	Customer name	
30-41	Purchase amount	Zero-suppress non-significant dollar position zeros. Insert commas and decimal point
46-55	Sales tax amount	Zero suppress non-significant dollar position zeros. Insert commas and decimal point
60-71	Transaction amount	Zero suppress non-significant dollar position zeros. Insert commas and decimal point

Total Line-1

Print positions	Field name	Comments
5-22		Print TOTAL TRANSACTIONS
24-27	Total number of transactions	Zero-suppress non-significant zeros
29-41	Total purchase amount	Zero-supress non-significant dollar position zeros. Insert commas and decimal point
42		Print an asterisk
44-55	Total sales tax amount	Zero-suppress non-significant dollar position zeros. Insert commas and decimal point
56		Print an asterisk
59-71	Total transaction amount	Zero-suppress non-significant dollar position zeros. Insert commas and decimal point
72		Print an asterisk

Total Line-2

Print positions	Field name	Comments
5-27		Print AVERAGE PURCHASE AMOUNT
30-41	Average purchase amount	Zero-suppress non-significant dollar position zeros. Insert commas and decimal point

Program operations

1. Read each input order record.
2. For each input order record, make the following computations:
   a. Compute the sales tax amount by applying a 6½% sales tax to the purchase amount.
   b. Compute the transaction amount by adding the purchase amount and the sales tax amount.
   c. Compute the total number of transactions by counting each input order record.
   d. Add the purchase amount to the total purchase amount.
   e. Add the sales tax amount to the total sales tax amount.
   f. Add the transaction amount to the total transaction amount.
3. Print an output sales report detail line as specified above for each order record.
4. Double-space each detail line.
5. After all input order records have been processed, print the first output sales report total line as specified above (triple-spaced from the last detail line).
6. Compute the average purchase amount by dividing the total purchase amount by the total number of transactions and print the second output sales report total line as specified above (double-space from the previous total line).

Programming Assignment 5-D: Discount Report

Program description

A discount report is to be printed from the order file. This report will contain detail lines and two total lines.

Input file

Order file

Input record format

Order record

Field location	Field name	Data class	Comments
1- 2	Record code	numeric	code "51"
6-29	Customer name	alphanumeric	
68-69	Discount percentage	numeric	
72-80	Purchase amount	numeric	assumed decimal point between positions 78 and 79

Output file

Discount report

Output report line formats

Print positions	Field name	Comments
	Detail Line	
3-26	Customer name	
30-41	Purchase amount	Zero-suppress non-significant dollar position zeros Insert commas and decimal point
46-55	Discount amount	Zero-suppress non-significant dollar position zeros Insert commas and decimal point
60-71	Net amount	Zero suppress non-significant dollar position zeros Insert commas and decimal point

Print positions	Field name	Comments
		Total Line-1
5–22		Print TOTAL TRANSACTIONS
24–27	Total number of transactions	Zero-suppress non-significant zeros
29–41	Total purchase amount	Zero-suppress non-significant dollar position zeros
		Insert commas and decimal point
42		Print an asterisk
44–55	Total discount amount	Zero-suppress non-significant dollar position zeros
		Insert commas and decimal point
56		Print an asterisk
58–71	Net purchase amount	Zero-suppress non-significant dollar position zeros
		Insert commas and decimal point
72		Print an asterisk
		Total Line-2
5–19		Print AVERAGE AMOUNTS
30–41	Average purchase amount	Zero-suppress non-significant dollar position zeros
		Insert commas and decimal point
46–55	Average discount amount	Zero-suppress non-significant dollar position zeros
		Insert commas and decimal point
59–71	Average net purchase amount	Zero-suppress non-significant dollar position zeros
		Insert commas and decimal point

Program operations

1. Read each input order record.

2. For each input order record, make the following computations:

   a. Compute the discount amount by multiplying the purchase amount by the discount percentage.

   b. Compute the net amount by subtracting the discount amount from the purchase amount.

   c. Compute the total number of transactions by counting each input order record.

   d. Add the purchase amount to the total purchase amount.

   e. Add the discount amount to the total discount amount.

   f. Add the net amount to the total net amount.

3. Print an output discount report detail line as specified above for each order record.

4. Double-space each detail line.

5. After all input order records have been processed, print the first output discount report total line as specified above (triple-spaced from the last detail line).

6. Compute the average amounts and print the second output sales report total line as specified above (double-spaced from the previous total line).

CHAPTER 6

STRUCTURED PROGRAM DEVELOPMENT

6

**STRUCTURED
PROGRAM DEVELOPMENT**

Now that you have had a chance to work with and assimilate some basics of the COBOL language, let's discuss structured programming. We will cover how it developed and what the term means today, and then we will look at structured design and documentation techniques, structured COBOL coding principles and conventions, and structured program development aids. These structured program development concepts will become more important as we proceed to more complex programs in later chapters.

The programming specifications for a mailing labels program are presented in Figure 6.1. We'll call this program LABELS and use it as an example for many of the topics discussed in this chapter.

The Development of Structured Programming

For the first quarter-century of computer programming (1950 to 1975, or so) most programmers designed and wrote programs on a linear basis. That is, the instructions that the program would execute first were placed at the front of the program and at the end of the program were the instructions that the program would execute last. A program designed and written on such a linear basis can be called an *unstructured program*. Figure 6.2 shows the PROCEDURE DIVISION for the LABELS program written on an unstructured basis. A fully structured version embodying many of the principles and conventions to be discussed in this chapter is shown in Figure 6.3.

By contrasting the unstructured code with the structured example, two significant differences can be identified:

1. The unstructured program does not have a concise mainline-type paragraph to direct the overall program flow.
2. The unstructured program contains GO TO statements to direct the flow of program control. The GO TO statement format is shown in Figure 6.4. It causes program control to be transferred to the procedure-name specified.

Unstructured programs can become exceedingly difficult to design, test, make operational, read, and maintain. Many deficiencies associated with unstructured programs are caused by the two characteristics mentioned above: no concise mainline routine and the use of GO TO statements.

The LABELS program is short and simple in relation to most actual business application programs. Consider a program with thousands of instructions and hundreds of GO TO statements. The control flow of such a program often winds through the PROCEDURE DIVISION statements like a strand of vermicelli in a plate of spaghetti. Indeed, programs of this type are often (not too fondly) referred to as "bowl-of-spaghetti" or "rat's nest" programs.

As practicing programmers and managers struggled with the problems presented by unstructured programs, certain computer scientists, educators and practitioners were doing research that contributed to a method of programming that has come to be called *structured programming*. We will briefly trace the important milestones in the development of structured programming. They are:

Program name: MAILING LABELS   Program ID: LABELS

Program description
>   This program prints subscriber mailing labels for
>   current subscribers from subscriber records.

Input file(s)
>   Subscriber file

Output file(s)
>   Subscriber labels

List of program operations

A. Read each input subscriber record.

B. For each record, the program should check the
    Expired—code field to see if the subscription is
    current or has expired.

>   1. If the subscription is current (Expired—code
>   = N):
>
>   a. Print a mailing label for the subscriber.
>   b. Add 1 to the Labels—printed count.
>
>   2. If the subscription has expired (Expired—code
>   = Y):
>
>   a. Do not print a mailing label.
>   b. Add 1 to the Expired—subscription count.

C. After all the input charge account records have
    been processed, the program should print the
    following total fields:

>   1. The Labels—printed count
>   2. The Expired—subscription count

Figure 6.1.   Programming specifications: Subscriber mailing labels program

1. The theoretical basis for structured programming
2. The identification of the harmful effects of the GO TO statement
3. The application of structured programming theory to a commercial data
    processing application
4. The adoption of structured programming concepts by the commercial data
    processing community

The Theoretical Basis for Structured Programming

In 1964, two mathematicians, Corrado Bohm and Guiseppe Jacopini, presented a paper at the International Colloquium on Algebraic Linguistics and Automata Theory in Israel. Bohm and Jacopini presented proof that any program logic—regardless of complexity — can be expressed by sequential processes and two control structures.

The concepts originally presented by Bohm and Jacopini have been developed and can be termed the *structure theorem*. According to the struc-

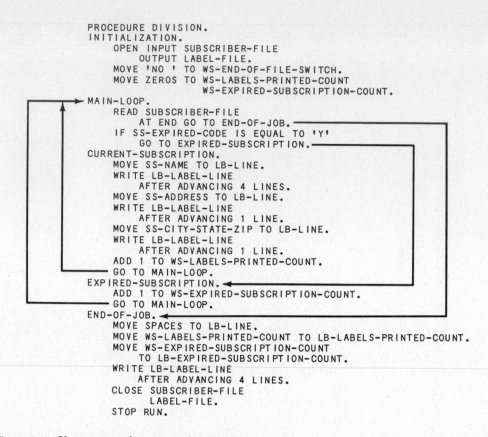

```
                              PROCEDURE DIVISION.
                              INITIALIZATION.
                                  OPEN INPUT SUBSCRIBER-FILE
                                       OUTPUT LABEL-FILE.
                                  MOVE 'NO ' TO WS-END-OF-FILE-SWITCH.
                                  MOVE ZEROS TO WS-LABELS-PRINTED-COUNT
                                                WS-EXPIRED-SUBSCRIPTION-COUNT.
                              MAIN-LOOP.
                                  READ SUBSCRIBER-FILE
                                      AT END GO TO END-OF-JOB.
                                  IF SS-EXPIRED-CODE IS EQUAL TO 'Y'
                                      GO TO EXPIRED-SUBSCRIPTION.
                              CURRENT-SUBSCRIPTION.
                                  MOVE SS-NAME TO LB-LINE.
                                  WRITE LB-LABEL-LINE
                                      AFTER ADVANCING 4 LINES.
                                  MOVE SS-ADDRESS TO LB-LINE.
                                  WRITE LB-LABEL-LINE
                                      AFTER ADVANCING 1 LINE.
                                  MOVE SS-CITY-STATE-ZIP TO LB-LINE.
                                  WRITE LB-LABEL-LINE
                                      AFTER ADVANCING 1 LINE.
                                  ADD 1 TO WS-LABELS-PRINTED-COUNT.
                                  GO TO MAIN-LOOP.
                              EXPIRED-SUBSCRIPTION.
                                  ADD 1 TO WS-EXPIRED-SUBSCRIPTION-COUNT.
                                  GO TO MAIN-LOOP.
                              END-OF-JOB.
                                  MOVE SPACES TO LB-LINE.
                                  MOVE WS-LABELS-PRINTED-COUNT TO LB-LABELS-PRINTED-COUNT.
                                  MOVE WS-EXPIRED-SUBSCRIPTION-COUNT
                                       TO LB-EXPIRED-SUBSCRIPTION-COUNT.
                                  WRITE LB-LABEL-LINE
                                      AFTER ADVANCING 4 LINES.
                                  CLOSE SUBSCRIBER-FILE
                                        LABEL-FILE.
                                  STOP RUN.
```

Figure 6.2. Unstructured version of LABELS program

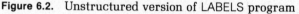

```
*
*
*
PROCEDURE DIVISION.
*
*
000-PRINT-MAILING-LABELS.
*
    OPEN INPUT SUBSCRIBER-FILE
         OUTPUT LABEL-FILE.
    PERFORM 100-INITIALIZE-VARIABLE-FIELDS.
    PERFORM 800-READ-SUBSCRIBER-RECORD.
    PERFORM 200-PROCESS-SUBSCRIBER-RECORD
        UNTIL WS-END-OF-FILE-SWITCH IS EQUAL TO 'YES'.
    PERFORM 700-PRINT-TOTAL-LINE.
    CLOSE SUBSCRIBER-FILE
          LABEL-FILE.
    STOP RUN.
*
*
100-INITIALIZE-VARIABLE-FIELDS.
*
    MOVE 'NO ' TO WS-END-OF-FILE-SWITCH.
    MOVE ZEROS TO WS-LABELS-PRINTED-COUNT
                  WS-EXPIRED-SUBSCRIPTION-COUNT.
*
*
200-PROCESS-SUBSCRIBER-RECORD.
*
    IF SS-EXPIRED-CODE IS EQUAL TO 'Y'
        ADD 1 TO WS-EXPIRED-SUBSCRIPTION-COUNT
    ELSE
        MOVE SS-NAME TO LB-LINE
        PERFORM 880-WRITE-LABEL-TOP-LINE
        MOVE SS-ADDRESS TO LB-LINE
        PERFORM 890-WRITE-LABEL-LINE
        MOVE SS-CITY-STATE-ZIP TO LB-LINE
        PERFORM 890-WRITE-LABEL-LINE
        ADD 1 TO WS-LABELS-PRINTED-COUNT.
    PERFORM 800-READ-SUBSCRIBER-RECORD.
```

```
*
*
700-PRINT-TOTAL-LINE.
*
    MOVE SPACES TO LB-LINE.
    MOVE WS-LABELS-PRINTED-COUNT TO LB-LABELS-PRINTED-COUNT.
    MOVE WS-EXPIRED-SUBSCRIPTION-COUNT
         TO LB-EXPIRED-SUBSCRIPTION-COUNT.
    PERFORM 880-WRITE-LABEL-TOP-LINE.
*
*
800-READ-SUBSCRIBER-RECORD.
*
    READ SUBSCRIBER-FILE
        AT END MOVE 'YES' TO WS-END-OF-FILE-SWITCH.
*
*
880-WRITE-LABEL-TOP-LINE.
*
    WRITE LB-LABEL-LINE
        AFTER ADVANCING 4 LINES.
*
*
890-WRITE-LABEL-LINE.
*
    WRITE LB-LABEL-LINE
        AFTER ADVANCING 1 LINE.
```

Figure 6.3. Structured version of LABELS program

Format:

GO TO procedure-name

Example:

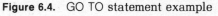

SEQUENCE		C O N T	A	B	COBOL STATEMENT	IDENTIFICATION

```
         GO TO MAIN-LOOP.
```

Figure 6.4. GO TO statement example

ture theorem, it is possible to write any computer program by using one or more of three basic control structures: sequence, selection, and iteration. Figure 6.5 illustrates these three structures.

Sequence structure

The *sequence* structure is the most basic of the three; it simply means that statements are executed in sequence, one after another, as they are coded. Figure 6.6 presents a COBOL example of the sequence structure.

Selection structure

This is sometimes termed the if-then-else structure. The *selection* structure presents a condition and two choices of actions depending upon whether the condition is true or false. In COBOL, the selection structure is achieved by use of the IF statement, which will be introduced in the next chapter and covered in detail in Chapter 8. A COBOL example of the selection structure is shown in Figure 6.7.

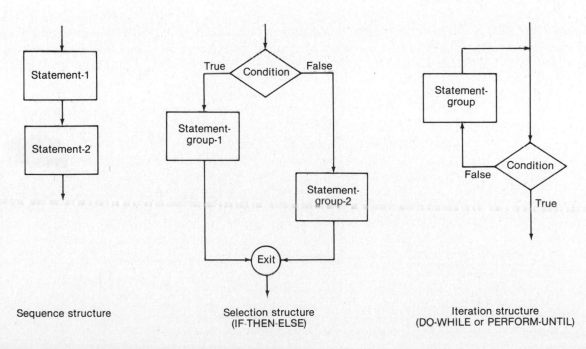

Sequence structure

Selection structure
(IF-THEN-ELSE)

Iteration structure
(DO-WHILE or PERFORM-UNTIL)

Figure 6.5. Structure theorem basic control structures

Iteration structure

Do-while is a name often given to the *iteration* structure since certain programming languages use those words to provide this structure. The iteration structure causes a set of instructions to be executed repeatedly as long as a given condition exists. COBOL does not have a statement that provides true do-while processing. However, the PERFORM/UNTIL statement that we have been using is related. There are two slight differences between the strict do-while interpretation of the iteration structure and the action of PERFORM/UNTIL.

First, the PERFORM/UNTIL statement causes a set of instructions to be repeatedly executed until—rather than *while*—a given condition exists. Second, the COBOL PERFORM/UNTIL statement tests the condition *before* instead of *after* the set of instructions is executed. Figure 6.8 presents a COBOL example of the iteration structure.

Harmful Effects of the GO TO Statement

Bohm and Jacopini's original paper was published in Italian. In 1966, an English translation was published in the United States. Due to its theoretical nature and complexity, the paper did not receive a great deal of attention.

In 1968, however, there was a letter to the editor of *Communications of ACM*, a publication of the Association for Computing Machinery, that did attract a good share of attention. This letter, titled "GO TO Statement Considered Harmful" was written by Professor Edsger W. Dijkstra of the Technological University at Eindhoven, Netherlands. Professor Dijkstra wrote: "For a number of years I have been familiar with the observation that the quality of programmers is a decreasing function of the density of GO TO statements in the programs they produce." He further suggested in this letter that "the GO TO statement should be abolished from all higher level programming languages . . . it is an invitation to make a mess of one's program."

At the time this letter was written, programmers felt no disdain for the GO TO statement. Most could not even conceive of a program written without it. Of course, the work of Bohm and Jacopini showed that it could be done. Thus, by 1968, the theoretical basis for structured programming was established and a spark of interest was ignited in the programming community.

A Commercial Application of Structured Programming Theory

Structured programming concepts, together with certain other methods—often termed *improved programming techniques*—were used by IBM Corporation on the "New York Times Project" from 1969 to 1971. This project is generally considered to be the first time structured programming concepts were applied to a large-scale data processing application.

In this project, the productivity and accuracy of programmers were measured so that the usefulness of various structured programming techniques could be evaluated. Programmers posted productivity figures from four to six times higher than those of an average programmer. The error—or program bug—rate was a phenomenally low .0004 per line of coding.

As the success of the structured programming techniques in the New York Times Project began surfacing within IBM and in written accounts, members of the data processing community began to show interest. By the mid-seventies, structured programming practices began emerging at many commercial data processing installations.

What "Structured Programming" Means Today

One of the most controversial and immediately identifiable aspects of the structure theorem is the concept that programs can be written without the use of GO TO statements. Thus, programmers and students often incorrectly

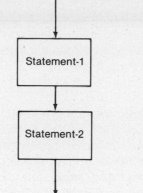

```
MOVE 'NO ' TO WS-END-OF-FILE-SWITCH.



MOVE ZEROS TO WS-LABELS-PRINTED-COUNT
             WS-EXPIRED-SUBSCRIPTION-COUNT.
```

Figure 6.6. Sequence structure and COBOL example

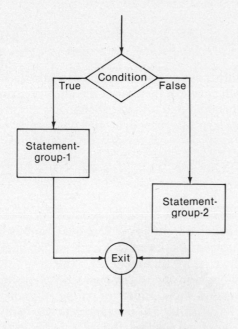

```
IF SS-EXPIRED-CODE IS EQUAL TO 'Y'


    ADD 1 TO WS-EXPIRED-SUBSCRIPTION-COUNT


ELSE

    MOVE SS-NAME TO LB-LINE
    PERFORM 880-WRITE-LABEL-TOP-LINE
    MOVE SS-ADDRESS TO LB-LINE
    PERFORM 890-WRITE-LABEL-LINE
    MOVE SS-CITY-STATE-ZIP TO LB-LINE
    PERFORM 890-WRITE-LABEL-LINE
    ADD 1 TO WS-LABELS-PRINTED-COUNT.
```

Figure 6.7. Selection structure and COBOL example

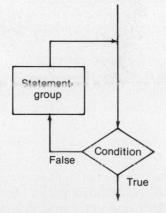

```
PERFORM 200-PROCESS-SUBSCRIBER-RECORD



UNTIL WS-END-OF-FILE-SWITCH IS EQUAL TO 'YES'.
```

Figure 6.8. Iteration structure and COBOL example

equate structured programming with "GO-TO-less" coding. The term structured programming actually means much more than that today. Studies have indicated that a typical programmer spends not even a quarter of the time on the job actually programming—that is, writing code. Most of the time is spent designing, documenting, and testing programs. In addition, programmers must attend meetings and do certain clerical tasks such as searching for and filing away program listings and the like.

So, a collection of improved programming techniques (IPT)—also known as *programmer productivity techniques* (PPT)—have evolved along with the application of the structure theorem to commercial programming in business and industry. Today, when members of the data processing community talk about structured programming, they generally mean not only the programming aspects, but also the structured design, documentation, testing, and organization precepts.

Structured programming, then, may be defined as a program design, documentation, coding, and testing methodology that utilizes techniques in program development to create proper, reliable, and maintainable software products on a cost-effective basis.

Survey of Structured Design and Documentation Techniques

Many techniques have been advanced to aid in the design and documentation of structured programs. We will survey a number of the more commonly known methods. An example of each technique will be shown for the LABELS program. Some of the techniques are addressed to overall program structure, whereas others are intended for the expression of more detailed program processing.

Overall Program Structure Design and Documentation Techniques

Data flow diagrams

The use of the data flow diagram for structural design and documentation has been advanced by Edward Yourdon and others within his organization. It can be used not only for individual program design but also for the design of complete systems. Alternately known as a "bubble chart," the data flow diagram (DFD) resembles a system flowchart in that it is primarily concerned with the flow of data through a program or system. However, rather than using special system flowcharting symbols to differentiate physical storage media, clerical activities, programs, subprograms, and the like, the DFD simply uses a circle—or bubble—symbol to represent all data flow steps.

The purpose of the DFD is to show only the logical flow of data, without regard for (1) the physical form (disk, tape, main storage, and so on) that the data will take; (2) the resources that will operate upon the data (people, computers, programs, and so on); or (3) the control logic (sequence, selection, or iteration) that will apply to the data. Thus, when used as a structured design technique, the DFD is used as a first step to proper design.

Although data flow diagrams are not ordinarily used with small, straightforward programs, an illustrative example for the LABELS program is shown in Figure 6.9. Use of the DFD is usually limited to the design of complete systems and large complex programs.

HIPO

In the early seventies, IBM Corporation introduced a program design and documentation technique called HIPO. HIPO is an acronym for *Hierarchy* plus *Input-Process-Output.* The objectives of HIPO are to (1) provide a structure by which the functions of a system can be understood, (2) state the functions to be

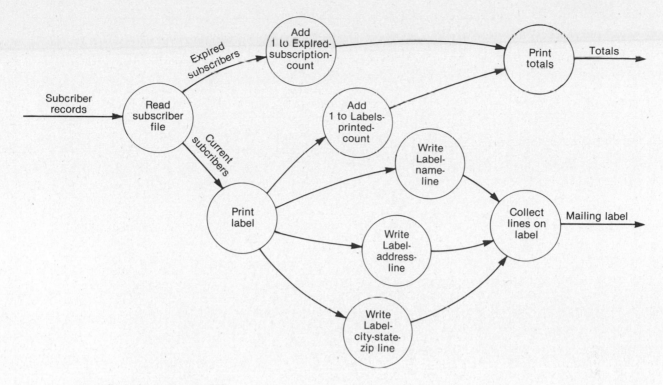

Figure 6.9. Data flow diagram example

accomplished by a program, and (3) provide a visual description of the inputs to be used and the outputs to be produced by each program function.

Typical HIPO documentation contains three kinds of diagrams: a visual table of contents (often abbreviated and called VTOC), overview diagrams, and detail diagrams. Figure 6.10 depicts and indicates relationships between these three diagrams. A partial HIPO documentation package for the LABELS program is shown in Figure 6.11.

HIPO is well suited to the design and development of structured programs because of its top-down modular approach. As a documentation technique, it is strong because it offers three levels of documentation, each of which might be used by different individuals. A manager might require only an overview of the system and thus consult the VTOC and overview diagrams. A programmer needing specific details would probably want information contained on the detail diagrams.

Although HIPO shows program function, it does not indicate detailed program organization and logic as flowcharts do. So, HIPO is often supplemented by pseudocode for program organization and for logic design and documentation.

Structure charts

We have been using structure charts in this text. They graphically show each module (COBOL procedure) required by the program, its hierarchical level, and its relationship to the other program modules. In appearance, a structure chart looks very much like the familiar organization chart that shows the hierarchy of positions within an organization. A structure chart is also referred to as a hierarchy chart or a visual table of contents (VTOC). These terms stem from HIPO, where the equivalent of a structure chart is the highest-level documentation item. A structure chart for the LABELS program is shown as Figure 6.12.

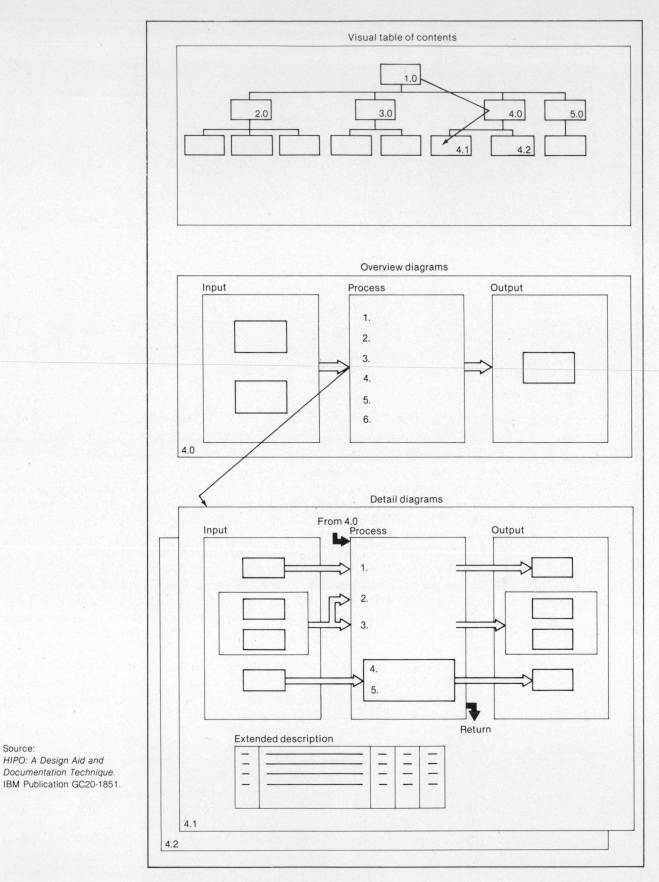

Figure 6.10. HIPO diagram relationships

Source:
*HIPO: A Design Aid and
Documentation Technique.*
IBM Publication GC20-1851.

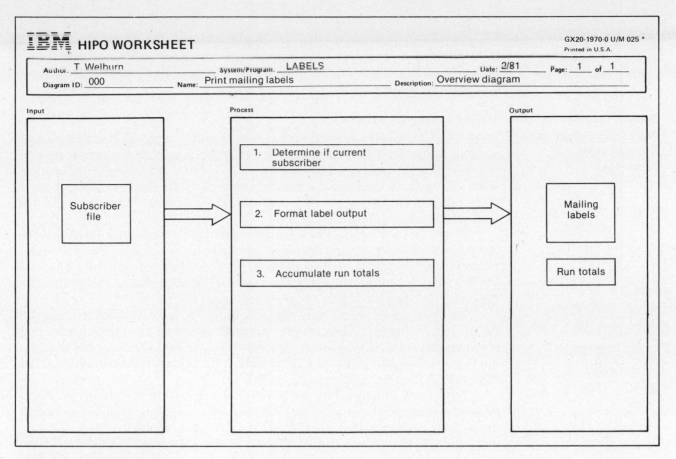

Figure 6.11. HIPO example

STRUCTURE CHART

Program name: MAILING LABELS   Program ID: LABELS

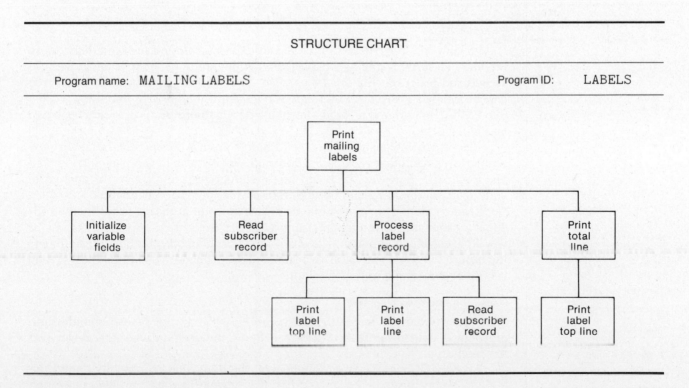

Figure 6.12. Structure chart example

Recognize that a structure chart does not show the sequence in which modules will be executed nor the conditional decisions that will cause modules to be performed or skipped. The purpose of a structure chart is to give a concise overview of module hierarchy and structure. It also serves as a table of contents to module location within a program.

Detailed Program Processing Design and Documentation Techniques

Traditional program flowcharts

It was recognized early in programmers' work with computers that there was a need to design and document computer operations so that a data processing function could be converted to computer instructions. A number of techniques were introduced and utilized: mathematical formulas, written textual material, process charts, decision tables, and flowcharts. Flowcharts quickly became the most widely used technique.

The program flowchart is a graphic technique specifically developed for the purpose of designing and documenting computer programs. One of the main reasons for the popularity of flowcharts is that they are graphic. That old adage, "a picture is worth a thousand words," applies also to the ability of a flowchart to convey complex program logic.

We have been using, and will continue to use, traditional program flowcharts in this text. Because they are understood by most data processing students and because they are "pictures," they will probably help you to grasp the logic of programs presented in this text. A traditional program flowchart of the LABELS program appears in Figure 6.13.

Traditional program flowcharts are often shunned in structured programming environments, however. Their drawbacks are: (1) they take a long time to draw; (2) once drawn, they are difficult and time-consuming to change; (3) they are bulky—their symbols and flowlines consume a significant amount of page space to show the program logic; and (4) frequently they do not depict selection or iteration logic in a manner that can be directly translated to structured COBOL code.

Pseudocode

Pseudocode has been used in this text to express detailed program logic in an English-like form. It has become a popular technique because it lends itself to structured programming documentation. That is, the three control structures can be easily represented by relative placement, indentation, and key words, like PERFORM, IF, and so forth. Pseudocode for the LABELS program is shown as Figure 6.14.

There are various pseudocode "dialects" in use. Some tend to be very exacting in usage; others are more informal. Regardless of the pseudocode conventions used, however, it should be (1) well-organized, (2) precise enough to code from, and (3) reasonably understandable to nonprogrammers.

One of the primary advantages of pseudocode is that it is well suited for speedy preparation and modification with the use of text-editing programs or word-processing equipment. However, since pseudocode can be very similar to the actual COBOL code, many experienced programmers complain that writing it is time-consuming and redundant.

Nassi-Shneiderman diagrams

Sometimes referred to as a structured flowchart, the Nassi-Shneiderman diagram is named for Isaac Nassi and Ben Shneiderman who first described the technique.

Like traditional program flowcharts, the diagrams graphically depict the logic to be performed. Unlike traditional program flowcharts, they contain no flowlines or arrowheads and do not use various symbol shapes to represent dif-

Program name: MAILING LABELS   Program ID: LABELS

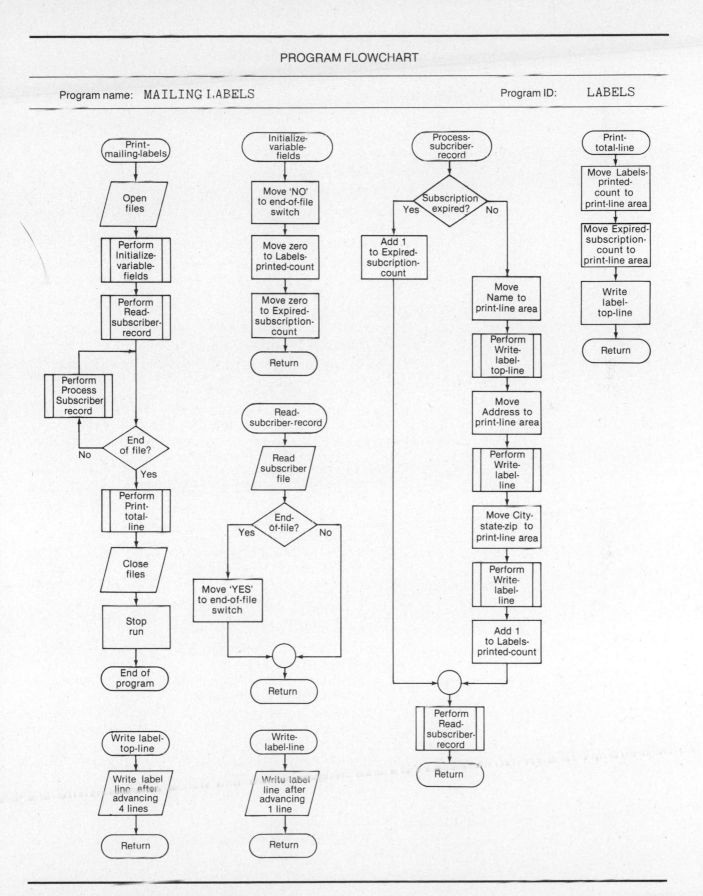

Figure 6.13. Program flowchart example

PSEUDOCODE

Program name: MAILING LABELS   Program ID: LABELS

Print—mailing—labels module

1. Open the files.
2. Perform Initialize—variable—fields module.
3. Perform Read—subscriber—record module.
4. Perform Process—subscriber—record module until no more records.
5. Perform Print—total—line module.
6. Close the files.
7. Stop the run.

Initialize—variable—fields module

1. Set the end—of—file indicator to "No".
2. Set the Labels—printed—count to zero.
3. Set the Expired—subscription—count to zero.

Process—subscriber—record module

1. If the Expired—code field is equal to "Y"
   Add 1 to the Expired—subscription—count.
2. If the Expired—code field is not equal to "Y"
   Move the Subscriber—name to the Label—line
   Perform the Write—label—top—line module
   Move the Subscriber—address to the Label—line
   Perform the Write—label—line module
   Move the Subscriber—city—state—zip to the Label—line
   Perform the Write—label—line module
   Add 1 to the Labels—printed—count.
3. Perform the Read—subscriber—record module.

Print—total—line module

1. Clear the output Label—line area.
2. Move the Labels—printed—count to the output Label—line area.
3. Move the Expired—subscription—count to the output Label—line area.
4. Perform the Write—label—top—line module.

Read—subscriber—record module

1. Read a record from the subscriber file.
2. If there are no more records
   Move "Yes" to the end—of—file—switch.

Write—label—top—line module

1. Write the Label—line after skipping to the next label.

Write—label—line module

1. Write the Label—line after single—spacing.

Figure 6.14. Pseudocode example

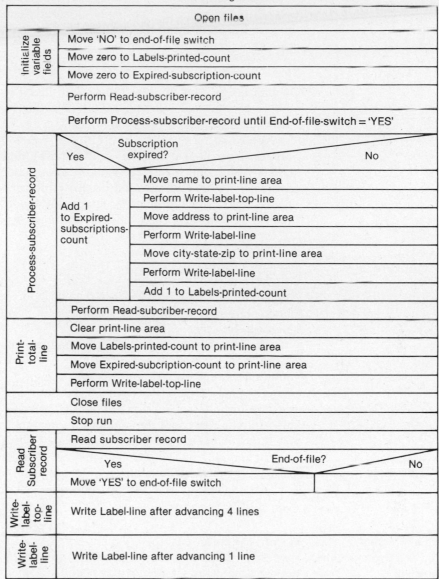

Print mailing labels

Open files		
Initialize variable fields	Move 'NO' to end-of-file switch	
	Move zero to Labels-printed-count	
	Move zero to Expired-subscription-count	
Perform Read-subscriber-record		
Perform Process-subscriber-record until End-of-file-switch = 'YES'		

Process-subscriber-record
Subscription expired?
Yes / No

Add 1 to Expired-subscriptions-count	Move name to print-line area
	Perform Write-label-top-line
	Move address to print-line area
	Perform Write-label-line
	Move city-state-zip to print-line area
	Perform Write-label-line
	Add 1 to Labels-printed-count
Perform Read-subcriber-record	

Print-total-line	Clear print-line area
	Move Labels-printed-count to print-line area
	Move Expired-subcription-count to print-line area
	Perform Write-label-top-line
Close files	
Stop run	

Read Subscriber record
Read subscriber record
End-of-file?
Yes / No
Move 'YES' to end-of-file switch

Write-label-top-line
Write Label-line after advancing 4 lines

Write-label-line
Write Label-line after advancing 1 line

Figure 6.15. Nassi-Shneiderman diagram example

ferent program functions (such as input/output, terminal, and so on). They are called structured flowcharts because they can depict only the three control structures: sequence, selection, and iteration. They have no provisions for the depiction of a GO TO statement. A Nassi-Shneiderman diagram for the LABELS program is shown in Figure 6.15.

Notice that each module is diagrammed as a series of rectangles. The rectangles can be of any size appropriate to depict the necessary logic. Module names are indicated within vertical rectangles that define the boundaries of the module. Conditions are depicted by inverted triangles drawn within a rectangle. The alternate logic paths are separated by vertical lines.

In comparison to traditional program flowcharts, Nassi-Shneiderman diagrams have the advantage of depicting program logic in a graphic form that can be directly translated to structured COBOL code. In addition, they are more compact, easier to draw, and allow for variable rectangle size to accomodate logic descriptions of different lengths. However, they are still difficult to modify easily and do not lend themselves to preparation with the aid of text-editing or word-processing equipment. Some detractors, not appreciating the graphic qualities of the method, dismiss the diagrams as "pseudocode with lines and rectangles around it."

Chapin charts

Originated by Ned Chapin, the Chapin chart is a structured flowchart very similar to the Nassi-Shneiderman diagram. Figure 6.16 presents a Chapin chart for the LABELS program logic.

What differentiates the Chapin chart in appearance from Nassi-Shneiderman diagrams is that module name identifiers and called modules are shown within the terminal symbol. Also, conditions are uniformly depicted within 45-degree triangles that identify the respective logic path.

As a program design and documentation technique, Chapin charts provide benefits and disadvantages similar to those of Nassi-Shneiderman diagrams.

Warnier diagrams

Named for Jean-Dominique Warnier, the Warnier diagram is a series of brackets used with a few other symbols to depict program logic. It can be thought of as a structure chart laid on its side. However, whereas the structure chart shows hierarchical relationships but not process flow, the Warnier diagram indicates both.

Warnier diagrams are often termed Warnier-Orr diagrams in recognition of the work done by Kenneth Orr in adapting and promulgating use of the technique in structured analysis and design.

The process flow of a Warnier diagram is presumed to be from left to right and top to bottom. The symbols in parentheses below the module and action descriptions represent the number of times that each module or action is to be executed. A horizontal line drawn above a description indicates a "not" or negated condition. The plus sign in a circle indicates that adjacent modules or actions are mutually exclusive; only one of the set will be executed.

An example of a Warnier diagram for the LABELS program is shown in Figure 6.17.

Recap of Program Design and Documentation Techniques

As you can infer from the number and range of techniques surveyed, there is a diversity of opinion over which method should be used. Most organizations choose a particular technique or combination of techniques. In this text, structure charts are used to indicate overall program organization and module definition. Traditional program flowcharts and pseudocode are both presented to show detailed processing logic. The former is presented because many students are already familiar and feel comfortable with flowcharts; the latter because it does a good job of expressing structured logic.

Probably less important than the specific design and documentation technique chosen is the process of taking two "cuts" at the program design. It is common with many human activities to feel that one could do a better job if it could be done all over again. Thus, the use of a program design technique provides the first "dry run" at tackling the problem; the actual program coding becomes the improved refinement. Of course, the same objective could perhaps be obtained by using none of the design techniques presented and merely coding the program twice. The problem with this approach is that the second coding would probably never happen, due to time requirements, schedule pressures, or just plain human laziness. By requiring submission of an initial design in a medium different than actual program code, enforcement of the two-step approach is simplified for most organizations. Of course, there are also many analytical benefits to be gained from each design technique.

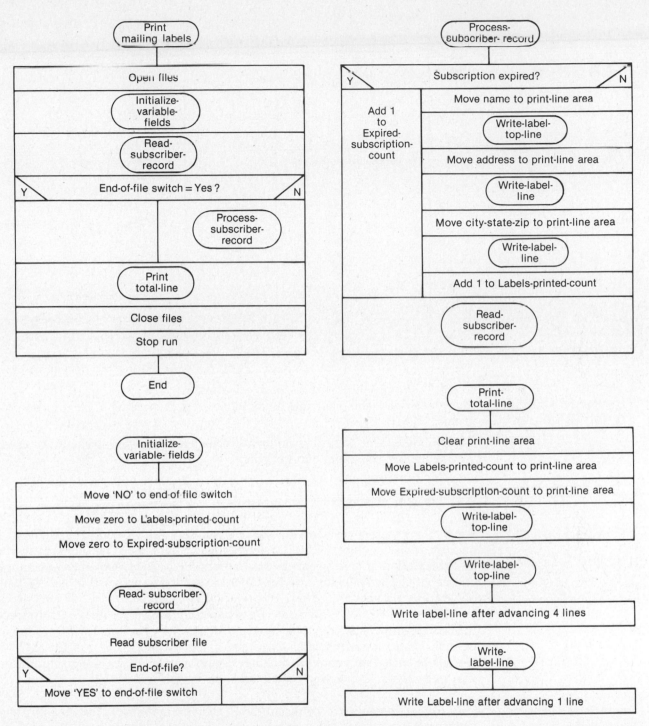

Figure 6.16. Chapin chart example

As documentation techniques, all must be maintained and updated concurrent with changes to the actual program code. This requirement is often preached but rarely practiced unless there are organizational standards and checkpoints that make such updating mandatory.

In the next chapter, as the programs become more complex—and as you become more familiar with structured COBOL coding—the structure chart preparation techniques will be refined and additional program design considerations will be introduced.

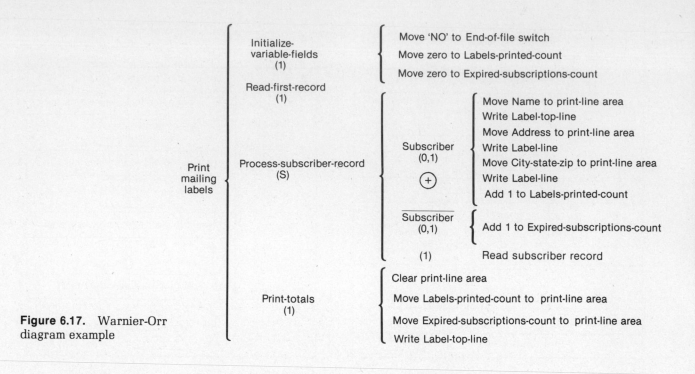

Figure 6.17. Warnier-Orr diagram example

Structured COBOL Coding Principles

There are two basic principles to be followed in the coding of structured programs:

1. Only the three control structures of the structure theorem should be used: sequence, selection, and iteration.
2. Each program module should have only one entry and one exit point.

Both these principles will be discussed.

Control Structures

For the programs covered in the first five chapters, we have used the sequence and iteration structures. (PERFORM/UNTIL is an iteration structure statement; the remainder of our program statements have been sequence structure statements.) The selection structure IF statement will be used in subsequent chapters.

Since the GO TO statement is not represented within the control structures, it generally should not be used in a structured program. However, due to COBOL syntax requirements, there are a few situations where the GO TO statement might be required. Further, some organizations adopt standards that permit GO TO usage in restricted situations.

Single Entry Point and Single Exit Point for Each Module

If GO TO statements are not used and PERFORM statements naming only one procedure-name are used, a program will be in compliance with this convention. That is, each module will be entered before the first statement and exited after the last statement of the module. Again, though, some organizations have standards that may permit relaxation of this rule.

Structured COBOL Coding Conventions

Module forming conventions

A program *module* may be defined as a contiguous group of statements that can be referred to as a unit. COBOL provides four ways of forming a module: as a single paragraph, as two or more contiguous paragraphs, as a single section, and as two or more contiguous sections. Each method will be discussed.

Format:

PERFORM procedure-name-1 $\left[\begin{Bmatrix} \underline{\text{THROUGH}} \\ \underline{\text{THRU}} \end{Bmatrix} \text{procedure-name-2} \right]$

Example:

SEQUENCE				COBOL STATEMENT	IDENTIFICATION
(PAGE) (SERIAL)	CONT	A	B		

```
PERFORM PRINT-NAME-LINE
    THRU PRINT-CITY-STATE-ZIP-LINE.
```

Figure 6.18. PERFORM/THRU statement example

Single-paragraph modules

In this text, we have been using and will continue to use, where possible, single-paragraph modules. Single-paragraph modules provide total compliance with the structured programming principle of the single entry point and single exit point. The advantages of single-paragraph modules can perhaps best be identified by discussing the disadvantages of the alternative methods.

Multiple-paragraph modules

To perform modules composed of more than one paragraph, the THRU option of the PERFORM verb is normally used. Its format and an example are shown in Figure 6.18. When PERFORM/THRU is specified, program control is transferred to the first procedure-name specified and is returned after execution of the last statement of the second procedure-name.

Prior to the adoption of structured programming concepts, the PERFORM/THRU statement was very popular. Indeed, many organizations recommended that the simple one-paragraph PERFORM statement never be used; the PERFORM/THRU statement was preferred. To allow the PERFORM/THRU to be used with what are actually single-paragraph modules, the programmer establishes a dummy last paragraph, as shown in Figure 6.19. The reserved word EXIT is a dummy statement that provides a null entry for the second paragraph. When EXIT is used in a COBOL program, it must be the only statement within the paragraph.

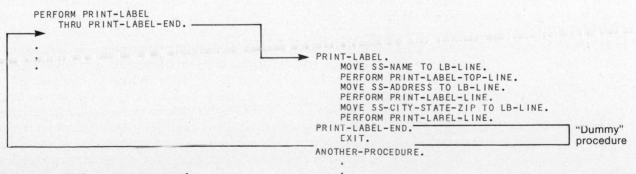

Figure 6.19. EXIT statement example

The reason that the PERFORM/THRU statement was recommended is that, if another paragraph-name is later required for a module, it can be added without having to change the PERFORM statement from a one-paragraph PER-FORM to a PERFORM/THRU. (Figure 6.20 shows a PERFORM/THRU statement with a multiple-paragraph module.) The main reason that another paragraph might be required, however, was that GO TO statements were used in the program. Hence, with structured programming, the PERFORM/THRU option provides few benefits while its disadvantages remain significant.

The main disadvantage is that, when a new module is added, it is often difficult to determine where PERFORM/THRU boundaries are located. Thus, a nonapplicable module added to a program might be unexpectedly executed by an unnoticed PERFORM/THRU statement. A second disadvantage, related to the first, is that the physical placement of modules in relationship to one another becomes significant. On the other hand, by using single-paragraph modules and a mainline control module specified as the first paragraph of the PROCEDURE DIVISION, the physical placement of modules (other than the mainline) does not affect program logic.

Single-section modules

One or more paragraphs may be organized into sections. An example is shown in Figure 6.21. A section can be thought of as a "super-paragraph"; a section-name may be referenced in a PERFORM statement just like a paragraph-name. When a section-name is specified as the procedure-name of a PERFORM statement, program control is transferred to the first statement of the section and continues through all paragraphs of that section. Control returns immediately prior to the next section-name (or, for the last section of the program, after the last source statement of the program).

The disadvantage of using sections is that not only can the section as a whole be referenced, but individual paragraphs within the sections can be performed. This situation can cause programming difficulties similar to the PER-FORM/THRU problems and is similarly in conflict with the convention of single entry point and single exit point.

According to COBOL syntax, however, there are three situations in which sections must be used: (1) when the SORT or MERGE verbs with input or output procedures are specified, (2) when program segmentation is called for, and (3) with declaratives. (The SORT and MERGE verbs will be discussed in Chapter 11; program segmentation and declaratives are not covered in this text.) Also, when the case structure is used in a COBOL program, it is appropriate to use sections. The case structure is mentioned in Appendix A.

Multiple-section modules

Just as two or more paragraphs may be performed by the PERFORM/THRU statement, two or more sections may also be specified as the procedure-names. The same disadvantages apply. Figure 6.22 provides an example of a multiple-section module.

READ/WRITE Module Conventions

It is a good idea to establish one READ module and/or one WRITE module for each file. Program logic and debugging are simplified when a common input or output operation for a file is handled in one place. When records are read or written, certain related functions frequently must be provided for: counting records, counting lines, testing for end-of-file, and so forth. Rather than writing separate READ or WRITE statements in-line, coding is more efficient and easier to debug when a separate module is established and performed whenever the appropriate input-output operation is required. For straightforwardness, in previous programs of this text, we have written two separate in-line READ

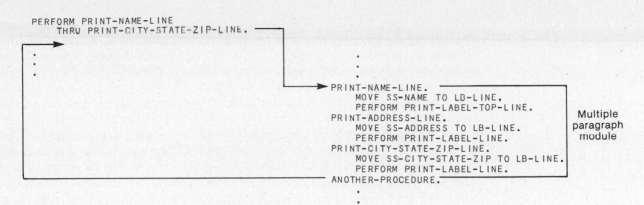

```
PERFORM PRINT-NAME-LINE
    THRU PRINT-CITY-STATE-ZIP-LINE.
                .
                .
                .
                                    PRINT-NAME-LINE.
                                        MOVE SS-NAME TO LB-LINE.
                                        PERFORM PRINT-LABEL-TOP-LINE.
                                    PRINT-ADDRESS-LINE.
                                        MOVE SS-ADDRESS TO LB-LINE.
                                        PERFORM PRINT-LABEL-LINE.
                                    PRINT-CITY-STATE-ZIP-LINE.
                                        MOVE SS-CITY-STATE-ZIP TO LB-LINE.
                                        PERFORM PRINT-LABEL-LINE.
                                    ANOTHER-PROCEDURE.
                                        .
                                        .
```

Multiple
paragraph
module

Figure 6.20. Multiple paragraph module example

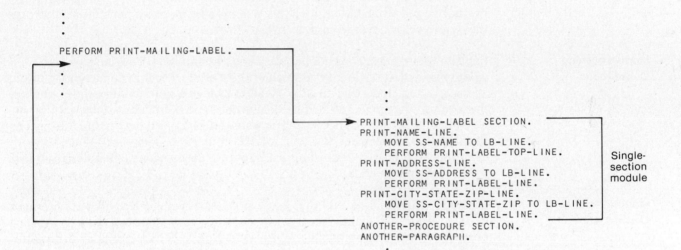

```
            .
            .
            .
PERFORM PRINT-MAILING-LABEL.
            .
            .
            .
                                    .
                                    .
                                    .
                                    PRINT-MAILING-LABEL SECTION.
                                    PRINT-NAME-LINE.
                                        MOVE SS-NAME TO LB-LINE.
                                        PERFORM PRINT-LABEL-TOP-LINE.
                                    PRINT-ADDRESS-LINE.
                                        MOVE SS-ADDRESS TO LB-LINE.
                                        PERFORM PRINT-LABEL-LINE.
                                    PRINT-CITY-STATE-ZIP-LINE.
                                        MOVE SS-CITY-STATE-ZIP TO LB-LINE.
                                        PERFORM PRINT-LABEL-LINE.
                                    ANOTHER-PROCEDURE SECTION.
                                    ANOTHER-PARAGRAPH.
                                        .
                                        .
```

Single-
section
module

Figure 6.21. Single section module example

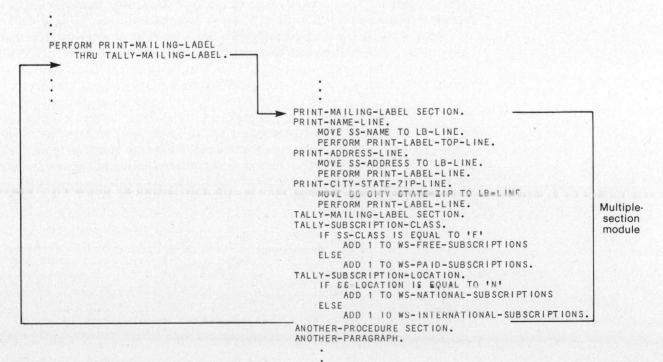

```
            .
            .
            .
PERFORM PRINT-MAILING-LABEL
    THRU TALLY-MAILING-LABEL.
            .
            .
            .
                                    .
                                    .
                                    .
                                    PRINT-MAILING-LABEL SECTION.
                                    PRINT-NAME-LINE.
                                        MOVE SS-NAME TO LB-LINE.
                                        PERFORM PRINT-LABEL-TOP-LINE.
                                    PRINT-ADDRESS-LINE.
                                        MOVE SS-ADDRESS TO LB-LINE.
                                        PERFORM PRINT-LABEL-LINE.
                                    PRINT-CITY-STATE-ZIP-LINE.
                                        MOVE SS-CITY-STATE-ZIP TO LB-LINE.
                                        PERFORM PRINT-LABEL-LINE.
                                    TALLY-MAILING-LABEL SECTION.
                                    TALLY-SUBSCRIPTION-CLASS.
                                        IF SS-CLASS IS EQUAL TO 'F'
                                            ADD 1 TO WS-FREE-SUBSCRIPTIONS
                                        ELSE
                                            ADD 1 TO WS-PAID-SUBSCRIPTIONS.
                                    TALLY-SUBSCRIPTION-LOCATION.
                                        IF SS-LOCATION IS EQUAL TO 'N'
                                            ADD 1 TO WS-NATIONAL-SUBSCRIPTIONS
                                        ELSE
                                            ADD 1 TO WS-INTERNATIONAL-SUBSCRIPTIONS.
                                    ANOTHER-PROCEDURE SECTION.
                                    ANOTHER-PARAGRAPH.
                                        .
                                        .
```

Multiple-
section
module

Figure 6.22. Multiple section module example

statements: one for the first record and one for all subsequent records. From now on, separate modules will be established and performed whenever an input/output operation is required for a file. (The structured version of the LABELS program shown in Figure 6.3 provides an example.)

There are certain cases where more than one WRITE module must be provided for a file. For instance, two WRITE modules are needed when a report file requires one WRITE statement to skip to the top of the next page to print report headings and another WRITE statement for normal line spacing in the body of the report. As we will cover in the next chapter, the statement to skip to the next page uses either the ADVANCING PAGE or the mnemonic-name option whereas the line-spacing statement uses the ADVANCING integer or identifier options. So, for report files, two WRITE modules are normally required.

Another situation where more than one WRITE module may be required is when variable-length records are written. Variable-length records are not used very often with COBOL programs (situations where they would be appropriate are usually handled by data base management systems now), and thus they will not be covered in this text.

Module Naming Conventions

Each program module should handle a specific function. The name chosen for a module should describe the function of the module. Module names that contain a single verb followed by an object tend to describe functional modules and are thus an aid to functional module design. So that the module name can be accommodated within the 30-character user-defined word maximum, it is recommended that, whenever possible, module names be composed of a one-word verb followed by a two-word object. Figure 6.23 provides examples of appropriate functional module names.

Module Numbering Conventions

Previous programs of this text have not used module numbers. For longer COBOL programs, though, module numbers are very helpful. Trying to locate a particular unnumbered module of an extensive program can pose difficulties similar to those encountered when trying to find a certain topic in a book without an index. Thus, module numbers can be used as a reference number to aid speedy location. For example, a three-digit sequence number can be assigned to each module-name and then the modules can be arranged in the program in ascending order according to this sequence number.

There are myriad module numbering systems that have been proposed. Some utilize three-digit numbers, others use four-digit numbers. Often a letter code is placed before the numbers to indicate the structure chart level (A = level-0, B = level-1, C = level-2, and so on). Sometimes decimal numbers are used; number 1.3.2 represents the second module subordinate to module 1.3, which in turn is the third module below block 1.0. (When this decimal numbering system is used, decimal points are usually expressed as hyphens in the COBOL program procedure-names; the decimal point cannot be used in the formation of user-defined words.) Some systems utilize significant numbers where certain types of modules are assigned specific number ranges; others use insignificant numbers.

INITIALIZE-VARIABLE-FIELDS
READ-INVENTORY-RECORD
PRINT-REPORT-HEADINGS
PRINT-TOTAL-LINE
WRITE-REPORT-LINE
VALIDATE-PRICE-FIELD

Figure 6.23. Module naming convention examples

Module number	Module function
000	Mainline
100-199	Initialization
200-699	General processing
700-799	End-of-program totals, statistics, and so on
800-849	Input (READ, ACCEPT)
850-869	General nonreport output (WRITE, REWRITE, DELETE, DISPLAY)
870-879	Report headings
880-889	Report top-line output (page skipping)
890-899	Report-line output (line spacing)
900-999	Inter-program communication

Figure 6.24. Module numbering convention examples

Generally, the use of numbers that reflect specific structure chart levels are cumbersome to use because structure chart placement for a module will sometimes change during program development or maintenance. Flexibility is increased, therefore, by not tying module numbers to structure chart levels so that the number need not be changed when placement changes.

Although specific number ranges for certain modules can also limit flexibility, it tends to retain commonality from one program to another and aids programmers in understanding the program structure. So, from this point in the text, the module numbering system described in Figure 6.24 will be used.

Structured Programming Development Aids

Chief Programmer Teams

A chief programmer team is often likened to a surgical team. The objective is to increase programmer productivity by assigning tasks to members that match their capabilities, training, experience, and specialties.

The chief programmer acts as team leader and is assisted by associate programmers, programmer trainees, librarians, administrators, technical writers, and secretaries. The number and range of personnel on a team will vary with the size of the project.

Structured Walkthroughs

A *structured walkthrough* is a group review of a programmer's work for the purpose of detecting errors or faulty design.

Structured walkthroughs can be conducted at various stages of the program development process; they can be conducted after programmer completion of program specifications, of the structure chart, of detailed design documentation, and of program testing.

Structured Testing

When programs are coded on a structured basis, it means that testing of the program can also be done on a structured basis. This is sometimes referred to as *top-down* or *stub* testing.

Since each module has a single entry and a single exit point, modules can be tested either one at a time or in a specific group of modules. Testing of top-level modules can begin before lower-level modules are completed.

To do top-down or stub testing, the programmer substitutes dummy modules consisting only of the procedure-name and the EXIT statement for the uncompleted or unincluded modules. This type of testing is of lesser value for smaller programs such as we are concerned with in this text. Structured testing offers considerable advantages for larger programs, however.

Regardless of whether or not structured testing is used, structured programs tend to have fewer bugs because the regimen of functional module design reduces program logic errors. Further, those bugs that do arise are usually easier to locate and correct.

Development Support Libraries

The purpose of a development support library is to keep a central library of program documentation, thereby reducing the clerical workload of the programmer. A development support library takes documentation out of the private domain of the programmer and makes it available for review by interested parties. It also facilitates management control of documentation.

Summary

The theoretical basis for structured programming was laid in 1964 by Bohm and Jacopini when they presented proof that any program logic can be expressed by using one or more of three basic control structures: sequence, selection, and iteration. This concept is termed the *structure theorem*. The *sequence structure* refers to statements that are executed in order, one after another. The *selection structure* (if-then-else) presents a condition and choices of action depending upon whether the condition is true or false. The *iteration structure* (do-while or perform-until) causes a set of instructions to be executed repeatedly as long as a given condition exists.

Publication of a letter by Dijkstra in 1968, titled "GO TO Statement Considered Harmful," attracted considerable attention in the programming community. This letter, together with proof of the structure theorem, led to a decline in use of the GO TO statement.

Along with other *improved programming techniques*, structured programming concepts were applied to a commercial application—the "New York Times Project"—from 1969 to 1971. The success of this application caused the data processing community to take note. By the mid-seventies, structured programming practices began emerging at many commercial data processing installations.

Today, the term *structured programming* may be defined as a program design, documentation, coding, and testing methodology that utilizes techniques in program development to create proper, reliable, and maintainable software products on a cost-effective basis.

Overall program structure design and documentation techniques include *data flow diagrams, HIPO,* and *structure charts. Traditional program flowcharts, pseudocode, Nassi-Shneiderman diagrams, Chapin charts,* and *Warnier diagrams* are commonly used detailed techniques.

Structured COBOL coding principles are:

1. Only the three control structures of the structure theorem should be used: sequence, selection, and iteration.
2. Each program module should have only one entry and one exit point.

In addition to the structured COBOL coding principles, there are certain conventions that should be followed in regard to module formation, READ/WRITE modules, module naming, and module numbering.

The improved programming techniques (IPT) and programmer productivity techniques (PPT) that aid structured program development include *chief programmer teams, structured walkthroughs, structured testing,* and *development support libraries.*

Style Summary

- Do not use the GO TO statement except where required for:
1. The SORT/MERGE statements with input or output procedures
2. The case structure

- Provide only a single entry point and a single exit point for each program module.

- To ensure a single entry and exit point, try to form each program module as a single paragraph except where it is necessary to form a program module as a single section for:

1. The SORT/MERGE statements with input or output procedures
2. Program segmentation
3. Declaratives
4. The case structure

- Establish one READ and/or WRITE module for each file. Conditions where more than one WRITE module will be required for a file are:

1. When a report file requires one WRITE module to skip to the top of the page and another to handle variable line spacing
2. When variable-length records are written

- Generally name each program module with a one-word verb and a two-word object.

- Number each program module in accordance with a module numbering system and arrange the program modules in order according to that number.

Exercises

Terms for Definition

structured program	traditional program flowchart
unstructured program	pseudocode
structure theorem	Nassi-Shneiderman diagram
sequence structure	structured flowchart
selection structure	Chapin chart
iteration structure	Warnier diagram
improved programming techniques	program module
programmer productivity techniques	chief programmer teams
structured programming	structured walkthroughs
data flow diagram	structured testing
HIPO	development support libraries
structure chart	

Review Questions

1. _____ programs are sometimes uncomplimentarily referred to as bowl-of-spaghetti programs.

2. Name two significant differences between structured and unstructured programs.

3. Proof of the structure theorem was documented by _____ and _____ .

4. The selection structure is sometimes referred to as the _____ _____ structure.

5. The iteration structure is sometimes referred to as the _____ _____ structure.

6. The academician who first drew attention to the structure theorem through his letter to the editor of a magazine widely read in the programming community is _____ _____ .

7. The first project that applied structured programming and improved programming techniques to large-scale data processing application is the _____ .

8. Match the structured design and documentation technique with its description.
      c data flow diagram
        HIPO
      h structure chart
      e traditional program flowchart
      b pseudocode
        Nassi-Shneiderman diagram
        Chapin chart
        Warnier diagram

   a. A structured flowchart with module name identifiers specified within terminal symbols.
   b. An English-like form of expressing program logic.
   c. A "bubble chart" depicting the logical flow of data.
   d. An overall program design and documentation technique introduced by IBM Corporation in the early seventies.
   e. A graphic technique for the design and documentation of program logic developed early in the computer age.
   f. A structured flowchart diagrammed as a series of rectangles with module names indicated in vertical rectangles which define the boundaries of the module.
   g. A method of expressing program logic with brackets and certain other symbols.
   h. A technique for graphically showing the relationship of program modules that resembles an organization chart in appearance.

9. Structured programs should be limited to the three control structures of the _____ .

10. A program module is a ___unit_____ .

11. Structured program modules should contain only one _____ _____ and one _____ .

12. List the four ways a module may be formed in a COBOL program.

13. Why are single paragraph modules recommended?

14. When the PERFORM statement with the THRU option is specified, program control is transferred to the first procedure-name specified and is returned after _____ .

15. Dummy paragraphs may be created by specifying the _____ statement as the only statement within the paragraph.

16. As an aid to functional module design, module names should generally be formed with a single _____ followed by a single _____ .

17. As an aid to program reference, module names should contain a _____ number.

18. A _____ is sometimes formed to increase programmer productivity through the assignment of program development tasks in accordance with an individual's capabilities, training, experience, and specialties.

19. A group review of a programmer's work for the purpose of detecting errors or faulty program design is referred to as a _____ .

20. Structured testing is sometimes referred to as _structured walkthrough_ or _development report_____ testing.

21. To reduce the clerical workload of the programmer and maintain central control of program documentation, _____ are established.

CHAPTER 7

DESIGNING AND WRITING A REPORT PROGRAM

**DESIGNING AND WRITING
A REPORT PROGRAM**

We will now design and code a complete report program—one that contains heading, detail, and total lines. In this chapter we will (1) introduce the program specifications, (2) design a structure chart for the program, (3) describe the pseudocode and flowchart design, and (4) explain the COBOL coding.

The following COBOL coding concepts will be covered in this chapter: (1) the REDEFINES clause, (2) the VALUE clause, (3) the definition of output and input records in the WORKING-STORAGE SECTION, (4) the handling of the operating system DATE, (5) the INTO phrase of the READ statement, (6) forms advancing with the PAGE phrase and the mnemonic-name options of the ADVANCING phrase, (7) the SPECIAL-NAMES paragraph of the ENVIRONMENT DIVISION, (8) the FROM phrase of the WRITE statement, and (9) an introduction to the IF statement.

Programming Specifications: Payroll Report Program

Universal Business Services Company has a requirement for a payroll report program. The input payroll record layout is shown in Figure 7.1, the output payroll report print chart appears in Figure 7.2, and Figure 7.3 presents the programming specifications. The system flowchart is depicted in Figure 7.4; sample output is shown in Figure 7.5. We will be writing a program that we will call PAYROLL to produce this report.

As depicted on the print chart, there are three heading-line formats, one detail-line format, and one total-line format.

Notice that the date must be obtained from the computer operating system and printed on the second heading-line together with a sequential page number to identify each report page.

There is one detail calculation required: rate times hours to equal gross pay. Three accumulations must be made for each detail record and printed on the total-line: total number of employee payroll records processed, total number of hours worked, and total gross pay.

Designing the Structure Chart

Step 1: List Functional Program Modules

To design a structure chart for a program, the programming specifications must be studied to determine the functional program modules to be included in the program. The programming specifications indicate that the PAYROLL program must print report headings, process each payroll record, and print a total-line. In accordance with the coding conventions described in the

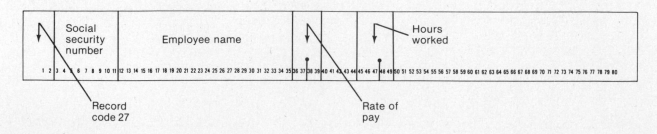

Figure 7.1. Record layout: Payroll record

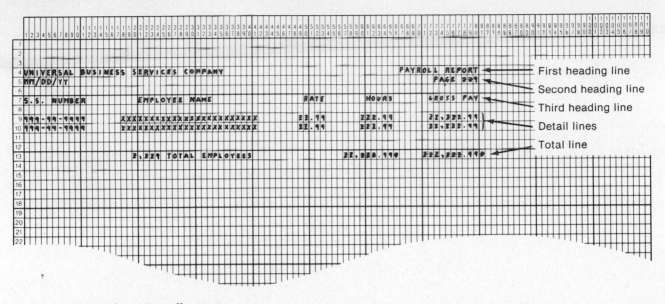

Figure 7.2. Print chart: Payroll report

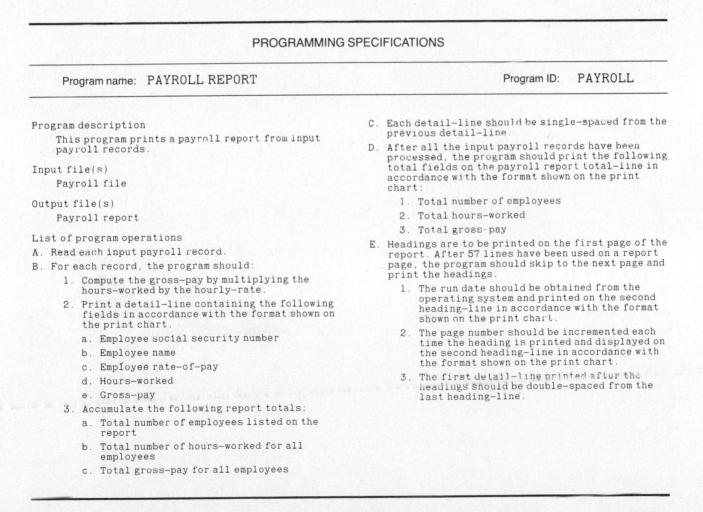

PROGRAMMING SPECIFICATIONS

Program name: PAYROLL REPORT

Program ID: PAYROLL

Program description

This program prints a payroll report from input payroll records.

Input file(s)

Payroll file

Output file(s)

Payroll report

List of program operations

A. Read each input payroll record.

B. For each record, the program should:

   1. Compute the gross-pay by multiplying the hours-worked by the hourly-rate.

   2. Print a detail-line containing the following fields in accordance with the format shown on the print chart.

     a. Employee social security number

     b. Employee name

     c. Employee rate-of-pay

     d. Hours-worked

     e. Gross-pay

   3. Accumulate the following report totals:

     a. Total number of employees listed on the report

     b. Total number of hours-worked for all employees

     c. Total gross-pay for all employees

C. Each detail-line should be single-spaced from the previous detail-line.

D. After all the input payroll records have been processed, the program should print the following total fields on the payroll report total-line in accordance with the format shown on the print chart:

   1. Total number of employees

   2. Total hours-worked

   3. Total gross-pay

E. Headings are to be printed on the first page of the report. After 57 lines have been used on a report page, the program should skip to the next page and print the headings.

   1. The run date should be obtained from the operating system and printed on the second heading-line in accordance with the format shown on the print chart.

   2. The page number should be incremented each time the heading is printed and displayed on the second heading-line in accordance with the format shown on the print chart.

   3. The first detail-line printed after the headings should be double-spaced from the last heading-line.

Figure 7.3. Programming specifications: Payroll report program

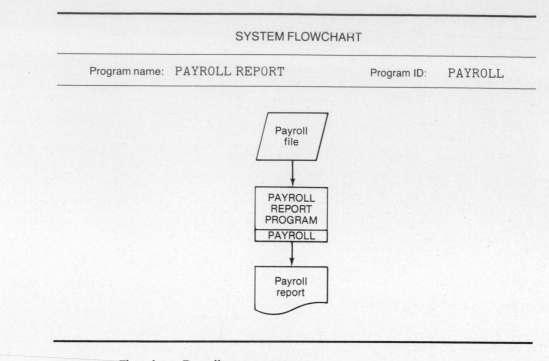

SYSTEM FLOWCHART

Program name: PAYROLL REPORT   Program ID: PAYROLL

Payroll
file

PAYROLL
REPORT
PROGRAM

PAYROLL

Payroll
report

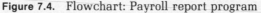

Figure 7.4. Flowchart: Payroll report program

preceding chapter, we will also need one module to read the payroll records and two modules to print report lines: one to print the first or top line of each page and one to print all other report lines. Further, a module to initialize the variable fields can be provided. Thus, a list of the PAYROLL program functions appears as shown in Figure 7.6. When listing functional program modules, they need not be arranged in any particular sequence. The purpose of listing them is for reference when the structure chart is drawn to ensure that all modules are included.

Notice also that the module-naming conventions covered in Chapter 6 were followed. Each module name begins with a verb and is followed by a two-word object.

Step 2: Describe Overall Program Function

In accordance with top-down program development concepts, the top level block on the structure chart is drawn to describe the overall program function: print payroll report. This is shown in Figure 7.7.

Step 3: Show Major Program Functions

The modules shown at level 1 of the structure chart are those that relate directly to the overall program function. These are the modules that will be performed from the mainline module. For the PAYROLL program, the following modules can be shown at the first level: Initialize-variable-fields, process-payroll-record, and print-total-line. Although the read-payroll-record module does not strictly qualify as a major program function, it will be shown on the first level because we will use a priming-read program to obtain the first record.

Remember that the purpose of a structure chart is to show how modules relate to one another hierarchically (or vertically); sequential (or horizontal) relationships are not necessarily indicated. However, it is usually easier to relate the structure chart to the program coding if the modules are arranged from left to right in the order in which the functions will probably occur during the program execution. This has been done in Figure 7.8, which shows the top and first level of the PAYROLL program structure chart.

```
UNIVERSAL BUSINESS SERVICES COMPANY                     PAYROLL REPORT
01/21/81                                                    PAGE   1

    S.S. NUMBER        EMPLOYEE NAME           RATE     HOURS      GROSS PAY

    901-50-4038       SMITH, JOHN M            8.57     40.00       342.80
    901-50-4639       ADAMS, DARLENE R         9.30     40.00       372.00
    901-50-5878       WALLACE, JANE            5.55     38.00       210.90
    905-43-4908       BROWNE, CARL S           6.78     40.00       271.20
    905-60-4897       GARCIA, ERNEST G         6.10     39.00       237.90
    905-60-5434       JOHNSON, ROBERT R        9.30     40.00       372.00
    908-50-1024       ROBERTSON, ALAN          7.77     40.00       310.80
    909-44-9877       DIXON, DONALD            5.03     39.50       198.69

              8 TOTAL EMPLOYEES                       316.50*     2,316.29*
```

Figure 7.5. Sample output: Payroll report program

Program function: Print payroll report

Functional modules: Print-report-headings
                     Process-payroll-record
                     Print-total-line
                     Initialize-variable-fields
                     Read-payroll-record
                     Write-report-top-line
                     Write-report-line

Figure 7.6 . List of functional program modules: Payroll report program

Figure 7.7. Top level of structure chart: Payroll program

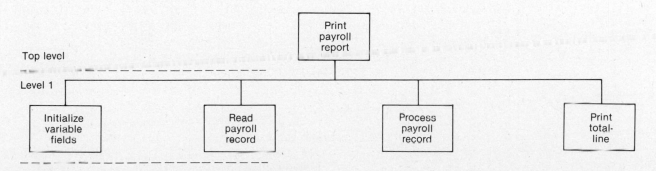
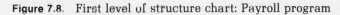

Figure 7.8. First level of structure chart: Payroll program

Those first-level modules that will perform other modules are expanded to show the performed modules. This is shown in Figure 7.9. Each first-level module is discussed below.

Initialize-variable-fields

This module is similar in function to that of previous programs. It does not perform any other modules.

Read-payroll-record

The sole function of this module is to read an input record (and set the end-of-file-switch when there are no remaining records). Rather than being established as a separate module, it could have been coded in-line as was done in previous programs. However, it is a better programming technique to set up a separate module for READ statements, as discussed in Chapter 6. No other modules are performed by this one.

Process-payroll-record

Three modules must be performed by this module: Print-report-headings when headings are required, print-report-line to print each detail-line, and read-payroll-record to obtain the next input record.

The print-report-headings module must in turn perform the print-report-top-line module, which prints the very first heading-line on each page, and the print-report-line module, which prints the second and third heading-lines.

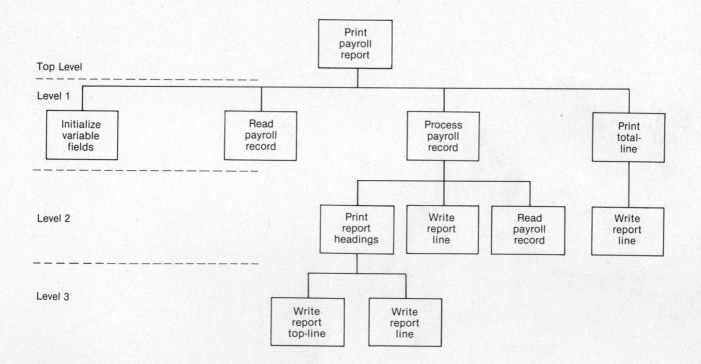

Figure 7.9. Full structure chart: Payroll report program

Print-total-line

This module performs one other module, write-report-line, to print the final total on the report.

Step 5: Identify Common Modules

The modules read-payroll-record and write-report-line are shown on the structure chart more than once. Such modules can be termed *common modules*. Identification of common modules aids analysis of the structure chart and program coding. To identify common modules, the upper right-hand corner of the block can be shaded.

Step 6: Review Structure Chart

Once the structure chart has been drawn, it should be reviewed to ensure that it is complete and correct.

Step 7: Number Each Module

Figure 7.10 shows the complete structure chart for the PAYROLL program. Common modules are identified and module numbers are assigned in accordance with the module numbering conventions presented in Chapter 6.

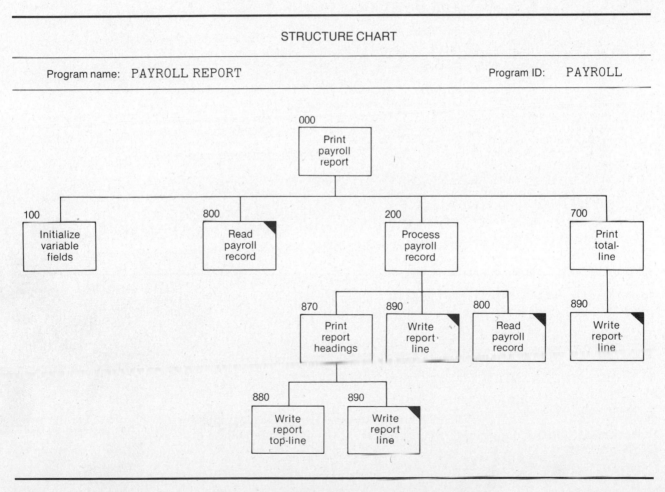

STRUCTURE CHART

Program name: PAYROLL REPORT   Program ID: PAYROLL

Figure 7.10. Complete structure chart with module numbers: Payroll report program

Program name: PAYROLL REPORT   Program ID: PAYROLL

000-Print-Payroll-Report module
1. Open the files.
2. Perform 100-Initialize-Variable-Fields.
3. Perform 800-Read-Payroll-Record.
4. Perform 200-Process-Payroll-Record until no more records.
5. Perform 700-Print-Total-Line.
6. Close the files.
7. Stop the run.

100-Initialize-Variable-Fields module
1. Set the end-of-file indicator to "No".
2. Set the page-count to zero.
3. Set the lines-used indicator so that headings for the first page will be triggered.
4. Obtain the date from the operating system and move it to the second heading-line.
5. Set the total-accumulator fields to zero.

200-Process-Payroll-Record module
1. If the report page is full, perform 870-Print-Report-Headings.
2. Move the input Social-security-number to the detail-line Social-security-number.
3. Move the input Employee-name to the detail-line employee-name.
4. Move the input Rate-of-pay to the detail-line Rate-of-pay.
5. Move the input Hours-worked to the detail-line Hours-worked.
6. Multiply the Rate-of-pay times the Hours-worked to equal Gross-pay.
7. Move the Gross-pay to the detail-line Gross-pay.
8. Move the detail-line to the output-line area.
9. Set the line-spacing for single-spacing.
10. Perform 890-Write-Report-Line.
11. Add 1 to Total-employees.
12. Add the Gross-pay to the Total-gross-pay.
13. Perform 800-Read-Payroll-Record.

700-Print-Total-Line module
1. Move the Total-employees to the total-line Total-employees.
2. Move the Total-hours-worked to the total-line Total-hours-worked.
3. Move the Total-gross-pay to the total-line Total-gross-pay.
4. Move the total-line to the output-line area.
5. Set the line-spacing for triple-spacing.
6. Perform 890-Write-Report-Line.

800-Read-Payroll-Record module
1. Read an input payroll record.

870-Print-Report-Headings module
1. Add 1 to the Page-count.
2. Move the Page-count to the heading-line-2 Page-number.
3. Move heading-line-1 to the output-line area.
4. Perform 880-Write-Report-Top-Line.
5. Move heading-line-2 to the output-line area.
6. Set the line-spacing for single-spacing.
7. Perform 890-Write-Report-Line.
8. Move heading-line-3 to the output-line area.
9. Set the line-spacing for double-spacing.
10. Perform 890-Write-Report-Line.
11. Clear the output-line area.
12. Set the line-spacing for single-spacing.
13. Perform 890-Write-Report-Line.

880-Write-Report-Top-Line module
1. Advance to the top of the next report page and write out the output-line area.
2. Set the Lines-used to 1.

890-Write-Report-Line module
1. Advance in accordance with the Line-spacing setting and write out the output-line area.
2. Add the Line-spacing to the Lines-used.

Figure 7.11. Pseudocode: Payroll report program

Writing the Pseudocode and Drawing the Program Flowchart

The pseudocode for the PAYROLL program is shown in Figure 7.11; the program flowchart is in 7.12. Each module will be discussed.

Program name: **PAYROLL REPORT**   Program ID: **PAYROLL**

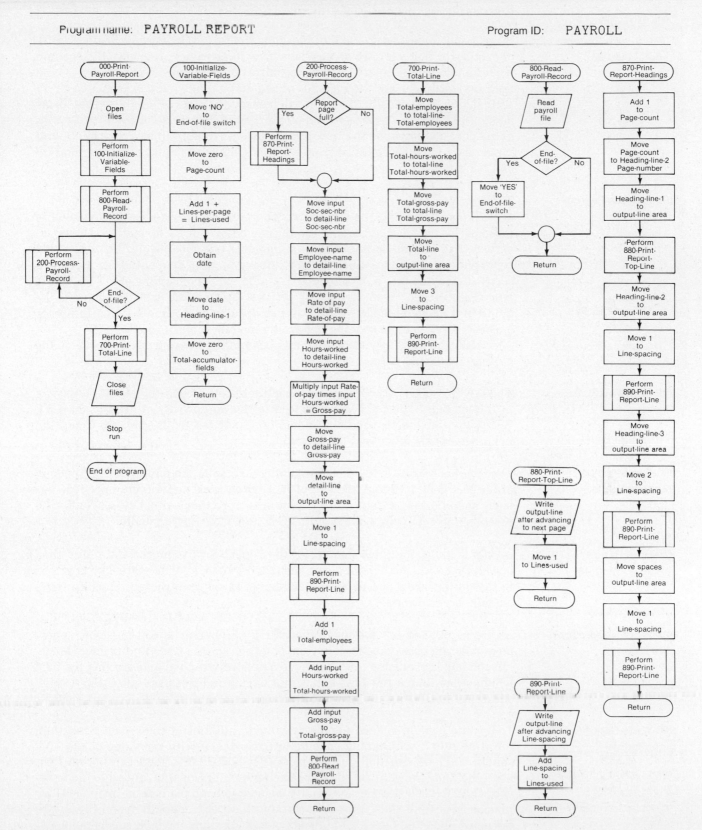

Figure 7.12. Program flowchart: Payroll report program

| **000-Print-Payroll-Report Module** | This is the mainline control module; after opening the files, it performs the four level-one modules of the structure chart: 100-Initialize-Variable-Fields, 200-Process-Payroll-Record, 700-Print-Total-Line, and 800-Read-Payroll-Record. |

100-Initialize-Variable-Fields Module

In addition to setting the end-of-file indicator to "NO" and setting the total-accumulator fields to zero as has been done in previous programs, this module must handle a few report heading initialization functions. Specifically, (1) the field that will be used to keep track of sequential page numbers must be set to zero; (2) the lines-used field, which will be used to detect when the report forms must be skipped to a new page and a report heading printed, must be set to trigger report headings for the first page before any detail-lines are printed; and (3) the date must be obtained from the operating system and placed in the second heading-line.

200-Process-Payroll-Record Module

The first thing that must be done in this module is to test the lines-used field to see if report headings are required. Then, as record-processing modules of previous programs have done, the output detail-line is formatted. However, rather than use an in-line WRITE statement, this module performs a write-report-line module so that we can adhere to the convention of having a separate module for READ and WRITE statements (as introduced in Chapter 6). Because different lines are being written by the line-printing module, the detail-line must be moved to the output area and the line-spacing indicator must be set for single-spacing before the module is performed.

After the line is written, the total accumulations are performed. Then, the next input record is read.

700-Print-Total-Line Module

The WORKING-STORAGE total-accumulations are moved to the total-line area in this module. The total-line is moved to the output record area in the FILE SECTION and the line-spacing indicator is set for triple-spacing. Then, the print-report-line module is performed.

800-Read-Payroll-Record Module

The function of this module is to read a record from the payroll file. If the end-of-file has been reached, the end-of-file-switch is set to indicate this. This has been specified as a separate module in accordance with the convention of establishing separate modules for READ and WRITE statements.

870-Print-Report-Headings Module

In this module, the page number of the report first is incremented and then moved to the second heading-line. Then, one by one, each heading-line is moved to the output area, the proper line spacing is set, and the appropriate write module is performed.

880-Write-Report-Top-Line Module

As we mentioned in Chapter 6, the WRITE statement to skip to a new report page must be coded separately from one that spaces lines and prints. Hence, this module is used only for skipping to a new report page and printing the first heading-line. Since the first line of the page has been used after this WRITE statement has been executed, the lines-used indicator is set to 1 in this module.

890-Write-Report-Line Module

This write module is used for the printing of all lines of the report other than the first one. It will handle spacing in accordance with the value of the line-spacing indicator at the time the module is being performed, and it will then print the line. The value of the line-spacing indicator is then added to the lines-used field to keep track of how many lines have been printed on the page. This lines-used count tells the process-payroll-record module when the page becomes filled and hence identifies the need to skip to the next report page and print headings.

Format:

Example:

SEQUENCE																

```
05  XX-PRICE                              PIC  ZZ,ZZZ.99.
05  XX-NC-PRICE REDEFINES  XX-PRICE       PIC  X(9).
```

Note: "Level-number" and "data-name-1" are shown in the above format to improve clarity. Level-number and data-name-1 are not part of the REDEFINES clause.

Figure 7.13. REDEFINES clause example

The REDEFINES Clause

The format of the REDEFINES clause is shown in Figure 7.13 together with an example. This clause is used in the DATA DIVISION where it is necessary to assign more than one name and/or more than one PICTURE clause to a given storage area.

The example depicts a situation where either a numeric edited price amount or the words NO CHARGE are to be printed. If the field were defined only as numeric edited, the words NO CHARGE could not be moved to the field. (Remember that an alphanumeric field cannot be moved to a numeric edited field.) On the other hand, if the field were defined as alphanumeric, then the editing could not be performed. By using the REDEFINES clause, the XX-PRICE field can be specified when the editing is desired and the XX-NC-PRICE can be referenced when the words are to be moved to the same area.

There are two primary rules to keep in mind when using the REDEFINES clause. First, the redefining field (in other words, the one with the REDEFINES clause—XX-NC-PRICE in the example) cannot be longer than the redefined field (XX-PRICE in the example). The redefining field must be equal or less than the length of the area being redefined. Second, the redefining entry must immediately follow, at that level-number, the area being redefined. Figure 7.14 shows examples of valid and invalid REDEFINES entries. A field may have multiple redefinitions, as shown in Figure 7.15.

The VALUE Clause

The VALUE clause is used to establish the initial contents of a field. Its format is shown in Figure 7.16. The VALUE clause may be specified in the data-item description entry of appropriate elementary items in the WORKING-STORAGE SECTION. The reserved word VALUE is required but the reserved word IS is optional and usually not included.

When establishing an initial value for a field, the programmer must make the literal specified in the VALUE clause consistent with the category of data defined by the PICTURE clause. That is, when the picture is numeric, a numeric literal must be specified. When the picture is alphanumeric, a non-numeric literal must be specified. Similarly, the length of the literal should be consistent with the length of the field. The literal cannot be longer than the field length as defined by the PICTURE clause. Also, when a numeric literal with a sign is used

Part A: Valid REDEFINES entries

```
Ø5    XX-FIELD-A                        PIC X(5).
Ø5    XX-FIELD-B REDEFINES XX-FIELD-A PIC X(3).
```

XX-FIELD-A

XX-FIELD-B

```
Ø5    XX-GROUP-FIELD-A.
      1Ø    XX-ELEMENTARY-FIELD-1        PIC X(3).
      1Ø    XX-ELEMENTARY-FIELD-2        PIC X(2).
Ø5    XX-ELEM-FIELD REDEFINES XX-GROUP-FIELD-A      PIC 9(5).
```

XX-GROUP-FIELD-A

XX-ELEMENTARY-FIELD-1   XX-ELEMENTARY-FIELD-2

XX-ELEM-FIELD

Part B: Invalid REDEFINES entries

The redefining field is longer than the redefined field.

```
Ø5    XX-FIELD-R                        PIC X(5).
Ø5    XX-FIELD-S REDEFINES XX-FIELD-R PIC X(6).
```

The redefining field does not immediately follow the redefined field.

```
Ø5    XX-FIELD-X                        PIC X(5).
Ø5    XX-FIELD-Y                        PIC X(5).
Ø5    XX-FIELD-Z REDEFINES XX-FIELD-X PIC X(5).
```

The redefining field is not at the same level as the redefined field.

```
1Ø    XX-LEVEL-1Ø-FIELD                        PIC X(5).
Ø5    XX-LEVEL-5-FIELD REDEFINES XX-LEVEL-1Ø-FIELD      PIC X(5).
```

Figure 7.14. Valid and invalid REDEFINES examples

```
05    XX-NUM-FLD                        PIC 9(5).
05    XX-SGN-FLD REDEFINES XX-NUM-FLD PIC S9(5).
05    XX-ALF-FLD REDEFINES XX-NUM-FLD PIC X(5).
```

Figure 7.15. Multiple redefinition example

Format:

VALUE IS literal

Example:

```
SEQUENCE        |C|A   |B                                   COBOL STATEMENT                                              | IDENTIFICATION
(PAGE) (SERIAL) |O|    |
1   3  4     6  |7|8   |12  16  20  24  28  32  36  40  44  48  52  56  60  64  68  72 | 76   80

               Ø5  XX-PI             PIC S9(1)V9999  VALUE +3.1416.
```

Figure 7.16. VALUE clause example

(+15 or −208, for example), the numeric PICTURE clause must contain the picture symbol S. Remember, too, that a numeric literal is limited to a length of 18 digits and a non-numeric literal is limited to a length of 120 characters.

A figurative constant such as ZERO or SPACE can be used as the literal of a VALUE clause. However, because a space is an alphanumeric character, SPACE or SPACES cannot be used with a numeric PICTURE clause. On the other hand, since a zero may be considered either numeric or alphanumerical, ZERO, ZEROS, or ZEROES may be used with either numeric or alphanumeric PICTURE clauses.

Places where the VALUE clause cannot be used are (1) in the FILE SECTION, (2) with a group field data-item description entry, (3) with a data-item description entry that contains an editing PICTURE clause, (4) with a data-item description entry that contains a REDEFINES clause, and (5) with a data-item description entry that contains an OCCURS clause (the OCCURS clause will be covered in Chapter 12). Examples of valid and invalid VALUE clauses are provided in Figure 7.17.

Valid VALUE clauses		*Comments*	*Invalid VALUE clauses*		*Reason invalid*
PIC X(3)	VALUE 'YES'		PIC X(2)	VALUE 'YES'	Literal longer then field length
PIC X(3)	VALUE 'NO'	For clarity it is better to make the non-numeric literal same length as the picture.	PIC 9(3)	VALUE '100'	Numeric field—non-numeric literal (due to quotation marks)
PIC X(3)	VALUE 'NO '	This is a better indication of actual data than previous example.	PIC 9(3)	VALUE +100	Unsigned field—signed literal
PIC 9(5)	VALUE 00010	For clarity it is better not to show non-significant zeros.	PIC 9(3)	VALUE −100	Unsigned field—signed literal
PIC 9(5)	VALUE 10	This is easier to read than previous example.	PIC 9(3)	VALUE 1000	Literal longer than field length
PIC S9(5)	VALUE 10		PIC ZZ9	VALUE 100	Numeric edited field
PIC S9(5)	VALUE +10	Remember a plus or minus sign must be leftmost in numeric literal.			can't use value clause on edited field
PIC S9(5)	VALUE −10				
PIC X(6)	VALUE '3.1416'	Remember that arithmetic cannot be done with non-numeric literals.			

Figure 7.17. Valid and invalid VALUE clause examples

```
001010 IDENTIFICATION DIVISION.
001020 PROGRAM-ID.       PAYROLL.
001030*AUTHOR.           WELBURN.
001040*INSTALLATION.     UNIVERSAL BUSINESS SERVICES.
001050*DATE-WRITTEN.     JAN 12.1981.
001060*DATE-COMPILED.    JAN 13.1981.
001070*SECURITY.         NONE.
001080*
001090*
001100*                  THIS PROGRAM READS PAYROLL RECORDS.
001110*                  COMPUTES THE GROSS PAY FOR EACH EMPLOYEE
001120*                  AND PRINTS AN EMPLOYEE DETAIL LINE
001130*                  FOR EACH PAYROLL RECORD.
001140*
001150*                  AFTER ALL INPUT PAYROLL RECORDS HAVE BEEN
001160*                  PROCESSED, A REPORT TOTAL LINE WILL BE PRINTED.
002010*
002020*
002030*
002040 ENVIRONMENT DIVISION.
002050*
002060*
002070 CONFIGURATION SECTION.
002080*
002090 SOURCE-COMPUTER.  IBM-370.
002100 OBJECT-COMPUTER.  IBM-370.
002110*
002120*
002130 INPUT-OUTPUT SECTION.
002140*
002150 FILE-CONTROL.
002160     SELECT PAYROLL-FILE
002170         ASSIGN TO UT-S-INFILE.
002180     SELECT PAYROLL-REPORT
002190         ASSIGN TO UT-S-PRTFILE.
```

Figure 7.18. IDENTIFICATION and ENVIRONMENT divisions: Payroll program

Coding the IDENTIFICATION and ENVIRONMENT Divisions

The coding for these two divisions is shown in Figure 7.18. There are no new concepts presented in these divisions.

Coding the DATA DIVISION

FILE SECTION

Coding for the FILE SECTION is shown in Figure 7.19. Observe for the PAYROLL-FILE that the fields of the input PAYROLL-RECORD have not been defined here in the FILE SECTION. Instead, a FILLER entry for 80 characters has been specified. Also, for the PAYROLL-REPORT file, only one 01-level record-description entry has been specified: PAYROLL-REPORT-LINE. There are no field descriptions for this record either—merely a FILLER specification

```
003010*
003020*
003030*
003040 DATA DIVISION.
003050*
003060*
003070 FILE SECTION.
003080*
003090 FD  PAYROLL-FILE
003100         RECORD CONTAINS 80 CHARACTERS
003110         LABEL RECORDS ARE OMITTED.
003120*
003130 01  PAYROLL-RECORD.
003140     05  FILLER                        PIC X(80).
004010*
004020 FD  PAYROLL-REPORT
004030         RECORD CONTAINS 133 CHARACTERS
004040         LABEL RECORDS ARE OMITTED.
004050*
004060 01  PAYROLL-REPORT-LINE.
004070     05  FILLER                        PIC X(133).
```

Figure 7.19. DATA DIVISION (FILE SECTION): Payroll program

for 133 characters. Actually, the PAYROLL-REPORT file has five record formats: three heading-line records, one detail-line record, and one total-line record.

The definition of these records has been omitted from the FILE SECTION because they will be described in the WORKING-STORAGE SECTION. This will introduce a commonly used programming technique: definition of output and input records in WORKING-STORAGE.

Definition of output records in the WORKING-STORAGE SECTION

In our previous programs, the output print lines have been described in the FILE SECTION. For this PAYROLL program, output record field descriptions are specified in the WORKING-STORAGE SECTION.

Previous programs used FILE SECTION specifications because that's the more direct, straightforward, simpler-to-understand method. However, WORKING-STORAGE definition is usually a better approach; it has the following advantages:

1. It allows VALUE clauses to be used for the initialization of fields with data (VALUE clauses to initialize fields cannot be specified in the FILE SECTION).
2. It eliminates double-buffering problems (as explained in Chapter 5).
3. It allows reference to fields of a record that has already been written to an output device. Data values for fields within records in the FILE SECTION are no longer available for a given record after the WRITE statement has been issued. In other words, once a record is written, the data in its fields can no longer be referenced. (This FILE SECTION restriction makes double-buffering possible.)
4. It makes it easier to determine the current output record being processed when referring to a storage dump. (A *storage dump* is a printout of the contents of computer storage. It serves as a snapshot of program conditions at the time a program error occurs.) Regarding this point, when input-output records are defined in the FILE SECTION, they are processed in the input-output buffer areas. Records are often blocked, so it is usually difficult for the programmer to determine exactly which record of the multiple record block is being processed at the specific time when the dump was taken. On the other hand, with the individual record in WORKING-STORAGE, the record being processed can be readily identified.

Specifying record-descriptions in the WORKING-STORAGE SECTION does have certain disadvantages: (1) it consumes more computer storage space (because FILE SECTION record-descriptions are implicitly redefined, as discussed in Chapter 5), and (2) it causes more data movement. Figure 7.20 diagrams these points.

The programming benefits of the WORKING-STORAGE definition technique usually outweigh the relatively minor efficiency advantages of FILE SECTION definition. Thus, the former approach is the preferred one for most current applications.

Definition of input records in the WORKING-STORAGE SECTION

Input records are frequently defined in the WORKING-STORAGE SECTION, too. There are two advantages to the definition of input records in WORKING-STORAGE:

1. It allows reference to fields of a record after the next record has been read. Actually, about the only time such reference is of particular value is

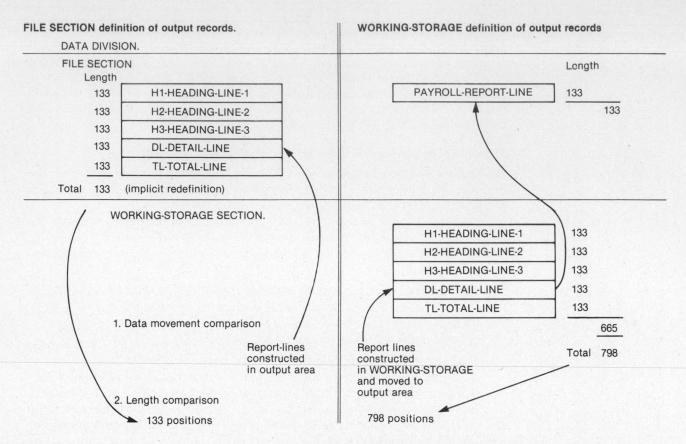

FILE SECTION definition of output records.　　|　**WORKING-STORAGE** definition of output records

DATA DIVISION.

FILE SECTION

Length

Length	
133	H1-HEADING-LINE-1
133	H2-HEADING-LINE-2
133	H3-HEADING-LINE-3
133	DL-DETAIL-LINE
133	TL-TOTAL-LINE

Total　133　(implicit redefinition)

PAYROLL-REPORT-LINE　133

133

WORKING-STORAGE SECTION.

	Length
H1-HEADING-LINE-1	133
H2-HEADING-LINE-2	133
H3-HEADING-LINE-3	133
DL-DETAIL-LINE	133
TL-TOTAL-LINE	133

665

1. Data movement comparison

Report-lines constructed in output area

Report lines constructed in WORKING-STORAGE and moved to output area

Total　798

2. Length comparison

133 positions　　　798 positions

Figure 7.20. Comparison of FILE SECTION and WORKING-STORAGE SECTION definition of output records

after the end-of-file has been reached. The last input record will remain in WORKING-STORAGE and control fields of that last record may be referred to. Such reference is useful in programs such as control-break applications (which will be discussed in Chapter 10).

2. When processing blocked records, the programmer can more easily determine the last input record that was read when referring to a storage dump.

WORKING-STORAGE SECTION

The first portion of the WORKING-STORAGE SECTION coding is shown in Figure 7.21. We will discuss the coding by 01-level record-description entry.

The WS-SWITCHES fields

As we have done in previous programs, an end-of-file switch—WS-END-OF-FILE-SWITCH—has been established to control input record processing.

The WS-REPORT-CONTROLS fields

Fields are required in WORKING-STORAGE to control the following report functions: sequential page numbers, page-skipping over the continuous form perforations to the top of the next report page, and variable line spacing with the identifier option of the WRITE statement.

The WS-PAGE-COUNT field will be used to keep track of the page number of the report page to be printed. It will be incremented each time a page is headed. Since the programming specifications call for a three-digit page number, WS-PAGE-COUNT has been specified as a three-digit signed numeric field.

```
005010*
005020*
005030 WORKING-STORAGE SECTION.
005040*
005050*
005060 01   WS-SWITCHES.
005070      05  WS-END-OF-FILE-SWITCH          PIC X(3).
006010*
006020 01   WS-REPORT-CONTROLS.
006030      05  WS-PAGE-COUNT                  PIC S9(3).
006040      05  WS-LINES-PER-PAGE              PIC S9(2)    VALUE +57.
006050      05  WS-LINES-USED                  PIC S9(2).
006060      05  WS-LINE-SPACING                PIC S9(2).
007010*
007020 01   WS-WORK-AREAS.
007030      05  WS-DATE-WORK                   PIC 9(6).
007040      05  WS-DATE-CONVERSION REDEFINES WS-DATE-WORK.
007050          10  WS-YEAR                    PIC 9(2).
007060          10  WS-MONTH                   PIC 9(2).
007070          10  WS-DAY                     PIC 9(2).
007080      05  WS-GROSS-PAY                   PIC S9(5)V99.
008010*
008020 01   WS-TOTAL-ACCUMULATORS.
008030      05  WS-TOTAL-EMPLOYEES-ACCUM       PIC S9(4).
008040      05  WS-TOTAL-HOURS-WORKED-ACCUM    PIC S9(5)V99.
008050      05  WS-TOTAL-GROSS-PAY-ACCUM       PIC S9(6)V99.
```

Figure 7.21. DATA DIVISION (first part of WORKING-STORAGE SECTION) payroll program

To print report headings, the program must define the line span of the report page so that a full page can be detected. Because the programming specifications call for (1) a one-half inch margin at the top of the report page and a one-inch margin at the bottom of the report, (2) six lines to be printed per inch, and (3) standard 11-inch-long forms to be used, the line span for each page is 57. See Figure 7.22 for an illustration of how this was computed. The WS-LINES-PER-PAGE field is used to hold this line span. The value of + 57 is placed in the field with a VALUE clause.

To accumulate a running total of the number of lines that have been used on each page, we define the WS-LINES-USED field. It must accommodate a running total of up to 57, so it has been defined as a two-digit signed numeric field.

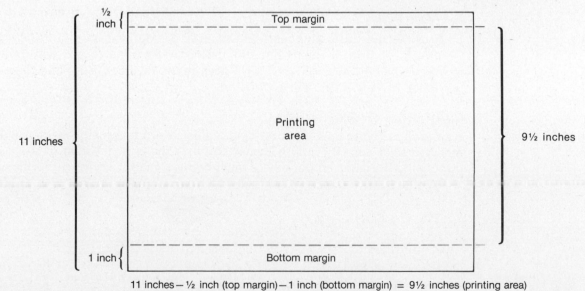

11 inches − ½ inch (top margin) − 1 inch (bottom margin) = 9½ inches (printing area)
9½ inches × 6 lines per inch = 57 lines per page

Figure 7.22. Computation of report line span

```
020010*
020020 01  PR-PAYROLL-RECORD.
020030     05   PR-RECORD-CODE               PIC X(2).
020040     05   PR-SOC-SEC-NBR.
020050          10   PR-SOC-SEC-NBR-1        PIC 9(3).
020060          10   PR-SOC-SEC-NBR-2        PIC 9(2).
020070          10   PR-SOC-SEC-NBR-3        PIC 9(4).
020080     05   PR-EMPLOYEE-NAME             PIC X(24).
020090     05   PR-RATE-OF-PAY               PIC 9(2)V99.
020100     05   FILLER                       PIC X(5).
020110     05   PR-HOURS-WORKED              PIC 9(3)V99.
020120     05   FILLER                       PIC X(31).
```

Figure 7.23. PR-PAYROLL-RECORD record definition

The WS-LINE-SPACING field will indicate whether single-, double-, or triple-spacing should occur. The function of this field will be discussed when the identifier option of the ADVANCING phrase is covered later in this chapter.

The WS-WORK-AREAS fields

The WS-DATE-WORK and the WS-DATE-CONVERSION data-names are needed to process the operating system DATE. Their function will be explained when system DATE handling is covered later in this chapter.

The WS-GROSS-PAY work field will be used to hold the product of the employee rate-times-hours calculation.

The WS-TOTAL-ACCUMULATORS fields

The programming specifications call for accumulations of the total number of employees, total hours worked, and total gross pay. Thus, the fields WS-TOTAL-EMPLOYEES-ACCUM, WS-TOTAL-HOURS-WORKED-ACCUM, and WS-TOTAL-GROSS-PAY-ACCUM have been established.

The PR-PAYROLL-RECORD fields

The input PAYROLL-RECORD is defined here in WORKING-STORAGE, as shown in Figure 7.23. After the record has been read into the FILE SECTION, it will be transferred to this area. The fields of the record will be processed in this PR-PAYROLL-RECORD area.

The report lines

Each of the five different report-line records are defined here in WORKING-STORAGE. To print a report line, the desired report-line record will first be moved to the PAYROLL-REPORT-LINE area in the FILE-SECTION and then the PAYROLL-REPORT-LINE will be written.

The H1-HEADING-LINE-1 fields

As shown in Figure 7.24, the first field of this record is a one-character alphanumeric field named FILLER. Remember that the first position of a record directed to a printer output device must be reserved for a vertical forms con-

```
030010*
030020 01  H1-HEADING-LINE-1.
030030     05   FILLER       PIC X(1).
030040     05   FILLER       PIC X(20)   VALUE 'UNIVERSAL BUSINESS S'.
030050     05   FILLER       PIC X(20)   VALUE 'ERVICES COMPANY     '.
030060     05   FILLER       PIC X(20)   VALUE '                    '.
030070     05   FILLER       PIC X(20)   VALUE '       PAYROLL REPORT'.
030080     05   FILLER       PIC X(20)   VALUE '                    '.
030090     05   FILLER       PIC X(20)   VALUE '                    '.
030100     05   FILLER       PIC X(12)   VALUE '            '.
```

Figure 7.24. H1-HEADING-LINE-1 record definition

trol character. In previous programs, we have given this one-character field a data-name. Here we could name it, say, H1-VERTICAL-FORMS-CONTROL. However, COBOL uses this first position for vertical forms control unconditionally, regardless of what it is named. So most programmers just assign the reserved word FILLER to this forms control position, as has been done in this PAYROLL program.

The first heading line contains what is termed *constant* data. Constant data is that which does not change during execution of the program. That is, the words UNIVERSAL BUSINESS SERVICES COMPANY and PAYROLL REPORT should be printed on the first heading line every time it is printed. The blank spaces between the words and through the end of the line can also be considered constant data. The VALUE clause is used to establish constant data in WORKING-STORAGE. When constant data is specified in WORKING-STORAGE record-descriptions and the individual fields are not referenced, the fields need not be assigned a data-name but can instead be specified as FILLER entries. Since the fields of the H1-HEADING-LINE-1 contain constant data and will never be referred to individually, specification of a data-name would serve no function, except perhaps as documentation. In this situation, though, further documentation is probably of little benefit.

Notice that the PICTURE clauses for the fields within the heading lines have been started in position 32. Previously in this text, we have begun the PICTURE clauses in position 48. However, when longer VALUE clauses must be used—as with heading lines—it is convenient to start the PICTURE clause earlier on the line so that the VALUE clause may be written on the same line. By starting the VALUE clause in position 44, a 20-character non-numeric literal can be specified.

There are other approaches to the writing of VALUE clauses, but the 20-character same-line method is probably the most readable and easily maintainable for specifying longer strings of constant data. Figure 7.25 shows alternate techniques.

The H2-HEADING-LINE-2 fields

The second heading line (see Figure 7.26) contains both constant and *variable* data. The constant data are the slashes within the date, the blank spaces, and the word PAGE. The variable data are the date and the page number.

Part A: Example using non-numeric literals for words and the figurative constant SPACE(S) for blank areas. Acceptable but somewhat difficult to read.

```
05  FILLER          PIC  X(35)
         VALUE  'UNIVERSAL  BUSINESS  SERVICES  COMPANY'.
05  FILLER          PIC  X(31)      VALUE  SPACES.
05  FILLER          PIC  X(14)      VALUE  'PAYROLL  REPORT'.
05  FILLER          PIC  X(52)      VALUE  SPACES.
```

Part B: Example using maximum-length (120 characters) non-numeric literal with continuation indicator. Continuation indicator is difficult to maintain and difficult to read.

```
05  FILLER          PIC  X(120)  VALUE  'UNIVERSAL  BUSINESS  SER
-                'VICES  COMPANY                   PAYROLL
-                'REPORT                           '.
05  FILLER          PIC  X(12)      VALUE  SPACES.
```

Figure 7.25. Alternate methods of formatting VALUE clauses for heading lines

```
031010*
031020 01  H2-HEADING-LINE-2.
031030     05  FILLER          PIC X(1).
031040     05  H2-MONTH        PIC 9(2).
031050     05  FILLER          PIC X(1)    VALUE '/'.
031060     05  H2-DAY          PIC 9(2).
031070     05  FILLER          PIC X(1)    VALUE '/'.
031080     05  H2-YEAR         PIC 9(2).
031090     05  FILLER          PIC X(64)   VALUE SPACES.
031100     05  FILLER          PIC X(5)    VALUE 'PAGE '.
031110     05  H2-PAGE-NBR     PIC ZZ9.
031120     05  FILLER          PIC X(52)   VALUE SPACES.
```

Figure 7.26. H2-HEADING-LINE-2 record definition

The constant fields have been named FILLER and appropriate VALUE clauses have been specified. The variable fields have been assigned data-names with the prefix H2. They do not contain VALUE clauses because their values must be acquired by the program. The date will be obtained from the operating system when the program begins executing; the page number must be incremented for each page.

The H3-HEADING-LINE-3 fields

This line contains all constant data and has been defined in accordance with the print chart. Its record-description appears in Figure 7.27.

The DL-DETAIL-LINE fields

This line appears in Figure 7.28 and is defined in accordance with the print chart. Fields that will have data moved to them have been assigned the prefix DL. They do not contain VALUE clauses because they will receive their values from the input payroll record or, in the case of the DL-GROSS-PAY field, from the product developed in the WS-GROSS-PAY field.

Those FILLER areas that represent blank spaces between columns have been assigned a VALUE by the figurative constant SPACES.

```
032010*
032020 01  H3-HEADING-LINE-3.
032030     05  FILLER      PIC X(1).
032040     05  FILLER      PIC X(20)   VALUE 'S.S. NUMBER         '.
032050     05  FILLER      PIC X(20)   VALUE 'EMPLOYEE NAME       '.
032060     05  FILLER      PIC X(20)   VALUE '          RATE      '.
032070     05  FILLER      PIC X(20)   VALUE 'HOURS      GROSS PAY'.
032080     05  FILLER      PIC X(20)   VALUE '                    '.
032090     05  FILLER      PIC X(20)   VALUE '                    '.
032100     05  FILLER      PIC X(12)   VALUE '            '.
```

Figure 7.27. H3-HEADING-LINE-3 record definition

```
033010*
033020 01  DL-DETAIL-LINE.
033030     05  FILLER                  PIC X(1).
033040     05  DL-SOC-SEC-NBR.
033050         10  DL-SOC-SEC-NBR-1    PIC 9(3).
033060         10  FILLER              PIC X(1)    VALUE '-'.
033070         10  DL-SOC-SEC-NBR-2    PIC 9(2).
033080         10  FILLER              PIC X(1)    VALUE '-'.
033090         10  DL-SOC-SEC-NBR-3    PIC 9(4).
033100     05  FILLER                  PIC X(6)    VALUE SPACES.
033110     05  DL-EMPLOYEE-NAME        PIC X(24).
033120     05  FILLER                  PIC X(7)    VALUE SPACES.
033130     05  DL-RATE-OF-PAY          PIC ZZ.99.
033140     05  FILLER                  PIC X(6)    VALUE SPACES.
033150     05  DL-HOURS-WORKED         PIC ZZZ.99.
033160     05  FILLER                  PIC X(6)    VALUE SPACES.
033170     05  DL-GROSS-PAY            PIC ZZ,ZZZ.99.
033180     05  FILLER                  PIC X(52)   VALUE SPACES.
```

Figure 7.28. DL-DETAIL-LINE record definition

```
034010*
034020 01  TL-TOTAL-LINE.
034030     05  FILLER                              PIC X(1).
034040     05  FILLER                              PIC X(19)    VALUE SPACES.
034050     05  TL-TOTAL-EMPLOYEES                  PIC Z,779.
034060     05  FILLER                              PIC X(32)
034070              VALUE ' TOTAL EMPLOYEES              '.
034080     05  TL-TOTAL-HOURS-WORKED               PIC ZZ,ZZZ.99.
034090     05  FILLER                              PIC X(1)     VALUE '*'.
034100     05  FILLER                              PIC X(4)     VALUE SPACES.
034110     05  TL-TOTAL-GROSS-PAY                  PIC ZZZ,ZZZ.99.
034120     05  FILLER                              PIC X(1)     VALUE '*'.
034120     05  FILLER                              PIC X(51)    VALUE SPACES.
```

Figure 7.29. TL-TOTAL-LINE record definition

The TL-TOTAL-LINE fields

The field descriptions are in accordance with the print chart definition. As shown in Figure 7.29, fields in this record have been assigned the data-name prefix TL.

Notice that the PICTURE and VALUE clauses for the DL-DETAIL-LINE and TL-TOTAL-LINE were started in positions 48 and 60, respectively, rather than 32 and 44 as they were for the heading-lines. Often, as with DL-DETAIL-LINE and TL-TOTAL-LINE, a record will contain mostly variable data but will have a few short fields of constant data. Starting the PICTURE clause in position 48 and the VALUE clause in 60 is appropriate here because it allows the specification of longer data-names and shorter VALUE clauses.

Coding the PROCEDURE DIVISION

The complete PAYROLL program including the PROCEDURE DIVISION is shown in Figure 7.30. It is coded in conformance with the pseudocode and flowchart. Most of the statements should be familiar to you because they have been used in previous programs. However, this program introduces four new PROCEDURE DIVISION considerations: (1) obtaining the date from the operating system; (2) the INTO phrase of the READ statement; (3) the WRITE statement using the identifier, mnemonic-name, and PAGE options; and (4) an introduction to the IF statement. Each of these items will be discussed.

Obtaining the Date from the Operating System

There are two commonly used methods of obtaining the date from the operating system in a COBOL program. The first, which we shall call ACCEPT/FROM DATE, is the standard COBOL method. It did not, however, become a COBOL standard until 1974, so, if you are using a pre-1974 compiler, you will not be able to use it. The second method, termed CURRENT-DATE, is not an ANS COBOL standard, but it is frequently used because it is available on most IBM and IBM-compatible compilers. If you are using a non-IBM, pre-1974 compiler, you may need to use another method to obtain the system date. In that case, you should consult the reference manual for the compiler you are using.

```
001010 IDENTIFICATION DIVISION.
001020 PROGRAM-ID.     PAYROLL.
001030*AUTHOR.         WELBURN.
001040*INSTALLATION.   UNIVERSAL BUSINESS SERVICES.
001050*DATE-WRITTEN.   JAN 12,1981.
001060*DATE-COMPILED.  JAN 13,1981.
001070*SECURITY.       NONE.
001080"
001090*
```

```
001100*          THIS PROGRAM READS PAYROLL RECORDS,
001110*          COMPUTES THE GROSS PAY FOR EACH EMPLOYEE
001120*          AND PRINTS AN EMPLOYEE DETAIL LINE
001130*          FOR EACH PAYROLL RECORD.
001140*
001150*          AFTER ALL INPUT PAYROLL RECORDS HAVE BEEN
001160*          PROCESSED, A REPORT TOTAL LINE WILL BE PRINTED.
002010*
002020*
002030*
002040 ENVIRONMENT DIVISION.
002050*
002060*
```

Figure 7.30. Complete program listing: Payroll program (continues)

```
002070 CONFIGURATION SECTION.                                033140      05  FILLER                  PIC X(6)    VALUE SPACES.
002080*                                                       033150      05  DL-HOURS-WORKED         PIC ZZZ.99.
002090 SOURCE-COMPUTER.  IBM-370.                             033160      05  FILLER                  PIC X(6)    VALUE SPACES.
002100 OBJECT-COMPUTER.  IBM-370.                             033170      05  DL-GROSS-PAY            PIC ZZ,ZZZ.99.
002110*                                                       033180      05  FILLER                  PIC X(52)   VALUE SPACES.
002120*                                                       034010*
002130 INPUT-OUTPUT SECTION.                                  034020 01  TL-TOTAL-LINE.
002140*                                                       034030      05  FILLER                  PIC X(1).
002150 FILE-CONTROL.                                          034040      05  FILLER                  PIC X(19)   VALUE SPACES.
002160     SELECT PAYROLL-FILE                                034050      05  TL-TOTAL-EMPLOYEES      PIC Z,ZZ9.
002170         ASSIGN TO UT-S-INFILE.                         034060      05  FILLER                  PIC X(32)
002180     SELECT PAYROLL-REPORT                              034070          VALUE ' TOTAL EMPLOYEES            '.
002190         ASSIGN TO UT-S-PRTFILE.                        034080      05  TL-TOTAL-HOURS-WORKED   PIC ZZ,ZZZ.99.
003010*                                                       034090      05  FILLER                  PIC X(1)    VALUE '*'.
003020*                                                       034100      05  FILLER                  PIC X(4)    VALUE SPACES.
003030*                                                       034110      05  TL-TOTAL-GROSS-PAY      PIC ZZZ,ZZZ.99.
003040 DATA DIVISION.                                         034120      05  FILLER                  PIC X(1)    VALUE '*'.
003050*                                                       034120      05  FILLER                  PIC X(51)   VALUE SPACES.
003060*                                                       050010*
003070 FILE SECTION.                                          050020*
003080*                                                       050030*
003090 FD  PAYROLL-FILE                                       050040 PROCEDURE DIVISION.
003100     RECORD CONTAINS 80 CHARACTERS                      050050*
003110     LABEL RECORDS ARE OMITTED.                         050060*
003120*                                                       050070 000-PRINT-PAYROLL-REPORT.
003130 01  PAYROLL-RECORD.                                    050080*
003140      05  FILLER                  PIC X(80).            050090     OPEN INPUT PAYROLL-FILE
004010*                                                       050100          OUTPUT PAYROLL-REPORT.
004020 FD  PAYROLL-REPORT                                     050110     PERFORM 100-INITIALIZE-VARIABLE-FIELDS.
004030     RECORD CONTAINS 133 CHARACTERS                     050130     PERFORM 800-READ-PAYROLL-RECORD.
004040     LABEL RECORDS ARE OMITTED.                         050140     PERFORM 200-PROCESS-PAYROLL-RECORD
004050*                                                       050150          UNTIL WS-END-OF-FILE-SWITCH IS EQUAL TO 'YES'.
004060 01  PAYROLL-REPORT-LINE.                               050160     PERFORM 700-PRINT-TOTAL-LINE.
004070      05  FILLER                  PIC X(133).           050170     CLOSE PAYROLL-FILE
005010*                                                       050180          PAYROLL-REPORT.
005020*                                                       050190     STOP RUN.
005030 WORKING-STORAGE SECTION.                               100010*
005040*                                                       100020*
005050*                                                       100030 100-INITIALIZE-VARIABLE-FIELDS.
005060 01  WS-SWITCHES.                                       100040*
005070      05  WS-END-OF-FILE-SWITCH   PIC X(3).             100050     MOVE 'NO ' TO WS-END-OF-FILE-SWITCH.
006010*                                                       100060     MOVE ZEROS TO WS-PAGE-COUNT.
006020 01  WS-REPORT-CONTROLS.                                100070     MOVE WS-LINES-PER-PAGE TO WS-LINES-USED.
006030      05  WS-PAGE-COUNT           PIC S9(3).            100080     ACCEPT WS-DATE-WORK FROM DATE.
006040      05  WS-LINES-PER-PAGE       PIC S9(2)   VALUE +57.100090     MOVE WS-MONTH TO H2-MONTH.
006050      05  WS-LINES-USED           PIC S9(2).            100100     MOVE WS-DAY TO H2-DAY.
006060      05  WS-LINE-SPACING         PIC S9(2).            100110     MOVE WS-YEAR TO H2-YEAR.
007010*                                                       100120     MOVE ZEROS TO WS-TOTAL-ACCUMULATORS.
007020 01  WS-WORK-AREAS.                                     200010*
007030      05  WS-DATE-WORK            PIC 9(6).             200020*
007040      05  WS-DATE-CONVERSION REDEFINES WS-DATE-WORK.    200030 200-PROCESS-PAYROLL-RECORD.
007050          10  WS-YEAR             PIC 9(2).             200040*
007060          10  WS-MONTH            PIC 9(2).             200050     IF WS-LINES-USED IS EQUAL TO WS-LINES-PER-PAGE
007070          10  WS-DAY              PIC 9(2).             200060          PERFORM 870-PRINT-REPORT-HEADINGS.
007080      05  WS-GROSS-PAY            PIC S9(5)V99.         200070     MOVE PR-SOC-SEC-NBR-1 TO DL-SOC-SEC-NBR-1.
008010*                                                       200080     MOVE PR-SOC-SEC-NBR-2 TO DL-SOC-SEC-NBR-2.
008020 01  WS-TOTAL-ACCUMULATORS.                             200090     MOVE PR-SOC-SEC-NBR-3 TO DL-SOC-SEC-NBR-3.
008030      05  WS-TOTAL-EMPLOYEES-ACCUM    PIC S9(4).        200100     MOVE PR-EMPLOYEE-NAME TO DL-EMPLOYEE-NAME.
008040      05  WS-TOTAL-HOURS-WORKED-ACCUM PIC S9(5)V99.     200110     MOVE PR-RATE-OF-PAY TO DL-RATE-OF-PAY.
008050      05  WS-TOTAL-GROSS-PAY-ACCUM    PIC S9(6)V99.     200120     MOVE PR-HOURS-WORKED TO DL-HOURS-WORKED.
020010*                                                       200130     MULTIPLY PR-RATE-OF-PAY BY PR-HOURS-WORKED
020020 01  PR-PAYROLL-RECORD.                                 200140          GIVING WS-GROSS-PAY ROUNDED.
020030      05  PR-RECORD-CODE          PIC X(2).             200150     MOVE WS-GROSS-PAY TO DL-GROSS-PAY.
020040      05  PR-SOC-SEC-NBR.                               200160     MOVE DL-DETAIL-LINE TO PAYROLL-REPORT-LINE.
020050          10  PR-SOC-SEC-NBR-1    PIC 9(3).             200170     MOVE 1 TO WS-LINE-SPACING.
020060          10  PR-SOC-SEC-NBR-2    PIC 9(2).             200180     PERFORM 890-WRITE-REPORT-LINE.
020070          10  PR-SOC-SEC-NBR-3    PIC 9(4).             200190     ADD 1 TO WS-TOTAL-EMPLOYEES-ACCUM.
020080      05  PR-EMPLOYEE-NAME        PIC X(24).            200200     ADD PR-HOURS-WORKED TO WS-TOTAL-HOURS-WORKED-ACCUM.
020090      05  PR-RATE-OF-PAY          PIC 9(2)V99.          200210     ADD WS-GROSS-PAY TO WS-TOTAL-GROSS-PAY-ACCUM.
020100      05  FILLER                  PIC X(5).             200220     PERFORM 800-READ-PAYROLL-RECORD.
020110      05  PR-HOURS-WORKED         PIC 9(3)V99.          700010*
020120      05  FILLER                  PIC X(31).            700020*
030010*                                                       700030 700-PRINT-TOTAL-LINE.
030020 01  H1-HEADING-LINE-1.                                 700040*
030030      05  FILLER      PIC X(1).                         700050     MOVE WS-TOTAL-EMPLOYEES-ACCUM TO TL-TOTAL-EMPLOYEES.
030040      05  FILLER      PIC X(20)   VALUE 'UNIVERSAL BUSINESS S'.700060     MOVE WS-TOTAL-HOURS-WORKED-ACCUM TO TL-TOTAL-HOURS-WORKED.
030050      05  FILLER      PIC X(20)   VALUE 'ERVICES COMPANY     '.700070     MOVE WS-TOTAL-GROSS-PAY-ACCUM TO TL-TOTAL-GROSS-PAY.
030060      05  FILLER      PIC X(20)   VALUE '                    '.700080     MOVE TL-TOTAL-LINE TO PAYROLL-REPORT-LINE.
030070      05  FILLER      PIC X(20)   VALUE '        PAYROLL REPORT'.700090     MOVE 3 TO WS-LINE-SPACING.
030080      05  FILLER      PIC X(20)   VALUE '                    '.700100     PERFORM 890-WRITE-REPORT-LINE.
030090      05  FILLER      PIC X(20)   VALUE '                    '.800010*
030100      05  FILLER      PIC X(12)   VALUE '            '.  800020*
031010*                                                       800030 800-READ-PAYROLL-RECORD.
031020 01  H2-HEADING-LINE-2.                                 800040*
031030      05  FILLER      PIC X(1).                         800050     READ PAYROLL-FILE INTO PR-PAYROLL-RECORD
031040      05  H2-MONTH    PIC 9(2).                         800060          AT END MOVE 'YES' TO WS-END-OF-FILE-SWITCH.
031050      05  FILLER      PIC X(1)    VALUE '/'.            870010*
031060      05  H2-DAY      PIC 9(2).                         870020*
031070      05  FILLER      PIC X(1)    VALUE '/'.            870030 870-PRINT-REPORT-HEADINGS.
031080      05  H2-YEAR     PIC 9(2).                         870040*
031090      05  FILLER      PIC X(64)   VALUE SPACES.         870050     ADD 1 TO WS-PAGE-COUNT.
031100      05  FILLER      PIC X(5)    VALUE 'PAGE '.        870060     MOVE WS-PAGE-COUNT TO H2-PAGE-NBR.
031110      05  H2-PAGE-NBR PIC ZZ9.                          870070     MOVE H1-HEADING-LINE-1 TO PAYROLL-REPORT-LINE.
031120      05  FILLER      PIC X(52)   VALUE SPACES.         870080     PERFORM 880-WRITE-REPORT-TOP-LINE.
032010*                                                       870090     MOVE H2-HEADING-LINE-2 TO PAYROLL-REPORT-LINE.
032020 01  H3-HEADING-LINE-3.                                 870100     MOVE 1 TO WS-LINE-SPACING.
032030      05  FILLER      PIC X(1).                         870110     PERFORM 890-WRITE-REPORT-LINE.
032040      05  FILLER      PIC X(20)   VALUE 'S.S. NUMBER         '.870120     MOVE H3-HEADING-LINE-3 TO PAYROLL-REPORT-LINE.
032050      05  FILLER      PIC X(20)   VALUE 'EMPLOYEE NAME       '.870130     MOVE 2 TO WS-LINE-SPACING.
032060      05  FILLER      PIC X(20)   VALUE '          RATE      '.870140     PERFORM 890-WRITE-REPORT-LINE.
032070      05  FILLER      PIC X(20)   VALUE 'HOURS      GROSS PAY'.870150     MOVE SPACES TO PAYROLL-REPORT-LINE.
032080      05  FILLER      PIC X(20)   VALUE '                    '.870160     MOVE 1 TO WS-LINE-SPACING.
032090      05  FILLER      PIC X(20)   VALUE '                    '.870170     PERFORM 890-WRITE-REPORT-LINE.
032100      05  FILLER      PIC X(12)   VALUE '            '.  880010*
033010*                                                       880020*
033020 01  DL-DETAIL-LINE.                                    880030 880-WRITE-REPORT-TOP-LINE.
033030      05  FILLER                  PIC X(1).             880040*
033040      05  DL-SOC-SEC-NBR.                               880050     WRITE PAYROLL-REPORT-LINE
033050          10  DL-SOC-SEC-NBR-1    PIC 9(3).             880060          AFTER ADVANCING PAGE.
033060          10  FILLER              PIC X(1)    VALUE '-'.880070     MOVE 1 TO WS-LINES-USED.
033070          10  DL-SOC-SEC-NBR-2    PIC 9(2).             890010*
033080          10  FILLER              PIC X(1)    VALUE '-'.890020*
033090          10  DL-SOC-SEC-NBR-3    PIC 9(4).             890030 890-WRITE-REPORT-LINE.
033100      05  FILLER                  PIC X(6)    VALUE SPACES.890040*
033110      05  DL-EMPLOYEE-NAME        PIC X(24).            890050     WRITE PAYROLL-REPORT-LINE
033120      05  FILLER                  PIC X(7)    VALUE SPACES.890060          AFTER ADVANCING WS-LINE-SPACING LINES.
033130      05  DL-RATE-OF-PAY          PIC ZZ.99.            890070     ADD WS-LINE-SPACING TO WS-LINES-USED.
```

Figure 7.30. (continued)

ACCEPT/FROM DATE method (1974 standard)

The format and an example of the ACCEPT/FROM DATE statement are shown in Figure 7.31. The identifier must be an unsigned integer numeric field six digits in length. The date will be stored in the identifier field in *yymmdd* format where *yy* is the year number of the century, *mm* is the month number, and *dd* is the day number.

Notice from the format that DAY and TIME can also be obtained. When DAY is specified, the identifier must be a five-digit unsigned numeric integer field. The DAY option provides the sequential day number of the year (often referred to as the *Julian date*) in *yyddd* format. The two-digit year number of the century is followed by the three-digit day of the year (from 001 to 365, or 366 for a leap year). For example, February 1, 1982, is represented as 82032 (see Figure 7.32).

When TIME is specified, the identifier must be an eight-digit integer numeric field. The TIME will be presented in *hhmmsscc* format where *hh* is the hour number from zero to 23, *mm* is the minute number from zero to 59, *ss* is the second number from zero to 59, and *cc* is the hundredths of a second from zero to 99. Thus, the minimum value of time—midnight—is represented as 00000000. The maximum value of time—11:59 p.m.—appears as 23595999 (see Figure 7.33).

In this PAYROLL program, as with most programs, we are concerned only with the DATE. So in the 100-INITIALIZE-VARIABLE-FIELDS module, the DATE is accepted from the operating system and placed in the WS-DATE-CONVERSION

Format:

```
ACCEPT identifier FROM  { DATE
                          DAY
                          TIME }
```

Example:

DATA DIVISION:

```
05  XX-DATE-AREA          PIC 9(6).
```

PROCEDURE DIVISION:

```
ACCEPT XX-DATE-AREA FROM DATE.
```

Before ACCEPT/FROM DATE:

```
A 0 3 * 5 X
```
XX-DATE-AREA

After ACCEPT/FROM DATE (on February 1, 1982):

```
8 2 0 2 0 1
```
XX-DATE-AREA

Figure 7.31. ACCEPT/FROM DATE example

DATA DIVISION:

SEQUENCE			A	D	COBOL STATEMENT	IDENTIFICATION
(PAGE)	(SERIAL)	CONT				

```
        Ø5  XX-DAY-AREA                          PIC  9(5).
```

PROCEDURE DIVISION:

```
            ACCEPT XX-DAY-AREA FROM DAY.
```

After ACCEPT/FROM DAY (on February 1, 1982):

8	2	0	3	2

XX-DAY-AREA

Figure 7.32. ACCEPT/FROM DAY example

field. Then the individual month, day, and year fields are moved to their respective locations in the H2-HEADING-LINE-2 area. Notice that the year, month, and day fields must be moved individually because DATE is represented in *yymmdd* sequence but, for the report, it must be printed in *mmddyy* sequence.

CURRENT-DATE method (IBM system-name extension)

CURRENT-DATE is an IBM system-name for an eight-character alphanumeric field that contains the date in *mm/dd/yy format*. Figure 7.34 compares the coding required for the ACCEPT/FROM DATE and the CURRENT-DATE methods. Notice that the slashes are already included in CURRENT-DATE.

Actually, to display dates on reports, the CURRENT-DATE method is more convenient to use (the slashes are already inserted and it is in the normally expressed *mmddyy* format) than the COBOL standard ACCEPT DATE/FROM statement. Even if the compiler you are using has both methods available, though, it is better to resist the temptation to use the non-ANS CURRENT-DATE; you should use ACCEPT/FROM DATE instead so that the program is in accordance with standard COBOL.

DATA DIVISION:

SEQUENCE			A	B	COBOL STATEMENT	IDENTIFICATION
(PAGE)	(SERIAL)	CONT				

```
        Ø5  XX-TIME-AREA                    PIC  9(8).
```

PROCEDURE DIVISION:

```
            ACCEPT XX-TIME-AREA FROM TIME.
```

After ACCEPT/FROM TIME (immediately before midnight):

2	3	5	9	5	9	9	9

XX-TIME-AREA

Figure 7.33. ACCEPT/FROM TIME example

Part A: ACCEPT/FROM DATE method:

DATA DIVISION:

```
05  WS-DATE-AREA                                    PIC 9(6).
05  WS-DATE-CONVERSION REDEFINES WS-DATE-AREA.
    10  WS-YEAR                                      PIC 9(2).
    10  WS-MONTH                                     PIC 9(2).
    10  WS-DAY                                       PIC 9(2).

05  H1-DATE.
    10  H1-MONTH      PIC 9(2).
    10  H1-SLASH-1    PIC X(1)      VALUE '/'.
    10  H1-DAY        PIC 9(2).
    10  H1-SLASH-2    PIC X(1)      VALUE '/'.
    10  H1-YEAR       PIC 9(2).
```

PROCEDURE DIVISION:

```
ACCEPT WS-DATE-AREA FROM DATE.
MOVE WS-MONTH TO H1-MONTH.
MOVE WS-DAY TO H1-DAY.
MOVE WS-YEAR TO H1-YEAR.
```

Part B: CURRENT-DATE method:

DATA DIVISION:

```
05  H1-DATE           PIC X(8).
```

PROCEDURE DIVISION:

```
MOVE CURRENT-DATE TO H1-DATE.
```

Figure 7.34. Comparison of ACCEPT/FROM DATE and CURRENT-DATE

The READ Statement INTO Phrase

The READ statement was introduced in Chapter 3. Its format is shown again in Figure 7.35 together with an example of the use of the INTO phrase taken from the PAYROLL program. A READ statement with the INTO phrase will read a record and transfer the data read from the file to the location written after the reserved word INTO. This INTO phrase is used when fields of the input record have been defined in WORKING-STORAGE, as has been done in the PAYROLL program. A READ statement without the INTO phrase followed by a MOVE statement would accomplish exactly the same result, as shown in Figure 7.36.

The WRITE Statement ADVANCING Phrase

The WRITE statement using the integer option of the ADVANCING phrase was introduced in Chapter 3. The format is shown again as Figure 7.37 for reference. With the integer option that has been used in previous programs of this text, it is possible to advance a fixed number (usually from 0 to 99) of lines. However, the integer option is not the one to use for structured programs with variable line-spacing requirements. The convention of having one line-spacing WRITE module per file cannot generally be adhered to when the integer form is used. For example, in the PAYROLL program, there are requirements for single-spacing (between the first and second heading-lines and between detail-

Example:

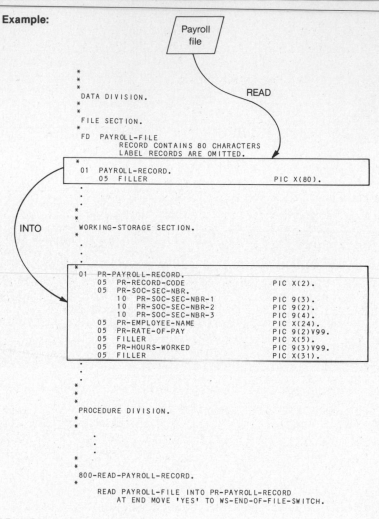

Figure 7.35. READ/INTO statement example

This READ/INTO statement

```
*
*
 800-READ-PAYROLL-RECORD.
*
      READ PAYROLL-FILE INTO PR-PAYROLL-RECORD
           AT END MOVE 'YES' TO WS-END-OF-FILE-SWITCH.
```

is equivalent to

these READ and MOVE statements

```
*
*
 800-READ-PAYROLL-RECORD.
*
      READ PAYROLL-FILE
           AT END MOVE 'YES' TO WS-END-OF-FILE-SWITCH.
      MOVE PAYROLL-RECORD TO PR-PAYROLL-RECORD.
```

Figure 7.36. Comparison of the READ/INTO statement with READ and MOVE statements

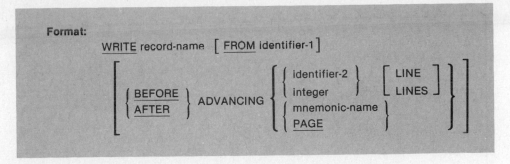

Format:

WRITE record-name [FROM identifier-1]

$$\left[\begin{Bmatrix} \underline{BEFORE} \\ \underline{AFTER} \end{Bmatrix} \text{ADVANCING} \begin{Bmatrix} identifier\text{-}2 \\ integer \\ mnemonic\text{-}name \\ \underline{PAGE} \end{Bmatrix} \begin{bmatrix} LINE \\ LINES \end{bmatrix} \right]$$

Figure 7.37. WRITE statement format

lines), double-spacing (between the second and third heading-lines), and triple-spacing (between the last detail-line and the total-line). If the integer form were used, three separate WRITE statements would be required.

Variable line spacing with the ADVANCING phrase

To provide variable line-spacing with just one WRITE statement, the identifier option must be used. Identifier-2 must be a one- or two-digit integer numeric field. When the WRITE statement is executed, the printer is advanced a number of lines equal to the current value of identifier-2. The PAYROLL program example is shown in Figure 7.38. By moving a 1, 2, or 3 to the WS-LINE-SPACING field, either single-, double-, or triple-spacing will occur when the WRITE statement in the 890-WRITE-REPORT-LINE module is executed. The reserved words ADVANCING and LINES are optional. When using the identifier option, programmers often omit the optional words because the phrase is sometimes more readable without them. Figure 7.39 shows examples.

Page skipping with the ADVANCING phrase

There are two commonly used methods to skip to the next report page with the ADVANCING phrase. The first method uses the reserved word PAGE and is the standard method. This PAGE option did not become a COBOL standard until

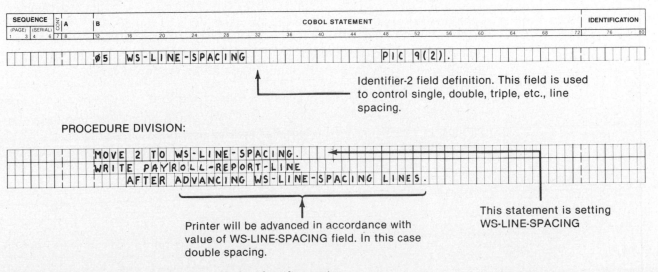

Figure 7.38. Variable line-spacing with the identifier option

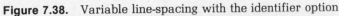

Part A: Written without words ADVANCING and LINES

SEQUENCE						

```
WRITE PAYROLL-REPORT-LINE
     AFTER WS-LINE-SPACING.
```

Part B: Written without word LINES

```
WRITE PAYROLL-REPORT-LINE
     AFTER ADVANCING WS-LINE-SPACING.
```

Part C: Written without word ADVANCING

```
WRITE PAYROLL-REPORT-LINE
     AFTER WS-LINE-SPACING LINES.
```

Figure 7.39. ADVANCING phrase without optional words

1974, however, so if you are using a pre-1974 compiler, you will not be able to use it.

The second method—the *mnemonic-name* option of the ADVANCING phrase—uses the SPECIAL-NAMES paragraph of the CONFIGURATION SECTION of the ENVIRONMENT DIVISION to associate the hardware top-of-page function with the mnemonic-name. The entries required to specify this top-of-page function in the SPECIAL-NAMES paragraph can vary with the COBOL compilers of various vendors.

We will cover the PAGE option for ANS-1974 compilers and the mnemonic-name option for IBM compilers. If you are using an ANS-1974 COBOL standard compiler, you should use the PAGE method because it is a COBOL standard and it does not require a SPECIAL-NAMES paragraph entry. With an ANS-1968 IBM-compatible COBOL compiler, you can use the mnemonic-name option as covered in this text. If you are using a pre-1974 non-IBM compiler, you should consult the reference manual for the top-of-forms requirements.

The PAGE option (1974 standard)

To cause the report to be advanced to the top of the next page, the programmer specifies the reserved word PAGE. An example is in the 880-WRITE-REPORT-TOP-LINE module of the PAYROLL program and is shown in Figure 7.40. When this statement is executed, the printer page will be advanced to the top of the next page in accordance with the printer setting for top-of-forms.

The mnemonic-name option (IBM implementor-name example)

This method requires a SPECIAL-NAMES paragraph entry. The format of the SPECIAL-NAMES paragraph together with an example is shown in Figure 7.41. The implementor-name is the implementor-defined name for the top of the

```
WRITE PAYROLL-REPORT-LINE
     AFTER ADVANCING PAGE.
```

Figure 7.40. ADVANCING phrase PAGE option

```
ENVIRONMENT DIVISION.
CONFIGURATION SECTION.
SOURCE-COMPUTER. computer-name
OBJECT-COMPUTER. computer-name
[ SPECIAL-NAMES. [implementor-name IS mnemonic name] ]
```

Example:

```
SEQUENCE  | C A | B                          COBOL STATEMENT                        IDENTIFICATION
(PAGE)(SERIAL) O N T
1    3 4   6 7 8   12    16    20    24    28    32    36    40    44    48    52    56    60    64    68    72    76    80

            SPECIAL-NAMES.
              C01 IS TO-TOP-OF-PAGE.
```

implementor name   mnemonic-name

Figure 7.41. SPECIAL-NAMES paragraph

page. For IBM COBOL compilers, the name that should be used is C01 (which is an abbreviation for Channel 01). Notice that the middle character is a zero, not an alphabetical O. The mnemonic-name is a user-defined word and thus created by the programmer. In our example, the mnemonic-name TO-TOP-OF-PAGE has been chosen.

Then, in the WRITE statement, the mnemonic-name is specified in the AD-VANCING phrase to cause the report to be advanced to the top of the next page.

Figure 7.42 compares the PAGE and the mnemonic-name forms of page advancing. In this text, the PAGE method is used. If you are using a compiler that does not have the PAGE option, it will be necessary for you to insert the proper SPECIAL-NAMES and mnemonic-name entries into your program.

Part A: Mnemonic-name option

ENVIRONMENT DIVISION — CONFIGURATION SECTION:

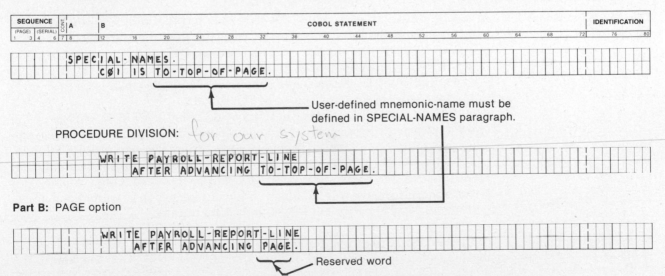

User-defined mnemonic-name must be defined in SPECIAL-NAMES paragraph.

PROCEDURE DIVISION: *for our system*

Part B: PAGE option

Reserved word

Figure 7.42. Comparison of page advancing: Mnemonic-name and PAGE options

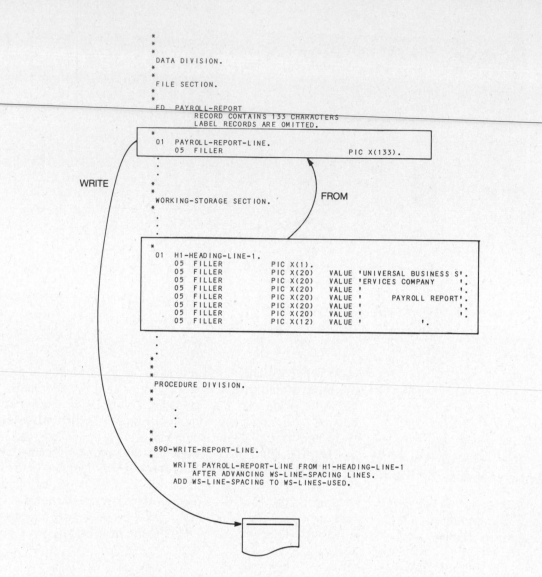

```
          *
          *
          *
          DATA DIVISION.
          *
          FILE SECTION.
          *
          FD  PAYROLL-REPORT
                    RECORD CONTAINS 133 CHARACTERS
                    LABEL RECORDS ARE OMITTED.
          *
          01  PAYROLL-REPORT-LINE.
              05  FILLER                            PIC X(133).
          .
          .
          *
          *
          WORKING-STORAGE SECTION.
          *
          .
          .
          .
          *
          01  H1-HEADING-LINE-1.
              05  FILLER        PIC X(1).
              05  FILLER        PIC X(20)    VALUE 'UNIVERSAL BUSINESS S'.
              05  FILLER        PIC X(20)    VALUE 'ERVICES COMPANY     '.
              05  FILLER        PIC X(20)    VALUE '                    '.
              05  FILLER        PIC X(20)    VALUE '        PAYROLL REPORT'.
              05  FILLER        PIC X(20)    VALUE '                    '.
              05  FILLER        PIC X(20)    VALUE '                    '.
              05  FILLER        PIC X(12)    VALUE '            '.
          .
          .
          *
          *
          *
          PROCEDURE DIVISION.
          *
          *
          .
          .
          *
          *
          890-WRITE-REPORT-LINE.
          *
              WRITE PAYROLL-REPORT-LINE FROM H1-HEADING-LINE-1
                  AFTER ADVANCING WS-LINE-SPACING LINES.
              ADD WS-LINE-SPACING TO WS-LINES-USED.
```

Figure 7.43. WRITE/FROM statement example

The WRITE Statement FROM Phrase

A WRITE statement with the FROM phrase is parallel to a READ/INTO statement. It causes the data to be moved from the identifier specified after the reserved word FROM to the record-name and then written. Thus, while READ/INTO is equivalent to a READ and a MOVE, WRITE/FROM corresponds to a MOVE and a WRITE. An example of how WRITE/FROM could have been used in the PAYROLL program is shown in Figure 7.43.

We recommend, however, that you avoid using the FROM phrase of the WRITE statement. It is usually not compatible with our structured programming convention of one WRITE statement per file. The use of WRITE/FROM creates one WRITE statement per record. Of course, if the file has only one record format, the convention objective could be satisfied. Often, though, different record formats will be added to files in accordance with changing requirements so it is better not to use the FROM phrase.

An Introduction to the IF Statement

In the PAYROLL program, the WS-LINES-USED field must be compared with the WS-LINES-PER-PAGE field. If the value of WS-LINES-USED is equal to the number of lines allotted to the page span, the 870-PRINT-REPORT-HEADINGS module should be performed. An IF statement is required to accomplish this

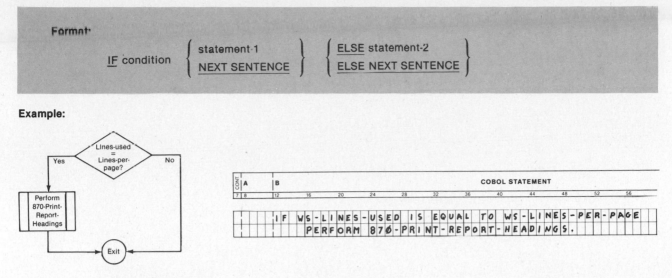

Format:

IF condition $\left\{ \begin{array}{l} \text{statement-1} \\ \underline{\text{NEXT SENTENCE}} \end{array} \right\}$ $\left\{ \begin{array}{l} \underline{\text{ELSE}} \text{ statement-2} \\ \underline{\text{ELSE NEXT SENTENCE}} \end{array} \right\}$

Example:

COBOL STATEMENT

```
IF WS-LINES-USED IS EQUAL TO WS-LINES-PER-PAGE
   PERFORM 870-PRINT-REPORT-HEADINGS.
```

Figure 7.44. IF statement example

comparison and conditional execution of the 870-PRINT-REPORT-HEADINGS module.

The IF statement format together with the example from the PAYROLL program is shown in Figure 7.44. When an IF statement is executed, the condition specified is tested. If the condition is true, the statements specified in the IF sentence before the period, or before the word ELSE if present, are executed. If the condition is false, those statements are skipped.

Questions You May Have about the PAYROLL Program Coding

Why were the WS-REPORT-CONTROLS *fields assigned an S in their picture character-string when there is no way that a negative value could develop in any of the fields?* If a numeric field is used in arithmetic operations or has a signed numeric field moved to it, and if its picture character-string does not contain an S, most COBOL compilers must provide an extra step in the program to strip the arithmetic sign from the field. Thus, it is more efficient to put the symbol S in the picture character-string for fields that will be used for arithmetic results or that will receive the contents of signed numeric fields—even if they will never contain a negative number.

Why weren't WORKING-STORAGE *fields, other than* WS-LINES-PER-PAGE, *initialized with* VALUE *clauses rather than being initialized by* MOVE *statements in the* 100-INITIALIZE-VARIABLE-FIELDS *module?* An example showing the alternative initialization methods is shown in Figure 7.45. The general convention recommended here is to initialize constant fields with VALUE clauses but to initialize variable fields in the PROCEDURE DIVISION. Following this convention allows one to review the WORKING-STORAGE SECTION of the program and to know immediately which fields never change in value and which are variables.

Why was the WS-DATE-WORK *field redefined as* WS-DATE-CONVERSION? *Why was that redefinition necessary?* Figure 7.46 illustrates the answer. The ACCEPT/FROM DATE statement requires that the identifier be an elementary field. The WS-DATE-CONVERSION field is required so that (1) WS-DATE-WORK may be defined as an elementary field with a PICTURE clause, and (2) the subordinate WS-YEAR, WS-MONTH, and WS-DAY fields can be defined for individual moves to the heading-line so that the date will be converted from *yymmdd* to *mmddyy* format.

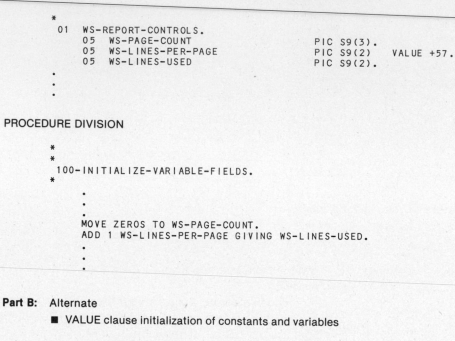

Part A: Recommended
- VALUE clause initialization of constants
- PROCEDURE DIVISION initialization of variables

DATA DIVISION

```
*
 01  WS-REPORT-CONTROLS.
     05  WS-PAGE-COUNT              PIC S9(3).
     05  WS-LINES-PER-PAGE         PIC S9(2)    VALUE +57.
     05  WS-LINES-USED             PIC S9(2).
 .
 .
 .
```

PROCEDURE DIVISION

```
*
*
 100-INITIALIZE-VARIABLE-FIELDS.
*
     .
     .
     .
     MOVE ZEROS TO WS-PAGE-COUNT.
     ADD 1 WS-LINES-PER-PAGE GIVING WS-LINES-USED.
     .
     .
     .
```

Part B: Alternate
- VALUE clause initialization of constants and variables

```
*
 01  WS-REPORT-CONTROLS.
     05  WS-PAGE-COUNT             PIC S9(3)    VALUE ZEROS.
     05  WS-LINES-PER-PAGE         PIC S9(2)    VALUE +57.
     05  WS-LINES-USED             PIC S9(2)    VALUE +57.
 .
 .
 .
```

Figure 7.45. Alternate initialization methods

Part A: Correct — required redefinition

```
 05  WS-DATE-WORK                  PIC 9(6).
 05  WS-DATE-CONVERSION REDEFINES WS-DATE-WORK.
     10  WS-YEAR                   PIC 9(2).
     10  WS-MONTH                  PIC 9(2).
     10  WS-DAY                    PIC 9(2).
```

Part B: Not correct — ACCEPT/FROM DATE requires an elementary 6-digit unsigned field as the identifier

```
 05  WS-DATE-WORK.
     10  WS-YEAR                   PIC 9(2).
     10  WS-MONTH                  PIC 9(2).
     10  WS-DAY                    PIC 9(2).
```

Part C: Invalid — this level relationship means that WS-DATE-WORK must be a group field and cannot contain a PICTURE clause

```
 05  WS-DATE-WORK                  PIC 9(6).
     10  WS-YEAR                   PIC 9(2).
     10  WS-MONTH                  PIC 9(2).
     10  WS-DAY                    PIC 9(2).
```

Figure 7.46. Example of need for redefinition

Why was the WS-PAGE-COUNT *field required? Why couldn't the page-number accumulation be done directly into the* H2-PAGE-NBR *field, which is also in* WORKING-STORAGE? The H2-PAGE-NBR field is a numeric edited field. Factors in arithmetic statements must be numeric. The accumulation is done in WS-PAGE-COUNT and then is moved to the H2-PAGE-NBR field for editing.

Summary

To design a structure chart for a program, the programmer should take the following steps:

1. List the functional program modules
2. Describe the overall program function on the top level of the structure chart
3. Show the major program functions on the first level of the structure chart
4. Expand these first-level modules
5. Identify common modules
6. Review structure chart
7. Number each module

The REDEFINES clause is used in the DATA DIVISION to assign more than one name and/or PICTURE clause to an area of storage. The redefining field must:

1. Be equal to or shorter than the field being redefined
2. Immediately follow, at that level number, the area being redefined

The VALUE clause is used in the DATA DIVISION to establish the initial contents of a field. The data class, length, and sign configuration (if applicable) must be consistent with the characteristics of the field as defined by its PICTURE clause. The VALUE clause cannot be used in the following situations:

1. In the FILE SECTION
2. With a group field data-item description entry
3. With a data-item description entry that contains an editing PICTURE clause
4. With a data-item description entry that contains a REDEFINES clause
5. With a data-item description entry that contains an OCCURS clause

The current date, day, or time may be obtained from the operating system by the statement: ACCEPT identifier FROM DATE, DAY, (or) TIME. When DATE is used, the identifier must be a six-digit unsigned integer field; the date will be returned in *yymmdd* format. When DAY is specified, the identifier must be a five-digit unsigned integer field; the day will be returned in *yyddd* format. For TIME, the identifier must be an eight-digit integer numeric field; the time will be returned in *hhmmsscc* format.

The statement READ file-name INTO record-name may be used to read a record into the FILE SECTION and then move it to the specified record-name. It is equivalent to a READ statement followed by a MOVE statement.

To obtain line-spacing for a variable number of lines with one WRITE statement, the programmer may use the *identifier* option of the ADVANCING phrase. The identifier must be a one- or two-digit numeric integer field. When the statement is executed, the printer forms are advanced a number of lines equivalent to the current value of the identifier field.

To skip printer forms to the next page, the programmer uses the PAGE option of the ADVANCING phrase. Alternately, the *mnemonic-name* option may be used. Its use requires an entry in the SPECIAL-NAMES paragraph of the CON-

FIGURATION SECTION of the ENVIRONMENT DIVISION to associate the mnemonic-name with the compiler's top-of-page function.

The statement WRITE record-name FROM record-name may be used to cause a record to be moved to the output record area and then written. It is equivalent to a MOVE statement followed by a WRITE statement.

An IF statement causes a condition to be tested and the following statements to be executed or skipped depending upon whether the condition is true or false.

Style Summary

- Do not use the optional word IS in the VALUE clause. It consumes space on the coding line and does not materially enhance program documentation.

- Define output records in the WORKING-STORAGE SECTION. It (1) allows VALUE clauses to be used for the initialization of constant fields within the record, (2) eliminates double-buffering problems, (3) allows reference to fields of a record that have already been written to an output device, and (4) makes it easier to determine the current output record being processed when referring to a storage dump.

- In most cases, define input records in the WORKING-STORAGE SECTION. The advantages of input record definition in WORKING-STORAGE are not as great as those for output record definition, but it (1) does allow reference to fields of a record after the next record has been read and (2) does make it easier to determine the last input record that was read when referencing to a storage dump.

- When describing records in WORKING-STORAGE that contain primarily constant values, start the PICTURE clauses in position 32 and the VALUE clauses in position 44.

- When describing longer records in WORKING-STORAGE that contain primarily non-numeric literal constant values, define such values in groups of 20 characters.

- When describing records in WORKING-STORAGE that contain primarily variable fields with short constant literals or figurative constants, start the PICTURE clause in position 48 and the VALUE clause in position 60.

- If available, use the COBOL standard ACCEPT/FROM DATE statement rather than other methods to acquire the current date.

- If available, use the COBOL standard PAGE option rather than the mnemonic-name option to advance printer forms to the next page.

- Avoid use of the WRITE/FROM statement because it limits WRITE module use.

- Initialize constant fields with VALUE clauses in the DATA DIVISION; initialize variable fields with PROCEDURE DIVISION statements. Doing so aids program documentation and tends to make modules reentrant.

1968 ANS COBOL Restrictions

- The ACCEPT/FROM DATE, DAY, and TIME statements are not available.
- The PAGE option of the ADVANCING phrase is not available.

Exercises

Terms for Definition

heading line
constant data
variable data

1. List the seven steps for preparation of a structure chart.

2. When using the REDEFINES clause, the redefining field (the one with the REDEFINES clause) must not be _greater_ than the redefined field. Also, the redefining entry must immediately _follow_ , at that level number, the field being redefined.

3. The literal specified in a VALUE clause should be consistent with the _____ clause of the data-item.

4. The VALUE clause cannot be specified in the following instances:
   a. In the _File_ SECTION of the DATA DIVISION
   b. With a _group field_ data-item
   c. With a data-item which contains a _redefines_ clause
   d. With a data-item which contains an _occurs_ clause.

5. Identify four reasons why it is usually preferable to define output records in the WORKING-STORAGE rather than the FILE SECTION.

6. Identify two reasons why it is usually preferable to define input records in the WORKING-STORAGE SECTION rather than the FILE SECTION.

7. Identify two usual disadvantages of WORKING-STORAGE definition of input and output records.

8. Most programs that provide for the printing of report headings require report control fields for which three functions?

9. When writing the ACCEPT/FROM DATE statement, the identifier must be a _____ -digit unsigned numeric integer field; the date is represented in _____ format.

10. With the non-ANS standard CURRENT-DATE, the date is represented in an _____ -character alphanumeric field in _____ format.

11. When writing the ACCEPT/FROM DAY statement, the identifier must be a _____ -digit unsigned numeric integer field; the day is represented in _____ format.

12. When writing the ACCEPT/FROM TIME statement, the identifier must be a _____ -digit unsigned numeric integer field; the time is represented in _____ format.

13. A READ statement specified with the INTO phrase is equivalent to the specification of a _____ statement followed by a _____ statement.

14. A WRITE statement specified with the FROM phrase is equivalent to the specification of a _____ statement followed by a _____ statement.

15. To provide variable line spacing with one WRITE statement, the _____ option of the ADVANCING phrase is used.

16. To provide for skipping to the top of the next report page, the reserved word _____ (1974-ANS only) or the _advancing_ option may be used.

17. When the _____ option of the ADVANCING phrase is used, the SPECIAL-NAMES paragraph is required in the _____ SECTION of the _____ DIVISION.

1. Some or all of the following data-item descriptions with VALUE clauses contain inconsistencies or syntax errors. Identify each inconsistent or erroneous description.
   a. 05 XX-AMT PIC S9(5) VALUE +0.
   b. 05 XX-AMT PIC S9(5) VALUE 00000.
   c. 05 XX-AMT PIC S9(5) VALUE ZEROS.
   d. 05 XX-AMT PIC S9(5) VALUE SPACES.
   e. 05 XX-AMT-2 REDEFINES XX-AMT VALUE 00100.
   f. 10 XX-FLD PIC X(3) VALUE SPACES.
   g. 10 XX-FLD PIC X(3) VALUE ZEROS.
   h. 10 XX-FLD PIC X(3) VALUE 'ABC'.

  i. 10 XX-FLD PIC X(3) VALUE '123'.
  j. 10 XX-FLD PIC X(3) VALUE 123.
  k. 01 XX-RECORD VALUE SPACES.

2. Some or all of the following data-item descriptions with REDEFINES clauses contain
   syntax errors. Identify the reason each erroneous clause is incorrect.

  a. 05 XX-FLD-A PIC X(5).
      05 XX-FLD-B REDEFINES XX-FLD-A PIC 9(5).
  b. 05 XX-FLD-A PIC X(5).
      05 XX-FLD-B REDEFINES XX-FLD-A PIC X(6).
  c. 05 XX-FLD-A PIC X(5).
      05 XX-FLD-B REDEFINES XX-FLD-B PIC 9(3).
  d. 05 XX-FLD-A.
          10 XX-FLD-1A PIC X(6).
          10 XX-FLD-1B PIC X(3).
      10 XX-FLD-B REDEFINES XX-FLD-A PIC X(9).

Programming
Assignment 7-A:
Price List

Program description
    A price list is to be printed from the part master file.

Input file
    Part master file

Input record format
    Part master record

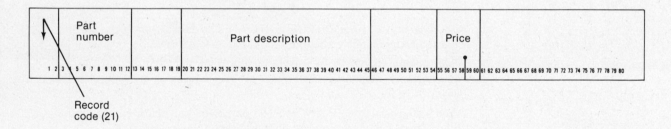

Record code (21)

Output file
    Price list

Output report format

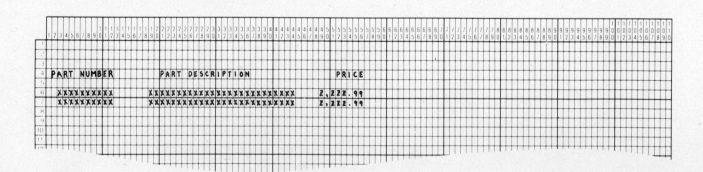

Program operations

1. Read each input part master record.

2. Print an output price list detail line as specified above for each part master record.

3. Single-space each detail line. Print the heading-line on the first page and each following page. Provide for a span of 57 lines per page.

Programming Assignment 7-B: Accounts Payable Report

Program description

An accounts payable report is to be printed from the accounts payable file.

Input file

Accounts payable file

Input record format

Vendor record

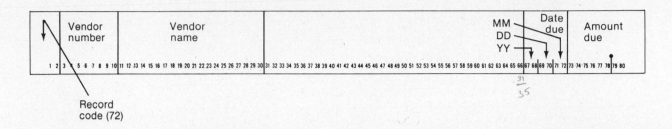

| | Vendor number | Vendor name | | MM DD YY | Date due | Amount due |

Record code (72)

31
—
35

Output file

Accounts payable report

Output record format

```
                ACCOUNTS PAYABLE REPORT

 DATE      VENDOR                       AMOUNT
 DUE       NUMBER      VENDOR NAME       DUE

99/99/99  XXXXXXXX   XXXXXXXXXXXXXXXXXXX  ZZZ,ZZZ.99
99/99/99  XXXXXXXX   XXXXXXXXXXXXXXXXXXX  ZZZ,ZZZ.99

          TOTAL ACCOUNTS PAYABLE   Z,ZZZ,ZZZ.99+
```

Program operations

1. Read each input accounts payable record.

2. For each input accounts payable record, do the following processing:
   a. Print an output detail line as specified above for each accounts payable record.

   b. Accumulate the total amount due.

3. Single-space each detail line. Print the heading-lines on the first page and each following page. Provide for a span of 57 lines per page.

4. After all input accounts payable records have been processed, print the total line.

Programming Assignment 7-C: Test Results Report

Program description

A test results report is to be printed from the test score file.

Input file

Test score file

Input record format

Test score record

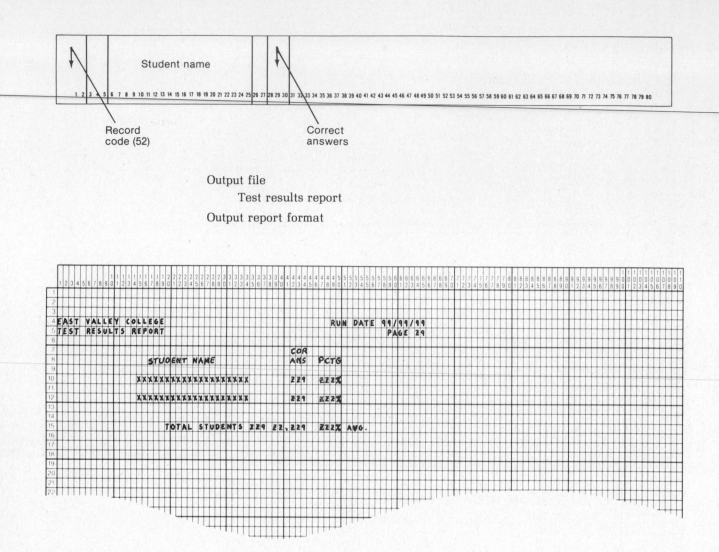

Output file
> Test results report

Output report format

```
EAST VALLEY COLLEGE                              RUN DATE 99/99/99
TEST RESULTS REPORT                                       PAGE 29

                                    COR
              STUDENT NAME          ANS   PCTG

         XXXXXXXXXXXXXXXXXXXXX      ZZ9   ZZZ%

         XXXXXXXXXXXXXXXXXXXXX      ZZ9   ZZZ%


         TOTAL STUDENTS ZZ9 ZZ,ZZ9  ZZZ% AVG.
```

Program operations

1. Read each input test score record.

2. For each input test score record, do the following:

   a. Compute the percentage of correct test answers (50 test questions were asked). Round to the nearest percentage point.

   b. Accumulate the total number of test score records processed and the total number of correct answers.

   c. Print an output detail line as specified above for each test score record.

3. Double-space each detail line. Print the heading-lines on the first page and each following page. Provide for a span of 57 lines per page.

4. After all input test score records have been processed, print the output report total line as specified above (triple-spaced from the last detail line).

Programming Assignment 7-D: Accounts Receivable Report

Program description
> An accounts receivable report is to be printed from the accounts receivable file.

Input file
> Accounts receivable file

Input record format
> Accounts receivable record

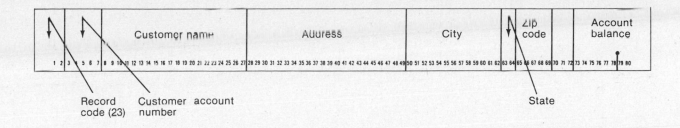

		Customer name	Address	City	Zip code	Account balance
1 2	3 5 6 7	8 9 10 11 12 13 14 15 16 17 18 19 20 21 22 23 24 25 26 27	28 29 30 31 32 33 34 35 36 37 38 39 40 41 42 43 44 45 46 47 48 49	50 51 52 53 54 55 56 57 58 59 60 61 62	63 64 65 66 67 68 69 70 71 72	73 74 75 76 77 78 79 80

Record code (23) Customer account number State

Output file

    Accounts receivable report

Output report format

```
 4 SILICON VALLEY MFG. CO.                    RUN TIME 99:99:99 RUN DATE 99/99/99
 5                                                              PAGE ZZZ9
 6
 8 CUST   CUSTOMER                                              ACCOUNT
 9 ACCT     NAME            ADDRESS            CITY     ST  ZIP  BALANCE
10
11 99999 XXXXXXXXXXXXXXXXXXXXXX  XXXXXXXXXXXXXXXXXXXXXXXX XXXXXXXXXXXXX XX 99999 ZZZ,ZZZ.99-
12 99999 XXXXXXXXXXXXXXXXXXXXXX  XXXXXXXXXXXXXXXXXXXXXXXX XXXXXXXXXXXXX XX 99999 ZZZ,ZZZ.99-
13
14                                           PAGE TOTAL      Z,ZZZ,ZZZ.99-*
15
16                                           REPORT TOTAL   ZZ,ZZZ,ZZZ.99-**
```

Program operations

1. Read each input accounts receivable record.

2. For each input accounts receivable record, do the following processing:

   a. Print an output report detail line.

   b. Accumulate required totals.

3. Single-space each detail line. Print the heading-lines on the first page and each following page. Provide for a span of 55 lines per page (not counting the page total line).

4. Print the accounts receivable page total at the bottom of each report page and after the last detail line has been printed.

5. After all input accounts receivable records have been processed, print the report total line (double-spaced from the page total line).

CHAPTER 8

THE IF STATEMENT AND DATA MANIPULATION

The IF statement is a powerful COBOL statement. This chapter will cover it in detail. In addition, COBOL character-manipulation statements—EXAMINE and INSPECT—will be presented in the latter part of the chapter.

The IF Statement

If-then-else is one of the three control structures of the structure theorem. Figure 8.1 depicts this structure. The COBOL IF statement is used for the if-then-else structure. The IF statement format is shown in Figure 8.2. With the IF statement, one or more conditions are tested and alternate statements are executed based upon the result of the test or tests. An IF statement may be written as either (1) a simple, one-condition statement, (2) a multiple-condition statement combined by logical operators (AND or OR), or (3) a multiple-condition nested IF statement. Each of these three IF statements types are covered here.

Simple IF Statements

There are three ways a simple IF statement can be written: with *true actions only*, *true and false actions*, and *false actions only*. Each will be discussed.

True Actions Only

An example of an IF statement with only true actions is shown and flowcharted in Figure 8.3. When the statement is executed, the XX-SEX-CODE field will be compared to the letter M. If the condition is true—that is, if the XX-SEX-CODE field contains an M—the statement ADD 1 TO XX-TOTAL-MALES-ACCUM will be executed. If the condition is false—XX-SEX-CODE does not contain an M—that statement will be skipped and execution of instructions will resume with the next statement after the period. The period terminates the IF sentence and is very important to the statement's effect. It controls where the IF sentence ends and where unconditional execution of instructions resumes.

The programmer is not limited to specification of just one statement of actions to be taken; Figure 8.4 shows an example with multiple (two, in this case) statements to be executed if the condition is true. Here, both the ADD 1 TO XX-TOTAL-MALES-ACCUM statement and the MOVE 'MALE' TO XX-SEX statement will be executed when the condition is true. When the condition is false, they will both be skipped and execution of instructions will resume with the next sentence after the period.

Both True and False Actions

Figure 8.5 shows an example of an IF statement specifying certain actions to be taken when the condition is true and other actions to be taken when the condition is false. If the XX-SEX-CODE field contains an M, the ADD 1 TO XX-TOTAL-MALES-ACCUM statement will be executed, but statements after the reserved word ELSE and before the period will be skipped. Should the condition be false—if there is any value other than M in the field—statements before the word ELSE will be skipped and the ADD 1 TO XX-TOTAL-FEMALES-ACCUM statement will be executed.

ions Only

Sometimes situations will occur where there are actions to be taken for false conditions but no actions required for true conditions. An example of this is

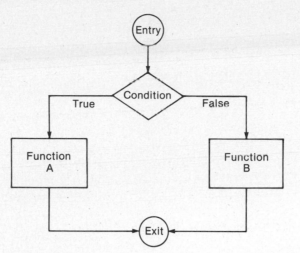

Figure 8.1. If-then-else control structure

Format:

$$\text{\underline{IF} condition} \begin{Bmatrix} \text{statement-1} \\ \text{\underline{NEXT SENTENCE}} \end{Bmatrix} \begin{Bmatrix} \text{\underline{ELSE} statement-2} \\ \text{\underline{ELSE NEXT SENTENCE}} \end{Bmatrix}$$

Figure 8.2. IF statement format

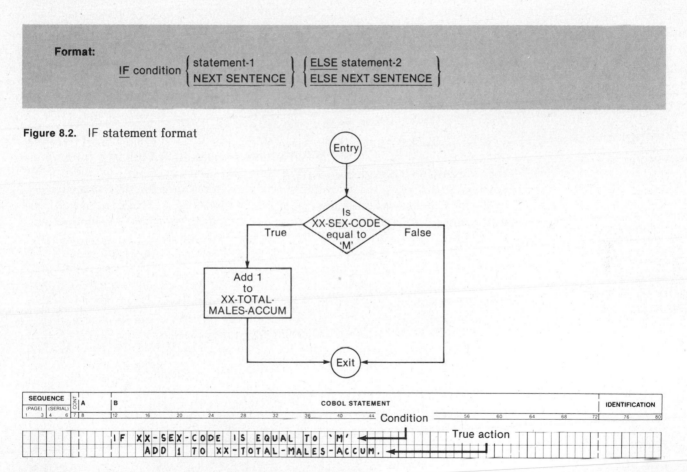

Figure 8.3. Simple IF statement example: True actions only

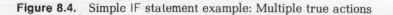

Figure 8.4. Simple IF statement example: Multiple true actions

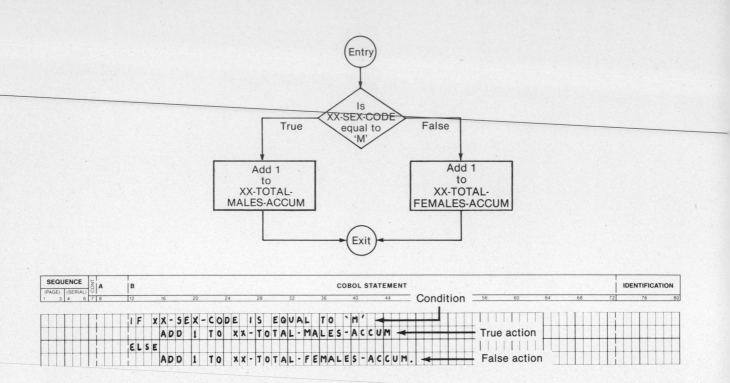

SEQUENCE	CONT	A	B	COBOL STATEMENT					IDENTIFICATION	

```
IF XX-SEX-CODE IS EQUAL TO 'M'          ← Condition
    ADD 1 TO XX-TOTAL-MALES-ACCUM       ← True action
ELSE
    ADD 1 TO XX-TOTAL-FEMALES-ACCUM.    ← False action
```

Figure 8.5. Simple IF statement example: Both true and false actions

shown in Figure 8.6. If there are no actions to be specified for true conditions, the words NEXT SENTENCE are written after the condition and before the word ELSE. Then, when the condition is true, program execution immediately resumes after the end-of-sentence period. The NEXT SENTENCE phrase acts as a placeholder or null statement. Notice that the phrase is not hyphenated.

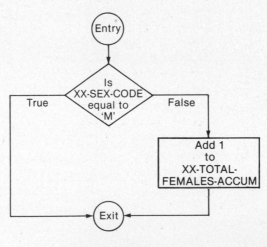

SEQUENCE	CONT	A	B	COBOL STATEMENT					IDENTIFICATION	

```
IF XX-SEX-CODE IS EQUAL TO 'M'          ← Condition
    NEXT SENTENCE                       ← NEXT SENTENCE statement
ELSE
    ADD 1 TO XX-TOTAL-FEMALES-ACCUM.    ← False action
```

Simple IF statement: False actions only

Part A: True actions only:

IF condition
      statements to be executed when statement is true.   ◄——— Period terminating last
                                                      true action statement

Part B: Both true and false actions:

IF condition
      statements to be executed when statement is true
ELSE
      statements to be executed when statement is false.

Part C: False actions only:

IF condition
      NEXT SENTENCE
ELSE
      statements to be executed when statement is false.

Period terminating last
false action statement

Figure 8.7. Recap of simple IF statement configurations

Recap of Simple IF Statement Configurations

When writing a simple IF statement, one of three configurations will apply. The pattern for each is shown in Figure 8.7. If there are only actions for true conditions, the condition is written and followed by one or more statements expressing those actions. The last statement must be terminated by a period.

If there are both true and false actions to be taken, the condition is written and followed by one or more statements to be executed when the condition is true. After the last true-action statement, the word ELSE is written and followed by one or more statements to be executed when the condition is false. The last false-action statement must be terminated by a period.

When there are only false actions to be taken, the condition is written and followed by the phrase NEXT SENTENCE. The word ELSE is then written and followed by one or more statements to be executed when the condition is false. The last false-action statement must be terminated by a period.

When writing simple IF statements, the programmer should do as has been done in the examples: start the words IF and ELSE in position 12 and indent the action statement verbs to position 16. Notice also that the word ELSE has been written on a line by itself. Since that looks like a waste of space, one might be inclined to write the word ELSE on the same line with the preceding or following statement. However, program modifications often require action statements to be added or deleted. Placing the ELSE on a separate line allows changes with minimum IF statement disruption and chance for error.

Recognize that IF statement indentation is provided only for program readability and does not affect the execution of the statement. IF statement control is determined solely by the location of the word ELSE and the end-of-sentence period.

Examples of incorrect and invalid simple IF statements are shown in Figure 8.8.

IF Statement Conditions

There are four types of conditions that may be expressed with an IF statement: relation, class, sign, and condition-name. Each of these will be covered.

Relation condition

Relation conditions are the most frequently used type. The IF statement in the PAYROLL program and the ones so far in this chapter have been relation conditions using the IS EQUAL TO operator. There are two other relation operators: IS GREATER THAN and IS LESS THAN. Figure 8.9 shows the relation condition

Part A: Incorrect IF statement:

SEQUENCE			A	B	COBOL STATEMENT	IDENTIFICATION

```
         IF  XX-SEX-CODE  IS  EQUAL  TO  'M'
             ADD  1  TO  XX-TOTAL-MALES-ACCUM
             MOVE  'MALE   '  TO  XX-SEX
         ELSE
             ADD  1  TO  XX-TOTAL-FEMALES-ACCUM.
             MOVE  'FEMALE'  TO  XX-SEX.
```

This period will end the IF statement.

This statement will be executed unconditionally.

Part B: Invalid IF statements:

```
         IF  XX-SEX-CODE  IS  EQUAL  TO  'M'
             ADD  1  TO  XX-TOTAL-MALES-ACCUM
             MOVE  'MALE   '  TO  XX-SEX.
         ELSE
             ADD  1  TO  XX-TOTAL-FEMALES-ACCUM
             MOVE  'FEMALE'  TO  XX-SEX.
```

This period will end the IF statement.

This then becomes an invalid sentence.

```
         IF  XX-SEX-CODE  IS  EQUAL  TO  'M'
         ELSE
             ADD  1  TO  XX-TOTAL-FEMALES-ACCUM
             MOVE  'FEMALE'  TO  XX-SEX.
```

This statement is invalid because there are no true actions or NEXT SENTENCE specifications.

Figure 8.8. Examples of incorrect and invalid simple IF statements

format. The element before the operator can be referred to as the *subject* of the condition; the element after the operator can be termed the *object*. Although the format shows a number of elements that may be used as subject and object, in this chapter—as in actual practice—the subject will usually be an identifier and the object will be either an identifier or a literal.

The subject can be examined to determine if it is greater than, less than, equal to, not greater than, not less than, or not equal to the object. Either the reserved words or the symbols (> , < , and =) may be used to specify the operator. In this text, the words will always be used. It's a good practice to refrain from using the symbols because (1) some computer printers do not contain the greater-than and less-than symbols, (2) the internal data representation of symbols varies with different makes of computers so program portability is diminished, and (3) most people understand the words more readily than the symbols.

Relation condition testing compares the subject and object values. The data class of the object of the relation condition should be consistent with the subject. That is, if the subject is numeric, the object should be numeric. If the

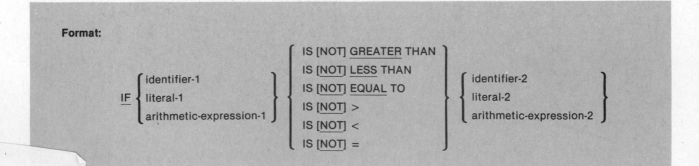

Format:

$$
IF \left\{ \begin{array}{l} \text{identifier-1} \\ \text{literal-1} \\ \text{arithmetic-expression-1} \end{array} \right\} \left\{ \begin{array}{l} \text{IS [NOT] } \underline{\text{GREATER}} \text{ THAN} \\ \text{IS [NOT] } \underline{\text{LESS}} \text{ THAN} \\ \text{IS [NOT] } \underline{\text{EQUAL}} \text{ TO} \\ \text{IS [NOT] } > \\ \text{IS [NOT] } < \\ \text{IS [NOT] } = \end{array} \right\} \left\{ \begin{array}{l} \text{identifier-2} \\ \text{literal-2} \\ \text{arithmetic-expression-2} \end{array} \right\}
$$

Relation condition format

Subject field	Object Field	
	Numeric data-item or Numeric literal	Alphanumeric data-item or Non-numeric literal or Group item
Numeric data-item or Numeric literal	Numeric (algebraic) comparison	Alphanumeric (character-by-character) comparison
Alphanumeric data-item or Non-numeric literal or Group item	Alphanumeric (character-by-character) comparison	Alphanumeric (character-by-character) comparison

Figure 8.10. Comparison processing table

subject is alphanumeric, the object should be alphanumeric. Certain other combinations are legal, but the programmer must understand the specific comparison processing that will occur. A table of comparison processing is shown in Figure 8.10. We will discuss the two types of comparisons: numeric and alphanumeric.

Numeric comparisons

When the subject and object are both numeric items, comparison of the two values is made according to their algebraic value. The relative length of the items does not matter. For example, a three-digit integer field containing 687 is equal to a seven-digit integer field containing 0000687. Similarly, a value of 0003.25 is equal to a value of 03.2500. Of course, the location of assumed decimal points does affect the comparison values. Figure 8.11 shows the effect of numeric comparisons.

DATA DIVISION entries:

```
05  XX-PURCHASE-AMOUNT              PIC S9(5)V99.
05  XX-AVAILABLE-CREDIT             PIC S9(5).
```

IF statement:

```
IF XX-PURCHASE-AMOUNT IS GREATER THAN XX-AVAILABLE-CREDIT
   PERFORM 999-IDENTIFY-OVER-LIMIT
ELSE
   PERFORM 999-POST-PURCHASE.
```

Value in XX-PURCHASE-AMOUNT field	Value in XX-AVAILABLE-CREDIT field	Condition test result	Statement executed
00198₄50 +	00580₄ +	False	999-POST-PURCHASE
01250₄00 +	00900₄ +	True	999-IDENTIFY-OVER-LIMIT
01000₄00 +	01000₄ +	False	999-POST-PURCHASE
01000₄05 +	01000₄ +	True	000 IDENTIFY-OVER-LIMIT
00098₄00 +	00100₄ −	True	999-IDENTIFY-OVER-LIMIT
00198₄00 −	00100₄ +	False	999-POST-PURCHASE

Note: ₄ — assumed decimal point

Figure 8.11. Numeric relation condition

	Collating sequence		
	EBCDIC	*ASCII*	
Low	Blank space	Blank space	Low
↓	Special characters	Special characters	↓
	Letters (A-Z)	Numbers (0-9)	
High	Numbers (0-9)	Letters (A-Z)	High

Figure 8.12. Common collating sequences

Alphanumeric comparisons

The result of alphanumeric comparisons depends upon the collating sequence of the computer being used. *Collating sequence* refers to the order of character values. Certainly a value of 3 is less than 7 and the letter R is greater than B. But, how does a dollar sign ($) compare to an E? Or which is higher—a letter or a number? Figure 8.12 shows two commonly used collating sequences. In this text we assume the EBCDIC collating sequence where numbers are considered higher values than letters. With alphanumeric fields, comparison begins at the leftmost character and proceeds until an unequal pair of characters is encountered or until the end of the longest field is reached. Figure 8.13 provides an example of an alphanumeric comparison that tests fields of equal length.

With an alphanumeric comparison, when the subject and object fields are of different lengths, the shorter field is internally extended on the right with blank spaces until it is the same length as the longer field. Then the comparison takes place. Figure 8.14 shows an example with unequal fields.

Class condition

The class condition determines whether a field contains only numeric digits or solely alphabetic characters. Its format is shown in Figure 8.15. To be con-

DATA DIVISION entries:

```
05  XX-TRANSACTION-NAME                    PIC X(24).
05  XX-MASTER-NAME                         PIC X(24).
```

IF statement:

```
IF XX-TRANSACTION-NAME IS LESS THAN XX-MASTER-NAME
   PERFORM 999-PROCESS-LOW-TRANSACTION.
```

Value in XX-TRANSACTION-NAME field	Value in XX-MASTER-NAME field	Condition test result	Statement executed
JONES	JONES	False	Next sentence
JONES	SMITH	True	999-PROCESS-LOW-TRANSACTION
SMITH	SMITHSON	True	999-PROCESS-LOW-TRANSACTION
THORPE	THORP	False	Next sentence

3. Alphanumeric relation condition: Equal length fields

DATA DIVISION entries:

SEQUENCE					COBOL STATEMENT	IDENTIFICATION
(PAGE)	(SERIAL)		A	B		

```
            Ø5   XX-TRANSACTION-UNIT-MEAS               PIC  X(2).
            Ø5   XX-MASTER-UNIT-MEAS                     PIC  X(5).
```

IF statement:

```
          IF  XX-TRANSACTION-UNIT-MEAS
              IS  EQUAL  TO  XX-MASTER-UNIT-MEAS
                  PERFORM  999-PROCESS-UNIT-MEAS
          ELSE
                  PERFORM  999-CHANGE-UNIT-MEAS.
```

Value in field			
XX-TRANSACTION-UNIT-MEAS	*XX-MASTER-UNIT-MEAS*	*Condition test result*	*Statement*
L B	L B	True	999-PROCESS-UNIT-MEAS
L B	L B S	False	999-CHANGE-UNIT-MEAS
Internal extension			

Figure 8.14. Alphanumeric relation condition example: Unequal length fields

sidered NUMERIC, a field must contain only values from 0 (zero) through 9. To be considered ALPHABETIC, the field must contain only characters from A through Z and blank spaces. NUMERIC tests may be made on alphanumeric and numeric fields. ALPHABETIC tests may be made on alphanumeric, alphabetic, and group fields. Figures 8.16 and 8.17 provide examples of class condition IF statements.

Because of ambiguities when the overpunch or embedded method of arithmetic sign representation is used, there are certain intricacies of the NUMERIC class test for IBM compilers that require further definition.

First, a field defined as unsigned numeric (PICTURE 9) or alphanumeric (PICTURE X) will test as NOT NUMERIC if the data in that field contains an explicit plus or minus sign. This usually isn't too much of a problem because an unsigned numeric field or an alphanumeric field does not normally contain explicitly signed fields. One notable exception is when input data is read directly into the field. If the input field were explicitly keyed with an arithmetic sign,

Format:

$$\text{IF identifier IS } \left[\underline{\text{NOT}} \right] \left\{ \begin{array}{l} \text{NUMERIC} \\ \text{ALPHABETIC} \end{array} \right\}$$

Figure 8.15. Class condition format

DATA DIVISION entry:

SEQUENCE		CONT	A	B	COBOL STATEMENT	IDENTIFICATION
(PAGE)	(SERIAL)					

```
Ø5  XX-PRICE                                    PIC 9(3)V99.
```

IF statement:

```
IF  XX-PRICE  IS  NUMERIC
    PERFORM 999-VALIDATE-PRICE
ELSE
    PERFORM 999-IDENTIFY-PRICE-ERROR.
```

Value in XX-PRICE field	Class	Condition test result	Statement executed
029ᵥ99	Numeric	True	999-VALIDATE-PRICE
29ᵥ99	Alphanumeric†	False	999-IDENTIFY-PRICE-ERROR
029ᵥ9R	Alphanumeric	False	999-IDENTIFY-PRICE-ERROR
	Alphabetic‡	False	999-IDENTIFY-PRICE-ERROR
000ᵥ00	Numeric	True	999-VALIDATE-PRICE

Note: ᵥ = assumed decimal point

†leading blank space
‡all blanks

Figure 8.16. NUMERIC class test example

DATA DIVISION entry:

SEQUENCE		CONT	A	B	COBOL STATEMENT	IDENTIFICATION
(PAGE)	(SERIAL)					

```
Ø5  XX-NAME                                     PIC X(11).
```

IF statement:

```
IF  XX-NAME  IS  ALPHABETIC
    NEXT SENTENCE
ELSE
    PERFORM 999-IDENTIFY-NAME-ERROR.
```

Value in XX-NAME field	Class	Condition test result	Statement executed
MIDDLEBROOK	Alphabetic	True	Next sentence
MIDDLETON	Alphabetic	True	Next sentence
MCDONALD	Alphabetic	True	Next sentence
MC DONALD	Alphabetic	True	Next sentence
O'BRIEN	Alphanumeric	False	999-IDENTIFY-NAME-ERROR
3M CORP	Alphanumeric	False	999-IDENTIFY-NAME-ERROR
	Alphabetic	True	Next sentence
ANN-MARGRET	Alphanumeric	False	999-IDENTIFY-NAME-ERROR
U.S. MFG.	Alphanumeric	False	999-IDENTIFY-NAME-ERROR

ALPHABETIC class test example

Even though a numeric field is defined without a sign:

SEQUENCE			A	B	COBOL STATEMENT		IDENTIFICATION

Ø5   XX-QUANTITY   PIC 9(5).

when a numeric sign is explicitly keyed or otherwise represented in the input, it will still be present in the field when it is transferred to computer storage.

XX-QUANTITY Field

If rightmost position contains either

– a twelve (Y) zone (explicitly positive field)
– an eleven (X) zone (negative field)

it will be transferred to computer storage.

So, this numeric class condition—IF XX-QUANTITY IS NUMERIC—will be considered false. Because this field was defined in the PICTURE clause without a sign, the rightmost position is considered an alphabetic character.

Figure 8.18. Class conditions with arithmetic sign considerations—part 1

the sign would remain in the field even if the field were defined as unsigned numeric or alphanumeric. Figure 8.18 depicts this situation.

    Second, a field defined as signed numeric (S9) may contain a sign in the rightmost position of the field and be considered numeric. Letters A through R in the rightmost position of the field will thus test as NUMERIC with a signed numeric field. Examples of this consideration are shown in Figure 8.19.

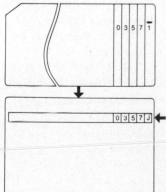

XX-QUANTITY field in input record is keyed as a negative value. Rightmost column contains an eleven (X) zone to indicate that the field is negative and a one-digit punch or representation.

XX-QUANTITY field in computer storage: The eleven (X) zone plus the one-digit representation are equivalent to the letter J.

The numeric condition test – IF XX-PRICE IS NUMERIC – will produce different results depending upon the PICTURE symbols specified for the data-item.

X(5)	FALSE	The J is considered a letter because arithmetic signs do not apply to alphanumeric fields.
9(5)	FALSE	The J is considered a letter because this numeric field is unsigned.
S9(5)	TRUE	The J is considered the digit 1 with a negative sign.

Figure 8.19. Class conditions with arithmetic sign considerations—part 2

DATA DIVISION entries:

SEQUENCE (PAGE) (SERIAL) 1 3 4 6	C O N T 7	A 8	B 12	COBOL STATEMENT	IDENTIFICATION 76 80

```
Ø5   XX-BANK-BALANCE                    PIC S9(8)V99.
```

Sign condition statements:

```
IF  XX-BANK-BALANCE  IS  POSITIVE
    PERFORM 999-PROCESS-CHECK.
```

```
IF  XX-BANK-BALANCE  IS  NEGATIVE
    PERFORM 999-PREPARE-OVERDRAFT-NOTICE.
```

```
IF  XX-BANK-BALANCE  IS  ZERO
    PERFORM 999-TEST-CLOSED-ACCOUNT.
```

Figure 8.20. Sign condition examples

Sign condition

The sign condition determines whether a numeric field is POSITIVE, NEGATIVE, or ZERO. Because the sign condition has narrower applicability, it is not used nearly as frequently as the relation and class conditions. Figure 8.20 shows the sign condition format and examples. When the value being tested is zero, it is considered to be a unique value that is neither positive or negative.

Condition-name condition

This is a special way of writing a relation condition that requires a level-88 entry in the DATA DIVISION. The format and an example of a level-88 item are shown in Figure 8.21. Each condition-name must be defined by a level-number 88 entry in the DATA DIVISION. After the level-number 88, the user-defined condition-name is specified and followed by a VALUE clause with the literal or literals that apply to the value of that condition. The level-88 item must immediately follow the definition of the field with which it is associated.

In the example, XX-MARITAL-STATUS is a one-character field that contains a code indicating whether or not the person is married. The level-88 item immediately following the field definition shows that the condition-name MAR-RIED has been assigned to a VALUE of M in the XX-MARITAL-STATUS field. That is, when there is an M in the field, the condition MARRIED is true.

The format of the condition-name condition and an example using the DATA DIVISION entries just discussed are shown in Figure 8.22. In the example, when the IF statement is executed and XX-MARITAL-STATUS contains a M the MARRIED condition is true and the PERFORM 999-APPLY-MARRIED-TAX-RATE statement will be executed. If there is anything other than M in the field, the PERFORM 999-APPLY-SINGLE-TAX-RATE statement will be executed.

The condition-name condition is actually just another way of expressing a relation condition. Since it can provide more descriptive documentation, though, the condition-name test is often preferable to the relation condition.

Format:

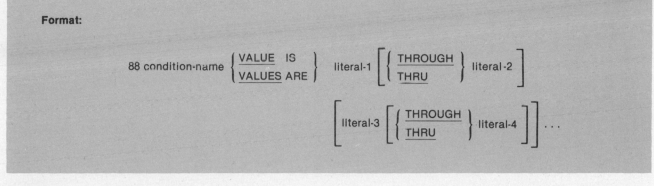

$$88 \text{ condition-name} \begin{Bmatrix} \underline{\text{VALUE}} \text{ IS} \\ \underline{\text{VALUES}} \text{ ARE} \end{Bmatrix} \text{literal-1} \left[\begin{Bmatrix} \underline{\text{THROUGH}} \\ \underline{\text{THRU}} \end{Bmatrix} \text{literal-2} \right]$$

$$\left[\text{literal-3} \left[\begin{Bmatrix} \underline{\text{THROUGH}} \\ \underline{\text{THRU}} \end{Bmatrix} \text{literal-4} \right] \right] \dots$$

Example:

SEQUENCE			A	B	COBOL STATEMENT	IDENTIFICATION
(PAGE)	(SERIAL)	CONT				
				05 XX-MARITAL-STATUS	PIC X(1).	
				88 SINGLE	VALUE 'S'.	
				88 MARRIED	VALUE 'M'.	

Figure 8.21. Level-number 88 format

The VALUE clause of a level-88 item may contain multiple values or a range of values. The reserved word THRU is used to define a range of values. Examples of multiple and of range VALUE clauses are shown in Figure 8.23.

There is some ambiguity caused by using the VALUE clause both with levels 01 through 49 WORKING-STORAGE fields to set initial values and with level-88 entries to associate values with a condition-name. Because different rules apply to the VALUE clause in each case, we will refer to the former as the *initializing* VALUE clause and the latter as the *condition-name* VALUE clause. Condition-name VALUE clauses differ from initializing VALUE clauses in the following ways: (1) they can be used in either the FILE or WORKING-STORAGE sections (they are not restricted to WORKING-STORAGE as the initializing VALUE clause is); (2) they may be associated with REDEFINES clauses; and (3) they may be associated with OCCURS clauses. Further, the condition-name VALUE clause may contain multiple values or a range of values. A condition-name VALUE clause is required for each level-88 item description.

Format:

IF condition-name

Example:

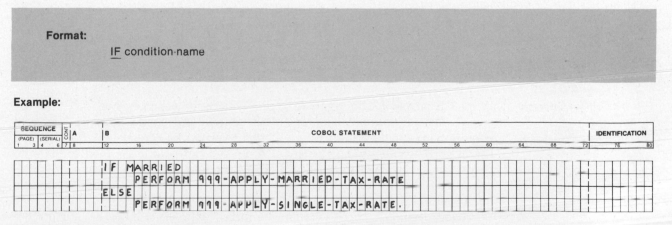

SEQUENCE			A	B	COBOL STATEMENT	IDENTIFICATION
(PAGE)	(SERIAL)	CONT				
				IF MARRIED		
				PERFORM 999-APPLY-MARRIED-TAX-RATE		
				ELSE		
				PERFORM 999-APPLY-SINGLE-TAX-RATE.		

Figure 8.22. Condition-name example

Part A: Level-88 items with multiple VALUE entries

SEQUENCE (PAGE) (SERIAL)	CONT	A	B	COBOL STATEMENT	IDENTIFICATION
		Ø5	XX-MONTH-ABBREV	PIC X(3).	
			88	3Ø-DAY-MONTH	VALUE 'APR'
					'JUN'
					'SEP'
					'NOV'.
			88	31-DAY-MONTH	VALUE 'JAN'
					'MAR'
					'MAY'
					'JUL'
					'AUG'
					'OCT'
					'DEC'.
			88	28-29-DAY-MONTH	VALUE 'FEB'.

Part B: Level-88 items with range VALUE entries

SEQUENCE	CONT	A	B	COBOL STATEMENT
		Ø5	XX-MONTH-NBR	PIC 9(2).
			88	QUARTER-1	VALUE Ø1 THRU Ø3.
			88	QUARTER-2	VALUE Ø4 THRU Ø6.
			88	QUARTER-3	VALUE Ø7 THRU Ø9.
			88	QUARTER-4	VALUE 1Ø THRU 12.

Figure 8.23. Conditional VALUE clause examples: Multiple range values

Combined IF Statements

A *combined* IF statement is one that contains multiple conditions connected with the reserved-word logical operators AND or OR. Combined IF statements are sometimes referred to as *combination* IF statements. Figure 8.24 presents the format of a combined IF statement.

The AND Logical Operator

When the AND operator is used, both conditions must be true for the combined condition to be considered true. If either one or both of the conditions is false, the combined condition is considered false. In the example shown in Figure 8.25, if a student is both taking more than 11 units *and* has a grade point average of 3.75 or better, the 999-PLACE-ON-DEANS-LIST module will be performed. If either one or both of those two conditions is not true, the 999-PLACE-ON-DEANS-LIST module will be skipped.

More than two conditions can be linked with the AND operator. Figure 8.26 provides an example where five conditions are checked. If all five are true, the 999-PROCESS-DATE module will be performed. If any one is false, the 999-IDENTIFY-DATE-ERROR module will be performed.

Notice that when the operator AND is used, the word IF is not repeated. Also, observe that different IF condition types may be combined. The last example includes class, relation, and condition-name conditions.

The OR Logical Operator

When OR is specified and either one or both of the conditions is true, then the combined condition is considered true. If neither one is true, then the combined condition is considered false. An example is shown in Figure 8.27. If either the credit card has been reported lost or if the account balance is greater than the credit limit, the 999-EXAMINE-ACCOUNT module will be performed. If both conditions are false, the 999-POST-CHARGE-TO-ACCOUNT module will be performed.

More than two conditions can be linked with OR. When OR is used, the word IF is not repeated.

Format:

$$\underline{\text{IF}} \text{ condition} \left\{ \left\{ \begin{array}{c} \underline{\text{AND}} \\ \underline{\text{OR}} \end{array} \right\} \text{condition} \right\} \dots$$

Figure 8.24. Combined IF statement format

SEQUENCE		CONT	A	B	COBOL STATEMENT	IDENTIFICATION
(PAGE)	(SERIAL)					

```
        IF XX-UNITS-THIS-SEMESTER IS GREATER THAN 11.0
        AND XX-GRADE-POINT-AVERAGE IS GREATER THAN 3.75
            PERFORM 999-PLACE-ON-DEANS-LIST.
```

Figure 8.25. Combined IF statement example: Logical operator AND

DATA DIVISION entries:

SEQUENCE		CONT	A	B	COBOL STATEMENT	IDENTIFICATION
(PAGE)	(SERIAL)					

```
        05  XX-DATE
            10  XX-MONTH                    PIC 9(2).
            10  XX-DAY                       PIC 9(2).
            10  XX-YEAR                      PIC 9(2).
                88  VALID-YEAR              VALUE 79 THRU 85.
```

Combined IF statement with more than one AND operator:

SEQUENCE		CONT	A	B	COBOL STATEMENT	IDENTIFICATION

```
        IF XX-DATE IS NUMERIC          ◄──── Class condition
        AND XX-MONTH IS GREATER THAN ZERO
        AND XX-MONTH IS LESS THAN 13         Relation
        AND XX-DAY IS GREATER THAN ZERO      conditions
        AND XX-DAY IS LESS THAN 32
        AND VALID-YEAR                 ◄──── Condition-name
                                             condition
            PERFORM 999-PROCESS-DATE   ◄──── All conditions true
        ELSE
            PERFORM 999-IDENTIFY-DATE-ERROR. ◄── One or more
                                                 conditions false
```

Figure 8.26. Combined IF statement example with multiple AND operators

SEQUENCE		CONT	A	B	COBOL STATEMENT	IDENTIFICATION
(PAGE)	(SERIAL)					

```
        IF CREDIT-CARD-LOST-OR-STOLEN
        OR XX-ACCOUNT-BALANCE IS GREATER THAN XX-CREDIT-LIMIT
            PERFORM 999-EXAMINE-ACCOUNT  ◄──── Either condition true
        ELSE
            PERFORM 999-POST-CHARGE-TO-ACCOUNT.  ◄── Both conditions false
```

Figure 8.27. Combined IF statement example: Logical operator OR

Part A: Compound condition written without parentheses (will be evaluated in accordance with COBOL combined condition evaluation rules)

SEQUENCE				COBOL STATEMENT	IDENTIFICATION

```
            IF  XX-RECORD-CODE  IS  EQUAL  TO  '23'
            OR  XX-UPDATE-CODE  IS  EQUAL  TO  'D'
            AND  XX-BALANCE  IS  ZERO
                    PERFORM  999-DELETE-RECORD.
```

Part B: Compound condition written with parentheses (this placement of parentheses has been made to be equivalent to the COBOL combined condition evaluation rules that are applied to the unparenthesized statement shown in Part A)

```
            IF  XX-RECORD-CODE  IS  EQUAL  TO  '23'
            OR  (XX-UPDATE-CODE  IS  EQUAL  TO  'D'
            AND  XX-BALANCE  IS  ZERO)
                    PERFORM  999-DELETE-RECORD.
```

Part C: Compound condition written with different parentheses placement (will cause processing different than that specified in Part A or B)

```
            IF  (XX-RECORD-CODE  IS  EQUAL  TO  '23'
            OR  XX-UPDATE-CODE  IS  EQUAL  TO  'D')
            AND  XX-BALANCE  IS  ZERO
                    PERFORM  999-DELETE-RECORD.
```

Figure 8.28. Compound condition IF statement examples

Compound Conditions

When the operators AND and OR are both used within the same IF statement, the resulting expression is referred to as a *compound condition*. Examples are shown in Figure 8.28.

Observe in Part A of the figure that ambiguity results when both AND and OR appear in an IF statement. (That is, it is not clear whether (1) the first two conditions are in an OR relationship, or (2) the first condition is in an OR relationship with the AND relationship of the second and third conditions.) Thus, COBOL combined condition evaluation rules call for AND condition pairs to be evaluated first, from left to right; then the OR conditions are evaluated, from left to right.

Part B of the figure shows that parentheses may be introduced into the statement to explicitly control the evaluation sequence. Part C of the figure demonstrates that different processing will occur depending on where the parentheses are placed.

Generally, compound conditions should be avoided because they tend to be confusing. Furthermore, the evaluation rules vary with different 1968 ANS COBOL compilers. When a compound condition is used, parentheses should be used, to make the condition more understandable and to explicitly specify the evaluation sequence.

Implied Subjects and Relation Operators

It is possible to compare one subject with two or more objects and not repeat the subject. This is shown in Figure 8.29, where XX-MONTH is the *implied subject* for the second and third comparisons. Similarly, *implied relation operators* are also permitted. Figure 8.30 provides an example.

However, it is recommended that implied subjects and relation operators not be used, for their use creates the same disadvantages mentioned for compound conditions. Implied subjects and relation operators apply only to relation conditions.

This combined IF statement relation condition

SEQUENCE		CONT	A	B	COBOL STATEMENT		IDENTIFICATION
(PAGE)	(SERIAL)						
1 3	4 6	7 8		12 16 20 24 28 32 36 40 44 48 52 56 60 64 68 72			76 80

```
        IF XX-MONTH IS GREATER THAN ZERO
        AND XX-MONTH IS LESS THAN '13'
        AND XX-MONTH IS NOT EQUAL TO 'Ø2'
           PERFORM 999-STANDARD-DAY-CHECK.
```

may be written with implied subjects as follows:

```
        IF XX-MONTH IS GREATER THAN ZERO
        AND LESS THAN '13'
        AND NOT EQUAL TO 'Ø2'
           PERFORM 999-STANDARD-DAY-CHECK.
```

Figure 8.29. Implied subject IF statement example

This combined IF statement relation condition

SEQUENCE		CONT	A	B	COBOL STATEMENT		IDENTIFICATION
(PAGE)	(SERIAL)						
1 3	4 6	7 8		12 16 20 24 28 32 36 40 44 48 52 56 60 64 68 72			76 80

```
        IF XX-BALANCE IS LESS THAN 1ØØØ.ØØ
        AND XX-BALANCE IS LESS THAN XX-CREDIT-LIMIT
           PERFORM 999-POST-PAYMENT.
```

may be written with an implied subject and relation operator as follows:

```
        IF XX-BALANCE IS LESS THAN 1ØØØ.ØØ
        AND XX-CREDIT-LIMIT
           PERFORM 999-POST-PAYMENT.
```

Figure 8.30 Implied subject and relation operator example

Nested IF Statements

When the reserved word IF is specified more than once within an IF statement, it is referred to as a *nested* IF. Nested IF statements can be classified as *linear* or *non-linear*, as discussed below.

Linear Nested IF Statements

The *linear* nested IF is relatively simple to write and understand, but its use is limited to situations where one condition applies to each action statement group, such as when one field is being tested for various values. Figure 8.31 shows an example. This form of nested IF is called linear because each ELSE immediately follows the IF condition, one after another. Comparisons are made until a true condition is encountered (or until the final ELSE or end-of-sentence is reached). When a true condition occurs, the specified action or actions are executed until the next ELSE statement is reached.

Indentation for the linear nested IF can be handled as shown in the example: The first IF and each ELSE are aligned, and each condition is specified on the same line with its respective ELSE. The actions are indented four places.

Non-linear Nested IF Statements

The relationship between the IF condition and the ELSE to which it is paired is readily apparent for the linear nested IF, since the ELSE immediately follows the IF with which it is associated. The non-linear nested IF is somewhat more complicated because (1) a combination of true and false conditions usually

```
IF XX-TRANSACTION-TYPE IS EQUAL TO 'NA'
    PERFORM 999-PROCESS-NAME-ADDRESS
ELSE IF XX-TRANSACTION-TYPE IS EQUAL TO 'WE'
    PERFORM 999-PROCESS-WEEKLY-EARNINGS
ELSE IF XX-TRANSACTION-TYPE IS EQUAL TO 'YE'
    PERFORM 999-PROCESS-YEARLY-EARNINGS
ELSE IF XX-TRANSACTION-TYPE IS EQUAL TO 'PD'
    PERFORM 999-PROCESS-PERSONNEL-DATA
ELSE
    PERFORM 999-PROCESS-ERROR-TRANSACTION.
```

Figure 8.31. Linear nested IF statement example

determines the specific action statement group executed, and (2) the ELSE statements may be separated from the IF statement with which it is paired. We will examine two general forms of non-linear IF statements: (1) all action statements after conditions and (2) interspersed conditions and action statements.

All action statements after conditions

Figure 8.32 provides two examples of non-linear nested IF statements, the first with two conditions and the second with three conditions. Logic for the three-condition example is shown in flowchart form in Figure 8.33. In non-linear nested IF statements each ELSE applies to the first IF that precedes it which has not already been paired with an ELSE. This concept is depicted in Figure 8.34. Indentation is important in making non-linear nested IF statements clear. Each ELSE statement should be vertically aligned with the IF condition to which it is paired.

Interspersed conditions and action statements

Figure 8.35 shows an example of this type of nested IF statement. Again, vertical alignment of paired IF and ELSE statements makes the statement more easily understandable.

```
IF HOURLY-EMPLOYEE
    IF REGULAR-WORKDAY
        PERFORM 999-COMPUTE-NORMAL-PAY
    ELSE
        PERFORM 999-COMPUTE-SUNDAY-HOLIDAY-PAY
ELSE
    PERFORM 999-COMPUTE-SALARY-PAY.
```

```
IF REGISTERED
    IF VOTED
        IF MALE
            ADD 1 TO XX-MALE-VOTERS
        ELSE
            ADD 1 TO XX-FEMALE-VOTERS
    ELSE
        ADD 1 TO XX-REGISTERED-NON-VOTERS
ELSE
    ADD 1 TO XX-NON-REGISTERED-CITIZENS.
```

-linear nested IF statement examples: All action statements after conditions

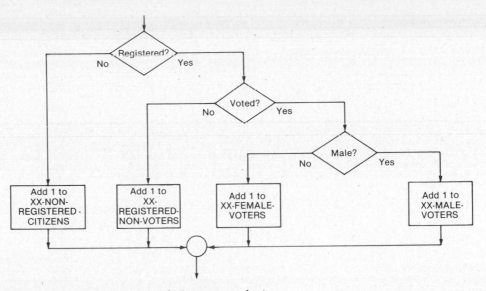

Figure 8.33. Non-linear nested IF statement logic

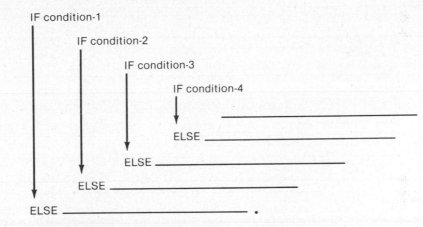

Figure 8.34. Depiction of IF/ELSE pairing

SEQUENCE		CONT	A	B	COBOL STATEMENT	IDENTIFICATION

```
          IF HOURLY-EMPLOYEE
             MULTIPLY XX-RATE BY XX-HOURS GIVING XX-REG-PAY
             IF XX-HOURS IS GREATER THAN 40
                SUBTRACT 40 FROM XX-HOURS GIVING XX-OT-HOURS
                MULTIPLY XX-RATE BY .5 GIVING XX-OT-RATE
                MULTIPLY XX-OT-RATE BY XX-OT-HOURS GIVING XX-OT-PAY
                IF XX-HOURS IS GREATER THAN 48
                   SUBTRACT 48 FROM XX-HOURS GIVING XX-PREM-HOURS
                   MULTIPLY XX-RATE BY XX-PREM-HOURS
                      GIVING XX-PREM-PAY
                   ADD XX-REG-PAY XX-OT-PAY XX-PREM-PAY
                      GIVING XX-GROSS-PAY
                ELSE
                   ADD XX-REG-PAY XX-OT-PAY GIVING XX-GROSS-PAY
             ELSE
                MOVE XX-REG-PAY TO XX-GROSS-PAY
          ELSE
             MOVE XX-SALARY TO XX-GROSS-PAY.
```

Figure 8.35. Non-linear nested IF statement example: Interspersed conditions and action statements

Simple IF statement:

```
IF condition
     true condition statement(s)
ELSE
     false condition statement(s).
```

Combined IF statement:

```
IF condition-1
AND/OR condition-2
     true condition statement(s)
ELSE
     false condition statement(s).
```

Linear nested IF statement:

```
IF condition-1
     true condition-1 statement(s)
ELSE IF condition-2
     true condition-2 statement(s)
ELSE IF condition-3
     true condition-3 statement(s)
ELSE IF condition-4
     true condition-4 statement(s)
ELSE
     all conditions false statement(s).
```

Non-linear nested IF statement
(all action statements after conditions):

```
IF condition-1
   IF condition-2
      IF condition-3
         all conditions true statement(s)
      ELSE
         false condition-3 statement(s)
   ELSE
      false condition-2 statement(s)
ELSE
   false condition-1 statement(s).
```

Non-linear nested IF statement
(interspersed conditions and action statements):

```
IF condition-1
   true condition-1 statement(s)
   IF condition-2
      true condition-2 statement(s)
      IF condition-3
         true condition-3 statement(s)
      ELSE
         false condition-3 statement(s)
   ELSE
      false condition-2 statement(s)
ELSE
   false condition-1 statement(s).
```

Figure 8.36. Summary of recommended IF statement indentation forms

Recap of nested IF statements

Before the development of structured programming concepts, use of nested IF statements was usually discouraged because they were considered complicated and difficult to understand. However, with structured programming, nested IF statements are often required to provide proper control of statement selection. The complexity of nested IF statements is reduced when (1) the programmer thoroughly understands how ELSE statements are paired with IF conditions, (2) proper indentation is used when the IF statement is written, and (3) the number of levels of nesting is limited to three or four. Figure 8.36 summarizes recommended nested IF statement indentation forms.

Character Manipulation Statements

For character manipulation, the EXAMINE and INSPECT statements are used. They are quite similar in function. In fact, the 1974 standard INSPECT statement is the "new, improved model" of the 1968 standard EXAMINE statement. If you are using a 1968 standard COBOL compiler, you must use the EXAMINE verb because INSPECT is not available. The INSPECT verb should be used if you have a 1974 standard compiler. You will want to read the EXAMINE statement material even if you are going to use INSPECT because (1) many of the concepts presented will apply to both statements, and (2) many existing programs contain the EXAMINE verb. Three major uses for the EXAMINE and INSPECT statements are data validation, character translation, and text editing.

Data validation means checking the fields of a record to ensure that they contain valid data. For example, numeric fields should contain only digits and perhaps a sign. Similarly, certain characters may be restricted from a particular alphanumeric field. The EXAMINE or INSPECT statements can be used to identify situations where, for instance, blank spaces occur in a numeric field or unwanted commas are present in a name field. Data validation will be covered in detail in the next two chapters.

Character translation refers to the conversion of characters within a field from one value to another value. For example, unkeyed characters of a numeric field are often translated from blank spaces to zeros. Or, suppose it is necessary to convert a COBOL program from the single quotation mark method of enclosing non-numeric literals to double quotation marks for another compiler. Making this change throughout a program is an example of character translation.

Text editing applications handle the manipulation of words or strings of words within fields or strings of data. It can be used, for example, to extract a surname from a full name field or to position a given name adjacent to the surname.

The EXAMINE Statement

There are two EXAMINE statement formats. The first format can be used for data validation, character translation, and text editing; the second can do character conversion only.

EXAMINE statement (Format-1)

The Format-1 EXAMINE statement with examples is shown in Figure 8.37. The first example will count the number of LEADING (non-significant) blank spaces in the XX-QUANTITY field and store the count in a special COBOL field called TALLY. Whenever the TALLYING phrase is used in a COBOL program, the TALLY field is automatically provided for; the programmer does not (and can-

Format:

<u>EXAMINE</u> identifier <u>TALLYING</u> { <u>UNTIL FIRST</u> | <u>ALL</u> | <u>LEADING</u> } literal-1

[<u>REPLACING BY</u> literal-2]

Examples:

SEQUENCE (PAGE) (SERIAL) 1 3 4 6	CONT 7	A 8	B 12	COBOL STATEMENT	IDENTIFICATION 73 80

```
       EXAMINE XX-QUANTITY
           TALLYING LEADING SPACES.
```

			2	8

XX-QUANTITY

3

TALLY

```
       EXAMINE XX-QUANTITY
           TALLYING LEADING SPACES
           REPLACING BY ZEROS.
```

Before EXAMINE

		2	0	6

XX-QUANTITY

After EXAMINE

0	0	2	0	6

XX-QUANTITY

2

TALLY

Figure 8.37. Format-1 EXAMINE statement examples

not) define the reserved word TALLY in the DATA DIVISION. (For many COBOL compilers, TALLY is a five integer digit signed numeric field; that is PIC S9(5).) TALLY is automatically initialized to ZEROS prior to execution of each EXAMINE statement. The second example shown not only counts the LEADING blank spaces but also converts them to zeros.

Although the identifier of the EXAMINE statement may be either a numeric or alphanumeric field, the literals specified must be consistent with the data class of the identifier field. That is, literal-1 (and literal-2, if the REPLACING phrase is specified) must be a numeric digit if the identifier field is numeric. Further, the literals must be a single character or digit. As shown in the examples, figurative constants can be used for the literals. When the identifier is a signed numeric field, the sign is not considered in the evaluation. Also, the identifier must be of DISPLAY usage. (All fields specified in this text thus far have been of DISPLAY usage; USAGE clauses are covered in Chapter 10.)

Notice that the Format-1 EXAMINE statement has three options: ALL, UNTIL FIRST, and LEADING. ALL applies to all occurrences of literal-1 in the field. UNTIL FIRST starts at the leftmost position of the field and applies to all positions that precede the first occurrence of literal-1. LEADING, as shown in the example, starts from the left and applies to all occurrences of literal-1 that are present before any other character is encountered. Other Format-1 EXAMINE statement examples are shown in Figure 8.38.

EXAMINE statement: Format-2

This second format, as shown in Figure 8.39, is similar to the first except that it does not provide for counting of the occurrences. Also, an additional option—FIRST—is available. Use of the FIRST option causes replacement, starting from the leftmost position, of only the first occurrence of the literal-1. Rules regarding the identifier and the literals are the same as for the Format-1 statement. Other examples of the Format-2 EXAMINE statement are shown in Figure 8.40.

The INSPECT Statement

The INSPECT statement is similar in function to the EXAMINE but offers more powerful character manipulation features—and is thus more complex. Figure 8.41 shows the three INSPECT statement formats and some examples.

Significant differences between the EXAMINE and INSPECT statement are the following:

1. The INSPECT statement does not use the automatically provided TALLY field; the identifier of a programmer-defined DATA DIVISION field must instead be specified when the TALLYING phrase is used. This identifier field must be defined as a numeric integer field. Also, although the EXAMINE statement automatically initializes TALLY to zero, with the INSPECT statement the programmer must explicitly initialize the TALLYING identifier when such initialization is required. This would normally be done by moving zeros to the TALLYING field.

2. Rather than offering an UNTIL FIRST option, the INSPECT statement provides specification of the reserved word CHARACTERS with either BEFORE INITIAL or AFTER INITIAL to provide, in effect, both "until first" and "after first" counting and replacement.

3. Although the EXAMINE statement is limited to the counting and replacement of single characters, the INSPECT statement allows strings of characters to be specified.

4. The character or character strings to be tallied or replaced can be specified as either literals or as the value contained within a field.

5. The INSPECT statement allows the specification of multiple tallies or replacements within one statement.

Statement	XX-FIELD before EXAMINE	XX-FIELD after EXAMINE	TALLY after EXAMINE

EXAMINE XX-FIELD
    TALLYING ALL '.'
    REPLACING BY SPACE.
	3.46.40	3 46 40	2

EXAMINE XX-FIELD
    TALLYING LEADING '0'
    REPLACING BY '*'.
	0009.08	***9.08	3

EXAMINE XX-FIELD TALLYING LEADING ZEROS.	0200.75	0200.75	1

EXAMINE XX-FIELD
    TALLYING UNTIL FIRST '/'
    REPLACING BY ' '.
	XR/S/TY	XR S/TY	2

Figure 8.38. Additional Format-1 EXAMINE statement examples

Format:

EXAMINE identifier REPLACING { ALL / LEADING / FIRST / UNTIL FIRST } literal-1 BY literal-2

Example:

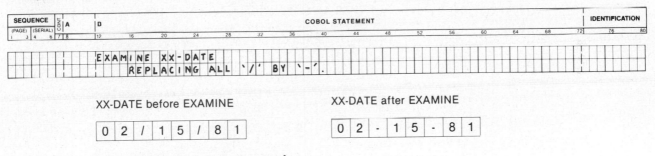

XX-DATE before EXAMINE

0 2 / 1 5 / 8 1

XX-DATE after EXAMINE

0 2 - 1 5 - 8 1

Figure 8.39. Format-2 EXAMINE statement example

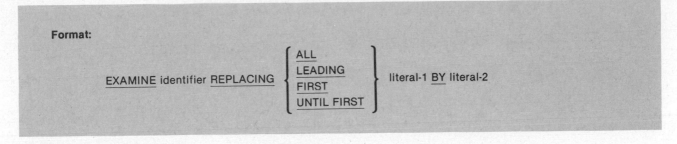

Statement	XX-FIELD before EXAMINE	XX-FIELD after EXAMINE
EXAMINE XX-QUANTITY REPLACING LEADING SPACES BY ZEROS.	bbbb7050	00007050
EXAMINE XX-DATE REPLACING ALL SPACES BY '-'.	02b28b81	02-28-81
EXAMINE XX-PRICE REPLACING FIRST ' ' BY '$'.	bb250.00	$ 250.00
EXAMINE XX-ACCOUNT REPLACING UNTIL FIRST '.' BY ZERO.	1100.410	0000.410

Note: b = blank space

Figure 8.40. Additional Format-2 EXAMINE statement examples

Format 1:

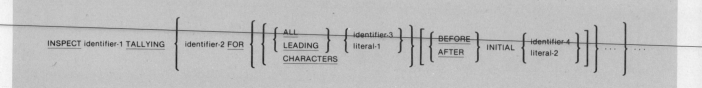

```
INSPECT identifier-1 TALLYING { identifier-2 FOR { { ALL      } { identifier-3 } } { { BEFORE }        { identifier-4 } } } ...  ...
                                              { LEADING   } { literal-1    }       { AFTER  } INITIAL { literal-2    }
                                              { CHARACTERS }
```

Format 2:

```
INSPECT identifier-1 REPLACING  { CHARACTERS BY { identifier-2 } [ { BEFORE } INITIAL { identifier-3 } ]                                                    }
                                {               { literal-1    }   { AFTER  }         { literal-2    }                                                      }
                                {                                                                                                                          } ...  ...
                                { { ALL     } { identifier-2 } BY { identifier-3 } [ { BEFORE } INITIAL { identifier-4 } ]                                  }
                                { { LEADING } { literal-1    }    { literal-2    }   { AFTER  }         { literal-3    }                                    }
                                { { FIRST   }                                                                                                              }
```

Format 3:

```
INSPECT identifier-1 TALLYING { identifier-2 FOR { { ALL      } { identifier-3 } } [ { BEFORE } INITIAL { identifier-4 } ] } ...  ...
                                                 { LEADING   } { literal-1    }     { AFTER  }         { literal-2    }
                                                 { CHARACTERS }

                     REPLACING { CHARACTERS BY { identifier-5 } [ { BEFORE } INITIAL { identifier-4 } ]                                           } ...  ...
                               {               { literal-3    }   { AFTER  }         { literal-2    }                                            }
                               { { ALL     } { identifier-5 } BY { identifier-6 } [ { BEFORE } INITIAL { identifier-7 } ]                         }
                               { { LEADING } { literal-3    }    { literal-4    }   { AFTER  }         { literal-5    }                           }
                               { { FIRST   }                                                                                                     }
```

Statement	XX-FIELD before INSPECT	XX-FIELD after INSPECT	XX-COUNT-A after INSPECT	XX-COUNT-B after INSPECT
INSPECT XX-FIELD REPLACING ALL SPACES BY ZEROS.	bb406b23	00406023		
INSPECT XX-FIELD TALLYING XX-COUNT-A FOR ALL '/'.	406/2087	406/2087	1	

INSPECT XX-FIELD
    TALLYING XX-COUNT-A FOR LEADING SPACES
    REPLACING ALL SPACES BY ZEROS.
	bbb20000	00020000	3	

INSPECT XX-FIELD
    TALLYING XX-COUNT-A FOR CHARACTERS BEFORE ','
             XX-COUNT-B FOR CHARACTERS AFTER ','.
	DOE,JOHN	DOE,JOHN	3	4

INSPECT XX-FIELD
    REPLACING LEADING ZEROS BY SPACES
             FIRST SPACE BY '$'
             ALL 'DB' BY 'DR'.
	002.56DB	$ 2.56DR		

Note: b = blank space.

Figure 8.41. INSPECT statement examples

Summary

An IF statement may be written as either (1) a simple, one-condition statement, (2) a multiple-condition statement combined by logical operators (AND or OR), or (3) a multiple condition nested IF statement.

A simple IF statement can be written with true actions only, true and false actions, and false actions only. The latter two forms require use of the reserved word ELSE; the last form also uses the reserved words NEXT SENTENCE.

Four types of conditions may be expressed with an IF statement: relation, class, sign, and condition-name. *Relation* conditions test whether the subject of the condition IS GREATER THAN, IS EQUAL TO, or IS LESS THAN the object. When the subject and the object are both numeric items, comparisons are made according to their algebraic value. Alphanumeric comparisons depend upon the *collating* sequence of the computer being used. With alphanumeric fields, comparison begins at the leftmost character and proceeds until an unequal pair of characters is encountered or until the end of the longest field is reached. *Class* conditions test whether a field contains only numeric digits or solely alphabetical characters. The former condition is considered NUMERIC; the latter ALPHABETIC. *Sign* conditions test whether a numeric field is POSITIVE, NEGATIVE, or ZERO. *Condition-name* tests are a special way of writing a relation condition that requires a level-88 item in the DATA DIVISION.

Each level-88 item requires a condition-name VALUE clause in the data-item description. Condition-name VALUE clauses differ from initializing VALUE clauses in that they:

1. can be used in either the FILE SECTION or WORKING-STORAGE SECTION
2. can be associated with REDEFINES clauses
3. can be associated with OCCURS clauses
4. can be specified with multiple values or a range of values.

A *combined* IF statement contains multiple conditions connected with the logical operators AND or OR. A *combined condition* is one that uses the operators AND and OR in the same IF statement.

A *nested* IF statement contains multiple IF statements. Nested IF statements may be *linear*—when ELSE actions immediately follow each IF condition—or *non-linear*—when multiple IF conditions precede ELSE actions.

The character manipulation statements EXAMINE and INSPECT can be used to handle *data validation*, *character translation*, and *text editing* functions.

Style Summary

- IF statement clarity is enhanced by providing appropriate indentation. Suggested indentation forms are shown in Figure 8.36.
- Compound conditions (the operator AND or OR used within the same IF statement) should be avoided because they are confusing. If used, parentheses should be inserted to make the condition understandable and explicitly specify the evaluation sequence.
- Implied subjects and relation operators should not be used. They tend to cause confusion.
- Nested IF statements should be limited to three or four levels to prevent them from becoming overly complex.

1968 ANS COBOL Restrictions

- The INSPECT statement is not available.
- Evaluation rules for compound conditions may vary with different COBOL compilers.

Exercises

Terms for Definition

simple IF statement
relation condition
~~class condition~~
sign condition
condition-name condition
combined IF statement
compound condition
implied subject

implied relation operator
nested IF statement
linear nested IF statement
non-linear nested IF statement
data validation
character translation
text editing

Review Questions

1. An IF statement containing only one condition is termed a _____ IF; an IF statement using the logical operators AND or OR is known as a _____ IF statement; an IF statement which contains more than one IF is called a _____ IF statement.

2. Name the four types of conditions that may be expressed with an IF statement.

3. Identify the three relation test operators.

4. With a relation condition, the element before the relation operator can be termed the _____ ; the element after the operator is called the _____.

5. When the subject and object of a relation test are both numeric, comparison of the two values is made according to their _____ value.

6. When the subject and/or object of a relation test is alphanumeric, comparison of the two values is made according to the _____ of the computer being used.

7. When an alphanumeric comparison is being made and the subject and object are of different lengths, the shorter field is *internally extended on the right* _____.

8. What are the two classes which a class condition may test?

9. What are the three sign condition tests?

10. A sign test can be made only with _____ fields.

11. A condition-name test requires an _____ -level entry in the _____ DIVISION.

12. A condition-name entry VALUE clause may contain one value, _____ values, or a _____ of values.

13. Condition-name VALUE clauses (can/cannot) be specified in the FILE SECTION of the DATA DIVISION.

14. When the logical operator _____ is specified in a combined IF statement, all conditions must be true for the true statements to be executed; when the logical operator _____ is specified, one or more conditions must be true for the true statements to be executed.

15. When the operators AND and OR are both used within the same IF statement, the resulting expression is referred to as a _____ condition.

16. When a nested IF statement contains an ELSE immediately following each IF condition, it is known as a _____ nested IF.

17. With nested IF statements, each ELSE applies to _____ _____.

18. Name the three TALLYING and REPLACING options of the Format-1 EXAMINE statement.

19. The additional REPLACING option provided by the Format-2 EXAMINE statement is _____ .

20. When counting occurrences, the INSPECT statement requires use of a programmer-defined field rather than _____ field provided by the EXAMINE statement.

Programming Assignment 8-A: Test Grades Report

Program description

A test grades report is to be printed from the test results file.

Input file

Test results file

Input record format

Test results record

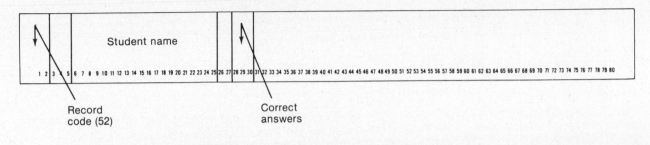

Record code (52)

Correct answers

Output file

Test grades report

Output report format

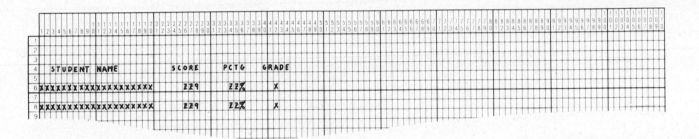

Program operations

1. Read each input test results record.

2. For each input test results record, do the following processing:

   a. Compute the percentage of correct test answers by dividing the test score by 50 (50 test questions were asked). Round to the nearest percentage point.

   b. Determine the letter grade as follows:

      A = 100% – 90%
      B = 89% – 80%
      C = 79% – 70%
      D = 69% – 60%
      F = 59% – 0%

   c. Print an output test grades report detail line as specified above for each test results record.

3. Double-space each detail line. Print the heading-line on the first page and each following page. Provide for a span of 57 lines per page.

Programming Assignment 8-B: Social Security Tax Report

Program description

A social security tax report is to be printed from the payroll file.

Input file

Payroll file

Input record format

Payroll record

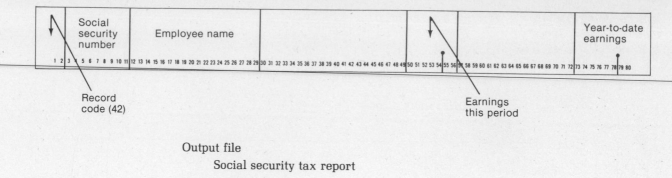

| Record code (42) | Social security number | Employee name | | Earnings this period | | Year-to-date earnings |

Record code (42) — columns 1 2 3

Social security number — columns 5 6 7 8 9 10 11

Employee name — columns 12–29

Earnings this period — columns around 51–56

Year-to-date earnings — columns 73–80

Output file

    Social security tax report

Output report format

```
    SOCIAL SECURITY TAX REPORT                          PAGE ZZ9

    SOC. SEC.        EMPLOYEE        YEAR-TO-DATE  EARNINGS   S.S. TAX
     NUMBER            NAME            EARNINGS    THIS PER.  THIS PER.

    999-99-9999   XXXXXXXXXXXXXXXXXXXX  ZZZ,ZZZ.99  ZZ,ZZZ.99-  Z,ZZZ.99

    999-99-9999   XXXXXXXXXXXXXXXXXXXX  ZZZ,ZZZ.99  ZZ,ZZZ.99-  Z,ZZZ.99
```

Program operations

1. Read each input payroll record.

2. For each input payroll record, do the following processing:

    a. Compute the social security tax this period as follows:
        —If the input year-to-date earnings is equal to or less than $29,700.00. social security tax = 6.65% of earnings this period
        —If the input year-to-date earnings is $29,700.00 or more, social security tax = 6.65% of that portion of earnings this period which is less than $29,700.00.

    b. Print an output detail line as specified above for each payroll record.

3. Double-space each detail line. Print the heading-lines on the first page and each following page. Provide for a span of 57 lines per page.

Programming Assignment 8-C: Earnings Report

Program description

    An earnings report is to be printed from the payroll file.

Input file

    Payroll file

Input record format

    Payroll record

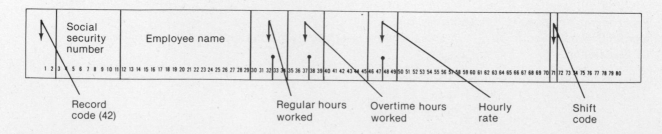

Record code (42) — columns 1 2 3

Social security number — columns 5 6 7 8 9 10 11

Employee name — columns 12–29

Regular hours worked — columns 30–34

Overtime hours worked — columns 35–39

Hourly rate — columns 46–49

Shift code — column 71

Output file
    Earnings report
Output report format

	EARNINGS REPORT										PAGE ZZ9
SOC. SEC. NUMBER	EMPLOYEE NAME	SHIFT CODE	HOURLY RATE	TOTAL HOURS	REG. HOURS	O.T. HOURS	SHIFT DIFF.	REGULAR EARNINGS	OVERTIME EARNINGS	TOTAL EARNINGS
999-99-9999	XXXXXXXXXXXXXXXXXXXX	9	ZZ.99	ZZZ.99-	ZZZ.99-	ZZZ.99-	ZZZ.99-	Z,ZZZ.99	Z,ZZZ.99-	Z,ZZZ.99-

Program operations

1. Read each input payroll record.
2. For each input payroll record, do the following:
   a. Compute the shift differential as follows:
      Shift code = 1: no shift differential
      Shift code = 2: shift differential = 10% of hourly rate times total hours worked
      Shift code = 3: shift differential = 12.5% of hourly rate times total hours worked
   b. Compute regular earnings = regular hours worked times hourly rate.
   c. Compute overtime earnings = overtime hours times hourly rate times 1.5 (time and one-half).
   d. Compute total earnings = shift differential plus regular earnings plus overtime earnings.
   e. Print an output detail line as specified above for each payroll record.
3. Single-space each detail line. Print the heading-lines on the first page and each following page. Provide for a span of 57 lines per page.

Programming Assignment 8-D: Accounts Receivable Report

Program description
    An aged analysis report is to be printed from the accounts receivable file.

Input file
    Accounts receivable file

Input record formats
    Accounts receivable record
    Aged account balance record

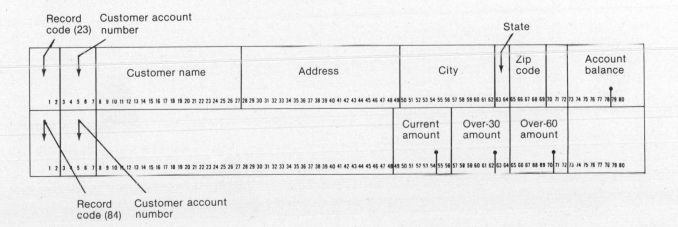

Output file

Aged analysis report

Output report format

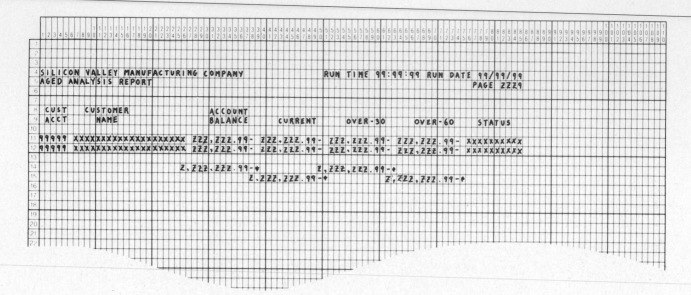

Program operations

1. Read each input accounts receivable record.

2. For each input accounts receivable record, do the following processing:

   a. Print an output report detail line as specified above.

   b. Print the account status as follows:
      - If the account balance is zero, leave the status blank.
      - If the over-30 amount and the over-60 amount are both equal to zero, print "CURRENT".
      - If the over-30 amount is not equal to zero but the over-60 amount is equal to zero, print "OVERDUE".
      - If the over-60 amount is not equal to zero, print "PAST DUE".

3. Single-space each detail line. Print the heading-lines on the first page and each following page. Provide for a span of 55 lines per page.

4. After all input accounts receivable records have been processed, print the report total lines (double-spaced from the last detail line).

SYSTEMS CHAPTER C

DATA VALIDATION CONCEPTS

The old cliche "G.I.G.O." (garbage in—garbage out) is all too familiar to data processing personnel and users alike. Although some may lamely try to enlist the phrase as a defense against an input data aberration, the professional programmer/analyst should rarely utter the words. Rather, the byword should be "G.D.G.I." (garbage doesn't get in). It is the programmer/analyst's responsibility to specify the safeguards and controls necessary to ensure data integrity within the system. This chapter discusses such aspects of control as they relate to data validation during initial input of the data to a computer system.

One of the most common mistakes made by the beginning programmer/analyst is failure to validate data completely at the time of its initial entry into the system. In the vernacular, this is known as letting "garbage," "junk," or "dirty data" into the system. The consequences are severe. Erroneous data spreads throughout the data files of the system like contagious germs. Data that enters the system has an increasing likelihood of becoming infected. As errors compound to epidemic proportions, the system's output is weakened until it is no longer viable. Since this sounds like a case for Marcus Welby, the programmer/analyst is well advised to practice preventive medicine—that is, institute programmed validation checks on data at initial input. There are three basic categories of programmed input validation checks: character testing, field checking, and record checking.

Character Testing

The most basic form of data validation control is the testing of individual character positions. There are two basic forms of *character tests*: class and sign.

Class Test

Class tests are concerned with determining whether data within a field is *numeric*, *alphabetic*, or *alphanumeric*. Figure C.1 categorizes character representations according to their class.

Generally, all numeric fields should be validated to ensure that they are purely numeric. If alphanumeric or special characters are present in a numeric field, the data is in error. Thus, a class test helps to ensure data integrity of the validated numeric fields and of any fields that hold the results of computations involving these numeric fields.

A two-letter state code (such as NY for New York, CA for California, and so forth) is an example of a data element that may be checked to ensure that it is alphabetic. In practice, characters are checked to ensure an alphabetic class less frequently than to ensure a numeric class. This is because strictly alphabetic fields rarely occur. An individual's name, for example, may validly contain an apostrophe or a hyphen. The apostrophe and hyphen are not alphabetic characters.

The term *alphanumeric* encompasses both the numeric and alphabetic classes of data and all special characters. By definition, therefore, all characters can be considered alphanumeric. Hence, there is no need to test for alphanumeric. See Figure C.2 for examples of class test determination.

Numeric	Alphabetic	Alphanumeric
0-9	A-Z	0-9
	Blank	A-Z
		Blank
		Special characters
		[(* $, . # ')] etc.

Figure C.1. Classes of data

Data element	Data	Class
Name	SMITH	Alphabetic
	JONES	Alphabetic
	O'BRIEN	Alphanumeric
	ANN-MARGRET	Alphanumeric
Maiden name	BROWNbbbbb	Alphabetic
	bbbbbbbbbb	Alphabetic
U.S. zip code	95129	Numeric
Canadian zip code	503R27	Alphanumeric
Bank balance	00051327	Numeric
	bbb51327	Alphanumeric
	00513.27	Alphanumeric
	b$513.27	Alphanumeric

Note: b = blank space

Figure C.2. Class test determinations

Medium	Positive sign	Negative sign	Unsigned
Punched card, 80 column	12-zone (Y-zone)	11-zone (X-zone)	No zone
Punched card, 96-column	B and A rows	B row	No B or A row
Computer memory (EBCDIC)	Hexadecimal C	Hexadecimal D	Hexadecimal F
Computer memory (binary)	Zero bit	One bit	—

Figure C.3. Common sign representations

Sign Test

A *sign test* is used with numeric data. Numeric fields can be categorized as containing either *absolute* or *algebraic* values. Most numeric codes (social security numbers, zip codes, and so on) are examples of absolute values. Quantities and dollar amounts usually require handling as algebraic values. If a number is operated on arithmetically, it should be treated as an algebraic value.

There are three normal arithmetic sign configurations: *positive*, *negative*, and *unsigned*. (Sometimes a positive sign is used in lieu of an unsigned representation, and vice versa.) Figure C.3 provides some examples of common sign representations. The location and data representation of the sign varies depending upon the data processing equipment, data representation method, and storage medium used. In punched cards, for example, the sign representation is located in the zone portion of the rightmost digit of the field. For an absolute value, the sign location position should be unsigned (or positive if there is no unsigned representation). An algebraic value should be unsigned (or explicitly signed positive) if it is a positive number; it should contain a negative sign if it is a negative number. Figure C.4 shows sign configurations for punched cards.

Field Checking

In addition to the basic character testing of input data fields, most data elements can be subjected to further, more rigorous checks. A discussion of various types of *field checks* follows.

Presence Check

A *presence check* is used to detect missing fields. Within many input records, there are usually both required and optional fields. A key field is a prime example of a required field—one that, if lacking, causes the input record to be immediately identified as an error. Some fields are used only when the data

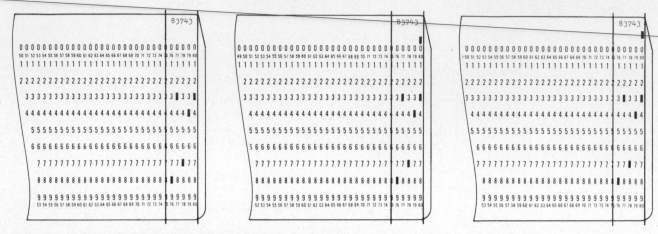

Part A: Unsigned or assumed positive value of 83743 (No zone punch in low-order column of the field)

Part B: Negative value of 83743 (11-zone–minus sign–in low-order column of the field)

Part C: Explicitly positive value of 83743 (12-zone–plus sign–in low-order column of the field)

Figure C.4. Sign representations in 80-column punched cards

elements they hold are applicable to the data entity. For instance, inclusion of data in the maiden-name field of an input record that applies to both males and females would be optional since it would not be used for men or unmarried women. A presence test should normally be performed on all required fields. Its power is limited, however, since it establishes only that there is data in a field. If possible, additional checks should be applied to the field to help ensure that the data is correct.

Absence Check

The converse of a presence check is an *absence check*, which is used to ensure that a data area is blank. It is appropriate in situations where there is an unassigned area of an input record. For example, assume positions 52 through 57 of a record are not to be used, but something is keyed in position 57. It is likely that the unexplained data belongs in the adjacent field starting in position 58. An absence test can signal such possible field-alignment errors. See Figure C.5 for examples of presence and absence checks.

Range Check

A *range check* is applied to code numbers to verify that the code numbers exist in the coding system used. As an example, the area identification codes assigned to social security numbers (the first three digits) currently range from 001 to 587 and from 700 to 728. A range check applied to these digits can identify certain transposed or otherwise erroneously coded entries. Figure C.6 provides some examples of range checks.

Limit Check

A *limit check* tests a field against maximum and/or minimum values. The limits can be either absolute amounts or percentages. An example of an absolute limit is where all expenditure transactions processed through a petty cash account must be less than $25.00. Similarly, product price changes may be validated against a percentage limit to ensure that a new price is not more than, say, 15 percent above or below the corresponding old price. An example of a limit check is shown in Figure C.7.

Reasonableness Check

A *reasonableness check* identifies abnormal data values. In a department store, for instance, a unit sales price of $800 in the notions department or a sales tag indicating a purchase of 10 diamond rings can be identified as excep-

SMITH	JOHN			2 000000b
Last name	First name	Middle name	Unassigned area	Monthly salary

Data element	Validation	Result of test on above data
Last name	Must be present	Passes presence test
First name	Must be present	Passes presence test
Middle name	Optional	Untested
Unassigned area	Must be blank	Fails absence test
Monthly salary	Must be present	Passes presence test
	Must be numeric	Fails numeric class test (because of blank)

Figure C.5. Presence/absence test examples

tion conditions. As another example, any discounts that are greater than 10 percent of the corresponding list prices can be flagged for investigation. The reasonableness check is similar to the limit check because it requires the establishment of parameters against which data is tested. It differs, however, because the parameters are norms rather than rigid limits. The programmer/analyst should recognize that experimentation may be required to set norms that will best detect invalid transactions but, at the same time, allow valid transactions to be processed routinely. Also, the parameters may need updating from time to time as conditions change. Figure C.8 shows examples of parameters for reasonableness checks.

One important consideration regarding the use of reasonableness checks is that certain exception conditions will be valid. Therefore, provisions must be included in the system to override reasonableness checks for re-entered, validated data.

Data element	Validation
Month number range	01-12
Social security number range (first three digits)	001-587, 700-728
U.S. telephone prefixes	221-998

Figure C.6. Range check examples

Data element	Minimum limit value	Maximum limit value
Individual social security tax (1981)	$ .00	$1975.05

Figure C.7. Limit check example

	Reasonable value	
Data element	Minimum	Maximum
Number of dependents	0	12
Adult height	58 inches	82 inches
Adult weight	90 pounds	299 pounds

Figure C.8. Examples of parameters for reasonableness checks

Consistency Check

A *consistency check* (sometimes called a *relationship check* or *combination check*) is the consideration of two or more data elements in relation to one another. It can be a powerful means of detecting erroneous data. Suppose that patient diagnosis data is input to a medical application and is checked. If the diagnosis code indicates pregnancy and the sex code specifies male, we have a prime example of inconsistent data. Note that the consistency check does not indicate which of the fields is incorrect. What it does indicate, though, is a discrepancy that requires resolution. Refer to Figure C.9 for examples of consistency checks.

Consistency checks find application not only in uncovering errors in data recording but also in monitoring operations. Consider a charge account system that uses credit limits of dollar amounts, beyond which customers are not privileged to incur further indebtedness. Suppose a customer's credit limit is correctly reflected at $500, and inputs correctly reflect $750 worth of merchandise charged to the account. In such a case, there are no data errors but there is an operational problem detected by checking the relationship of one field to another.

Justification Check

A *justification check* is used to assure proper alignment or adjustment of data within a field. Alphabetic and alphanumeric fields are normally left-justified (with the first character in the leftmost position of the field); numeric fields are justified to the right or decimal-point aligned. An alphanumeric field that is present but has a blank in the leftmost character position fails a normal justification check.

Justification checks are not normally performed on numeric fields. Instead a numeric field with blank positions would usually be flagged as erroneous by the numeric class test. The numeric class test is more powerful because it (1) detects both blank *and* non-numeric characters and (2) checks *all* positions of the field.

Embedded Blank Check

An *embedded blank check* is used to check certain key alphanumeric fields and code fields to ensure that blank positions have not been entered inadvertently. An embedded blank is one that has data characters represented within the field both to the left and the right of the blank position. For example, a part number field is an alphanumeric field that often serves as a key field for inventory records and the like. It would not be prudent to allow embedded blanks in

Quantity ordered	Item	Consistency determination
1 place setting	Sterling silver tableware	Consistent
8 place settings	Sterling silver tableware	Consistent
93 place settings	Sterling silver tableware	Inconsistent

Department	Amount of sale	Consistency determination
Major appliances	$1286.43	Consistent
Major appliances	.79	Inconsistent
Notions	998.00	Inconsistent
Notions	.89	Consistent

Figure C.9. Consistency check examples

Part A: Example of Part-number field with data not left-justified:

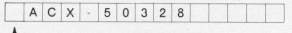

Part-number not left-justified

Part B: Example of Part-number field with embedded blank:

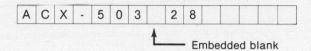

Embedded blank

Figure C.10. Justification and embedded blank check error examples

part numbers because it would probably cause confusion when entering and retrieving data. So, if embedded blank positions are restricted, detection of an embedded blank will identify an erroneous entry. Figure C.10 shows examples of justification and embedded blank error conditions.

Date Check

A *date check* is used to ensure the validity of calendar dates reflected in input transactions. There are two basic methods used to record dates: Gregorian and Julian. The *Gregorian* method is the familiar one that we use daily. July 4, 1776, is an example of a Gregorian date representation—it is a date based upon our Gregorian calendar. When a day is not identified as within a certain month but rather is identified by a sequential day number, the representation is commonly termed a *Julian date*.

Common date representations are shown in Figure C.11. Gregorian dates are most frequently used in data processing applications because they are common to our everyday lives and therefore much easier for us to use and understand. Gregorian dates can be represented in any of several formats. The most familiar one is the traditional *mmddyy* format. The leftmost two digits represent a month number from 01 to 12, the middle two digits indicate a day number from 01 to 31, and the rightmost two digits identify the year of the century from 00 to 99. The programmer/analyst should be aware, however, that the U.S. military and the people of Europe usually represent six-digit dates in *ddmmyy* format. Also, *yymmdd* dates are often used within data processing systems because such a format simplifies the identification of an earlier or later date in comparison to another date.

Generally, in a Gregorian date, month numbers are checked to see that they range from 01 through 12, and day numbers are validated against a range

Date	Type	Data class
FEBRUARY 15, 1980	Gregorian	Alphanumeric
FEB. 15, 1980	Gregorian	Alphanumeric
021580	Gregorian *mmddyy* format	Numeric
150280	Gregorian *ddmmyy* format	Numeric
800215	Gregorian *yymmdd* format	Numeric
80046	Julian *yyddd* format	Numeric

Note: d = day digit, m = month digit, y = year digit

Figure C.11. Date representations

of 01 through 31. If increased data integrity is required, a consistency check of day in relation to month can be made. That is, the day range for April, June, September, and November can be limited to from 01 to 30. February presents a special day-range problem. A precise date check for February involves dividing the year by four. If the remainder is zero, the year is a leap year and the acceptable range is then, of course, from 01 through 29—rather than from 01 to 28. There is one exception to this rule, however. If the year ends in 00 (1900, for example) the year is not a leap year unless it is evenly divisible by 400. Thus, 1600 was a leap year, and 2000 will be a leap year, but 1700, 1800, and 1900 were not. Figure C.12 provides examples of date checks.

In addition to checking a date for a valid month/day combination, it is generally advisable to validate the date for recency. Input transactions to be processed at any given time can usually be expected to be dated near that date. The further in the past or future the date, the greater the likelihood that a date error has been made. Thus, it is wise to establish a reasonableness check as to how much variance will be tolerated before identifying the distant date as an exception condition. Although any time-limit selection is somewhat arbitrary, it should depend on the data processing application and processing schedule. Usually the length of time allowed for past dates is greater than that tolerated for future dates. For example, a sales transaction dated seven days into the future will probably be suspect. Remember that, with all reasonableness checks, a re-entry override must be provided to allow exception conditions to be accepted by the system.

Self-Checking Numbers

Self-checking numbers are often used to validate account codes. A self-checking number is a code number with a calculated digit—called a *check digit*—suffixed to it so that transcription, data-entry, and transmission errors can be detected through recalculation. As an example, suppose that five-digit sequence codes are used to identify customer accounts in a charge account application. Whenever any charges, payments, returns, or adjustments are made to an account, it is necessary to identify the account to which they should be posted. Unless some control is exercised over the accuracy of the account code numbers, it is probable that undetected errors in recording will occur. This could cause misapplication of debits and credits or other customer problems. The types of errors that can be expected to arise are:

1. *Substitutional error*—The wrong digit is written, such as 7 instead of 9.
2. *Transpositional error*—The correct digits are written but their positional placement is reversed, as if code number 56789 were entered as 57689.
3. *Double transpositional error*—The digits are transposed across one or more columns, as if 56789 were written 58769.
4. *Compound error*—Two or more of the above errors occurs with the same data.

Date (mm-dd-yy) format	Validity determination
10-31-79	Valid
10-00-79	Invalid
00-31-79	Invalid
03-16-00	Valid
02-29-81	Invalid
02-29-80	Valid
02-30-80	Invalid

Figure C.12. Date check validity determination examples

Basic code	7	5	3	8	1
1. Units and alternate positions	7		3		1
Multiply by 2	14		6		2
2. Cross-foot		14 + 5 + 6 + 8 + 2 = 35			
3. Next higher number ending in zero					40
Subtract					− 35
4. Check digit					5
Self-checking number = 753815					

Figure C.13. Self-checking number computation—modulus 10 example

If any of these recording errors occur without detection, they are apt to introduce serious processing problems; transactions will be posted to the wrong accounts. To counter this, the programmer can form a check digit by summing the individual digits of each account number. For account number 40212, say, the check digit is 9 (4 + 0 + 2 + 1 + 2 = 9). With this check digit suffixed to the original code, the full self-checking account number is 402129. If a clerk makes an error in transcribing or keying any of the digits (for example, 401129), the sum of the individual digits will not be equal to the check digit 9 (4 + 0 + 1 + 1 + 2 = 8). Therefore, the test will show that an error has occurred.

A simple sum-of-the-digits check-digit system can aid in detecting a substitution error in which the wrong digit is recorded, as in the example above. It is not recommended or often used, however, because it fails to reveal transposition and double transposition errors. To identify transposition errors, a self-checking system employing weights and modulus must be used. The modulus-10 method is an example of such a system. It can be described as follows (see Figure C.13):

1. The units position and every second position of the basic code number are multiplied by 2.
2. The products of the multiplication and the unchanged alternate digit positions are added.
3. The sum is subtracted from the next highest number ending in 0.
4. The difference becomes the check digit.

The modulus-10 method detects simple transposition errors. It was often adopted in the past because of its compatibility with punched-card data processing equipment. However, it does not always detect double transposition errors. If the transposed digits are both multiplied by the same weight (2 or 1), the erroneous number still checks.

A more effective system is the modulus-11 method. It is implemented as follows (see Figure C.14):

1. Starting with the units position, each digit of the basic code number is assigned a weight or checking factor in the range from 2 to 7. The checking factor is 2 for the units position, 3 for the tens position, 4 for the hundreds position, and so forth. If the checking factor reaches 7 and there are still remaining positions of the code number, the checking factor starts again at 2. Assignments continue until the full basic code number has been assigned.
2. Multiply each digit by its checking factor.
3. Add the products.
4. Divide the sum of the products by 11.

Basic code	5	0	8	8	7	3	2	9
1. Checking factors	3	2	7	6	5	4	3	2
2. Multiply	15	0	56	48	35	12	6	18
3. Cross-foot	$15 + 0 + 56 + 48 + 35 + 12 + 6 + 18 = 190$							
4. Divide by 11	$190 \div 11 = 17$ Remainder $= 3$							
5. Subtract from 11	$11 - 3 = 8$							
6. Check digit	8							
Self-checking number = 508873298								

Figure C.14. Self-checking number computation—modulus 11

5. Subtract the remainder from 11.
6. The difference becomes the check digit.

The modulus-11 method catches approximately 97 percent of all substitution, transposition, and double transposition errors. An example is shown in Figure C.15.

On the negative side, all self-checking numbers slightly increase the length of the code values. In doing so, they somewhat increase the possibility of transcription errors. Also, a precalculated index of valid code values, including the check digit, is needed for code assignment. Nevertheless, the code validation power of a self-checking number far outweighs these minor disadvantages.

Although rarely done in practice, it is possible to do check-digit validation for alphabetic codes. Here the binary or binary coded decimal values of each character would be used.

Name-Correspondence Check

A *name-correspondence check* is sometimes used in lieu of a self-checking number. For example, social security numbers are not self-checking. When posting annual earnings, the Social Security Administration experiences an error rate of up to 10 percent on number alone. To assure that earnings are posted to the right accounts, each number is verified by checking the first six positions of the last name in the transaction record for correspondence with the name in the master file record. The name-correspondence check does not require computations like self-checking numbers do. An obvious disadvantage is that it does require, in addition to the code, a correspondence field in each transaction record. Further, the master file record must be available when the verification is performed. A self-checking number, on the other hand, can be validated independently. Examples of name-correspondence checks appear in Figure C.16.

	Entered check digit	Computed check digit	Validity determination
Basic account number: 87329			
Full account number with check digit: 873292			
Number correctly entered as: 873292	2	2	Valid
Number entered with transposition as: 872392	2	3	Invalid

Figure C.15. Self-checking number validation—modulus 11

| Master record | | Transaction record | | Correspondence determination |
Account number	Name	Account number	Name†	
40360	THOMAS	40368	THOMAS	Corresponds
40369	WALLACE	40369	WALLAC	Corresponds
40370	CARPENTER	40370	ABRAMS	Does not correspond
40380	ADAMS	40380	ADAMS	Corresponds

†First six characters

Figure C.16. Name-correspondence check examples

Code-Existence Check

A *code-existence check* is used to assure that a particular code is valid. Many codes can be validated through use of the range check mentioned earlier. Some codes require positive matches against a table of valid codes maintained within a program or data file. Each input code must be matched by the program against this table (this is often termed a *table lookup*). If there is a match, the input code is assumed to be valid; if not, the code is identified as in error. Figure C.17 provides an example of a code existence check table.

Record Checking

Not only must the character position and field values of fields be validated, but it is also often necessary to check the completeness and status of record group relationships.

For example, in a student registration system, there may be one student name-and-address record and from one to seven class records (one for each course in which the student is enrolled) required for each student. As shown in Figure C.18, errors which can be detected by record checking in this example are (1) student name-and-address record present but no class record(s) present; (2) one or more class records present but no name-and-address record present; or (3) too many (over seven) class records present for one name-and-address record.

Design Considerations

A representative transaction record is shown in Figure C.19. Its fields are keyed to the types of validation checks to which each may be subjected. Within these types of checks, there are of course additional decisions about the specific validations that should be made for each field.

The programmer/analyst must study actual conditions carefully before establishing a data validation plan. The checks must be rigorous enough to reject invalid data but flexible enough to accept all legitimate conditions.

| Fluid container units-of-measure | |
Code	Meaning
HP	Half-pint
PT	Pint
QT	Quart
HG	Half-gallon
GL	Gallon

Figure C.17. Code-existence check table example

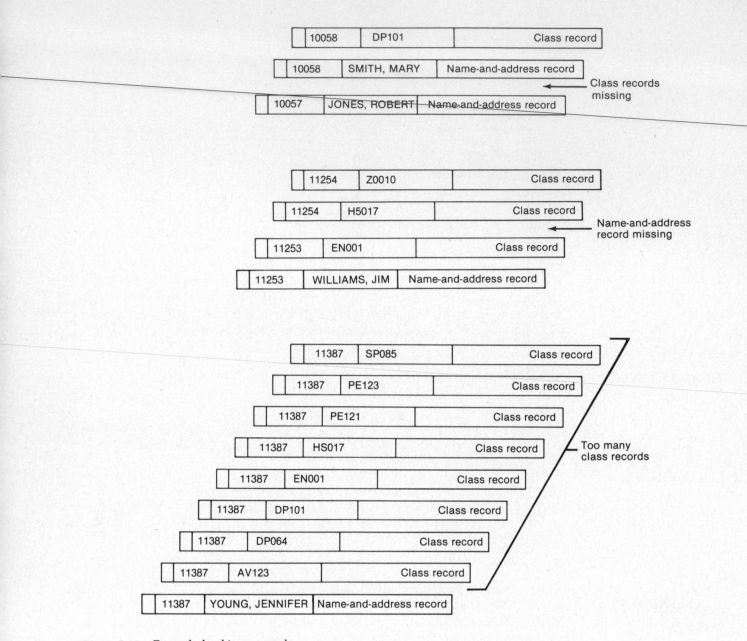

Figure C.18. Record checking example

Summary

Data processing systems should have safeguards and controls to aid in ensuring the integrity of data within the system. There are three general categories of programmed validation of input data: *character testing, field checking,* and *record checking.*

Character Testing

Class tests determine whether positions within a field contain numeric, alphabetic, or alphanumeric data. A *sign test* checks whether the value of a numeric field is positive, negative, or unsigned.

Field Checking

Presence checks are used to detect missing fields; *absence checks* identify extraneous or possibly misaligned data fields. *Range checks* are applied to code

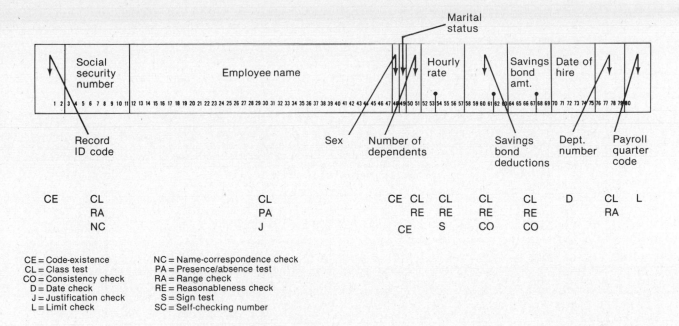

Figure C.19. Validation checks on input record fields

numbers to verify that a code number is valid. A *limit check* tests fields against maximum and/or minimum values. *Reasonableness checks* identify abnormal (though not necessarily incorrect) values. A *consistency check* is the consideration of two or more data elements in relation to one another. Proper alignment of data within alphanumeric fields are checked by *justification* and *embedded blank* tests. A *date check* tests the validity of calendar dates. *Self-checking numbers* contain check digits that allow validation of code numbers. A *name-correspondence check* checks a name field in a transaction to ensure that it corresponds to the name field in the master record; if it does not, the code number upon which the two records were matched may be in error. To assure that a particular code is valid, *code-existence checks* are used.

Record Checking

When a situation exists where multiple records are required, the completeness and status of record relationships should be validated.

CHAPTER 9

DESIGNING AND WRITING A DATA VALIDATION PROGRAM

Data validation programs check fields of an input record to help ensure that only valid data enters the system. Sometimes such programs are called *edit* programs or *front-end edits*. The latter term arises because data validation programs are usually run at the beginning of a batch system job stream or as data entry time routines for on-line programs. Figure 9.1 gives an example of a batch payroll system flowchart showing typical front-end placement of a data validation program.

As the system flowchart indicates, most batch data validation programs read a transaction input file and write an audit list and an error list. Often a combined audit/error list is produced. An audit list prints out the contents of each record input to the system; it is usually retained merely for control purposes. The audit list provides an accounting trail should it be necessary to determine where, or in what form, data originated. An error list, on the other

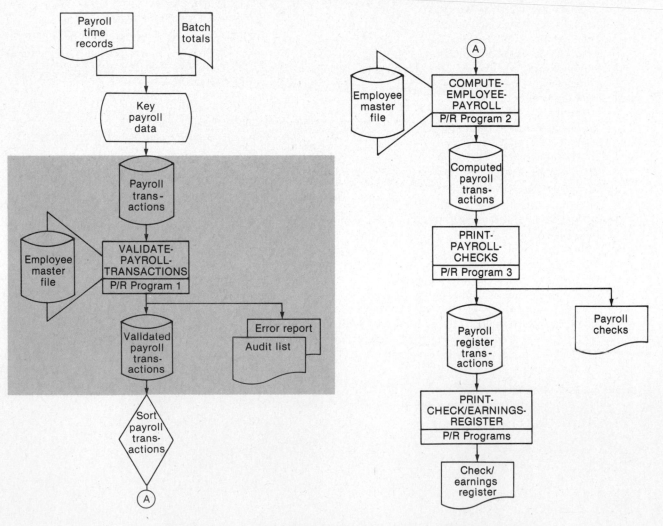

Figure 9.1. Typical front-end placement of data validation program

hand, is an action document that reports what error or discrepancy conditions have entered the system. Error reports usually require action to correct or confirm identified conditions whereas audit lists need only be retained for reference over a specified period of time. A combined audit/error list serves both functions. Voluminous audit lists are frequently stored on microfiche or some other nonprint storage medium to conserve printing time and costs.

An error list is usually designed so that the fields of the input records are displayed on the left hand side of the report; this may be referred to as the *record image* area. To the right of the record image area, error messages—or perhaps just error codes—are printed. Identification of errors by meaningful error messages is obviously preferable to the use of the more cryptic error codes. Whenever a code is used, reference to a legend is required to comprehend the meaning. Sometimes, though, space limitations may require the use of error codes. In addition to messages or codes, the data in error is often highlighted in the record-image area by printing asterisks alongside or below the field in error. Examples of commonly used audit/error list formats are depicted in Figure 9.2.

There are two general ways that erroneous transaction records (those containing fields with errors) are handled. We can term these methods *error-rejecting* and *error-abeyance*. Their effect is depicted in Figure 9.3. The error-rejecting approach—commonly used in smaller, simpler, less sophisticated, and less critical systems—writes the "good" validated records to a validated transaction file and drops the erroneous records. The error records must, of course, be corrected and then reentered into the system in a later run. The error-abeyance method writes the error records to an *abeyance*, or *suspense*, file that keeps track of all outstanding transaction records. Then, when an error is corrected, the original error record is removed from the abeyance file. The obvious advantage of the error-abeyance approach is that error records are kept to ensure that each error is corrected and that the correction is reentered into the system. Of course, this approach requires more programming effort than the error-rejecting approach.

Often, a data validation program will require accessing of a master file for some validations. For example, the validation of payroll time records would normally require reference to the employee master file: the employee number must be checked to ensure that it is a correct number assigned to an active employee. (The payroll system example in Figure 9.1 depicts master file reference for the data validation program.)

Audit/error report with error messages and error fields identified:

```
                     AUDIT/ERROR REPORT
 **-------------RECORD IMAGE--------------**
 STATE  S.S. NUMBER    NAME                ERROR MESSAGE
 -----  -----------    --------------      ----------------------
  AX    997438475     SMITH, JOHN          INVALID STATE CODE
  **
  AK    998765678     JOHNSON, ROBERT
  AZ    938374 49     JONES, BILL          INVALID SOC. SEC. NBR.
                      *********
  CA    998474647                          NAME NOT PRESENT
                      *********************
  CA    904567828     WALLACE, RUTH
```

Audit/error report with error codes:

```
                     AUDIT/ERROR REPORT
 **-------------RECORD IMAGE--------------**
 STATE  S.S. NUMBER    NAME                ERROR CODES
 -----  -----------    --------------      ----------------------
  AX    997438475     SMITH, JOHN          S
  AK    998765678     JOHNSON, ROBERT
  AZ    938374 49     JONES, BILL          X
  CA    998474647                          N
  CA    904567828     WALLACE, RUTH
```

Figure 9.2. Commonly-used audit/error report formats

Part A: Error-rejecting data validation program: Part B: Error-abeyance data validation program:

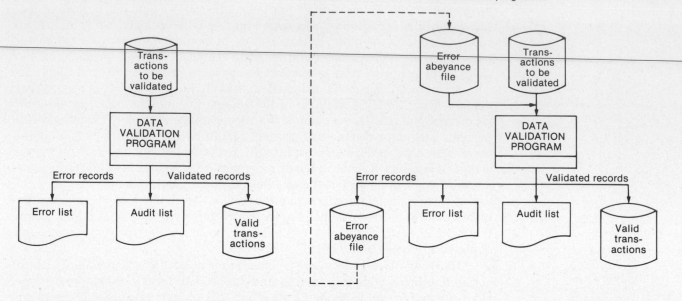

Figure 9.3.   Error handling methods for data validation programs

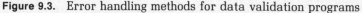

In this chapter, a sample sales transaction validation program, called DATA-VAL, will be presented. It may be thought of as a model batch data validation program. That is, the general program logic used in this example can be applied to practically any data validation program, regardless of the specific application and type of record being validated. To minimize program complexity, we will make DATA-VAL an error-rejecting—rather than error-abeyance—program; it will not reference any master files or provide for marking erroneous fields with asterisks on the error list.

Programming Specifications: Sales Transaction Validation Program

System Flowchart

The system flowchart for the DATA-VAL program is shown in Figure 9.4. Observe that there is an input sales transaction record file and two output files: an audit/error list and a valid sales transaction disk file.

Input Record Layout

The input sales transaction record is defined in Figure 9.5. It contains a number of fields applicable to individual retail sales.

Print Chart

The DATA-VAL program will produce a combined audit/error list as depicted in Figure 9.6. Notice that the input record fields are to be printed for each record processed. If any fields of the record are in error, an error message is to be printed to the right of the record-image area. Observe in the program output of Figure 9.7 that, when there is more than one error for an input record, the second and all subsequent errors are printed on a separate line following the preceding error. The record-image area is not repeated, however. After all input records have been processed, record counts are printed at the end of the report.

Programming Specifications

The programming specifications are presented in Figure 9.8.

SYSTEM FLOWCHART

Program name: SALES TRANSACTION VALIDATION   Program ID: DATA—VAL

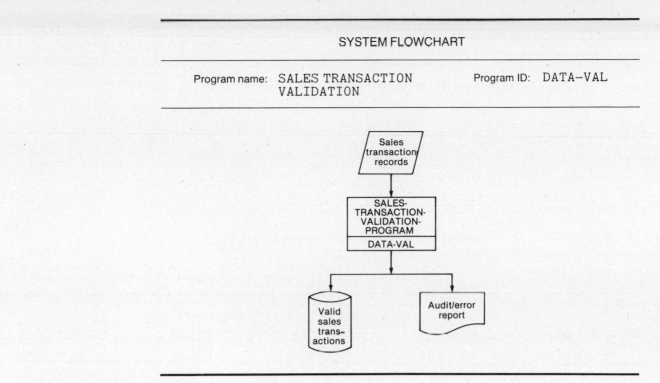

Figure 9.4. System flowchart: Sales transaction validation program

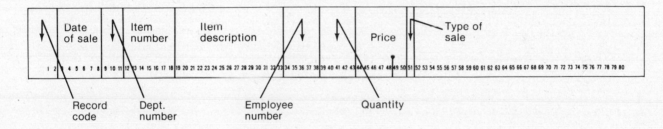

Figure 9.5. Record layout: Sales transaction record

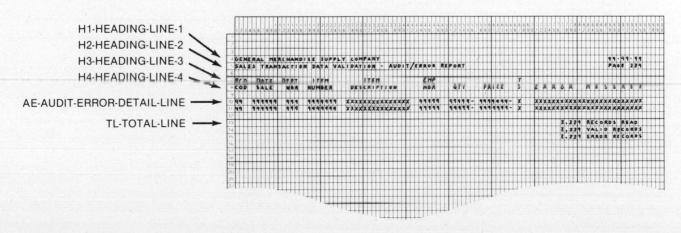

Figure 9.6. Print chart: Audit/error report

```
                            AUDIT/ERROR REPORT

          ************ RECORD IMAGE ************    ** ERROR MESSAGE **

          -------Record Image for 1st Record-------   Error message-1
          _____
          -------Record Image for 2nd record-------

          -------Record Image for 3rd record-------   Error message-1
                                                       Error message-2
                                                       Error message-3
                                                       Error message-4

          -------Record Image for 4th record-------

          -------Record Image for 5th record-------   Error message-1
                                                       Error message-2

          -------Record Image for 6th record-------
```

Figure 9.7. Example of audit/error list for records with multiple errors

---

PROGRAMMING SPECIFICATIONS

Program name: SALES TRANSACTION VALIDATION   Program ID: DATA-VAL

Program Description

This program reads input sales transaction records and makes certain field validations on each record. An audit/error list is prepared listing each record and each error detected. Validated records are written to a disk file. At the conclusion of the run, record count totals are printed.

Input File(s)

Sales transaction file

Output File(s)

Validated sales transaction file
Audit/error list

List of Program Operations

A. Read each input sales transaction record.

B. For each sales transaction record, the program is to validate the fields as shown below:

C. For each record that passes all the validation tests, the program is to:

1. Write the record to the validated sales transaction file. The validated sales transaction file is a disk file; the sales transaction record format remains the same and the blocking factor is 10. (If a record does not pass one or more validation tests, do not write that record to the disk file.)

2. Write an audit-line on the audit/error report containing the record image.

D. For each record that has one or more errors, write an error-line on the audit-error report for each error detected for that record.

1. The first error-line for each record is to contain the record image and the error message.

2. Successive error-lines for the same record (if any) should contain only the error message.

E. Accumulate the following record counts and, after all input sales transaction records have been processed, print each on a separate line in accordance with the print chart:

   a. Total number of records read

   b. Total number of valid records

   c. Total number of error records

F. Headings are to be printed on the first page of the report. After 54 lines have been used on a report page, the program is to skip to the next page and print the report headings.

1. The run date is to be obtained from the operating system and printed on the second heading-line in accordance with the format shown on the print chart.

2. The page number is to be incremented each time the heading is printed and displayed on the second heading-line in accordance with the format shown on the print chart.

G. Line-spacing is to be handled as follows:

1. The first detail-line printed after the headings is to be double-spaced from the last heading-line.

2. Second and successive error-lines for the same sales transaction record are to be single-spaced from one another.

3. The first audit or error line for each sales transaction record is to be double-spaced from the previous line.

4. The record count total-lines are to be single-spaced from one another. The first record count total-line is to be triple spaced from the last detail-line.

Figure 9.8. Programming specifications: Sales transaction validation program

Field	Validation Type	Validation	Error Message
Record-code	code-existence	27	INVALID RECORD CODE
Date-of-sale	date/range	month range 01–12	INVALID MONTH
	date/range	day range 01–31	INVALID DAY
	date/class	year numeric	YEAR NOT NUMERIC
Department-number	class	numeric	DEPT. NO. NOT NUMERIC
	presence	not equal to zero	DEPT. NO. NOT PRESENT
Item-number	class	numeric	ITEM NO. NOT NUMERIC
	presence	not equal to zero	ITEM NO. NOT PRESENT
Item-description	presence	not equal to spaces	ITEM DESC. NOT PRESENT
	justification	if present, first position not equal to space	ITEM DESC. NOT LEFT JUST.
Employee-number	range	10001–79999	INVALID EMPLOYEE NUMBER
Quantity	class	numeric	QUANTITY NOT NUMERIC
	presence	not equal to zero	QUANTITY NOT PRESENT
Price	class	numeric	PRICE NOT NUMERIC
	presence	not equal to zero	PRICE NOT PRESENT
	sign	not negative	PRICE NOT POSITIVE
	consistency	if Dept. No. less than 500, price must be less than one thousand dollars	PRICE NOT CONSISTENT
Type-of-sale	code-existence	must be equal to "$", "C" or "R"	INVALID TYPE OF SALE CODE

Program name: SALES TRANSACTION VALIDATION   Program ID: DATA-VAL

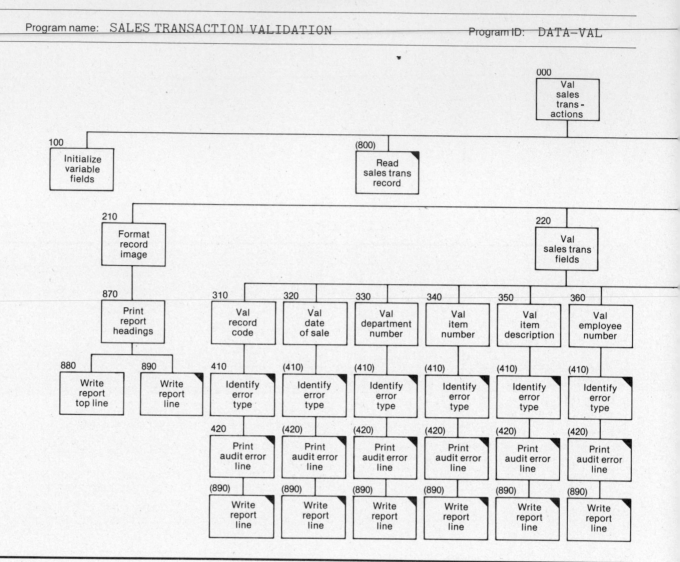

Figure 9.9. Structure chart: Sales transaction validation program

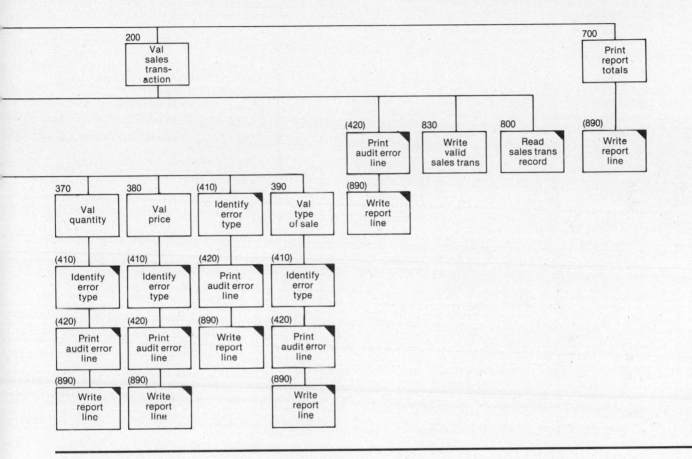

Design Documentation

Structure Chart

Pseudocode and Program Flowchart

The structure chart shown in Figure 9.9 conforms to the general patterns set by previous programs presented in this text. It does, however, have more modules and is a bit more complex than the other programs.

The pseudocode for the DATA-VAL program is shown in Figure 9.10; the program flowchart appears in Figure 9.11. A review of each module follows.

000-Val-sales-transactions module

This is the mainline control module and it performs the four level-one modules of the structure chart: 100-Initialize-Variable-Fields, 800-Read-Sales-Transaction, 200-Val-Sales-Transaction, and 700-Print-Report-Totals. The 200-Val-Sales-Transaction module is performed repeatedly as long as there are input records, so it is performed by a PERFORM/UNTIL statement. After the total-lines have been printed and the files have been closed, the run will be stopped.

Program name: VALIDATE SALES TRANSACTIONS   Program ID: DATA-VAL

000-Val-Sales-Transactions module
1. Open the files.
2. Perform 100-Initialize-Variable-Fields.
3. Perform 800-Read-Sales-Trans-Record.
4. Perform 200-Val-Sales-Transaction until no more records.
5. Perform 700-Print-Report-Totals.
6. Close the files.
7. Stop the run.

100-Initialize-Variable-Fields module
1. Set the end-of-file indicator to "No".
2. Set the page-count to zero.
3. Set the record count fields to zero.
4. Set the lines-per-page so that headings for the first page will be triggered.
5. Obtain the date from the operating system and move it to the first heading-line run-date.

200-Val-Sales-Transaction module
1. Move "No" to the error-switch.
2. Perform 210-Format-Record-Image.
3. Perform 220-Val-Sales-Trans-Fields.
4. If errors have not been detected in the input sales transaction record
    Add 1 to the Valid-record count
    Perform 420-Print-Audit-Error-Line
    Move the input Sales Transaction record to the output Validated sales transaction record area
    Perform 830-Write-Valid-Sales-Trans
   Else
    Add 1 to the Error-record count.
5. Perform 800-Read-Sales-Trans-Record.

210-Format-Record-Image module
1. If the Lines-used is greater than the Lines-per-page.
    Perform 870-Print-Report-Headings.
2. Move spaces to the detail print-line area.
3. Move each input field to the print-line area.

220-Val-Sales-Trans-Fields module
1. Perform 310-Val-Record-Code.
2. Perform 320-Val-Date-Of-Sale.
3. Perform 330-Val-Dept-Number.
4. Perform 340-Val-Item-Number.
5. Perform 350-Val-Item-Description.
6. Perform 360-Val-Employee-Number.
7. Perform 370-Val-Quantity.
8. Perform 380-Val-Price.
9. Perform 390-Val-Type-Of-Sale.

310-Val-Record-Code module

320-Val-Date-Of-Sale module

330-Val-Dept-Number module

340-Val-Item-Number module

350-Val-Item-Description module

360-Val-Employee-Number module

370-Val-Quantity module

380-Val-Price module

390-Val-Type-Of-Sale module
For each of the above modules the following general logic is used:
1. The validations illustrated in Figure 9.8, the programming specifications, are made.
2. If an error is detected
    Move the respective error-message to the detail print-line area.
    Perform 410-Identify-Error-Type.

410-Identify-Error-Type module
1. If this is not the first error-line for this sales transaction record
    Move Spaces to the Record-image-area.
2. Move "Yes" to the error-switch.

420-Print-Audit-Error-Line module
1. Move the Audit-error-line to the output print-line area.
2. If this is the first line to be printed for this sales transaction record
    Set the line-spacing indicator for double-spacing
   Else
    Set the line-spacing indicator for single-spacing.

700-Print-Report-Totals module
1. Move spaces to the total-line area.
2. Move the Records-read count field to the output Record-count field.
3. Move the words "Records read" to the output Record-count-description field.
4. Move the Total-line to the output print-line area.
5. Set the line-spacing indicator for triple-spacing.
6. Perform 890-Write-Report-Line.
7. Move the Valid-records count field to the output Record-count field.
8. Move the words "Valid records" to the output Record-count-description field.
9. Move the Total-line to the output print-line area.
10. Set the line-spacing indicator for single-spacing.
11. Perform 890-Write-Report-Line.
12. Move the Error-record count field to the output Record-count-description field.
13. Move the words "Error records" to the output Record-count-description field.
14. Move the Total-line to the output print-line area.
15. Perform 890-Write-Report-Line.

800-Read-Sales-Trans-Record module
1. Read an input sales transaction record.
2. If there are no more records
    Move "Yes" to the end-of-file indicator.
3. If a record has been read (not end-of-file)
    Add 1 to the Records-read count.

Figure 9.10. Pseudocode: Sales transaction validation program

830-Write-Valid-Sales-Trans module

1. Write the output Valid sales transaction record area.

870-Print-Report-Headings module

1. Add 1 to the Page-count.
2. Move the Page-count to the second heading-line Page-number.
3. Move heading-line-1 to the output print-line area.
4. Perform 880-Write-Report-Top-Line.
5. Move heading-line-2 to the output print-line area.
6. Set the line-spacing indicator for single-spacing.
7. Perform 890-Write-Report-Line.
8. Move heading-line-3 to the output print-line area.
9. Set the line-spacing indicator for double-spacing.

10. Perform 890-Write-Report-Line.
11. Move heading-line-4 to the output print-line area.
12. Set the line-spacing indicator for single-spacing.
13. Perform 890-Write-Report-Line.

880-Write-Report-Top-Line module

1. Advance to the top of the next report page and write the output print-line area.
2. Set the Lines-used to 1.

890-Write-Report-Line module

1. Advance in accordance with the setting of the line-spacing indicator and write the output print-line area.
2. Add the line-spacing indicator to the Lines-used.

Figure 9.10. (continued)

100-Initialize-variable-fields module

The end-of-file switch must be initialized to 'NO'. The page-count field and the fields used for the accumulation of the record-count totals must be set to zeros. The lines-used field is set to a value greater than the line span of the page so that headings for the first page of the audit/error list will be triggered. The date is obtained from the system and moved to the date area of the first heading-line.

200-Val-sales-transaction module

This module performs the 210-Format-Record-Image and 220-Val-Sales-Trans-Fields modules. If the input sales transaction record has no errors, the valid-record count is incremented and the 420-Print-Audit-Error-Line module is performed to cause an audit line to be printed. If an error has been detected, the invalid-record count is incremented. Finally, the 800-Read-Sales-Trans-Record module is performed to obtain the next input record.

210-Format-record-image module

If this is the first page of the report or if the present report page is full, the 870-Print-Report-Headings module is performed. Each of the input fields is moved to its specified location in the record-image area of the output audit/error list.

220-Val-sales-trans-fields module

Because no fields have been validated yet for the present input record, the error-switch is set to 'NO' to indicate that no errors have yet been found. Then each of the validation modules is performed to test each field of the current input sales transaction record for errors.

310-Val-record-code through 390-Val-type-of-sale modules

Each of these nine modules makes the specified validations of its respective input field. When an error is detected, the appropriate error message is moved to the error message area of the audit/error list detail-line. Then the 410-Identify-Error-Type module is performed.

410-Identify-error-type module

This module controls the printing of the record-image area of each detail-line. The first time this module is performed for each record, the record-image area

Program name: SALES TRANSACTION VALIDATION   Program ID: DATA—VAL

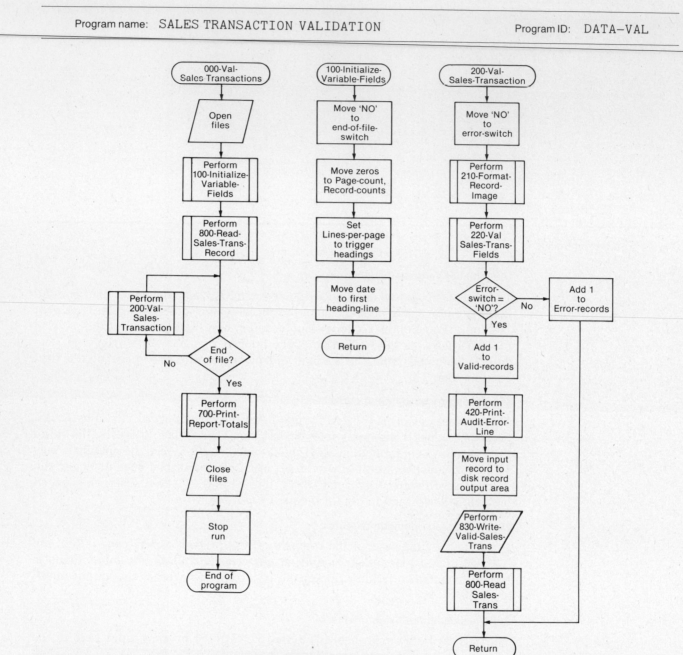

Figure 9.11. Program flowchart: Sales transaction validation program

For each of the validation modules, the following general approach is used:

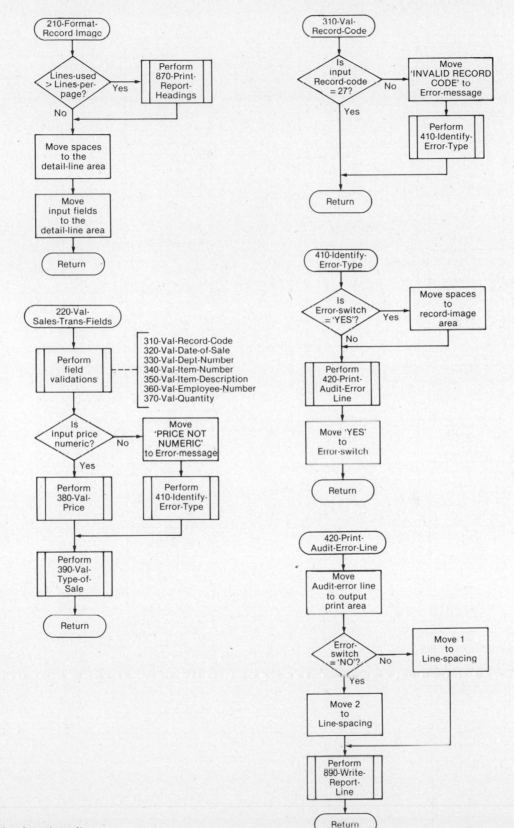

Figure 9.11. (continued)

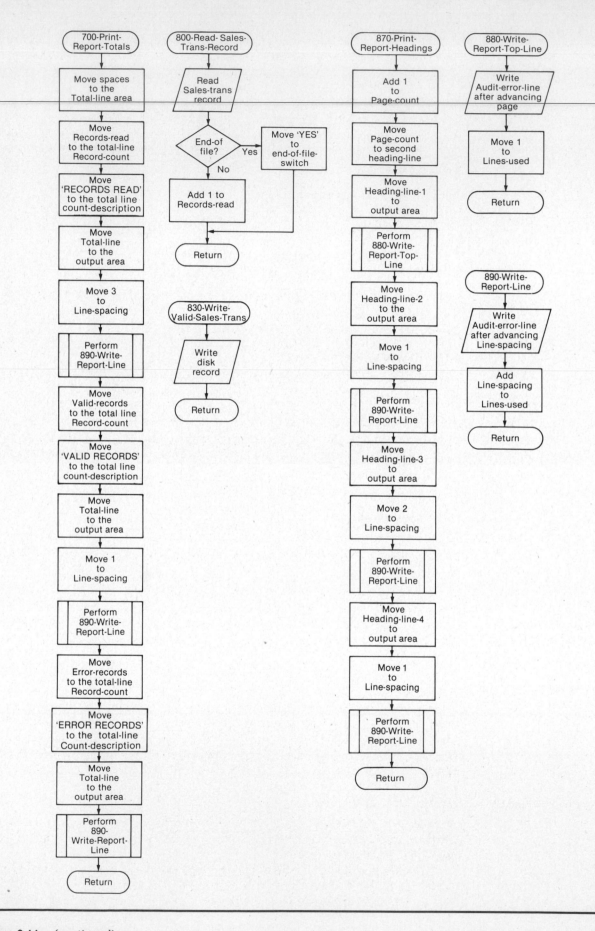

Figure 9.11. (continued)

is to be printed. For successive times, however, the record-image area is not to be printed and must therefore be blanked out. The logic of this module controls such processing.

420-Print-audit-error-line module

Both audit lines and error lines are printed through this module. The audit-error-detail-line is moved to the print area. If this is the first line for this input sales transaction record, the line-spacing indicator is set for double-spacing; if not, single-spacing is set. The 890-Write-Report-Line module is then performed.

800-Read-sales-trans-record module

This module causes the next record to be read from the input sales transaction file. Each record is then counted.

830-Write-valid-sales-trans module

The valid sales transaction disk record is in the exact same format as the input sales transaction record. This module simply moves the entire input record to the output valid sales transaction record area. Then the valid sales transaction record is written to disk.

870-Print-report-headings module

The page-count is incremented in this module and it is moved to the second heading-line. Then each of the four heading-lines is printed.

880-Write-report-top-line module

This print module is used to write only the first heading-line on the report. It causes the form to skip to the top of the next page before the line is printed. Since this module uses the first line of the report page, the lines-used indicator is set to 1.

890-Write-report-line module

This print module is used for all lines of the report other than the first heading-line. It provides for variable spacing in accordance with the value of the line-spacing field.

COBOL Coding Considerations

The COBOL coding for the DATA-VAL program is shown in Figure 9.12. We will discuss the new techniques and considerations introduced by this data validation program.

ENVIRONMENT DIVISION Coding

Three files

The previous programs in this text have been limited to two files: one input and one output. This program is an example of one with multiple output files; thus, there are three SELECT statements. Having three SELECT statements means, of course, that there must be three FD entries specified in the FILE SECTION of the DATA DIVISION.

DATA DIVISION Coding

BLOCK CONTAINS clause

This program presents an example of a situation where logical records are blocked into longer physical records. The subject of blocked records was discussed in Systems Chapter A.

The program specifications call for the records of the valid sales transactions disk file to have a blocking factor of 10. When records are blocked, the BLOCK CONTAINS clause should generally be specified in the FD for the file.

```
001010 IDENTIFICATION DIVISION.
001020 PROGRAM-ID.      DATA-VAL.
001030*AUTHOR.          WELBURN.
001040*INSTALLATION.    GENERAL MERCHANDISE SUPPLY COMPANY.
001050*DATE-WRITTEN.    MAR 5,1981.
001060*DATE-COMPILED.   MAR 5,1981.
001070*SECURITY.        NONE.
001080*
001090*
001100*               THIS PROGRAM WILL READ INPUT SALES TRANSACTION
001110*               RECORDS AND MAKE CERTAIN FIELD VALIDATIONS ON EACH
001120*               RECORD.  AN AUDIT-ERROR REPORT WILL BE PREPARED.
001130*               EACH VALIDATED RECORD WILL BE WRITTEN TO A DISK
001140*               FILE.  EACH RECORD WILL BE PRINTED ON THE AUDIT-
001150*               ERROR REPORT.  IF ANY ERRORS ARE DETECTED FOR A
001160*               RECORD, EACH WILL BE IDENTIFIED ON THE AUDIT-ERROR
001170*               REPORT.  AT THE CONCLUSION OF THE RUN, RECORD COUNT
001180*               TOTALS WILL BE PRINTED.
002010*
002020*
002030*
002040 ENVIRONMENT DIVISION.
002050*
002060*
002070 CONFIGURATION SECTION.
002080*
002090 SOURCE-COMPUTER.  IBM-370.
002100 OBJECT-COMPUTER.  IBM-370.
002110*
002120*
002130 INPUT-OUTPUT SECTION.
002140 FILE-CONTROL.
002150     SELECT SALES-TRANSACTION-FILE
002160         ASSIGN TO UT-S-INFILE.
002170     SELECT AUDIT-ERROR-REPORT
002180         ASSIGN TO UT-S-PRTFILE.
002190     SELECT VALID-SALES-TRANSACTION-FILE
002200         ASSIGN TO UT-S-OUTFILE.
003010*
003020*
003030*
003040 DATA DIVISION.
003050*
003060*
003070 FILE SECTION.
003080*
003090 FD  SALES-TRANSACTION-FILE
003100         RECORD CONTAINS 80 CHARACTERS
003110         LABEL RECORDS ARE OMITTED.
004010*
004020 01  SALES-TRANSACTION-RECORD.
004030     05  FILLER                      PIC X(80).
005010*
005020 FD  AUDIT-ERROR-REPORT
005030         RECORD CONTAINS 133 CHARACTERS
005040         LABEL RECORDS ARE OMITTED.
005050*
005060 01  AUDIT-ERROR-LINE.
005070     05  FILLER                      PIC X(133).
005110*
005120 FD  VALID-SALES-TRANSACTION-FILE
005130         RECORD CONTAINS 80 CHARACTERS
005140         BLOCK CONTAINS 10 RECORDS
005150         LABEL RECORDS ARE STANDARD.
005160*
005170 01  VALID-SALES-TRANSACTION-RECORD.
005180     05  FILLER                      PIC X(80).
006010*
006020*
006030 WORKING-STORAGE SECTION.
006040*
006050*
006060 01  WS-SWITCHES.
006070     05  WS-END-OF-FILE-SWITCH       PIC X(3).
006080         88  END-OF-FILE                         VALUE 'YES'.
006090     05  WS-ERROR-SWITCH             PIC X(3).
006100         88  VALID-SALES-TRANS                   VALUE 'NO '.
006110         88  INVALID-SALES-TRANS                 VALUE 'YES'.
008010*
008020 01  WS-REPORT-CONTROLS.
008030     05  WS-PAGE-COUNT               PIC S9(3).
008040     05  WS-LINES-PER-PAGE           PIC S9(2)   VALUE +54.
008050     05  WS-LINES-USED               PIC S9(2).
008060     05  WS-LINE-SPACING             PIC 9(2).
009010*
009020 01  WS-WORK-AREAS.
009030     05  WS-DATE-WORK                PIC 9(6).
009040     05  WS-DATE-CONVERSION REDEFINES WS-DATE-WORK.
009050         10  WS-YEAR                 PIC 9(2).
009060         10  WS-MONTH                PIC 9(2).
009070         10  WS-DAY                  PIC 9(2).
010010*
010020 01  WS-TOTAL-ACCUMULATORS.
010030     05  WS-RECORDS-READ             PIC S9(4).
010040     05  WS-VALID-RECORDS            PIC S9(4).
010050     05  WS-ERROR-RECORDS            PIC S9(4).
020010*
020020 01  ST-SALES-TRANSACTION-RECORD.
020030     05  ST-RECORD-CODE              PIC X(2).
020040     05  ST-DATE-OF-SALE.
020050         10  ST-MONTH-OF-SALE        PIC X(2).
020060         10  ST-DAY-OF-SALE          PIC X(2).
020070         10  ST-YEAR-OF-SALE         PIC X(2).
020080     05  ST-DEPARTMENT-NUMBER        PIC X(3).
020090     05  ST-ITEM-NUMBER              PIC X(7).
020100     05  ST-ITEM-DESCRIPTION.
020110         10  ST-ITEM-DESC-FIRST-POS  PIC X(1).
020120         10  ST-ITEM-DESC-REST-POS   PIC X(14).
020130     05  ST-EMPLOYEE-NUMBER          PIC X(5).
020140     05  ST-QUANTITY-X               PIC X(5).
020150     05  ST-QUANTITY REDEFINES ST-QUANTITY-X
020160                                     PIC S9(5).
020170     05  ST-PRICE-X                  PIC X(7).
020180     05  ST-PRICE REDEFINES ST-PRICE-X  PIC S9(5)V99.
020190     05  ST-TYPE-OF-SALE             PIC X(1).
020200     05  FILLER                      PIC X(29).
030010*
030020 01  H1-HEADING-LINE-1.
030030     05  FILLER              PIC X(1).
030040     05  FILLER              PIC X(20)  VALUE 'GENERAL MERCHANDISE '.
030050     05  FILLER              PIC X(20)  VALUE 'SUPPLY COMPANY       '.
030060     05  FILLER              PIC X(20)  VALUE '                    '.
030070     05  FILLER              PIC X(20)  VALUE '                    '.
030080     05  FILLER              PIC X(7)   VALUE '       '.
030090     05  H1-MONTH            PIC X(2).
030100     05  FILLER              PIC X(1)   VALUE '-'.
030110     05  H1-DAY              PIC X(2).
030120     05  FILLER              PIC X(1)   VALUE '-'.
030130     05  H1-YEAR             PIC X(2).
030140     05  FILLER              PIC X(5)   VALUE '     '.
030150     05  FILLER              PIC X(20)  VALUE '                    '.
030160     05  FILLER              PIC X(12)  VALUE '            '.
031010*
031020 01  H2-HEADING-LINE-2.
031030     05  FILLER              PIC X(1).
031040     05  FILLER              PIC X(20)  VALUE 'SALES TRANSACTION DA'.
031050     05  FILLER              PIC X(20)  VALUE 'TA VALIDATION - AUDI'.
031060     05  FILLER              PIC X(20)  VALUE 'T/ERROR REPORT      '.
031070     05  FILLER              PIC X(20)  VALUE '                    '.
031080     05  FILLER              PIC X(12)  VALUE '       PAGE '.
031090     05  H2-PAGE-NBR         PIC ZZ9.
031100     05  FILLER              PIC X(5)   VALUE '     '.
031110     05  FILLER              PIC X(20)  VALUE '                    '.
031120     05  FILLER              PIC X(12)  VALUE '            '.
032010*
032020 01  H3-HEADING-LINE-3.
032030     05  FILLER              PIC X(1).
032040     05  FILLER              PIC X(20)  VALUE 'RCD DATE   DEPT   IT'.
032050     05  FILLER              PIC X(20)  VALUE 'EM          ITEM    '.
032060     05  FILLER              PIC X(20)  VALUE '            EMP     '.
032070     05  FILLER              PIC X(20)  VALUE '          T         '.
032080     05  FILLER              PIC X(20)  VALUE '                    '.
032090     05  FILLER              PIC X(20)  VALUE '                    '.
032100     05  FILLER              PIC X(12)  VALUE '            '.
033010*
033020 01  H4-HEADING-LINE-4.
033030     05  FILLER              PIC X(1).
033040     05  FILLER              PIC X(20)  VALUE 'COD SALE  NBR   NUM '.
033050     05  FILLER              PIC X(20)  VALUE 'BER    DESCRIPTION  '.
033060     05  FILLER              PIC X(20)  VALUE '        NBR    QTY  P'.
033070     05  FILLER              PIC X(20)  VALUE 'ICE   S  ERROR      '.
033080     05  FILLER              PIC X(20)  VALUE '  MESSAGE           '.
033090     05  FILLER              PIC X(20)  VALUE '                    '.
033100     05  FILLER              PIC X(20)  VALUE '                    '.
034010*
034020 01  AE-AUDIT-ERROR-DETAIL-LINE.
034030     05  FILLER                      PIC X(1).
034040     05  AE-RECORD-IMAGE-AREA.
034050         10  AE-RECORD-CODE          PIC X(2).
034060         10  FILLER                  PIC X(2).
034070         10  AE-DATE-OF-SALE         PIC X(6).
034080         10  FILLER                  PIC X(2).
034090         10  AE-DEPARTMENT-NUMBER    PIC X(3).
034100         10  FILLER                  PIC X(2).
034110         10  AE-ITEM-NUMBER          PIC X(7).
034120         10  FILLER                  PIC X(2).
034130         10  AE-ITEM-DESCRIPTION     PIC X(15).
034140         10  FILLER                  PIC X(2).
034150         10  AE-EMPLOYEE-NUMBER      PIC X(5).
034160         10  FILLER                  PIC X(2).
034170         10  AE-QUANTITY             PIC 99999-.
034180         10  AE-QUANTITY-X REDEFINES AE-QUANTITY
034190                                     PIC X(5).
034200         10  FILLER                  PIC X(1).
034210         10  AE-PRICE                PIC 99999V99-.
034220         10  AE-PRICE-X REDEFINES AE-PRICE
034230                                     PIC X(7).
034240         10  FILLER                  PIC X(1).
034250         10  AE-TYPE-OF-SALE         PIC X(1).
034260     05  FILLER                      PIC X(3).
034270     05  AE-ERROR-MESSAGE            PIC X(25).
034280     05  FILLER                      PIC X(37).
035010*
035020 01  TL-TOTAL-LINE.
035030     05  FILLER                      PIC X(1).
035040     05  FILLER                      PIC X(76).
035050     05  TL-RECORD-COUNT             PIC Z,ZZ9.
035060     05  FILLER                      PIC X(1).
035070     05  TL-RECORD-COUNT-DESCRIPTION PIC X(13).
035080     05  FILLER                      PIC X(37).
050010*
050020*
050030*
050040 PROCEDURE DIVISION.
050050*
050060*
050070 000-VAL-SALES-TRANSACTIONS.
050080*
050090     OPEN INPUT SALES-TRANSACTION-FILE
050100          OUTPUT AUDIT-ERROR-REPORT
050110                 VALID-SALES-TRANS-FILE.
050120     PERFORM 100-INITIALIZE-VARIABLE-FIELDS.
050130     PERFORM 800-READ-SALES-TRANS-RECORD.
050140     PERFORM 200-VAL-SALES-TRANSACTION
050150         UNTIL END-OF-FILE.
050160     PERFORM 700-PRINT-REPORT-TOTALS.
050170     CLOSE SALES-TRANSACTION-FILE
050180           AUDIT-ERROR-REPORT
050190           VALID-SALES-TRANS-FILE.
050200     STOP RUN.
100010*
100020*
100030 100-INITIALIZE-VARIABLE-FIELDS.
100040*
100050     MOVE 'NO ' TO WS-END-OF-FILE-SWITCH.
100060     MOVE ZEROS TO WS-PAGE-COUNT
100070                   WS-TOTAL-ACCUMULATORS.
100080     ADD 1 WS-LINES-PER-PAGE GIVING WS-LINES-USED.
100090     ACCEPT WS-DATE-WORK FROM DATE.
100100     MOVE WS-MONTH TO H1-MONTH.
100110     MOVE WS-DAY TO H1-DAY.
100120     MOVE WS-YEAR TO H1-YEAR.
200010*
200020*
```

Figure 9.12. COBOL coding: DATA-VAL program

```
200030 200-VAL-SALES-TRANSACTION.                                  360030 360-VAL-EMPLOYEE-NUMBER.
200040*                                                            360040*
200050     MOVE 'NO ' TO WS-ERROR-SWITCH.                          360050     IF ST-EMPLOYEE-NUMBER IS NOT NUMERIC
200060     PERFORM 210-FORMAT-RECORD-IMAGE.                        360060     OR ST-EMPLOYEE-NUMBER IS LESS THAN '10001'
200070     PERFORM 220-VAL-SALES-TRANS-FIELDS.                     360070     OR ST-EMPLOYEE-NUMBER IS GREATER THAN '79999'
200080     IF VALID-SALES-TRANS                                    360080        MOVE 'INVALID EMPLOYEE NUMBER' TO AE-ERROR-MESSAGE
200090        ADD 1 TO WS-VALID-RECORDS                            360090        PERFORM 410-IDENTIFY-ERROR-TYPE.
200100        PERFORM 420-PRINT-AUDIT-ERROR-LINE                   360100*
200110        MOVE ST-SALES-TRANSACTION-RECORD                     360110*
200120           TO VALID-SALES-TRANSACTION-RECORD                 360120 370-VAL-QUANTITY.
200130        PERFORM 830-WRITE-VALID-SALES-TRANS                  360130*
200140     ELSE                                                    360140     IF ST-QUANTITY IS NOT NUMERIC
200150        ADD 1 TO WS-ERROR-RECORDS.                           360150        MOVE 'QUANTITY NOT NUMERIC' TO AE-ERROR-MESSAGE
200160     PERFORM 800-READ-SALES-TRANS-RECORD.                    360160        PERFORM 410-IDENTIFY-ERROR-TYPE.
210010*                                                            380010*
210020*                                                            380020*
210030 210-FORMAT-RECORD-IMAGE.                                    380030 380-VAL-PRICE.
210040*                                                            380040*
210050     IF WS-LINES-USED IS GREATER THAN WS-LINES-PER-PAGE      380050     IF ST-PRICE-X IS EQUAL TO ZERO
210060        PERFORM 870-PRINT-REPORT-HEADINGS.                   380060        MOVE 'PRICE NOT PRESENT' TO AE-ERROR-MESSAGE
210070     MOVE SPACES TO AE-AUDIT-ERROR-DETAIL-LINE.              380070        PERFORM 410-IDENTIFY-ERROR-TYPE.
210080     MOVE ST-RECORD-CODE TO AE-RECORD-CODE.                  380080     IF ST-PRICE IS NOT POSITIVE
210090     MOVE ST-DATE-OF-SALE TO AE-DATE-OF-SALE.                380090        MOVE 'PRICE NOT POSITIVE' TO AE-ERROR-MESSAGE
210100     MOVE ST-DEPARTMENT-NUMBER TO AE-DEPARTMENT-NUMBER.      380100        PERFORM 410-IDENTIFY-ERROR-TYPE.
210110     MOVE ST-ITEM-NUMBER TO AE-ITEM-NUMBER.                  380110     IF ST-DEPARTMENT-NUMBER IS LESS THAN '500'
210120     MOVE ST-ITEM-DESCRIPTION TO AE-ITEM-DESCRIPTION.        380120     AND ST-PRICE IS GREATER THAN +00999.99
210130     MOVE ST-EMPLOYEE-NUMBER TO AE-EMPLOYEE-NUMBER.          380130        MOVE 'PRICE NOT CONSISTENT' TO AE-ERROR-MESSAGE
210140     INSPECT ST-QUANTITY-X                                   380140        PERFORM 410-IDENTIFY-ERROR-TYPE.
210150        REPLACING LEADING SPACES BY ZEROS.                   390010*
210160     IF ST-QUANTITY IS NUMERIC                               390020*
210170        MOVE ST-QUANTITY TO AE-QUANTITY                      390030 390-VAL-TYPE-OF-SALE.
210180     ELSE                                                    390040*
210190        MOVE ST-QUANTITY-X TO AE-QUANTITY-X.                 390050     IF ST-TYPE-OF-SALE IS NOT EQUAL TO '$'
210200     INSPECT ST-PRICE-X                                      390060     AND ST-TYPE-OF-SALE IS NOT EQUAL TO 'C'
210210        REPLACING LEADING SPACES BY ZEROS.                   390070     AND ST-TYPE-OF-SALE IS NOT EQUAL TO 'R'
210220     IF ST-PRICE IS NUMERIC                                  390080        MOVE 'INVALID TYPE OF SALE CODE' TO AE-ERROR-MESSAGE
210230        MOVE ST-PRICE TO AE-PRICE                            390090        PERFORM 410-IDENTIFY-ERROR-TYPE.
210240     ELSE                                                    410010*
210250        MOVE ST-PRICE-X TO AE-PRICE-X.                       410020*
210260     MOVE ST-TYPE-OF-SALE TO AE-TYPE-OF-SALE.                410030 410-IDENTIFY-ERROR-TYPE.
220010*                                                            410040*
220020*                                                            410050     IF INVALID-SALES-TRANS
220030 220-VAL-SALES-TRANS-FIELDS.                                 410060        MOVE SPACES TO AE-RECORD-IMAGE-AREA.
220040*                                                            410070     PERFORM 420-PRINT-AUDIT-ERROR-LINE.
220050     PERFORM 310-VAL-RECORD-CODE.                            410080     MOVE 'YES' TO WS-ERROR-SWITCH.
220060     PERFORM 320-VAL-DATE-OF-SALE.                           420010*
220070     PERFORM 330-VAL-DEPARTMENT-NUMBER.                      420020*
220080     PERFORM 340-VAL-ITEM-NUMBER.                            420030 420-PRINT-AUDIT-ERROR-LINE.
220090     PERFORM 350-VAL-ITEM-DESCRIPTION.                       420040*
220100     PERFORM 360-VAL-EMPLOYEE-NUMBER.                        420050     MOVE AE-AUDIT-ERROR-DETAIL-LINE TO AUDIT-ERROR-LINE.
220110     PERFORM 370-VAL-QUANTITY.                               420060     IF VALID-SALES-TRANS
220120     IF ST-PRICE IS NUMERIC                                  420070        MOVE 2 TO WS-LINE-SPACING
220130        PERFORM 380-VAL-PRICE                                420080     ELSE
220140     ELSE                                                    420090        MOVE 1 TO WS-LINE-SPACING.
220150        MOVE 'PRICE NOT NUMERIC' TO AE-ERROR-MESSAGE         420100     PERFORM 890-WRITE-REPORT-LINE.
220160        PERFORM 410-IDENTIFY-ERROR-TYPE.                     700010*
220170     PERFORM 390-VAL-TYPE-OF-SALE.                           700020*
310010*                                                            700030 700-PRINT-REPORT-TOTALS.
310020*                                                            700040*
310030 310-VAL-RECORD-CODE.                                        700050     MOVE SPACES TO TL-TOTAL-LINE.
310040*                                                            700060     MOVE WS-RECORDS-READ TO TL-RECORD-COUNT.
310050     IF ST-RECORD-CODE IS NOT EQUAL TO '27'                  700070     MOVE 'RECORDS READ' TO TL-RECORD-COUNT-DESCRIPTION.
310060        MOVE 'INVALID RECORD CODE' TO AE-ERROR-MESSAGE       700080     MOVE TL-TOTAL-LINE TO AUDIT-ERROR-LINE.
310070        PERFORM 410-IDENTIFY-ERROR-TYPE.                     700090     MOVE 3 TO WS-LINE-SPACING.
320010*                                                            700100     PERFORM 890-WRITE-REPORT-LINE.
320020*                                                            700110     MOVE WS-VALID-RECORDS TO TL-RECORD-COUNT.
320030 320-VAL-DATE-OF-SALE.                                       700120     MOVE 'VALID RECORDS' TO TL-RECORD-COUNT-DESCRIPTION.
320040*                                                            700130     MOVE TL-TOTAL-LINE TO AUDIT-ERROR-LINE.
320050     IF ST-MONTH-OF-SALE IS NOT NUMERIC                      700140     MOVE 1 TO WS-LINE-SPACING.
320060     OR ST-MONTH-OF-SALE IS LESS THAN '01'                   700150     PERFORM 890-WRITE-REPORT-LINE.
320070     OR ST-MONTH-OF-SALE IS GREATER THAN '12'                700160     MOVE WS-ERROR-RECORDS TO TL-RECORD-COUNT.
320080        MOVE 'INVALID MONTH' TO AE-ERROR-MESSAGE             700170     MOVE 'ERROR RECORDS' TO TL-RECORD-COUNT-DESCRIPTION.
320090        PERFORM 410-IDENTIFY-ERROR-TYPE.                     700180     MOVE TL-TOTAL-LINE TO AUDIT-ERROR-LINE.
320100     IF ST-DAY-OF-SALE IS NOT NUMERIC                        700190     PERFORM 890-WRITE-REPORT-LINE.
320110     OR ST-DAY-OF-SALE IS LESS THAN '01'                     800010*
320120     OR ST-DAY-OF-SALE IS GREATER THAN '31'                  800020*
320130        MOVE 'INVALID DAY' TO AE-ERROR-MESSAGE               800030 800-READ-SALES-TRANS-RECORD.
320140        PERFORM 410-IDENTIFY-ERROR-TYPE.                     800040*
320150     IF ST-YEAR-OF-SALE IS NOT NOT NUMERIC                   800050     READ SALES-TRANSACTION-FILE INTO ST-SALES-TRANSACTION-RECORD
320160        MOVE 'YEAR NOT NUMERIC' TO AE-ERROR-MESSAGE          800060        AT END MOVE 'YES' TO WS-END-OF-FILE-SWITCH.
320170        PERFORM 410-IDENTIFY-ERROR-TYPE.                     800070     IF NOT END-OF-FILE
330010*                                                            800080        ADD 1 TO WS-RECORDS-READ.
330020*                                                            830010*
330030 330-VAL-DEPT-NUMBER.                                        830020*
330040*                                                            830030 830-WRITE-VALID-SALES-TRANS.
330050     INSPECT ST-DEPARTMENT-NUMBER                            830040*
330060        REPLACING LEADING SPACES BY ZEROS.                   830050     WRITE VALID-SALES-TRANSACTION-RECORD.
330070     IF ST-DEPARTMENT-NUMBER IS NOT NUMERIC                  870010*
330080        MOVE 'DEPT. NO. NOT NUMERIC' TO AE-ERROR-MESSAGE     870020*
330090        PERFORM 410-IDENTIFY-ERROR-TYPE.                     870030 870-PRINT-REPORT-HEADINGS.
330100     IF ST-DEPARTMENT-NUMBER IS EQUAL TO ZERO                870040*
330110        MOVE 'DEPT. NO. NOT PRESENT' TO AE-ERROR-MESSAGE     870050     ADD 1 TO WS-PAGE-COUNT.
330120        PERFORM 410-IDENTIFY-ERROR-TYPE.                     870060     MOVE WS-PAGE-COUNT TO H2-PAGE-NBR.
340010*                                                            870070     MOVE H1-HEADING-LINE-1 TO AUDIT-ERROR-LINE.
340020*                                                            870080     PERFORM 880-WRITE-REPORT-TOP-LINE.
340030 340-VAL-ITEM-NUMBER.                                        870090     MOVE H2-HEADING-LINE-2 TO AUDIT-ERROR-LINE.
340040*                                                            870100     MOVE 1 TO WS-LINE-SPACING.
340050     INSPECT ST-ITEM-NUMBER                                  870110     PERFORM 890-WRITE-REPORT-LINE.
340060        REPLACING LEADING SPACES BY ZEROS.                   870120     MOVE H3-HEADING-LINE-3 TO AUDIT-ERROR-LINE.
340070     IF ST-ITEM-NUMBER IS NOT NUMERIC                        870130     MOVE 2 TO WS-LINE-SPACING.
340080        MOVE 'ITEM NO. NOT NUMERIC' TO AE-ERROR-MESSAGE      870140     PERFORM 890-WRITE-REPORT-LINE.
340090        PERFORM 410-IDENTIFY-ERROR-TYPE.                     870150     MOVE H4-HEADING-LINE-4 TO AUDIT-ERROR-LINE.
340100     IF ST-ITEM-NUMBER IS EQUAL TO ZERO                      870160     MOVE 1 TO WS-LINE-SPACING.
340110        MOVE 'ITEM NO. NOT PRESENT' TO AE-ERROR-MESSAGE      870170     PERFORM 890-WRITE-REPORT-LINE.
340120        PERFORM 410-IDENTIFY ERROR-TYPE.                     880010*
350010*                                                            880020*
350020*                                                            880030 880-WRITE-REPORT-TOP-LINE.
350030 350-VAL-ITEM-DESCRIPTION.                                   880040*
350040*                                                            880050     WRITE AUDIT-ERROR-LINE
350050     IF ST-ITEM-DESCRIPTION IS EQUAL TO SPACES               880060        AFTER ADVANCING PAGE.
350060        MOVE 'ITEM DESC. NOT PRESENT' TO AE-ERROR-MESSAGE    880070     MOVE 1 TO WS-LINES-USED.
350070        PERFORM 410-IDENTIFY-ERROR-TYPE.                     890010*
350080     IF ST-ITEM-DESC-FIRST-POS IS EQUAL TO SPACE             890020*
350090     AND ST-ITEM-DESC-REST-POS IS NOT EQUAL TO SPACES        890030 890-WRITE-REPORT-LINE.
350100        MOVE 'ITEM DESC. NOT LEFT JUST.' TO AE-ERROR-MESSAGE 890040*
350110        PERFORM 410-IDENTIFY-ERROR-TYPE.                     890050     WRITE AUDIT-ERROR-LINE
360010*                                                            890060        AFTER ADVANCING WS-LINE-SPACING.
360020*                                                            890070     ADD WS-LINE-SPACING TO WS-LINES-USED.
```

Figure 9.12. (continued)

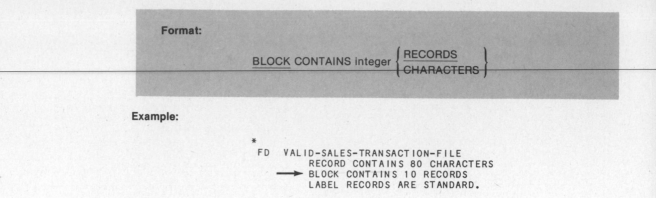
Example:

```
*
FD  VALID-SALES-TRANSACTION-FILE
        RECORD CONTAINS 80 CHARACTERS
  ----> BLOCK CONTAINS 10 RECORDS
        LABEL RECORDS ARE STANDARD.
```

Figure 9.13. BLOCK CONTAINS clause example

The BLOCK CONTAINS clause format and the example from the DATA-VAL program are shown in Figure 9.13.

Notice that the block size can be expressed as either the number of records (the blocking factor) or as the character length of the block (the block size or block length). It is usually more readily understandable and thus preferable to specify blocking as the number of RECORDS rather than as the number of CHARACTERS.

Some computer operating systems allow the specification of the blocking factor, or block size, in the job control language for the operating system. It is generally advisable to provide record blocking specifications in the job control language because, should it be necessary to change the blocking factor, modifications to the block size can be made without recompiling the COBOL program. When blocking information is specified in the job control language, depending upon the operating system, it may be necessary to either (1) omit the BLOCK CONTAINS clause from the COBOL program or (2) specify a "dummy" clause: BLOCK CONTAINS 0 RECORDS.

Alphanumeric definition of all input fields

Notice in Figure 9.14 that each field of the input sales transaction record has been defined as an alphanumeric field with the picture symbol X, even if it is actually a numeric field. For example, ST-DEPARTMENT-NUMBER is specified

```
*
01  ST-SALES-TRANSACTION-RECORD.
    05  ST-RECORD-CODE                          PIC X(2).
    05  ST-DATE-OF-SALE.
        10  ST-MONTH-OF-SALE                    PIC X(2).
        10  ST-DAY-OF-SALE                      PIC X(2).
        10  ST-YEAR-OF-SALE                     PIC X(2).
    05  ST-DEPARTMENT-NUMBER                    PIC X(3).
    05  ST-ITEM-NUMBER                          PIC X(7).
    05  ST-ITEM-DESCRIPTION.
        10  ST-ITEM-DESC-FIRST-POS              PIC X(1).
        10  ST-ITEM-DESC-REST-POS               PIC X(14).
    05  ST-EMPLOYEE-NUMBER                      PIC X(5).
    05  ST-QUANTITY-X                           PIC X(5).
    05  ST-QUANTITY REDEFINES ST-QUANTITY-X
                                                PIC S9(5).
    05  ST-PRICE-X                              PIC X(7).
    05  ST-PRICE REDEFINES ST-PRICE-X           PIC S9(5)V99.
    05  ST-TYPE-OF-SALE                         PIC X(1).
    05  FILLER                                  PIC X(29).
```

Numeric redefinition

Figure 9.14. Alphanumeric definition of all input fields and numeric redefinition of required numeric fields

with a picture character string of X(3), although it is defined in the program specifications as a numeric field. It is a good practice to define non-arithmetic integer numeric fields as alphanumeric rather than numeric. This is because (1) numeric PICTURE clauses are usually somewhat less efficient to work with because the COBOL compiler must generate extra instructions for MOVE and IF statements to provide for arithmetic sign handling and (2) since data exceptions only occur with numeric operations, abnormal program terminations can be minimized by using alphanumeric specifications.

Redefinition of input quantity and price fields

Sometimes, however, numeric field definition will be required. Observe that the alphanumeric ST-QUANTITY-X field has been redefined as a numeric field: ST-QUANTITY. Similarly, ST-PRICE-X has been redefined as ST-PRICE. These redefinitions are required because, since these two fields could be entered as positive or negative values, we will want to print a minus sign on the audit/error list for a negative value. The PICTURE for that field on the output audit/error line, then, must be numeric edited. Remember that an alphanumeric sending field cannot be moved to a numeric edited receiving field. Hence, the numeric ST-QUANTITY and ST-PRICE data-names must be used for the move to the output report line.

    The program specifications also call for a validation of the price field to ensure that it is positive. A convenient way to make such a validation is to use the sign test form of the IF statement. When making a sign test, a numeric data-name must be specified. The ST-PRICE data-name will be used in the IF sign test when validating the field in the PROCEDURE DIVISION.

Condition-name for WS-END-OF-FILE-SWITCH

In previous programs, we have not affixed a condition-name to the end-of-file switch. The test for end-of-file was thus made with the relation test. Figure 9.15 shows that by assigning a condition-name in the DATA DIVISION, we can use the convenient and self-documenting condition-name test form of the IF statement in the PROCEDURE DIVISION.

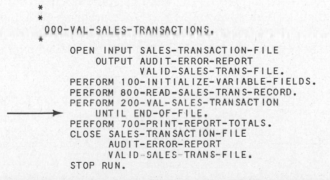

DATA DIVISION:

```
*
01  WS-SWITCHES.
    05  WS-END-OF-FILE-SWITCH              PIC X(3).
        88  END-OF-FILE                               VALUE 'YES'.
```

PROCEDURE DIVISION:

```
*
*
000-VAL-SALES-TRANSACTIONS.
*
    OPEN INPUT SALES-TRANSACTION-FILE
         OUTPUT AUDIT-ERROR-REPORT
                VALID-SALES-TRANS-FILE.
    PERFORM 100-INITIALIZE-VARIABLE-FIELDS.
    PERFORM 800-READ-SALES-TRANS-RECORD.
    PERFORM 200-VAL-SALES-TRANSACTION
        UNTIL END-OF-FILE.
    PERFORM 700-PRINT-REPORT-TOTALS.
    CLOSE SALES-TRANSACTION-FILE
          AUDIT-ERROR-REPORT
          VALID-SALES-TRANS-FILE.
    STOP RUN.
```

Figure 9.15. Condition-name entry for WS-END-OF-FILE-SWITCH

DATA DIVISION:

```
05   WS-ERROR-SWITCH                    PIC X(3).
     88   VALID-SALES-TRANS                            VALUE 'NO '.
     88   INVALID-SALES-TRANS                          VALUE 'YES'.
```

PROCEDURE DIVISION:

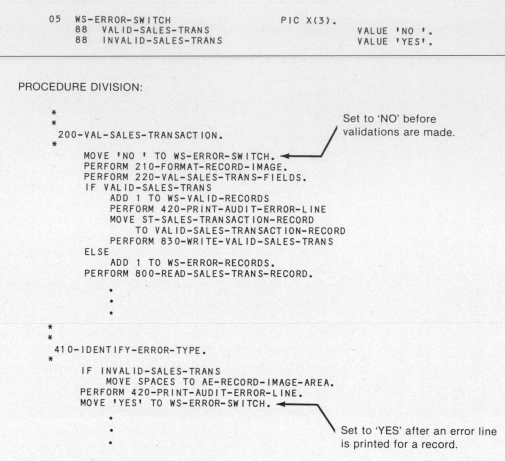

```
*
*
 200-VAL-SALES-TRANSACTION.
*
     MOVE 'NO ' TO WS-ERROR-SWITCH.
     PERFORM 210-FORMAT-RECORD-IMAGE.
     PERFORM 220-VAL-SALES-TRANS-FIELDS.
     IF VALID-SALES-TRANS
         ADD 1 TO WS-VALID-RECORDS
         PERFORM 420-PRINT-AUDIT-ERROR-LINE
         MOVE ST-SALES-TRANSACTION-RECORD
             TO VALID-SALES-TRANSACTION-RECORD
         PERFORM 830-WRITE-VALID-SALES-TRANS
     ELSE
         ADD 1 TO WS-ERROR-RECORDS.
     PERFORM 800-READ-SALES-TRANS-RECORD.
                     .
                     .
                     .

*
*
 410-IDENTIFY-ERROR-TYPE.
*
     IF INVALID-SALES-TRANS
         MOVE SPACES TO AE-RECORD-IMAGE-AREA.
     PERFORM 420-PRINT-AUDIT-ERROR-LINE.
     MOVE 'YES' TO WS-ERROR-SWITCH.
                     .
                     .
                     .
```

Set to 'NO' before validations are made.

Set to 'YES' after an error line is printed for a record.

Figure 9.16. Error switch control logic

WS-ERROR-SWITCH field

The WS-ERROR-SWITCH field, as shown in Figure 9.16, will be used to keep track of whether or not an error has occurred for each input sales transaction record. In the PROCEDURE DIVISION, before validation begins for each record, the field will be set to 'NO '. If an error is detected, the switch will be set to 'YES'.

WS-LINES-PER-PAGE field

As shown in Figure 9.17, the line span has been set to a value of +54, rather than +57 as it was in the PAYROLL program. The line span has been shortened because we don't want to continue error messages for the same record from one page to the next. This idea will be further explained below.

```
*
01   WS-REPORT-CONTROLS.
     05   WS-PAGE-COUNT              PIC S9(3).
→    05   WS-LINES-PER-PAGE          PIC S9(2)   VALUE +54.
     05   WS-LINES-USED              PIC S9(2).
     05   WS-LINE-SPACING            PIC 9(2).
```

Figure 9.17. Line span setting

```
      *
   01  AE-AUDIT-ERROR-DETAIL-LINE.
       05  FILLER                           PIC X(1).
       05  AE-RECORD-IMAGE-AREA.
           10  AE-RECORD-CODE               PIC X(2).
           10  FILLER                       PIC X(2).
           10  AE-DATE-OF-SALE              PIC X(6).
           10  FILLER                       PIC X(2).
           10  AE-DEPARTMENT-NUMBER         PIC X(3).
           10  FILLER                       PIC X(2).
           10  AE-ITEM-NUMBER               PIC X(7).
           10  FILLER                       PIC X(2).
           10  AE-ITEM-DESCRIPTION          PIC X(15).
           10  FILLER                       PIC X(2).
           10  AE-EMPLOYEE-NUMBER           PIC X(5).
           10  FILLER                       PIC X(2).
           10  AE-QUANTITY                  PIC 99999-.
    ───▶   10  AE-QUANTITY-X REDEFINES AE-QUANTITY
                                            PIC X(5).
           10  FILLER                       PIC X(1).
           10  AE-PRICE                     PIC 99999V99-.
    ───▶   10  AE-PRICE-X REDEFINES AE-PRICE
                                            PIC X(7).
           10  FILLER                       PIC X(1).
           10  AE-TYPE-OF-SALE              PIC X(1).
       05  FILLER                           PIC X(3).
       05  AE-ERROR-MESSAGE                 PIC X(25).
       05  FILLER                           PIC X(37).
```

Figure 9.18. Redefinition of quantity and price fields on audit/error line

Redefinition of quantity and price fields on audit/error line

As mentioned above, if the quantity or price fields are negative, we want to print a minus sign as documentation on the audit/error list. The PICTURE character-strings for AE-QUANTITY and AE-PRICE provide for this specification. If, however, the ST-QUANTITY or ST-PRICE fields are incorrectly keyed with non-numeric values, the non-numeric values must be moved to the AE-QUANTITY-X and the AE-PRICE-X fields. This will be discussed further below.

Notice in Figure 9.18 that AE-QUANTITY has been defined before AE-QUANTITY-X and AE-PRICE before AE-PRICE-X. AE-QUANTITY is six print positions in length; AE-PRICE is eight positions long. However, because the alphanumeric definitions do not provide for the minus sign, AE-QUANTITY-X and AE-PRICE-X are one position shorter than their respective numeric edited definitions. Remember, a field redefining another field cannot be longer than the field being redefined. Thus, we had to define the longer AE-QUANTITY and AE-PRICE fields first.

PROCEDURE DIVISION Coding

Valid/error record control

If no errors have been detected in an input sales transaction record, the WS-ERROR-SWITCH field will contain a value of 'NO'; if one or more errors have been identified, it will have a value of 'YES'. As Figure 9.19 shows, these values have been associated with the condition-names of VALID-SALES-TRANS and INVALID-SALES-TRANS, respectively. For a VALID-SALES-TRANS, the functions that must be accomplished are: (1) counting the record as valid; (2) writing an audit-line on the audit/error list; and (3) writing the record to the output disk file.

For an INVALID-SALES-TRANS, the record need only be counted as being in error. The record is not written to the output disk file because the specifications call for only the valid records to be stored there. A line is not written to the audit/error list at this time because the record-image and applicable error messages were written whenever errors were detected and the 410-IDENTIFY-ERROR-TYPE module was performed.

DATA DIVISION:

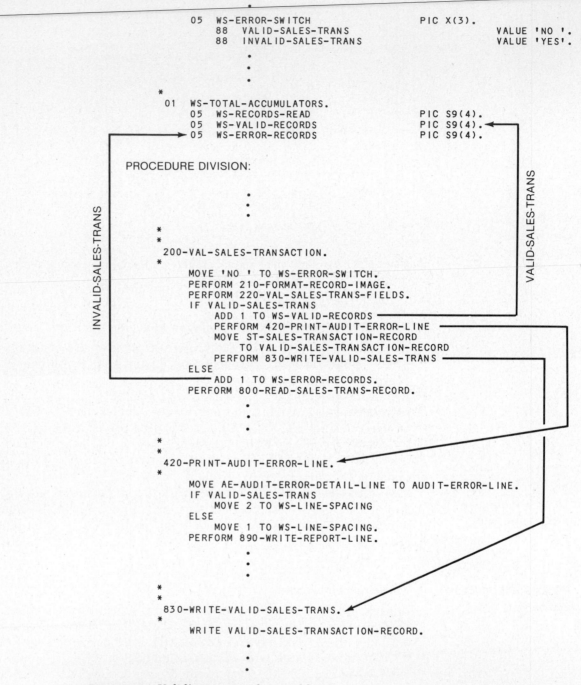

```
                    •
                    •
                    •
        05   WS-ERROR-SWITCH                 PIC X(3).
             88   VALID-SALES-TRANS                          VALUE 'NO '.
             88   INVALID-SALES-TRANS                         VALUE 'YES'.
                    •
                    •
                    •
    *
    01   WS-TOTAL-ACCUMULATORS.
        05   WS-RECORDS-READ                 PIC S9(4).
        05   WS-VALID-RECORDS                PIC S9(4).
        05   WS-ERROR-RECORDS                PIC S9(4).

    PROCEDURE DIVISION:

                    •
                    •
                    •
    *
    *
    200-VAL-SALES-TRANSACTION.
    *
        MOVE 'NO ' TO WS-ERROR-SWITCH.
        PERFORM 210-FORMAT-RECORD-IMAGE.
        PERFORM 220-VAL-SALES-TRANS-FIELDS.
        IF VALID-SALES-TRANS
            ADD 1 TO WS-VALID-RECORDS
            PERFORM 420-PRINT-AUDIT-ERROR-LINE
            MOVE ST-SALES-TRANSACTION-RECORD
                TO VALID-SALES-TRANSACTION-RECORD
            PERFORM 830-WRITE-VALID-SALES-TRANS
        ELSE
            ADD 1 TO WS-ERROR-RECORDS.
        PERFORM 800-READ-SALES-TRANS-RECORD.
                    •
                    •
                    •
    *
    *
    420-PRINT-AUDIT-ERROR-LINE.
    *
        MOVE AE-AUDIT-ERROR-DETAIL-LINE TO AUDIT-ERROR-LINE.
        IF VALID-SALES-TRANS
            MOVE 2 TO WS-LINE-SPACING
        ELSE
            MOVE 1 TO WS-LINE-SPACING.
        PERFORM 890-WRITE-REPORT-LINE.
                    •
                    •
                    •
    *
    *
    830-WRITE-VALID-SALES-TRANS.
    *
        WRITE VALID-SALES-TRANSACTION-RECORD.
                    •
                    •
                    •
```

Figure 9.19.   Valid/error record control logic

Testing for end-of-page

Often an end-of-page test will be done before printing each line. By specifying the end-of-page test at the beginning of module 210-FORMAT-RECORD-IMAGE, we are instead testing prior to each error-line group rather than prior to each line. That is, if one sales transaction record has four errors, four lines will be printed but the end-of-page test is made only for the first line.

Let's say we checked for end-of-page before printing each error-message. And then suppose the end-of-page condition was met between the second and third error messages. That would cause the program to skip to the next page and print the headings. Then, the third error line would be printed as the first line of the new page, and the record-image area would not be repeated. If the reader were looking at the last record-image on the preceding page, for instance, he or she might overlook the errors printed on the following page; when viewing the continuation page, the reader would be forced to refer to the preceding page to determine which record the errors pertained to.

Some programs solve this problem by printing a note that indicates that the errors continue on the next page and by then repeating the record-image on the continuation page. Alternatively, the note indicating continuation may be printed on the continuation page itself. Either method would require more program logic and so neither has been specified for the DATA-VAL program.

The choice of 54 lines as the page span is somewhat arbitrary. The value of 54 should, however, allow a span that (1) does not provide too much unused space at the bottom of the report and (2) provides sufficient space to contain all lines on the page when the last record has many errors.

Replacing blank spaces with zeros in numeric fields

Unused positions of numeric fields will be input either as blank spaces or as zeros. When there is no data for a particular numeric field and zero-filling is not done, a blank numeric field will result. If the number of significant digits required for the field is less than the field length and if the field is not zero-filled, spaces will be present in the leftmost positions.

To guard against these two occurrences, which would result in the presence of non-numeric data (the blank spaces) in numeric fields, programmers often force blank spaces to become zeros in numeric fields with an INSPECT (or EXAMINE) statement. This statement can replace all spaces within the field with zeros, as shown in Figure 9.20.

Although this technique of replacing all spaces by zeros in numeric fields is often used, it should be recognized that it handles successfully only those situations where a numeric field is input as an entirely blank field or without leftmost zero-filling. It has two serious problem areas.

First, if the numeric data within a field is misaligned and contains a blank space either within the actual correct digits or to the right of the value, then the replacement of blank spaces with zeros will cause the numeric value of the field to be erroneously represented. For example, if the value 1856 is misaligned one position to the left within a field, the value will be converted to

Part A: A commonly used technique to replace blank spaces with zeros in numeric fields (which may cause erroneous values for miskeyed data):

```
INSPECT ST-QUANTITY-X
      REPLACING ALL SPACES BY ZEROS.
```

Part B: A better technique to replace blank spaces with zeros in numeric fields:

```
INSPECT ST-QUANTITY-X
      REPLACING LEADING SPACES BY ZEROS.
```

Figure 9.20. Replacing blank spaces with zeros

18560. One way to counter this problem is to specify the operator LEADING rather than ALL in the INSPECT (or EXAMINE) statement. Then only nonsignificant zeros will be inserted.

Second, if the replacement of blank spaces by zeros is used in lieu of a numeric class test, data exceptions may still occur should a special character, such as an asterisk or dollar sign, be erroneously represented in the field.

In summary then, *leading* blank spaces should be replaced by zeros when numeric fields have not previously been zero-filled. This replacement does not eliminate the need for a numeric class test, however. If all blank spaces are replaced by zeros, misplaced blank spaces will be converted to valid—even though erroneous—data.

Alternate MOVE statements to edited numeric or unedited alphanumeric fields

If the ST-QUANTITY field of the ST-SALES-TRANSACTION-RECORD is numeric, it should of course be moved to the AE-QUANTITY field of the AE-AUDIT-ERROR-DETAIL-LINE. (It is not possible to move ST-QUANTITY-X to AE-QUANTITY because the compiler does not allow an alphanumeric field to be moved to a numeric edited field.) However, if the ST-QUANTITY field contained non-numeric data and it was moved to the AE-QUANTITY field, a data exception would occur at execution time.

The IF statement shown in Figure 9.21 is used to achieve the result we're after: print a minus sign if the field is negative and avoid a data exception if the field contains non-numeric data.

Parallel logic is used for the ST-PRICE and AE-PRICE fields in subsequent program statements.

Error-checking logic

Figure 9.22 indicates the common approach used when checking each field for errors: (1) the error condition is tested; (2) if an error is detected, the appropriate error message is moved to the AE-ERROR-MESSAGE field so that it will be printed on the audit/error list and the module 410-IDENTIFY-ERROR-TYPE is performed to control the audit/error line printing; and (3) the program flows to the next sequential statement (or the module end).

Reason for numeric class test prior to performing 380-VAL-PRICE module

Notice in Figure 9.23 that, unlike the other field validation modules, the 380-VAL-PRICE module is not performed unless the ST-PRICE field is numeric. If the ST-PRICE field contains non-numeric data, the error is identified and the 380-VAL-PRICE module is skipped.

This conditional performance of the 380-VAL-PRICE module is specified to ensure that a data exception does not occur when making numeric comparisons in the module. Of course, protection against data exceptions could also be provided by construction of appropriate nested IF statements. However, the logic shown provides correct handling and simplifies the 380-VAL-PRICE module.

410-IDENTIFY-ERROR-TYPE module logic

The basic purpose of this module is to control the printing of the record-image area. The logic is shown in Figure 9.24. Remember that the record-image is to be printed only on the first error-line. If there are multiple errors, the second and subsequent lines should thus be blank in the record-image area.

The first time this module is executed for each record the WS-ERROR-SWITCH will contain the value of 'NO'. The first time through, then, the program logic will leave the record-image data in the record-image area and set the WS-ERROR-SWITCH to 'YES', since an error has now been detected. Thus,

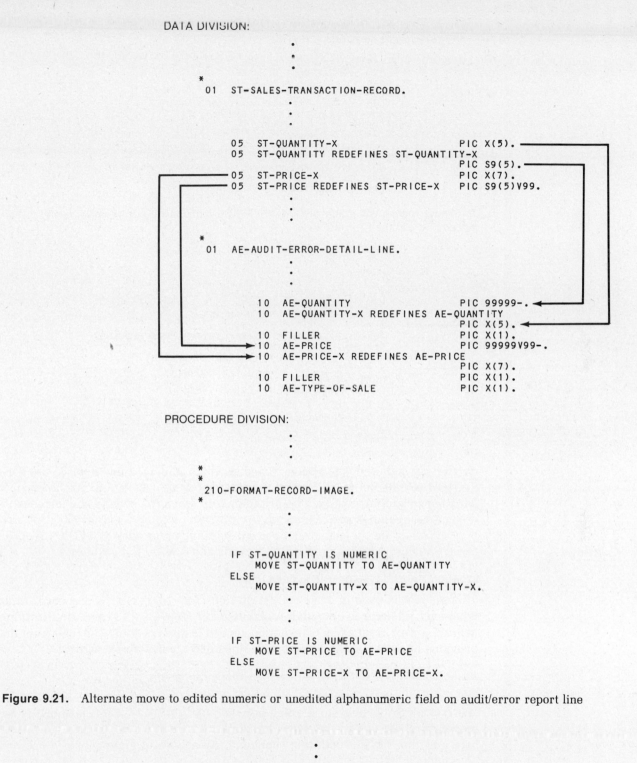

```
DATA DIVISION:
                                       •
                                       •
                                       •
                *
                01    ST-SALES-TRANSACTION-RECORD.
                                       •
                                       •
                                       •
                     05   ST-QUANTITY-X                    PIC X(5).
                     05   ST-QUANTITY REDEFINES ST-QUANTITY-X
                                                           PIC S9(5).
                     05   ST-PRICE-X                       PIC X(7).
                     05   ST-PRICE REDEFINES ST-PRICE-X    PIC S9(5)V99.
                                       •
                                       •
                                       •
                *
                01    AE-AUDIT-ERROR-DETAIL-LINE.
                                       •
                                       •
                                       •
                          10   AE-QUANTITY                 PIC 99999-.
                          10   AE-QUANTITY-X REDEFINES AE-QUANTITY
                                                           PIC X(5).
                          10   FILLER                      PIC X(1).
                          10   AE-PRICE                     PIC 99999V99-.
                          10   AE-PRICE-X REDEFINES AE-PRICE
                                                           PIC X(7).
                          10   FILLER                      PIC X(1).
                          10   AE-TYPE-OF-SALE             PIC X(1).

PROCEDURE DIVISION:
                                       •
                                       •
                                       •
                *
                *
                210-FORMAT-RECORD-IMAGE.
                *
                                       •
                                       •
                                       •
                     IF ST-QUANTITY IS NUMERIC
                          MOVE ST-QUANTITY TO AE-QUANTITY
                     ELSE
                          MOVE ST-QUANTITY-X TO AE-QUANTITY-X.
                                       •
                                       •
                                       •
                     IF ST-PRICE IS NUMERIC
                          MOVE ST-PRICE TO AE-PRICE
                     ELSE
                          MOVE ST-PRICE-X TO AE-PRICE-X.
```

Figure 9.21.   Alternate move to edited numeric or unedited alphanumeric field on audit/error report line

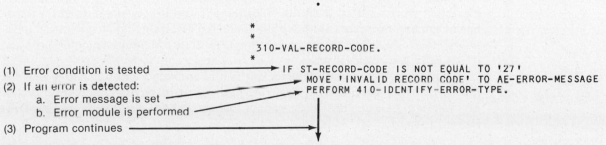

```
                                       •
                                       •
                                       •
                     *
                     *
                     310-VAL-RECORD-CODE.
                     *
```

(1) Error condition is tested ——————→ IF ST-RECORD-CODE IS NOT EQUAL TO '27'
(2) If an error is detected: MOVE 'INVALID RECORD CODE' TO AE-ERROR-MESSAGE
    a. Error message is set ———————→ PERFORM 410-IDENTIFY-ERROR-TYPE.
    b. Error module is performed ——→
(3) Program continues ————————————————→

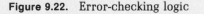

Figure 9.22.   Error-checking logic

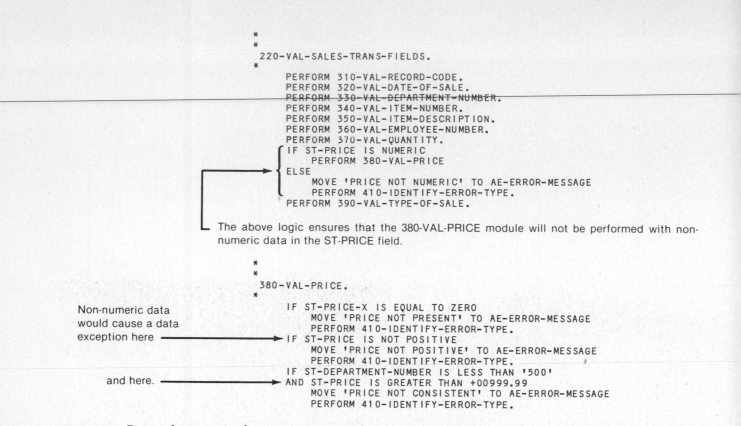

```
     *
     *
     220-VAL-SALES-TRANS-FIELDS.
     *
           PERFORM 310-VAL-RECORD-CODE.
           PERFORM 320-VAL-DATE-OF-SALE.
           PERFORM 330-VAL-DEPARTMENT-NUMBER.
           PERFORM 340-VAL-ITEM-NUMBER.
           PERFORM 350-VAL-ITEM-DESCRIPTION.
           PERFORM 360-VAL-EMPLOYEE-NUMBER.
           PERFORM 370-VAL-QUANTITY.
           IF ST-PRICE IS NUMERIC
              PERFORM 380-VAL-PRICE
           ELSE
              MOVE 'PRICE NOT NUMERIC' TO AE-ERROR-MESSAGE
              PERFORM 410-IDENTIFY-ERROR-TYPE.
           PERFORM 390-VAL-TYPE-OF-SALE.
```

The above logic ensures that the 380-VAL-PRICE module will not be performed with non-numeric data in the ST-PRICE field.

```
     *
     *
     380-VAL-PRICE.
     *
           IF ST-PRICE-X IS EQUAL TO ZERO
              MOVE 'PRICE NOT PRESENT' TO AE-ERROR-MESSAGE
              PERFORM 410-IDENTIFY-ERROR-TYPE.
           IF ST-PRICE IS NOT POSITIVE
              MOVE 'PRICE NOT POSITIVE' TO AE-ERROR-MESSAGE
              PERFORM 410-IDENTIFY-ERROR-TYPE.
           IF ST-DEPARTMENT-NUMBER IS LESS THAN '500'
           AND ST-PRICE IS GREATER THAN +00999.99
              MOVE 'PRICE NOT CONSISTENT' TO AE-ERROR-MESSAGE
              PERFORM 410-IDENTIFY-ERROR-TYPE.
```

Non-numeric data would cause a data exception here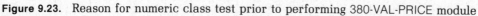

and here.

Figure 9.23. Reason for numeric class test prior to performing 380-VAL-PRICE module

on the second and successive times through the module, the WS-ERROR-SWITCH will be set to 'YES', and the program logic will blank out the record-image area so that it will not be printed again when the second and successive error message lines are displayed.

Whether this is the first or a subsequent error, the 420-PRINT-AUDIT-ERROR-LINE module is performed to write the line on the audit/error list.

420-PRINT-AUDIT-ERROR-LINE module logic

This module is used to print both audit-lines for valid records and error-lines whenever an error is detected. As the logic of Figure 9.25 shows, the first line printed for an input sales transaction record is always double-spaced from the previous line; second and successive lines are always single-spaced.

Numeric class test combined with alphanumeric range test

One might question why the numeric class test is made while checking the ST-MONTH-OF-SALE field for a value between '01' and '12'. This class test is required for IBM larger-scale systems and others with byte-oriented architecture and the EBCDIC collating sequence. As shown in Figure 9.26, there are non-numeric values present between the range of '01' and '12'. If the numeric class test were omitted from the IF statement and if by some data entry error one of the non-numeric values within the range just happened to get into the ST-MONTH-OF-SALE field, then the erroneous data would not be detected because it is within the correct range.

Notice that the numeric class test is also included with the range test for the ST-DAY-OF-SALE field within this module. It is similarly specified in the 360-VAL-EMPLOYEE-NUMBER module, when validating the ST-EMPLOYEE-NUMBER field.

The second and successive times through this module will cause AE-RECORD-IMAGE-AREA to be set to SPACES.

```
     *
     *
      410-IDENTIFY-ERROR-TYPE.
     *
          IF INVALID-SALES-TRANS
              MOVE SPACES TO AE-RECORD-IMAGE-AREA.
          PERFORM 420-PRINT-AUDIT-ERROR-LINE.
          MOVE 'YES' TO WS-ERROR-SWITCH.
```

Figure 9.24. 410-IDENTIFY-ERROR-TYPE logic

WS-ERROR-SWITCH is set to INVALID-SALE-TRANS condition *after* the first error line is printed for each record.

The first line printed for each input sales transaction is double-spaced.

```
  *
  *
   420-PRINT-AUDIT-ERROR-LINE.
  *
       MOVE AE-AUDIT-ERROR-DETAIL-LINE TO AUDIT-ERROR-LINE.
       IF VALID-SALES-TRANS
           MOVE 2 TO WS-LINE-SPACING
       ELSE
           MOVE 1 TO WS-LINE-SPACING.
       PERFORM 890-WRITE-REPORT-LINE.
```

Figure 9.25. 420-PRINT-AUDIT-ERROR-LINE logic

The successive lines printed for each input sales transaction are single-spaced.

```
  *
  *
   320-VAL-DATE-OF-SALE.
  *
       IF ST-MONTH-OF-SALE IS NOT NUMERIC
       OR ST-MONTH-OF-SALE IS LESS THAN '01'
       OR ST-MONTH-OF-SALE IS GREATER THAN '12'
           MOVE 'INVALID MONTH' TO AE-ERROR-MESSAGE
           PERFORM 410-IDENTIFY-ERROR-TYPE.
       IF ST-DAY-OF-SALE IS NOT NUMERIC
       OR ST-DAY-OF-SALE IS LESS THAN '01'
       OR ST-DAY-OF-SALE IS GREATER THAN '31'
           MOVE 'INVALID DAY' TO AE-ERROR-MESSAGE
           PERFORM 410-IDENTIFY-ERROR-TYPE.
       IF ST-YEAR-OF-SALE IS NOT NOT NUMERIC
           MOVE 'YEAR NOT NUMERIC' TO AE-ERROR-MESSAGE
           PERFORM 410-IDENTIFY-ERROR-TYPE.
```

Values '01' through '12'

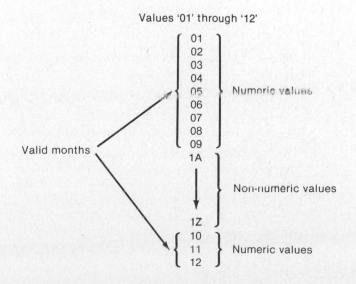

Figure 9.26. Need for numeric class test combined with alphanumeric range test

DATA DIVISION:

```
05  ST-ITEM-DESCRIPTION.
    10  ST-ITEM-DESC-FIRST-POS          PIC X(1).
    10  ST-ITEM-DESC-REST-POS           PIC X(14).
```

PROCEDURE DIVISION:

```
*
*
 350-VAL-ITEM-DESCRIPTION.
*
      IF ST-ITEM-DESCRIPTION IS EQUAL TO SPACES
          MOVE 'ITEM DESC. NOT PRESENT' TO AE-ERROR-MESSAGE
          PERFORM 410-IDENTIFY-ERROR-TYPE.
      IF ST-ITEM-DESC-FIRST-POS IS EQUAL TO SPACE
      AND ST-ITEM-DESC-REST-POS IS NOT EQUAL TO SPACES
          MOVE 'ITEM DESC. NOT LEFT JUST.' TO AE-ERROR-MESSAGE
          PERFORM 410-IDENTIFY-ERROR-TYPE.
```

Part A: Properly left-justified example (not in error):

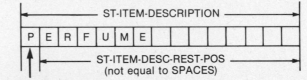

Part B: Improperly justified example (error):

Part C: Blank description example (not justification error):

Figure 9.27. Checking for left justification of alphanumeric fields

Checking for left justification of alphanumeric fields

The logic depicted in Figure 9.27 shows an easy, efficient way to test to ensure that an alphanumeric field is left justified. If the first position is blank and any one of the remaining positions is not blank, the field is not left justified.

Notice that when the field is completely blank, no justification error is identified. This error condition is identified only by the previous validation, which causes the error message "ITEM DESC. NOT PRESENT" to be printed.

```
*
*
 390-VAL-TYPE-OF-SALE.
 *
```

		Examples with	
		Valid code "$"	Invalid code "T"

Part A: Correct combined IF test using operator AND and negated conditions

```
IF ST-TYPE-OF-SALE IS NOT EQUAL TO '$'
AND ST-TYPE-OF-SALE IS NOT EQUAL TO 'C'
AND ST-TYPE-OF-SALE IS NOT EQUAL TO 'R'
    MOVE 'INVALID TYPE OF SALE CODE' TO AE-ERROR-MESSAGE
    PERFORM 410-IDENTIFY-ERROR-TYPE.
```

	Valid code "$"	Invalid code "T"
	False	True
	True	True
	True	True
	Correct logic: no error identified	Correct logic: error identified

Part B: Incorrect combined IF test using operator OR and negated conditions

```
IF ST-TYPE-OF-SALE IS NOT EQUAL TO '$'
OR ST-TYPE-OF-SALE IS NOT EQUAL TO 'C'
OR ST-TYPE-OF-SALE IS NOT EQUAL TO 'R'
    MOVE 'INVALID TYPE OF SALE CODE' TO AE-ERROR-MESSAGE
    PERFORM 410-IDENTIFY-ERROR-TYPE.
```

	Valid code "$"	Invalid code "T"
	False	True
	True	True
	True	True
	Incorrect logic: error identified	Correct logic: error identified

Part C: Correct combined IF test using operator OR

```
IF ST-TYPE-OF-SALE IS EQUAL TO '$'
OR ST-TYPE-OF-SALE IS EQUAL TO 'C'
OR ST-TYPE-OF-SALE IS EQUAL TO 'R'
    NEXT SENTENCE
ELSE
    MOVE 'INVALID TYPE OF SALE CODE' TO AE-ERROR-MESSAGE
    PERFORM 410-IDENTIFY-ERROR-TYPE.
```

	Valid code "$"	Invalid code "T"
	True	False
	False	False
	False	False
	Correct logic: no error identified	Correct logic: error identified

Part D: Incorrect combined IF test using operator AND and negated conditions

```
IF ST-TYPE-OF-SALE IS NOT EQUAL TO '$'
AND ST-TYPE-OF-SALE IS NOT EQUAL TO 'C'
AND ST-TYPE-OF-SALE IS NOT EQUAL TO 'R'
    NEXT SENTENCE
ELSE
    MOVE 'INVALID TYPE OF SALE CODE' TO AE-ERROR-MESSAGE
    PERFORM 410-IDENTIFY-ERROR-TYPE.
```

	Valid code "$"	Invalid code "T"
	False	True
	True	True
	True	True
	Correct logic: error identified	Incorrect logic: no error identified

Figure 9.28. Use of the combined IF operators

Use of combined IF operators

When a number of IF condition tests are combined, beginning programmers often make errors when selecting the operator AND or OR. Figure 9.28 contrasts correct and incorrect combinations for the ST-TYPE-OF-SALE field validation.

Writing records to disk or tape

The WRITE statement of the 830-WRITE-VALID-SALES-TRANS provides an example of writing a record to a non-printer file such as the disk file specified in this program. If this record were being written to a tape file, the WRITE statement would be identical. It is similar in format to the WRITE statements that we have constructed for printer files in that the reserved word WRITE is specified and followed by the user-defined record-name; the ADVANCING phrase applies only to printer files and is thus omitted.

```
       .
       .
       .
 *
 01   WS-ERROR-MESSAGES.
       05   WS-220-ERR-1 PIC X(25) VALUE 'PRICE NOT NUMERIC         '.
       05   WS-310-ERR-1 PIC X(25) VALUE 'INVALID RECORD CODE       '.
       05   WS-320-ERR-1 PIC X(25) VALUE 'INVALID MONTH             '.
       05   WS-320-ERR-2 PIC X(25) VALUE 'INVALID DAY               '.
       05   WS-320-ERR-3 PIC X(25) VALUE 'YEAR NOT NUMERIC          '.
       05   WS-330-ERR-1 PIC X(25) VALUE 'DEPT. NO. NOT NUMERIC     '.
       05   WS-330-ERR-2 PIC X(25) VALUE 'DEPT. NO. NOT PRESENT     '.
       05   WS-340-ERR-1 PIC X(25) VALUE 'ITEM NO. NOT NUMERIC      '.
       05   WS-340-ERR-2 PIC X(25) VALUE 'ITEM NO. NOT PRESENT      '.
       05   WS-350-ERR-1 PIC X(25) VALUE 'ITEM DESC. NOT PRESENT    '.
       05   WS-350-ERR-2 PIC X(25) VALUE 'ITEM DESC. NOT LEFT JUST. '.
       05   WS-360-ERR-1 PIC X(25) VALUE 'INVALID EMPLOYEE NUMBER   '.
       05   WS-370-ERR-1 PIC X(25) VALUE 'QUANTITY NOT NUMERIC      '.
       05   WS-380-ERR-1 PIC X(25) VALUE 'PRICE NOT PRESENT         '.
       05   WS-380-ERR-2 PIC X(25) VALUE 'PRICE NOT POSITIVE        '.
       05   WS-380-ERR-3 PIC X(25) VALUE 'PRICE NOT CONSISTENT      '.
       05   WS-390-ERR-1 PIC X(25) VALUE 'INVALID TYPE OF SALE CODE'.
       .
       .
       .
```

Figure 9.29. Specification of error messages in the WORKING-STORAGE SECTION

```
 *
 01   ST-SALES-TRANSACTION-RECORD.
       05   ST-RECORD-CODE                   PIC X(2).
             88   VALID-RECORD-CODE                VALUE '27'.

       05   ST-DATE-OF-SALE.
             10   ST-MONTH-OF-SALE            PIC X(2).
                   88   VALID-MONTH                VALUE '01' THRU '12'.
             10   ST-DAY-OF-SALE              PIC X(2).
                   88   VALID-DAY                  VALUE '01' THRU '31'.
             10   ST-YEAR-OF-SALE             PIC X(2).

       05   ST-DEPARTMENT-NUMBER             PIC X(3).
             88   DEPT-NO-NOT-PRESENT              VALUE ZERO.
             88   DEPT-NO-LESS-THAN-500            VALUE '001'
                                                     THRU '499'.

       05   ST-ITEM-NUMBER                   PIC X(7).
             88   ITEM-NO-NOT-PRESENT             VALUE ZERO.

       05   ST-ITEM-DESCRIPTION.
             88   ITEM-DESC-NOT-PRESENT          VALUE SPACES.
             10   ST-ITEM-DESC-FIRST-POS      PIC X(1).
                   88   ITEM-DESC-FIRST-POS-BLANK  VALUE SPACE.
             10   ST-ITEM-DESC-REST-POS       PIC X(14).
                   88   ITEM-DESC-REST-POS-BLANK   VALUE SPACES.

       05   ST-EMPLOYEE-NUMBER               PIC X(5).
             88   VALID-EMPLOYEE-NUMBER           VALUE '10001'
                                                     THRU '79999'.

       05   ST-QUANTITY-X                    PIC X(5).
       05   ST-QUANTITY REDEFINES ST-QUANTITY-X
                                             PIC S9(5).
       05   ST-PRICE-X                       PIC X(7).
             88   PRICE-NOT-PRESENT              VALUE ZEROS.
       05   ST-PRICE REDEFINES ST-PRICE-X    PIC S9(5)V99.
             88   PRICE-1000-DLRS-OR-MORE        VALUE +01000.00
                                                     THRU +99999.99.
       05   ST-TYPE-OF-SALE                  PIC X(1).
             88   VALID-TYPE-OF-SALE             VALUE '$'
                                                     'C'
                                                     'R'.

       05   FILLER                           PIC X(29).
```

Figure 9.30. Specification of 88-level condition-names in
ST-SALES-TRANSACTION-RECORD

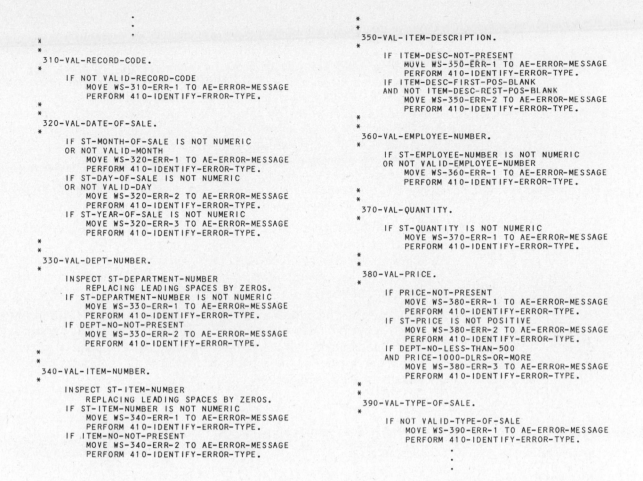

```
                .                                   *
                .                                   *
                .                  350-VAL-ITEM-DESCRIPTION.
  *                                                 *
  *                                    IF ITEM-DESC-NOT-PRESENT
   310-VAL-RECORD-CODE.                   MOVE WS-350-ERR-1 TO AE-ERROR-MESSAGE
  *                                       PERFORM 410-IDENTIFY-ERROR-TYPE.
       IF NOT VALID-RECORD-CODE           IF ITEM-DESC-FIRST-POS-BLANK
          MOVE WS-310-ERR-1 TO AE-ERROR-MESSAGE  AND NOT ITEM-DESC-REST-POS-BLANK
          PERFORM 410-IDENTIFY-ERROR-TYPE.       MOVE WS-350-ERR-2 TO AE-ERROR-MESSAGE
  *                                              PERFORM 410-IDENTIFY-ERROR-TYPE.
  *                                   *
   320-VAL-DATE-OF-SALE.              *
  *                                    360-VAL-EMPLOYEE-NUMBER.
       IF ST-MONTH-OF-SALE IS NOT NUMERIC  *
       OR NOT VALID-MONTH                    IF ST-EMPLOYEE-NUMBER IS NOT NUMERIC
          MOVE WS-320-ERR-1 TO AE-ERROR-MESSAGE  OR NOT VALID-EMPLOYEE-NUMBER
          PERFORM 410-IDENTIFY-ERROR-TYPE.          MOVE WS-360-ERR-1 TO AE-ERROR-MESSAGE
       IF ST-DAY-OF-SALE IS NOT NUMERIC             PERFORM 410-IDENTIFY-ERROR-TYPE.
       OR NOT VALID-DAY                   *
          MOVE WS-320-ERR-2 TO AE-ERROR-MESSAGE  *
          PERFORM 410-IDENTIFY-ERROR-TYPE.   370-VAL-QUANTITY.
       IF ST-YEAR-OF-SALE IS NOT NUMERIC  *
          MOVE WS-320-ERR-3 TO AE-ERROR-MESSAGE  IF ST-QUANTITY IS NOT NUMERIC
          PERFORM 410-IDENTIFY-ERROR-TYPE.          MOVE WS-370-ERR-1 TO AE-ERROR-MESSAGE
  *                                                 PERFORM 410-IDENTIFY-ERROR-TYPE.
  *                                   *
   330-VAL-DEPT-NUMBER.               *
  *                                    380-VAL-PRICE.
       INSPECT ST-DEPARTMENT-NUMBER   *
          REPLACING LEADING SPACES BY ZEROS.  IF PRICE-NOT-PRESENT
       IF ST-DEPARTMENT-NUMBER IS NOT NUMERIC    MOVE WS-380-ERR-1 TO AE-ERROR-MESSAGE
          MOVE WS-330-ERR-1 TO AE-ERROR-MESSAGE  PERFORM 410-IDENTIFY-ERROR-TYPE.
          PERFORM 410-IDENTIFY-ERROR-TYPE.    IF ST-PRICE IS NOT POSITIVE
       IF DEPT-NO-NOT-PRESENT                    MOVE WS-380-ERR-2 TO AE-ERROR-MESSAGE
          MOVE WS-330-ERR-2 TO AE-ERROR-MESSAGE  PERFORM 410-IDENTIFY-ERROR-TYPE.
          PERFORM 410-IDENTIFY-ERROR-TYPE.    IF DEPT-NO-LESS-THAN-500
  *                                          AND PRICE-1000-DLRS-OR-MORE
  *                                             MOVE WS-380-ERR-3 TO AE-ERROR-MESSAGE
   340-VAL-ITEM-NUMBER.                          PERFORM 410-IDENTIFY-ERROR-TYPE.
  *                                   *
       INSPECT ST-ITEM-NUMBER         *
          REPLACING LEADING SPACES BY ZEROS.  390-VAL-TYPE-OF-SALE.
       IF ST-ITEM-NUMBER IS NOT NUMERIC   *
          MOVE WS-340-ERR-1 TO AE-ERROR-MESSAGE  IF NOT VALID-TYPE-OF-SALE
          PERFORM 410-IDENTIFY-ERROR-TYPE.          MOVE WS-390-ERR-1 TO AE-ERROR-MESSAGE
       IF ITEM-NO-NOT-PRESENT                       PERFORM 410-IDENTIFY-ERROR-TYPE.
          MOVE WS-340-ERR-2 TO AE-ERROR-MESSAGE            .
          PERFORM 410-IDENTIFY-ERROR-TYPE.               .
                                                         .
```

Figure 9.31. Use of WORKING-STORAGE error messages and 88-level condition-names in field validation modules

Alternate Coding Techniques

The coding presented for this DATA-VAL program has been written to best explain the logic of such a program. There are a couple of other coding techniques that could be incorporated in such a program.

Specification of Error Messages in the WORKING-STORAGE SECTION

Rather than coding the error messages as non-numeric literals in the PROCEDURE DIVISION, we could establish the error messages as data-items in the WORKING-STORAGE SECTION, as shown in Figure 9.29. This groups all the error messages in one location for easy reference.

Notice that, as a reference aid, the data-names for each error message reflect the module number in which the related condition is tested. Observe also that each error message has been specified as 25 characters long to conform to the length of the AE-ERROR-MESSAGE field. Remember that processing efficiency is optimized when the sending and receiving fields of an alphanumeric MOVE statement are of equal length.

Use of 88-Level Condition-Name Entries for Applicable Validations

As shown in Figure 9.30, condition-names may be specified within the record-description specifications for the ST-SALES-TRANSACTION-RECORD to provide convenient program documentation and PROCEDURE DIVISION coding.

Use of these condition-names with the WORKING-STORAGE error messages in PROCEDURE DIVISION modules 310-VAL-RECORD-CODE through 390-VAL-TYPE-OF-SALE is shown in Figure 9.31.

Summary

Data validation programs check fields of an input record to help ensure that only valid data enters the system. They are alternately termed *edit* or *front-end* edit programs. Most batch data validation programs read a transaction input file and write an audit list and an error list; combined audit/error lists are sometimes produced. Error records are usually handled by either the *error-rejecting* or the *error-abeyance* approach. With the former, errors are rejected from the validated file; with the latter, they are maintained in an error-abeyance file until corrected. Often, data validation programs will access an existing master file for some validations.

Style Summary

- Specify blocking by using the easier to comprehend RECORDS option of the BLOCK CONTAINS clause rather than the CHARACTERS option.

- When possible, it is generally advisable to provide record blocking specifications through the computer operating system job control language rather than the COBOL BLOCK CONTAINS clause. This allows changes to the blocking factor without requiring recompilation of the COBOL program.

- Define non-arithmetic integer numeric fields as alphanumeric rather than numeric. Numeric PICTURE clauses are usually less efficient because of the need for arithmetic sign handling. Also, on some computer systems, numeric fields introduce the possibility that data exceptions may occur and cause abnormal program termination.

Exercises

Terms for Definition

data validation program
edit program
front-end edit program
record image
error-rejecting data validation program

error-abeyance data validation program
abeyance file
suspense file
master file

Review Questions

1. Why are data validation programs alternately referred to as front-end edits?

2. Why is the error-abeyance method of handling erroneous records superior to the error-rejecting approach?

3. Why is it better to specify record blocking specifications in the job control language (when supported by the operating system) rather than through the BLOCK CONTAINS clause of the COBOL program?

4. Identify two reasons why non-arithmetic numeric integer fields should generally be specified as alphanumeric rather than numeric fields.

5. For numeric fields which are not zero-filled, why is it advisable to replace LEADING SPACES BY ZEROS rather than ALL SPACES BY ZEROS?

6. Explain why a numeric field should be tested for NUMERIC even though all SPACES have been replaced by ZEROS.

7. Explain why a numeric range test made with non-numeric literals also requires a NUMERIC class test (for the EBCDIC collating sequence).

Programming Assignment 9-A: Test Result Validation

Program description

The test results file is to be validated. An audit/error report is to be prepared that lists each record and identifies each error detected by an error code.

Input file

Test results file

Input record format

Test results record

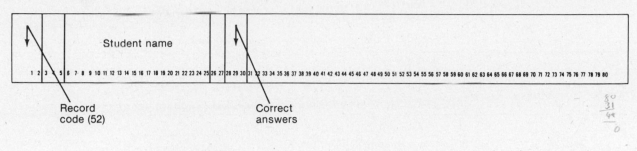

Record code (52)

Correct answers

Output file

Student test result validation audit/error report

Output report format

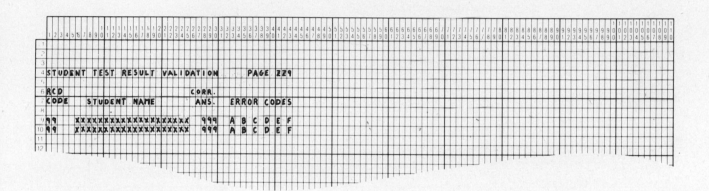

Program operations

1. Read each input test results record.

2. For each input test results record, make the following field validations:

   a. (Error code A) Validate the record code field to ensure that it is equal to 52.

   b. (Error code B) Validate the student name field to ensure that it is present.

   c. (Error code C) If the student name field is present, validate it to ensure that it is left justified.

   d. (Error code D) Validate the correct answer field to ensure that it is present.

   e. (Error code E) If the correct answer field is present, validate to ensure that it is numeric.

   f. (Error code F) If the correct answer field is present and numeric, validate to ensure that it contains a value within the range of 0 to 50.

3. For each input test results record, print the fields of the record and the error codes for any errors identified for that record.

4. Single-space each detail line. Print the heading-line on the first page and each following page. Print the page number on the first heading line. Provide for a span of 57 lines per page.

Programming Assignment 9-B: Student Test Result Validation with Error Field Marking

Program description

The test results file is to be validated. An audit/error report is to be prepared that lists each record and identifies each error detected by an error code. The field in error is to be identified by marking asterisks beneath the audit/error report line field image.

Input file
    Test results file
Input record format
    Test results record

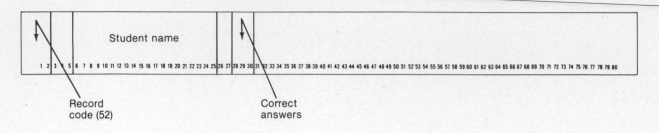

Record code (52)

Correct answers

Output file
    Student test result validation audit/error report
Output report format

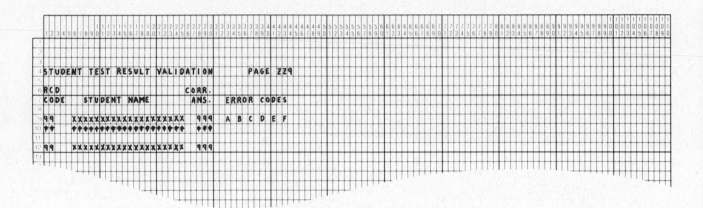

Program operations

1. Read each input test results record.

2. For each input test results record, make the following field validations:

    a. (Error code A) Validate the record code field to ensure that it is equal to 52.

    b. (Error code B) Validate the student name field to ensure that it is present.

    c. (Error code C) If the student name field is present, validate to ensure that it is left justified.

    d. (Error code D) Validate the correct answer field to ensure that it is present.

    e. (Error code E) If the correct answer field is present, validate to ensure that it is numeric.

    f. (Error code F) If the correct answer field is present and numeric, validate to ensure that it contains a value within the range of 0 to 50.

3. For each input test results record, print the fields of the record and the error codes for any errors identified for that record.

4. If errors were detected for the record, print a line (single-spaced from the audit/error line for that record) with asterisks beneath each field that contains errors.

5. Double-space each audit/error line from the previous audit/error or asterisk line. Print the heading-line on the first page and each following page. Print the page number on the first heading line. Provide for a span of no more than 57 lines per page. (Always print the asterisk line on the same page as the audit/error line to which it applies.)

Programming Assignment 9-C: Part Master File Validation

Program description

The part master file is to be validated. An audit/error report is to be prepared that lists each record and identifies each error detected by an error message.

Input file

Part master file

Input record format

Part master record

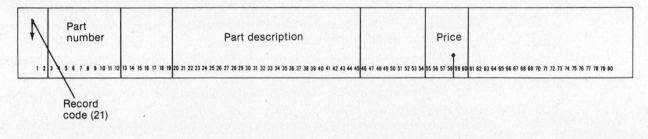

Output file

Part master validation audit/error report

Output report format

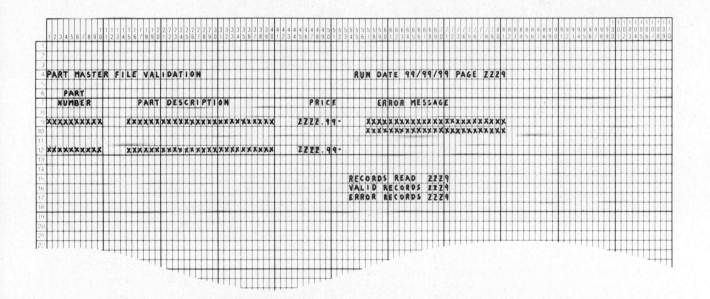

Program operations

1. Read each input part master record.

2. For each input part master record, make the following field validations:

   a. Validate the record code to ensure that it is equal to 21. If it is not, print the error message INVALID RECORD CODE.

   b. Validate the part number field to ensure that it is present. If it is not, print the error message PART NUMBER MISSING.

   c. If the part number field is present, validate it to ensure that it contains no embedded blank spaces (a blank space followed by any non-blank space within the field). If it does, print the error message INVALID PART NUMBER.

   d. Validate the part description field to ensure that it is present. If it is not, print the error message PART DESCRIPTION MISSING.

e. If the part description field is present, validate it to ensure that it is left justified. If it is not, print the error message PART DESC. NOT LEFT JUST.

f. Validate the price field to ensure that it is present. If it is not, print the error message PRICE MISSING.

g. If the price field is present, validate it to ensure that it is numeric. If it is not, print the error message PRICE NOT NUMERIC.

h. If the price field is numeric, validate it to ensure that it is not negative. If it is, print the error message NEGATIVE PRICE.

i. If the price field is numeric, validate it to ensure that it is not greater than 4999.99. If it is, print the error message UNREASONABLE PRICE.

3. For each record that passes all the validation tests, write an audit-line on the audit/error report containing the record image.

4. For each record that has one or more errors, write an error-line on the audit/error report for each error detected for that record.

a. The first error-line for each record is to contain the record image and the error message.

b. Successive error-lines for the same record (if any) should contain only the error message.

5. Accumulate the following record counts and, after all input sales transaction records have been processed, print each on a separate line in accordance with the print chart:

a. Total number of records read.

b. Total number of valid records.

c. Total number of error records.

6. Headings are to be printed on the first page of the report. After 54 lines have been used on a report page and a new part master record is to be printed, the program is to skip to the next page and print the report headings. (Do not continue lines for one part master record from one page to another.)

a. The run date is to be obtained from the operating system and printed on the first heading-line in accordance with the format shown on the print chart.

b. The page number is to be incremented each time the heading is printed and displayed on the second heading-line in accordance with the format shown on the print chart.

7. Line-spacing is to be handled as follows:

a. The first detail-line after the headings is to be double-spaced from the last heading-line.

b. Second and successive error-lines for the same sales transaction record are to be single-spaced from one another.

c. The first audit or error line for each sales transaction record is to be double-spaced from the previous line.

d. The record count total-lines are to be single-spaced from one another. The first record count total-line is to be triple-spaced from the last detail-line.

Programming Assignment 9-D: Accounts Receivable Validation

Program description

The accounts receivable file is to be validated. An audit/error report is to be prepared that lists each record and identifies each error detected by an error message. Validated records are written to a disk file. At the conclusion of the file, record count totals are printed.

Input file

Accounts receivable customer file

Input record format

Accounts receivable customer record

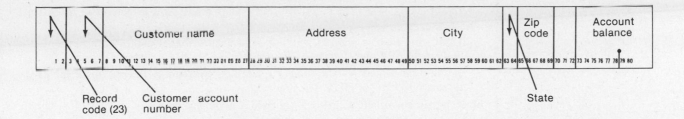

Output file

Accounts receivable customer record audit/error report

Output report format

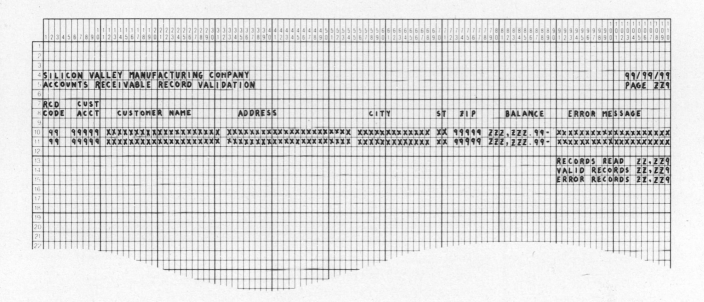

Program operations

1. Read each input accounts receivable customer record.

2. For each input accounts receivable customer record, make the following field validations:

   a. Validate the record code field to ensure that it is equal to 23. If it is not, print the error message INVALID RECORD CODE.

   b. Validate the customer account field to ensure that it is present. If it is not, print the error message ACCT. NBR. MISSING.

   c. If the customer account number field is present, validate it to ensure that it is numeric. If it is not, print the error message ACCT. NOT NUMERIC.

   d. Validate the customer name field to ensure that it is present. If it is not, print the error message CUST. NAME MISSING.

   e. If the customer name field is present, validate it to ensure that it is left justified. If it is not, print the error message CUST NAME NOT L.J.

   f. Validate the address field to ensure that it is present. If it is not, print the error message ADDRESS MISSING.

   g. If the address field is present, validate it to ensure that it is left justified. If it is not, print the error message ADDRESS NOT L.J.

   h. Validate the city field to ensure that it is present. If it is not, print the error message CITY MISSING.

   i. If the city field is present, validate it to ensure that it is left justified. If it is not, print the error message CITY NOT L.J.

j. Validate the state field to ensure that it is present. If it is not, print the error message STATE MISSING.

k. If the state field is present, validate it to ensure that it contains two alphabetic characters. If it does not, print the error message INVALID STATE.

l. Validate the zip code field to ensure that it is present. If it is not, print the error message ZIP CODE MISSING.

m. If the zip code field is present, validate it to ensure that it is numeric. If it is not, print the error message ZIP NOT NUMERIC.

n. Validate the account balance field to ensure that it is numeric. If it is not, print the error message BALANCE NOT NUMERIC.

o. If the account balance field is numeric, validate it to ensure that it is positive or zero. If it is not, print the error message WARNING NEG. BAL.

p. If the first digit of the account number is equal to 9, validate to ensure that the account balance is less than 10,000.00. If it is not, print the error message OVER CREDIT LIMIT.

3. For each record that passes all the validation tests:

a. Write the record to the validated accounts receivable customer file. If a record does not pass one or more validation tests, do not write that record to the validated accounts receivable customer file.

b. Write an audit-line on the audit/error report containing the record image.

4. For each record that has one or more errors, write an error-line on the audit-error report for each error detected for that record.

a. The first error-line for each record is to contain the record image and the error message.

b. Successive error-lines for the same record (if any) should contain only the error message.

5. Accumulate the following record counts and, after all input customer records have been processed, print each on a separate line in accordance with the print chart:

a. Total number of records read.

b. Total number of valid records.

c. total number of error records.

6. Headings are to be printed on the first page of the report. After 54 lines have been used on a report page and a new customer record is to be printed, the program is to skip to the next page and print the report headings. (Do not continue lines for one customer record from one page to another.)

a. The run date is to be obtained from the operating system and printed on the first heading-line in accordance with the format shown on the print chart.

b. The page number is to be incremented each time the heading is printed and displayed on the second heading-line in accordance with the format shown on the print chart.

7. Line-spacing is to be handled as follows:

a. The first detail-line after the headings is to be double-spaced from the last heading-line.

b. Second and successive error-lines for the same sales transaction record are to be single-spaced from one another.

c. The first audit or error line for each sales transaction record is to be double-spaced from the previous line.

d. The record count total-lines are to be single-spaced from one another. The first record count total-line is to be triple-spaced from the last detail-line.

SYSTEMS CHAPTER D

SORTING AND CONTROL BREAK CONCEPTS

Sorting Concepts
    The sort key
        Multiple field sort keys
        Significance of fields within the sort key
        Sequence of sort key fields
    Merging

Report Control Break Concepts
    Single-level control break reports
    Multiple-level control break reports

Summary

Sorting Concepts

Sorting is the process of arranging items according to a certain order or sequence. Records in a file are generally stored according to a certain predefined sequence. Consider the example of a telephone company. They must maintain a file of subscriber records so that they can keep track of the charges and credits to each telephone number account. Such an accounts receivable file would probably be maintained in telephone number sequence. A hypothetical indication of such a file is shown in Figure D.1.

The Sort Key

The field, or group of fields, that contains the value used to sequence the file is called the *sort key*. In the telephone company accounts receivable file, the sort key is thus the telephone number field.

Multiple field sort keys

Often, a file will be sorted in different sequence to produce different outputs. For example, when the telephone company publishes a white-page telephone directory, they will have a need to sort the file into name sequence. In addition to sorting by name, they will also probably want to provide for the arrangement of duplicate names into a prescribed sequence. When two names are the same, perhaps they want to list the duplicate names in address sequence. Such would be an example of a multiple field sort key—one containing two or more fields.

Significance of fields within the sort key

When a sort key contains more than one field, the most significant field—the one that determines the overall sequence of the file—is termed the *major* field. The least significant field is called the *minor* field. In the white-page directory, then, the subscriber's listing name (last name first) is the major field and the subscriber's address is the minor field. Figure D.2 depicts this relationship.

Often, a sort key will contain more than just two fields. For example, the sort key for the yellow-page directory might contain three fields: classified heading, listing name, and address. In this case, the major field is the classified heading, for that determines the overall sequence of the listings. The address field is still the minor field. The name field can now be termed an *intermediate* field. If there is more than one intermediate field in the sort key, they are sometimes termed intermediate-1, intermediate-2, and so on.

Sequence of sort key fields

Each sort key field can be arranged according to either *ascending* or *descending* values within the field. It is far more common that sort key fields are arranged according to ascending order, since that pertains to our normal numerical and alphabetical orders. For some purposes, though, it is convenient to arrange items in descending order. For example, perhaps the telephone company would like to see the names of subscribers who owe them money for overdue bills. They might want this report in descending order by amount owed, so that the larger past-due amounts are at the top of the list. Figure D.3 shows an example of how such a report would look.

When descending order is used, there will often be both ascending and descending fields in the sort key. An example is shown in Figure D.4, which

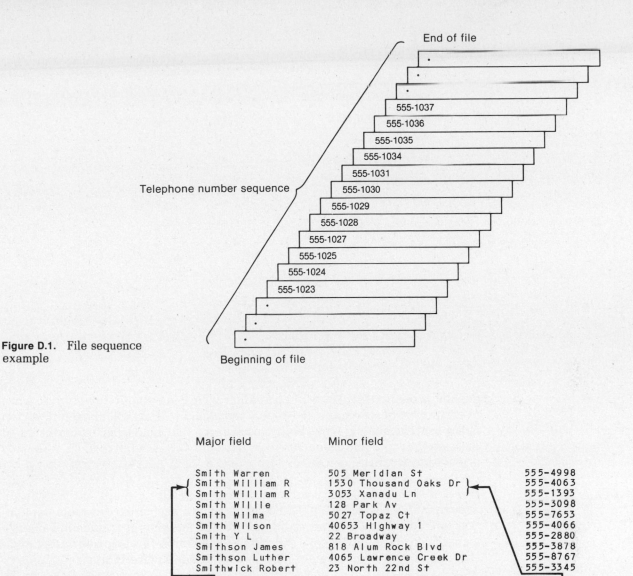

Figure D.1. File sequence example

End of file

Telephone number sequence

555-1037
555-1036
555-1035
555-1034
555-1031
555-1030
555-1029
555-1028
555-1027
555-1025
555-1024
555-1023

Beginning of file

Major field | Minor field

Smith Warren	505 Meridian St	555-4998
Smith William R	1530 Thousand Oaks Dr	555-4063
Smith William R	3053 Xanadu Ln	555-1393
Smith Willie	128 Park Av	555-3098
Smith Wilma	5027 Topaz Ct	555-7653
Smith Wilson	40653 Highway 1	555-4066
Smith Y L	22 Broadway	555-2880
Smithson James	818 Alum Rock Blvd	555-3878
Smithson Luther	4065 Lawrence Creek Dr	555-8767
Smithwick Robert	23 North 22nd St	555-3345

Figure D.2. Multiple field sort key example

When major field is the same, records are sequenced in accordance with minor field.

OVERDUE ACCOUNT BALANCES

TEL. NO.	SUBSCRIBER	AMOUNT DUE	
555-8037	JONES, JOHN	486.23	
555-7610	CHINN, A	460.98	
555-1087	DOUGHERTY, JANE	456.22	
555-3308	JOHNSON, ROBERT	402.80	Descending sequence
555-4585	SMITH, JONATHAN	333.28	
555-4044	ADAMS, ALBERT	310.77	
555-5782	BOYD, THOMAS	298.10	
555-6089	BUTLER, VERNA	286.27	

Figure D.3. Descending sequence sort key example

351

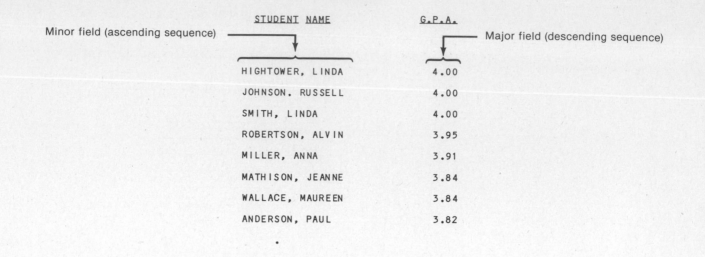

Minor field (ascending sequence)	STUDENT NAME	G.P.A.	Major field (descending sequence)
	HIGHTOWER, LINDA	4.00	
	JOHNSON, RUSSELL	4.00	
	SMITH, LINDA	4.00	
	ROBERTSON, ALVIN	3.95	
	MILLER, ANNA	3.91	
	MATHISON, JEANNE	3.84	
	WALLACE, MAUREEN	3.84	
	ANDERSON, PAUL	3.82	

Figure D.4. Ascending and descending sequence sort key example

depicts a dean's list. Here is a situation where the major field, grade-point average, is in descending order so that the highest G.P.A. will appear at the top of the list. The student-name field is used as a minor field in ascending order so that, when two or more students have the same G.P.A., alphabetical order will prevail for identical averages.

Merging

Merging is the process of combining two or more files already in the same sequence into one sequenced file. For example, an accounts receivable application for a department store might call for the merging of the month's charge transaction file and the cash payments transaction file before printing each customer's monthly statement. This is depicted in Figure D.5.

Report Control Break Concepts

Records are often sorted prior to preparing reports. The main reason they are sorted is so that they are easier for the user to understand and refer to. It is common that control totals are also provided on reports prepared from sorted records.

Consider the sales transaction record of a department store chain depicted in Figure D.6. Even without sorting the records, a sales report could be prepared with a report total as shown in Figure D.7.

Single-Level Control Break Reports

It is likely, though, that the general manager of the department store chain would also want to know the total sales revenue from each individual store. The most efficient way to process such a report would be to sort the sales transaction records by store number and print totals whenever all the records for one store had been printed. This would be an example of a *single-level control break report* with the store number as the control field; it would appear as shown in Figure D.8.

Multiple-Level Control Break Reports

Perhaps the general manager then distributes the report to each store manager. The store manager would probably be interested in looking at the sales revenue from each of his departments. Thus a report sorted by department number within store number (the major field is the store number; the

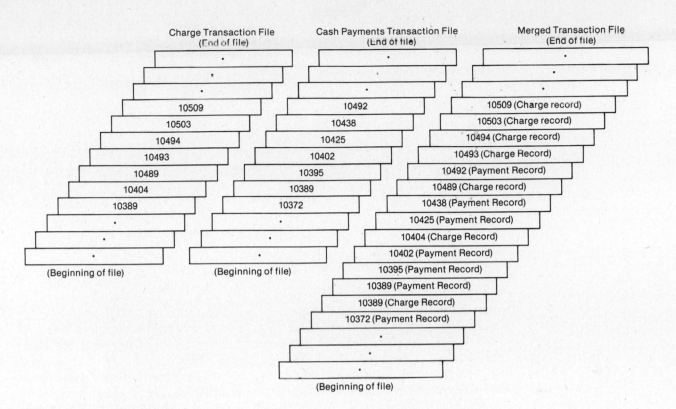

Charge Transaction File
(End of file)

Cash Payments Transaction File
(End of file)

Merged Transaction File
(End of file)

Charge Transaction File:
- 10509
- 10503
- 10494
- 10493
- 10489
- 10404
- 10389

(Beginning of file)

Cash Payments Transaction File:
- 10492
- 10438
- 10425
- 10402
- 10395
- 10389
- 10372

(Beginning of file)

Merged Transaction File:
- 10509 (Charge record)
- 10503 (Charge record)
- 10494 (Charge record)
- 10493 (Charge Record)
- 10492 (Payment Record)
- 10489 (Charge record)
- 10438 (Payment Record)
- 10425 (Payment Record)
- 10404 (Charge Record)
- 10402 (Payment Record)
- 10395 (Payment Record)
- 10389 (Payment Record)
- 10389 (Charge Record)
- 10372 (Payment Record)

(Beginning of file)

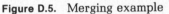

Figure D.5. Merging example

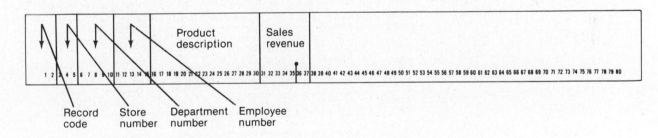

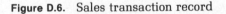

Record code   Store number   Department number   Employee number   Product description   Sales revenue

Figure D.6. Sales transaction record

STORE NUMBER	DEPARTMENT NUMBER	PRODUCT DESCRIPTION	SALES REVENUE
002	50000	PERFUME	18.95
001	60000	WASHER	398.00
001	50000	COLOGNE	9.98
002	70000	VIDEO RECORDER	698.00
002	60000	MICROWAVE OVEN	569.00
001	60000	REFRIGERATOR	498.00
001	50000	PERFUME	29.95
002	60000	WASHER	379.00
002	70000	TELEVISION	598.00
		REPORT TOTAL	3,198.88*

Figure D.7. Sales report without control breaks

```
STORE      DEPARTMENT       PRODUCT            SALES
NUMBER       NUMBER       DESCRIPTION         REVENUE

 001         50000        PERFUME              29.95
 001         50000        COLOGNE               9.98
 001         60000        WASHER              398.00
 001         60000        REFRIGERATOR        498.00

                    TOTAL FOR STORE 001       935.93*

 002         50000        PERFUME              18.95
 002         60000        WASHER              379.00
 002         60000        MICROWAVE OVEN      569.00
 002         70000        TELEVISION          598.00
 002         70000        VIDEO RECORDER      698.00

                    TOTAL FOR STORE 002     2,262.95*

                           REPORT TOTAL     3,198.88**
```

Figure D.8. Single level control break example

minor field is the department number), as shown in Figure D.9, would be appropriate. This is an example of a *multiple-level control break report*. The control fields are store number and department number. Notice that the store totals are a summation of all the department totals.

If the store manager then sent a copy of the report to the department managers, the department managers would probably like to see the report sequenced by salesperson number within department within store. This would allow the department managers to identify easily how each of their salespeople is performing. Similarly, buyers at the main office might be interested in seeing the report organized by product within department regardless of salesperson

```
STORE      DEPARTMENT       PRODUCT            SALES
NUMBER       NUMBER       DESCRIPTION         REVENUE

 001         50000        PERFUME              29.95
 001         50000        COLOGNE               9.98

            TOTAL FOR STORE 001 DEPT. 50000    39.93*

 001         60000        WASHER              398.00
 001         60000        REFRIGERATOR        498.00

            TOTAL FOR STORE 001 DEPT. 60000   896.00*

                    TOTAL FOR STORE 001       935.93**

 002         50000        PERFUME              18.95

            TOTAL FOR STORE 002 DEPT. 50000    18.95*

 002         60000        WASHER              379.00
 002         60000        MICROWAVE OVEN      569.00

            TOTAL FOR STORE 002 DEPT. 60000   948.00*

 002         70000        TELEVISION          598.00
 002         70000        VIDEO RECORDER      698.00

            TOTAL FOR STORE 002 DEPT. 70000  1.296.00*

                    TOTAL FOR STORE 002     2.262.95**

                           REPORT TOTAL     3,198.88***
```

Figure D.9. Multiple level control break example

or store, so they could more easily spot product sales trends. Then too, maybe someone in the advertising department would like to see sales totals sequenced by product within date so that they could judge the effectiveness of advertising programs.

For practically all data processing applications, a given set of records may require sequencing and reporting in a variety of formats, depending upon the user of the report. Most business reports have control totals based upon the sequence of the report. Thus, control break programs are very common. The next chapter will present material on how to design and program them.

Summary

Sorting is the process of arranging items according to a certain order or sequence. Records of a file are generally stored according to a certain predefined sequence. The field, or group of fields, that contains the value used to sequence the file is called the *sort key*. When a sort key contains more than one field, the most significant field is termed the *major* field; the least significant field is called the *minor* field. Other fields of the sort key are known as *intermediate* fields. Each sort key field can be arranged according to either *ascending* or *descending* values within the field.

Merging is the process of combining two or more files already in the same sequence into one sequenced file.

The *control break* is an important data processing concept often used in the preparation of reports with control totals. A report with just one control field is a *single-level* control break; a *multiple-level* control break report has two or more control fields.

CHAPTER 10

DESIGNING AND WRITING A CONTROL BREAK PROGRAM

In previous programs of this text, we have been concerned only with individual records of a file; the relationship of one record to another record in the file was not a factor. Control break programs require the records to be in proper sequence and the program logic must test the control field of each record in relation to the control field of the previous record. Although control break programs are not overly complex, they can be very difficult to program for one not trained in their design and coding.

In this chapter, we will cover (1) the design and coding of a single-level control break program (2) the USAGE clause, (3) the handling of period-ending date records, and (4) the design and coding of a multiple-level control break program.

Programming a Single-Level Control Break Program: The Single-Level Sales Report Program

Programming Specifications

Pyramid Sales Company has a need for a single-level Sales Report. The print chart for the single-level Sales Report is shown in Figure 10.1. Notice that there are four heading-line formats, one detail-line format, one sales representative total-line format, and one report total-line format specified. The sales representative total-line is the *control break* line. Whenever the sales representative number changes, the sales representative total-line is to be printed.

Figure 10.2 shows the input record layout for the sales record. The sales representative number is the control field for this Sales Report. An illustration of control breaks for the sales record is depicted in Figure 10.3.

The complete programming specifications for the single-level Sales Report is shown in Figure 10.4. Figure 10.5 presents the system flowchart. A sample of the program output appears in Figure 10.6.

Program Design

There are two tricky things about a control break program: (1) bypassing the "false" or null control break, which will occur when the first record is

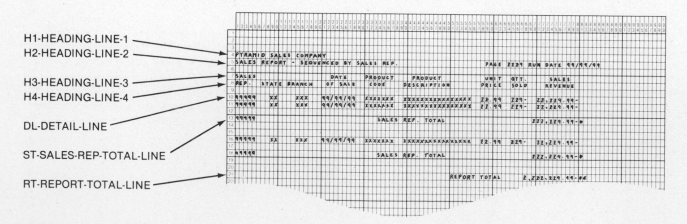

Figure 10.1. Print chart: Single-level sales report

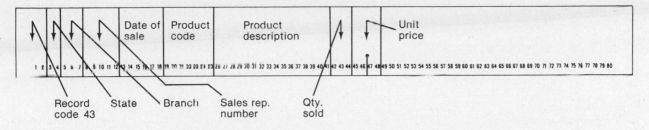

Figure 10.2. Record layout: Sales record

processed, and (2) forcing out the last control break after all records have been processed. The effect that these common errors have on the output from a single-level control break program is shown in Figure 10.7.

Remember that input records for a control break program must be sorted into the correct sequence for the control breaks. For this single-level Sales Report, the sales records must be sorted in ascending order according to the sales representative number field. When designing this program, we will assume that the sales records have already been properly sequenced by a previous sort routine.

The single-level Sales Report structure chart appears in Figure 10.8. The pseudocode and program flowchart are shown in Figures 10.9 and 10.10, respectively.

So that the exact processing of a single-level control break program can be understood, we will walk through the steps in the processing of the sales records shown in Figure 10.3.

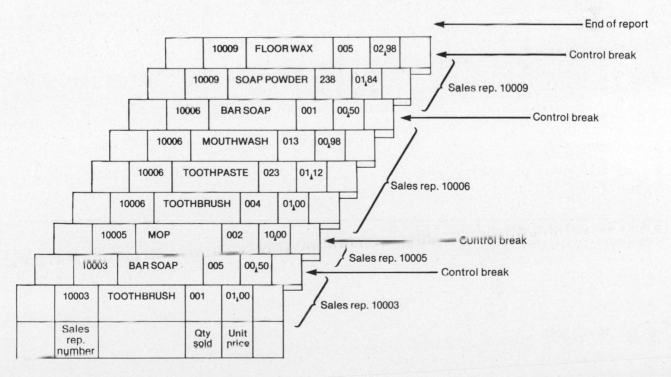

Figure 10.3. Sales record control break example

Program name: SINGLE—LEVEL SALES REPORT   Program ID: S—SLSRPT

Program Description

This program reads sales records, computes the sales revenue for each sales record and prints a sales report detail—line for each sales record.

When the sales representative number changes a sales representative total—line is printed.

After all input sales record have been processed, a report total—line is printed.

Input File(s)

Sales file

Output File(s)

Sales report

List of Program Operations

A. Read records from the input sales file.

B. For each sales record, the program is to:

1. Compute the sales—revenue by multiplying the unit—price by the quantity—sold.

2. Print a detail—line containing the following fields in accordance with the format shown on the print—chart:

   a. Sales—representative number
   b. State
   c. Branch
   d. Date—of—sale
   e. Product—code
   f. Product—description
   g. Unit—price
   h. Quantity—sold
   i. Sales—revenue

3. Accumulate the following totals:

   a. Total sales—revenue for each sales—representative
   b. Total sales—revenue for all sales—representatives

C. Whenever the sales—representative number changes, the program is to print a sales—representative total—line containing the following fields in accordance with the format shown on the print chart:

1. Sales—representative number

2. The words "sales rep. total"

3. Total sales—revenue for that sales—representative

4. One asterisk

D. After all the input sales records have been processed, the program is to print the following total fields on the sales report total—line in accordance with the format shown on the print chart:

1. The words "report total"

2. Total sales—revenue for all sales—representatives

3. Two asterisks

E. Headings are to be printed on the first page of the report. After 54 lines have been used on a report page, the program is to skip to the next page and print the report headings.

1. The run date is to be obtained from the operating system and printed on the second heading—line in accordance with the format shown on the print chart.

2. The page number is to be incremented each time the heading is printed and displayed on the second heading—line in accordance with the format shown on the print chart.

F. Line—spacing is to be handled as follows:

1. The first detail—line printed after the headings is to be double—spaced from the last heading—line.

2. Detail—lines for the same sales—representative are to be single—spaced from one another.

3. Each sales—representative total—line is to be double—spaced from the previous detail—line.

4. The first detail—line for each sales—representative is to be triple—spaced from the previous sales—representative total—line.

5. The report total—line is to be triple—spaced from the last sales—representative total—line.

Figure 10.4. Programming specifications: Single-level sales report program

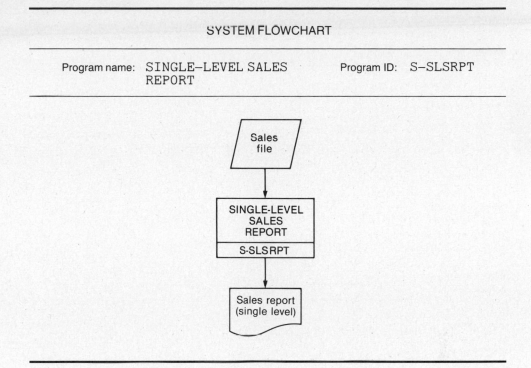

Program name: SINGLE–LEVEL SALES
REPORT   Program ID: S–SLSRPT

```
                        ┌──────────┐
                       /  Sales   /
                      /   file   /
                     └──────────┘
                          │
                          ▼
                 ┌──────────────────┐
                 │  SINGLE-LEVEL    │
                 │     SALES        │
                 │    REPORT        │
                 ├──────────────────┤
                 │    S-SLSRPT      │
                 └──────────────────┘
                          │
                          ▼
                 ┌──────────────────┐
                 │  Sales report    │
                 │  (single level)  │
                 └─────────────────╮
```

Figure 10.5.   System flowchart: Single-level sales report program

```
PYRAMID SALES COMPANY
SALES REPORT - SEQUENCED BY SALES REP.                    PAGE    1 RUN DATE 05/10/81

SALES                      DATE    PRODUCT  PRODUCT           UNIT  QTY.    SALES
REP.    STATE BRANCH     OF SALE   CODE     DESCRIPTION       PRICE SOLD    REVENUE

10003   CA    001        05/07/81  TB001    TOOTHBRUSH        1.00   1      1.00
10003   CA    001        05/07/81  SB005    BAR SOAP           .50   5      2.50

10003                              SALES REP. TOTAL                        3.50*


10005   CA    001        05/07/81  MP070    MOP              10.00   2     20.00

10005                              SALES REP. TOTAL                       20.00*


10006   CA    001        05/07/81  TB001    TOOTHBRUSH        1.00   4      4.00
10006   CA    001        05/07/81  TP002    TOOTHPASTE        1.12  23     25.76
10006   CA    001        05/07/81  MW004    MOUTHWASH          .98  13     12.74
10006   CA    001        05/07/81  SB005    BAR SOAP           .50   1       .50

10006                              SALES REP. TOTAL                       43.00*


10009   CA    001        05/07/81  SP000    SOAP POWDER       1.89  238   449.82
10009   CA    001        05/07/81  WF080    FLOOR WAX         2.98   5     14.90

10009                              SALES REP. TOTAL                      464.72*


                                            REPORT TOTAL               531.22**
```

Figure 10.6.   Single-level sales report output example

```
                    PYRAMID SALES COMPANY
                    SALES REPORT - SEQUENCED BY SALES REP.                    PAGE   1 RUN DATE 05/10/81

                    SALES                    DATE   PRODUCT  PRODUCT              UNIT   QTY.   SALES
                    REP.   STATE BRANCH   OF SALE   CODE     DESCRIPTION          PRICE  SOLD   REVENUE
False control                                               SALES REP. TOTAL                    .00
break triggered  ──────────────────────►
by first record

                    10003   CA    001    05/07/81  TB001    TOOTHBRUSH           1.00    1      1.00
                    10003   CA    001    05/07/81  SB005    BAR SOAP              .50     5      2.50

                    10003                                   SALES REP. TOTAL                    3.50*

                    10005   CA    001    05/07/81  MP070    MOP                  10.00   2      20.00

                    10005                                   SALES REP. TOTAL                    20.00*

                    10006   CA    001    05/07/81  TB001    TOOTHBRUSH           1.00    4      4.00
Missing control     10006   CA    001    05/07/81  TP002    TOOTHPASTE           1.12    23     25.76
break for last      10006   CA    001    05/07/81  MW004    MOUTHWASH            .98     13     12.74
control group       10006   CA    001    05/07/81  SB005    BAR SOAP             .50     1      .50
(Sales rep 10009)   10006                                   SALES REP. TOTAL                    43.00*

May cause           10009   CA    001    05/07/81  SP008    SOAP POWDER          1.89    238    449.82
erroneous           10009   CA    001    05/07/81  WF080    FLOOR WAX            2.98    5      14.90
report total  ──────────────────────►                      REPORT TOTAL                       66.50**
```

Figure 10.7. Common control-break programming error examples

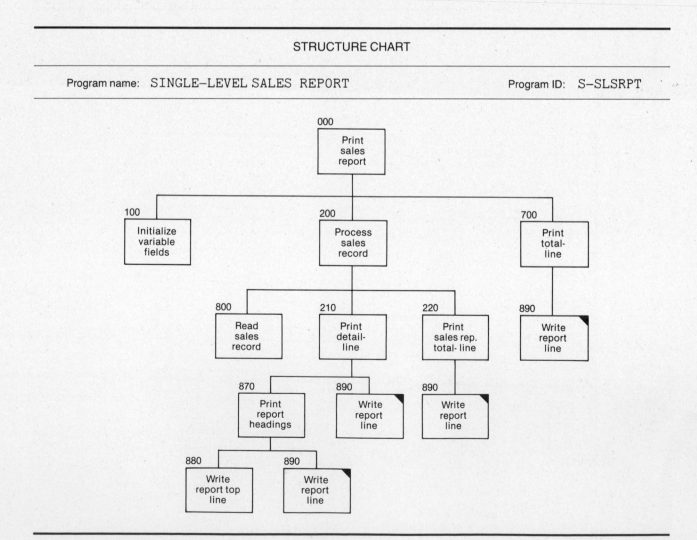

Figure 10.8. Structure chart: Single-level sales report program

PSEUDOCODE

Program name: SINGLE–LEVEL SALES REPORT   Program ID: S–SLSRPT

000–Print–Sales–Report module
1. Open the files.
2. Perform 100–Initialize–Variable–Fields.
3. Perform 200–Process–Sales–Record until no more records.
4. Perform 700–Print–Report–Total–Line.
5. Close the files.
6. Stop the run.

100–Initialize–Variable–Fields module
1. Set the end–of–file indicator to "No".
2. Set the first–record indicator to "Yes".
3. Set the page–count to zero.
4. Set the lines–per–page so that headings for the first page will be triggered.
5. Obtain the date from the operating system and move it to the second heading–line run–date.
6. Set the total–accumulator fields to zero.

200–Process–Sales–Record module
1. Perform 800–Read–Sales–Record. *(Test)*
2. If this is the first input record
   Move the input Sales–rep to the Previous–sales–rep *(Section–number / Section–number)*
   Set the First–record indicator to "No".
3. If the input record Sales–rep is not the same as the Previous–sales–rep *(Section–number)*
   Perform 220–Print–Sales–Rep–Total–Line. *(Student–Total)*
4. If there is an input record
   Perform 210–Print–Detail–Line.

210–Print–Detail–Line module
1. If the Lines–used is greater than the Lines–per–page,
   Perform 870–Print–Report–Headings.
2. Move the input Sales–rep field *(Section–number)* to the detail–line Sales–rep field *(Section–number)*
3. Move the input State field to the detail–line State field.
4. Move the input Branch field to the detail–line Branch field.
5. Move the input Date–of–sale field to the detail–line Date–of–sale field.
6. Move the input Product–code field to the detail–line Product–code field.
7. Move the input Product–description field *(Student–name)* to the detail–line Product–description field.
8. Move the input Quantity–sold field *(correct–answers)* to the detail–line Quantity–sold field.
9. Move the input Unit–price field to the detail–line Unit–price field.
10. Multiply the input Unit–price field by the input Quantity–sold field to equal the detail–line Sales–revenue field.
11. Move the detail–line to the output print–line area.
12. Perform 890–Write–Report–Line.
13. Set the line–spacing indicator for single–spacing.
14. Add the Sales–revenue for this record *(correct–answers)* to the Total–sales–rep–sales–revenue. *(Total correct–answers)*

(handwritten left margin: 13. add one to Total / No. of Students)

220–Print–Sales–Rep–Total–Line module *(Student–Totals)*
1. Move the Previous–sales–rep *(section–number)* to the sales–rep–total–line Sales–rep. *(Student–Total–Line section–number)*

2. Move the total–sales–rep–sales–revenue *(No, Students–In)* to the sales–rep–total–line Sales–revenue. *(Total–No. = Students out)*
3. Move the sales–rep–total–line *(Total–correct–ans)* to the output print–line area. *(To Total–correct–ans out)*
4. Set the line–spacing indicator for double–spacing.
5. Perform 890–Write–Report–Line.
6. Add the Total–sales–rep–sales–revenue *(Divide Total correct answer by Total student)* to the Total–report–sales–revenue. *(giving average dat)*
7. Move zero to the Total–sales–rep–sales–revenue. *(Total correct–answers / Total–students–in.)*
8. Move the input Sales–rep *(section–number)* to the Previous–sales–rep.

700–Print–Report–Total–Line module
1. Move the Total–report–sales–revenue to the total–line Sales–revenue.
2. Move the total–line to the output print–line area.
3. Perform 890–Write–Report–Line.

800–Read–Sales–Record module
1. Read an input sales record. *(Test–record–in)*
2. If there are no more records
   Move "Yes" to the end–of–file indicator
   Move high–values to the input record Sales–rep. *(section–number)*

870–Print–Report–Headings module
1. Add 1 to the Page–count.
2. Move the Page–count to the second heading–line Page–number.
3. Move heading–line–1 to the output print–line area.
4. Perform 880–Write–Report–Top–Line.
5. Move heading–line–2 to the output print–line area.
6. Set the line–spacing indicator for single–spacing. *(Double)*
7. Perform 890–Write–Report–Line.
8. Move heading–line–3 to the output print–line area.
9. Set the line–spacing indicator for double–spacing. *(Single)*
10. Perform 890–Write–Report–Line.
11. Move heading–line–4 to the output print–line area.
12. Set the line–spacing indicator for single–spacing.
13. Perform 890–Write–Report–Line.
14. Set the line–spacing indicator for double–spacing.

880–Write–Report–Top–Line module
1. Advance to the top of the next report page and write the output print–line area.
2. Set the Lines–used to 1.

890–Write–Report–Line module
1. Advance in accordance with the setting of the line–spacing indicator and write the output print–line area.
2. Add the line–spacing indicator to the Lines–used.

Figure 10.9. Pseudocode: Single-level sales report program   363

Program name: SINGLE—LEVEL SALES REPORT   Program ID: S—SLSRPT

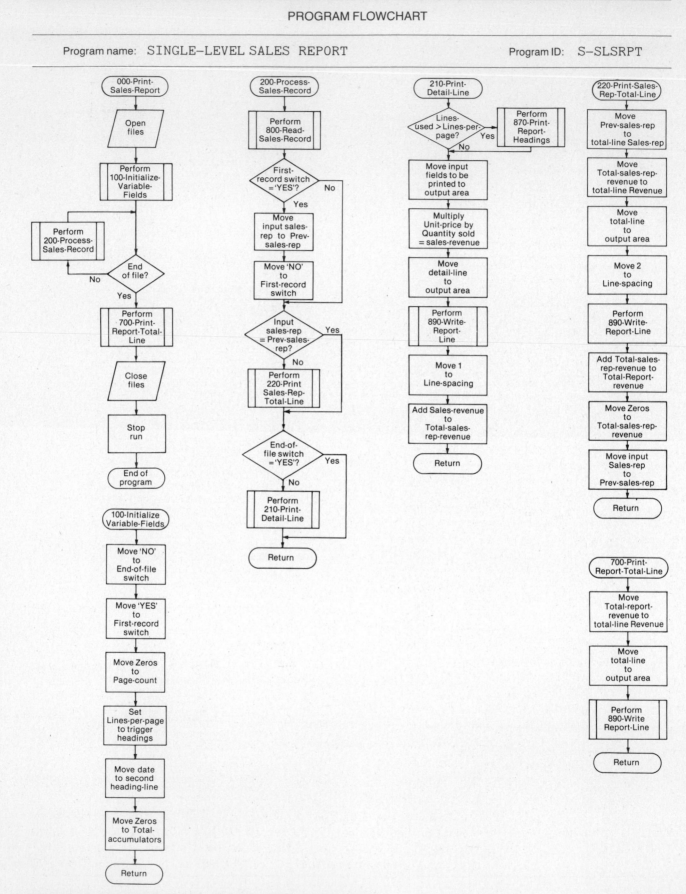

Figure 10.10. Program flowchart: Single-level sales report program

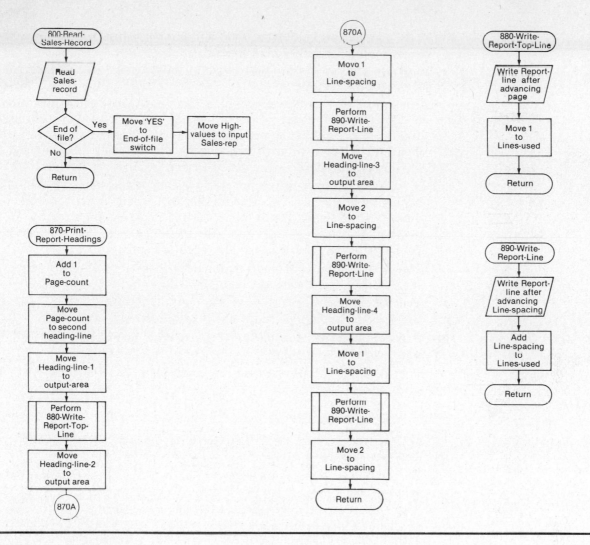

Figure 10.10. (continued)

Step A: Initialize control break fields

Figure 10.11 depicts the actions taken for the control break fields in the 100-Initialize-Variable-Fields module.

1. The First-record-indicator is set to 'YES.'
2. The Total-accumulators for the Sales-representative-revenue-total and the Report-revenue-total are set to zero.

Step B: Process first record

As depicted in Figure 10.12, the following actions (described in modules 200-Process-Sales-Record and 210-Print-Detail-Line of the pseudocode and flowchart) are taken:

1. The first record is read. (In this example, this is the first record for sales representative 10003.)
2. The First-record-indicator is equal to 'YES' so the Previous-sales-representative-number is initialized to be the same as the Sales-representative-number of this first input record. (This will eliminate the problem of getting an erroneous control break on the first input record.)

3. The First-record-indicator is set to 'NO' so the Previous-sales-representative-number field will not be initialized again to the value of the current record. This initialization to the current Sales-representative-number value is only wanted for the first record of the file.

4. The Sales-representative-number of the input record (10003) is compared to the Previous-sales-representative-number field (which also contains 10003 as a result of the previous step). They are equal, so the program logic knows that a sales representative control break line is not required for this input record.

5. If an input record has been read—which it has—the Print-detail-line module is performed. This module checks to see if report headings are required. Since this is the first record, headings are required for the first page of the report. The Print-report-headings module is performed and headings for the first page of the report are printed.

6. The Print-detail-line module then moves these input fields to be printed from this first record to the detail-line area.

7. The Sales-revenue is computed by multiplying the Quantity-sold by the Unit-price; it is then moved to the detail-line area.

8. The detail-line is then moved to the output print area and the line is written.

9. The computed Sales-revenue is added to the Sales-representative-revenue-total field.

Step C: Process second record

This processing is depicted in Figure 10.13.

1. The second record is read.

2. The First-record-indicator is now equal to 'NO' so first-record processing is bypassed.

3. The Sales-representative-number of the input record (10003) is compared to the Previous-sales-representative field (which also contains 10003). They are equal, so control break processing is bypassed.

4. An input record has been read, so the Print-detail-line module is performed and the detail-line is written.

5. The Sales-revenue for that line is added to the Sales-representative-revenue-total field.

Step D: Process control break

The control break is processed upon detecting the first record for sales representative 10005. This processing is shown in Figure 10.14.

1. The third record is read.

2. The First-record-indicator is equal to 'NO' so first-record processing is bypassed.

3. The Sales-representative-number of the input record (10005) is compared to the Previous-sales-representative-number field (which contains 10003). They are unequal, so control break processing takes place as described in module 220-Print-Sales-Rep-Total-Line.

4. The Previous-sales-representative-number field is moved to the Sales-representative-total-line.

5. The Sales-representative-revenue-total field is moved to the Sales-representative-total-line.

6. The Sales-representative-total-line is moved to the output report-line area and the line is written.

7. The Sales-representative-revenue-total is added to the Report-revenue-total.

8. The Sales-representative-revenue-total is then set back to zero to ready it for accumulation of the next sales representative's revenues.

9. The Sales-representative-number of the current input record (10005) is then moved to the Previous-sales-representative-number field. This Previous-sales-representative-number field keeps track of the sales representative for which the *next* control break will be printed.

Step E: Process third record

The processing of the first record for sales representative 10005 is illustrated in Figure 10.15. This input record has already been read (in Step D.1). The Print-detail-line module is performed and the detail-line is written.

Continuing steps

This control break processing will continue until all records have been processed. It may be summarized as follows:

1. The next input record will be read.

2. If the input control field (Sales-representative-number) is not the same as that of the previous record (Previous-sales-representative-number), control break processing to print the Sales-representative-total-line will occur.

3. The detail-line processing will be performed.

Last step: End-of-file processing

See Figure 10.16.

1. Reading of a sales record is attempted, but there are no remaining records so the End-of-file-indicator is set to 'YES.'

2. The Sales-representative-number field of the input record area is set to high-values to force a control break the next time a control break test is made.

3. The Sales-representative-number field of the input record area (which has just been set to high-values) is compared to the Previous-sales-representative-number field (which now contains 10009).

4. They are not equal, so control break processing to print the Sales-representative-total-line for sales representative 10009 occurs.

5. It is end-of-file, so detail-line processing does not occur. The program logic returns to the mainline Print-sales-report module where the Print-report-total-line module is performed, the files are closed, and the run is stopped.

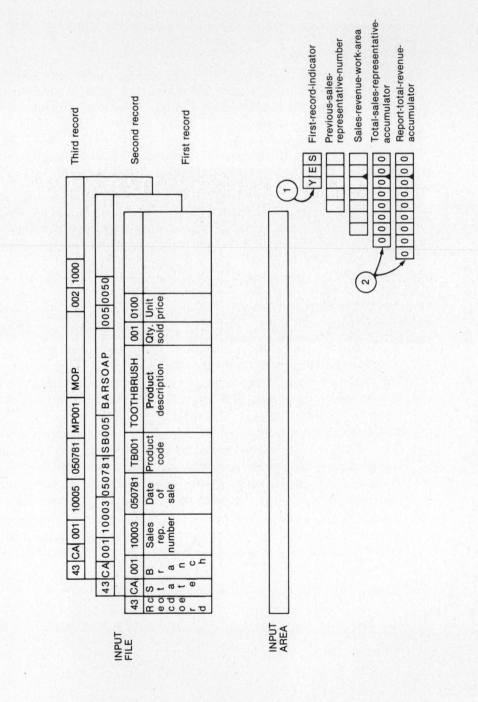

Figure 10.11. Control break processing example: Step A

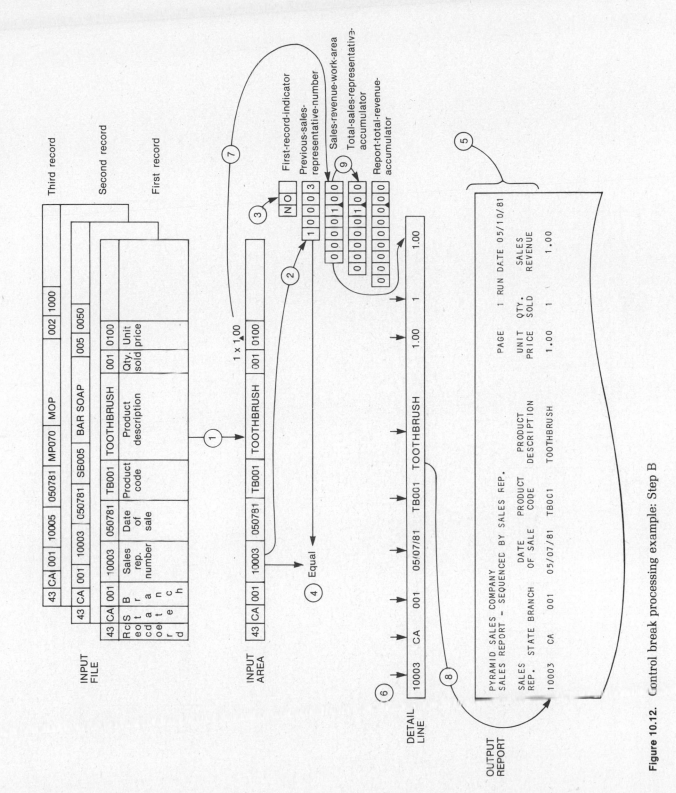

Figure 10.12. Control break processing example: Step B

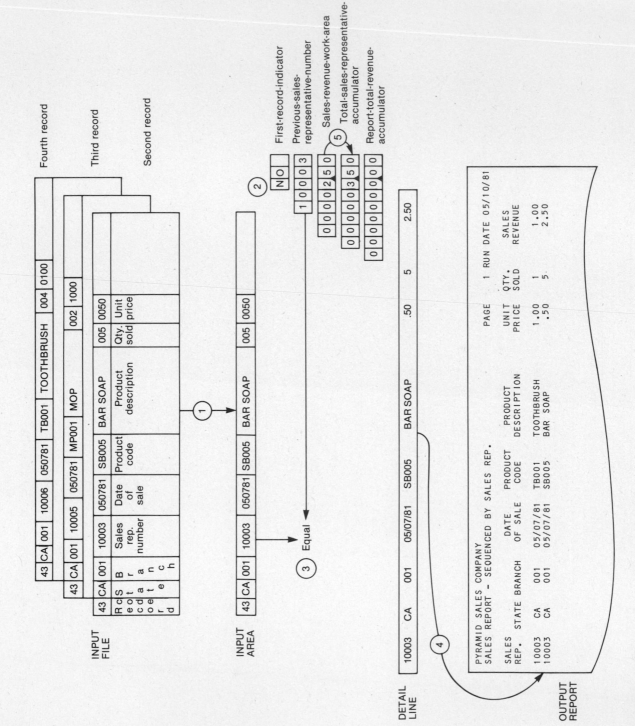

Figure 10.13. Control break processing example: Step C

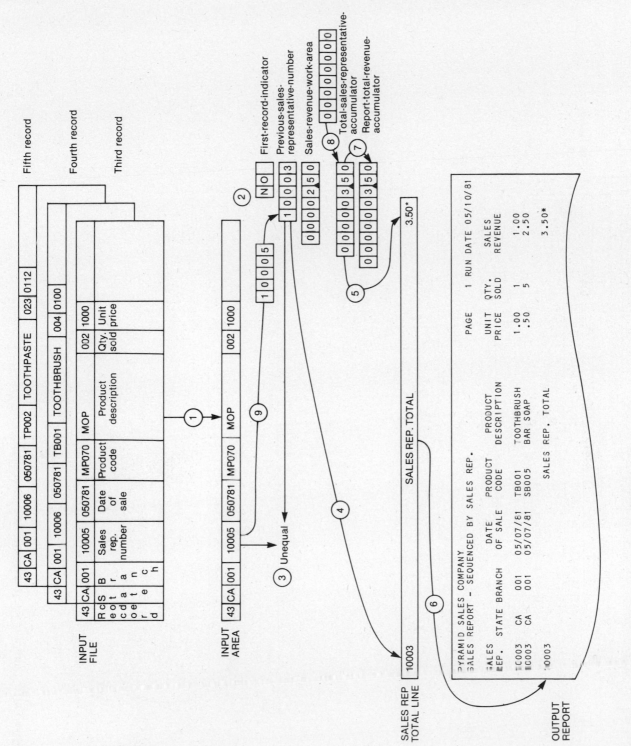

Figure 10.14. Control break processing example: Step D

Figure 10.15. Control break processing example: Step E

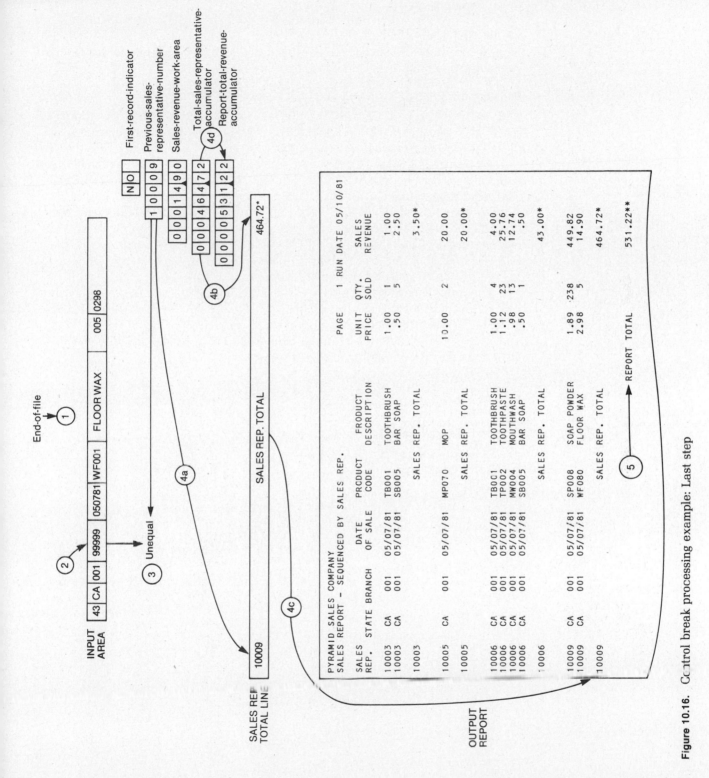

Figure 10.16. Control break processing example: Last step

Coding the IDENTIFICATION and ENVIRONMENT DIVISIONS

The IDENTIFICATION and ENVIRONMENT DIVISIONS of the S-SLSRPT program are shown in Figure 10.17. There are no new concepts introduced in these two divisions.

Coding the FILE SECTION of the DATA DIVISION

Entries for the FILE SECTION have been coded in accordance with the programming specifications and are shown in Figure 10.18.

Coding the WORKING-STORAGE SECTION of the DATA DIVISION

The WORKING-STORAGE SECTION is shown in Figure 10.19. In the WS-SWITCHES area, the WS-FIRST-RECORD-SWITCH has been established to indicate when the first record is being processed.

An additional level-01 entry—WS-CONTROL-FIELDS—has been specified and the WS-PREVIOUS-SALES-REP field has been created to hold the Sales-representative-number of the previously processed record.

In the WS-WORK-AREAS, the WS-SALES-REVENUE field has been specified to hold the product of the Quantity-sold times the Unit-price of each input record. The fields WS-TOTAL-SALES-REP-ACCUM and WS-TOTAL-REPORT-ACCUM have been entered in the WS-TOTAL-ACCUMULATORS area to contain their respective running totals.

The input record-description—SR-SALES-RECORD—and the seven output record formats—H1-HEADING-LINE-1, H2-HEADING-LINE-2, H3-HEADING-LINE-3, H4-HEADING-LINE-4, DL-DETAIL-LINE, ST-SALES-REP-TOTAL-LINE, and RT-REPORT-TOTAL-LINE—have been coded in accordance with the programming specifications.

```
001010 IDENTIFICATION DIVISION.
001020 PROGRAM-ID.       S-SLSRPT.
001030*AUTHOR.           WELBURN.
001040*INSTALLATION.     PYRAMID SALES COMPANY.
001050*DATE-WRITTEN.     FEB 27,1981.
001060*DATE-COMPILED.    MAR 10,1981.
001070*SECURITY.         NONE.
001080*
001090*
001100*                  THIS PROGRAM READS SALES RECORDS,
001110*                  COMPUTES THE SALES REVENUE FOR EACH SALES RECORD
001120*                  AND PRINTS A SALES DETAIL LINE
001130*                  FOR EACH SALES RECORD.
001140*
001150*                  WHEN THE SALES REP NUMBER CHANGES,
001160*                  A SALES-REP TOTAL LINE IS PRINTED.
001170*
001180*                  AFTER ALL INPUT SALES RECORDS HAVE BEEN PROCESSED,
001190*                  A REPORT TOTAL LINE WILL BE PRINTED.
002010*
002020*
002030*
002040 ENVIRONMENT DIVISION.
002050*
002060*
002070 CONFIGURATION SECTION.
002080*
002090 SOURCE-COMPUTER.  IBM-370.
002100 OBJECT-COMPUTER.  IBM-370.
002110*
002120*
002130 INPUT-OUTPUT SECTION.
002140*
002150 FILE-CONTROL.
002160     SELECT SALES-FILE
002170         ASSIGN TO UT-S-INFILE.
002180     SELECT SALES-REPORT
002190         ASSIGN TO UT-S-PRTFILE.
```

Figure 10.17. IDENTIFICATION and ENVIRONMENT divisions: S-SLSRPT program

```
003010*
003020*
003030*
003040 DATA DIVISION.
003050*
003060*
003070 FILE SECTION.
003080*
003090 FD   SALES-FILE
003100          RECORD CONTAINS 80 CHARACTERS
003110          LABEL RECORDS ARE OMITTED.
004010*
004020 01   SALES-RECORD.
004030       05  FILLER                          PIC X(80).
005010*
005020 FD   SALES-REPORT
005030          RECORD CONTAINS 133 CHARACTERS
005040          LABEL RECORDS ARE OMITTED.
005050*
005060 01   SALES-REPORT-LINE.
005070       05  FILLER                          PIC X(133).
```

Figure 10.18. FILE SECTION of the DATA DIVISION: S-SLSRPT program

Coding the PROCEDURE DIVISION

The PROCEDURE DIVISION appears in Figure 10.20. Each module that introduces new concepts will be covered. In addition, an explanation of the variable-line-spacing logic employed in this program will be discussed.

000-PRINT-SALES-REPORT module

In this program the priming-read method of READ statement placement is not being used; thus the READ module is *not* being performed prior to the PERFORM/UNTIL statement as has been the case in previous programs of this text. The method of READ statement handling being used in this program can be termed *conditional-processing* and will be further explained when the 200-PROCESS-SALES-RECORD module is described.

100-INITIALIZE-VARIABLE-FIELDS module

Here, the WS-FIRST-RECORD-SWITCH is set to 'YES' to indicate that the next record to be processed will be the first record. The remaining statements in this module are similar to those of previous programs.

Notice that initialization of the WS-PREVIOUS-SALES-REP field has not been specified. It certainly could be initialized to SPACES or ZEROS here, but it would serve no purpose since the WS-FIRST-RECORD-SWITCH will be used to control WS-PREVIOUS-SALES-REP initialization in the 200-PROCESS-SALES-RECORD module.

200-PROCESS-SALES-RECORD module

With the conditional-processing method of READ statement handling, placement of the READ statement is at the start, rather than the end (as for the priming-read method) of the record processing procedure. Hence, the statement PERFORM 800-READ-SALES-RECORD has been specified at the beginning of this procedure. Then, for the first record—and only the first record—of the file, the program initializes the WS-PREVIOUS-SALES-REP field by moving the input SR-SALES-REP number to it and then sets the WS-FIRST-RECORD-SWITCH to 'NO'. These two statements—MOVE SR-SALES-REP TO WS-PREVIOUS-SALES-REP and MOVE 'NO' TO WS-FIRST-RECORD-SWITCH—will be executed only once during the entire program run. That's because the condition FIRST-RECORD will be false after the first time those two statements are executed.

```
006010*
006020*
006030 WORKING-STORAGE SECTION.
006040*
006050*
006060 01  WS-SWITCHES.
006070     05  WS-END-OF-FILE-SWITCH        PIC X(3).
006080         88  END-OF-FILE                          VALUE 'YES'.
006090     05  WS-FIRST-RECORD-SWITCH       PIC X(3).
006100         88  FIRST-RECORD                         VALUE 'YES'.
007010*
007020 01  WS-CONTROL-FIELDS.
007050     05  WS-PREVIOUS-SALES-REP        PIC X(5).
008010*
008020 01  WS-REPORT-CONTROLS.
008030     05  WS-PAGE-COUNT                PIC S9(4).
008040     05  WS-LINES-PER-PAGE            PIC S9(2)    VALUE +54.
008050     05  WS-LINES-USED                PIC S9(2).
008060     05  WS-LINE-SPACING              PIC S9(2).
009010*
009020 01  WS-WORK-AREAS.
009030     05  WS-DATE-WORK                 PIC 9(6).
009040     05  WS-DATE-CONVERSION REDEFINES WS-DATE-WORK.
009050         10  WS-YEAR                  PIC 9(2).
009060         10  WS-MONTH                 PIC 9(2).
009070         10  WS-DAY                   PIC 9(2).
009080     05  WS-SALES-REVENUE             PIC S9(5)V99.
010010*
010020 01  WS-TOTAL-ACCUMULATORS.
010030     05  WS-TOTAL-SALES-REP-ACCUM     PIC S9(6)V99.
010060     05  WS-TOTAL-REPORT-ACCUM        PIC S9(7)V99.
020010*
020020 01  SR-SALES-RECORD.
020030     05  SR-RECORD-CODE               PIC X(2).
020040     05  SR-STATE                     PIC X(2).
020050     05  SR-BRANCH                    PIC X(3).
020060     05  SR-SALES-REP                 PIC X(5).
020070     05  SR-DATE-OF-SALE              PIC X(6).
020080     05  SR-PRODUCT-CODE              PIC X(7).
020090     05  SR-PRODUCT-DESCRIPTION       PIC X(16).
020100     05  SR-QUANTITY-SOLD             PIC S9(3).
020110     05  SR-UNIT-PRICE                PIC 9(2)V99.
020120     05  FILLER                       PIC X(32).
030010*
030020 01  H1-HEADING-LINE-1.
030030     05  FILLER          PIC X(1).
030040     05  FILLER          PIC X(20)   VALUE 'PYRAMID SALES COMPAN'.
030050     05  FILLER          PIC X(20)   VALUE 'Y                   '.
030060     05  FILLER          PIC X(20)   VALUE '                    '.
030070     05  FILLER          PIC X(20)   VALUE '                    '.
030080     05  FILLER          PIC X(20)   VALUE '                    '.
030090     05  FILLER          PIC X(20)   VALUE '                    '.
030100     05  FILLER          PIC X(12)   VALUE '            '.
031010*
031020 01  H2-HEADING-LINE-2.
031030     05  FILLER          PIC X(1).
031040     05  FILLER          PIC X(20)   VALUE 'SALES REPORT - SEQUE'.
031050     05  FILLER          PIC X(20)   VALUE 'NCED BY SALES REP   '.
031060     05  FILLER          PIC X(20)   VALUE '                 PA'.
031070     05  FILLER          PIC X(03)   VALUE 'GE '.
031080     05  H2-PAGE-NBR     PIC ZZZ9.
031090     05  FILLER          PIC X(10)   VALUE '  RUN DATE '.
031100     05  H2-MONTH        PIC 9(2).
031110     05  FILLER          PIC X(1)    VALUE '/'.
031120     05  H2-DAY          PIC 9(2).
031130     05  FILLER          PIC X(1)    VALUE '/'.
031140     05  H2-YEAR         PIC 9(2).
031150     05  FILLER          PIC X(47)   VALUE SPACES.
032010*
032020 01  H3-HEADING-LINE-3.
032030     05  FILLER          PIC X(1).
032040     05  FILLER          PIC X(20)   VALUE 'SALES               '.
032050     05  FILLER          PIC X(20)   VALUE ' DATE      PRODUCT  '.
032060     05  FILLER          PIC X(20)   VALUE ' PRODUCT         UN'.
032070     05  FILLER          PIC X(20)   VALUE 'IT QTY.      SALES '.
032080     05  FILLER          PIC X(20)   VALUE '                   '.
032090     05  FILLER          PIC X(20)   VALUE '                   '.
032100     05  FILLER          PIC X(12)   VALUE '           '.
033010*
033020 01  H4-HEADING-LINE-4.
033030     05  FILLER          PIC X(1).
033040     05  FILLER          PIC X(20)   VALUE 'REP. STATE BRANCH  '.
033050     05  FILLER          PIC X(20)   VALUE ' OF SALE    CODE  D'.
033060     05  FILLER          PIC X(20)   VALUE 'ESCRIPTION        PRI'.
033070     05  FILLER          PIC X(20)   VALUE 'CE  SOLD     REVENUE'.
033080     05  FILLER          PIC X(20)   VALUE '                   '.
033090     05  FILLER          PIC X(20)   VALUE '                   '.
033100     05  FILLER          PIC X(12)   VALUE '           '.
034010*
034020 01  DL-DETAIL-LINE.
034030     05  FILLER                 PIC X(1).
034040     05  DL-SALES-REP           PIC X(5).
034050     05  FILLER                 PIC X(3)    VALUE SPACES.
034060     05  DL-STATE               PIC X(2).
034070     05  FILLER                 PIC X(4)    VALUE SPACES.
034080     05  DL-BRANCH              PIC X(3).
034090     05  FILLER                 PIC X(3)    VALUE SPACES.
034100     05  DL-DATE-OF-SALE        PIC XX/XX/XX.
034110     05  FILLER                 PIC X(2)    VALUE SPACES.
034120     05  DL-PRODUCT-CODE        PIC X(7).
034130     05  FILLER                 PIC X(2)    VALUE SPACES.
034140     05  DL-PRODUCT-DESCRIPTION PIC X(16).
034150     05  FILLER                 PIC X(2)    VALUE SPACES.
034160     05  DL-UNIT-PRICE          PIC ZZ.99.
034170     05  FILLER                 PIC X(2)    VALUE SPACES.
034180     05  DL-QUANTITY-SOLD       PIC ZZ9-.
034190     05  FILLER                 PIC X(2)    VALUE SPACES.
034200     05  DL-SALES-REVENUE       PIC ZZ,ZZZ.99-.
034210     05  FILLER                 PIC X(52)   VALUE SPACES.
035010*
035020 01  ST-SALES-REP-TOTAL-LINE.
035030     05  FILLER              PIC X(1).
035040     05  ST-SALES-REP        PIC X(5).
035050     05  FILLER              PIC X(28)   VALUE SPACES.
035060     05  FILLER              PIC X(16)   VALUE 'SALES REP. TOTAL'.
035130     05  FILLER              PIC X(20)   VALUE SPACES.
035140     05  ST-SALES-REVENUE    PIC ZZZ,ZZZ.99-.
035150     05  FILLER              PIC X(1)    VALUE '*'.
035160     05  FILLER              PIC X(51)   VALUE SPACES.
036010*
036020 01  RT-REPORT-TOTAL-LINE.
036030     05  FILLER              PIC X(1).
036040     05  FILLER              PIC X(50)   VALUE SPACES.
036090     05  FILLER              PIC X(12)   VALUE 'REPORT TOTAL'.
036100     05  FILLER              PIC X(5)    VALUE SPACES.
036110     05  RT-SALES-REVENUE    PIC Z,ZZZ,ZZZ.99-.
036120     05  FILLER              PIC X(2)    VALUE '**'.
036130     05  FILLER              PIC X(50)   VALUE SPACES.
```

Figure 10.19. WORKING-STORAGE SECTION of the DATA DIVISION: S-SLSRPT program

The relationship of the control field of the present record (SR-SALES-REP) to the control field of the previous record (WS-PREVIOUS-SALES-REP) is then checked. If they are equal, detail-processing should take place. If they are not equal, this means that a control break has occurred and that the ST-SALES-REP-TOTAL-LINE should be prepared and written.

Observe that one of the potential program bugs—the printing of total lines prior to the first record—was avoided by taking the SR-SALES-REP field of the first record and placing it in the WS-PREVIOUS-SALES-REP field prior to making the comparison for the first record. This forced the control field test to show an equal condition on the first record. Recognize that this initialization of the WS-PREVIOUS-SALES-REP field could not have been done in the 100-INITIALIZE-VARIABLE-FIELDS module because the first record had not yet been read when that module was performed.

The last statement of this module is the conditional-processing required for the READ statement handling of this program. That is, when there are no more records in the SALES-FILE, the condition NOT END-OF-FILE will be false. Hence, the processing of module 210-PRINT-DETAIL-LINE will not be performed.

Observe, however, that the previous statement, which tests for a control break (IF SR-SALES-REP IS NOT EQUAL TO WS-PREVIOUS-SALES-REP PERFORM 220-PRINT-SALES-REP-TOTAL-LINE), must be executed one time after the end of file has been reached to force out the SR-REP-TOTAL-LINE for the

```
050010*                                        220020*
050020*                                        220030 220-PRINT-SALES-REP-TOTAL-LINE.
050030*                                        220040*
050040 PROCEDURE DIVISION.                      220070     MOVE WS-PREVIOUS-SALES-REP TO ST-SALES-REP.
050050*                                        220090     MOVE WS-TOTAL-SALES-REP-ACCUM TO ST-SALES-REVENUE.
050060*                                        220110     MOVE ST-SALES-REP-TOTAL-LINE TO SALES-REPORT-LINE.
050070 000-PRINT-SALES-REPORT.                 220120     MOVE 2 TO WS-LINE-SPACING.
050080*                                        220130     PERFORM 890-PRINT-REPORT-LINE.
050090     OPEN INPUT SALES FILE                220140     MOVE 3 TO WS-LINE-SPACING.
050100          OUTPUT SALES-REPORT.            220150     ADD WS-TOTAL-SALES-REP-ACCUM TO WS-TOTAL-REPORT-ACCUM.
050110     PERFORM 100-INITIALIZE-VARIABLE-FIELDS. 220160     MOVE ZEROS TO WS-TOTAL-SALES-REP-ACCUM.
050120     PERFORM 200-PROCESS-SALES-RECORD       220170     MOVE SR-SALES-REP TO WS-PREVIOUS-SALES-REP.
050130          UNTIL WS-END-OF-FILE-SWITCH IS EQUAL TO 'YES'. 700010*
050140     PERFORM 700-PRINT-REPORT-TOTAL-LINE    700020*
050150     CLOSE SALES-FILE                       700030 700-PRINT-REPORT-TOTAL-LINE.
050160          SALES-REPORT.                      700040*
050170     STOP RUN.                              700050     MOVE WS-TOTAL-REPORT-ACCUM TO RT-SALES-REVENUE.
100010*                                        700060     MOVE RT-REPORT-TOTAL-LINE TO SALES-REPORT-LINE.
100020*                                        700080     PERFORM 890-PRINT-REPORT-LINE.
100030 100-INITIALIZE-VARIABLE-FIELDS.         800010*
100040*                                        800020*
100050     MOVE 'NO ' TO WS-END-OF-FILE-SWITCH.  800030 800-READ-SALES-RECORD.
100060     MOVE 'YES' TO WS-FIRST-RECORD-SWITCH. 800040*
100070     MOVE ZEROS TO WS-PAGE-COUNT.          800050     READ SALES-FILE INTO SR-SALES-RECORD
100080     ADD 1 WS-LINES-PER-PAGE GIVING WS-LINES-USED. 800060          AT END MOVE 'YES' TO WS-END-OF-FILE-SWITCH
100090     ACCEPT WS-DATE-WORK FROM DATE.        800070               MOVE HIGH-VALUES TO SR-SALES-REP.
100100     MOVE WS-MONTH TO H2-MONTH.            870010*
100110     MOVE WS-DAY TO H2-DAY.                870020*
100120     MOVE WS-YEAR TO H2-YEAR.              870030 870-PRINT-REPORT-HEADINGS.
100130     MOVE ZEROS TO WS-TOTAL-ACCUMULATORS.  870040*
200010*                                        870050     ADD 1 TO WS-PAGE-COUNT.
200020*                                        870060     MOVE WS-PAGE-COUNT TO H2-PAGE-NBR.
200030 200-PROCESS-SALES-RECORD.               870070     MOVE H1-HEADING-LINE-1 TO SALES-REPORT-LINE.
200040*                                        870080     PERFORM 880-PRINT-REPORT-TOP-LINE.
200050     PERFORM 800-READ-SALES-RECORD.        870090     MOVE H2-HEADING-LINE-2 TO SALES-REPORT-LINE.
200060     IF FIRST-RECORD                       870100     MOVE 1 TO WS-LINE-SPACING.
200090          MOVE SR-SALES-REP TO WS-PREVIOUS-SALES-REP 870110     PERFORM 890-PRINT-REPORT-LINE.
200100          MOVE 'NO ' TO WS-FIRST-RECORD-SWITCH. 870120     MOVE H3-HEADING-LINE-3 TO SALES-REPORT-LINE.
200180     IF SR-SALES-REP IS NOT EQUAL TO WS-PREVIOUS-SALES-REP 870130     MOVE 2 TO WS-LINE-SPACING.
200190          PERFORM 220-PRINT-SALES-REP-TOTAL-LINE. 870140     PERFORM 890-PRINT-REPORT-LINE.
200200     IF NOT END-OF-FILE                    870150     MOVE H4-HEADING-LINE-4 TO SALES-REPORT-LINE.
200210          PERFORM 210-PRINT-DETAIL-LINE.    870160     MOVE 1 TO WS-LINE-SPACING.
210010*                                        870170     PERFORM 890-PRINT-REPORT-LINE.
210020*                                        870180     MOVE 2 TO WS-LINE-SPACING.
210030 210-PRINT-DETAIL-LINE.                  880010*
210040*                                        880020*
210050     IF WS-LINES-USED IS GREATER THAN WS-LINES-PER-PAGE 880030 880-PRINT-REPORT-TOP-LINE.
210060          PERFORM 870-PRINT-REPORT-HEADINGS. 880040*
210070     MOVE SR-SALES-REP TO DL-SALES-REP.    880050     WRITE SALES-REPORT-LINE
210080     MOVE SR-STATE TO DL-STATE.            880060          AFTER ADVANCING PAGE.
210090     MOVE SR-BRANCH TO DL-BRANCH.          880070     MOVE 1 TO WS-LINES-USED.
210100     MOVE SR-DATE-OF-SALE TO DL-DATE-OF-SALE. 890010*
210110     MOVE SR-PRODUCT-CODE TO DL-PRODUCT-CODE. 890020*
210120     MOVE SR-PRODUCT-DESCRIPTION TO DL-PRODUCT-DESCRIPTION. 890030 890-PRINT-REPORT-LINE.
210120     MOVE SR-UNIT-PRICE TO DL-UNIT-PRICE.  890040*
210130     MOVE SR-QUANTITY-SOLD TO DL-QUANTITY-SOLD. 890050     WRITE SALES-REPORT-LINE
210140     MULTIPLY SR-UNIT-PRICE BY SR-QUANTITY-SOLD 890060          AFTER ADVANCING WS-LINE-SPACING.
210150          GIVING WS-SALES-REVENUE ROUNDED. 890070     ADD WS-LINE-SPACING TO WS-LINES-USED.
210160     MOVE WS-SALES-REVENUE TO DL-SALES-REVENUE.
210170     MOVE DL-DETAIL-LINE TO SALES-REPORT-LINE.
210180     PERFORM 890-PRINT-REPORT-LINE.
210190     MOVE 1 TO WS-LINE-SPACING.
210200     ADD WS-SALES-REVENUE TO WS-TOTAL-SALES-REP-ACCUM.
220010*
```

Figure 10.20. PROCEDURE DIVISION: S-SLSRPT program

last sales representative in the file. Thus, the second common error when programming control break programs—the failure to print the last control break after the last record—is prevented by the logic of this module.

210-PRINT-DETAIL-LINE module

This module conforms to the general logic used in the record processing modules of previous programs. The following functions are handled: (1) an end-of-page test is made and if headings are required, the report-headings module is performed; (2) the input fields to be printed are moved to the detail-line area; (3) the detail-line calculation (Unit-price times Quantity-sold to equal Sales-revenue) is made, placed in WORKING-STORAGE, and moved to the detail-line area; (4) the detail-line area is moved to the print area and the Print-report-line module is performed; (5) the line-spacing is set; and (6) the sales revenue for the detail record is added to the total sales revenue for that sales representative.

One difference from previous programs, however, is that the line-spacing is set *after* rather than *before* the line is printed. This will be discussed in more detail later when the subject of variable line-spacing is covered.

220-PRINT-SALES-REP-TOTAL-LINE module

The ST-SALES-REP-TOTAL-LINE is formatted in this module. Remember that the present record caused the control break; thus the control break is for the sales representative of the previous record. So, the field WS-PREVIOUS-SALES-REP (not the input SR-SALES-REP field) is moved to the ST-SALES-REP-TOTAL-LINE for printing. The total sales revenue for the sales representative (WS-TOTAL-SALES-REP-ACCUM) field is also moved for printing, the entire line is moved to the output print line area, the line-spacing is set to double-spacing and the Print-report-line module is performed.

Then, after the line-spacing has been set for triple-spacing (more on this later), the WS-TOTAL-SALES-REP-ACCUM field is added to the WS-TOTAL-REPORT-ACCUM field to accumulate the total revenue for all sales representatives printed on the report. After this accumulation has been made, the WS-TOTAL-SALES-REP-ACCUM field must be set back to zero so that a fresh accumulation can be started for the records of the next sales representative. Finally, the WS-PREVIOUS-SALES-REP field must be reset to the sales representative number of the new sales representative. This new sales representative number is the one from the input record currently read, hence the statement: MOVE SR-SALES-REP TO WS-PREVIOUS-SALES-REP.

700-PRINT-REPORT-TOTAL-LINE module

This module is executed only once, after all input records have been processed and all sales representative total lines have been printed. The WS-TOTAL-REPORT-ACCUM field is moved to the RT-REPORT-TOTAL-LINE, the RT-REPORT-TOTAL-LINE is moved to the output report-line area, and the Print-report-line module is performed.

800-READ-SALES-RECORD module

At end-of-file, in addition to setting the WS-END-OF-FILE-SWITCH, the program also sets the SR-SALES-REP field to HIGH-VALUES. Remember that HIGH-VALUES is a figurative constant that can be used to set a field to the highest possible value. This setting will be used to force out the SR-SALES-REP-TOTAL-LINE for the last record.

Line-spacing logic

The line-spacing logic for this program is a bit more complicated than that of previous programs. The complicating factor is that, although detail lines are normally single-spaced, the first detail-line after the sales representative total-line is to be triple-spaced. Figure 10.21 diagrams the logic used to accomplish this.

At points A, B, C, and D of the figure, the WS-LINE-SPACING field has been set prior to performing the 890-WRITE-REPORT-LINE module, in accordance with the handling of previous programs. However, at point E (in the 220-PRINT-SALES-REP-TOTAL-LINE module), notice that WS-LINE-SPACING is set to 3 *after* the line to be printed in that module has already been written. The setting is made at this time so that, when the next detail line is written in the 210-PRINT-DETAIL-LINE module, WS-LINE-SPACING will properly indicate triple-spacing.

Of course, this means that WS-LINE-SPACING cannot be set for single-spacing before performing the print module in the 210-PRINT-DETAIL-LINE module, because all detail-lines would then be unconditionally single-spaced. Hence, at point F of the figure, WS-LINE-SPACING is set to 1 after 890-PRINT-REPORT-LINE has been performed. This will set the detail-line to single-spacing for subsequent detail-lines before the next sales representative total-line.

Observe also at point G in the 870-PRINT-REPORT-HEADINGS module that this type of logic has obviated the need for the printing of a dummy blank line between the last heading-line and the first detail-line, as was coded for the PAYROLL and DATA-VAL programs. By setting WS-LINE-SPACING to 2 in the headings module, double-spacing will occur for the first detail-line printed after the report headings.

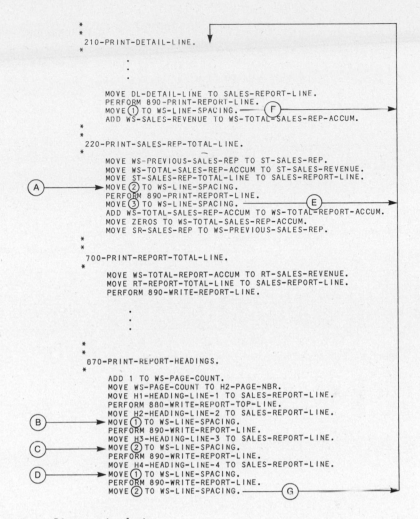

```
*
*                       ┌──────────────────────────────────────────────────────┐
  210-PRINT-DETAIL-LINE.                                                         │
*                                                                                │
            .                                                                    │
            .                                                                    │
            .                                                                    │
                                                                                 │
      MOVE DL-DETAIL-LINE TO SALES-REPORT-LINE.                                   │
      PERFORM 890-PRINT-REPORT-LINE.                                              │
      MOVE ①  TO WS-LINE-SPACING. ────────⦿F                                    │
      ADD WS-SALES-REVENUE TO WS-TOTAL-SALES-REP-ACCUM.                           │
*                                                                                │
*                                                                                │
  220-PRINT-SALES-REP-TOTAL-LINE.                                                 │
*                                                                                │
      MOVE WS-PREVIOUS-SALES-REP TO ST-SALES-REP.                                 │
      MOVE WS-TOTAL-SALES-REP-ACCUM TO ST-SALES-REVENUE.                          │
      MOVE ST-SALES-REP-TOTAL-LINE TO SALES-REPORT-LINE.                          │
   A─▶MOVE ②  TO WS-LINE-SPACING.                                               │
      PERFORM 890-PRINT-REPORT-LINE.                                              │
      MOVE ③  TO WS-LINE-SPACING. ───────────────⦿E                            │
      ADD WS-TOTAL-SALES-REP-ACCUM TO WS-TOTAL-REPORT-ACCUM.                      │
      MOVE ZEROS TO WS-TOTAL-SALES-REP-ACCUM.                                     │
      MOVE SR-SALES-REP TO WS-PREVIOUS-SALES-REP.                                 │
*                                                                                │
*                                                                                │
  700-PRINT-REPORT-TOTAL-LINE.                                                    │
*                                                                                │
      MOVE WS-TOTAL-REPORT-ACCUM TO RT-SALES-REVENUE.                             │
      MOVE RT-REPORT-TOTAL-LINE TO SALES-REPORT-LINE.                             │
      PERFORM 890-WRITE-REPORT-LINE.                                              │
                                                                                 │
            .                                                                    │
            .                                                                    │
            .                                                                    │
*                                                                                │
*                                                                                │
  870-PRINT-REPORT-HEADINGS.                                                      │
*                                                                                │
      ADD 1 TO WS-PAGE-COUNT.                                                     │
      MOVE WS-PAGE-COUNT TO H2-PAGE-NBR.                                          │
      MOVE H1-HEADING-LINE-1 TO SALES-REPORT-LINE.                               │
      PERFORM 880-WRITE-REPORT-TOP-LINE.                                          │
      MOVE H2-HEADING-LINE-2 TO SALES-REPORT-LINE.                               │
   B─▶MOVE ①  TO WS-LINE-SPACING.                                               │
      PERFORM 890-WRITE-REPORT-LINE.                                              │
      MOVE H3-HEADING-LINE-3 TO SALES-REPORT-LINE.                               │
   C─▶MOVE ②  TO WS-LINE-SPACING.                                               │
      PERFORM 890-WRITE-REPORT-LINE.                                             │
      MOVE H4-HEADING-LINE-4 TO SALES-REPORT-LINE.                               │
   D─▶MOVE ①  TO WS-LINE-SPACING.                                               │
      PERFORM 890-WRITE-REPORT-LINE.                                             │
      MOVE ②  TO WS-LINE-SPACING. ───────⦿G─────────────────────────────────────┘
```

Figure 10.21. Line-spacing logic

Although it would be acceptable and it would provide better documentation, notice that it is not necessary to set WS-LINE-SPACING to 3 in the 700-PRINT-REPORT-TOTAL-LINE module. This is because a sales representative total-line must always be printed prior to the total-line. Thus, the line-spacing setting at point E will provide for the correct triple-spacing of the report total-line.

The USAGE Clause

The USAGE clause may be specified with the data-item description entry of a field in the DATA DIVISION. It defines the form in which data fields are to be stored, or the *data representation* method. The USAGE clause is always an optional entry. However, its judicious use can contribute to program and storage-media efficiency. The format and examples of the USAGE clause are shown in Figure 10.22. There are three usages commonly used in commercial data processing programs: DISPLAY, COMPUTATIONAL, and COMPUTATIONAL-3. Examples of data representation for each are shown in Figure 10.23.

When specifying usage, notice that the reserved words USAGE and IS are optional. They impart little meaning to the data-item description but do consume space on the coding line, so it is recommended that they be omitted.

Format:

$$\text{[\underline{USAGE} IS]} \left\{ \begin{array}{l} \underline{\text{COMPUTATIONAL}} \\ \underline{\text{COMP}} \\ \underline{\text{DISPLAY}} \end{array} \right\}$$

$$\left\{ \begin{array}{l} \text{COMPUTATIONAL-3} \\ \text{COMP-3} \end{array} \right\} \text{Non-ANS extensions}$$

Example:

Part A: Full specification of USAGE clause reserved words

```
05  XX-ALPHA-FIELD    PIC  X(24)        USAGE  IS  DISPLAY.
05  XX-NUMERIC-FLD    PIC  S9(8)        USAGE  IS  COMPUTATIONAL.
05  XX-DECIMAL-FLD    PIC  S9(7)V99     USAGE  IS  COMPUTATIONAL-3.
```

Part B: Recommended specification of USAGE clause with abbreviations and implicit DISPLAY usage

```
05  XX-ALPHA-FIELD    PIC  X(24).
05  XX-NUMERIC-FLD    PIC  S9(8)                           COMP  SYNC.
05  XX-DECIMAL-FLD    PIC  S9(7)V99                               COMP-3.
```

Implicit DISPLAY usage

Figure 10.22. USAGE clause examples

DISPLAY Usage

When USAGE IS DISPLAY is specified or the USAGE clause is omitted, the DISPLAY form of data representation is provided. Since USAGE clauses have not been used previously in this text, USAGE IS DISPLAY has been assumed for the data representation of all fields.

DISPLAY usage is the basic form in which each computer or storage-medium position (storage positions are often termed *bytes*) contains one character of data. That is, one letter, one numeric digit, or one special character can be stored in each storage position. Data fields of punched cards or of report lines to be printed must be of DISPLAY usage. Non-COBOL synonyms for DISPLAY usage are *character* format, *zoned decimal* format, or *external decimal* format.

Rather than explicitly coding the USAGE clause for DISPLAY usage, it is recommended that the clause be omitted and implicit specification of DISPLAY usage be used.

COMPUTATIONAL Usage

COMPUTATIONAL usage is limited to numeric fields. With this form of data representation, more than one decimal digit is usually stored in one storage position. Most computer systems do arithmetic in the COMPUTATIONAL format. A non-COBOL term that usually corresponds to the COMPUTATIONAL format is *binary* representation.

The reserved word COMPUTATIONAL may be abbreviated as COMP. Since the abbreviation takes less space on the coding line and is just as understandable, it is recommended that the abbreviation COMP be used.

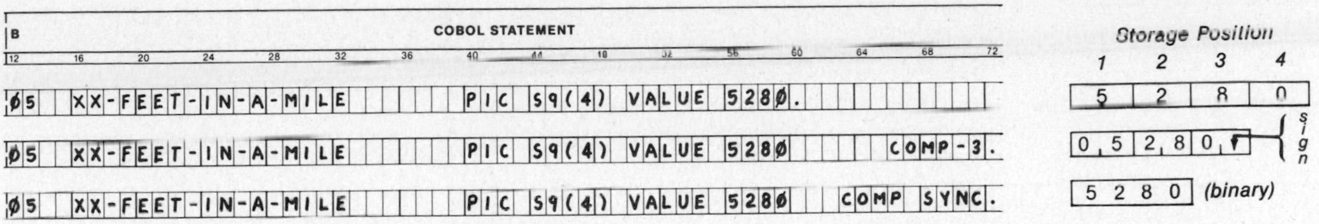

Figure 10.23. Data representation of common usages

```
B            COBOL STATEMENT                                    Storage Position
                                                                 1   2   3   4
05  XX-FEET-IN-A-MILE        PIC S9(4) VALUE 5280.               5   2   8   0
05  XX-FEET-IN-A-MILE        PIC S9(4) VALUE 5280      COMP-3.   0 5 2 8 0 {sign}
05  XX-FEET-IN-A-MILE        PIC S9(4) VALUE 5280  COMP SYNC.    5 2 8 0  (binary)
```

The SYNCHRONIZED clause

Notice in Figure 10.23 that the reserved word SYNC was specified after the USAGE clause. SYNC is an abbreviation for the SYNCHRONIZED clause. This clause should usually be specified for COMP fields in WORKING-STORAGE that are not contained within input or output records. It provides proper internal field alignment (synchronization) to optimize arithmetic processing efficiency. (However, if a COMP field is within an input or output record, use of the SYNC clause may cause improper field alignment within the record. For more information on the SYNC clause, you should check the reference manual for the compiler you are using.)

A convenient place to specify the word COMP is in position 63 when the SYNC clause is specified or in position 66 when SYNC is not coded.

COMPUTATIONAL-3 Usage This usage is not an ANS COBOL standard but a commonly used IBM-originated method of data representation. Hence, this usage is often found in COBOL programs written for IBM and IBM-compatible COBOL compilers.

COMPUTATIONAL-3 usage is also limited to numeric fields. With this method of data representation, two numeric digits are generally stored in each storage position (the one exception is the rightmost storage position of each field, which is used for one digit and the arithmetic sign). This data representation method is, for non-COBOL purposes, sometimes termed *packed decimal* or *internal decimal* format.

The abbreviation COMP-3 may be used and is recommended to save space on the coding line. Position 66 is a convenient place to start the word.

Choosing the Most Efficient Usage for Numeric Fields Because arithmetic is usually executed internally in COMP or COMP-3 usage, it is usually more efficient to specify explicitly COMP or COMP-3 usage for WORKING-STORAGE fields involved in arithmetic calculations or numeric comparisons.

However, input data from punched cards or certain other input devices must be of DISPLAY usage in their initial record-description entry.

Similarly, data fields to be printed on reports or displayed on video-display terminal screens must be converted to DISPLAY usage for print-out or display. Thus, fields within the record descriptions for report and screen lines must be of DISPLAY usage.

Conversion from one usage to another takes place during a MOVE statement or as a result of the GIVING clause of an arithmetic statement. For example, conversion of data from COMP usage to DISPLAY usage occurs when a MOVE statement is specified that has a sending field of COMP usage and a receiving field of DISPLAY usage. Such conversion takes time, though, and this can have a degrading effect on processing time.

Conversion of data from COMP-3 usage, when available, to DISPLAY usage, or vice versa, also consumes processing time, although usually not as

Digit length of field	Storage positions required			Digit length of field	Storage positions required			Digit length of field	Storage positions required		
	DISPLAY usage	COMP-3 usage	COMP usage		DISPLAY usage	COMP-3 usage	COMP usage		DISPLAY usage	COMP-3 usage	COMP usage
1	1	1	2	7	7	4	4	13	13	7	8
2	2	2	2	8	8	5	4	14	14	8	8
3	3	2	2	9	9	5	4	15	15	8	8
4	4	3	2	10	10	6	8	16	16	9	8
5	5	3	4	11	11	6	8	17	17	9	8
6	6	4	4	12	12	7	8	18	18	10	8

Note: These usages are compatible with IBM 370 computers. The binary representation (COMP usage) on these computers requires 2, 4, or 8 bytes as indicated.

Figure 10.24. Storage positions consumed for various field lengths with common usages (IBM-370-compatible data representation)

much as the COMP-to-DISPLAY conversion. On the other hand, arithmetic is usually processed faster with COMP usage rather than COMP-3 usage.

Both COMP and COMP-3 usages can be expected to store longer numeric fields in less space on the storage medium (such as tape or disk) than with DISPLAY usage. Figure 10.24 shows a table of relative storage positions consumed using data representation formats compatible with an IBM 370-compatible computer.

Although it is sometimes difficult to determine which usage will be best, the following guidelines are usually applied:

1. When it is desired to reduce record storage space requirements on a tape or disk, longer numeric fields may be stored in COMP or COMP-3 usage (see Figure 10.25).

   a. If the field has decimal positions, choose COMP-3 usage, when available, rather than COMP. This is because COMP fields are usually stored in binary format. Fractional decimal values will usually require rounding to a binary equivalent. This may introduce minor rounding discrepancies.

Fields of hypothetical earnings record	Length		
	DISPLAY usage	COMP-3 usage	COMP usage
Record code	2	2	2
Social security number	9	5	4
Employee name	28	28 (DISPLAY)	28 (DISPLAY)
Earnings quarter-1	7	4	4
Earnings quarter-2	7	4	4
Earnings quarter-3	7	4	4
Earnings quarter-4	7	4	4
Year-to-date earnings	8	5	4
Federal income tax withheld	7	4	4
F.I.C.A. tax withheld	7	4	4
State income tax withheld	7	4	4
State disability insurance	7	4	4
State unemployment tax	7	4	4
Total record length	110	76	74

Figure 10.25. Effect of USAGE upon record length

b. If the field has no decimal positions, COMP usage may provide more efficient storage and processing than COMP-3.

2. When WORKING-STORAGE fields are involved in arithmetic or many numeric comparisons, specify COMP or COMP-3 usage.

   a. Choose COMP (in preference to COMP-3) for integer fields that will not be moved to fields with DISPLAY or COMP-3 usage and will not be frequently compared to DISPLAY or COMP-3 fields.

   b. Choose COMP-3, when available, in preference to COMP when the field will be moved to or from DISPLAY or COMP-3 fields and/or will be compared to DISPLAY or COMP-3 usage fields.

In the multiple-level control break program presented in the next part of this chapter, examples of the USAGE clause will be presented.

Choosing Field Lengths for COMP and COMP-3 Fields

As indicated in Figure 10.24, COMP-3 fields of an odd number of positions occupy the same storage space as a field of the next lower even number. That is, a seven-digit and a six-digit COMP-3 field both require four storage positions. Thus, COMP-3 fields should generally be specified as an odd number of digit positions.

Similarly, COMP fields from one to four digits in length require the same number of storage positions; five to nine digits require the same number; and ten to eighteen digits require a like number of storage positions. So, COMP fields should usually be specified as four, nine, or eighteen digits.

Because COMP and COMP-3 fields are considered algebraic, the PICTURE symbol S should normally be specified.

Programming for Multiple-Level Control Breaks: The Multiple-Level Sales Report Program

When there is more than one control level, the control break program logic complexity is increased in two areas: in the test for control breaks and in the need to provide additional control-break line-printing modules.

To illustrate multiple-level control breaks, we will use the single-level Sales Report program as a base. The following additional topics will be introduced in the program: the USAGE clause and the processing of date records. Since much of the programming specifications, design documentation, and coding for this multiple-level control break program will duplicate those of the single-level version, changes are shaded in each figure.

Programming Specifications

Rather than just printing control totals by sales representative, this multiple-level control break program will print sales representative totals within branch office totals within state totals. A report total will also be printed.

Print chart

The print chart for the output multiple-level Sales Report is shown in Figure 10.26. A period-ending date together with the descriptive words have been added to the first heading-line of the report. Thus, this report will show both the period-ending date to which the report applies and the run-date on which the report is actually printed.

Notice that the arrangement of the sales representative number, office, and state fields has been changed to show them in major to minor sequence, from left to right. Reports are usually easier to read and comprehend when arranged this way. (The single-level Sales Report program showed its major field—Sales-Representative-number—on the left for ease of reference, also.)

The additional total-lines for branch and state totals are also shown on the print chart.

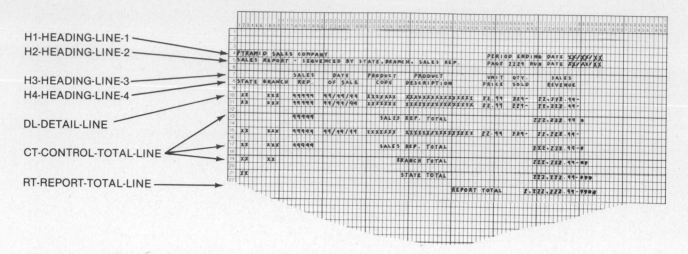

H1-HEADING-LINE-1

H2-HEADING-LINE-2

H3-HEADING-LINE-3

H4-HEADING-LINE-4

DL-DETAIL-LINE

CT-CONTROL-TOTAL-LINE

RT-REPORT-TOTAL-LINE

Figure 10.26. Print chart: Multiple-level sales report program

Input record layouts

The input sales record format is exactly the same as it is for the single-level Sales Report program. But another input record to carry the period-ending date must be provided. Its format is shown in Figure 10.27.

Programming specifications

The programming specifications have been expanded to define the additional requirements. They are shown in Figure 10.28. An example of the report output appears in Figure 10.29.

Design Documentation

Structure chart

The multiple-level Sales Report structure chart is shown in Figure 10.30. Notice that the Initialize-variable-fields module will perform the Read-sales-record module (to obtain the period-ending date record). Also the Process-sales-record module will perform the additional modules Print-sales-total and Print-branch-total.

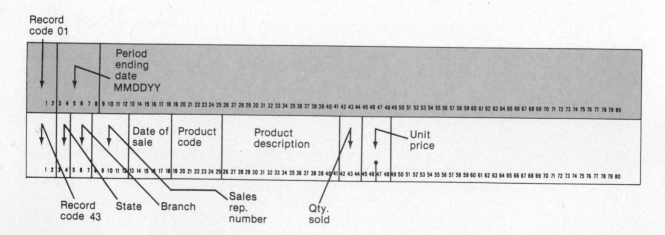

Figure 10.27. Printed layout: Period-ending date and sales records

Program name. MULTIPLE–LEVEL SALES REPORT   Program ID: M–SLSRPT

Program Description

This program reads sales records, computes the sales revenue for each sales record and prints a sales report detail–line for each sales record.

Sales representative total–lines are printed for each sales representative within each branch within each state. Branch total–lines are printed for each branch within each state. A state total–line is printed for each state.

After all input sales record have been processed, a report total–line is printed.

Input File(s)

Sales file

Output File(s)

Sales report

List of Program Operations

A. Read records from the input sales file.

B. The first record is to be a period–ending–date record.

1. The period–ending–date is to be extracted from the date record and stored in the first heading–line period–ending–date.

2. If the first record is not a date record, the program processing should terminate.

C. For each sales record, the program is to:

1. Compute the sales–revenue by multiplying the unit–price by the quantity–sold.

2. Print a detail–line containing the following fields in accordance with the format shown on the print–chart:

   a. Sales–representative number
   b. State
   c. Branch
   d. Date–of–sale
   e. Product–code
   f. Product–description
   g. Unit–price
   h. Quantity–sold
   i. Sales–revenue

3. Accumulate the following totals:

   a. Total sales–revenue for each sales–representative
   b. Total sales–revenue for each branch
   c. Total sales–revenue for each state
   d. Total sales–revenue for all sales–representatives

D. Whenever the sales–representative number (within branch and within state) changes, the program should print a sales representative total–line containing the following fields in accordance with the format shown on the print chart:

   a. State
   b. Branch
   c. Sales–representative number
   d. The words "sales rep. total"
   e. Total sales–revenue for that sales–representative

   f. One asterisk

E. Whenever the branch (within state) changes, the program should print a branch total–line containing the following fields in accordance with the format shown on the print chart:

   a. State
   b. Branch
   c. The words "branch total"
   d. Total sales–revenue for that branch
   e. Two asterisks

F. Whenever the state changes, the program should print a state total–line containing the following fields in accordance with the format shown on the print chart:

   a. State
   b. The words "state total"
   c. Total sales–revenue for that state
   d. Three asterisks

G. After all the input sales records have been processed, the program should print the following total fields on the sales report total–line in accordance with the format shown on the print chart:

1. The words "report total"
2. Total sales–revenue for all sales–representatives
3. Four asterisks

H. Headings are to be printed on the first page of the report. After 54 lines have been used on a report page, the program should skip to the next page and print the report headings.

1. The period–ending date is to be obtained from the date record as described above and printed on the first heading–line in accordance with the format shown on the print chart.

2. The page number is to be incremented each time the heading is printed and displayed on the second heading–line in accordance with the format shown on the print chart.

3. The run date is to be obtained from the operating system and printed on the second heading–line in accordance with the format shown on the print chart.

I. Line–spacing is to be handled as follows:

1. The first detail–line printed after the headings is to be double–spaced from the last heading–line.

2. Detail–lines for the same sales–representative are to be single–spaced from one another.

3. Each sales–representative total–line is to be double–spaced from the previous detail–line.

4. The first detail–line for each sales–representative is to be triple–spaced from the previous sales–representative total–line.

5. The report total–line is to be triple–spaced from the last sales–representative total–line.

Figure 10.28. Programming specifications: Multiple-level sales report program

```
PYRAMID SALES COMPANY                                    PERIOD ENDING DATE 05/07/81
SALES REPORT - SEQUENCED BY STATE, BRANCH, SALES REP.    PAGE    1 RUN DATE 05/10/81

              SALES    DATE     PRODUCT   PRODUCT            UNIT  QTY.    SALES
STATE BRANCH  REP.     OF SALE  CODE      DESCRIPTION        PRICE SOLD    REVENUE

CA    001     10003    05/07/81 TB001     TOOTHBRUSH         1.00  1       1.00
CA    001     10003    05/07/81 SB005     BAR SOAP            .50  5       2.50

CA    001     10003                       SALES REP. TOTAL                3.50*


CA    001     10005    05/07/81 MP070     MOP               10.00  2       20.00

CA    001     10005                       SALES REP. TOTAL                20.00*

CA    001                                 BRANCH TOTAL                    23.50**


CA    002     10063    05/07/81 SB005     BAR SOAP            .50  5       2.50

CA    002     10063                       SALES REP. TOTAL                2.50*


CA    002     10069    05/07/81 SP008     SOAP POWDER        1.89  238     449.82
CA    002     10069    05/07/81 WF080     FLOOR WAX          2.98  5       14.90

CA    002     10069                       SALES REP. TOTAL                464.72*

CA    002                                 BRANCH TOTAL                    467.22**

CA                                        STATE TOTAL                     490.72***


NV    017     20006    05/07/81 SB005     BAR SOAP            .50  1        .50

NV    017     20006                       SALES REP. TOTAL                 .50*


NV    017     20009    05/07/81 SP008     SOAP POWDER        1.89  1       1.89
NV    017     20009    05/07/81 WF080     FLOOR WAX          2.98  1       2.98

NV    017     20009                       SALES REP. TOTAL                4.87*

NV    017                                 BRANCH TOTAL                    5.37**


NV    018     20033    05/07/81 TB001     TOOTHBRUSH         1.00  1       1.00
NV    018     20033    05/07/81 SB005     BAR SOAP            .50  5       2.50

NV    018     20033                       SALES REP. TOTAL                3.50*


NV    018     20039    05/07/81 WF080     FLOOR WAX          2.98  2       5.96

NV    018     20039                       SALES REP. TOTAL                5.96*

NV    018                                 BRANCH TOTAL                    9.46**

NV                                        STATE TOTAL                     14.83***


                                          REPORT TOTAL                    505.55****
```

Figure 10.29. Multiple-level sales report output example

Program name: MULTIPLE–LEVEL SALES REPORT   Program ID: M–SLSRPT

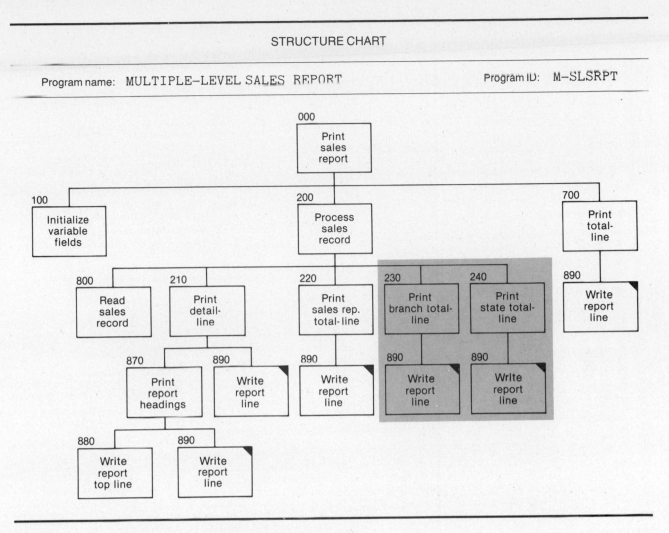

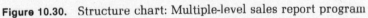

Figure 10.30.   Structure chart: Multiple-level sales report program

Pseudocode and program flowchart

The pseudocode is shown in Figure 10.31; the program flowchart is shown in Figure 10.32. In addition to providing for the additional modules, additional logic was added to the Initialize-variable-fields module to handle the period-ending date record and to the Process-sales-record module to test the multiple control breaks.

Program Coding

We'll assign a program identification of M-SLSRPT to this program. The first three divisions of the program are shown in Figure 10.33.

Coding the IDENTIFICATION and ENVIRONMENT DIVISIONS

Except for the comment lines, there are no changes to these two divisions.

Coding the FILE SECTION of the DATA DIVISION

There are no changes required to the FILE SECTION coding.

Program name: MULTIPLE–LEVEL SALES REPORT   Program ID: M–SLSRPT

000–Print–Sales–Report module

1. Open the files.
2. Perform 100–Initialize–Variable–Fields.
3. Perform 200–Process–Sales–Record until no more records.
4. Perform 700–Print–Report–Total–Line.
5. Close the files.
6. Stop the run.

100–Initialize–Variable–Fields module

1. Set the end–of–file indicator to "No".
2. Set the first–record indicator to "Yes".
3. Set the page–count to zero.
4. Set the lines–per–page so that headings for the first page will be triggered.
5. Obtain the date from the operating system and move it to the second heading–line Run–date.
6. Set the total–accumulator fields to zero.
7. Perform 800–Read–Sales–Record.
8. If a Date–record has been read

   Move the period–ending–date to the first heading–line period–ending–date

   Else

   Move "Yes" to the end–of–file indicator.

200–Process–Sales–Record module

1. Perform 800–Read–Sales–Record.
2. If this is the first input record

   Move the input State to the Previous–state
   Move the input Branch to the Previous–branch
   Move the input Sales–rep to the Previous–sales–rep
   Set the First–record indicator to "No".

3. If the input record State is not the same as the Previous–state

   Perform 220–Print–Sales–Rep–Total–Line
   Perform 230–Print–Branch–Total–Line
   Perform 240–Print–State–Total–Line
   Else if the input record Branch is not the same as the Previous–branch
   Perform 220–Print–Sales–Rep–Total–Line
   Perform 230–Print–Branch–Total–Line
   Else if the input record Sales–Rep is not the same as the Previous–sales–rep

   Perform 220–Print–Sales–Rep–Total–Line.

4. If there is an input record
   Perform 210–Print–Detail–Line.

210–Print–Detail–Line module

1. If the Lines–used is greater than the lines–per–page Perform 870–Print–Report–Headings.
2. Move the input Sales–rep field to the detail–line Sales–rep field.
3. Move the input State field to the detail–line State field.
4. Move the input Branch field to the detail–line Branch field.
5. Move the input Date–of–sale field to the detail–line Date–of–sale field.
6. Move the input Product–code field to the detail–line Product–code field.
7. Move the input Product–description field to the detail–line Product–description field.

8. Move the input Quantity–sold field to the detail–line Quantity–sold field.
9. Move the input Unit–price field to the detail–line Unit–price field.
10. Multiply the input Unit–price field by the input Quantity–sold field to equal the detail–line Sales–revenue field.
11. Move the detail–line to the output print–line area.
12. Perform 890–Write–Report–Line.
13. Set the line–spacing indicator for single–spacing.
14. Add the sales–revenue for this record to the Total–sales–rep–sales–revenue.

220–Print–Sales–Rep–Total–Line module

1. Move the Previous–state to the control break total–line State.
2. Move the Previous–Branch to the control break total–line Branch.
3. Move the Previous–sales–rep to the control break total–line Sales–rep.
4. Move the description "sales rep." to the control break total–line Description.
5. Move the Total–sales–rep–sales–revenue to the control break total–line Sales–revenue.
6. Move one asterisk to the control break total–line Asterisk–area.
7. Move the control break total–line to the output print–line area.
8. Set the line–spacing indicator for double–spacing.
9. Perform 890–Write–Report–Line.
10. Set the line–spacing indicator for triple–spacing.
11. Add the Total–sales–rep–sales–revenue to the Total–branch–sales–revenue.
12. Move zero to the Total–sales–rep–sales–revenue.
13. Move the input Sales–rep to the Previous–sales–rep.

230–Print–Branch–Total–Line module

1. Move spaces to the control break total–line Sales–rep.
2. Move the description "branch" to the control break total–line Description.
3. Move the Total–branch–sales–revenue to the control break total–line Sales–revenue.
4. Move two asterisks to the control break total–line Asterisk–area.
5. Move the control break total–line to the output print–line area.
6. Set the line–spacing indicator for double–spacing.
7. Perform 890–Write–Report–Line.
8. Set the line–spacing indicator for triple–spacing.
9. Add the Total–branch–sales–revenue to the Total–state–sales–revenue.
10. Move zero to the Total–branch–sales–revenue.
11. Move the input Branch to the Previous–branch.

Figure 10.31. Pseudocode: Multiple-level sales report program

240-Print-State-Total-Line module

1. Move spaces to the control break total-line Branch

2. Move the description "state" to the control break total-line Description.

3. Move the Total-state-sales-revenue to the control break total-line Sales-revenue.

4. Move three asterisks to the control break total-line Asterisk-area.

5. Move the control break total-line to the output print-line area.

6. Set the line-spacing indicator for double-spacing.

7. Perform 890-Write-Report-Line.

8. Set the line-spacing indicator for triple-spacing.

9. Add the Total-state-sales-revenue to the Total-report-sales-revenue.

10. Move zero to the Total-state-sales-revenue.

11. Move the input State to the Previous-state.

700-Print-Report-Total-Line module

1. Move the Total-report-sales-revenue to the total-line Sales-revenue.

2. Move the total-line to the output print-line area.

3. Set the line-spacing indicator for triple-spacing.

4. Perform 890-Write-Report-Line.

800-Read-Sales-Record module

1. Read an input sales record.

2. If there are no more records
   Move "Yes" to the end-of-file indicator
   Move high-values to the input record
   State, Branch, and Sales-rep.

870-Print-Report-Headings module

1. Add 1 to the Page-count.

2. Move the page-count to the second heading-line Page-number.

3. Move heading-line-1 to the output print-line area.

4. Perform 880-Write-Report-Top-Line.

5. Move heading-line-2 to the output print-line area.

6. Set the line-spacing indicator for single-spacing.

7. Perform 890-Write-Report-Line.

8. Move heading-line-3 to the output print-line area.

9. Set the line-spacing indicator for double-spacing.

10. Perform 890-Write-Report-Line.

11. Move heading-line-4 to the output print-line area.

12. Set the line-spacing indicator for single-spacing.

13. Perform 890-Write-Report-Line.

14. Set the line-spacing indicator for double-spacing.

880-Write-Report-Top-Line module

1. Advance to the top of the next report page and write the output print-line area.

2. Set Lines-used to 1.

890-Write-Report-Line module

1. Advance in accordance with the setting of the Line-spacing indicator and write the output print-line area.

2. Add the line-spacing indicator to Lines-used.

Figure 10.31. (continued)

Program name: MULTIPLE–LEVEL SALES REPORT   Program ID: Ṁ–SLSRPT

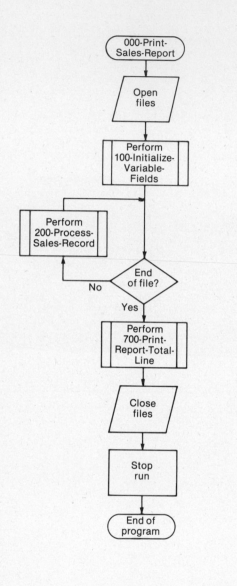

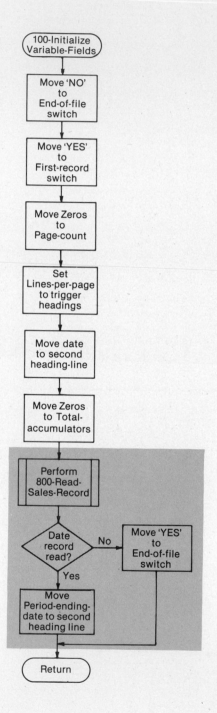

Figure 10.32.   Program flowchart: Multiple-level sales report program

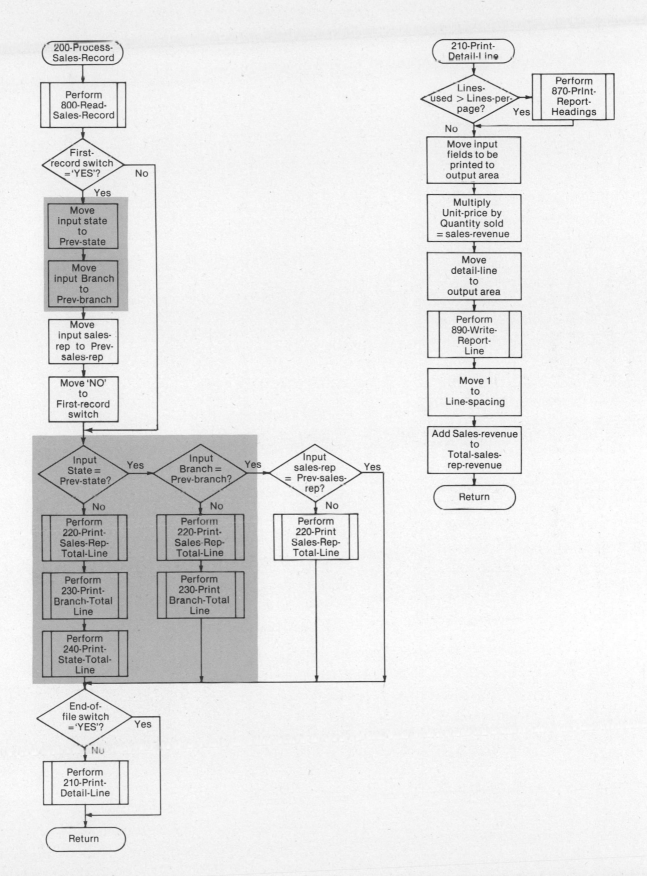

Figure 10.32. (continued)

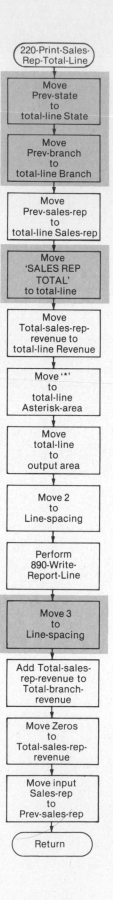

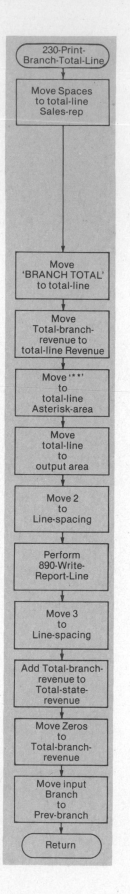

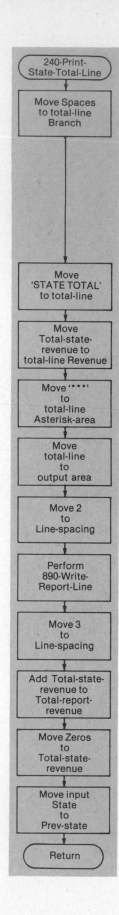

Figure 10.32. (continued)

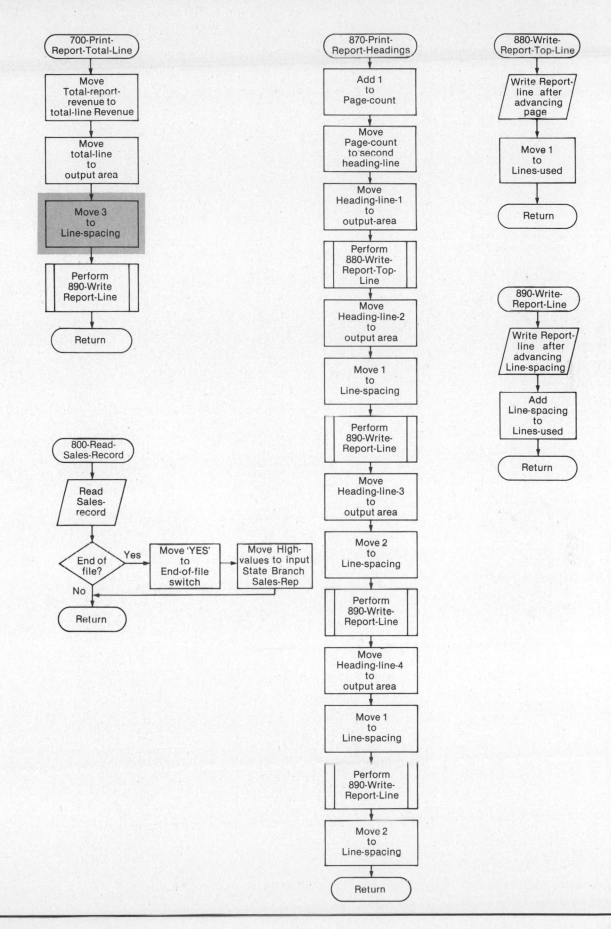

700-Print-Report-Total-Line

- Move Total-report-revenue to total-line Revenue
- Move total-line to output area
- Move 3 to Line-spacing
- Perform 890-Write Report-Line
- Return

800-Read-Sales-Record

- Read Sales-record
- End of file?
  - Yes → Move 'YES' to End-of-file switch → Move High-values to input State Branch Sales-Rep
  - No → Return

870-Print-Report-Headings

- Add 1 to Page-count
- Move Page-count to second heading-line
- Move Heading-line-1 to output-area
- Perform 880-Write-Report-Top-Line
- Move Heading-line-2 to output area
- Move 1 to Line-spacing
- Perform 890-Write-Report-Line
- Move Heading-line-3 to output area
- Move 2 to Line-spacing
- Perform 890-Write-Report-Line
- Move Heading-line-4 to output area
- Move 1 to Line-spacing
- Perform 890-Write-Report-Line
- Move 2 to Line-spacing
- Return

880-Write-Report-Top-Line

- Write Report-line after advancing page
- Move 1 to Lines-used
- Return

890-Write-Report-Line

- Write Report-line after advancing Line-spacing
- Add Line-spacing to Lines-used
- Return

Figure 10.32. (continued)

393

```
001010 IDENTIFICATION DIVISION.
001020 PROGRAM-ID.       M-SLSRPT.
001030*AUTHOR.           WELBURN.
001040*INSTALLATION.     PYRAMID SALES COMPANY.
001050*DATE-WRITTEN.     FEB 27,1981.
001060*DATE-COMPILED.    MAR 10,1981.
001070*SECURITY.         NONE.
001080*
001090*
001100*               THIS PROGRAM READS SALES RECORDS,
001110*               COMPUTES THE SALES REVENUE FOR EACH SALES RECORD
001120*               AND PRINTS A SALES DETAIL LINE
001130*               FOR EACH SALES RECORD.
001140*
001150*               TOTAL LINES ARE PRINTED BY SALES-REP
001160*               WITHIN BRANCH WITHIN STATE.
001170*
001180*               AFTER ALL INPUT SALES RECORDS HAVE BEEN PROCESSED,
001190*               A REPORT TOTAL LINE WILL BE PRINTED.
002010*
002020*
002030*
002040 ENVIRONMENT DIVISION.
002050*
002060*
002070 CONFIGURATION SECTION.
002080*
002090 SOURCE-COMPUTER.  IBM-370.
002100 OBJECT-COMPUTER.  IBM-370.
002110*
002120*
002130 INPUT-OUTPUT SECTION.
002140*
002150 FILE-CONTROL.
002160     SELECT SALES-FILE
002170         ASSIGN TO UT-S-INFILE.
002180     SELECT SALES-REPORT
002190         ASSIGN TO UT-S-PRTFILE.
003010*
003020*
003040 DATA DIVISION.
003050*
003060*
003070 FILE SECTION.
003080*
003090 FD  SALES-FILE
003100     RECORD CONTAINS 80 CHARACTERS
003110     LABEL RECORDS ARE OMITTED.
004010*
004020 01  SALES-RECORD.
004030     05  FILLER                    PIC X(80).
005010*
005020 FD  SALES-REPORT
005030     RECORD CONTAINS 133 CHARACTERS
005040     LABEL RECORDS ARE OMITTED.
005050*
005060 01  SALES-REPORT-LINE.
005070     05  FILLER                    PIC X(133).
006010*
006020*
006030 WORKING-STORAGE SECTION.
006040*
006050*
006060 01  WS-SWITCHES.
006070     05  WS-END-OF-FILE-SWITCH     PIC X(3).
006080         88  END-OF-FILE                         VALUE 'YES'.
006090     05  WS-FIRST-RECORD-SWITCH    PIC X(3).
006100         88  FIRST-RECORD                         VALUE 'YES'.
007010*
007020 01  WS-CONTROL-FIELDS.
007030     05  WS-PREVIOUS-STATE         PIC X(2).
007040     05  WS-PREVIOUS-BRANCH        PIC X(3).
007050     05  WS-PREVIOUS-SALES-REP     PIC X(5).
008010*
008020 01  WS-REPORT-CONTROLS.
008030     05  WS-PAGE-COUNT             PIC S9(4)      COMP-3.
008040     05  WS-LINES-PER-PAGE         PIC S99 VALUE +54
008050                                                  COMP SYNC.
008060     05  WS-LINES-USED             PIC S9(2)      COMP SYNC.
008070     05  WS-LINE-SPACING           PIC S9(2).
009010*
009020 01  WS-WORK-AREAS.
009030     05  WS-DATE-WORK              PIC 9(6).
009040     05  WS-DATE-CONVERSION REDEFINES WS-DATE-WORK.
009050         10  WS-YEAR               PIC 9(2).
009060         10  WS-MONTH              PIC 9(2).
009070         10  WS-DAY                PIC 9(2).
009080     05  WS-SALES-REVENUE          PIC S9(5)V99   COMP-3.
010010*
010020 01  WS-TOTAL-ACCUMULATORS.
010030     05  WS-TOTAL-SALES-REP-ACCUM  PIC S9(6)V99   COMP-3.
010040     05  WS-TOTAL-BRANCH-ACCUM     PIC S9(6)V99   COMP-3.
010050     05  WS-TOTAL-STATE-ACCUM      PIC S9(6)V99   COMP-3.
010060     05  WS-TOTAL-REPORT-ACCUM     PIC S9(7)V99   COMP-3.

020010*
020020 01  SR-SALES-RECORD.
020030     05  SR-RECORD-CODE            PIC X(2).
020040     05  SR-STATE                  PIC X(2).
020050     05  SR-BRANCH                 PIC X(3).
020060     05  SR-SALES-REP              PIC X(5).
020070     05  SR-DATE-OF-SALE           PIC X(6).
020080     05  SR-PRODUCT-CODE           PIC X(7).
020090     05  SR-PRODUCT-DESCRIPTION    PIC X(16).
020100     05  SR-QUANTITY-SOLD          PIC S9(3).
020110     05  SR-UNIT-PRICE             PIC 9(2)V99.
020120     05  FILLER                    PIC X(32).
021010*
021020 01  DR-DATE-RECORD REDEFINES SR-SALES-RECORD.
021030     05  DR-RECORD-CODE            PIC X(2).
021040         88  DATE-RECORD                         VALUE '01'.
021050     05  DR-PERIOD-ENDING-DATE     PIC X(6).
021060     05  FILLER                    PIC X(72).
030010*
030020 01  H1-HEADING-LINE-1.
030030     05  FILLER           PIC X(1).
030040     05  FILLER           PIC X(20)  VALUE 'PYRAMID SALES COMPAN'.
030050     05  FILLER           PIC X(20)  VALUE 'Y                   '.
030060     05  FILLER           PIC X(20)  VALUE '                  PE'.
030070     05  FILLER           PIC X(17)  VALUE 'RIOD ENDING DATE '.
030080     05  H1-PER-END-DATE PIC XX/XX/XX.
030090     05  FILLER           PIC X(47)  VALUE SPACES.
031010*
031020 01  H2-HEADING-LINE-2.
031030     05  FILLER           PIC X(1).
031040     05  FILLER           PIC X(20)  VALUE 'SALES REPORT - SEQUE'.
031050     05  FILLER           PIC X(20)  VALUE 'NCED BY STATE, BRANC'.
031060     05  FILLER           PIC X(20)  VALUE 'H, SALES REP.     PA'.
031070     05  FILLER           PIC X(03)  VALUE 'GE '.
031080     05  H2-PAGE-NBR      PIC ZZZ9.
031090     05  FILLER           PIC X(10)  VALUE     ' RUN DATE '.
031100     05  H2-MONTH         PIC 9(2).
031110     05  FILLER           PIC X(1)   VALUE '/'.
031120     05  H2-DAY           PIC 9(2).
031130     05  FILLER           PIC X(1)   VALUE '/'.
031140     05  H2-YEAR          PIC 9(2).
031150     05  FILLER           PIC X(47)  VALUE SPACES.
032010*
032020 01  H3-HEADING-LINE-3.
032030     05  FILLER           PIC X(1).
032040     05  FILLER           PIC X(20)  VALUE '            SALES   '.
032050     05  FILLER           PIC X(20)  VALUE '   DATE    PRODUCT  '.
032060     05  FILLER           PIC X(20)  VALUE ' PRODUCT         UN '.
032070     05  FILLER           PIC X(20)  VALUE 'IT QTY.    SALES    '.
032080     05  FILLER           PIC X(20)  VALUE '                   '.
032090     05  FILLER           PIC X(20)  VALUE '                   '.
032100     05  FILLER           PIC X(12)  VALUE '           '.
033010*
033020 01  H4-HEADING-LINE-4.
033030     05  FILLER           PIC X(1).
033040     05  FILLER           PIC X(20)  VALUE 'STATE BRANCH REP.   '.
033050     05  FILLER           PIC X(20)  VALUE ' OF SALE   CODE    D'.
033060     05  FILLER           PIC X(20)  VALUE 'ESCRIPTION       PRI'.
033070     05  FILLER           PIC X(20)  VALUE 'CE SOLD    REVENUE  '.
033080     05  FILLER           PIC X(20)  VALUE '                   '.
033090     05  FILLER           PIC X(20)  VALUE '                   '.
033100     05  FILLER           PIC X(12)  VALUE '           '.
034010*
034020 01  DL-DETAIL-LINE.
034030     05  FILLER                    PIC X(1).
034040     05  FILLER                    PIC X(1)   VALUE SPACES.
034050     05  DL-STATE                  PIC X(2).
034060     05  FILLER                    PIC X(4)   VALUE SPACES.
034070     05  DL-BRANCH                 PIC X(3).
034080     05  FILLER                    PIC X(3)   VALUE SPACES.
034090     05  DL-SALES-REP              PIC X(5).
034100     05  FILLER                    PIC X(2)   VALUE SPACES.
034110     05  DL-DATE-OF-SALE           PIC XX/XX/XX.
034120     05  FILLER                    PIC X(2)   VALUE SPACES.
034130     05  DL-PRODUCT-CODE           PIC X(7).
034140     05  FILLER                    PIC X(2)   VALUE SPACES.
034150     05  DL-PRODUCT-DESCRIPTION    PIC X(16).
034160     05  FILLER                    PIC X(2)   VALUE SPACES.
034170     05  DL-UNIT-PRICE             PIC ZZ.99.
034180     05  FILLER                    PIC X(2)   VALUE SPACES.
034190     05  DL-QUANTITY-SOLD          PIC ZZ9-.
034200     05  FILLER                    PIC X(2)   VALUE SPACES.
034210     05  DL-SALES-REVENUE          PIC ZZ,ZZZ.99-.
034220     05  FILLER                    PIC X(52)  VALUE SPACES.
035010*
035020 01  CT-CONTROL-TOTAL-LINE.
035030     05  FILLER                    PIC X(1).
035040     05  FILLER                    PIC X(1)   VALUE SPACES.
035050     05  CT-STATE                  PIC X(2).
035060     05  FILLER                    PIC X(4)   VALUE SPACES.
035070     05  CT-BRANCH                 PIC X(3).
035080     05  FILLER                    PIC X(3)   VALUE SPACES.
035090     05  CT-SALES-REP              PIC X(5).
035100     05  FILLER                    PIC X(15)  VALUE SPACES.
035110     05  CT-TOTAL-DESCRIPTION      PIC X(10) JUSTIFIED RIGHT.
035120     05  FILLER                    PIC X(6)   VALUE ' TOTAL'.
035130     05  FILLER                    PIC X(20)  VALUE SPACES.
035140     05  CT-SALES-REVENUE          PIC ZZZ,ZZZ.99-.
035150     05  CT-ASTERISKS              PIC X(3).
035160     05  FILLER                    PIC X(49)  VALUE SPACES.
036010*
036020 01  RT-REPORT-TOTAL-LINE.
036030     05  FILLER                    PIC X(1).
036040     05  FILLER                    PIC X(50)  VALUE SPACES.
036090     05  FILLER                    PIC X(12) VALUE 'REPORT TOTAL'.
036100     05  FILLER                    PIC X(5)   VALUE SPACES.
036110     05  RT-SALES-REVENUE          PIC Z,ZZZ,ZZZ.99-.
036120     05  FILLER                    PIC X(4)   VALUE '****'.
036130     05  FILLER                    PIC X(48)  VALUE SPACES.
```

Figure 10.33. IDENTIFICATION, ENVIRONMENT, and DATA divisions: M-SLSRPT program

```
        *
        01  WS-REPORT-CONTROLS.
            05  WS-PAGE-COUNT                       PIC S9(4)           COMP-3.
            05  WS-LINES-PER-PAGE                   PIC S99 VALUE +54
                                                                        COMP SYNC.
            05  WS-LINES-USED                       PIC S9(2)           COMP SYNC.
            05  WS-LINE-SPACING                     PIC S9(2).
        *
        01  WS-WORK-AREAS.
            05  WS-DATE-WORK                        PIC 9(6).
            05  WS-DATE-CONVERSION REDEFINES WS-DATE-WORK.
                10  WS-YEAR                         PIC 9(2).
                10  WS-MONTH                        PIC 9(2).
                10  WS-DAY                          PIC 9(2).
            05  WS-SALES-REVENUE                    PIC S9(5)V99        COMP-3.
        *
        01  WS-TOTAL-ACCUMULATORS.
            05  WS-TOTAL-SALES-REP-ACCUM            PIC S9(6)V99        COMP-3.
            05  WS-TOTAL-BRANCH-ACCUM               PIC S9(6)V99        COMP-3.
            05  WS-TOTAL-STATE-ACCUM                PIC S9(6)V99        COMP-3.
            05  WS-TOTAL-REPORT-ACCUM               PIC S9(7)V99        COMP-3.
```

Figure 10.34. USAGE clause selection

Coding the WORKING-STORAGE SECTION of the DATA DIVISION

Two additional fields have been added to the WS-CONTROL-FIELDS area: WS-PREVIOUS-STATE and WS-PREVIOUS-BRANCH. Observe that the individual control fields have been sequenced in major to minor order. That is, the major control field, WS-PREVIOUS-STATE, is specified first; the intermediate control field, WS-PREVIOUS-BRANCH, is second; and the minor control field, WS-PREVIOUS-SALES-REP is specified last. Although such major through minor ordering is not really necessary in this program, it is logically sound to specify the fields in such sequence. Further, such placement of control or sort fields can simplify coding should sequence-checking of the control or sort fields be required.

To the WS-TOTAL-ACCUMULATORS area, the additional total fields of WS-TOTAL-BRANCH-ACCUM and WS-TOTAL-STATE-ACCUM have been added. Here, the control total accumulation fields have been specified in minor to major order. Again, a specific arrangement is not necessary, but such minor to major sequence best depicts the hierarchy of totals as it will appear on the report.

USAGE clauses

USAGE clauses have been specified for appropriate numeric fields. Figure 10.34 indicates how such usages were chosen. Notice that all the WS-TOTAL-ACCUMULATORS fields have been assigned a COMP-3 usage. As shown in Figure 10.35, the exact same usage specifications could be obtained by assigning the USAGE clause to the group field WS-TOTAL-ACCUMULATORS and omitting the USAGE clause from the elementary item descriptions. Such specification at the group level causes all elementary fields within the group to be of the specified usage.

Date record

The format of the date record has been specified as the DR-DATE-RECORD record-description. These data-item descriptions will be used to obtain the period-ending date from the date record. Notice that the DR-DATE-RECORD has been specified with a REDEFINES clause, which causes it to occupy the same storage locations as the SR-SALES-RECORD. This has been done because (1) the READ statement INTO phrase causes all records from the input file to be placed in the SR-SALES-RECORD area, and (2) since the date record should

Part A: USAGE specified on elementary items:

```
01   WS-TOTAL-ACCUMULATORS.
     05   WS-TOTAL-SALES-REP-ACCUM              PIC  S9(6)V99        COMP-3.
     05   WS-TOTAL-BRANCH-ACCUM.                PIC  S9(6)V99        COMP-3.
     05   WS-TOTAL-STATE-ACCUM                  PIC  S9(6)V99        COMP-3.
     05   WS-TOTAL-REPORT-ACCUM                 PIC  S9(7)V99        COMP-3.
```

Part B: USAGE specified on group item (applies to each elementary item in the group):

```
01   WS-TOTAL-ACCUMULATORS                                          COMP-3.
     05   WS-TOTAL-SALES-REP-ACCUM              PIC  S9(6)V99.
     05   WS-TOTAL-BRANCH-ACCUM                 PIC  S9(6)V99.
     05   WS-TOTAL-STATE-ACCUM                  PIC  S9(6)V99.
     05   WS-TOTAL-REPORT-ACCUM                 PIC  S9(7)V99.
```

Figure 10.35. Comparison of elementary and group item USAGE clause specification

always be the first record of the file and because it will not be required after the date has been obtained from it, there is no need to retain the date record in storage. Hence, the same storage area can be used to process both the date record and the sales records.

Report line changes

The following changes have been made to the report lines.

H1-HEADING-LINE-1   The constant words "PERIOD ENDING DATE" have been added, together with the variable field H1-PER-END-DATE.

H2-HEADING-LINE-2   The report title has been changed to indicate the multiple-level control sequence.

DL-DETAIL-LINE   The arrangement of the DL-SALES-REP, DL-STATE, and DL-BRANCH fields have been changed to reflect the sequence specified in the print chart.

CT-CONTROL-TOTAL-LINE   This line is equivalent to the ST-SALES-REP-TOTAL-LINE of the single-level sales report. The prefix has been changed to CT and the CT-STATE and CT-BRANCH fields have been added to show the applicable state and branch on the total-line. Also, the constant describing the total: "SALES REP TOTAL" has been shortened to just "TOTAL". A variable field, CT-TOTAL-DESCRIPTION, has been added to contain the description of which total is being printed: state, branch, or sales representative.

Of course, instead of specifying just one control break-total-line, a separate line for each of the three control totals could have been specified as shown in Figure 10.36. By providing for all three lines with just one line definition, a bit of a coding shortcut has been taken. In the PROCEDURE DIVISION, though, additional statements must be provided to move the correct description and asterisks to the line.

Such a shortcut is acceptable, given these specifications. If the three total-lines had been significantly different in format, however, it would have been better to describe each separately.

RT-REPORT-TOTAL-LINE   The number of asterisks following the report total has been increased in accordance with the print chart specifications. The length of the FILLER area has been correspondingly decreased.

Part A: Common control break total-line record-definition:

```
*
01  CT-CONTROL-TOTAL-LINE.
    05  FILLER                 PIC X(1).
    05  FILLER                 PIC X(1)    VALUE SPACES.
    05  CT-STATE               PIC X(2).
    05  FILLER                 PIC X(4)    VALUE SPACES.
    05  CT-BRANCH              PIC X(3).
    05  FILLER                 PIC X(3)    VALUE SPACES.
    05  CT-SALES-REP           PIC X(5).
    05  FILLER                 PIC X(15)   VALUE SPACES.
    05  CT-TOTAL-DESCRIPTION   PIC X(10) JUSTIFIED RIGHT.
    05  FILLER                 PIC X(6)    VALUE ' TOTAL'.
    05  FILLER                 PIC X(20)   VALUE SPACES.
    05  CT-SALES-REVENUE       PIC ZZZ,ZZZ.99-.
    05  CT-ASTERISKS           PIC X(3).
    05  FILLER                 PIC X(49)   VALUE SPACES.
```

Part B: Separate control break total-line record-definitions:

```
*
01  RT-SALES-REP-TOTAL-LINE.
    05  FILLER                 PIC X(1).
    05  FILLER                 PIC X(1)    VALUE SPACES.
    05  RT-STATE               PIC X(2).
    05  FILLER                 PIC X(4)    VALUE SPACES.
    05  RT-BRANCH              PIC X(3).
    05  FILLER                 PIC X(3)    VALUE SPACES.
    05  RT-SALES-REP           PIC X(5).
    05  FILLER                 PIC X(15)   VALUE SPACES.
    05  FILLER                 PIC X(16)
                               VALUE 'SALES REP. TOTAL'.
    05  FILLER                 PIC X(20)   VALUE SPACES.
    05  RT-SALES-REVENUE       PIC ZZZ,ZZZ.99-.
    05  FILLER                 PIC X(1)    VALUE '*'.
    05  FILLER                 PIC X(51)   VALUE SPACES.
*
01  BT-BRANCH-TOTAL-LINE.
    05  FILLER                 PIC X(1).
    05  FILLER                 PIC X(1)    VALUE SPACES.
    05  BT-STATE               PIC X(2).
    05  FILLER                 PIC X(4)    VALUE SPACES.
    05  BT-BRANCH              PIC X(8).
    05  FILLER                 PIC X(3)    VALUE SPACES.
    05  FILLER                 PIC X(18)   VALUE SPACES.
    05  FILLER                 PIC X(16)
                               VALUE '   BRANCH TOTAL'.
    05  FILLER                 PIC X(20)   VALUE SPACES.
    05  BT-SALES-REVENUE       PIC ZZZ,ZZZ.99-.
    05  FILLER                 PIC X(2)    VALUE '**'.
    05  FILLER                 PIC X(50)   VALUE SPACES.
*
01  ST-STATE-TOTAL-LINE.
    05  FILLER                 PIC X(1).
    05  FILLER                 PIC X(1)    VALUE SPACES.
    05  ST-STATE               PIC X(2).
    05  FILLER                 PIC X(30)   VALUE SPACES.
    05  FILLER                 PIC X(16)
                               VALUE '   STATE TOTAL'.
    05  FILLER                 PIC X(20)   VALUE SPACES.
    05  ST-SALES-REVENUE       PIC ZZZ,ZZZ.99-.
    05  FILLER                 PIC X(3)    VALUE '***'.
    05  FILLER                 PIC X(49)   VALUE SPACES.
```

Figure 10.36. Alternate methods of handling control break total lines

Coding the PROCEDURE DIVISION

The PROCEDURE DIVISION for the M-SLSRPT program is shown in Figure
10.37. Each of the modules that contains changes will be discussed.

100-INITIALIZE-VARIABLE-FIELDS

There are two important changes in this module: the initialization of the
COMP-3 fields and the date record processing.

COMP-3 (and COMP) field initialization   Previous programs of this text have used
only DISPLAY usage. When there were multiple elementary DISPLAY usage
fields to be initialized to zero within one group item, it was accomplished by
moving zeros to the group item. With COMP-3 and COMP usages, however,
moving zeros to the group item will not produce the correct effect. This is
because of the MOVE statement rules. That is, when data is moved to a group
field, it is treated as an alphanumeric move. This causes alphanumeric—not
numeric—zeros to be moved to the group field. Alphanumeric zeros do not have
the same data representation as numeric zeros within COMP-3 and COMP

```
050010*                                          220090      MOVE WS-TOTAL-SALES-REP-ACCUM TO CT-SALES-REVENUE.
050020*                                          220100      MOVE '*  ' TO CT-ASTERISKS.
050030*                                          220110      MOVE CT-CONTROL-TOTAL-LINE TO SALES-REPORT-LINE.
050040 PROCEDURE DIVISION.                        220120      MOVE 2 TO WS-LINE-SPACING.
050050*                                          220130      PERFORM 890-PRINT-REPORT-LINE.
050060*                                          220140      MOVE 3 TO WS-LINE-SPACING.
050070 000-PRINT-SALES-REPORT.                   220150      ADD WS-TOTAL-SALES-REP-ACCUM TO WS-TOTAL-BRANCH-ACCUM.
050080*                                          220160      MOVE ZEROS TO WS-TOTAL-SALES-REP-ACCUM.
050090      OPEN INPUT SALES-FILE                 220170      MOVE SR-SALES-REP TO WS-PREVIOUS-SALES-REP.
050100           OUTPUT SALES-REPORT.            230010*
050110      PERFORM 100-INITIALIZE-VARIABLE-FIELDS.  230020*
050120      PERFORM 200-PROCESS-SALES-RECORD      230030 230-PRINT-BRANCH-TOTAL-LINE.
050130           UNTIL WS-END-OF-FILE-SWITCH IS EQUAL TO 'YES'.  230040*
050140      PERFORM 700-PRINT-REPORT-TOTAL-LINE.  230050      MOVE SPACES TO CT-SALES-REP.
050150      CLOSE SALES-FILE                      230060      MOVE 'BRANCH' TO CT-TOTAL-DESCRIPTION.
050160           SALES-REPORT.                   230070      MOVE WS-TOTAL-BRANCH-ACCUM TO CT-SALES-REVENUE.
050170      STOP RUN.                             230080      MOVE '** ' TO CT-ASTERISKS.
100010*                                          230090      MOVE CT-CONTROL-TOTAL-LINE TO SALES-REPORT-LINE.
100020*                                          230100      MOVE 2 TO WS-LINE-SPACING.
100030 100-INITIALIZE-VARIABLE-FIELDS.           230110      PERFORM 890-PRINT-REPORT-LINE.
100040*                                          230120      MOVE 3 TO WS-LINE-SPACING.
100050      MOVE 'NO ' TO WS-END-OF-FILE-SWITCH.  230130      ADD WS-TOTAL-BRANCH-ACCUM TO WS-TOTAL-STATE-ACCUM.
100060      MOVE 'YES' TO WS-FIRST-RECORD-SWITCH.  230140      MOVE ZEROS TO WS-TOTAL-BRANCH-ACCUM.
100070      MOVE ZEROS TO WS-PAGE-COUNT.          230150      MOVE SR-BRANCH TO WS-PREVIOUS-BRANCH.
100080      ADD 1 WS-LINES-PER-PAGE GIVING WS-LINES-USED.  240010*
100090      ACCEPT WS-DATE-WORK FROM DATE.        240020*
100100      MOVE WS-MONTH TO H2-MONTH.            240030 240-PRINT-STATE-TOTAL-LINE.
100110      MOVE WS-DAY TO H2-DAY.                240040*
100120      MOVE WS-YEAR TO H2-YEAR.              240050      MOVE SPACES TO CT-BRANCH.
100130      MOVE ZEROS TO WS-TOTAL-SALES-REP-ACCUM  240060      MOVE 'STATE' TO CT-TOTAL-DESCRIPTION.
100140                    WS-TOTAL-BRANCH-ACCUM   240070      MOVE WS-TOTAL-STATE-ACCUM TO CT-SALES-REVENUE.
100150                    WS-TOTAL-STATE-ACCUM    240080      MOVE '***' TO CT-ASTERISKS.
100160                    WS-TOTAL-REPORT-ACCUM.  240090      MOVE CT-CONTROL-TOTAL-LINE TO SALES-REPORT-LINE.
100170      PERFORM 800-READ-SALES-RECORD.        240100      MOVE 2 TO WS-LINE-SPACING.
100180      IF DATE-RECORD                        240110      PERFORM 890-PRINT-REPORT-LINE.
100190           MOVE DR-PERIOD-ENDING-DATE TO H1-PER-END-DATE  240120      MOVE 3 TO WS-LINE-SPACING.
100200      ELSE                                  240130      ADD WS-TOTAL-STATE-ACCUM TO WS-TOTAL-REPORT-ACCUM.
100210           MOVE 'YES' TO WS-END-OF-FILE-SWITCH.  240140      MOVE ZEROS TO WS-TOTAL-STATE-ACCUM.
200010*                                          240150      MOVE SR-STATE TO WS-PREVIOUS-STATE.
200020*                                          700010*
200030 200-PROCESS-SALES-RECORD.                 700020*
200040*                                          700030 700-PRINT-REPORT-TOTAL-LINE.
200050      PERFORM 800-READ-SALES-RECORD.        700040*
200060      IF FIRST-RECORD                       700050      MOVE WS-TOTAL-REPORT-ACCUM TO RT-SALES-REVENUE.
200070           MOVE SR-STATE TO WS-PREVIOUS-STATE  700060      MOVE RT-REPORT-TOTAL-LINE TO SALES-REPORT-LINE.
200080           MOVE SR-BRANCH TO WS-PREVIOUS-BRANCH  700070      MOVE 3 TO WS-LINE-SPACING.
200090           MOVE SR-SALES-REP TO WS-PREVIOUS-SALES-REP  700080      PERFORM 890-PRINT-REPORT-LINE.
200100           MOVE 'NO ' TO WS-FIRST-RECORD-SWITCH.  800010*
200110      IF SR-STATE IS NOT EQUAL TO WS-PREVIOUS-STATE  800020*
200120           PERFORM 220-PRINT-SALES-REP-TOTAL-LINE  800030 800-READ-SALES-RECORD.
200130           PERFORM 230-PRINT-BRANCH-TOTAL-LINE  800040*
200140           PERFORM 240-PRINT-STATE-TOTAL-LINE  800050      READ SALES-FILE INTO SR-SALES-RECORD
200150      ELSE IF SR-BRANCH IS NOT EQUAL TO WS-PREVIOUS-BRANCH  800060           AT END MOVE 'YES' TO WS-END-OF-FILE-SWITCH.
200160           PERFORM 220-PRINT-SALES-REP-TOTAL-LINE  800070                MOVE HIGH-VALUES TO SR-STATE
200170           PERFORM 230-PRINT-BRANCH-TOTAL-LINE  800080                                    SR-BRANCH
200180      ELSE IF SR-SALES-REP IS NOT EQUAL TO WS-PREVIOUS-SALES-REP  800090                                    SR-SALES-REP.
200190           PERFORM 220-PRINT-SALES-REP-TOTAL-LINE  870010*
200200      IF NOT END-OF-FILE                    870020*
200210           PERFORM 210-PRINT-DETAIL-LINE.   870030 870-PRINT-REPORT-HEADINGS.
210010*                                          870040*
210020*                                          870050      ADD 1 TO WS-PAGE-COUNT.
210030 210-PRINT-DETAIL-LINE.                    870060      MOVE WS-PAGE-COUNT TO H2-PAGE-NBR.
210040*                                          870070      MOVE H1-HEADING-LINE-1 TO SALES-REPORT-LINE.
210050      IF WS-LINES-USED IS GREATER THAN WS-LINES-PER-PAGE  870080      PERFORM 880-WRITE-REPORT-TOP-LINE.
210060           PERFORM 870-PRINT-REPORT-HEADINGS.  870090      MOVE H2-HEADING-LINE-2 TO SALES-REPORT-LINE.
210070      MOVE SR-SALES-REP TO DL-SALES-REP.    870100      MOVE 1 TO WS-LINE-SPACING.
210080      MOVE SR-STATE TO DL-STATE.            870110      PERFORM 890-WRITE-REPORT-LINE.
210090      MOVE SR-BRANCH TO DL-BRANCH.          870120      MOVE H3-HEADING-LINE-3 TO SALES-REPORT-LINE.
210100      MOVE SR-DATE-OF-SALE TO DL-DATE-OF-SALE.  870130      MOVE 2 TO WS-LINE-SPACING.
210110      MOVE SR-PRODUCT-CODE TO DL-PRODUCT-CODE.  870140      PERFORM 890-WRITE-REPORT-LINE.
210120      MOVE SR-PRODUCT-DESCRIPTION TO DL-PRODUCT-DESCRIPTION.  870150      MOVE H4-HEADING-LINE-4 TO SALES-REPORT-LINE.
210120      MOVE SR-UNIT-PRICE TO DL-UNIT-PRICE.  870160      MOVE 1 TO WS-LINE-SPACING.
210130      MOVE SR-QUANTITY-SOLD TO DL-QUANTITY-SOLD.  870170      PERFORM 890-WRITE-REPORT-LINE.
210140      MULTIPLY SR-UNIT-PRICE BY SR-QUANTITY-SOLD  870180      MOVE 2 TO WS-LINE-SPACING.
210150           GIVING WS-SALES-REVENUE ROUNDED.  880010*
210160      MOVE WS-SALES-REVENUE TO DL-SALES-REVENUE.  880020*
210170      MOVE DL-DETAIL-LINE TO SALES-REPORT-LINE.  880030 880-WRITE-REPORT-TOP-LINE.
210180      PERFORM 890-PRINT-REPORT-LINE.        880040*
210190      MOVE 1 TO WS-LINE-SPACING.            880050      WRITE SALES-REPORT-LINE
210200      ADD WS-SALES-REVENUE TO WS-TOTAL-SALES-REP-ACCUM.  880060           AFTER ADVANCING PAGE.
220010*                                          880070      MOVE 1 TO WS-LINES-USED.
220020*                                          890010*
220030 220-PRINT-SALES-REP-TOTAL-LINE.           890020*
220040*                                          890030 890-WRITE-REPORT-LINE.
220050      MOVE WS-PREVIOUS-STATE TO CT-STATE.   890040*
220060      MOVE WS-PREVIOUS-BRANCH TO CT-BRANCH.  890050      WRITE SALES-REPORT-LINE
220070      MOVE WS-PREVIOUS-SALES-REP TO CT-SALES-REP.  890060           AFTER ADVANCING WS-LINE-SPACING.
220080      MOVE 'SALES REP.' TO CT-TOTAL-DESCRIPTION.  890070      ADD WS-LINE-SPACING TO WS-LINES-USED.
```

Figure 10.37. PROCEDURE DIVISION: M-SLSRPT program

fields and thus the elementary fields will not be initialized correctly to zero. This concept is illustrated in Figure 10.38.

So, to properly initialize COMP-3 and COMP fields to zero, the zeros must be moved to each elementary field, not to the group field.

Date record handling   Date records are often used to provide a period-ending date for report headings; it is common for them to be specified as the first record of a file. Since the date record is expected to be the first record of the file, the READ module is performed from this 100-INITIALIZE-VARIABLE-FIELDS module.

Part A: Result of moving ZEROS to a group field
(incorrect initialization of COMP-3 fields with alphanumeric zeros):

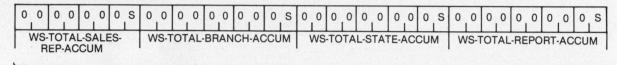

| Z | 0 | Z | 0 | Z | 0 | Z | 0 | Z | 0 | Z | 0 | Z | 0 | Z | 0 | Z | 0 | Z | 0 | Z | 0 | Z | 0 | Z | 0 | Z | 0 | Z | 0 | Z | 0 | Z | 0 | Z | 0 |

| WS-TOTAL-SALES-REP-ACCUM | WS-TOTAL-BRANCH-ACCUM | WS-TOTAL-STATE-ACCUM | WS-TOTAL-REPORT-ACCUM |

WS-TOTAL-ACCUMULATORS

Part B: Result of moving ZEROS to the elementary COMP-3 fields
(correct initialization in accordance with COMP-3 format):

| 0 | 0 | 0 | 0 | 0 | 0 | 0 | S | 0 | 0 | 0 | 0 | 0 | 0 | 0 | 0 | 0 | S | 0 | 0 | 0 | 0 | 0 | 0 | 0 | 0 | 0 | S | 0 | 0 | 0 | 0 | 0 | 0 | 0 | 0 | 0 | S |

| WS-TOTAL-SALES-REP-ACCUM | WS-TOTAL-BRANCH-ACCUM | WS-TOTAL-STATE-ACCUM | WS-TOTAL-REPORT-ACCUM |

WS-TOTAL-ACCUMULATORS

S = Sign representation
Z = Alphanumeric zero zone representation
0 = Zero

Figure 10.38. Initialization of COMP-3 fields to zero

The program then checks to see if a date record has actually been read. This is accomplished by the IF DATE-RECORD test. If the first record read is correctly coded as a date record (DR-RECORD-CODE = 01), the date will be moved from the DR-PERIOD-ENDING-DATE field to the H1-PER-END-DATE field. If the record is not coded as a date record, WS-END-OF-FILE switch will be set to "YES"; this will abnormally terminate the program, preventing it from processing the current record or any other records in the file.

When a date record is required within a program, it is very important to ensure that it is actually present. If, for example, the program did not provide for such record checking and, through oversight or error, the date record was omitted for a particular program run, the first sales record would be processed as a date record. This would, of course, cause serious processing errors.

Actually, rather than just cause the program to terminate as has been done in this program, we should print a message explaining why the program has been terminated. For simplicity within this example, however, this has not been done.

200-PROCESS-SALES-RECORD module

When there are multiple control fields, each one of the previous control fields must be set when the first record is processed, as has been done in this module.

The test for a control break in a multiple-level control break program is more complicated than that for a single-level control break. A proper nested IF statement must be established and the control totals must be performed in the proper sequence.

Establishment of a proper nested IF for multiple-level control break programs This nested IF can be written as either a linear or a nonlinear IF. Figure 10.39 contrasts the two forms. A linear IF is usually easier to understand, so it has been used in the M-SLSRPT program.

The tricky aspect of establishing the control break test is the determination of which control field should be tested first. The rule is simple, though: always test the major field first and then proceed testing each field in descend-

Part A: Linear IF control break test:

```
IF SR-STATE IS NOT EQUAL TO WS-PREVIOUS-STATE
    PERFORM 220-PRINT-SALES-REP-TOTAL-LINE
    PERFORM 230-PRINT-BRANCH-TOTAL-LINE
    PERFORM 240-PRINT-STATE-TOTAL-LINE
ELSE IF SR-BRANCH IS NOT EQUAL TO WS-PREVIOUS-BRANCH
    PERFORM 220-PRINT-SALES-REP-TOTAL-LINE
    PERFORM 230-PRINT-BRANCH-TOTAL-LINE
ELSE IF SR-SALES-REP IS NOT EQUAL TO WS-PREVIOUS-SALES-REP
    PERFORM 220-PRINT-SALES-REP-TOTAL-LINE.
```

Part B: Non-linear IF control break test:

```
IF SR-STATE IS EQUAL TO WS-PREVIOUS-STATE
    IF SR-BRANCH IS EQUAL TO WS-PREVIOUS-BRANCH
        IF SR-SALES-REP IS EQUAL TO WS-PREVIOUS-SALES-REP
            NEXT SENTENCE
        ELSE
            PERFORM 220-PRINT-SALES-REP-TOTAL-LINE
    ELSE
        PERFORM 220-PRINT-SALES-REP-TOTAL-LINE
        PERFORM 230-PRINT-BRANCH-TOTAL-LINE
ELSE
    PERFORM 220-PRINT-SALES-REP-TOTAL-LINE
    PERFORM 230-PRINT-BRANCH-TOTAL-LINE
    PERFORM 240-PRINT-STATE-TOTAL-LINE.
```

Figure 10.39. Comparison of multiple-level control break test with linear and non-linear IF statements

ing significance down through the minor field. Thus, in this M-SLSRPT program, the major field SR-STATE is tested first; the intermediate field SR-BRANCH is tested second; and the minor field SR-SALES-REP is tested last.

Someone who is not familiar with this rule regarding multiple-level control break tests might incorrectly construct the test from minor to major rather than major to minor. The erroneous effect of constructing the test from minor to major is shown in Figure 10.40.

This erroneous control break test:

```
IF SR-SALES-REP IS NOT EQUAL TO WS-PREVIOUS-SALES-REP
    PERFORM 220-PRINT-SALES-REP-TOTAL-LINE
ELSE IF SR-BRANCH IS NOT EQUAL TO WS-PREVIOUS-BRANCH
    PERFORM 220-PRINT-SALES-REP-TOTAL-LINE
    PERFORM 230-PRINT-BRANCH-TOTAL-LINE
ELSE IF SR-STATE IS NOT EQUAL TO WS-PREVIOUS-STATE
    PERFORM 220-PRINT-SALES-REP-TOTAL-LINE
    PERFORM 230-PRINT-BRANCH-TOTAL-LINE
    PERFORM 240-PRINT-STATE-TOTAL-LINE.
```

will not detect a State or Branch control break such as this:

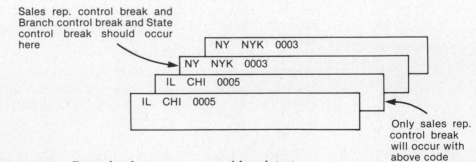

Sales rep. control break and Branch control break and State control break should occur here

```
                    NY  NYK  0003
                NY  NYK  0003
            IL  CHI  0005
        IL  CHI  0005
```

Only sales rep. control break will occur with above code

Figure 10.40. Example of erroneous control break test

Control total sequence   Although the control break test is done in major to minor sequence, the printing of the control totals must be performed in minor to major sequence. Each of the control breaks, starting with the minor control field, should be performed up to the level of the control break detected.

For example, when a Branch control break occurs, first the module 220-PRINT-SALES-REP-TOTAL-LINE is performed and then the 230-PRINT-BRANCH-TOTAL-LINE module is performed.

220-PRINT-SALES-REP-TOTAL-LINE, 230-PRINT-BRANCH-TOTAL-LINE, and 240-PRINT-STATE-TOTAL-LINE modules

Each of these modules handles the following:

1. Indication of the proper control fields (CT-SALES-REP, CT-BRANCH, CT-STATE) on the CT-CONTROL-TOTAL-LINE is provided.

2. The type of control break line (SALES REP, BRANCH, STATE) is moved to the CT-CONTROL-TOTAL-LINE.

3. The proper number of asterisks to indicate the respective control break total is moved to the CT-CONTROL-TOTAL-LINE.

4. The respective control break total accumulation (WS-TOTAL-SALES-REP-ACCUM, WS-TOTAL-BRANCH-ACCUM, or WS-TOTAL-STATE-ACCUM) is moved to the CT-CONTROL-TOTAL-LINE.

5. The CT-CONTROL-TOTAL-LINE is moved to the output SALES-REPORT-LINE.

6. The WS-LINE-SPACING field is set to double-space the control break total-line from the previous report line.

7. The 890-WRITE-REPORT-LINE module is performed.

8. The WS-LINE-SPACING field is set to triple-spacing for the next detail-line (or report total-line).

9. The respective control break total accumulation is added to the next more major control total accumulation (WS-TOTAL-BRANCH-ACCUM, WS-TOTAL-STATE-ACCUM, or WS-TOTAL-REPORT-ACCUM).

10. The respective control break total accumulation, which has just been printed, is set to zero.

11. The respective previous control break key (WS-PREVIOUS-SALES-REP, WS-PREVIOUS-BRANCH, or WS-PREVIOUS-STATE) is set from the current input record that caused the control break.

Items 1 and 8, above, deserve a bit more explanation.

Indication of the proper control fields   A Sales-representative control break line applies to that sales-representative number within that branch within that state; a Branch control break total-line applies to that branch within that state; a State control break total-line applies to that state. Hence, on the Sales-representative control break total-line, the state, branch and sales representative number should be printed for identification; on the Branch control break total-line the state and branch—but not the sales-representative number—should be displayed; and, on the State control break total-line, only the state should be printed.

This is accomplished by moving all three control fields (WS-PREVIOUS-STATE, WS-PREVIOUS-BRANCH, and WS-PREVIOUS-SALES-REP) to the respective CT-CONTROL-TOTAL-LINE field (CT-STATE, CT-BRANCH, and CT-SALES-REP) at the time of the Sales-representative control break total-line. Then, when a Branch control break total-line is to be printed, the state and branch are already in the CT-STATE and CT-BRANCH fields of the line; the sales-representative number is blanked out by moving SPACES to the CT-SALES-REP field. Similarly, when a State control break total-line is required, the CT-BRANCH is blanked.

Setting of WS-LINE-SPACING for triple-spacing of the next detail-line (or report total-line)   The first detail-line for a particular sales representative is to be triple-spaced from the last control break total-line printed. Therefore, the WS-LINE-SPACING field is set for triple-spacing immediately after a control break total-line is printed in case there are no subsequent control break total-lines to be printed prior to the next detail-line. If there are one or more control break total-lines to be printed, each control break total module resets the WS-LINE-SPACING field back to double-spacing before the control break total-line is printed.

This logic also ensures that the report total-line is triple-spaced from the last control break total-line. Also, it handles properly the situation where the first detail-line for a particular sales representative occurs as the first line after the headings. When this happens, it is visually appropriate to retain the normal condition where the first detail-line is double-spaced from the last heading-line.

800-READ-SALES-RECORD module

Upon detecting end-of-file, each of the control fields (SR-STATE, SR-BRANCH, and SR-SALES-REP) must be set to HIGH-VALUES to trigger the control breaks for the last record.

Summary

Input records for a control break program must be sorted into the correct sequence for the control breaks. When programming a control break program, the programmer must provide logic to (1) bypass the false or null control break that will occur when the first record is processed, and (2) force the last control break after all records have been processed.

Multiple-level control break programs show increased complexity over single-level control break programs in two areas: in the test for a control break and in the need to provide additional control break line-printing modules. When making the test for a multiple-level control break program, always test the major control field first and then proceed testing each field in descending significance down through the minor field. The sequence in which the control break modules should be performed is in minor through major order up to the level of the control break detected.

Date records are frequently used to provide a period-ending date for report headings and the like. When a date record is required within a program, the program logic must test the record code to ensure that the date record is actually present. Otherwise, erroneous processing may occur.

The USAGE clause may be specified with the data-item description entry of a field in the DATA DIVISION. Commonly used usages are DISPLAY, COMPUTATIONAL (COMP), and COMPUTATIONAL-3 (COMP-3). Although COMPUTATIONAL-3 is not an ANS COBOL standard, it is frequently specified with IBM-compatible COBOL compilers. If no USAGE clause is specified with a data-item description entry, USAGE IS DISPLAY is assumed.

DISPLAY usage is the basic form in which each computer or storage medium position contains one character of data. Both alphanumeric and numeric data can be represented with DISPLAY usage. COMP and COMP-3 usage may be specified for numeric fields. When COMP is specified for fields in WORKING-STORAGE that are not part of input or output records, the SYNC clause should be specified to obtain optimum processing efficiency.

It is usually more efficient to specify COMP or COMP-3 usage for WORKING-STORAGE fields involved in arithmetic calculations or numeric comparisons. Input data from punched cards or certain other input devices must be of DISPLAY usage within their initial record description entry. Data fields to be printed on reports or displayed on video-display terminal screens must be ultimately converted to DISPLAY usage for print-out or display.

When initializing COMP or COMP-3 fields by moving zeros to them in the PROCEDURE DIVISION, be certain to move the zero value to each elementary, not the group, data-item description. Moving zeros to a group field will not provide proper COMP or COMP-3 numeric zeros.

Style Summary

- When specifying the USAGE clause for data-item descriptions, omit the optional words USAGE and IS. They consume valuable space on the coding line but impart little additional meaning.

- Rather than explicitly coding the USAGE clause for DISPLAY usage, omit the USAGE clause; implicit DISPLAY usage will be provided.

- Use of the abbreviations COMP for COMPUTATIONAL and COMP-3 for COMPUTATIONAL-3 conserves space on the coding line and is equally understandable.

- When specifying COMP usage for WORKING-STORAGE fields which are not part of an input or output record, include the SYNC clause to ensure proper internal alignment for optimum processing efficiency.

- A convenient position to start the USAGE clause words COMP (when SYNC is not specified) or COMP-3 is in position 66. When COMP and SYNC are both specified, position 63 is an appropriate starting position.

- Choose field lengths of an odd number of digits when specifying the length of COMP-3 fields. Also, assign the PICTURE symbol S.

- Specify COMP fields as 4, 9, or 18 digits in length. Assign the PICTURE symbol S.

- When specifying fields used to hold the control fields of the previous record, it is logical to list them in major through minor sequence.

- When specifying control total accumulation fields, it is logical to list them in minor through major sequence.

Exercises

Terms for Definition

control break program
control field
single-level control break
multiple-level control break
control total
control break line
conditional-processing
data representation method
zoned decimal

external decimal
character
binary
packed decimal
internal decimal
date record
major control field
minor control field

Review Questions

1. Control break programs require that records be in the proper _Sequence_ and the program logic must test the control field(s) of the _relationship_ to the control field(s) of the _previous record_

2. Control field accumulations are termed _control-break-line_

3. The line which contains the control field accumulations is called the _____ line.

4. Name the two control break logic considerations that, unless provided for, will cause erroneous control break reports.

5. How many control fields apply to a single-level control break report?

6. How many control fields apply to a multiple-level control break report?

7. For multiple-level control breaks, the _____ control field should be tested first.

8. Match the following USAGE clause specifications with the descriptions below:
   a. DISPLAY
   b. COMP
   c. COMP-3

   __*a*__ Assumed USAGE when no USAGE clause is specified
   __*c*__ Non-ANS COBOL USAGE
   __*a*__ Allows representation of both alphanumeric and numeric data
   __*b*__ Generally refers to storage of numeric values in binary format
   __*b*__ USAGE that refers to method of representation where two digits are stored in each byte (except for low-order byte that contains one digit and the arithmetic sign representation)
   _____ USAGE for data punched in cards, printed on a printer or displayed on a screen
   _____ Packed decimal
   _____ External decimal
   _____ Character
   _____ Internal decimal
   _____ Binary
   _____ Zoned decimal

9. Explain the effect of specifying a USAGE clause at the group level.

10. To provide proper internal alignment of COMP fields in WORKING-STORAGE, the _____ clause should be specified.

11. When a date record is contained within a file, it is generally specified to be present as the _____ record of the file.

12. When a date record is contained within a file, the program logic should check for its _____ .

Programming Assignment 10-A: Section Test Results

Program description

A section test results report is to be printed from the test results file. It is to provide totals for each section number.

Input file

Test results file (Records are in ascending sequence according to the section number field).

Input record format

Test results record

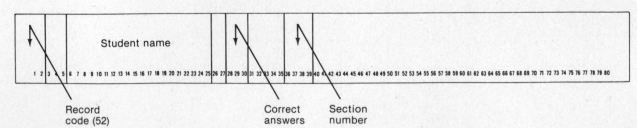

Record code (52)   Correct answers   Section number

Output file

Section test results report

Output report format

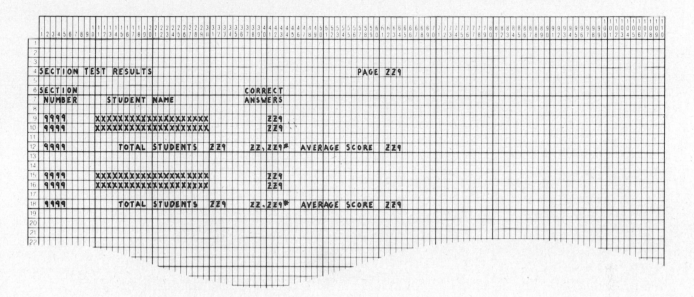

Program operations

1. Read each input results record.

2. For each test results record, do the following processing:

   a. Print a detail line as specified above for each test results record.

   b. Accumulate the total correct answers and the total number of students in each section.

3. Whenever the section number changes, print a control break section total line in accordance with the print chart specifications containing the following:

   a. The section number

   b. Total number of students

   c. Total number of correct answers

   d. Average score (total number of correct answers divided by total number of students)

   e. Descriptive words and an asterisk as specified on the print chart.

4. Headings are to be printed on the first page of the report. After 54 lines have been used on a report page and a new test results record is to be printed, the program is to skip to the next page and print the report headings. (Do not allow the control break line to be printed on a report page which does not contain at least one detail line for the section number to which it applies.)

   a. The page number is to be incremented each time the heading is printed and displayed on the first heading-line in accordance with the format shown on the print chart.

5. Line-spacing is to be handled as follows:

   a. The first detail-line after the headings is to be double-spaced from the last heading-line.

   b. Second and successive detail-lines for the same section number are to be single-spaced from one another.

   c. Each control break section total-line is to be double-spaced from the previous detail-line.

   d. The first detail-line following a control break section total-line is to be triple-spaced from the section total-line.

Programming Assignment 10-B: Invoice Register

Program description

An invoice register is to be printed from the invoice file. It is to provide control break totals for each invoice.

Input file

Invoice file (Records are in ascending sequence according to the invoice number field. The first record in the file is an invoice date record.)

Input record formats

Invoice date record
Invoice record

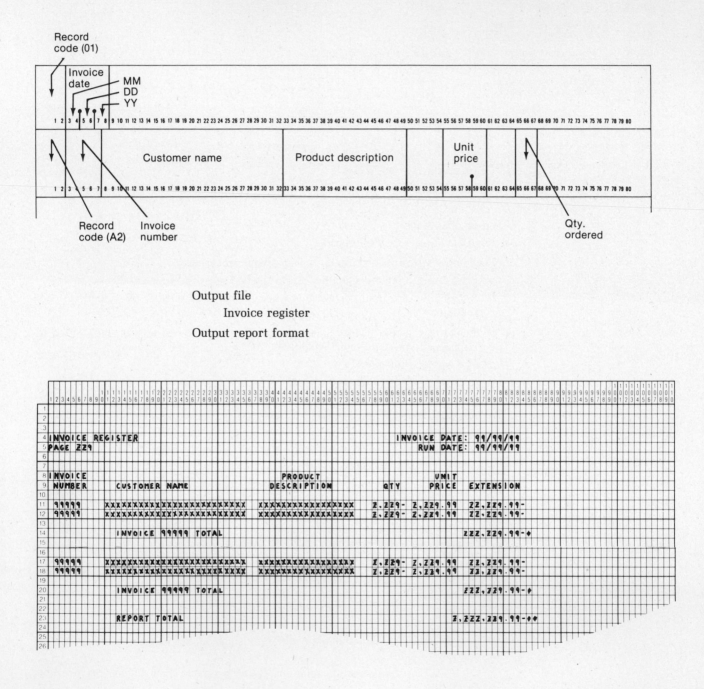

Output file

Invoice register

Output report format

Program operations

1. Read each input record.

2. The first record is to be an invoice date record.
   a. The date is to be extracted from the invoice date record and stored in the first heading line as specified on the print chart.
   b. If the first record is not an invoice date record, the program processing should terminate.

3. For each invoice record, do the following processing:
   a. Compute the extension amount by multiplying the unit price by the quantity ordered.
   b. Print a detail line in accordance with the print chart specifications.
   c. Accumulate the invoice total.

4. Whenever the invoice number changes, print a control break invoice total line in accordance with the print chart specifications containing the following:
   a. The invoice number
   b. Total invoice amount (total of extension amounts)
   c. Descriptive words and an asterisk as specified on the print chart.

5. After all the input records have been processed, print a report total line containing the total of all invoice totals printed.

6. Headings are to be printed on each page of the report. After 54 lines have been used on a report page and a new invoice record is to be printed, the program is to skip to the next page and print the report headings. (Do not allow the control break line to be printed on a report page which does not contain at least one detail line for the invoice number to which it applies.)
   a. The page number is to be incremented each time the heading is printed and displayed on the second heading-line in accordance with the format shown on the print chart.
   b. The run date is to be obtained from the operating system and printed on the second heading-line in accordance with the format shown on the print chart.

7. Line spacing is to be handled as follows:
   a. The first detail-line after the headings is to be double-spaced from the last heading line.
   b. Second and successive detail-lines for the same invoice number are to be single-spaced from one another.
   c. Each control break invoice total-line is to be double-spaced from the previous detail-line.
   d. The first detail-line following a control break invoice total-line is to be triple-spaced from the invoice total-line.

Programming Assignment 10-C: Departmental Earnings Report

Program description

A departmental earnings report is to be printed from the payroll file. It is to provide control break totals for each department within each plant. A report total is also to be printed.

Input file

Payroll file (Records are in ascending sequence according to the following sort key: major field = plant; intermediate field = departmental number; minor field = social security number. The first record in the file is a period-ending date record.)

Input record formats

Period ending date record
Payroll record

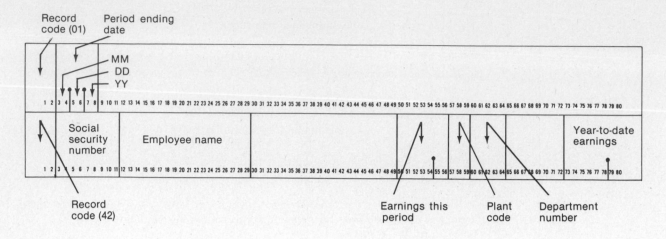

Output file
Departmental earnings report
Output report format

```
 4 DEPARTMENTAL EARNINGS REPORT                    PERIOD ENDING DATE 99/99/99
 5 PAGE ZZ9                                              RUN DATE 99/99/99
 7 PLANT    DEPT.   SOCIAL SEC.                    EARNINGS       YEAR-TO-DATE
 8 CODE     NBR     NUMBER        EMPLOYEE NAME     THIS PER.       EARNINGS
10 XXX      99999   999-99-9999   XXXXXXXXXXXXXXXXXXXX   ZZ,ZZZ.99-      ZZZ,ZZZ.99-
11 XXX      99999   999-99-9999   XXXXXXXXXXXXXXXXXXXX   ZZ,ZZZ.99-      ZZZ,ZZZ.99-
13 XXX      99999   DEPARTMENT TOTAL                ZZZ,ZZZ.99-*   Z,ZZZ,ZZZ.99-*
15 XXX              PLANT TOTAL                      ZZZ,ZZZ.99-**  Z,ZZZ,ZZZ.99-**
17                  REPORT TOTAL                    ZZZ,ZZZ.99-*** Z,ZZZ,ZZZ.99-***
```

Program operations

1. Read each input record.

2. The first record is to be a period-ending date record.

    a. The date is to be extracted from the period-ending date record and stored in the first heading-line as specified on the print chart.

    b. If the first record is not a period-ending date record, the program processing should terminate.

3. For each payroll record, do the following processing:

    a. Print a detail line in accordance with the print chart specifications.

    b. Accumulate the department earnings this period and the department year-to-date earnings.

4. Whenever the department (within plant) changes, print a control break department total line in accordance with the print chart specifications containing the following:

    a. The plant code

    b. The department number

c. Department earnings this period

d. Department year-to-date earnings

5. Whenever the plant code changes, print a control break plant total line in accordance with the print chart specifications containing the following.

a. The plant code

b. Plant earnings this period

c. Plant year-to-date earnings

6. After all the input records have been processed, print a report total line containing the total earnings this period and year-to-date earnings of all departments printed.

7. Headings are to be printed on each page of the report. After 50 lines have been used on a report page and a new payroll record is to be printed, the program is to skip to the next page and print the report headings. (Do not allow a control break line to be printed on a report page which does not contain at least one detail line for the control group to which it applies.)

a. The page number is to be incremented each time the heading is printed and displayed on the second heading-line in accordance with the format shown on the print chart.

b. The run date is to be obtained from the operating system and printed on the second heading-line in accordance with the format shown on the print chart.

8. Line spacing is to be handled as follows:

a. The first detail-line after the headings is to be double-spaced from the last heading line.

b. Second and successive detail-lines for the same department number are to be single-spaced from one another.

c. Each control break total-line is to be double-spaced from the previous line.

d. The first detail-line following a control break total-line is to be double-spaced from the previous control break total-line.

Programming Assignment 10-D: Store Revenue Report

Program description

A store revenue report is to be printed from the sales transaction file. It is to provide control break totals for each employee within department within store. A report total is also to be printed.

Input file

Sales transaction file (Records are in ascending sequence according to the following sort key: major field = store number; intermediate field = department; minor field = employee number. The first record in the file is a period-ending date record.)

Input record formats

Period ending date record

Sales transaction record

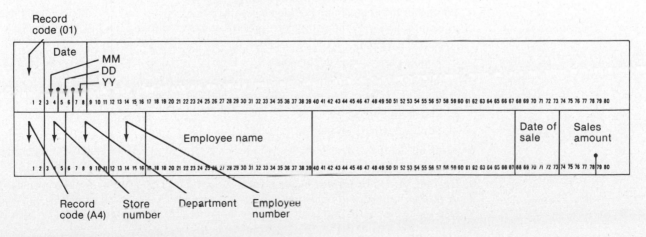

Output file

Store revenue report

Output report format

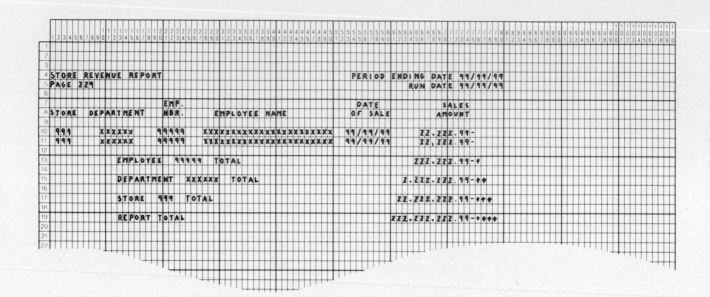

Program operations

1. Read each input record.

2. The first record is to be a period-ending date record.

   a. The date is to be extracted from the date record and stored in the first heading-line as specified on the print chart.

   b. If the first record is not a period-ending date record, the program processing should terminate.

3. For each sales transaction record, do the following processing:

   a. Print a detail line in accordance with the print chart specifications.

   b. Accumulate the sales amount.

4. Whenever the employee number (within department within store) changes, print a control break employee total line in accordance with the print chart specifications containing the following:

   a. The employee number

   b. Total sales for that employee

5. Whenever the department (within store) changes, print a control break plant total line in accordance with the print chart specifications containing the following:

   a. The department

   b. Total sales for that department

6. Whenever the store number changes, print a control break store total line in accordance with the print chart specifications containing the following:

   a. The store number

   b. Total sales for that store

7. After all the input records have been processed, print a report total line containing the total sales for all stores.

8. Headings are to be printed on each page of the report. After 50 lines have been used on a report page and a new sales transaction record is to be printed, the program is to skip to the next page and print the report headings. (Do not allow a control break line

to be printed on a report page which does not contain at least one detail line for the control group to which it applies.)

    a. The page number is to be incremented each time the heading is printed and displayed on the second heading-line in accordance with the format shown on the print chart.

    b. The run date is to be obtained from the operating system and printed on the second heading-line in accordance with the format shown on the print chart.

9. Line spacing is to be handled as follows:

    a. The first detail-line after the headings is to be double-spaced from the last heading line.

    b. Second and successive detail-lines for the same employee number are to be single-spaced from one another.

    c. Each control break total-line is to be double-spaced from the previous line.

    d. The first detail-line following a control break total-line is to be double-spaced from the previous control break total-line.

CHAPTER 11

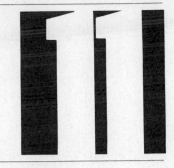

SORTING AND MERGING

11

SORTING AND MERGING

Sorting is a common program function within all commercial data processing installations because records of files must be frequently arranged and re-arranged in certain sequences for reports, record matching, and the like. The actual sort program logic is usually written as a generalized utility program so that it can sort various types of records and can sequence them according to different fields. To sort a specific group of records into a given sequence, the programmer supplies specifications to the utility sort program regarding the length of the records to be sorted, the location of the sort-key fields within the record, and so forth.

For example, to sort the sales transaction records into the proper sequence for the M-SLSRPT program of the previous chapter, the programmer would supply the sort program with specifications, often termed *parameters*, showing that (1) the sales records are 80 characters in length; (2) the major field for this sort is the state field and it is located in positions 3 and 4 of the record; (3) the intermediate field is the branch field, located in positions 5 through 7 of the record; and (4) the minor field is the sales representative number, located in positions 8 through 12 of the record.

A utility sort program is typically supplied with each computer operating system. However, because sorting is such a common and time-consuming program function, certain independent software companies offer sort programs that provide processing speed and other enhancements over those provided with the operating system.

Regardless of whether the standard operating system sort program or the independent software company sort program is used, there are two general approaches to handling sorts within a COBOL-oriented data processing installation. Some installations prefer to specify sort parameters directly to the utility sort program. These sorts are usually termed *external* or *stand-alone* sorts. Other installations use the COBOL SORT statement within a COBOL program; such a sort is often termed an *internal* sort. (Unfortunately, confusion sometimes arises with the term "internal sort" because it is also used to refer to programmer-written sort logic that has nothing to do with the COBOL SORT feature. However, with the increasing availability of the COBOL SORT feature, programmer-written internal sorts are becoming rather rare.)

Both external and internal COBOL sorts normally use the same sort program to actually accomplish the sorting; the difference is whether the parameters are specified directly by the programmer or passed by the COBOL program to the sort program.

In this chapter we will cover the COBOL statements required to handle the sorting and merging functions. The formats for all the COBOL SORT-related statements are provided in Figure 11.1. To introduce the statements, an inventory program application will be described. When using the COBOL SORT statement, there are four possible sort program variations. They may be described as (1) SORT-only, (2) SORT with preprocessing of the input file, (3) SORT with preprocessing of the input file and postprocessing of the sorted output file, and (4) SORT with postprocessing of the sorted output file. We will cover each by utilizing four slightly different inventory program specifications.

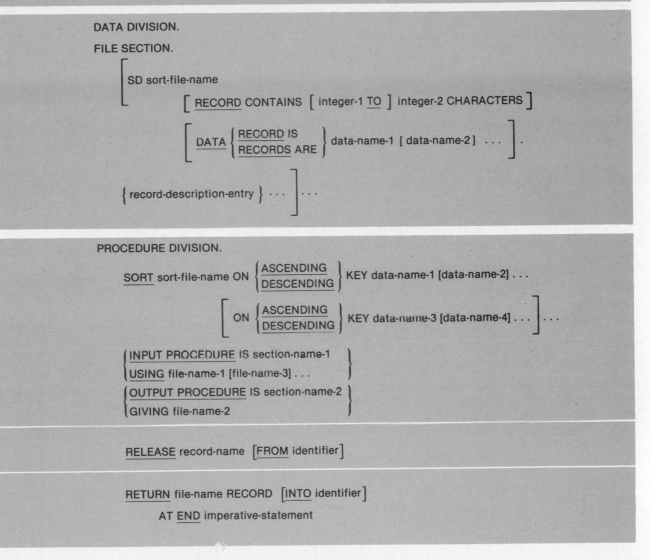

SORT Formats:

ENVIRONMENT DIVISION.
INPUT-OUTPUT SECTION.
FILE CONTROL.
    SELECT sort-file-name
        ASSIGN TO implementor-name.

DATA DIVISION.
FILE SECTION.
    [SD sort-file-name
        [RECORD CONTAINS [integer-1 TO] integer-2 CHARACTERS]
        [DATA { RECORD IS / RECORDS ARE } data-name-1 [data-name-2] ...] .
    { record-description-entry } ...] ...

PROCEDURE DIVISION.
    SORT sort-file-name ON { ASCENDING / DESCENDING } KEY data-name-1 [data-name-2] ...
        [ON { ASCENDING / DESCENDING } KEY data-name-3 [data-name-4] ...] ...
    { INPUT PROCEDURE IS section-name-1 / USING file-name-1 [file-name-3] ... }
    { OUTPUT PROCEDURE IS section-name-2 / GIVING file-name-2 }

    RELEASE record-name [FROM identifier]

    RETURN file-name RECORD [INTO identifier]
        AT END imperative-statement

Figure 11.1. SORT-related statement formats

Since the purpose of this chapter is to train you in SORT program coding, and because you should by now be experienced with general program design and coding concepts, the inventory program specifications and design documentation will be somewhat abbreviated. Thus, you will be better able to concentrate on the SORT statement itself—how to use it and how use of it affects program design.

Part A: System flowchart:

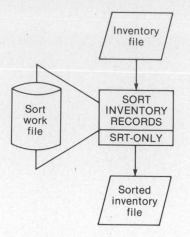

Part B: Record layout — inventory record (blocking factor = 20):

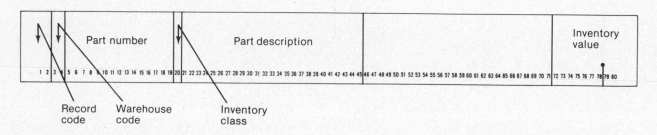

Part C: Programming specifications:

1. Sort the inventory file in sequence according to the following sort-key:
   a. Major field: Warehouse-code (ascending sequence)
   b. Intermediate field: Inventory-value (descending sequence)
   c. Minor field: Part-number   (ascending sequence)
2. Write the sorted output to the sorted inventory file (blocking factor = 20).

Figure 11.2. Programming documentation: Sort-only inventory program

A Sort-only Program

The sort-only inventory program system flowchart, record layout, and programming specifications appear in Figure 11.2. Notice that the only function of this program is to sort each of the records of the inventory file in sequence according to the Warehouse-code, Inventory-value, and Part-number fields. Examples of input and output for this sort-only inventory program are shown in Figure 11.3.

We will call the program SRT-ONLY to indicate that this is an example of a *sort-only* program. Figure 11.4 presents the program coding for this SRT-ONLY program. We will cover the ENVIRONMENT, DATA, and PROCEDURE DIVISION statements required for such a sort program.

ENVIRONMENT DIVISION Coding

Notice in the system flowchart (shown in Figure 11.2) that a *sort work file* has been depicted. This is because sort programs require an area in which to rearrange the records to be sorted during the sorting process. This sort work file must be specified in the COBOL program.

Unsorted Inventory records (input)

Record code	Warehouse code	Part number	Inventory class	Part description	Inventory value
23	PA	D40783	A	DESK	000203768
23	PA	A50365	A	CREDENZA	000405897
23	AT	R789654	B	STENO CHAIR	000200115
23	AT	E309287	C	WASTE RECEPTACLE	000032580
23	AT	X502987	B	EXEC CHAIR	000200115
23	AT	Q302765	C	TYPEWRITER STAND	000050082
23	PA	T50398767	A	EXEC DESK	000550000

Sorted inventory records (output)

Major field	Minor field				Intermediate field
23	AT	R789654	B	STENO CHAIR	000200115
23	AT	X502987	B	EXEC CHAIR	000200115
23	AT	Q302765	C	TYPEWRITER STAND	000050082
23	AT	E309287	C	WASTE RECEPTACLE	000032580
23	PA	T50398767	A	EXEC DESK	000550000
23	PA	A50365	A	CREDENZA	000405897
23	PA	D40783	A	DESK	000203768

Figure 11.3.   Input and output data example

```
001010 IDENTIFICATION DIVISION.
001020 PROGRAM-ID.      SRT-ONLY.
001030*AUTHOR.          WELBURN.
001040*INSTALLATION.    SILICON VALLEY MANUFACTURING COMPANY.
001050*DATE-WRITTEN.    MAR 28,1981.
001060*DATE-COMPILED.   MAR 28,1981.
001070*SECURITY.        NONE.
001080*
001090*
001100*                 THIS IS A SORT-ONLY PROGRAM.
001110
001120*                 THE FOLLOWING SORT STATEMENT PHRASES ARE SPECIFIED
001130*                     USING
001140*                     GIVING
002010*
002020*
002030*
002040 ENVIRONMENT DIVISION.
002050*
002060*
002070 CONFIGURATION SECTION.
002080*
002090 SOURCE-COMPUTER.  IBM-370.
002100 OBJECT-COMPUTER.  IBM-370.
002110*
002120*
002130 INPUT-OUTPUT SECTION.
002140*
002150 FILE-CONTROL.
002160     SELECT INVENTORY-FILE
002170         ASSIGN TO UT-S-INFILE.
002180     SELECT SORTED-INVENTORY-FILE
002190         ASSIGN TO UT-S-OUTFILE.
002220     SELECT SORT-FILE
002230         ASSIGN TO UT-S-SORTWORK.
003010*
003020*
003030*
003040 DATA DIVISION.
003050*
003060*
003070 FILE SECTION.
```

```
003080*
003090 FD  INVENTORY-FILE
003100         RECORD CONTAINS 80 CHARACTERS
003110         BLOCK CONTAINS 20 RECORDS
003120         LABEL RECORDS ARE STANDARD.
003130*
003140 01  IR-INVENTORY-RECORD.
003150     05  FILLER                  PIC X(80).
004010*
004020 FD  SORTED-INVENTORY-FILE
004030         RECORD CONTAINS 80 CHARACTERS
004040         BLOCK CONTAINS 20 RECORDS
004050         LABEL RECORDS ARE STANDARD.
004060*
004070 01  SI-INVENTORY-RECORD.
004080     05  FILLER                  PIC X(80).
007010*
007020 SD  SORT-FILE
007030         RECORD CONTAINS 80 CHARACTERS.
007040*
007050 01  SR-SORT-RECORD.
007060     05  FILLER                  PIC X(2).
007070     05  SR-WAREHOUSE-CODE       PIC X(2).
007080     05  SR-PART-NUMBER          PIC X(15).
007090     05  FILLER                  PIC X(52).
007100     05  SR-INVENTORY-VALUE      PIC S9(7)V99.
050010*
050020*
050030*
050040 PROCEDURE DIVISION.
050050*
050060*
050070 000-SORT-INVENTORY-RECORDS.
050080*
050160     SORT SORT-FILE
050170         ASCENDING KEY  SR-WAREHOUSE-CODE
050180         DESCENDING KEY SR-INVENTORY-VALUE
050190         ASCENDING KEY  SR-PART-NUMBER
050200         USING  INVENTORY-FILE
050210         GIVING SORTED-INVENTORY-FILE.
050220     STOP RUN.
```

Figure 11.4.   COBOL coding: SRT-ONLY program

| 0 0 2 2 2 0 | | | | SELECT SORT-FILE | | | SRT-ONLY |
| 0 0 2 2 3 0 | | | | ASSIGN TO UT-S-SORTWORK. | | | SRT-ONLY |

Figure 11.5. SELECT statement for the sort work file

SELECT statement for the sort work file

As Figure 11.5 shows, the SELECT statement for a sort work file is coded like any other SELECT statement. However, some computer operating systems have a special implementor-name that must be specified in the ASSIGN clause. Your particular COBOL reference manual should be checked for this requirement. Because most COBOL programs using the SORT feature contain only one sort work file per program, and because an application-dependent file-name does not offer much meaning for this file, the user-defined name SORT-FILE is often chosen for the sort work file.

DATA DIVISION Coding

As with any other COBOL file, the sort work file must be described in the FILE SECTION of the DATA DIVISION. However, whereas an FD statement is used for other files, an SD (sort-file description) statement is required for a sort work file.

The SD statement

The SD statement, as shown in Figure 11.6, is very similar to the FD statement except that the programmer does not specify the BLOCK CONTAINS or LABEL RECORDS clauses. This is because (1) the sort program determines the optimum block size for the sort work file and (2) the label record handling is predefined by the operating system.

As in the FD statement, the RECORD CONTAINS clause is optional. However, as described in Chapter 2, the benefits of the RECORD CONTAINS clause suggest its inclusion.

The record-description entry

Just as one or more 01-level record-description entries follow the FD statement, record-description entries follow the SD statement. There are certain special considerations for sort-file record-descriptions, however.

Field specifications

Within the record-description for a sort file, each of the fields that will be used in determining the record sequence (the sort-key fields) must be specified. Notice that the key fields for the SRT-ONLY program—SR-WAREHOUSE-CODE, SR-PART-NUMBER, and SR-INVENTORY-VALUE—have been specified within the SR-SORT-RECORD.

As shown for the SR-SORT-RECORD, often the sort file record descriptions will contain data-names for only the sort-key fields; all other areas will be defined as FILLER. This is because the sort file record area is usually used only for the sort; hence definitions for fields that are not part of the sort-key—although they may be specified—are usually not required.

Multiple record definitions

Although a sort file may contain multiple 01-level record-descriptions, the sort-key fields must be in the same relative position for each record. This requirement for record sorting was discussed in Systems Chapter B. Because of this

Format:

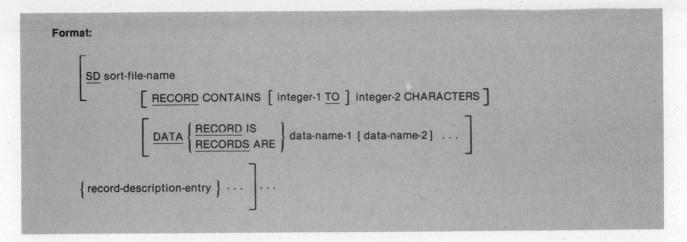

Example:

SEQUENCE		C O N T	A	B							COBOL STATEMENT													IDENTIFICATION	
(PAGE)	(SERIAL)																								

```
0 0 7 0 1 0  *                                                                    SRT-ONLY
      0 2   SD  SORT-FILE
      0 3           RECORD CONTAINS 80 CHARACTERS.
      0 4   *
      0 5   01  SR-SORT-RECORD.
      0 6       05  FILLER                        PIC X(2).
      0 7       05  SR-WAREHOUSE-CODE             PIC X(2).
      0 8       05  SR-PART-NUMBER                PIC X(15).
      0 9       05  FILLER                        PIC X(52).
0 0 7 1 0 0   05  SR-INVENTORY-VALUE              PIC S9(7)V99.            SRT-ONLY
```

Figure 11.6. SD statement example

requirement, and because non-sort-key fields are not usually defined in sort records, multiple record definitions are rarely specified within a sort file.

PROCEDURE DIVISION Coding

The PROCEDURE DIVISION for the SRT-ONLY program is very short. It contains only two statements: SORT and STOP.

The SORT statement

The SORT statement is used to specify the name of the sort file, the sort-key, input file handling, and output file handling. After the verb SORT, the name of the sort work file is specified, as shown in Figure 11.7.

The ASCENDING KEY and DESCENDING KEY phrase

After the sort file name, the phrase ASCENDING KEY or DESCENDING KEY is specified, depending upon whether the sort-key field is to be sequenced in ascending or descending order, and this phrase is followed by the major sort-key field. When there is more than one sort-key field, the additional fields are listed in order of decreasing significance. That is, sort-key fields are always listed with the major field first and the minor field last, regardless of the ASCENDING KEY or DESCENDING KEY specifications.

ASCENDING KEY and DESCENDING KEY sort-key fields may be mixed within the same SORT statement, as has been done in the SRT-ONLY program. The reserved words ASCENDING KEY and DESCENDING KEY may be specified for each field or merely written for the first field and whenever there is a

Format:

$$\text{SORT sort-file-name ON} \begin{Bmatrix} \underline{\text{ASCENDING}} \\ \underline{\text{DESCENDING}} \end{Bmatrix} \text{KEY data-name-1 [data-name-2]} \dots$$

$$\left[\text{ON} \begin{Bmatrix} \underline{\text{ASCENDING}} \\ \underline{\text{DESCENDING}} \end{Bmatrix} \text{KEY data-name-3 [data-name-4]} \dots \right] \dots$$

$$\begin{Bmatrix} \underline{\text{INPUT PROCEDURE}} \text{ IS section-name-1} \\ \underline{\text{USING}} \text{ file-name-1 [file-name-3]} \dots \end{Bmatrix}$$

$$\begin{Bmatrix} \underline{\text{OUTPUT PROCEDURE}} \text{ IS section-name-2} \\ \underline{\text{GIVING}} \text{ file-name-2} \end{Bmatrix}$$

Example:

Major field   Minor field

SEQUENCE		CONT	A	B	COBOL STATEMENT			IDENTIFICATION

```
Ø5Ø16Ø        SORT  SORT-FILE                                              SRT-ONLY
    17            ASCENDING  KEY    SR-WAREHOUSE-CODE  ◄──┐                  
    18            DESCENDING KEY    SR-INVENTORY-VALUE    │◄─────┐
    19            ASCENDING  KEY    SR-PART-NUMBER        │      │◄──
    2Ø                USING   INVENTORY-FILE
Ø5Ø21Ø                GIVING  SORTED-INVENTORY-FILE.                        SRT-ONLY
```

Figure 11.7. SORT statement example

change. Notice in the SORT statement format that, although the optional reserved word ON may be specified, it contributes little and is usually omitted. KEY phrase examples are shown in Figure 11.8.

Although the COBOL standard does not place a limit on the number of KEY fields that may be specified, the sort program used by the compiler will probably have some limit—perhaps a dozen or so. Should you need this information, the COBOL reference manual for your compiler should be checked.

When specifying KEY fields for numeric values with mixed positive, negative, and unsigned representations, the programmer should be certain that the data-item description referenced is an elementary item and contains a numeric PICTURE. If it is defined as a group field or with an alphanumeric PICTURE, it will be sorted according to its character value; this may cause positive values to be considered lower than negative values and unsigned numbers higher than negative values. When a numeric field is referenced in the KEY phrase, algebraic sequence is provided; negative numbers are considered lower in sequence than positive or unsigned numbers. Similarly, if the correct USAGE is not associated with data-items referenced by the KEY phrase, incorrect sorting may occur.

The USING phrase

After the sort-key is listed, the USING phrase may be specified to name the input file that is to be sorted. When the USING phrase is specified, the SORT statement will cause the named file to be opened, transferred to the sort work file, and closed. In the SRT-ONLY program, the INVENTORY-FILE was called for by the USING phrase. Observe that OPEN and CLOSE statements have not been coded for the INVENTORY-FILE. That's because the SORT statement handles these functions; thus they must not be present.

Part A: Example with ASCENDING KEY specified once:

```
SORT SORT-FILE
     ASCENDING KEY XX-DEPARTMENT-NUMBER
                   XX-EMPLOYEE-NUMBER
                      .
                      .
                      .
```

Part B: Example with ASCENDING KEY specified for each sort-key field:

```
SORT SORT-FILE
     ASCENDING KEY XX-TERRITORY-CODE
     ASCENDING KEY XX-SALES-REP-NUMBER
     ASCENDING KEY XX-PRODUCT-CODE
                      .
                      .
                      .
```

Part C: Example with both ASCENDING KEY and DESCENDING KEY phrases:

```
SORT SORT-FILE
     DESCENDING KEY XX-GRADE-POINT-AVERAGE
     ASCENDING KEY  XX-LAST-NAME
                    XX-FIRST-NAME
                    XX-MIDDLE-NAME
                      .
                      .
                      .
```

Figure 11.8. KEY phrase examples

Observe from the format of the USING phrase that, according to the standard, multiple input files to be sorted may be specified. However, many COBOL compilers do not actually provide this capability. This is another example of an area where the reference manual for your particular compiler should be checked.

The GIVING phrase

The GIVING phrase is specified to name the output sorted file that is to be created. When the GIVING phrase is specified, the SORT statement will cause the named file to be opened, the sorted records from the sort work file will be transferred to it, and the newly created sort file will be closed.

As with the USING clause, OPEN and CLOSE statements must not be included for a GIVING file. In the SRT-ONLY program, the SORTED-INVENTORY-FILE will be created containing the sorted inventory records.

Recap of Sort-only Programs

Sort-only programs utilize the USING and GIVING phrases of the SORT statement. Actually, a program such as this SRT-ONLY program would rarely be written; it would be much quicker to write this as an external sort.

Sometimes, though, the SORT statement will be specified within a program to sort a file that has previously been opened, processed, and closed (the USING file) or one that will subsequently be opened, processed, and closed (the GIVING file).

A Sort Program with Preprocessing of the Input File

Specifications for the sort program with preprocessing of the input inventory file are shown in Figure 11.9. Notice that the specifications for this program are identical to those of the SRT-ONLY program except that only inventory

Part A: System flowchart:

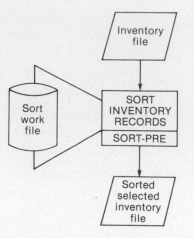

Part B: Record layout: Inventory record (blocking factor = 20)

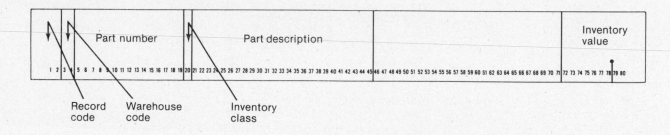

Part C: Programming specifications:

1. Inventory class codes are coded as "A", "B", or "C". Select and sort those inventory records from the inventory file that have an Inventory-class-code equal to "A".
2. Write the sorted output to the sorted selected inventory file (blocking factor = 20).

Figure 11.9. Programming documentation: Sort with preprocessing of input inventory file program

records containing an inventory class code of "A" are to be sorted and written to the output sorted inventory file.

The structure chart for this program is shown in Figure 11.10. When a structure chart is prepared for a program using the SORT statement, a dummy block will result.

We'll call this program SRT-PRE to indicate that it is an example of a sort with preprocessing of the input file. Figure 11.11 presents the program coding for the first three divisions of the SRT-PRE program.

DATA DIVISION Coding

The DATA DIVISION for SRT-PRE differs from that of SRT-ONLY in just two ways. First, the IR-INVENTORY-RECORD record-description has been specified with the IR-INVENTORY-CLASS-CODE data-item defined rather than appearing as FILLER. This definition is required because the inventory class code field must be tested to determine whether or not the record should be written on the output sorted inventory file. Of course, if desired, all the fields of the IR-INVENTORY-RECORD could have been defined.

Second, the WS-END-OF-FILE-SWITCH will be required and has thus been defined in WORKING-STORAGE.

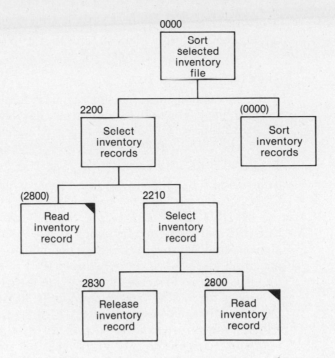

Figure 11.10. Structure chart: Sort with preprocessing of input inventory file program

```
001010 IDENTIFICATION DIVISION.
001020 PROGRAM-ID.    SRT-PRE.
001030*AUTHOR.        WELBURN.
001040*INSTALLATION.  SILICON VALLEY MANUFACTURING COMPANY.
001050*DATE-WRITTEN.  MAR 28,1981.
001060*DATE-COMPILED. MAR 28,1981.
001070*SECURITY.      NONE.
001080*
001090*
001100*            THIS IS A SORT PROGRAM WITH PRE-PROCESSING
001110*                OF THE INPUT FILE.
001120*
001130*            THE FOLLOWING SORT STATEMENT PHRASES ARE SPECIFIED
001140*                INPUT PROCEDURE
001150*                GIVING
002010*
002020*
002030*
002040 ENVIRONMENT DIVISION.
002050*
002060*
002070 CONFIGURATION SECTION.
002080*
002090 SOURCE-COMPUTER.  IBM-370.
002100 OBJECT-COMPUTER.  IBM-370.
002110*
002120*
002130 INPUT-OUTPUT SECTION.
002140*
002150 FILE-CONTROL.
002160     SELECT INVENTORY-FILE
002170         ASSIGN TO UT-S-INFILE.
002180     SELECT SORTED-INVENTORY-FILE
002190         ASSIGN TO UT-S-OUTFILE.
002200     SELECT SORT-FILE
002210         ASSIGN TO UT-S-SORTWORK.
003010*
003020*
003030*
003040 DATA DIVISION.
```

```
003050*
003060*
003070 FILE SECTION.
003080*
003090 FD  INVENTORY-FILE
003100         RECORD CONTAINS 80 CHARACTERS
003110         BLOCK CONTAINS 20 RECORDS
003120         LABEL RECORDS ARE STANDARD.
004010*
004020 01  IR-INVENTORY-RECORD.
004030     05  FILLER                        PIC X(19).
004040     05  IR-INVENTORY-CLASS-CODE        PIC X(1).
004050     05  FILLER                        PIC X(60).
006010*
006020 FD  SORTED-INVENTORY-FILE
006030         RECORD CONTAINS 80 CHARACTERS
006040         BLOCK CONTAINS 20 RECORDS
006050         LABEL RECORDS ARE STANDARD.
006060*
006070 01  SI-INVENTORY-RECORD.
006080     05  FILLER                        PIC X(80).
007010*
007020 SD  SORT-FILE
007030         RECORD CONTAINS 80 CHARACTERS.
007040*
007050 01  SR-SORT-RECORD.
007060     05  FILLER                        PIC X(2).
007070     05  SR-WAREHOUSE-CODE             PIC X(2).
007080     05  SR-PART-NUMBER                PIC X(15).
007090     05  FILLER                        PIC X(52).
007100     05  SR-INVENTORY-VALUE            PIC S9(7)V99.
020010*
020020*
020030 WORKING-STORAGE SECTION.
020040*
020050*
020060 01  WS-SWITCHES.
020070     05  WS-END-OF-FILE-SWITCH         PIC X(3).
020080         88  END-OF-FILE                          VALUE 'YES'.
```

Figure 11.11. COBOL coding: First three divisions of SRT-PRE program

Although definition of input and output records in the WORKING-STORAGE SECTION has generally been recommended in this text, we have used FILE SECTION definition in this chapter to keep these sort programs shorter and more straightforward. However, should you be writing more complex sort programs, we recommend record definition in the WORKING-STORAGE SECTION.

PROCEDURE DIVISION Coding

The PROCEDURE DIVISION for the SRT-PRE program, as shown in Figure 11.12, is considerably longer than that of the SRT-ONLY program.

The SORT statement

The SORT statement for this program is identical to that for the SRT-ONLY program except that the USING phrase has been replaced by the INPUT PROCEDURE phrase.

The INPUT PROCEDURE phrase

To provide for processing of input records before they are sorted, the INPUT PROCEDURE phrase must be specified. The SORT statement gives control to the INPUT PROCEDURE before the actual SORT is made. The INPUT PROCEDURE phrase acts very much like a PERFORM statement. However, one significant difference is that a section-name—not a paragraph-name—must be specified after the reserved words INPUT PROCEDURE IS.

There are a few rules that apply to the INPUT PROCEDURE. It can only be referenced by a SORT statement; that is, it cannot be named in a PERFORM or GO TO statement. Within the INPUT PROCEDURE, program control cannot be transferred to procedures outside it. In other words, PERFORM or GO TO statements within the procedure must not name a SECTION or a paragraph that is not included within the INPUT PROCEDURE itself. Also, an INPUT PROCEDURE cannot contain a SORT statement.

Notice that, unlike the USING phrase, OPEN and CLOSE statements for the input file to be sorted must be coded when INPUT PROCEDURE is specified.

Structured programming problems introduced by the INPUT PROCEDURE phrase

There are three items introduced by the INPUT PROCEDURE phrase that are in conflict with good structured programming practices as presented in this text: the need for sections, the requirements for module structure and numbering, and the need for GO TO and EXIT statements.

Need for sections

Because the INPUT PROCEDURE must be a section-name, it is logical (and sometimes necessary) to group the other paragraphs of the program into sections. In the SRT-PRE program, notice that there are two sections: 0000-ML-SORT-INV-RECORDS and 2000-IP-SELECT-INV-RECORDS. (The letters ML and IP following the module numbers are used to identify these sections as mainline and input procedure, respectively.)

Module structure and numbering

SORT statement syntax and SECTION requirements impose certain structure requirements that do not lend themselves to optimal structured code. The need to keep all INPUT PROCEDURE paragraphs within the SECTION also causes module numbering problems. When the SORT statement is used, notice that we have modified the module numbering system by prefixing a digit to the recommended three-digit module number to indicate the SECTION sequence ($1xxx$ = first SECTION, $2xxx$ = second SECTION, and so on). Then, the three-digit module numbering system previously used in this text appears.

Need for GO TO and EXIT statements

To structure the coding within the INPUT PROCEDURE, we must use the GO TO and EXIT statements, as will be explained below.

```
050010*
050020*
050030*
050040 PROCEDURE DIVISION.
050050*
050060*
050070 0000-ML-SORT-INV-RECORDS SECTION.
050080*
050090*
050100 0000-SORT-INV-RECORDS.
050110*
050120     OPEN INPUT INVENTORY-FILE.
050130     SORT SORT-FILE
050140         ASCENDING KEY   SR-WAREHOUSE-CODE
050150         DESCENDING KEY SR-INVENTORY-VALUE
050160         ASCENDING KEY   SR-PART-NUMBER
050170             INPUT PROCEDURE IS  2000-IP-SELECT-INV-RECORDS
050180             GIVING SORTED-INVENTORY-FILE.
050190     CLOSE INVENTORY-FILE.
050100     STOP RUN.
200010*
200020*
200030 2000-IP-SELECT-INV-RECORDS SECTION.
220010*
220020*
220030 2200-SELECT-INVENTORY-RECORDS.
220040*
220050     MOVE 'NO ' TO WS-END-OF-FILE-SWITCH.
220060     PERFORM 2800-READ-INVENTORY-RECORD.
220070     PERFORM 2210-SELECT-INVENTORY-RECORD
220080         UNTIL END-OF-FILE.
220090     GO TO 2999-EXIT.
221010*
221020*
221030 2210-SELECT-INVENTORY-RECORD.
221040*
221050     IF IR-INVENTORY-CLASS-CODE IS EQUAL TO 'A'
221060         MOVE IR-INVENTORY-RECORD TO SR-SORT-RECORD
221070         PERFORM 2830-RELEASE-INVENTORY-RECORD.
221080     PERFORM 2800-READ-INVENTORY-RECORD.
280010*
280020*
280030 2800-READ-INVENTORY-RECORD.
280040*
280050     READ INVENTORY-FILE
280060         AT END MOVE 'YES' TO WS-END-OF-FILE-SWITCH.
283010*
283020*
283030 2830-RELEASE-INVENTORY-RECORD.
283040*
283050     RELEASE SR-SORT-RECORD.
299010*
299020*
299030 2999-EXIT.
299040*
299050     EXIT.
```

Figure 11.12. COBOL coding: PROCEDURE DIVISION of SRT-PRE program

The INPUT PROCEDURE Logic: 2000-IP-SELECT-INV-RECORDS SECTION

This section is similar to a little program of its own. Figure 11.13 depicts its logic. After the SORT statement of module 0000-SORT-INV-RECORDS is encountered, this SECTION is invoked. It reads each record from the input INVENTORY-FILE, tests to see if it is one of the records to be sorted (IR-INVENTORY-CLASS CODE = A), and, if so, transfers the record to the SORT-FILE. After end-of-file has been reached, program control transfers back to the SORT statement and the actual sorting of the SORT-FILE occurs.

Notice in paragraphs 2200-SELECT-INVENTORY-RECORDS and 2210-SELECT-INVENTORY-RECORD that a priming-read is used. Observe also that a GO TO statement has been placed at the end of the 2200-SELECT-INV-RECORDS module. After end-of-file has been detected, this GO TO statement is required to skip over the remainder of the modules in the SECTION in order to return to the SORT statement. Since a module name is therefore needed at the end of the SECTION to GO TO, the module 2999-EXIT has been created. Because it is a null module—there are no operations to be executed there—the dummy statement EXIT has been specified for it.

```
           *
           *
           *
            PROCEDURE DIVISION.
           *
           *
            0000-ML-SORT-INV-RECORDS SECTION.
           *
           *
            0000-SORT-INV-RECORDS.
           *
                OPEN INPUT INVENTORY-FILE.
                SORT SORT-FILE
                    ASCENDING KEY   SR-WAREHOUSE-CODE
                    DESCENDING KEY  SR-INVENTORY-VALUE
                    ASCENDING KEY   SR-PART-NUMBER
                        INPUT PROCEDURE IS  2000-IP-SELECT-INV-RECORDS
                        GIVING SORTED-INVENTORY-FILE.
                CLOSE INVENTORY-FILE.
                STOP RUN.
           *
           *
            2000-IP-SELECT-INV-RECORDS SECTION.
           *
           *
            2200-SELECT-INVENTORY-RECORDS.
           *
                MOVE 'NO ' TO WS-END-OF-FILE-SWITCH.
                PERFORM 2800-READ-INVENTORY-RECORD.
                PERFORM 2210-SELECT-INVENTORY-RECORD
                    UNTIL END-OF-FILE.
                GO TO 2999-EXIT.
           *
           *
            2210-SELECT-INVENTORY-RECORD.
           *
                IF IR-INVENTORY-CLASS-CODE IS EQUAL TO 'A'
                    MOVE IR-INVENTORY-RECORD TO SR-SORT-RECORD
                    PERFORM 2830-RELEASE-INVENTORY-RECORD.
                PERFORM 2800-READ-INVENTORY-RECORD.
           *
           *
            2800-READ-INVENTORY-RECORD.
           *
                READ INVENTORY-FILE
                    AT END MOVE 'YES' TO WS-END-OF-FILE-SWITCH.
           *
           *
            2830-RELEASE-INVENTORY-RECORD.
           *
                RELEASE SR-SORT-RECORD.
           *
           *
            2999-EXIT.
           *
                EXIT.
```

Before sort

After end-of-file

Figure 11.13. INPUT PROCEDURE logic: 2000-IP-SELECT-INV-RECORDS SECTION

The RELEASE statement

The RELEASE statement, shown in Figure 11.14, transfers the record in the sort work file record area to the sort work file; it is equivalent to a WRITE statement for an output file. Like the WRITE statement, it has a FROM option. In accordance with our structured programming conventions, it should be coded as a separate module. The RELEASE statement can only be specified within an INPUT PROCEDURE.

Notice that the IR-INVENTORY-RECORD was moved to the SR-SORT-RECORD area in module 2210-SELECT-INVENTORY-RECORD before performing 2830-RELEASE-INVENTORY-RECORD. That is, before releasing the record, the programmer must either MOVE the input record to the sort work record area or use the FROM option of the RELEASE statement. Many times the record formats of the input file and the sort file will not be the same. When this situation exists, MOVE statements for individual fields must be used (see Figure 11.15).

Format:

RELEASE record-name [FROM identifier]

Example:

SEQUENCE									COBOL STATEMENT								IDENTIFICATION	

```
283050      RELEASE SR-SORT-RECORD.                              SRT-PRE
                                   or
283050      RELEASE SR-SORT-RECORD FROM IR-INVENTORY-RECORD.     SRT-P-P
```

Figure 11.14. RELEASE statement examples

Recap of Sort Programs with Preprocessing of the Input File

Sort programs that preprocess the input file are coded with the INPUT PROCEDURE phrase of the SORT statement. Preprocessing of the input file is usually called for when any of the following program functions is required: (1) to select certain records from the input file and to sort only those selected records (as the SRT-PRE program does); (2) to create additional records to augment the input file and to sort the augmented file; (3) to change the record (record length, field size, field values, field locations, or the like) prior to sorting; (4) to edit or validate the records prior to sorting; (5) to list the input records prior to sorting; or (6) to count the records of one or more input files.

DATA DIVISION:

```
*
 01  IR-INPUT-RECORD.
     05   IR-RECORD-CODE           PIC X(2).
     05   IR-NAME                  PIC X(24).
     05   IR-SOC-SEC-NUMBER        PIC X(9).
     05   IR-DATE-OF-BIRTH         PIC X(6).
     05   IR-REST-OF-RECORD        PIC X(37).


*
 01  SR-SORT-RECORD.
     05   SR-RECORD-CODE           PIC X(2).
     05   SR-SOC-SEC-NUMBER        PIC X(9).
     05   SR-NAME                  PIC X(24).
     05   SR-DATE-OF-BIRTH         PIC X(6).
     05   SR-REST-OF-RECORD        PIC X(37).
```

PROCEDURE DIVISION:

```
     MOVE IR-RECORD-CODE TO SR-RECORD-CODE.
     MOVE IR-NAME TO SR-NAME.
     MOVE IR-SOC-SEC-NUMBER TO SR-SOC-SEC-NUMBER.
     MOVE IR-DATE-OF-BIRTH TO SR-DATE-OF-BIRTH.
     MOVE IR-REST-OF-RECORD TO SR-REST-OF-RECORD.
     RELEASE SR-SORT-RECORD.
```

Figure 11.15. Example of sort file record format modification from input record

Part A: System flowchart:

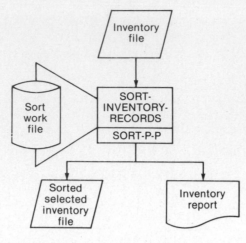

Part B: Record layout: Inventory record (blocking factor = 20)

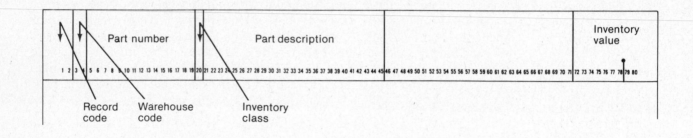

Part C: Print chart: Inventory report

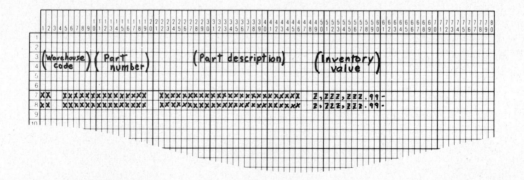

Part D: Programming specifications:

1. Inventory-class-codes are coded as "A", "B", or "C". Select and sort those inventory records from the inventory file that have an Inventory-class-code equal to "A".

2. After sorting, print each selected inventory record in accordance with the print chart specifications for the inventory report.

3. Write the sorted output to the sorted selected inventory file (blocking factor = 20).

Figure 11.16. Programming documentation: Sort with preprocessing of input inventory file and postprocessing of the sorted output file

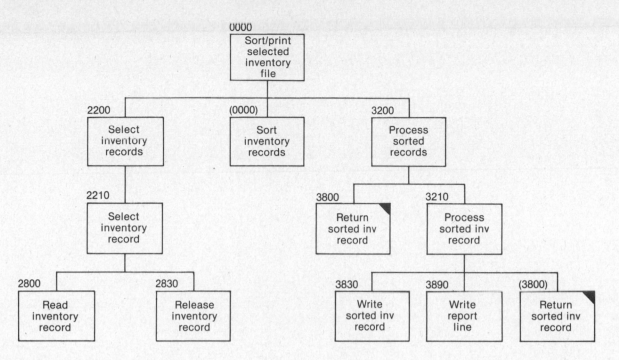

Figure 11.17. Structure chart: Sort with preprocessing of input inventory and postprocessing of the sorted output inventory file

A Sort Program with Preprocessing of the Input File and Postprocessing of the Sorted Output File

Specifications for the sort with preprocessing and postprocessing of inventory records are shown in Figure 11.16. These specifications are similar to those for the SRT-PRE program except that the sorted inventory records are to be printed. For program simplicity, no headings or page-skipping is specified.

The structure chart is shown in Figure 11.17. This program will be called SRT-P-P to indicate that it is an example of a sort with preprocessing of the input file and postprocessing of the sorted output file. Figure 11.18 presents the program coding for the first three divisions of the SRT-P-P program.

ENVIRONMENT and DATA DIVISION Coding

Because this program calls for an output report, an ASSIGN clause for the INVENTORY-REPORT-FILE has been specified in the FILE-CONTROL paragraph of the ENVIRONMENT DIVISION.

In the DATA DIVISION, an FD has been established for the INVENTORY-REPORT-FILE. Also, each field of the inventory record has been defined in the SI-INVENTORY-RECORD record-description. Most of these fields are required for moving to the RL-REPORT-LINE. Alternately, they could have been defined in the SR-SORT-RECORD.

PROCEDURE DIVISION Coding

Figure 11.18 presents the PROCEDURE DIVISION coding for the SRT-P-P program.

The SORT statement

In this program the GIVING phrase has been replaced by the OUTPUT PROCEDURE phrase.

The OUTPUT PROCEDURE phrase

To provide for processing of the sorted output records, the OUTPUT PROCEDURE phrase is specified. The SORT statement gives control to the output procedure after the sort has been completed.

```
001010 IDENTIFICATION DIVISION.                          004020 01  IR-INVENTORY-RECORD.
001020 PROGRAM-ID.      SRT-P-P.                          004030     05  FILLER                    PIC X(19).
001030*AUTHOR.          WELBURN.                          004040     05  IR-INVENTORY-CLASS-CODE   PIC X(1).
001040*INSTALLATION.    SILICON VALLEY MANUFACTURING COMPANY.    004050     05  FILLER                    PIC X(60).
001050*DATE-WRITTEN.    MAR 28,1981.                      005010*
001060*DATE-COMPILED.   MAR 28,1981.                      005020 FD  INVENTORY-REPORT-FILE
001070*SECURITY.        NONE.                             005030     RECORD CONTAINS 133 CHARACTERS
001080*                                                   005040     LABEL RECORDS ARE OMITTED.
001090*                                                   005050*
001100*              THIS IS A SORT PROGRAM WITH PRE-PROCESSING    005060 01  RL-REPORT-LINE.
001110*                    OF THE INPUT FILE              005070     05  FILLER                    PIC X(1).
001120*              AND POST-PROCESSING OF THE SORTED OUTPUT FILE  005080     05  RL-WAREHOUSE-CODE         PIC X(2).
001130*                                                   005090     05  FILLER                    PIC X(2).
001140*              THE FOLLOWING SORT STATEMENT PHRASES ARE SPECIFIED    005100     05  RL-PART-NUMBER            PIC X(15).
001150*                    INPUT PROCEDURE                005110     05  FILLER                    PIC X(2).
001160*                    OUTPUT PROCEDURE               005120     05  RL-PART-DESCRIPTION       PIC X(25).
002010*                                                   005130     05  FILLER                    PIC X(2).
002020*                                                   005140     05  RL-INVENTORY-VALUE        PIC Z,ZZZ,ZZZ.99-.
002030*                                                   005150     05  FILLER                    PIC X(71).
002040 ENVIRONMENT DIVISION.                              006010*
002050*                                                   006020 FD  SORTED-INVENTORY-FILE
002060*                                                   006030     RECORD CONTAINS 80 CHARACTERS
002070 CONFIGURATION SECTION.                             006040     BLOCK CONTAINS 20 RECORDS
002080*                                                   006050     LABEL RECORDS ARE STANDARD.
002090 SOURCE-COMPUTER.  IBM-370.                         006060*
002100 OBJECT-COMPUTER.  IBM-370.                         006070 01  SI-INVENTORY-RECORD.
002110*                                                   006080     05  SI-RECORD-CODE            PIC X(2).
002120*                                                   006090     05  SI-WAREHOUSE-CODE         PIC X(2).
002130 INPUT-OUTPUT SECTION.                              006100     05  SI-PART-NUMBER            PIC X(15).
002140*                                                   006110     05  SI-INVENTORY-CLASS-CODE   PIC X(1).
002150 FILE-CONTROL.                                      006120     05  SI-DESCRIPTION            PIC X(25).
002160     SELECT INVENTORY-FILE                          006130     05  FILLER                    PIC X(26).
002170          ASSIGN TO UT-S-INFILE.                    006140     05  SI-INVENTORY-VALUE        PIC S9(7)V99.
002180     SELECT INVENTORY-REPORT-FILE                   007010*
002190          ASSIGN TO UT-S-PRTFILE.                   007020 SD  SORT-FILE
002200     SELECT SORTED-INVENTORY-FILE                   007030     RECORD CONTAINS 80 CHARACTERS.
002210          ASSIGN TO UT-S-OUTFILE.                   007040*
002220     SELECT SORT-FILE                               007050 01  SR-SORT-RECORD.
002230          ASSIGN TO UT-S-SORTWORK.                  007060     05  FILLER                    PIC X(2).
003010*                                                   007070     05  SR-WAREHOUSE-CODE         PIC X(2).
003020*                                                   007080     05  SR-PART-NUMBER            PIC X(15).
003030*                                                   007090     05  FILLER                    PIC X(52).
003040 DATA DIVISION.                                     007100     05  SR-INVENTORY-VALUE        PIC S9(7)V99.
003050*                                                   020010*
003060*                                                   020020*
003070 FILE SECTION.                                      020030 WORKING-STORAGE SECTION.
003080*                                                   020040*
003090 FD  INVENTORY-FILE                                 020050*
003100     RECORD CONTAINS 80 CHARACTERS                  020060 01  WS-SWITCHES.
003110     BLOCK CONTAINS 20 RECORDS                      020070     05  WS-END-OF-FILE-SWITCH     PIC X(3).
003120     LABEL RECORDS ARE STANDARD.                    020080         88  END-OF-FILE                     VALUE 'YES'.
004010*
```

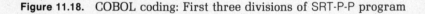

(handwritten annotations: "input file — major", "output file", "output file for sorted stuff", "work file")

Figure 11.18. COBOL coding: First three divisions of SRT-P-P program

```
050010*                                                   299010*
050020*                                                   299020*
050030*                                                   299030 2999-EXIT.
050040 PROCEDURE DIVISION.                                299040*
050050*                                                   299050     EXIT.
050060*                                                   300010*
050070 0000-ML-SORT-INV-RECORDS SECTION.                  300020*
050080*                                                   300030 3000-OP-PROCESS-SORTED-RECORDS SECTION.
050090*                                                   320040*
050100 0000-SORT-INV-RECORDS.                             320050*
050110*                                                   320060 3200-PROCESS-SORTED-RECORDS.
050120     OPEN INPUT INVENTORY-FILE                      320070*
050130          OUTPUT INVENTORY-REPORT-FILE              320080     MOVE 'NO ' TO WS-END-OF-FILE-SWITCH.
050140               SORTED-INVENTORY-FILE.               320090     PERFORM 3800-RETURN-SORTED-INV-RECORD.
050150     SORT SORT-FILE                                 320100     PERFORM 3210-PROCESS-SORTED-INV-RECORD
050160          ASCENDING KEY  SR-WAREHOUSE-CODE          320110          UNTIL END-OF-FILE.
050170          DESCENDING KEY SR-INVENTORY-VALUE         320120     GO TO 3999-EXIT.
050180          ASCENDING KEY  SR-PART-NUMBER             321010*
050190          INPUT PROCEDURE IS  2000-IP-SELECT-INV-RECORDS    321020*
050200          OUTPUT PROCEDURE IS 3000-OP-PROCESS-SORTED-RECORDS.    321030 3210-PROCESS-SORTED-INV-RECORD.
050210     CLOSE INVENTORY-FILE                           321040*
050220          INVENTORY-REPORT-FILE                     321050     MOVE SR-SORT-RECORD TO SI-INVENTORY-RECORD.
050230          SORTED-INVENTORY-FILE.                    321060     MOVE SPACES TO RL-REPORT-LINE.
050240     STOP RUN.                                      321070     MOVE SI-WAREHOUSE-CODE TO RL-WAREHOUSE-CODE.
200010*                                                   321080     MOVE SI-PART-NUMBER TO RL-PART-NUMBER.
200020*                                                   321090     MOVE SI-INVENTORY-CLASS-CODE TO RL-INVENTORY-CLASS-CODE.
200030 2000-IP-SELECT-INV-RECORDS SECTION.                321100     MOVE SI-INVENTORY-VALUE TO RL-INVENTORY-VALUE.
220010*                                                   321110     PERFORM 3830-WRITE-SORTED-INV-RECORD.
220020*                                                   321120     PERFORM 3890-WRITE-REPORT-LINE.
220030 2200-SELECT-INVENTORY-RECORDS.                     321130     PERFORM 3800-RETURN-SORTED-INV-RECORD.
220040*                                                   380010*
220050     MOVE 'NO ' TO WS-END-OF-FILE-SWITCH.           380020*
220060     PERFORM 2210-SELECT-INVENTORY-RECORD           380030 3800-RETURN-SORTED-INV-RECORD.
220080          UNTIL END-OF-FILE.                        380040*
220090     GO TO 2999-EXIT.                               380050     RETURN SORT-FILE
221010*                                                   380060          AT END MOVE 'YES' TO WS-END-OF-FILE-SWITCH.
221020*                                                   383010*
221030 2210-SELECT-INVENTORY-RECORD.                      383020*
221040*                                                   383030 3830-WRITE-SORTED-INV-RECORD.
221050     PERFORM 2800-READ-INVENTORY-RECORD.            383040*
221060     IF NOT END-OF-FILE                             383050     WRITE SI-INVENTORY-RECORD.
221070     AND IR-INVENTORY-CLASS-CODE IS EQUAL TO 'A'    383060*
221080          PERFORM 2830-RELEASE-INVENTORY-RECORD.    383070*
280010*                                                   383080 3890-WRITE-REPORT-LINE.
280020*                                                   383090*
280030 2800-READ-INVENTORY-RECORD.                        383100     WRITE RL-REPORT-LINE
280040*                                                   383110          AFTER ADVANCING 1 LINE.
280050     READ INVENTORY-FILE                            399010*
280060          AT END MOVE 'YES' TO WS-END-OF-FILE-SWITCH.    399020*
283010*                                                   399030 3999-EXIT.
283020*                                                   399040*
283030 2830-RELEASE-INVENTORY-RECORD.                     399050     EXIT.
283040*
283050     RELEASE SR-SORT-RECORD FROM IR-INVENTORY-RECORD.
```

Figure 11.19. COBOL coding: PROCEDURE DIVISION of SRT-P-P program

An output procedure is parallel to an input procedure. The section specified in this statement is performed after the sort has been completed. The output procedure cannot be referenced by any other statements. Within the output procedure, program control cannot be transferred to a procedure outside it and no SORT statements may be coded. Any output files created by the output procedure must be explicitly opened and closed by the programmer. Output procedures introduce structured programming problems identical to those of input procedures.

The OUTPUT PROCEDURE logic: 3000-OP-PROCESS-SORTED-RECORDS SECTION

After the SORT statement of module 0000-SORT-INV-RECORDS has completed the sort, this section is invoked. Its logic obtains each record from the sort work file, transfers it to the output SORTED-INVENTORY-FILE record area, moves specified fields to the report-line area, and writes the output sorted inventory record and report-line. After end-of-file has been reached on the sort work file, program control is transferred back to the next sequential statement following the SORT statement.

The RETURN statement

This statement, shown in Figure 11.20, is used to transfer the record from the sort work file to the sort work file record area; it is equivalent to a READ statement for an input file. Like the READ statement, it has an INTO option. In accordance with our structured programming conventions, it should be coded as a separate module. The RETURN statement can only be specified within an OUTPUT PROCEDURE.

Notice that the WS-END-OF-FILE-SWITCH is used for both the input INVENTORY-FILE and the SORT-FILE. Normally, separate end-of-file switches should be established for multiple files. However, since these two files cannot be processed at the same time, such multi-use is acceptable. Observe that it is necessary to re-initialize the switch to 'NO' at the beginning of the OUTPUT PROCEDURE.

Notes regarding the INPUT PROCEDURE

The INPUT PROCEDURE for the SRT-P-P program is identical in function to that of the SRT-PRE program. Just to show alternate approaches, the conditional-processing structure is used and the RELEASE statement contains the FROM phrase.

Format:

RETURN file-name RECORD [INTO identifier]

    AT END Imperative-statement

Example:

```
SEQUENCE                                          COBOL STATEMENT                                    IDENTIFICATION
(PAGE) (SERIAL)  A   B
1    3  4   6 7 8   12    16   20   24   28   32   36   40   44   48   52   56   60   64   68  72     76          80

380050          RETURN SORT-FILE                                                                    SRT-P-P
380060              AT END MOVE 'YES' TO WS-END-OF-FILE-SWITCH.                                      SRT-P-P
                                                  or
380050          RETURN SORT-FILE INTO SI-INVENTORY-RECORD                                           SRT-POST
380060              AT END MOVE 'YES' TO WS-END-OF-FILE-SWITCH.                                      SRT-POST
```

Figure 11.20. RETURN statement examples

431

Recap of Sort Programs with Postprocessing of the Sorted Output File

Sort programs that process the sorted output file are coded with the OUTPUT PROCEDURE phrase of the SORT statement. Processing of the sorted output file is appropriate when any of the following program functions are required: (1) to create more than one sorted output file; (2) to select or summarize records after sorting and before writing them to the sorted output file; (3) to create additional records to augment the sorted output file; (4) to change the record (record length, field size, field values, field locations, or the like) after sorting; (5) to list the sorted records (as the SORT-P-P program does); or (6) to count records of the output file or files.

A Sort Program with Postprocessing of the Sorted Output File

To provide an example of each of the four possible variations of USING, GIVING, INPUT PROCEDURE, and OUTPUT PROCEDURE clauses, we show an example of a program with a USING clause and an OUTPUT PROCEDURE in Figure 11.21. The program has been named SRT-POST. Although the output procedure for this program is similar in function to that of the SRT-P-P program, here the conditional-processing structure is used and the RETURN statement contains the INTO phrase. Also, to show an example of a SORT program with a totaling routine, this program provides for the printing of a total of inventory values at the end of the report.

The MERGE Statement

Utility sort programs are usually designed and written to handle the related function of merging. Figure 11.22 shows the COBOL statements that provide for the merging of two or more files. Recognize that, to merge files, each must already be in sequence according to the merge-key fields.

As you can infer from the similarity of the statements, merge programs follow the same general pattern as sort programs. However, there is one important difference. Notice from the MERGE statement format that an INPUT PROCEDURE phrase is not provided. That, in turn, means that RELEASE operations cannot be handled since the USING phrase of the MERGE statement must be used.

Without the INPUT PROCEDURE phrase, it is difficult to count the records from various input files being merged. When files are combined, however, it is a common data processing requirement to know how many records originated from each of the input files. Because of this limitation and because the MERGE statement is not available on all compilers, some programmers handle merges by coding the SORT statement with an INPUT PROCEDURE phrase, as shown in Figure 11.23. Notice that this coding also provides for the counting of records from each file.

In actual practice, the MERGE statement is rarely used because of (1) its generally limited applicability (merging situations are encountered only occasionally whereas sorting ones are common), (2) the INPUT PROCEDURE limitation, and (3) its restricted availability with COBOL compilers.

A Discussion of COBOL Sorts Versus External Sorts

On few COBOL subjects is there such a divergence of opinion as on the use of COBOL versus external sorts. Those programmers and organizational standards that recommend external sorts contend that external sorts (1) are quicker to write, (2) are easier to modify when sort-key specifications, field location, record size, or blocking factors change because they do not require recompilation of the COBOL program, and (3) eliminate the adverse effect upon program structure that the SORT statement's INPUT and OUTPUT PROCEDURE phrases introduce.

```
001010 IDENTIFICATION DIVISION.
001020 PROGRAM-ID.    SRT-POST.
001030*AUTHOR.        WELBURN.
001040*INSTALLATION.  SILICON VALLEY MANUFACTURING COMPANY.
001050*DATE-WRITTEN.  MAR 28,1981.
001060*DATE-COMPILED. MAR 28,1981.
001070*SECURITY.      NONE.
001080*
001090*
001100*          THIS IS A SORT PROGRAM WITH POST-PROCESSING
001110*               OF THE SORTED OUTPUT FILE
001120*
001130*          THE FOLLOWING SORT STATEMENT PHRASES ARE SPECIFIED
001140*               USING
001150*               OUTPUT PROCEDURE
002010*
002020*
002030*
002040 ENVIRONMENT DIVISION.
002050*
002060*
002070 CONFIGURATION SECTION.
002080*
002090 SOURCE-COMPUTER.  IBM-370.
002100 OBJECT-COMPUTER.  IBM-370.
002110*
002120*
002130 INPUT-OUTPUT SECTION.
002140*
002150 FILE-CONTROL.
002160     SELECT INVENTORY-FILE
002170         ASSIGN TO UT-S-INFILE.
002180     SELECT INVENTORY-REPORT-FILE
002190         ASSIGN TO UT-S-PRTFILE.
002200     SELECT SORTED-INVENTORY-FILE
002210         ASSIGN TO UT-S-OUTFILE.
002220     SELECT SORT-FILE
002230         ASSIGN TO UT-S-SORTWORK.
003010*
003020*
003030*
003040 DATA DIVISION.
003050*
003060*
003070 FILE SECTION.
003080*
003090 FD  INVENTORY-FILE
003100     RECORD CONTAINS 80 CHARACTERS
003110     BLOCK CONTAINS 20 RECORDS
003120     LABEL RECORDS ARE STANDARD.
004010*
004020 01  IR-INVENTORY-RECORD.
004030     05  FILLER                     PIC X(19).
004040     05  IR-INVENTORY-CLASS-CODE     PIC X(1).
004050     05  FILLER                     PIC X(60).
005010*
005020 FD  INVENTORY-REPORT-FILE
005030     RECORD CONTAINS 133 CHARACTERS
005040     LABEL RECORDS ARE OMITTED.
005050*
005060 01  RL-REPORT-LINE.
005070     05  FILLER                     PIC X(1).
005080     05  RL-WAREHOUSE-CODE          PIC X(2).
005090     05  FILLER                     PIC X(2).
005100     05  RL-PART-NUMBER             PIC X(15).
005110     05  FILLER                     PIC X(2).
005120     05  RL-PART-DESCRIPTION        PIC X(25).
005130     05  FILLER                     PIC X(2).
005140     05  RL-INVENTORY-VALUE         PIC Z,ZZZ,ZZZ.99-.
005150     05  FILLER                     PIC X(71).
006010*
006020 FD  SORTED-INVENTORY-FILE
006030     RECORD CONTAINS 80 CHARACTERS
006040     BLOCK CONTAINS 20 RECORDS
006050     LABEL RECORDS ARE STANDARD.
006060*
006070 01  SI-INVENTORY-RECORD.
006080     05  SI-RECORD-CODE             PIC X(2).
006090     05  SI-WAREHOUSE-CODE          PIC X(2).
006100     05  SI-PART-NUMBER             PIC X(15).
006110     05  SI-INVENTORY-CLASS-CODE     PIC X(1).
006120     05  SI-DESCRIPTION             PIC X(25).
006130     05  FILLER                     PIC X(26).
006140     05  SI-INVENTORY-VALUE         PIC S9(7)V99.
007010*
007020 SD  SORT-FILE
007030     RECORD CONTAINS 80 CHARACTERS.
007040*
007050 01  SR-SORT-RECORD.
007060     05  FILLER                     PIC X(2).
007070     05  SR-WAREHOUSE-CODE          PIC X(2).
007080     05  SR-PART-NUMBER             PIC X(15).
007090     05  FILLER                     PIC X(52).
007100     05  SR-INVENTORY-VALUE         PIC S9(7)V99.
```

```
020010*
020020*
020030 WORKING-STORAGE SECTION.
020040*
020050*
020060 01  WS-SWITCHES.
020070     05  WS-END-OF-FILE-SWITCH      PIC X(3).
020080         88  END-OF-FILE                        VALUE 'YES'.
021010*
021020 01  WS-TOTAL-ACCUMULATORS.
021030     05  WS-INVENTORY-VALUE-ACCUM    PIC S9(9)V99.
022010*
022020 01  TL-TOTAL-LINE.
022030     05  FILLER                     PIC X(1).
022040     05  FILLER                     PIC X(46) VALUE SPACES.
022050     05  TL-INVENTORY-VALUE         PIC ZZZ,ZZZ,ZZZ.99-.
022060     05  FILLER                     PIC X(1)  VALUE '*'.
022070     05  FILLER                     PIC X(70) VALUE SPACES.
050010*
050020*
050030*
050040 PROCEDURE DIVISION.
050050*
050060*
050070 0000-ML-SORT-INV-RECORDS SECTION.
050080*
050090*
050100 0000-SORT-INV-RECORDS.
050110*
050120     OPEN OUTPUT INVENTORY-REPORT-FILE
050130                 SORTED-INVENTORY-FILE.
050140     MOVE ZEROS TO WS-INVENTORY-VALUE-ACCUM.
050150     SORT SORT-FILE
050160         ASCENDING KEY SR-WAREHOUSE-CODE
050170         DESCENDING KEY SR-INVENTORY-VALUE
050180         ASCENDING KEY SR-PART-NUMBER
050190             USING INVENTORY-FILE
050200             OUTPUT PROCEDURE IS 3000-OP-PROCESS-SORTED-RECORDS.
050210     PERFORM 7000-PRINT-TOTAL-LINE.
050220     CLOSE INVENTORY-REPORT-FILE
050230           SORTED-INVENTORY-FILE.
050240     STOP RUN.
300010*
300020*
300030 3000-OP-PROCESS-SORTED-RECORDS SECTION.
320040*
320050*
320060 3200-PROCESS-SORTED-RECORDS.
320070*
320080     MOVE 'NO ' TO WS-END-OF-FILE-SWITCH.
320090     PERFORM 3210-PROCESS-SORTED-INV-RECORD
320100         UNTIL END-OF-FILE.
320110     GO TO 3999-EXIT.
321010*
321020*
321030 3210-PROCESS-SORTED-INV-RECORD.
321040*
321050     PERFORM 3800-RETURN-SORTED-INV-RECORD.
321060     IF NOT END-OF-FILE
321070         MOVE SPACES TO RL-REPORT-LINE
321080         MOVE SI-WAREHOUSE-CODE TO RL-WAREHOUSE-CODE
321090         MOVE SI-PART-NUMBER TO RL-PART-NUMBER
321100         MOVE SI-INVENTORY-VALUE TO RL-INVENTORY-VALUE
321110         ADD SI-INVENTORY-VALUE TO WS-INVENTORY-VALUE-ACCUM
321120         PERFORM 3830-WRITE-SORTED-INV-RECORD
321130         PERFORM 3890-WRITE-REPORT-LINE.
380010*
380020*
380030 3800-RETURN-SORTED-INV-RECORD.
380040*
380050     RETURN SORT-FILE INTO SI-INVENTORY-RECORD
380060         AT END MOVE 'YES' TO WS-END-OF-FILE-SWITCH.
383010*
383020*
383030 3830-WRITE-SORTED-INV-RECORD.
383040*
383050     WRITE SI-INVENTORY-RECORD.
383060*
383070*
383080 3890-WRITE-REPORT-LINE.
383090*
383100     WRITE RL-REPORT-LINE
383110         AFTER ADVANCING 1 LINE.
399010*
399020*
399030 3999-EXIT.
399040*
399050     EXIT.
700010*
700020*
700030 7000-PRINT-TOTAL-LINE SECTION.
770010*
770020*
770030 7700-PRINT-TOTAL-LINE.
770040*
770050     MOVE WS-INVENTORY-VALUE-ACCUM TO TL-INVENTORY-VALUE.
770060     MOVE TL-TOTAL-LINE TO RL-REPORT-LINE.
770070     PERFORM 3890-WRITE-REPORT-LINE.
```

Figure 11.21. COBOL coding: SRT-POST

On the other hand, those who favor COBOL sorts argue that they are standard and portable from one computer system to another; external sorts usually have different parameter statements for each operating system. This standardization and portability has the dual effect of easing future conversions and reducing the need for programmer training and retraining. Further, when field locations, record size, or blocking factors change, applicable COBOL programs must usually be modified and recompiled anyway, so sort

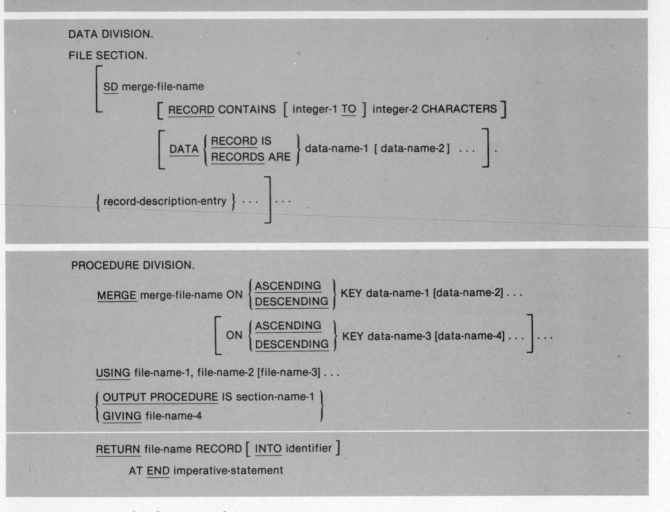

MERGE Formats:

ENVIRONMENT DIVISION.

INPUT-OUTPUT SECTION.

FILE CONTROL.

      SELECT merge-file-name

      ASSIGN TO implementor-name.

DATA DIVISION.

FILE SECTION.

    [SD merge-file-name

        [RECORD CONTAINS [integer-1 TO] integer-2 CHARACTERS]

        [DATA { RECORD IS / RECORDS ARE } data-name-1 [data-name-2] ...] .

      { record-description-entry } ...] ...

PROCEDURE DIVISION.

    MERGE merge-file-name ON { ASCENDING / DESCENDING } KEY data-name-1 [data-name-2] ...

      [ON { ASCENDING / DESCENDING } KEY data-name-3 [data-name-4] ...] ...

    USING file-name-1, file-name-2 [file-name-3] ...

    { OUTPUT PROCEDURE IS section-name-1 / GIVING file-name-4 }

    RETURN file-name RECORD [INTO identifier]

      AT END imperative-statement

Figure 11.22. Merge-related statement formats

modifications almost occur automatically as a byproduct. Probably most important, COBOL sort advocates point out that use of the SORT statement with IN-PUT and/or OUTPUT PROCEDURE phrases can enhance processing efficiency since INPUT and OUTPUT PROCEDURE sections process the records "on the fly" to and from the sort work area. Within a group of programs, this can have the effect of eliminating one read of the records from a file when INPUT PROCEDURE is used and one write of the records to a file when OUTPUT PROCEDURE is used. Figure 11.24 illustrates this situation.

Those who recommend the COBOL sorts are probably in the majority now because their arguments are more compatible with current views on program

Part A: Example of merging by specification of multiple USING files:

```
SORT SORT-FILE
    ASCENDING KEY SR-SORT-KEY-FIELD
    USING  FIRST-FILE
           SECOND-FILE
    GIVING MERGED-FILE.
```

Part B: Example of merging with an INPUT PROCEDURE:

```
*
*
 0000-ML-MERGE-TWO-FILES SECTION.
*
*
 0000-MERGE-TWO-FILES.
*
     OPEN INPUT FIRST-FILE
                SECOND-FILE.
     SORT SORT-FILE
          ASCENDING KEY SR-SORT-KEY-FIELD
          INPUT PROCEDURE 2000-IP-MERGE-FILES
          GIVING MERGED-FILE.
     CLOSE FIRST-FILE
           SECOND-FILE.
     STOP RUN.
*
*
 2000-IP-MERGE-FILES SECTION.
*
     MOVE 'NO ' TO WS-END-OF-FILE-SWITCH.
     MOVE ZEROS TO WS-FIRST-FILE-RECORDS
                   WS-SECOND-FILE-RECORDS.
     PERFORM 2200-PROCESS-FIRST-FILE
         UNTIL END-OF-FILE.
     MOVE 'NO ' TO WS-END-OF-FILE-SWITCH.
     PERFORM 2210-PROCESS-SECOND-FILE
         UNTIL END-OF-FILE.
     GO TO 2999-EXIT.
*
*
 2200-PROCESS-FIRST-FILE.
*
     PERFORM 2800-READ-FIRST-FILE-RECORD.
     IF NOT END-OF-FILE
         MOVE FF-FIRST-FILE-RECORD TO SR-SORT-RECORD
         ADD 1 TO WS-FIRST-FILE-RECORDS
         PERFORM 2830-RELEASE-MERGE-RECORD.
*
*
 2210-PROCESS-SECOND-FILE.
     PERFORM 2810-READ-SECOND-FILE-RECORD.
     IF NOT END-OF-FILE
         MOVE SF-SECOND-FILE-RECORD TO SR-SORT-RECORD
         ADD 1 TO WS-SECOND-FILE-RECORDS
         PERFORM 2830-RELEASE-MERGE-RECORD.
*
*
 2800-READ-FIRST-FILE-RECORD.
*
     READ FIRST-FILE
         AT END MOVE 'YES' TO WS-END-OF-FILE-SWITCH.
*
*
 2810-READ-SECOND-FILE-RECORD.
*
     READ SECOND-FILE
         AT END MOVE 'YES' TO WS-END-OF-FILE-SWITCH.
*
*
 2830-RELEASE-MERGE-RECORD.
*
     RELEASE SR-SORT-RECORD.
*
*
 2999-EXIT.
*
     EXIT.
```

Figure 11.23. Examples of merging with the SORT statement

portability and standardized data definition concepts. However, when writing programs for a particular data processing installation, the COBOL programmer must be aware of and follow organizational standards regarding sort program specifications.

Part A: External sort prior to COBOL report program:

Part B: COBOL SORT in report program:

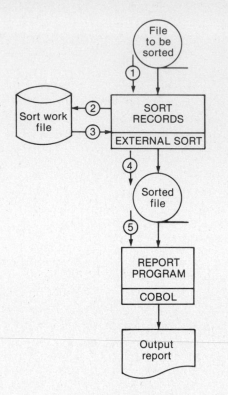

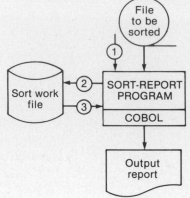

Part C: Input/output operation comparison

1. Read record from file to be sorted	1. Read record from file to be sorted.
2. Write to sort-work file	2. Write to sort-work file
3. Read record from sorted sort-work file	3. Read record from sorted sort-work file.
4. Write to sorted file	
5. Read record from sorted file	

Figure 11.24. Depiction of SORT statement efficiencies

Summary

The sorting of records may be handled either by the *external* (or *stand-alone*) sort program supplied with most computer operating systems or by an *internal* COBOL sort. When internal COBOL sorts are used, the COBOL program will take one of the four following variations: (1) sort only, (2) sort with preprocessing of the input file, (3) sort with preprocessing of the input file and postprocessing of the sorted output file, or (4) sort with postprocessing of the sorted output file.

Sort-only programs are specified with the USING and GIVING phrases of the SORT statement. They are not frequently written. However, sort programs that do other processing by preopening the USING file or reopening the GIVING file are sometimes encountered. Rather than preopening or reopening, though, the programmer should use the INPUT PROCEDURE or OUTPUT PROCEDURE phrases.

A *sort program with preprocessing of the input file* is coded with the IN-PUT PROCEDURE phrase of the SORT statement. This type of sort program is useful in the following ways: (1) to select and sort only certain records from the input file; (2) to create additional records to be included in the output sorted file; (3) to make changes to the input record; (4) to edit or validate records prior to sorting; (5) to list the input records prior to sorting; and (6) to count the input records and/or the records to be sorted.

A *sort program with preprocessing of the input file and postprocessing of the sorted output file* contains the INPUT PROCEDURE and OUTPUT PROCEDURE phrases of the SORT statement.

A *sort program with postprocessing of the sorted output file* is used for the following: (1) to create more than one sorted output file; (2) to select or summarize records after sorting and before writing them to the sorted output file; (3) to create additional records after sorting to be included in the output sorted file; (4) to change the record after sorting; (5) to list the sorted records; and (6) to count sorted output records.

When either INPUT PROCEDURE or OUTPUT PROCEDURE is specified for a SORT statement, three situations are introduced that are in conflict with generally accepted structured programming conventions: (1) the need for the use of sections, (2) the constraints on module structure and numbering; and (3) the need for the use of GO TO and EXIT statements.

Utility sort programs generally handle the related function of merging two or more input files that are already in the sequence specified by the merge-key. The INPUT PROCEDURE phrase is not available with the MERGE statement.

Those who recommend the use of external sorts rather than COBOL sorts contend that external sorts are quicker to write, easier to modify, and eliminate adverse effects upon COBOL program structure. Those who favor COBOL sorts argue for their portability, standardized data definition and modification qualities, and processing efficiencies.

1968 ANS COBOL Restrictions

- Multiple files cannot be specified in the USING clause.
- The MERGE statement is not available.

Exercises

Terms for Definition

parameter
external sort
stand-alone sort
internal sort
sort work file

Review Questions

1. When a SORT or MERGE statement is specified in a COBOL program, a _____Select_____ statement for the sort work file is required in the ENVIRONMENT DIVISION.

2. When a SORT or MERGE statement is specified in a COBOL program, an _____SD_____ entry is required in the FILE SECTION of the DATA DIVISION.

3. Sort key fields are specified by _Ascending_ KEY or _descending_ KEY phrases.

4. An input file to be sorted without preprocessing of the input records is specified with the _using_ phrase.

5. To create an output sorted file without postprocessing of the sorted records, the _Giving_ phrase is specified.

6. When preprocessing of the input file to be sorted is required, the _input procedure_ _____ phrase must be specified.

7. When postprocessing of the sorted file is required, the _output procedure_ phrase must be specified.

8. List six sort program requirements that call for specification of an INPUT PROCEDURE phrase. *427—*

9. List six sort program requirements that call for specification of an OUTPUT PROCEDURE phrase. *432—*

10. A RETURN statement is similar in function to a _read_ statement.

11. A RELEASE statement is similar in function to a _write_ statement.

12. Identify the three situations that are in conflict with generally accepted structured programming conventions but are introduced by use of the SORT or MERGE statements. *424—*

13. When files are merged, each file must already be _sequenced_.

14. In contrast to the SORT statement, the MERGE statement does not provide for specification of an _input procedure_ phrase.

Programming Assignment 11-A: Sort Accounts Receivable File

Program description

The accounts receivable file is to be sorted so that the accounts receivable records are sequenced by the customer name field in alphabetical order.

Input file

Accounts receivable file

Input record format

Accounts receivable record

Output file

Sorted accounts receivable file

Program operations

1. Sort the accounts receivable file so that the accounts receivable records are arranged in alphabetical order according to the customer name field.

2. When the customer name fields are identical, the duplicate records should be arranged in ascending sequence according to the customer account number.

Programming Assignment 11-B: Sort Active Accounts Receivable Records

Program description

Accounts receivable records containing a non-zero balance are to be selected from the accounts receivable file and sorted so that the accounts receivable records are sequenced by the customer name field in alphabetical order.

Input file

Accounts receivable file

Input record format

Accounts receivable record

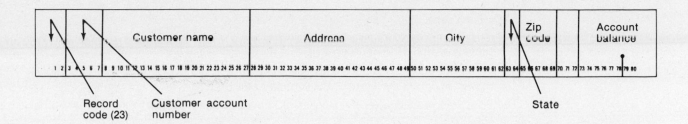

Record   Customer account   State
code (23)   number

Output file

 Sorted active accounts receivable file

Program operations

1. Extract accounts receivable records that contain an account balance that is not equal to zero and sort the selected records so that the accounts receivable records are arranged in alphabetical order according to the customer name field.

2. When the customer name fields are identical, the duplicate records should be arranged in ascending sequence according to the customer account number.

Programming Assignment 11-C: Sort and Print Customer List

Program description

 A customer list sequenced in alphabetical order by customer name is to be prepared from the accounts receivable file.

Input file

 Accounts receivable file

Input record format

 Accounts receivable record

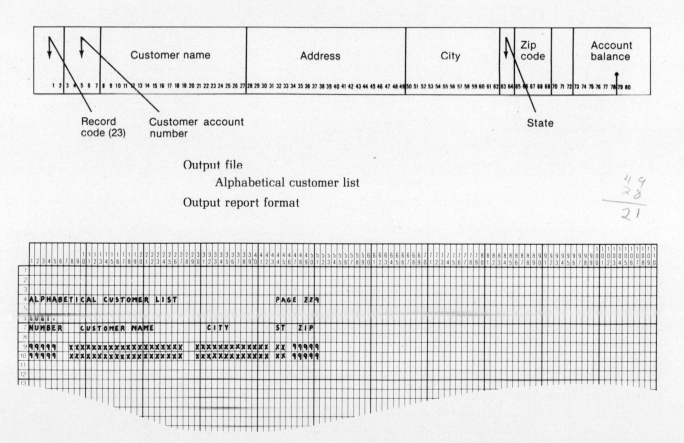

Record   Customer account   State
code (23)   number

Output file

 Alphabetical customer list

Output report format

Program operations

1. Sort the accounts receivable file so that the accounts receivable records are arranged in alphabetical order according to the customer name field.

2. When the customer name fields are identical, the duplicate records should be arranged in ascending sequence according to the customer account number.

3. Print each accounts receivable record in accordance with the format shown on the print chart.

4. Headings are to be printed on each page of the report. After 57 lines have been used on a report page, the program is to skip to the next page and print the report headings.

   a. The page number is to be incremented each time the heading is printed and displayed on the first heading-line in accordance with the format shown on the print chart.

5. Line spacing is to be handled as follows:

   a. The first detail-line after the headings is to be double-spaced from the last heading line.

   b. Detail lines are to be single-spaced.

Programming Assignment 11-D: Sort Active Accounts Receivable Records and Print Customer Account Balance Report

Program description

A customer account balanced report sequenced in descending order according to account balance is to be prepared from the accounts receivable file.

Input file

Accounts receivable file

Input record format

Accounts receivable record

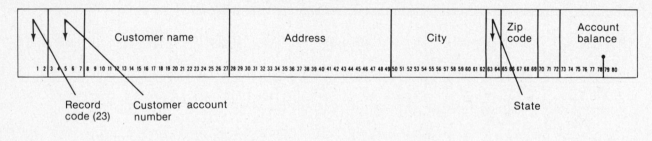

Output file

Customer account balance report

Output report format

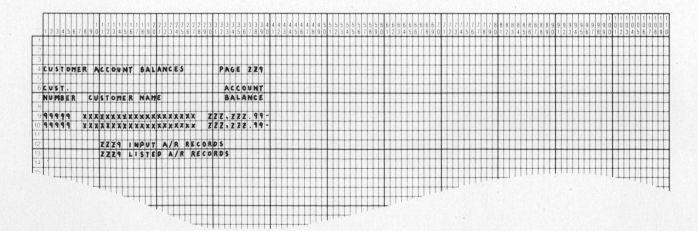

Program operations

1. Extract accounts receivable records that contain an account balance that is not equal to zero and sort the selected records so that the accounts receivable records are arranged in descending sequence according to the account balance field.

2. When the account balance fields are identical, the duplicate records should be arranged in ascending sequence according to the customer account number.

3. Print each sorted active accounts receivable record in accordance with the format shown on the print chart.

4. Count all input accounts receivable records (active and inactive) and each listed (active) accounts receivable record.

5. After all active accounts receivable records have been listed, print the record counts in accordance with the print chart specifications.

6. Headings are to be printed on each page of the report. After 57 lines have been used on a report page, the program is to skip to the next page and print the report headings.

   a. The page number is to be incremented each time the heading is printed and displayed on the first heading-line in accordance with the format shown on the print chart.

7. Line spacing is to be handled as follows:

   a. The first detail-line after the headings is to be double-spaced from the last heading line.

   b. Detail-lines are to be single-spaced.

   c. The record count total-lines are to be single-spaced from one another and double spaced from the last detail-line.

SYSTEMS CHAPTER E

TABLE HANDLING CONCEPTS

443

TABLE HANDLING CONCEPTS

The word "table" has a number of meanings in the English language. In data processing terminology, a *table* is "a collection of data in which each item is uniquely identified by a label, by its position relative to the other items, or by some other means." (This definition is taken from the *American National Dictionary for Information Processing*, published by the American National Computer and Business Equipment Manufacturers Association in 1977.)

Consider the familiar income tax table, a logarithmic table, a mileage table, or an airlines schedule. These are all tables used to present information in tabular form for a common reason: to provide data that is concise yet easy to read and understand.

Tables are used similarly in programming. They allow data to be stored compactly and referenced or retrieved efficiently by a program.

Let's take an example. Suppose we have input records containing a month-number field in which months are represented by two-digit codes. On output, however, we want to print the month names in alphabetic format as three-character abbreviations. A program table can be established to accomplish this task. Figure E.1 shows how the table could be formed and indicates the terminology used for its components.

A table contains *table entries*. A table entry may contain a *table argument* and one or more *table functions*. In the month-table example, there are 12 table entries. Each table entry contains a table argument—the month number—and one table function—the month-name abbreviation for the month represented by the month number. The field used to locate the appropriate table entry—in this case, the month-number field of the input record—is termed the *search argument*.

Table entries may have more than one table function. For example, in addition to the month abbreviation, suppose that the maximum number of days in each month is required for data validation purposes. A table can be constructed with two table functions, as shown in Figure E.2.

Table Organization Methods

When a program table is designed, there are four methods by which the table entry arguments can be organized: randomly, sequentially, by frequency of usage, and positionally.

Random Organization

A table of hypothetical soft-drink product codes together with their associated product names, or flavors, is shown in Figure E.3. The code numbers are the table arguments; the flavor names are the table functions. The table entries have been placed in the table in random product code-number order. Thus, random organization establishes table entry location haphazardly without concern for the values or characteristics of the table arguments.

Sequential Organization

Figure E.4 shows the same soft-drink product table, but this time the table entries are arranged in ascending sequence according to the value of the product code. Although arrangement could be made in descending sequence, ascending arguments are more common for sequentially organized tables.

Month number	Month name abbreviation
01	JAN
02	FEB
03	MAR
04	APR
05	MAY
06	JUN
07	JUL
08	AUG
09	SEP
10	OCT
11	NOV
12	DEC

Table entries

↑ Table argument   ↑ Table function

Figure E.1. Table components

Month number	Month name abbreviation	Maximum days in month
01	JAN	31
02	FEB	29
03	MAR	31
04	APR	30
05	MAY	31
06	JUN	30
07	JUL	31
08	AUG	31
09	SEP	30
10	OCT	31
11	NOV	30
12	DEC	31

Table entries

↑ Table argument   ↑ Table function-1   ↑ Table function-2

Figure E.2. Table with two functions

Usage-Frequency Organization

Sometimes a table will have some entries that are frequently referred to and others that receive only occasional reference. If a few table entries are expected to receive a significant percentage of references in relation to all other entries, it may optimize program processing efficiency to place the frequently used entries at the beginning of the table. For example, the soft-drink table can be arranged in the order of normal sales frequency patterns, as shown in Figure E.5.

Positional Organization

A positionally organized table is a sequential table with an unbroken sequence of numerical table arguments. Thus, if a table argument contains alphabetic or other non-numeric characters, or if it has large gaps between numerical codes (as the soft-drink product table does), the table is not a suitable candidate for positional organization. Such tables usually would require too many null entries to maintain the positional organization—that is, unused code numbers would require "dummy" table entries.

Product code (Table argument)	Soft drink flavor (Table function)
110	ORANGE
300	GINGER ALE
320	CREME SODA
120	CHERRY COLA
200	ROOT BEER
310	LIME RICKEY
500	COLA
100	LEMON-LIME
150	FRUIT PUNCH
140	GRAPE
130	STRAWBERRY

Figure E.3. Random table organization example

Product code (Table argument)	Soft drink flavor (Table function)
100	LEMON-LIME
110	ORANGE
120	CHERRY COLA
130	STRAWBERRY
140	GRAPE
150	FRUIT PUNCH
200	ROOT BEER
300	GINGER ALE
310	LIME RICKEY
320	CREME SODA
500	COLA

Figure E.4. Sequential table organization example

Product code (Table argument)	Soft drink flavor (Table function)
500	COLA
100	LEMON-LIME
200	ROOT BEER
120	CHERRY COLA
110	ORANGE
300	GINGER ALE
140	GRAPE
150	FRUIT PUNCH
130	STRAWBERRY
320	CREME SODA
310	LIME RICKEY

Figure E.5. Usage-frequency organization table example

Month name abbreviation	Maximum days in month
JAN	31
FEB	29
MAR	31
APR	30
MAY	31
JUN	30
JUL	31
AUG	31
SEP	30
OCT	31
NOV	30
DEC	31

| ↑ | ↑ |
| Table function-1 | Table function-2 |

Figure E.6. Positional organization table example

The month table discussed earlier can be considered a positionally organized table. It contains an unbroken sequence of numerical table arguments from 01 to 12. When a table is organized positionally, there is no need to store explicitly the table argument in the table; the table argument value can be determined implicitly by its relative position in the table. In other words, the ninth table entry can be considered to have a table argument of nine. Figure E.6 shows the month table as a positionally organized table without an explicit table argument.

Table Lookup Methods

A table is established and organized so that a program can efficiently access and retrieve data fields that relate to a given search argument. The process of locating the specific data fields is termed *table lookup*. There are three general table-lookup methods: serial search, binary search, and positional addressing.

Serial Search

A *serial search* compares the search argument with the argument of the first table entry. If they are equal, the appropriate table entry has been located. If they do not match, the program logic causes the search argument to be compared to the remaining table arguments, one by one, until either (1) a table argument that matches the search argument is encountered, or (2) the end of the table is reached. This logic is diagrammed in Figure E.7.

A serial search is the only lookup method that can be used with tables of random or usage-frequency organization. Serial searches are frequently used with sequentially organized tables, also.

There is a programming enhancement that can be incorporated into a serial search of a sequentially organized table. It can be termed the *serial search with early exit*.

For certain applications, a search argument may have no matching table argument. This can happen when (1) there are erroneously coded or keyed search arguments, or (2) the table contains only exception entries for items that require special handling.

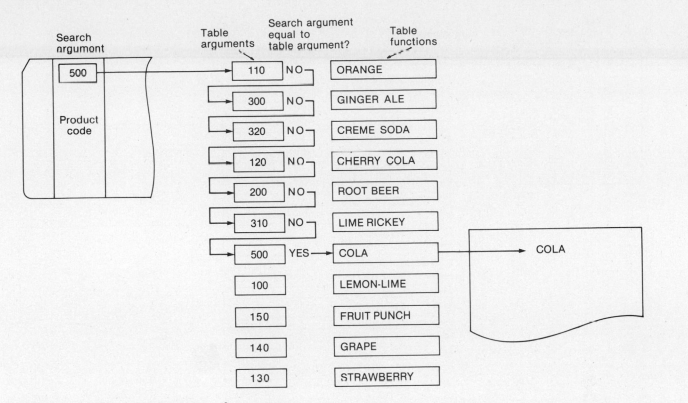

Figure E.7. Serial search logic example

For a table with random or usage-frequency organization, the entire table must be searched before it can be determined that a search argument has no corresponding table argument. Figure E.8 illustrates this requirement. The length of time required to make the search increases with the number of comparisons required between search and table arguments. That is, the longer the table, the longer the time required to reach the end of the table and thus to determine that there is no corresponding table argument.

Figure E.9 shows how a sequentially organized table using a serial search with early exit can reduce the number of comparisons required to determine that a search argument has no corresponding table argument. Rather than just check for an equal condition between search and table arguments, the program logic tests to see if the search argument is lower than the table argument. If it is, the equal table argument has clearly not yet been reached in the table. If the search argument is not lower than the table argument, however, the program logic then checks to see if it is equal to the table argument. If it is equal, the table entry has been located. If the search argument and table argument are not equal, not only has the table entry *not* been found, but—since the table arguments are organized in ascending sequence—it follows that the search argument does not have a corresponding table argument and the lookup may be terminated. This early-exit processing means that fewer comparisons are made and thus less time is expended for lookups.

Binary Search

When a table contains numerous table entries, a serial search for arguments whose entries are located deep in the table becomes time-consuming. For longer sequentially organized tables, the programmer can use a *binary search* instead of a serial search. A binary search can substantially reduce the average amount of time required to locate a table entry.

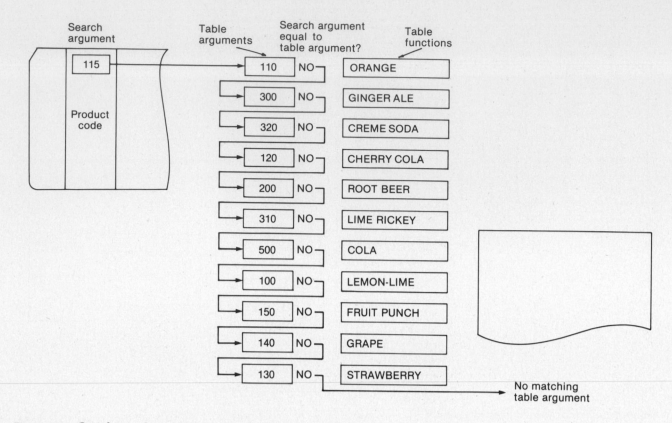

Figure E.8. Serial search with no corresponding table argument

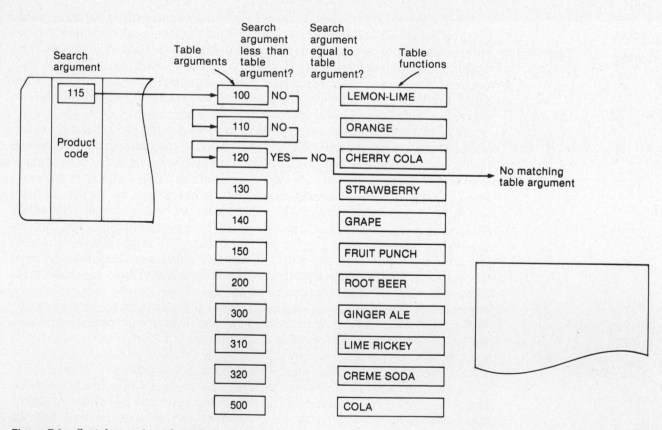

Figure E.9. Serial search with early exit example

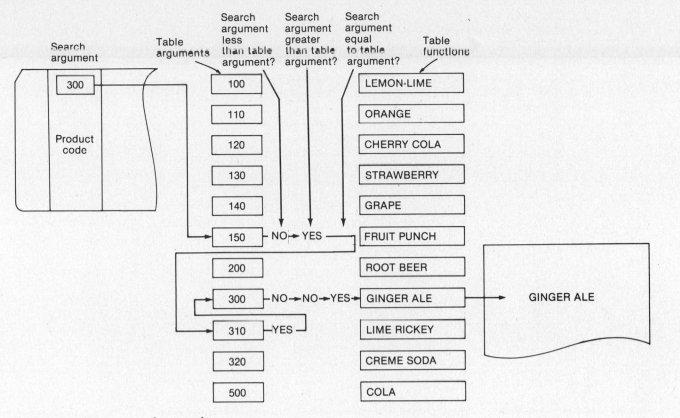

Figure E.10. Binary search example

The binary search technique is diagrammed in Figure E.10. Notice that the first comparison is made against the table argument in the middle of the table (rather than the first argument as is done with the serial search). Then either the top half or the bottom half of the table is searched, depending upon the relationship of the search argument to that midpoint table argument. If the search argument is less than the middle table argument, the lower half of the table must be checked. Conversely, if the search argument is greater than the middle table argument, the upper half of the table becomes the search area.

Next the search argument is compared with the argument of the middle entry in the selected half of the table to determine their relationship. Depending upon the result of that comparison, the table is again split in half and the middle entry of that portion of the table is checked. This halving process is repeated until an equal table argument is found or there are no remaining portions of the table to divide.

Recognize that a binary search cannot, of course, be used with a table organized randomly or by usage-frequency. There is no need to use a binary search for a positionally organized table.

Positional Addressing

Positional addressing requires no search. It is thus a rapid table-lookup method. With positional addressing, the search argument specifies the relative position (or an indication of the relative position) of the corresponding table entry. An example is shown in Figure E.11.

Remember that positional addressing applies only to positionally organized tables. Such tables require an unbroken sequence of numerical table arguments. However, the argument values need not start at 0 or 1. If the first table entry corresponded to a table argument value of 27, the matching table

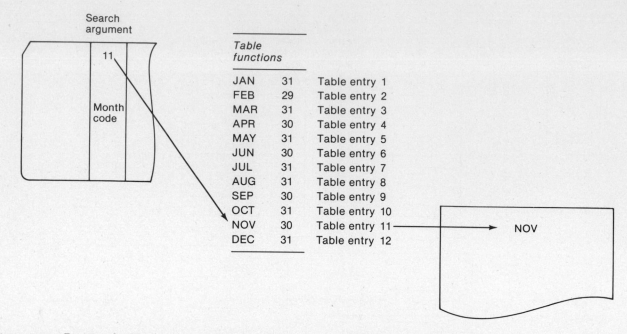

Figure E.11. Positional addressing example

Part A: Example of positional addressing when first table entry value is greater than a value of 1.

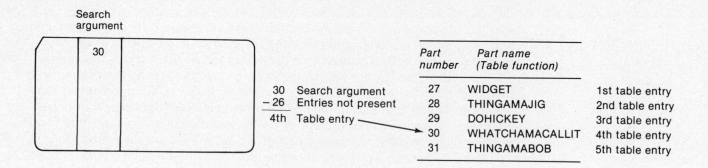

Part B: Example of positional addressing when first table entry value is less than a value of 1.

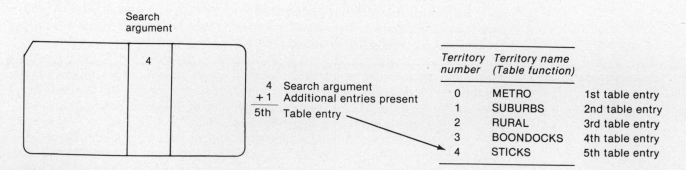

Figure E.12. Other positional addressing examples

Table organization	Lookup method			
	Serial search	Serial search with early exit	Binary search	Positional addressing
Random	Same lookup efficiency as for sequential organization			
Sequential	Lookup may be slow if number of table entries is large	Improves serial search when many search arguments do not have matching table argument	Most efficient sequential lookup for longer tables (differential increases as table gets longer)	
Usage-frequency	Efficient lookup if great majority of search arguments are just a few table entries			
Positionally				Immediate lookup

Figure E.13. Summary of table organization and lookup characteristics

entry could be determined by subtracting a value of 26 from the search argument value. Figure E.12 provides examples.

Before attempting to access a positionally addressed table, however, the programmer must validate to ensure that the search argument is within the range of the table. For example, when positionally addressing the month-name table, it is mandatory that the search argument value be greater than 0 and less than 13. If an out-of-range value is used, erroneous processing occurs.

Figure E.13 summarizes table organization and lookup characteristics.

Multiple-Level Tables

The tables discussed so far are all examples of *single-level*, or *one-dimensional*, tables. Some applications require tables with two or more dimensions. Such tables can be termed *multiple-level*, or *multidimensional* tables. A multiple-level table has, in effect, tables within each table entry.

A federal income tax withholding table, as shown in Figure E. 14, is an example of a two-level table. The first level pertains to amount of earnings ("wages"); the second level applies to number of exemptions ("withholding allowances") claimed.

An example of a three-level table is shown in Figure E.15.

WEEKLY PAYROLL PERIOD
SINGLE PERSONS – UNMARRIED HEADS OF HOUSEHOLD
WAGES: $135 — $670 and over

And the wages are—		And the number of withholding allowances claimed is—										
At least	Less than	0	1	2	3	4	5	6	7	8	9	10 or more
		The amount of income tax to be withheld shall be—										
$135	$140	$19.00	$15.30	$11.80	$8.40	$5.00	$2.10					
140	145	20.00	16.20	12.70	9.30	5.80	2.90					
145	150	21.10	17.10	13.60	10.20	6.70	3.60	$ .70				
150	160	22.60	18.60	15.00	11.50	8.10	4.70	1.80				
160	170	24.70	20.70	16.80	13.30	9.90	6.40	3.30	$ .50			
170	180	26.80	22.80	18.80	15.10	11.70	8.20	4.80	2.00			
180	190	28.90	24.90	20.90	16.90	13.50	10.00	6.50	3.50	$ .60		
190	200	31.00	27.00	23.00	18.90	15.30	11.80	8.30	5.00	2.10		
200	210	33.60	29.10	25.10	21.00	17.10	13.60	10.10	6.70	3.60	$ .70	
210	220	36.20	31.20	27.20	23.10	19.10	15.40	11.90	8.50	5.10	2.20	

Level-1 table arguments — Level-2 table arguments

Figure E.14. Two-level table example

Product-code	Quantity ordered							
	1		2-6		7-12		13-up	
	Customer-type-1	Customer-type-2	Customer-type-1	Customer-type-2	Customer-type-1	Customer-type-2	Customer-type-1	Customer-type-2
A1818	$110.00	$102.00	$100.00	$ 92.00	$ 95.00	$ 86.00	$ 90.00	$ 81.00
A2418	128.00	115.00	117.00	105.00	111.00	100.00	106.00	95.00
A3018	139.00	125.00	127.00	114.00	120.00	108.00	114.00	103.00
A2424	149.00	134.00	136.00	122.00	129.00	116.00	123.00	111.00
A3024	161.00	146.00	146.00	132.00	139.00	125.00	131.00	118.00
A3624	173.00	158.00	157.00	141.00	149.00	144.00	142.00	128.00
A4824	200.00	180.00	182.00	164.00	173.00	156.00	164.00	148.00

Level-1
table arguments

Level-3
table arguments

Figure E.15. Three-level table example

Part A: Hard-coded table   **Part B:** Input-loaded table

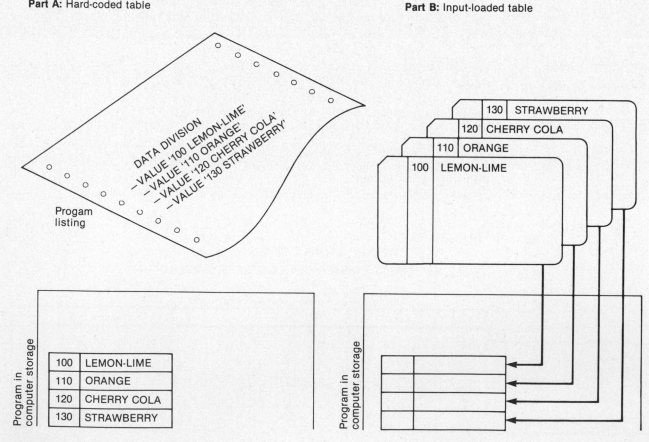

Figure E.16. Hard-coded and input-loaded tables

CHAPTER 12

TABLE PROCESSING

12

TABLE PROCESSING

Table processing is a very important COBOL subject. In this chapter, a number of table processing topics will be covered. The following COBOL elements will be introduced: (1) the OCCURS clause, (2) subscripts, (3) the VARYING phrase of the PERFORM statement, (4) the INDEXED BY clause, (5) the SET statement, (6) index data-items, and (7) the SEARCH statement.

Establishing and Accessing a Positionally Organized Table

Tables are defined in the WORKING-STORAGE SECTION of the DATA DIVISION and accessed in the PROCEDURE DIVISION. Suppose, for example, that we want to define a table of three-letter month abbreviations so that input records containing a month number from 01 to 12 can be processed and printed out with the month abbreviation. This can be done efficiently by establishing a *positionally organized* table in WORKING-STORAGE and then writing PROCEDURE DIVISION statements to handle the logic.

Establishing the Table in the WORKING-STORAGE SECTION

To establish a "hard-coded" storage table, the programmer must first define the abbreviations with VALUE clauses as shown in Figure 12.1. Notice that each one of the twelve table elements has been specified as a separate data-item. Such separate definition is not actually necessary. The table could be defined with multiple table elements within a data-item, as shown in Figure 12.2. The approach of using separate data-items for each table element is recommended, though, because (1) the table entries are easier to read; (2) the table is easier to modify when additions, changes, or deletions to the table become necessary; (3) when COMP and COMP-3 usage is desired for the storage of numeric table arguments or functions, each field *must* be specified as a separate data-item (to provide for proper data representation and sign handling).

After the table data have been specified with VALUE clauses, the table must be redefined with an OCCURS clause, as shown in Figure 12.3.

The OCCURS clause

The OCCURS clause is used to indicate how many times a particular field or group of fields is repeated. Its format is shown in Figure 12.4. The integer specified in the OCCURS clause specifies the number of repetitions. The OCCURS clause can be used with any data-item description that has a level number from 02 though 49; it cannot be used with an 01-level or 77-level item. One other restriction is that a data-item with an OCCURS clause cannot contain a VALUE clause.

The prohibition that a data-item cannot contain both an OCCURS and a VALUE clause explains why the table must first be defined with the appropriate VALUE clause data and then redefined with the OCCURS clause.

So, as depicted in Figure 12.5, the coding for the MT-MONTH-ABBREVIATION-DATA specifies 36 character positions containing the 12 three-letter month abbreviations. The MT-MONTH-ABBREVIATION-TABLE redefines those 36 storage positions as 12 occurrences of a three-character field called MT-MONTH-ABBREVIATION.

```
SEQUENCE  C A  B                              COBOL STATEMENT                        IDENTIFICATION
(PAGE)(SERIAL) O
1    3 4   6 7 8  12   16   20   24   28   32   36   40   44   48   52   56   60   64   68  72    76    80

         Ø1  MT-MONTH-ABBREVIATION-DATA.
             Ø5   FILLER            PIC  X(3)      VALUE  'JAN'.
                                                         'FEB'.
                                                         'MAR'.
                                                         'APR'.
                                                         'MAY'.
                                                         'JUN'.
                                                         'JUL'.
                                                         'AUG'.
                                                         'SEP'.
                                                         'OCT'.
                                                         'NOV'.
             Ø5   FILLER            PIC  X(3)      VALUE  'DEC'.
```

Figure 12.1. Establishing table data in WORKING-STORAGE: Recommended method

```
SEQUENCE  C A  B                              COBOL STATEMENT                        IDENTIFICATION
(PAGE)(SERIAL) O
1    3 4   6 7 8  12   16   20   24   28   32   36   40   44   48   52   56   60   64   68  72    76    80

         Ø1  MT-MONTH-ABBREVIATION-DATA.
             Ø5   FILLER            PIC  X(36)
                  VALUE  'JANFEBMARAPRMAYJUNJULAUGSEPOCTNOVDEC'.
```

Figure 12.2. Establishing table data in WORKING-STORAGE: Not recommended method

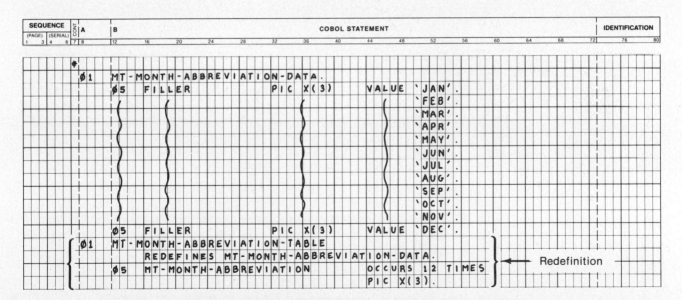

Figure 12.3. Redefinition of table data using the OCCURS clause

Format:

OCCURS Integer TIMES

Figure 12.4. OCCURS clause format

JAN	MT-MONTH-ABBREVIATION occurrence 1
FEB	MT-MONTH-ABBREVIATION occurrence 2
MAR	MT-MONTH-ABBREVIATION occurrence 3
APR	MT-MONTH-ABBREVIATION occurrence 4
MAY	MT-MONTH-ABBREVIATION occurrence 5
JUN	MT-MONTH-ABBREVIATION occurrence 6
JUL	MT-MONTH-ABBREVIATION occurrence 7
AUG	MT-MONTH-ABBREVIATION occurrence 8
SEP	MT-MONTH-ABBREVIATION occurrence 9
OCT	MT-MONTH-ABBREVIATION occurrence 10
NOV	MT-MONTH-ABBREVIATION occurrence 11
DEC	MT-MONTH-ABBREVIATION occurrence 12

Figure 12.5. Depiction of table specifications

Accessing the Table in the PROCEDURE DIVISION

Whenever an OCCURS clause is associated with a data-item, either a *subscript* or an *index* must be used when referring to that item in the PROCEDURE DIVISION. Subscripts will be covered at this time; indexes will be discussed later in this chapter.

Subscripts

Subscripts are used to reference a specific occurrence of a repeated field defined with the OCCURS clause. The subscript indicates which occurrence of the field is being referenced. For example, in the month abbreviation table, JAN is occurrence 1, FEB is occurrence 2, MAR is occurrence 3, and so forth. There are two forms of subscripts, *literal* and *variable*.

Literal Subscripts

Figure 12.6 shows how the month abbreviation AUG would be extracted from the table with a literal subscript and placed in an output report line field called RL-MONTH-ABBREVIATION. The occurrence number—8, in this case—is simply placed in parentheses following the data-name MT-MONTH-ABBREVIATION.

Literal subscripts have limited use because they must be precoded in the program. For example, to convert an input field that is called IN-MONTH-NUMBER to its three-letter abbreviation and to place it in the RL-MONTH-ABBREVIATION field, the programmer must use rather lengthy literal subscript logic, as shown in Figure 12.7. As we will see, variable subscripts are much more powerful and thus more frequently used.

Variable subscripts

Variable subscripts use the value contained in a field to indicate the occurrence number. Like the literal subscript, it is coded within parentheses and follows the data-name being referenced. As shown in Figure 12.8, the actual value contained in the IN-MONTH-NUMBER field will be used to identify which of the 12 occurrences of MT-MONTH-ABBREVIATION is to be moved to the RL-MONTH-ABBREVIATION field.

Observe how this one statement with a variable subscript—MOVE MT-MONTH-ABBREVIATION (IN-MONTH-NUMBER) TO RL-MONTH-ABBREVIATION—replaces the lengthy IF statement of Figure 12.7, which used literal subscripts.

MT-MONTH-ABBREVIATION
number occurrence

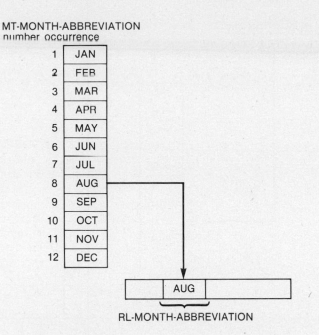

RL-MONTH-ABBREVIATION

Literal subscript example:

SEQUENCE		CONT	A	B	COBOL STATEMENT	IDENTIFICATION
(PAGE)	(SERIAL)					

```
MOVE MT-MONTH-ABBREVIATION (8) TO RL-MONTH-ABBREVIATION.
```

Figure 12.6. Example of table accessing with a literal subscript

```
                .
                .
                .
      IF IN-MONTH-NUMBER IS EQUAL TO 01
          MOVE MT-MONTH-ABBREVIATION (1) TO RL-MONTH-ABBREVIATION
      ELSE IF IN-MONTH-NUMBER IS EQUAL TO 02
          MOVE MT-MONTH-ABBREVIATION (2) TO RL-MONTH-ABBREVIATION
      ELSE IF IN-MONTH-NUMBER IS EQUAL TO 03
          MOVE MT-MONTH-ABBREVIATION (3) TO RL-MONTH-ABBREVIATION
      ELSE IF IN-MONTH-NUMBER IS EQUAL TO 04
          MOVE MT-MONTH-ABBREVIATION (4) TO RL-MONTH-ABBREVIATION
      ELSE IF IN-MONTH-NUMBER IS EQUAL TO 05
          MOVE MT-MONTH-ABBREVIATION (5) TO RL-MONTH-ABBREVIATION
      ELSE IF IN-MONTH-NUMBER IS EQUAL TO 06
          MOVE MT-MONTH-ABBREVIATION (6) TO RL-MONTH-ABBREVIATION
      ELSE IF IN-MONTH-NUMBER IS EQUAL TO 07
          MOVE MT-MONTH-ABBREVIATION (7) TO RL-MONTH-ABBREVIATION
      ELSE IF IN-MONTH-NUMBER IS EQUAL TO 08
          MOVE MT-MONTH-ABBREVIATION (8) TO RL-MONTH-ABBREVIATION
      ELSE IF IN-MONTH-NUMBER IS EQUAL TO 09
          MOVE MT-MONTH-ABBREVIATION (9) TO RL-MONTH-ABBREVIATION
      ELSE IF IN-MONTH-NUMBER IS EQUAL TO 10
          MOVE MT-MONTH-ABBREVIATION (10) TO RL-MONTH-ABBREVIATION
      ELSE IF IN-MONTH-NUMBER IS EQUAL TO 11
          MOVE MT-MONTH-ABBREVIATION (11) TO RL-MONTH-ABBREVIATION
      ELSE IF IN-MONTH-NUMBER IS EQUAL TO 12
          MOVE MT-MONTH-ABBREVIATION (12) TO RL-MONTH-ABBREVIATION.
                .
                .
                .
```

Figure 12.7. Coding for table accessing with literal subscripts

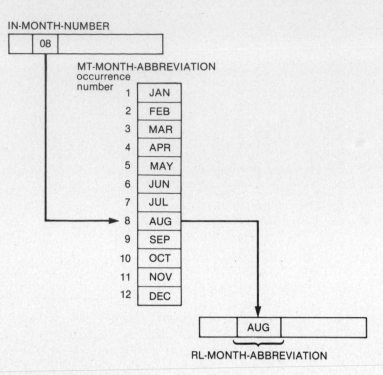

IN-MONTH-NUMBER

MT-MONTH-ABBREVIATION
occurrence
number

1	JAN
2	FEB
3	MAR
4	APR
5	MAY
6	JUN
7	JUL
8	AUG
9	SEP
10	OCT
11	NOV
12	DEC

RL-MONTH-ABBREVIATION

Variable subscript example:

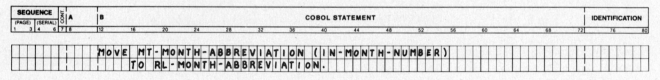

```
MOVE MT-MONTH-ABBREVIATION (IN-MONTH-NUMBER)
     TO RL-MONTH-ABBREVIATION.
```

Figure 12.8. Example of table accessing with a variable subscript

Variable subscripts must be elementary numeric integer data-items defined in the DATA DIVISION. The length of the subscript field must be sufficient to contain the number of occurrences specified in the OCCURS clause. They may be of any USAGE, but subscripts that are of COMP usage are most efficient. So, when subscripts are established within WORKING-STORAGE, they should be specified with COMP usage. Sometimes, however, a subscript will be an existing field within a record, as is the case with our IN-MONTH-NUMBER field. In such cases, the pre-existing usage of the field must, of course, be maintained.

When the program is executing the statement containing the subscript, the value of the subscript field should be greater than zero and not greater than the number of occurrences of the field being referenced, as specified in the OCCURS clause. For example, if IN-MONTH-NUMBER contained a value of zero or of 13 the subscript would be outside the range of the table and hence provide erroneous results or program termination (depending upon the compiler and computer system). So, when an input field is being used for a subscript, it is imperative that its value be validated before it is used (or by a prior data validation program). Figure 12.9 provides an example of a validation for the IN-MONTH-NUMBER field. With this logic, whenever an invalid month number is detected in the IN-MONTH-NUMBER field, the error condition will be identified by the printing of three asterisks in the RL-MONTH-ABBREVIATION field.

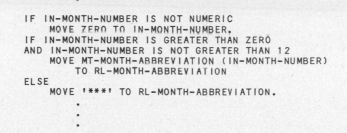

```
         IF IN-MONTH-NUMBER IS NOT NUMERIC
             MOVE ZERO TO IN-MONTH-NUMBER.
         IF IN-MONTH-NUMBER IS GREATER THAN ZERO
         AND IN-MONTH-NUMBER IS NOT GREATER THAN 12
             MOVE MT-MONTH-ABBREVIATION (IN-MONTH-NUMBER)
                 TO RL-MONTH-ABBREVIATION
         ELSE
             MOVE '***' TO RL-MONTH-ABBREVIATION.
```

Figure 12.9. Example of validation of variable subscript range

Other Table Establishment Considerations

Uniform field lengths

Often, data for table elements will not be of equal lengths. For example, if we established a table of full month names, the shortest table entry (MAY) would contain three characters and the longest (SEPTEMBER) would be nine positions in length. So that the OCCURS clause can properly identify the repetition of fields, each table entry must be as long as the longest entry. Figure 12.10 shows an example of such coding; here, shorter month names are padded with rightmost blank spaces to equal the length of the longest month name.

Naming the table data-items that contain the data value

In the month abbreviation table and the month name table, notice that each of the data-items was not given a user-defined name but instead named FILLER. This is usually appropriate because the data is normally referred to only by the redefined data-name associated with the OCCURS clause. User-defined names could be specified, though, if desired. For instance, if certain table elements are referred to with variable subscripts and also referred to specifically with a literal subscript, a user-defined descriptive data-name can be used for the specific references instead of a subscript. This technique also minimizes required program maintenance if the occurrence number of the table entry is changed due to additions or deletions. Figure 12.11 provides an example.

SEQUENCE		CONT	A	B	COBOL STATEMENT	IDENTIFICATION

```
     Ø1  MT-MONTH-NAME-DATA.
         Ø5  FILLER              PIC  X(9)    VALUE 'JANUARY  '.
                                               'FEBRUARY '.
                                               'MARCH    '.
                                               'APRIL    '.
                                               'MAY      '.
                                               'JUNE     '.
                                               'JULY     '.
                                               'AUGUST   '.
                                               'SEPTEMBER'.
                                               'OCTOBER  '.
                                               'NOVEMBER '.
         Ø5  FILLER              PIC  X(9)    VALUE 'DECEMBER '.
     Ø1  MT-MONTH-NAME-TABLE  REDEFINES MT-MONTH-NAME-DATA.
         Ø5  MT-MONTH-NAME               OCCURS 12 TIMES
                                         PIC  X(9).
```

Figure 12.10 Example of a table with data of varying length padded to uniform length

DATA DIVISION:

```
*
  01   TT-TAX-RATE-DATA.
       05   FILLER         PIC V9999    VALUE .0600.
       05   FILLER         PIC V9999    VALUE .0610.
       05   TT-DEFAULT-RATE PIC V9999   VALUE .0625.
       05   FILLER         PIC V9999    VALUE .0633.
       05   FILLER         PIC V9999    VALUE .0650.
  01   TT-TAX-RATE-TABLE REDEFINES TT-TAX-RATE-DATA.
       05   TT-TAX-RATE                 OCCURS 5 TIMES
                                        INDEXED BY TT-INDEX
                                          PIC V9999.
```

PROCEDURE DIVISION:

```
                    .
                    .
                    .
       IF IN-TAX-RATE-CODE IS GREATER THAN ZERO
       AND IN-TAX-RATE-CODE IS NOT GREATER THAN 5
           MULTIPLY XX-PURCHASE-AMOUNT BY TT-TAX-RATE (TT-INDEX)
       ELSE
           MULTIPLY XX-PURCHASE-AMOUNT BY TT-DEFAULT-RATE.
                    .
                    .
                    .
```

Figure 12.11. Example of table data using a data-name in the data-item description

---

Serial Table Lookups Using Subscripts

Positionally organized tables, such as the month abbreviation and month name tables, do not contain a table argument (implicitly, it is the entry's relative occurrence number). When a table is to be used with a *serial lookup*, however, each table entry will usually contain one table argument and one or more table functions. For example, if we had input records with two-character state abbreviations and wished to look up the complete state name, a 51-entry (50 states plus the District of Columbia) table containing a table argument of state abbreviation and a table function of the complete state name could be defined as shown in Figure 12.12. Each of the 51 entries contains the two-letter state abbreviation followed immediately by the state name. The entries are in alphabetical sequence according to the table arguments: state abbreviation. Notice that the OCCURS clause has been specified at the group level for the ST-STATE-ENTRY data-item. Specification of the OCCURS clause at the group level causes all elementary fields within the group to occur that number of times.

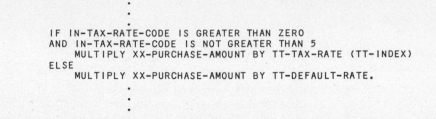

```
*
  01  ST-STATE-DATA.
      05  FILLER    PIC X(22) VALUE 'AKALASKA             '.      05  FILLER    PIC X(22) VALUE 'NDNORTH DAKOTA       '.
      05  FILLER    PIC X(22) VALUE 'ALALABAMA            '.      05  FILLER    PIC X(22) VALUE 'NENEBRASKA           '.
      05  FILLER    PIC X(22) VALUE 'ARARKANSAS           '.      05  FILLER    PIC X(22) VALUE 'NHNEW HAMPSHIRE      '.
      05  FILLER    PIC X(22) VALUE 'AZARIZONA            '.      05  FILLER    PIC X(22) VALUE 'NJNEW JERSEY         '.
      05  FILLER    PIC X(22) VALUE 'CACALIFORNIA         '.      05  FILLER    PIC X(22) VALUE 'NMNEW MEXICO         '.
      05  FILLER    PIC X(22) VALUE 'COCOLORADO           '.      05  FILLER    PIC X(22) VALUE 'NVNEVADA             '.
      05  FILLER    PIC X(22) VALUE 'CTCONNECTICUT        '.      05  FILLER    PIC X(22) VALUE 'NYNEW YORK           '.
      05  FILLER    PIC X(22) VALUE 'DCDISTRICT OF COLUMBIA'.     05  FILLER    PIC X(22) VALUE 'OHOHIO               '.
      05  FILLER    PIC X(22) VALUE 'DEDELAWARE           '.      05  FILLER    PIC X(22) VALUE 'OKOKLAHOMA           '.
      05  FILLER    PIC X(22) VALUE 'FLFLORIDA            '.      05  FILLER    PIC X(22) VALUE 'OROREGON             '.
      05  FILLER    PIC X(22) VALUE 'GAGEORGIA            '.      05  FILLER    PIC X(22) VALUE 'PAPENNSYLVANIA       '.
      05  FILLER    PIC X(22) VALUE 'HIHAWAII             '.      05  FILLER    PIC X(22) VALUE 'RIRHODE ISLAND       '.
      05  FILLER    PIC X(22) VALUE 'IAIOWA               '.      05  FILLER    PIC X(22) VALUE 'SCSOUTH CAROLINA     '.
      05  FILLER    PIC X(22) VALUE 'IDIDAHO              '.      05  FILLER    PIC X(22) VALUE 'SDSOUTH DAKOTA       '.
      05  FILLER    PIC X(22) VALUE 'ILILLINOIS           '.      05  FILLER    PIC X(22) VALUE 'TNTENNESSEE          '.
      05  FILLER    PIC X(22) VALUE 'ININDIANA            '.      05  FILLER    PIC X(22) VALUE 'TXTEXAS              '.
      05  FILLER    PIC X(22) VALUE 'KSKANSAS             '.      05  FILLER    PIC X(22) VALUE 'UTUTAH               '.
      05  FILLER    PIC X(22) VALUE 'KYKENTUCKY           '.      05  FILLER    PIC X(22) VALUE 'VAVIRGINIA           '.
      05  FILLER    PIC X(22) VALUE 'LALOUISIANA          '.      05  FILLER    PIC X(22) VALUE 'VTVERMONT            '.
      05  FILLER    PIC X(22) VALUE 'MAMASSACHUSETTS      '.      05  FILLER    PIC X(22) VALUE 'WAWASHINGTON         '.
      05  FILLER    PIC X(22) VALUE 'MDMARYLAND           '.      05  FILLER    PIC X(22) VALUE 'WIWISCONSIN          '.
      05  FILLER    PIC X(22) VALUE 'MEMAINE              '.      05  FILLER    PIC X(22) VALUE 'WVWEST VIRGINIA      '.
      05  FILLER    PIC X(22) VALUE 'MIMICHIGAN           '.      05  FILLER    PIC X(22) VALUE 'WYWYOMING            '.
      05  FILLER    PIC X(22) VALUE 'MNMINNESOTA          '.  01  ST-STATE-TABLE REDEFINES ST-STATE-DATA.
      05  FILLER    PIC X(22) VALUE 'MOMISSOURI           '.      05  ST-STATE-ENTRY             OCCURS 51 TIMES.
      05  FILLER    PIC X(22) VALUE 'MSMISSISSPI          '.          10  ST-STATE-ABBREVIATION  PIC X(2).
      05  FILLER    PIC X(22) VALUE 'MTMONTANA            '.          10  ST-STATE-NAME          PIC X(20).
      05  FILLER    PIC X(22) VALUE 'NCNORTH CAROLINA     '.
```

Figure 12.12. Establishing a table with a table argument and a table function

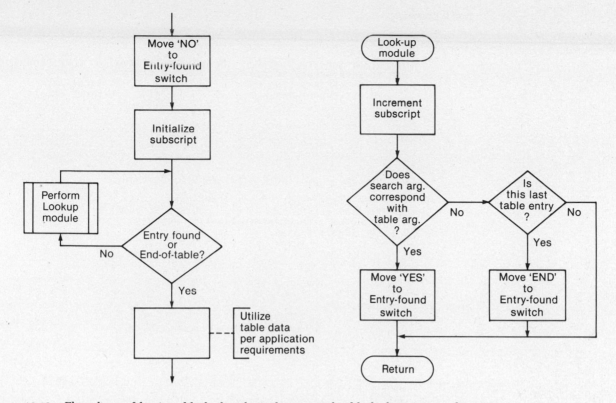

Figure 12.13. Flowchart of basic table lookup logic for a serial table lookup using subscripts

A Basic Serial Lookup for a Table with Random, Sequential, or Usage-Frequency Organization

To do a serial table lookup using subscripts, the program must provide for the following functions: (1) the initialization of the subscript, (2) the incrementation of the subscript, (3) the testing for correspondence between the search argument and the table argument, and (4) the testing to see if the end of the table has been reached. This logic is shown in the flowchart of Figure 12.13.

A COBOL coding example for the ST-STATE-TABLE look-up is shown in Figure 12.14. Notice that an additional 01-level item, ST-TABLE-CONTROLS has been created to contain the necessary table control fields: ST-SUBSCRIPT and ST-ENTRY-FOUND-SWITCH. Then, in the PROCEDURE DIVISION, ST-ENTRY-FOUND-SWITCH is initialized to 'NO' and ST-SUBSCRIPT is initialized to ZERO. The 999-LOOKUP-STATE-NAME module is performed until the table argument ST-STATE-ABBREVIATION occurrence indicated by the ST-SUBSCRIPT value matches the search argument IN-STATE-ABBREVIATION. Incrementation of the subscript and testing for end-of-table are handled in the lookup module.

There are two ways in which this table lookup coding can be improved. First, it is preferable to store the table entry limit—51 in the case of the state table—as a field in WORKING-STORAGE rather than to use a literal value in the PROCEDURE DIVISION. This is because should table entries be added to or deleted from the table, it is much easier to change one table size value within the DATA DIVISION rather than to hunt through the PROCEDURE DIVISION looking for places where the table size has been specified with the literal 51. So, the ST-NUMBER-OF-ENTRIES field has been added to the ST-TABLE-CONTROLS.

The second improvement is minor but is a good defensive programming practice. Rather than using an equal condition for the end-of-table test, it is safer to make a relationship test that will also end table searching should the

DATA DIVISION:

```
        *
        01    ST-TABLE-CONTROLS.
              05    ST-SUBSCRIPT                    PIC S9(4)      COMP SYNC.
              05    ST-ENTRY-FOUND-SWITCH           PIC X(3).
                    88    ST-ENTRY-FOUND                           VALUE 'YES'.
                    88    ST-END-OF-TABLE                          VALUE 'END'.
        *
        01    ST-STATE-DATA.
              05    FILLER          PIC X(22) VALUE 'AKALASKA            '.
                              .
                              .
                              .
              05    FILLER          PIC X(22) VALUE 'WYWYOMING          '.
        *
        01    ST-STATE-TABLE REDEFINES ST-STATE-DATA.
              05    ST-STATE-ENTRY                  OCCURS 51 TIMES.
                    10    ST-STATE-ABBREVIATION     PIC X(2).
                    10    ST-STATE-NAME             PIC X(20).
                              .
                              .
                              .
```

PROCEDURE DIVISION:

```
                              .
                              .
                              .
Initialization ─────▶ { MOVE 'NO ' TO ST-ENTRY-FOUND-SWITCH.
                      { MOVE ZERO TO ST-SUBSCRIPT.
                        PERFORM 999-LOOKUP-STATE-NAME
                            UNTIL ST-ENTRY-FOUND
                            OR ST-END-OF-TABLE.
                        IF ST-ENTRY-FOUND
                            MOVE ST-STATE-NAME (ST-SUBSCRIPT) TO RL-STATE-NAME
                        ELSE
                            MOVE SPACES TO RL-STATE-NAME.
                              .
                              .
                              .
        *
        *
        999-LOOKUP-STATE-NAME.
        *
Incrementation ─────▶   ADD 1 TO ST-SUBSCRIPT.
Test for correspondence ─────▶ { IF IN-STATE-ABBREVIATION
                               {     IS EQUAL TO ST-STATE-ABBREVIATION (ST-SUBSCRIPT)
                                         MOVE 'YES' TO ST-ENTRY-FOUND-SWITCH
Test for end-of-table ─────▶ { ELSE IF ST-SUBSCRIPT IS EQUAL TO 51
                             {     MOVE 'END' TO ST-ENTRY-FOUND-SWITCH.
```

Figure 12.14. COBOL coding of basic serial table lookup using subscripts

subscript erroneously—due to a programming error—get set to a value beyond the range of the table. Both these features are embodied in the improved sequential lookup logic of Figure 12.15.

A Serial Lookup with Early Exit for a Sequentially Organized Table

When a rather lengthy table has sequential organization and there are a significant number of search arguments that are not represented in the table arguments, it is efficient to code the lookup module with early exit logic. Such coding is shown in Figure 12.16.

For optimum efficiency, a dummy end-of-table entry is coded at the end of the table and set to HIGH-VALUES. This dummy entry will ensure that end-of-table will always be correctly detected. Notice that when a dummy end-of-table entry is used with appropriate lookup logic, there is no need for a field to

DATA DIVISION:

```
        *
         01   ST-TABLE-CONTROLS.
Table limit      05   ST-SUBSCRIPT                      PIC S9(4)      COMP SYNC.
in working-storage ───────▶ 05   ST-NUMBER-OF-ENTRIES            PIC S9(4)      VALUE +51
                                                                                COMP SYNC.
             05   ST-ENTRY-FOUND-SWITCH            PIC X(3).
                  88   ST-ENTRY-FOUND                             VALUE 'YES'.
                  88   ST-END-OF-TABLE                            VALUE 'END'.
        *
         01   ST-STATE-DATA.
             05   FILLER          PIC X(22) VALUE 'AKALASKA            '.
                                    .
                                    .
                                    .
             05   FILLER          PIC X(22) VALUE 'WYWYOMING           '.
        *
         01   ST-STATE-TABLE REDEFINES ST-STATE-DATA.
             05   ST-STATE-ENTRY                   OCCURS 51 TIMES.
                  10   ST-STATE-ABBREVIATION       PIC X(2).
                  10   ST-STATE-NAME               PIC X(20).
                                    .
                                    .
                                    .

PROCEDURE DIVISION:

                                    .
                                    .
                                    .

             MOVE 'NO ' TO ST-ENTRY-FOUND-SWITCH.
             MOVE ZERO TO ST-SUBSCRIPT.
             PERFORM 999-LOOKUP-STATE-NAME
                 UNTIL ST-ENTRY-FOUND
                 OR ST-END-OF-TABLE.
             IF ST-ENTRY-FOUND
                 MOVE ST-STATE-NAME (ST-SUBSCRIPT) TO RL-STATE-NAME
             ELSE
                 MOVE SPACES TO RL-STATE-NAME.
                                    .
                                    .
                                    .

        *
        *
         999-LOOKUP-STATE-NAME.
        *
             ADD 1 TO ST-SUBSCRIPT.
             IF IN-STATE-ABBREVIATION
                 IS EQUAL TO ST-STATE-ABBREVIATION (ST-SUBSCRIPT)
                     MOVE 'YES' TO ST-ENTRY-FOUND-SWITCH
Improved
end-of-table test ───────▶ ELSE IF ST-SUBSCRIPT IS NOT LESS THAN ST-NUMBER-OF-ENTRIES
                 MOVE 'END' TO ST-ENTRY-FOUND-SWITCH.
```

Figure 12.15. Improved COBOL coding of basic serial table lookup using subscripts

specify the number of table entries (such as ST-NUMBER-OF-ENTRIES). A dummy end-of-table entry can be used for serial searches without early exit, also. The advantage of a dummy end-of-table entry is that it minimizes the chance that a change to the field specifying the number of entries will be overlooked when entries are added to or deleted from the table.

A Serial Lookup Using the PERFORM Statement with the VARYING Phrase

Sequential lookup coding can be minimized by using the PERFORM statement with the VARYING phrase. Its format and an example for the state name lookup are shown in Figure 12.17.

The PERFORM/VARYING statement logic is depicted in the flowchart of Figure 12.18. Notice that subscript initialization and incrementation are handled by the FROM and BY phrases respectively.

DATA DIVISION:

```
               *
               01  ST-TABLE-CONTROLS.
No table limit field ──→ 05  ST-SUBSCRIPT                      PIC S9(4)     COMP SYNC.
               05  ST-ENTRY-FOUND-SWITCH            PIC X(3).
                   88  ST-ENTRY-FOUND                         VALUE 'YES'.
                   88  ST-END-OF-TABLE                        VALUE 'END'.
               *
               01  ST-STATE-DATA.
               05  FILLER          PIC X(22) VALUE 'AKALASKA                '.
                       .
                       .
                       .
Dummy end-of-table     05  FILLER          PIC X(22) VALUE 'WYWYOMING               '.
     entry        ──→  05  FILLER          PIC X(22) VALUE HIGH-VALUES.
               *
               01  ST-STATE-TABLE REDEFINES ST-STATE-DATA.
               05  ST-STATE-ENTRY               OCCURS 52 TIMES.
                   10  ST-STATE-ABBREVIATION        PIC X(2).
                   10  ST-STATE-NAME                PIC X(20).
                       .
                       .
                       .
```

PROCEDURE DIVISION:

```
                       .
                       .
                       .
               MOVE 'NO ' TO ST-ENTRY-FOUND-SWITCH.
               MOVE ZERO TO ST-SUBSCRIPT.
               PERFORM 999-LOOKUP-STATE-NAME
                   UNTIL ST-ENTRY-FOUND
                   OR ST-END-OF-TABLE.
               IF ST-ENTRY-FOUND
                   MOVE ST-STATE-NAME (ST-SUBSCRIPT) TO RL-STATE-NAME
               ELSE
                   MOVE SPACES TO RL-STATE-NAME.
                       .
                       .
                       .
               *
               *
                999-LOOKUP-STATE-NAME.
               *
               ADD 1 TO ST-SUBSCRIPT.
               IF IN-STATE-ABBREVIATION
                   IS GREATER THAN ST-STATE-ABBREVIATION (ST-SUBSCRIPT)
               NEXT SENTENCE
               ELSE IF IN-STATE-ABBREVIATION
                   IS EQUAL TO ST-STATE-ABBREVIATION (ST-SUBSCRIPT)
               MOVE 'YES' TO ST-ENTRY-FOUND-SWITCH
               ELSE
                   MOVE 'END' TO ST-ENTRY-FOUND-SWITCH.
```

Lookup logic for early exit ──→

Figure 12.16. COBOL coding of basic serial table lookup with early exit using subscripts

Format:

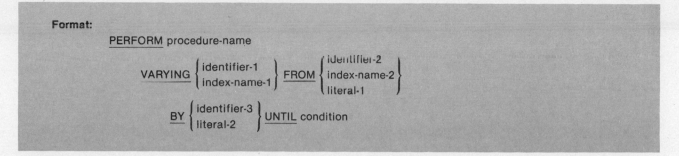

PERFORM procedure-name

VARYING $\left\{ \begin{array}{l} \text{identifier-1} \\ \text{index-name-1} \end{array} \right\}$ FROM $\left\{ \begin{array}{l} \text{identifier-2} \\ \text{index-name-2} \\ \text{literal-1} \end{array} \right\}$

BY $\left\{ \begin{array}{l} \text{identifier-3} \\ \text{literal-2} \end{array} \right\}$ UNTIL condition

Example:

SEQUENCE		CONT	A	B	COBOL STATEMENT	IDENTIFICATION
(PAGE)	(SERIAL)					

```
            PERFORM 999-LOOKUP-STATE-NAME
                VARYING ST-SUBSCRIPT
                FROM 1
                BY 1
                    UNTIL ST-ENTRY-FOUND
                    OR ST-TABLE-END.
```

Figure 12.17. PERFORM statement with VARYING phrase example

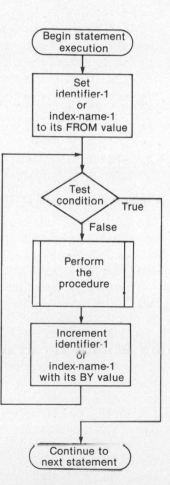

Figure 12.18. Flowchart of PERFORM/VARYING statement logic

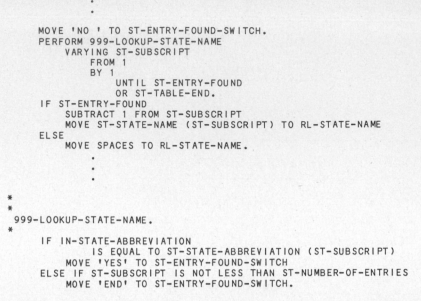

```
                              .
                              .
                              .
         MOVE 'NO ' TO ST-ENTRY-FOUND-SWITCH.
         PERFORM 999-LOOKUP-STATE-NAME
             VARYING ST-SUBSCRIPT
                 FROM 1
                 BY 1
                       UNTIL ST-ENTRY-FOUND
                       OR ST-TABLE-END.
         IF ST-ENTRY-FOUND
             SUBTRACT 1 FROM ST-SUBSCRIPT
             MOVE ST-STATE-NAME (ST-SUBSCRIPT) TO RL-STATE-NAME
         ELSE
             MOVE SPACES TO RL-STATE-NAME.
                              .
                              .
                              .

 *
 *
   999-LOOKUP-STATE-NAME.
 *
         IF IN-STATE-ABBREVIATION
             IS EQUAL TO ST-STATE-ABBREVIATION (ST-SUBSCRIPT)
             MOVE 'YES' TO ST-ENTRY-FOUND-SWITCH
         ELSE IF ST-SUBSCRIPT IS NOT LESS THAN ST-NUMBER-OF-ENTRIES
             MOVE 'END' TO ST-ENTRY-FOUND-SWITCH.
```

Figure 12.19.   COBOL coding of basic serial table lookup using the PERFORM/VARYING statement

It is important to note that, once the match between search and table arguments has been located, the subscript must be decremented by one to cause it to reflect the proper table occurrence number. This is because the subscript has been incremented one time after the matching condition has been identified. This is shown in the coding for the state table lookup in Figure 12.19.

Table Lookups Using Indexes and the SEARCH Statement

To increase processing efficiency and simplify lookup coding, the SEARCH statement may be used. It requires the use of indexes rather than subscripts.

The Use of Indexes

The INDEXED BY clause

The INDEXED BY clause format and an example of its use with the state table are shown in Figure 12.20. When the INDEXED BY clause is written, a user-defined index-name is specified. This index-name is then used like a variable subscript for identification of a specific occurrence.

There are three important differences between subscripts and indexes. First, when an index-name is specified in the INDEXED BY clause, the index is automatically provided for by the compiler; the programmer does not establish a data-name in the DATA DIVISION as would be done for a variable subscript.

Second, subscripts are used for the storage of occurrence values whereas indexes contain displacement values. Displacement refers to the number of positions from the starting position of the table. Figure 12.21 compares subscript occurrence numbers to index displacement values.

Third, since index values are different than normal data values, initialization of the index cannot be done with a MOVE statement as can the initialization of subscripts. Similarly, arithmetic statements, such as ADD and SUBTRACT, cannot be used for incrementation and decrementation of an index. Instead the SET statement is used for index initialization, incrementation, decrementation, or other modification.

Format:

OCCURS integer TIMES

[INDEXED BY index-name-1 [index-name-2] . . .]

Example:

```
SEQUENCE       |C| A  | B                                                          | IDENTIFICATION
(PAGE) (SERIAL)|O|    |           COBOL STATEMENT                                  |
1   3 4     6  |7| 8  |12  16  20  24  28  32  36  40  44  48  52  56  60  64  68 72| 76        80

          Ø1  ST-STATE-TABLE REDEFINES ST-STATE-DATA.
              Ø5  ST-STATE-ENTRY              OCCURS 51 TIMES
                                              INDEXED BY ST-INDEX.
                  1Ø  ST-STATE-ABBREVIATION       PIC X(2).
                  1Ø  ST-STATE-NAME               PIC X(2Ø).
```

Figure 12.20. INDEXED BY clause example

The SET statement

Formats and examples of the SET statement are shown in Figure 12.22. Format-1 is used for index initialization; Format-2 is used for index incrementation or decrementation. The SET statement takes occurrence numbers and converts them to index displacement values, and vice versa. Figure 12.23 presents a table of its operation.

Index data-items

As shown in Figure 12.24, index data-items may be specified in the DATA DIVISION to allow for the storage of index displacement values for later use without their conversion to occurrence numbers. To specify an index data-item, the USAGE IS INDEX clause is written. Notice that PICTURE and VALUE clauses are not allowed with INDEX usage; index lengths are uniform and always assigned by the compiler.

Recognize the distinction between indexes and index data-items. Indexes are specified with the INDEXED BY phrase and are used, like a subscript, to

Table entry	*Occurrence number (subscript value)*	*Displacement (index value)*
JAN	1	0
FEB	2	3
MAR	3	6
APR	4	9
MAY	5	12
JUN	6	15
JUL	7	18
AUG	8	21
SEP	9	24
OCT	10	27
NOV	11	30
DEC	12	33

Figure 12.21. Comparison of subscript occurrence numbers and index displacement values

Formats:

Format-1

$$\text{SET} \left\{ \begin{array}{l} \text{identifier-1 [identifier-2] } \dots \\ \text{index-name-1 [index-name-2] } \dots \end{array} \right\} \text{TO} \left\{ \begin{array}{l} \text{identifier-3} \\ \text{index-name-3} \\ \text{integer-1} \end{array} \right\}$$

Format-2

$$\text{SET index-name-1 [index-name-2] } \dots \left\{ \begin{array}{l} \underline{\text{UP BY}} \\ \underline{\text{DOWN BY}} \end{array} \right\} \left\{ \begin{array}{l} \text{identifier-1} \\ \text{integer-1} \end{array} \right\}$$

Examples:

SEQUENCE		CONT	A	B	COBOL STATEMENT		IDENTIFICATION

```
SET ST-INDEX TO 1.          ← Initializes index
SET ST-INDEX UP BY 1.       ← Increments index
SET ST-INDEX DOWN BY 1.     ← Decrements index
```

Figure 12.22. SET statement examples

Form: SET receiving-field TO sending-field

	Sending-field		
Receiving-field	Integer or numeric identifier	Index	Index data-item
Index	Index set to index value corresponding to occurrence number of sending-field	Index set to index value corresponding to occurrence number of sending-field's occurrence	Index data-item moved to index without conversion
Numeric identifier	Illegal	Numeric identifier set to occurrence number corresponding to index value	Illegal
Index data-item	Illegal	Index moved to index data-item without conversion	Index data-item moved to index data-item without conversion

Figure 12.23. Table of SET statement processing

Format:

$$[\underline{\text{USAGE IS}}] \ \underline{\text{INDEX}}$$

Example:

SEQUENCE		CONT	A	B	COBOL STATEMENT		IDENTIFICATION

```
Ø5  XX-INDEX-ITEM                          USAGE IS INDEX.

Ø5  XX-INDEX-ITEM                                    INDEX.
```

Figure 12.24. Index data-item examples

Format:

Format-1

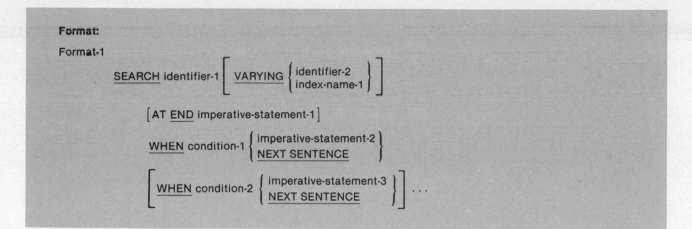

Example:

SEQUENCE			A	B	COBOL STATEMENT	IDENTIFICATION

```
SEARCH ST-STATE-ENTRY
    AT END MOVE 'NO ' TO ST-ENTRY-FOUND-SWITCH
WHEN ST-STATE-ABBREVIATION (ST-INDEX)
        IS EQUAL TO IN-STATE-ABBREVIATION
    MOVE 'YES' TO ST-ENTRY-FOUND-SWITCH.
```

Figure 12.25. Format-1 SEARCH statement example

refer to a certain occurrence of a data-item containing an OCCURS clause. The only function of an index data-item is to store, without conversion, the contents of an index. Hence, index data-items are required only occasionally and not commonly used.

In the PROCEDURE DIVISION, index data-items can only be used in a SET statement or in a relation condition test with an index or another index data-item.

The SEARCH Statement

After a table has been established with the INDEXED BY clause, the SEARCH statement can be used to look up table entries.

Serial searches

The Format-1 SEARCH statement and an example are shown in Figure 12.25. When a Format-1 SEARCH statement is encountered, the table specified as identifier-1 is stepped through, entry by entry, until the condition expressed in the WHEN phrase is satisfied. As soon as the condition is satisfied, the SEARCH ends. If the end-of-table is reached, the condition has not been satisfied, and the action or actions specified by the AT END phrase are executed.

Thus, with the SEARCH statement, index incrementation is handled automatically, condition testing is accomplished by the WHEN phrase, and the AT END phrase specifies end-of-table processing. Initialization of the index must be handled by coding a SET statement prior to the SEARCH.

Coding for the state table lookup using a serial SEARCH appears in Figure 12.26.

Specification of multiple WHEN phrases causes the SEARCH to end whenever any WHEN condition is satisfied; its effect is similar to that of an OR operator. A serial search with early exit for a sequentially organized table can be handled by coding multiple WHEN phrases, as shown in Figure 12.27.

```
                                    .
                                    .
                                    .
              PERFORM 999-LOOKUP-STATE-NAME.
              IF  ST-ENTRY-FOUND
                  MOVE ST-STATE-NAME (ST-INDEX) TO RL-STATE-NAME
              ELSE
                  MOVE SPACES TO RL-STATE-NAME.
                                    .
                                    .
                                    .

         *
         *
          999-LOOKUP-STATE-NAME.
         *
              SET ST-INDEX TO 1.
              SEARCH ST-STATE-ENTRY
                  AT END MOVE 'NO ' TO ST-ENTRY-FOUND-SWITCH
                  WHEN ST-STATE-ABBREVIATION (ST-INDEX)
                          IS EQUAL TO IN-STATE-ABBREVIATION
                      MOVE 'YES' TO ST-ENTRY-FOUND-SWITCH.
```

Figure 12.26. COBOL coding for serial SEARCH

```
         *
         *
          999-LOOKUP-STATE-NAME.
         *
              SET ST-INDEX TO 1.
              SEARCH ST-STATE-ENTRY
                  AT END MOVE 'NO ' TO ST-ENTRY-FOUND-SWITCH
                  WHEN ST-STATE-ABBREVIATION (ST-INDEX)
                          IS GREATER THAN IN-STATE-ABBREVIATION
                      MOVE 'NO ' TO ST-ENTRY-FOUND-SWITCH
                  WHEN ST-STATE-ABBREVIATION (ST-INDEX)
                          IS EQUAL TO IN-STATE-ABBREVIATION
                      MOVE 'YES' TO ST-ENTRY-FOUND-SWITCH.
```

Figure 12.27. COBOL coding for serial SEARCH with early exit

Binary searches

The SEARCH statement can also be used for a binary search. A binary search requires the use of the KEY clause in the DATA DIVISION and of the ALL phrase in the SEARCH statement of the PROCEDURE DIVISION.

The KEY clause

When a table is used in a binary search, the KEY clause must be specified to indicate whether the table arguments are arranged in ASCENDING or DESCENDING sequence. The format and an example of the KEY clause are shown in Figure 12.28.

Recognize that the use of the KEY clause does not ensure that the table arguments are actually in ascending or descending order. It is the programmer's responsibility to make certain that the table is actually arranged in accordance with the KEY clause specifications.

The ALL phrase

The Format-2 SEARCH statement is used to provide a binary search. Its format and an example are shown in Figure 12.29. Specification of the reserved word ALL triggers the binary search logic. Because a binary search is more complicated than a serial one, the Format-2 SEARCH statement imposes some coding restrictions that do not apply to the Format-1 SEARCH. The WHEN phrase requires specification of the indexed-key field as the first entry, and the

Format:

OCCURS integer TIMES

$\left[\begin{array}{c}\underline{\text{ASCENDING}}\\\underline{\text{DESCENDING}}\end{array}\right]$ KEY IS data-name-2 [data-name-3] ...

[INDEXED BY index-name-1 [index-name-2] ...]

Example:

SEQUENCE		CONT	A	B	COBOL STATEMENT	IDENTIFICATION

```
Ø1   ST-STATE-TABLE REDEFINES ST-STATE-DATA.
     Ø5  ST-STATE-ENTRY              OCCURS 51 TIMES
                                     ASCENDING KEY
                                         ST-STATE-ABBREVIATION
                                     INDEXED BY ST-INDEX.
         1Ø  ST-STATE-ABBREVIATION   PIC X(2).
         1Ø  ST-STATE-NAME           PIC X(2Ø).
```

Figure 12.28. KEY clause example

Format:

Format-2

SEARCH ALL identifier-1 [AT END imperative-statement-1]

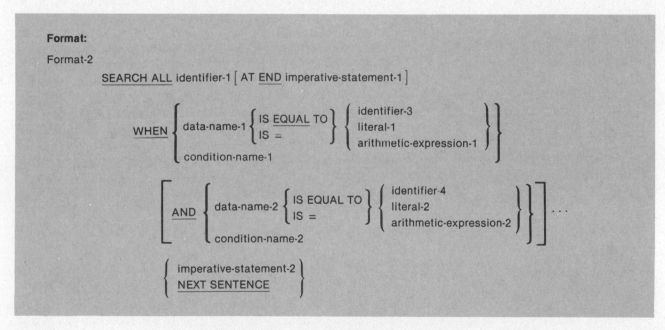

Example:

SEQUENCE		CONT	A	B	COBOL STATEMENT	IDENTIFICATION

```
SEARCH ALL ST-STATE-ENTRY
    AT END MOVE 'NO' TO ST-ENTRY-FOUND-SWITCH
    WHEN ST-STATE-ABBREVIATION (ST-INDEX)
        IS EQUAL TO IN-STATE-ABBREVIATION
    MOVE 'YES' TO ST-ENTRY-FOUND-SWITCH.
```

Figure 12.29. Format-2 SEARCH statement example

condition test is limited to an EQUAL relationship. Should multiple WHEN conditions be written, they must be specified with AND connectors. This means that *all* WHEN conditions must be satisfied for the SEARCH to end prior to end-of-table.

When ALL is specified to obtain a binary search, the SEARCH statement handles index initialization. Thus, the programmer need not code a SET statement as must be done for a serial SEARCH.

The Format-1 serial SEARCH versus the Format-2 binary SEARCH

A binary search is much quicker than a serial search. Notice in Figure 12.30 that the average number of comparisons required for the serial SEARCH of a 1000-entry table is 500 whereas the maximum number of comparisons for a binary SEARCH is only 10. However, since there is some "overhead" required to initialize and execute the search, it is not as efficient for smaller tables. So, as a rule of thumb, binary searches should be applied only to tables with over thirty table entries. Remember that a binary search requires that the table arguments be in sequential order.

Other Table Lookup Techniques

Table Arguments with Range Steps

Sometimes there will not be a one-to-one correspondence between the search argument and the table entry. This situation occurs when one table function (or group of table functions) applies to a range of arguments. A common example of this is an income tax table where a range of earned income dollar amounts apply to a specific tax bracket or percentage.

Similarly, each one of the twelve signs of the zodiac applies to a range of dates, as shown in Figure 12.31. Suppose we wanted to use an individual's month and day of birth as contained in a field called IN-BIRTH-MONTH-DAY as a search argument to look up his or her sign. This would be an example of a lookup for a *range-step* table, since each table function—the sunsign name—applies to a range of dates, which are the table arguments.

Such a range-step lookup is simply a variation of a serial lookup. When defining the table, the highest numerical value for each month/day entry should be arranged in numerical order and used as the table argument, as shown in Figure 12.32. Also, since the range for Capricorn spans from one year to the next, it has been represented both at the start and at the end of the table. Then, rather than testing for an equal condition in the lookup module, the match is made when the ZT-SIGN-END-DATE table argument is greater than or equal to the IN-BIRTH-MONTH-DAY search argument. To minimize SEARCH coding and comparisons, the relationship is specified with the NOT LESS THAN operator.

Lookups for Separately Defined Table Arguments and Functions

In the state table and the sunsign table, each table argument was defined adjacent to the table function. This is a good approach because the physically adjacent placement of argument and function makes it relatively easy for the programmer to see the correspondence and thus helps to ensure that the correct table function is associated with each table argument when creating or modifying the table. However, sometimes arguments and functions will be defined separately. An example is shown in Figure 12.33 where the model number arguments are defined in a table separate from the price functions.

When subscripts are used, such separate definition does not affect programming because the occurrence numbers must still correspond and thus the same subscript could be used for both tables. If indexes are used, the SEARCH statement with a VARYING phrase can be used as shown in Figure 12.34. As shown here, the VARYING phrase causes the PT-PRICE-INDEX occurrence to be maintained relative to the MT-MODEL-INDEX occurrence.

| Number of Table entries | Serial search | | Binary search |
	Maximum number of comparisons	Average number of comparisons	Maximum number of comparisons
50	50	25	6
100	100	50	7
500	500	250	9
1000	1000	500	10
2000	2000	1000	11

Figure 12.30. Number of comparisons required for serial and binary searches

Birth date	Zodiac sign name	Birth date	Zodiac sign name
Mar. 21 - Apr. 19	Aries	Sep. 23 - Oct. 22	Libra
Apr. 20 - May 20	Taurus	Oct. 23 - Nov. 21	Scorpio
May 21 - Jun. 20	Gemini	Nov. 22 - Dec. 21	Sagittarius
Jun. 21 - Jul. 22	Cancer	Dec. 22 - Jan. 19	Capricorn
Jul. 23 - Aug. 22	Leo	Jan. 20 - Feb. 18	Aquarius
Aug. 23 - Sep. 22	Virgo	Feb. 19 - Mar. 20	Pisces

Figure 12.31. Table of zodiac signs

DATA DIVISION:

```
     *
     01   ZT-TABLE-CONTROLS.
          05   ZT-ENTRY-FOUND-SWITCH           PIC X(3).
               88   ZT-ENTRY-FOUND                         VALUE 'YES'.
     *
     01   ZT-ZODIAC-SIGN-DATA.
          05   FILLER         PIC X(15)   VALUE '0119CAPRICORN  '.
          05   FILLER         PIC X(15)   VALUE '0218AQUARIUS   '.
          05   FILLER         PIC X(15)   VALUE '0320PISCES     '.
          05   FILLER         PIC X(15)   VALUE '0419ARIES      '.
          05   FILLER         PIC X(15)   VALUE '0520TAURUS     '.
          05   FILLER         PIC X(15)   VALUE '0620GEMINI     '.
          05   FILLER         PIC X(15)   VALUE '0722CANCER     '.
          05   FILLER         PIC X(15)   VALUE '0822LEO        '.
          05   FILLER         PIC X(15)   VALUE '0922VIRGO      '.
          05   FILLER         PIC X(15)   VALUE '1022LIBRA      '.
          05   FILLER         PIC X(15)   VALUE '1121SCORPIO    '.
          05   FILLER         PIC X(15)   VALUE '1221SAGITTARIUS'.
          05   FILLER         PIC X(15)   VALUE '1231CAPRICORN  '.
     01   ZT-ZODIAC-SIGN-TABLE REDEFINES ZT-ZODIAC-SIGN-DATA.
          05   ZT-ZODIAC-SIGN-ENTRY          OCCURS 13 TIMES
                                             INDEXED BY ZT-INDEX.
               10   ZT-SIGN-END-DATE         PIC X(4).
               10   ZT-SIGN-NAME             PIC X(11).
```

PROCEDURE DIVISION:

```
     *
     *
     999-LOOKUP-SIGN-NAME.
     *
          SET ZT-INDEX TO 1.
          SEARCH ZT-ZODIAC-SIGN-ENTRY
               AT END MOVE 'NO ' TO ZT-ENTRY-FOUND-SWITCH
               WHEN ZT-SIGN-END-DATE (ZT-INDEX)
                    IS NOT LESS THAN IN-BIRTH-MONTH-DAY
               MOVE 'YES' TO ZT-ENTRY-FOUND-SWITCH.
```

Figure 12.32. COBOL coding for zodiac sign lookup

```
     *
     01  MT-TABLE-CONTROLS.
         05  MT-ENTRY-FOUND-SWITCH              PIC X(3).
             88  MT-ENTRY-FOUND                             VALUE 'YES'.
     *
     01  MT-MODEL-DATA.
         05  FILLER          PIC X(7)   VALUE 'RS16   '.
         05  FILLER          PIC X(7)   VALUE 'RS20   '.
         05  FILLER          PIC X(7)   VALUE 'RS24   '.
         05  FILLER          PIC X(7)   VALUE 'LS12-12'.
         05  FILLER          PIC X(7)   VALUE 'L212-16'.
         05  FILLER          PIC X(7)   VALUE 'LS16-16'.
         05  FILLER          PIC X(7)   VALUE 'LS16-20'.
     01  MT-MODEL-TABLE REDEFINES MT-MODEL-DATA.
         05  MT-MODEL-CODE                   OCCURS 7 TIMES
                                             INDEXED BY MT-MODEL-INDEX
                                                PIC X(7).
     *
     01  PT-PRICE-DATA.
         05  FILLER          PIC 9(3)V99 VALUE 041.00.
         05  FILLER          PIC 9(3)V99 VALUE 047.00.
         05  FILLER          PIC 9(3)V99 VALUE 051.00.
         05  FILLER          PIC 9(3)V99 VALUE 035.00.
         05  FILLER          PIC 9(3)V99 VALUE 038.00.
         05  FILLER          PIC 9(3)V99 VALUE 039.00.
         05  FILLER          PIC 9(3)V99 VALUE 043.00.
     01  PT-PRICE-TABLE REDEFINES PT-PRICE-DATA.
         05  PT-MODEL-PRICE                  OCCURS 7 TIMES
                                             INDEXED BY PT-PRICE-INDEX
                                                PIC 9(3)V99.
```

Figure 12.33.   Separately defined model and price tables

```
          SET MT-MODEL-INDEX TO 1.
          SET PT-PRICE-INDEX TO 1.
          SEARCH MT-MODEL-CODE VARYING PT-PRICE-INDEX
              AT END MOVE 'NO ' TO MT-ENTRY-FOUND-SWITCH
              WHEN MT-MODEL-CODE (MT-MODEL-INDEX)
                     IS EQUAL TO IN-MODEL-CODE
                  MOVE 'YES' TO MT-ENTRY-FOUND-SWITCH.
```

Figure 12.34.   COBOL coding for model price lookup

Multiple-Level Tables

The tables we have been defining are all examples of single-level or one-dimensional tables. Single-level tables are encountered much more frequently but there are certain multiple-level table applications. In addition to single-level tables, COBOL can handle multiple-level tables of two or three dimensions.

Multiple-level tables contain tables within table entries. Do not confuse a table that has multiple functions with a multiple-level table. For example, a table containing a part number, part description, and part price is a single-level table with one table argument and two table functions.

Defining a two-level table

An example of a two-level table of pay rates for various job classifications during each of three shifts is shown in Part A of Figure 12.35. The hourly pay rate depends upon two factors: job classification and shift worked. Notice that there is a three-occurrence shift rate table within each of the seven job classification entries.

Part B of Figure 12.35 shows the occurrence notation for each rate-of-pay table function. The first number within the parentheses refers to the job classification occurrence number; the second to the shift pay rate occurrence number.

As shown in Part A of Figure 12.36, a two-level table contains two OCCURS clauses and, when indexes are used, two INDEXED BY clauses. Notice

Part A: Rate-of-pay table data | | | | **Part B:** Rate-of-pay table occurrences

Job classification	Rate of pay Shift 1 (days)	Shift 2 (swing)	Shift 3 (grave)	Job classification	Rate of pay Shift 1 (days)	Shift 2 (swing)	Shift 3 (grave)
A1	9.64	10.60	11.09	A1	(1, 1)	(1, 2)	(1, 3)
A2	8.93	9.82	10.27	A2	(2, 1)	(2, 2)	(2, 3)
B1	7.12	7.83	8.19	B1	(3, 1)	(3, 2)	(3, 3)
C1	6.80	7.48	7.82	C1	(4, 1)	(4, 2)	(4, 3)
C2	6.07	6.68	6.98	C2	(5, 1)	(5, 2)	(5, 3)
C3	5.41	5.95	6.22	C3	(6, 1)	(6, 2)	(6, 3)
C4	4.39	4.83	5.04	C4	(7, 1)	(7, 2)	(7, 3)

Figure 12.35. Rate-of-pay table

that the RT-JOB-ENTRY table has been specified as an 05-level data-item whereas the RT-JOB-CLASSIFICATION and the subordinate RT-RATE-ENTRY table have been specified at level number 10.

To refer to a particular pay rate, the RT-RATE-OF-PAY field must be specified with two subscripts or, as in this case, two indexes. Part B of Figure 12.36 shows how they are written in one set of parentheses with the hierarchically more significant (numerically lower level number) subscript or index placed first and the less significant one last. A comma must separate the subscripts or indexes for 1968 ANS COBOL; the comma is optional with the 1974 standards.

Defining and accessing a three-level table

Part A of Figure 12.37 shows an example of a three-level table of prices for various products according to the quantity ordered and whether the customer is a regular private-industry or governmental-agency customer. There is a two-occurrence customer-type table within the four-occurrence quantity-ordered table for each of the product entries. In Part B of Figure 12.37, the occurrence notation for each product code table function is shown. The first number within the parentheses refers to the job classification occurrence number, the second indicates the quantity-ordered classification, and the third reflects the customer-type. Figure 12.38 shows the sample coding for the defining and accessing of this three-level table.

Part A: Table definition:

```
*
01  RT-RATE-DATA.
    05  FILLER                       PIC X(14)    VALUE 'A1096410601109'.
    05  FILLER                       PIC X(14)    VALUE 'A2089309821027'.
    05  FILLER                       PIC X(14)    VALUE 'B1071207830819'.
    05  FILLER                       PIC X(14)    VALUE 'C1068007480782'.
    05  FILLER                       PIC X(14)    VALUE 'C2060706680698'.
    05  FILLER                       PIC X(14)    VALUE 'C3054105950622'.
    05  FILLER                       PIC X(14)    VALUE 'C4043904830504'.
01  RT-RATE-TABLE REDEFINES RT-RATE-DATA.
    05  RT-JOB-ENTRY                              OCCURS 7 TIMES
                                                  INDEXED BY RT-JOB-INDEX.
        10  RT-JOB-CLASSIFICATION       PIC X(2).
        10  RT-RATE-ENTRY                         OCCURS 3 TIMES
                                                  INDEXED BY RT-RATE-INDEX.
            15  RT-RATE-OF-PAY            PIC 99V99.
```

Part B: Reference to table entry: RT-RATE-OF-PAY (RT-JOB-INDEX, RT-RATE-INDEX)

Figure 12.36. Definition of rate-of-pay table

Part A: Quantity-ordered/Customer-type price table data

	Quantity-ordered							
	1		2-6		7-12		13-up	
Product-code	Customer-type-1	Customer-type-2	Customer-type-1	Customer-type-2	Customer-type-1	Customer-type-2	Customer-type-1	Customer-type-2
A1818	$110.00	$102.00	$100.00	$ 92.00	$ 95.00	$ 86.00	$ 90.00	$ 81.00
A2418	128.00	115.00	117.00	105.00	111.00	100.00	106.00	95.00
A3018	139.00	125.00	127.00	114.00	120.00	108.00	114.00	103.00
A2424	149.00	134.00	136.00	122.00	129.00	116.00	123.00	111.00
A3024	161.00	146.00	146.00	132.00	139.00	125.00	131.00	118.00
A3624	173.00	158.00	157.00	141.00	149.00	144.00	142.00	128.00
A4824	200.00	180.00	182.00	164.00	173.00	156.00	164.00	148.00

Part B: Quantity-ordered/Customer-type price table occurrences

	Quantity-ordered							
	1		2-6		7-12		13-up	
Product-code	Customer-type-1	Customer-type-2	Customer-type-1	Customer-type-2	Customer-type-1	Customer-type-2	Customer-type-1	Customer-type-2
A1818	(1, 1, 1)	(1, 1, 2)	(1, 2, 1)	(1, 2, 2)	(1, 3, 1)	(1, 3, 2)	(1, 4, 1)	(1, 4, 2)
A2418	(2, 1, 1)	(2, 1, 2)	(2, 2, 1)	(2, 2, 2)	(2, 3, 1)	(2, 3, 2)	(2, 4, 1)	(2, 4, 2)
A3018	(3, 1, 1)	(3, 1, 2)	(3, 2, 1)	(3, 2, 2)	(3, 3, 1)	(3, 3, 2)	(3, 4, 1)	(3, 4, 2)
A2424	(4, 1, 1)	(4, 1, 2)	(4, 2, 1)	(4, 2, 2)	(4, 3, 1)	(4, 3, 2)	(4, 4, 1)	(4, 4, 2)
A3024	(5, 1, 1)	(5, 1, 2)	(5, 2, 1)	(5, 2, 2)	(5, 3, 1)	(5, 3, 2)	(5, 4, 1)	(5, 4, 2)
A3624	(6, 1, 1)	(6, 1, 2)	(6, 2, 1)	(6, 2, 2)	(6, 3, 1)	(6, 3, 2)	(6, 4, 1)	(6, 4, 2)
A4824	(7, 1, 1)	(7, 1, 2)	(7, 2, 1)	(7, 2, 2)	(7, 3, 1)	(7, 3, 2)	(7, 4, 1)	(7, 4, 2)

Figure 12.37. Three-level product/quantity/customer table

Input-Loaded Tables

Rather than coding table data directly into the program with VALUE clauses, the programmer may have the table data loaded into the program at execution time from records stored on a card, tape, or disk file. When tables are loaded from input records, each record normally contains the data for one table entry. A program with an input-loaded table must contain program logic to read the table records and move the table data to the table area of WORKING-STORAGE.

Separate Table File or Combined Table and Data File

The use of card input for both the table file and the data file to be processed produces a combined table/data file. For instance, a part-number/description table and a series of inventory records could be read into a program as one file. However, when a disk or tape input is used, usually the table and the data will comprise separate files.

When a combined table/data file is being used, the table data must, of course, physically precede the data to be processed. Then the program logic must check the record codes of the input records carefully so that it can determine (1) if the table data is actually present and (2) when the table data has ended and processing of regular data is to begin.

When table data is being loaded from a separate file, all additional definitions and the processing statements for that file must be provided (namely the SELECT, FD, OPEN, READ and CLOSE statements).

Part A: Depiction of table definition:

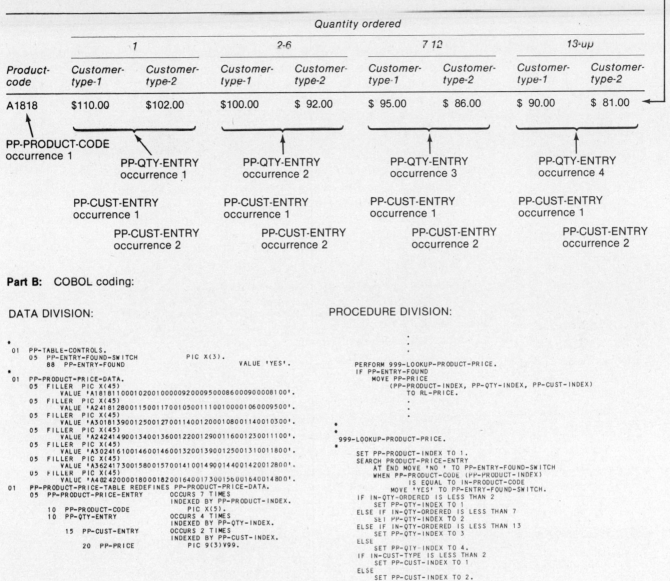

Figure 12.38. COBOL coding for product/quantity/customer table definition and lookup

Part B: COBOL coding:

DATA DIVISION:

```
*
  01  PP-TABLE-CONTROLS.
      05  PP-ENTRY-FOUND-SWITCH          PIC X(3).
          88  PP-ENTRY-FOUND                       VALUE 'YES'.
*
  01  PP-PRODUCT-PRICE-DATA.
      05  FILLER PIC X(45)
          VALUE 'A1818110001020010000092000950008600090000 81 00'.
      05  FILLER PIC X(45)
          VALUE 'A2418128001150011700105001110010000010600 09500'.
      05  FILLER PIC X(45)
          VALUE 'A3018139001250012700114001200010800114001 0300'.
      05  FILLER PIC X(45)
          VALUE 'A2424149001340013600122001290011600123001 1100'.
      05  FILLER PIC X(45)
          VALUE 'A3024161001460014600132001390012500131001 1800'.
      05  FILLER PIC X(45)
          VALUE 'A3624173001580015700141001490014400142001 2800'.
      05  FILLER PIC X(45)
          VALUE 'A4024200001800018200164001730015600164001 4800'.
  01  PP-PRODUCT-PRICE-TABLE REDEFINES PP-PRODUCT-PRICE-DATA.
      05  PP-PRODUCT-PRICE-ENTRY         OCCURS 7 TIMES
                                         INDEXED BY PP-PRODUCT-INDEX.
          10  PP-PRODUCT-CODE            PIC X(5).
          10  PP-QTY-ENTRY               OCCURS 4 TIMES
                                         INDEXED BY PP-QTY-INDEX.
              15  PP-CUST-ENTRY          OCCURS 2 TIMES
                                         INDEXED BY PP-CUST-INDEX.
                  20  PP-PRICE           PIC 9(3)V99.
```

PROCEDURE DIVISION:

```
          .
          .
          .
      PERFORM 999-LOOKUP-PRODUCT-PRICE.
      IF PP-ENTRY-FOUND
          MOVE PP-PRICE
              (PP-PRODUCT-INDEX, PP-QTY-INDEX, PP-CUST-INDEX)
              TO RL-PRICE.
          .
          .
          .
*
*
  999-LOOKUP-PRODUCT-PRICE.
*
      SET PP-PRODUCT-INDEX TO 1.
      SEARCH PRODUCT-PRICE-ENTRY
          AT END MOVE 'NO ' TO PP-ENTRY-FOUND-SWITCH
          WHEN PP-PRODUCT-CODE (PP-PRODUCT-INDEX)
              IS EQUAL TO IN-PRODUCT-CODE
              MOVE 'YES' TO PP-ENTRY-FOUND-SWITCH.
      IF IN-QTY-ORDERED IS LESS THAN 2
          SET PP-QTY-INDEX TO 1
      ELSE IF IN-QTY-ORDERED IS LESS THAN 7
          SET PP-QTY-INDEX TO 2
      ELSE IF IN-QTY-ORDERED IS LESS THAN 13
          SET PP-QTY-INDEX TO 3
      ELSE
          SET PP-QTY-INDEX TO 4.
      IF IN-CUST-TYPE IS LESS THAN 2
          SET PP-CUST-INDEX TO 1
      ELSE
          SET PP-CUST-INDEX TO 2.
```

Table Sequence

If the table organization is sequential or positional, it is imperative that the input be in the proper sequence. Sometimes the table data records will already be in the correct sequence on the table file; sometimes the table file will be used for other purposes and be in a different sequence.

Even though the records are expected to be in the correct sequence, the table-loading routine should contain sequence checking logic to ensure that the table records actually are in the required sequence.

When the table file is of a different sequence, sorting of the table records will be required. This could be handled by a SORT statement with the GIVING phrase and an OUTPUT PROCEDURE in which the table loading is accomplished.

Table Limits

When a table is loaded from input data, there is always the chance that, through additions to the table, the table data will exceed the limits of the table as defined in the program. If additional table entries are expected to be introduced in the future, the number of occurrences specified in the OCCURS clause should be a value large enough to accommodate a reasonable number of additions.

Then, to prevent overloading of the table, the program should always check the table limits before adding each table entry. For example, if 105 table entries were present for a table defined with an OCCURS clause specifying 100 entries, severe processing problems would result unless the program logic diagnosed and reported the error.

Program Example

A stock status report program containing an input-loaded table will be presented. The program, which we are naming STOCK, reads model description table records and model inventory balance records from a combined table/data file to print a stock status report.

The stock status report program is defined in the following figures:

Figure 12.39—Record layout: model inventory record
Figure 12.40—Print chart: stock status report
Figure 12.41—Programming specifications
Figure 12.42—System flowchart
Figure 12.43—Structure chart
Figure 12.44—Pseudocode
Figure 12.45—Program flowchart
Figure 12.46—COBOL coding

Notice in the STOCK program that, since the input-loaded table is coded in WORKING-STORAGE and requires no VALUE clauses, there is no need for a REDEFINES clause. Also, observe that when the table is loaded, logic is provided to check for the presence of table data, the table record sequence, the table limits, and the end of the table data.

Part A: Model description table record:

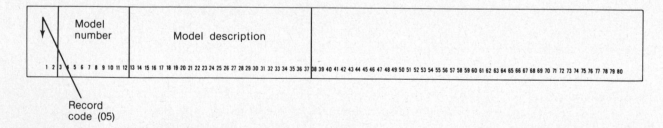

Record
code (05)

Part B: Model inventory balance record:

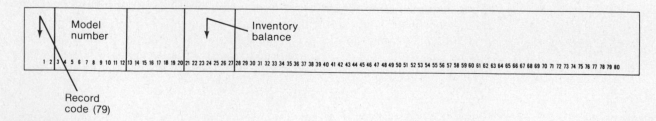

Record
code (79)

Figure 12.39. Record layout: Model description and model inventory balance records

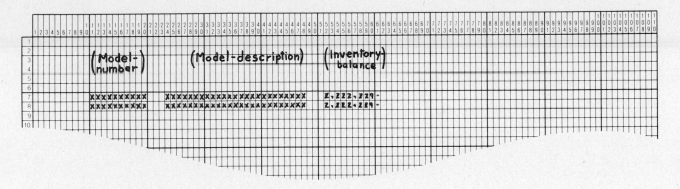

Figure 12.40. Print chart: Stock status report

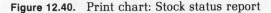

Program name: STOCK STATUS REPORT   Program ID: STOCK

Program Description

This program prints an inventory stock status report from inventory model records. Before reading inventory model balance records, inventory description table records are read from the combined inventory description table record/ inventory model balance record file and stored in the model description table.

Input File(s)

Inventory model file

Output File(s)

Stock status report

List of Program Operations

A. Read each input inventory model file record.

B. The first records read from the file should be inventory description table records. For each inventory description table record, the program should store the model number and the inventory description in the model description table.

1. If there are less than 10 inventory description table records, the program is to print an error message "incomplete inventory description table file" and terminate processing.

2. If there are more than 100 inventory description table records, the program is to print an error message "inventory description table cannot hold all entries" and terminate processing.

3. If the inventory description table records are not in sequence by inventory model number, the program is to print an error message "inventory description table records not in sequence" and terminate processing.

4. If an inventory description table record is read after an inventory model record has been processed, the program is to print an error message "inventory description table record follows inventory model record" and terminate processing.

C. For each inventory model record, the program should:

1. Look up the model description for the input model number on the model description table.

a. If the input model number cannot be located in the model description table, print "model desc. not on file" as the model description.

2. Print a single-spaced detail-line containing the following fields in accordance with the format shown on the print-chart:

a. Model number
b. Model description
c. Inventory balance

Figure 12.41. Programming specifications: Stock status report program

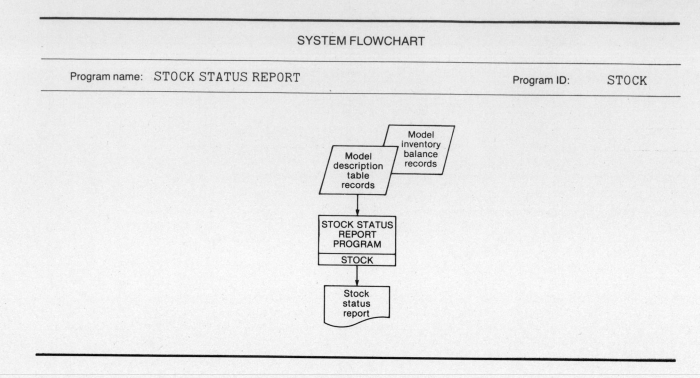

Figure 12.42. System flowchart: Stock status report program

STRUCTURE CHART

Program name: STOCK STATUS REPORT   Program ID: STOCK

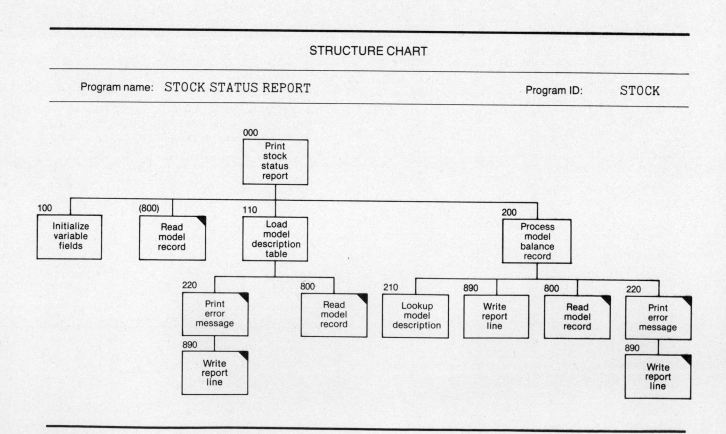

Figure 12.43. Structure chart: Stock status report program

Program name: STOCK STATUS REPORT   Program ID: STOCK

000-Print-Stock-Status-Report module
1. Open the files.
2. Perform 100-Initialize-Variable-Fields.
3. Perform 800-Read-Model-Record.
4. Move input Model-number field to the Previous-Model-number field.
5. Perform 110-Load-Description-Table until a model balance record has been read or no more records.
6. If less than 10 table records have been read
    Move "Incomplete inventory description table file" to Error-message
    Perform 220-Print-Error-Message.
7. Perform 200-Process-Balance-Record until no more records.
8. Close the files.
9. Stop the run.

100-Initialize-Variable-Fields module
1. Set the end-of-file indicator to "No".
2. Set the Table-index to 1.

110-Load-Description-Table module
1. If Table-index is greater than 100
    Move "Inventory description table cannot hold all entries" to Error-message
    Perform 220-Print-Error-Message.
2. If the input record Model-number is not greater than the Previous-model-number
    Move "Inventory description table records not in sequence" to Error-message
    Perform 220-Print-Error-Message.
3. Move the input record Model-number to the table Model-number (Table-index occurrence).
4. Move the input record Model-description to the table Model-description (in accordance with the Table-index).
5. Move the input record Model-number field to the Previous-model-number field.
6. Increment the Table-index by 1.
7. Perform 800-Read-Model-Record.

200-Process-Balance-Record module
1. Move the input Model-number field to the detail-line Model-number field.
2. Perform 210-Lookup-Model-Description.
3. If the Entry-found indicator is equal to "Yes"
    Move the table Model-description (Table-index occurrence) to the detail-line Model-description field
   Else
    Move "Model desc. not on file" to the detail-line Model-description field
4. Move the input Inventory-balance field to the detail-line Inventory-balance field.
5. Move the detail-line to the output print-line area.
6. Perform 890-Write-Report-Line.
7. Perform 800-Read-Model-Record.
8. If the input record is a table record
    Move "Inventory description table record follows inventory model record" to Error-message
    Perform 220-Print-Error-Message.

210-Lookup-Model-Description module
1. Set the Table-index to 1.
2. Search for the table Model-number that matches the input record Model-number.
3. If a matching table-argument entry is found
    Move "Yes" to the Entry-found indicator
   Else
    If end of table is reached
     Move "No" to the Entry-found indicator.

220-Print-Error-Message module
1. Move the Error-message field to the detail-line Error-message field.
2. Perform 890-Write-Report-Line.
3. Move "Yes" to the end-of-file indicator.

800-Read-Model-Record module
1. Read an input model record.
2. If there are no more records
    Set the end-of-file indicator to "Yes".

890-Write-Report-Line module
1. Write the output print-line area after single-spacing.

Figure 12-44   Pseudocode: Stock status report program

Program name: STOCK STATUS REPORT   Program ID: STOCK

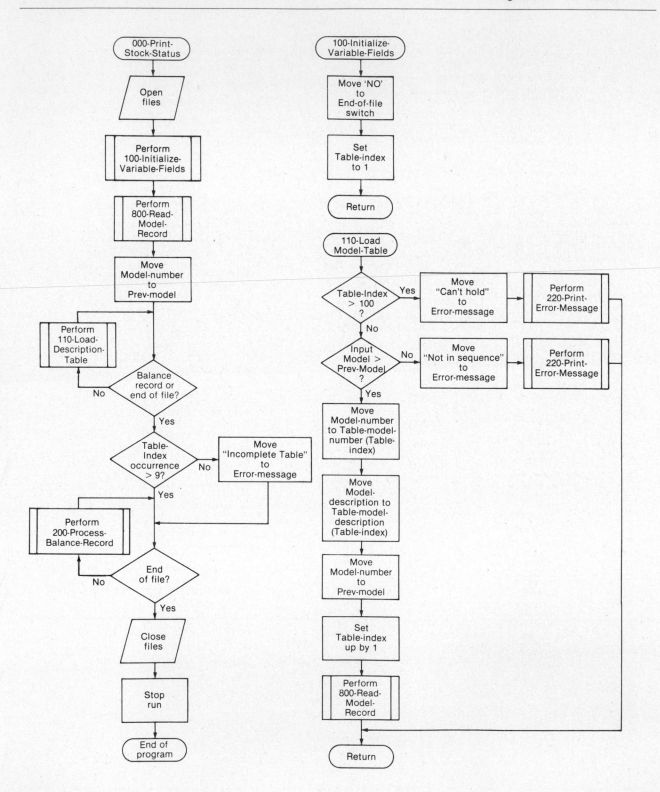

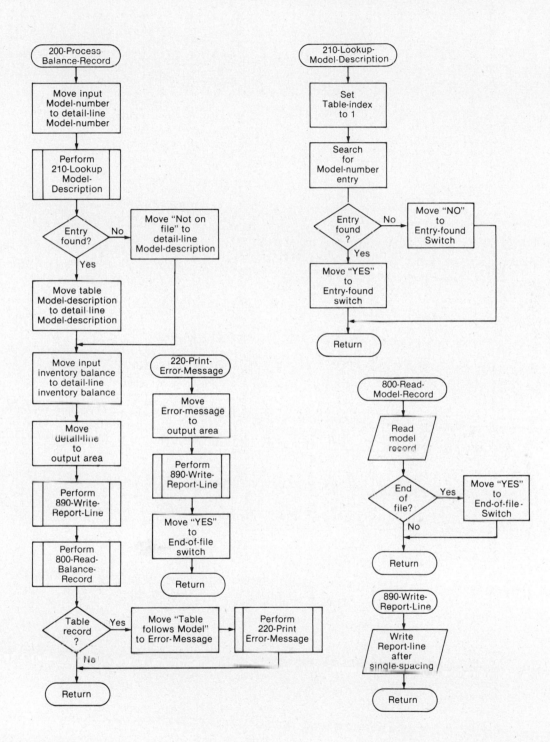

Figure 12.45. Program flowchart: Stock status report program

```
001010 IDENTIFICATION DIVISION.
001020 PROGRAM-ID.     STOCK.
001030*AUTHOR.         WELBURN.
001040*INSTALLATION.   SILICON VALLEY MANUFACTURING COMPANY.
001050*DATE-WRITTEN.   APR 12,1981.
001060*DATE-COMPILED.  APR 13,1981.
001070*SECURITY.       NONE.
001080*
001090*
001100*             THIS PROGRAM READS MODEL TABLE RECORDS
001110*             AND MODEL BALANCE RECORDS FROM THE MODEL FILE.
001120*             FIRST, THE MODEL TABLE RECORDS ARE PROCESSED
001130*             TO LOAD THE MODEL DESCRIPTION TABLE.
001140*
001150*             THEN THE MODEL BALANCE RECORDS ARE READ TO PRINT
001160*             A STOCK STATUS REPORT.
002010*
002020*
002030*
002040 ENVIRONMENT DIVISION.
002050*
002060*
002070 CONFIGURATION SECTION.
002080*
002090 SOURCE-COMPUTER.   IBM-370.
002100 OBJECT-COMPUTER.   IBM-370.
002110*
002120*
002130 INPUT-OUTPUT SECTION.
002140*
002150 FILE-CONTROL.
002160     SELECT MODEL-FILE
002170         ASSIGN TO UT-S-INFILE.
002180     SELECT STOCK-STATUS-REPORT
002190         ASSIGN TO UT-S-PRTFILE.
003010*
003020*
003030*
003040 DATA DIVISION.
003050*
003060*
003070 FILE SECTION.
003080*
003090 FD  MODEL-FILE
003100         RECORD CONTAINS 80 CHARACTERS
003110         LABEL RECORDS ARE OMITTED.
003120*
003130 01  MODEL-RECORD.
003140     05  FILLER                    PIC X(80).
004010*
004020 FD  STOCK-STATUS-REPORT
004030         RECORD CONTAINS 133 CHARACTERS
004040         LABEL RECORDS ARE OMITTED.
004050*
004060 01  STOCK-STATUS-REPORT-LINE.
004070     05  FILLER                    PIC X(133).
005010*
005020*
005030 WORKING-STORAGE SECTION.
005040*
005050*
005060 01  WS-SWITCHES.
005070     05  WS-END-OF-FILE-SWITCH     PIC X(3).
005080         88  END-OF-FILE                     VALUE 'YES'.
007010*
007020 01  WS-CONTROL-FIELDS.
007030     05  WS-PREVIOUS-MODEL-NUMBER  PIC X(10).
020010*
020020 01  MD-MODEL-RECORD.
020030     05  MD-RECORD-CODE            PIC X(2).
020040         88  MODEL-DESCR-TABLE-RECORD        VALUE '05'.
020050     05  MD-MODEL-NUMBER           PIC X(10).
020060     05  MD-MODEL-DESCRIPTION      PIC X(25).
020070     05  FILLER                    PIC X(43).
021010*
021020 01  MB-MODEL-BALANCE-RECORD REDEFINES MD-MODEL-RECORD.
021030     05  MB-RECORD-CODE            PIC X(2).
021040         88  MODEL-BALANCE-RECORD            VALUE '79'.
021050     05  MB-MODEL-NUMBER           PIC X(10).
021060     05  FILLER                    PIC X(8).
021070     05  MB-INVENTORY-BALANCE      PIC S9(7).
021080     05  FILLER                    PIC X(53).
033010*
033020 01  DL-DETAIL-LINE.
033030     05  FILLER                    PIC X(1).
033040     05  FILLER                    PIC X(10)   VALUE SPACES.
033050     05  DL-MODEL-NUMBER           PIC X(10).
033060     05  FILLER                    PIC X(3)    VALUE SPACES.
033070     05  DL-MODEL-DESCRIPTION      PIC X(25).
033080     05  FILLER                    PIC X(3)    VALUE SPACES.
033090     05  DL-INVENTORY-BALANCE      PIC Z,ZZZ,ZZ9-.
033100     05  FILLER                    PIC X(3)    VALUE SPACES.
033110     05  DL-ERROR-MESSAGE          PIC X(50)   VALUE SPACES.
033120     05  FILLER                    PIC X(18)   VALUE SPACES.
040010*
040020 01  MT-TABLE-CONTROLS.
040030     05  MT-ENTRY-FOUND-SWITCH     PIC X(3).
040040         88  MT-ENTRY-FOUND                  VALUE 'YES'.
040050     05  MT-NUMBER-OF-ENTRIES      PIC S9(4)   VALUE +100.
040060*
040070 01  MT-MODEL-DESCRIPTION-TABLE.
040080     05  MT-MODEL-DESCRIPTION-ENTRY   OCCURS 100 TIMES
040090                                      INDEXED BY MT-INDEX.
040100         10  MT-MODEL-NUMBER          PIC X(10).
040110         10  MT-MODEL-DESCRIPTION     PIC X(25).
```

```
050010*
050020*
050030*
050040 PROCEDURE DIVISION.
050050*
050060*
050070 000-PRINT-STOCK-STATUS-REPORT.
050080*
050090     OPEN INPUT MODEL-FILE
050100          OUTPUT STOCK-STATUS-REPORT.
050110     PERFORM 100-INITIALIZE-VARIABLE-FIELDS.
050120     PERFORM 800-READ-MODEL-RECORD.
050130     MOVE MD-MODEL-NUMBER TO WS-PREVIOUS-MODEL-NUMBER.
050140     PERFORM 110-LOAD-DESCRIPTION-TABLE
050150         UNTIL MODEL-BALANCE-RECORD
050160         OR END-OF-FILE.
050170     IF MT-INDEX IS NOT GREATER THAN 9
050180         MOVE 'INCOMPLETE INVENTORY DESCRIPTION TABLE FILE'
050190             TO DL-ERROR-MESSAGE
050200         PERFORM 220-PRINT-ERROR-MESSAGE.
050210     PERFORM 200-PROCESS-BALANCE-RECORD
050220         UNTIL END-OF-FILE.
050230     CLOSE MODEL-FILE
050240           STOCK-STATUS-REPORT.
050250     STOP RUN.
100010*
100020*
100030 100-INITIALIZE-VARIABLE-FIELDS.
100040*
100050     MOVE 'NO ' TO WS-END-OF-FILE-SWITCH.
100060     SET MT-INDEX TO 1.
110010*
110020*
110030 110-LOAD-DESCRIPTION-TABLE.
110040*
110050     IF MT-INDEX IS GREATER THAN MT-NUMBER-OF-ENTRIES
110060         MOVE 'MODEL DESCRIPTION TABLE CANNOT HOLD ALL ENTRIES'
110070             TO DL-ERROR-MESSAGE
110080         PERFORM 220-PRINT-ERROR-MESSAGE
110090     ELSE IF MD-MODEL-NUMBER
110100             IS NOT GREATER THAN WS-PREV-MODEL-NUMBER
110110         MOVE 'MODEL DESCRIPTION TABLE RECORDS NOT IN SEQUENCE'
110120             TO DL-ERROR-MESSAGE
110130         PERFORM 220-PRINT-ERROR-MESSAGE
110140     ELSE
110150         MOVE MD-MODEL-NUMBER TO MT-MODEL-NUMBER (MT-INDEX)
110160         MOVE MD-MODEL-DESCRIPTION
110170             TO MT-MODEL-DESCRIPTION (MT-INDEX)
110180         MOVE MD-MODEL-NUMBER TO WS-PREVIOUS-MODEL-NUMBER
110190         SET MT-INDEX UP BY 1
110200         PERFORM 800-READ-MODEL-RECORD.
200010*
200020*
200030 200-PROCESS-BALANCE-RECORD.
200040*
200050     MOVE MB-MODEL-NUMBER TO DL-MODEL-NUMBER.
200060     PERFORM 210-LOOKUP-MODEL-DESCRIPTION.
200070     IF MT-ENTRY-FOUND
200080         MOVE MT-MODEL-DESCRIPTION (MT-INDEX)
200090             TO DL-MODEL-DESCRIPTION
200100     ELSE
200110         MOVE 'MODEL DESC. NOT ON FILE' TO DL-MODEL-DESCRIPTION.
200120     MOVE MB-INVENTORY-BALANCE TO DL-INVENTORY-BALANCE.
200130     MOVE DL-DETAIL-LINE TO STOCK-STATUS-REPORT-LINE.
200140     PERFORM 890-WRITE-REPORT-LINE.
200150     PERFORM 800-READ-MODEL-RECORD.
200160     IF MODEL-DESCR-TABLE-RECORD
200170         MOVE 'TABLE RECORD FOLLOWS BALANCE RECORD'
200180             TO DL-ERROR-MESSAGE
200190         PERFORM 220-PRINT-ERROR-MESSAGE.
210010*
210020*
210030 210-LOOKUP-MODEL-DESCRIPTION.
210040*
210050     SET MT-INDEX TO 1.
210060     SEARCH MT-MODEL-DESCIPTION-ENTRY
210070         AT END MOVE 'NO ' TO MT-ENTRY-FOUND-SWITCH
210080         WHEN MT-MODEL-NUMBER (MT-INDEX)
210090             IS EQUAL TO MB-MODEL-NUMBER
210100             MOVE 'YES' TO MT-ENTRY-FOUND-SWITCH.
220010*
220020*
220030 220-PRINT-ERROR-MESSAGE.
220040*
220050     MOVE SPACES TO DL-MODEL-NUMBER
220060                    DL-MODEL-DESCRIPTION.
220070     MOVE DL-DETAIL-LINE TO STOCK-STATUS-REPORT-LINE.
220080     PERFORM 890-WRITE-REPORT-LINE.
220090     MOVE 'YES' TO WS-END-OF-FILE-SWITCH.
800010*
800020*
800030 800-READ-MODEL-RECORD.
800040*
800050     READ MODEL-FILE INTO MD-MODEL-RECORD
800060         AT END MOVE 'YES' TO WS-END-OF-FILE-SWITCH.
890010*
890020*
890030 890-WRITE-REPORT-LINE.
890040*
890050     WRITE STOCK-STATUS-REPORT-LINE
890060         AFTER ADVANCING 1 LINE.
```

Figure 12.46. COBOL coding: STOCK program

Table Processing Guidelines

This section provides guidelines for table processing, which are drawn from the material already covered as well as certain additional considerations.

Table Source

1. Table data should be hard-coded in the program when it is high security data or if it changes only infrequently.
2. Tables should be loaded from input records when they consist of volatile or voluminous data.

Table Establishment

1. Determine the optimum method of table organization for the table: random, sequential, usage-frequency, or positional.
2. Arrange the table arguments adjacent to the table function or functions to ease programmer checking, debugging, and maintenance functions.
3. When hard-coding the table data with VALUE clauses, try to specify a separate data-item for each table entry. This will also ease programmer checking and maintenance functions. (If the table entries are long or of varying usages, separate data-items may be required for certain fields of each table entry.)
4. The table description definition must contain a REDEFINES clause when the table data has been hard-coded with VALUE clauses. It will always contain one or more OCCURS clauses.
5. It is generally more efficient processing to use indexes rather than subscripts. In most cases, then, the programmer should specify the IN-DEXED BY clause.
6. If the table is organized sequentially and contains over 30 table entries, consider specifying the ASCENDING KEY or DESCENDING KEY phrase in accordance with its sequence so that a binary search may be made.
7. If the table is organized sequentially, consider providing a dummy end-of-table entry containing either HIGH-VALUES or LOW-VALUES (depending upon whether the table is arranged in ascending or descending sequence) to maximize processing efficiency and eliminate maintenance of a number-of-entries field.
8. For ease of reference, establish table control fields immediately before the table. Such fields include: (1) a subscript field (when an index is not used); (2) a number-of-table-entries field (unless a dummy end-of-table entry and its appropriate logic are used); and (3) an entry-found switch.
9. When a subscript is used, processing efficiency will usually be enhanced by specifying COMP usage and the SYNC clause. Specify a PICTURE clause of S9(4).

Table Lookup

1. If SEARCH is available with the COBOL compiler and if no special lookup logic is required, use the SEARCH statement for serial and binary lookups.
   a. If the table is organized sequentially and contains over 30 table entries, use SEARCH ALL to obtain a binary search.
   b. When doing a serial search, remember to set the index to 1 immediately before specifying the SEARCH statement.
   c. If table arguments and functions are defined separately, use the VARY-ING phrase of the SEARCH statement.
2. When using the PERFORM/VARYING statement for a lookup, remember to decrement the subscript or index by 1 after the matching arguments have been found.
3. Since lookups must sometimes be made at multiple locations in a program, always code the lookup logic as an independent module. This is similar to

the convention that calls for READ and WRITE statements to be coded as separate modules.

Table Loading

1. When loading a table from a combined table/data file, the table data must precede the regular data to be processed. Then the program logic must check the input record codes to determine if the table data is actually present and to determine when the table data has ended and processing of regular data is to begin.

2. If the table organization is sequential the program logic should ensure that the table records are actually in the required sequence.

3. The program logic should always check the table limit to see that the number of table entries provided in the program is not exceeded by the number of input table entries.

Summary

Tables are defined in the WORKING-STORAGE SECTION of the DATA DIVISION and accessed in the PROCEDURE DIVISION. To establish hard-coded table data, it is specified with VALUE clauses and then redefined with an OCCURS clause.

The OCCURS clause is used to indicate how many times a particular field or group of fields is repeated. The integer specified in the OCCURS clause indicates the number of repetitions. The OCCURS clause: (1) can be used with any data-item description that has a level number from 02 through 49 (it cannot be used with an 01-level or 77-level item); (2) cannot be used with a data-item that contains a VALUE clause.

Whenever an OCCURS clause is associated with a data-item, either a subscript or an index must be used when referring to that item in the PROCEDURE DIVISION. *Subscripts* are used to reference a specific occurrence of a repeated field defined with the OCCURS clause. Subscripts are always enclosed in parentheses and may be of either literal or variable form. *Literal* subscripts are an actual occurrence number coded in the parentheses. *Variable* subscripts are much more powerful and thus more frequently used. They use the value contained in a field to indicate the occurrence number.

A field used for a variable subscript must be: (1) an elementary numeric integer data-item defined in the DATA DIVISION and (2) of sufficient length to contain the number of occurrences specified in the OCCURS clause for the field being referenced.

At execution time, the subscript field should contain a value greater than zero but not greater than the number of occurrences of the field being referenced.

Indexes are used much like subscripts, but there are three important differences:

1. When an index-name is specified in the INDEXED BY clause, the index is automatically provided for by the compiler; the programmer does not establish a data-item in the DATA DIVISION as would be done for a variable subscript.

2. Subscripts contain occurrence values; indexes contain *displacement* values.

3. Initialization, incrementation, and decrementation of an index must be done with a SET statement.

The SET statement has two formats: Format-1 is used for index initialization; Format-2 is used for index incrementation or decrementation.

Index data-items may be specified in the DATA DIVISION to allow for the storage of index displacement values that may be used without being converted to occurrence numbers. To specify an index data-item, the programmer codes the USAGE IS INDEX clause.

Table lookups can be accomplished using the PERFORM/UNTIL statement, the PERFORM/VARYING statement, or the SEARCH statement.

The SEARCH statement can be used for a serial search or a binary search. To provide for a binary search, the ASCENDING KEY or DESCENDING KEY clause must be coded in the DATA DIVISION and the ALL phrase must be coded for the SEARCH statement.

Multiple-level tables contain tables within table entries. COBOL can handle multiple-level tables of two or three dimensions.

When processing input-loaded tables, the programmer must provide appropriate logic to handle separate or combined table/data files, table sequence considerations, and table limits.

Style Summary

- When establishing table data in WORKING-STORAGE, try to define each table element as a separate data-item. Such definition makes the table entries easier to read and modify.

- When an entry has more than one element (an argument and one or more functions, for example), define the elements adjacent to one another rather than as separate tables. Again, such definition makes the table entries easier to read and modify.

- More efficient processing is generally provided by indexes than subscripts. So, normally specify the INDEXED BY clause.

- For a sequential table, consider providing a dummy end-of-table entry to maximize processing efficiency and eliminate maintenance of a number-of-entries field.

- For ease of reference, establish table control fields immediately before the table. Such fields include: (1) a subscript field (when an index is not used); (2) a number-of-table-entries field (unless a dummy end-of-table entry and its appropriate logic are used); and (3) an entry-found switch.

- When a subscript is used, processing efficiency will usually be enhanced by specifying COMP usage and the SYNC clause with a PICTURE of S9(4).

- Use the SEARCH statement for serial and binary lookups (providing it is available with the COBOL compiler and appropriate for the required lookup logic).

- Since lookups must sometimes be made at multiple locations in a program, always code the lookup logic as an independent module.

1968 ANS COBOL Restrictions

- When multiple subscripts or indexes appear within a set of parentheses, they must be separated by commas.

Exercises

Terms for Definition

subscript	displacement value
literal subscript	range step table arguments
variable subscript	separately defined table arguments and functions
index	separate table file
dummy end-of-table entry	combined table/data file
occurrence number	

1. To establish a "hard-coded" table, the table data is entered with _Value_ clauses in the _working storage_ SECTION of the DATA DIVISION.

2. After "hard-coded" table data has been established, it must be _redefined_ with data-item descriptions containing an _occurs_ clause.

3. The OCCURS statement can be specified with level-numbers _2_ through _49_ .

4. A data-item containing an OCCURS clause cannot contain a _value_ clause.

5. When an OCCURS clause is associated with a data-item, either a _subscript_ or an _index_ must be used when referring to that field in the PROCEDURE DIVISION.

6. Subscripts may be expressed as _literal_ or _variable_ .

7. The value of a subscript is used to identify which _occurrence_ of the data-item is being referred to.

8. It is generally most efficient to define subscripts of _computational_ usage.

9. When a program is executing the statement containing the subscript, the value of the subscript should be greater than _0_ and less than _# of entries_ .

10. Specification of the OCCURS clause at the group level causes _____ .

11. When the PERFORM/VARYING clause is used for a table lookup, the subscript or index must be _decremented by 1_ after the match between search and table arguments has been located.

12. For efficiency, it is generally preferable to use an _index_ rather than a subscript.

13. Index-names are established by the _indexed by_ clause.

14. Subscripts are used for the storage of _____ numbers; indexes contain _____ values.

15. Subscripts are usually initialized by a _move_ statement; indexes are initialized by a _set_ statement.

16. Index data-items may be established by specifying _index_ usage.

17. Index data-names cannot be specified with _picture_ or _value_ clauses.

18. When a SEARCH statement reaches the end of the table and the condition expressed in the WHEN phrase is not satisfied, the _at end_ phrase is executed.

19. Execution of a SEARCH statement ends when _condition is satisfied_ .

20. To cause a binary search, the _search all_ phrase of the SEARCH statement is specified.

21. A binary search requires that the _ascending/descending key_ phrase be specified for the table in the DATA DIVISION.

22. In addition to single-level tables, COBOL can handle multiple-level tables of _2_ or _3_ dimensions.

23. A three-level table requires _3_ subscripts (and/or indexes).

24. Rather than "hard-coding" a table, it may be loaded from _a file_ .

Programming Assignment 12-A: Department Name Lookup

Program description

An employee/department list is to be prepared from the payroll file. A hard-coded table of department numbers/names will be required.

Input file

Payroll file

Input record format
Payroll record

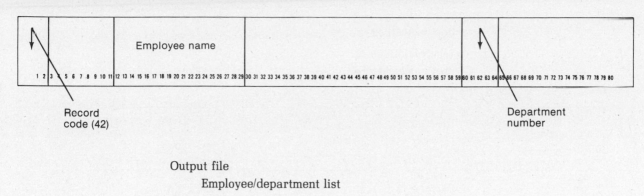

Record
code (42)

Department
number

Output file

Employee/department list

Output report format

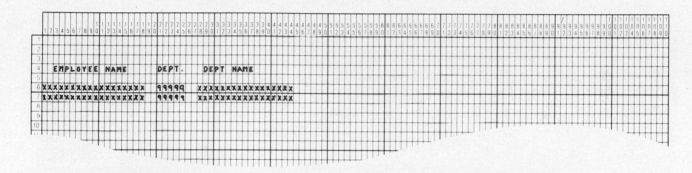

Table data

Department number	Department name
1000	ADMINISTRATION
1100	PURCHASING
1200	PERSONNEL
1300	ADVERTISING
1350	PUBLIC RELATIONS
1900	TRAINING
2000	RESEARCH & DEVEL.
3000	FINANCE
3500	DATA PROCESSING
4000	MANUFACTURING

Program operations

1. Read each input payroll record.

2. For each payroll record, do the following processing:

   a. Use the input department number to lookup the department name. If the input department number cannot be located in the table, print "DEPT NOT IN TABLE" in the department name field of the output record.

   b. Print a detail line in accordance with the print chart specifications.

3. Headings are to be printed on each page of the report. After 57 lines have been used on a report page, the program is to skip to the next page and print the report headings.

4. Line spacing is to be handled as follows:

   a. The first detail-line after the headings is to be double-spaced from the last heading line.

   b. Single-space each detail-line.

*Programming
Assignment 12-B: Part
Data Lookup*

Program description

A part data list is to be printed from part number records. A hard-coded table of part numbers/unit of measures/part descriptions/prices will be required.

Input file

Part number file

Input records formats

Part number record

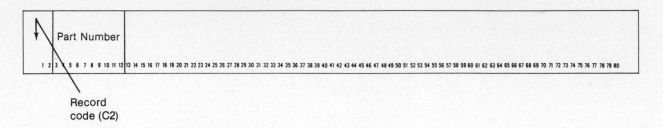

Record
code (C2)

Output file

Part data list

Output report format

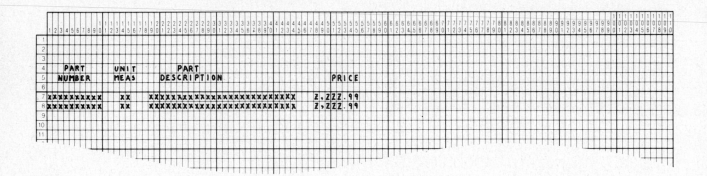

Table data

Part number	Part description	Price	Unit Meas.
E5900	DATA STAND	115.00	EA
E5950	CRT CHAIR	128.00	EA
E5972	PRINTER STAND	107.00	EA
E5980	ANTI-STATIC MAT	168.00	EA
E6102	FILE CASE	31.75	EA
E6111	PRINTWHEEL CASE	10.95	EA
T85590	FLEXIBLE DISK, SOFT SECTOR	385.00	C
T85591	FLEXIBLE DISK, HARD SECTOR	385.00	C
X50634	CONTINUOUS FORM PAPER	28.50	BX
X78055	NYLON POST BINDERS	2.86	EA

Program operations

1. Read each input part number record.

2. For each part number record, do the following processing:

   a. Use the part number field to lookup the unit of measure, part description, and price for that part. If the input part number cannot be located in the table, print "PART NOT IN TABLE" as the part description and print asterisks in the unit of measure and price fields.

   b. Print a detail line in accordance with the print chart specifications.

3. Line spacing is to be handled as follows:

   a. The first detail-line after the headings is to be double-spaced from the last heading line.

   b. Single-space each detail-line.

Programming Assignment 12-C: Federal Income Tax Register

Program description

   A federal income tax register is to be printed from the payroll file. A hard-coded federal withholding tax table will be required.

Input file

   Payroll file

Input record format

   Payroll record

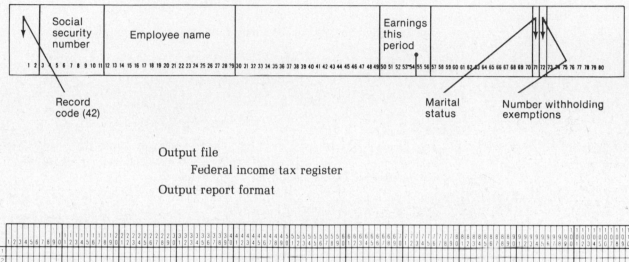

Output file

   Federal income tax register

Output report format

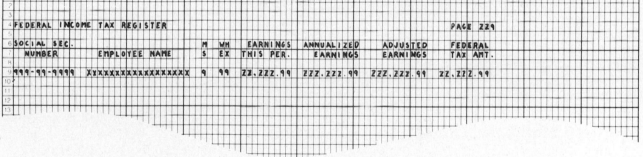

Table data

TABLE 7. ANNUAL Payroll Period

(a) SINGLE person—including head of household:

If the amount of wages is:	The amount of income tax to be withheld shall be:	
Not over $1,420	0	
Over— But not over—		**of excess over—**
$1,420 —$3,300	15%	—$1,420
$3,300 —$6,800	$282.00 plus 18%	—$3,300
$6,800 —$10,200	$912.00 plus 21%	—$6,800
$10,200 —$14,200	$1,626.00 plus 26%	—$10,200
$14,200 —$17,200	$2,666.00 plus 30%	—$14,200
$17,200 —$22,500	$3,566.00 plus 34%	—$17,200
$22,500	$5,368.00 plus 39%	—$22,500

(b) MARRIED person—

If the amount of wages is:	The amount of income tax to be withheld shall be:	
Not over $2,400	0	
Over— But not over—		**of excess over—**
$2,400 —$6,600	15%	—$2,400
$6,600 —$10,900	$630.00 plus 18%	—$6,600
$10,900 —$15,000	$1,404.00 plus 21%	—$10,900
$15,000 —$19,200	$2,265.00 plus 24%	—$15,000
$19,200 —$23,600	$3,273.00 plus 28%	—$19,200
$23,600 —$28,900	$4,505.00 plus 32%	—$23,600
$28,900	$6,201.00 plus 37%	—$28,900

Program operations
1. For each input payroll record, do the following processing:
   a. Compute the annualized earnings by multiplying the earnings this period by 26 (the pay period is two weeks; there are 26 two-week periods in a year).
   b. Compute the adjusted earnings by multiplying the number of withholding exemptions by $1000.00 (standard deduction) and subtract the product from the annualized earnings.
   c. Compute the federal tax amount in accordance with the employee's marital status from the tax table.
   d. Print a detail line in accordance with the print chart specifications.
2. Headings are to be printed on each page of the report. After 57 lines have been used on a report page, the program is to skip to the next page and print the report headings.
   a. The page number is to be incremented each time the heading is printed and displayed on the first heading-line in accordance with the format shown on the print chart.
3. Line spacing is to be handled as follows:
   a. The first detail-line after the headings is to be double-spaced from the last heading line.
   b. Double-space each detail-line.

*Programming
Assignment 12-D:
Section Data Lookup*

Program description

A section test results report is to be printed from the test results file. It is to provide control break totals for each section. An input-loaded table of section numbers/course names/instructors will be required.

Input file

Test results file

Input record formats

Section table record
Test results record

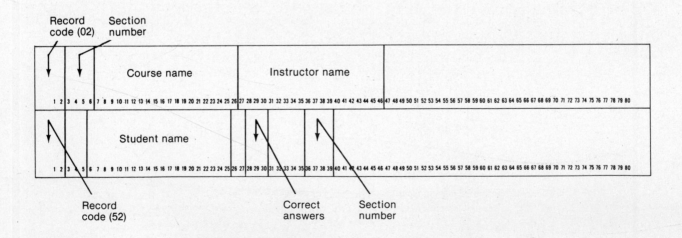

Output file

Section test results report

Output report format

```
 1|
 2|
 3|
 4|SECTION TEST RESULTS                                                              PAGE ZZ9
 5|
 6|SECTION                                                            CORRECT
 7| NUMBER      COURSE NAME          INSTRUCTOR         STUDENT NAME   ANSWERS
 8|
 9| 9999    XXXXXXXXXXXXXXXXXXXX  XXXXXXXXXXXXXXXXXXXX  XXXXXXXXXXXXXXXXXXXX   ZZ9
10|                                                     XXXXXXXXXXXXXXXXXXXX   ZZ9
11|
12| 9999    XXXXXXXXXXXXXXXXXXXX  XXXXXXXXXXXXXXXXXXXX  TOTAL STUDENTS ZZ9     ZZ9*  AVG. ZZ9
13|
14|
15|
16|
```

Program operations

1. For each section table record, do the following processing:
   a. Store the section number, course name, and instructor name in the section table.
   b. If there are more than 100 section table records, print an error message "TOO MANY TABLE RECORDS" and terminate processing.

2. If there are no section table records in the input file, print an error message "TABLE RECORDS MISSING" and terminate processing.

3. If a section table record follows a test results record, print "TABLE RECORD FOLLOWS TEST RECORD" and terminate processing.

4. For each test results record, do the following processing:
   a. Use the section number field of the input test results record to lookup the course name and instructor name from the section table. If the input section number cannot be located in the section table, print asterisks in the course name and instructor fields on the output record.
   b. Print a detail line in accordance with the print chart specifications. Notice that the course name and instructor name are to be printed only on the first line for a section number (unless the section is continued to a new page in which case the course name and instructor name should be printed on the next page).

5. Whenever the section number changes, print a control break section total line in accordance with the print chart specifications containing the following:
   a. The section number
   b. Total number of students
   c. Total number of correct answers
   d. Average score (total number of correct answers divided by total number of students).
   e. Descriptive words and an asterisk as specified on the print chart.

6. Headings are to be printed on each page of the report. After 54 lines have been used on a report page and a new test results record is to be printed, the program is to skip to the next page and print the report headings. (Do not allow the control break line to be printed on a report page which does not contain at least one detail line for the section number to which it applies.)
   a. The page number is to be incremented each time the heading is printed and displayed on the first heading-line in accordance with the format shown on the print chart.

7. Line spacing is to be handled as follows:
    a. The first detail-line after the headings is to be double-spaced from the last heading line.
    b. Second and successive detail-lines for the same section number are to be single-spaced from one another.
    c. Each control break section total-line is to be double-spaced from the previous detail-line.
    d. The first detail-line following a control break section total-line is to be double-spaced from the section total-line.

APPENDICES AND INDEX

OTHER COBOL CLAUSES AND STATEMENTS

There are a number of additional COBOL clauses and statements that are either not frequently used, outdated, or their use is generally discouraged. Though this text does not cover clauses and statements used with the Relative I-O, Indexed I-O, Report Writer, Debug, Inter-program Communication module, or Communication modules, the following additional COBOL clauses and statements are covered in this appendix:

Division	Clause or statement
IDENTIFICATION	REMARKS
DATA	OCCURS/DEPENDING ON
	RENAMES
PROCEDURE	ACCEPT
	DISPLAY
	ALTER
	GO TO/DEPENDING ON
	MOVE CORRESPONDING
	ADD CORRESPONDING
	SUBTRACT CORRESPONDING
	ON SIZE ERROR
	NOTE
	PERFORM/TIMES
	STRING
	UNSTRING

IDENTIFICATION DIVISION

The REMARKS Paragraph

The REMARKS paragraph was included in the 1968 ANS COBOL standards to provide the facility for general documentation in the IDENTIFICATION DIVISION but was removed from the language prior to the 1974 standards. It is still found in older programs and is sometimes still used by programmers. Under the 1974 standards, comment lines (* in position 7) should be used rather than the REMARKS paragraph. Figure A.1 depicts the two methods.

DATA DIVISION

The OCCURS/DEPENDING ON Clause

This clause is seldom used but is valuable when an input-table is defined as a generous number of entries that are only partially filled. An example is shown in Figure A.2. Notice that the IT-ITEM-TABLE is defined to hold a maximum of 200 table entries. Suppose, though, that there were only 45 table entries loaded. By keeping count of the number of table entries loaded—and storing that count in the object of the DEPENDING ON clause (IT-NBR-ENTRIES in the example)—table lookup processing for unmatched entries is made faster. When a SEARCH statement does a lookup on the table, it will consider the table to be 45 entries long rather than 200.

The Level 66 RENAMES Clause

Though rarely used, this clause is similar to the REDEFINES clause in that it permits one or more data-items to be assigned alternate data-names. It is different because (1) it does not provide for assigning an alternate PICTURE clause, (2) it allows multiple fields to be renamed, and (3) the clause must be placed at the end of the record-description to which it applies. Examples of the RENAMES clause are provided in Figure A.3.

Example:

```
REMARKS.   THE REMARKS PARAGRAPH WAS PROVIDED SO THAT OVERALL
           PROGRAM DOCUMENTATION COMMENTS COULD BE PROVIDED
           IN THE IDENTIFICATION DIVISION.
```

1974 ANS method:

```
*              THE REMARKS PARAGRAPH HAS BEEN DROPPED FROM THE 1974
*              ANS COBOL STANDARDS.  COMMENT LINES
*              (* IN POSITION 7) SHOULD INSTEAD BE USED.
```

Figure A.1.   REMARKS paragraph example

The following rules apply to the RENAMES clause:

- It must be a level-number 66 entry and must be specified immediately following the record-description to which it applies.
- It cannot be used to rename level 01, 66, 77, or 88 entries.
- The identifiers specified in a RENAMES clause cannot contain an OCCURS clause.
- Identifier-3 (the THRU identifier) must physically follow identifier-2 in the record-description and cannot be subordinate to identifier-2.

Format:

OCCURS integer-1 TO integer-2 TIMES

   DEPENDING ON data-name-1

Example:

```
*
01  IT-TABLE-CONTROLS.
    05  IT-NBR-ENTRIES                    PIC S9(4)       COMP SYNC.
*

01  IT-ITEM-TABLE.

    05  IT-ITEM-ENTRY                     OCCURS 1 TO 200 TIMES
                                          DEPENDING ON IT-NBR-ENTRIES.
        10  IT-ITEM-CODE                  PIC X(8).
        10  IT-ITEM-DESCRIPTION           PIC X(20).
```

Figure A.2.   OCCURS/DEPENDING ON example

Format:

$$66 \text{ data-name-1 } \underline{\text{RENAMES}} \text{ data-name-2 } \left[\left\{ \begin{array}{l} \underline{\text{THROUGH}} \\ \underline{\text{THRU}} \end{array} \right\} \text{ data name-3} \right] .$$

Example:

```
*
 01  NA-NAME-ADDRESS-RECORD.
     05  NA-FIRST-NAME                 PIC X(10).
     05  NA-MIDDLE-INITIAL             PIC X(1).
     05  NA-LAST-NAME                  PIC X(12).
     05  NA-ADDRESS                    PIC X(24).
     05  NA-CITY                       PIC X(13).
     05  NA-STATE                      PIC X(2).
     05  NA-ZIP-CODE                   PIC X(5).
*
     66  NA-FULL-NAME RENAMES NA-FIRST-NAME THRU NA-LAST-NAME.
     66  NA-STREET-ADDRESS RENAMES NA-ADDRESS.
     66  NA-DESTINATION RENAMES NA-CITY THRU NA-ZIP-CODE.
```

Figure A.3.   RENAMES clause examples

PROCEDURE DIVISION

The ACCEPT Statement

The ACCEPT statement obtains low-volume input data (such as dates, control numbers, etc.) from an input device or the computer operator console. It is similar in function to a READ statement but it differs in that it does not require an FD entry (or a SELECT statement or an OPEN and CLOSE). Examples of its use are shown in Figure A.4.

The identifier may be either an elementary item of DISPLAY usage or a group item. The maximum length of the data transfer for each type of input device is defined by the implementor of the COBOL compiler. (Often, the maximum length is set at 80 characters.) One physical record is read from the input device. If the data length of the transferred data is greater than the identifier length, the excess leftmost positions are truncated.

Format:

$$\underline{\text{ACCEPT}} \text{ identifier } \left[\underline{\text{FROM}} \text{ mnemonic-name} \right]$$

Examples:

Part A: ACCEPT from input device

```
        ACCEPT WS-PERIOD-ENDING-DATE.
```

Part B: ACCEPT from console

   ENVIRONMENT DIVISION

```
    SPECIAL-NAMES.
        CONSOLE IS TYPEWRITER.
```

   PROCEDURE DIVISION

```
        ACCEPT WS-PERIOD-ENDING DATE FROM TYPEWRITER.
```

Figure A.4.   ACCEPT statement examples

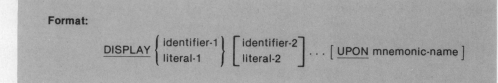

Format:

$$\text{DISPLAY} \left\{ \begin{array}{l} \text{identifier-1} \\ \text{literal-1} \end{array} \right\} \left[\begin{array}{l} \text{identifier-2} \\ \text{literal-2} \end{array} \right] \dots [\ \underline{\text{UPON}}\ \text{mnemonic-name}\ ]$$

Examples:

Part A: DISPLAY upon output device

```
DISPLAY 'RUN CANCELLED DUE TO ' WS-ERROR-MESSAGE.
```

Part B: DISPLAY upon console

ENVIRONMENT DIVISION

```
SPECIAL-NAMES.
    CONSOLE IS TYPEWRITER.
```

PROCEDURE DIVISION

```
DISPLAY 'ENTER PERIOD ENDING DATE' UPON TYPEWRITER.
```

Figure A.5. DISPLAY statement examples

When the FROM phrase is used, the mnemonic-name usually refers to the operator console.

Use of the ACCEPT statement is generally discouraged. It is better to use READ statements for normal input devices and to avoid accepting data from the operator console. Entry of data at the operator console tends to slow down operations and places a burden on the computer operator who may be tending to a number of operations requirements at one time. Thus, to minimize the chance for error and optimize computer run time, it is preferable to provide for the input of variable data (such as dates, starting check numbers, etc.) to be entered via a control record which is prepared by personnel responsible for data control.

The DISPLAY Statement

The DISPLAY statement transfers low-volume output data to an output device. It is similar in function to a WRITE statement but it differs in that it does not require an FD entry (or a SELECT statement or an OPEN and CLOSE). Examples of its use are shown in Figure A.5.

The identifier may be either an elementary item of DISPLAY usage or a group item. Literals may also be displayed. Notice from the format notation that multiple identifiers and/or literals may be displayed by one DISPLAY statement. The maximum length of the data transfer for each type of output device is defined by the implementor of the COBOL compiler. (Often, the maximum length is 120 or 132 characters.)

When the FROM phrase is used, the mnemonic-name usually refers to the operator console.

Use of the DISPLAY statement is generally discouraged. It is better to use WRITE statements for normal output devices and to avoid displaying data to the operator console. However, some programmers use the DISPLAY statement for temporary program statements to aid in program debugging.

The ALTER Statement

The ALTER statement alters the path of program control. It is used in conjunction with the GO TO statement. There is a general consensus throughout the data processing community that the ALTER statement should not be used in COBOL programs, since its use makes it difficult to determine from the program listing what procedures program con-

Example:

```
*
*
  999-CONTROL-PROCEDURE.
*
      GO TO 999-PROCESS-DETAIL-RECORD.
*
*
  999-NEXT-PROCEDURE.
*
          .
          .
          .

          .
          .
          .

      ALTER 999-CONTROL-PROCEDURE
            TO PROCEED TO 999-PROCESS-CONTROL-BREAK.
          .
          .
          .
```

Figure A.6. ALTER statement example

trol is or has been transferred to. Thus, debugging is complicated and maintenance becomes perplexing. The ALTER statement is scheduled to be removed from the next COBOL standard.

The ALTER statement can sometimes still be found in older COBOL programs so it is briefly covered here. An example is shown in Figure A.6. Procedure-name-1 must be a paragraph containing only one GO TO statement, as is 999-CONTROL-PROCEDURE. After the ALTER statement is executed, the GO TO statement will transfer control to the 999-PROCESS-CONTROL-BREAK procedure rather than the 999-PROCESS-DETAIL-RECORD. (Usually, there will be another ALTER statement elsewhere in the program to change control back to the 999-PROCESS-DETAIL-RECORD when required.)

The GO TO/DEPENDING ON Statement

The Format-1 GO TO statement is discussed in Chapter 6. The Format-2 GO TO statement contains the DEPENDING ON phrase and provides the ability to branch to various procedures depending on the value of a numeric identifier, as shown in Figure A.7. The program branches to the relative procedure in conformance with the value of the identifier. That is, if the identifier contains a 1, the branch is to the first procedure named; if the identifier contains a 2, the branch is to the second procedure named, and so forth. If the identifier contains a value which is less than 1 or greater than the number of procedures specified, no branch is taken and the program continues with the next sequential instruction.

The GO TO/DEPENDING ON statement is not used often because it has limited applicability and because use of the GO TO statement is generally avoided for structured coding. However, in addition to the three control structures of the structure theorem, there is another generally accepted structure, the *case structure*, within which the GO TO/DEPENDING ON statement is useful, as shown in Figure A.8. The group of modules is formed as a SECTION with the GO TO/DEPENDING ON as the first statement. Notice that this structure contains only one entry point and one exit point in accordance with structured programming precepts.

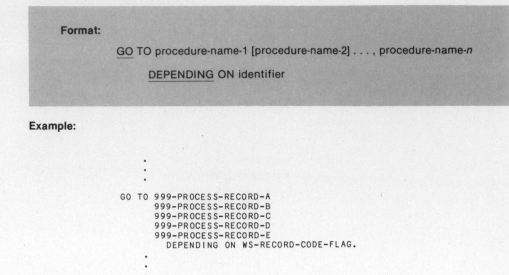

Format:

<u>GO</u> TO procedure-name-1 [procedure-name-2] . . . , procedure-name-*n*

<u>DEPENDING</u> ON identifier

Example:

```
                .
                .
                .
     GO TO 999-PROCESS-RECORD-A
           999-PROCESS-RECORD-B
           999-PROCESS-RECORD-C
           999-PROCESS-RECORD-D
           999-PROCESS-RECORD-E
              DEPENDING ON WS-RECORD-CODE-FLAG.
                .
                .
                .
```

Figure A.7. GO TO/DEPENDING ON statement example

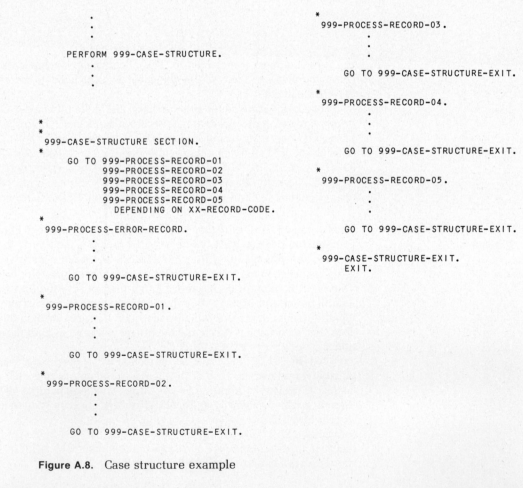

```
        .                              *
        .                               999-PROCESS-RECORD-03.
        .                                        .
     PERFORM 999-CASE-STRUCTURE.                 .
        .                                        .
        .                                      GO TO 999-CASE-STRUCTURE-EXIT.
        .
                                        *
                                         999-PROCESS-RECORD-04.
 *                                               .
 *                                               .
  999-CASE-STRUCTURE SECTION.                    .
 *                                             GO TO 999-CASE-STRUCTURE-EXIT.
     GO TO 999-PROCESS-RECORD-01
           999-PROCESS-RECORD-02          *
           999-PROCESS-RECORD-03           999-PROCESS-RECORD-05.
           999-PROCESS-RECORD-04                   .
           999-PROCESS-RECORD-05                   .
              DEPENDING ON XX-RECORD-CODE.         .
 *                                              GO TO 999-CASE-STRUCTURE-EXIT.
  999-PROCESS-ERROR-RECORD.
        .                                  *
        .                                   999-CASE-STRUCTURE-EXIT.
        .                                       EXIT.
     GO TO 999-CASE-STRUCTURE-EXIT.

 *
  999-PROCESS-RECORD-01.
        .
        .
        .
     GO TO 999-CASE-STRUCTURE-EXIT.

 *
  999-PROCESS-RECORD-02.
        .
        .
        .
     GO TO 999-CASE-STRUCTURE-EXIT.
```

Figure A.8. Case structure example

Format:

MOVE { CORRESPONDING | CORR } identifier-1 TO identifier-2

Example:

DATA DIVISION:

```
*
 01  RECORD-A.
     05  FIELD-AA                               PIC X(2).
     05  FIELD-BB                               PIC S9(5).
     05  FIELD-CC                               PIC X(12).
     05  FIELD-DD                               PIC S9(5).
     05  FIELD-EE                               PIC X(2).
     05  FIELD-FF                               PIC 9(6).
*
 01  RECORD-B.
     05  FIELD-AA                               PIC X(2).
     05  FIELD-CC                               PIC X(12).
     05  FIELD-DD                               PIC S9(5).
     05  FIELD-FF                               PIC 9(6).
     05  FIELD-GG                               PIC X(25).
```

PROCEDURE DIVISION:

```
     MOVE CORRESPONDING RECORD-A TO RECORD-B.
```

Figure A.9. MOVE CORRESPONDING example

The MOVE CORRESPONDING Statement

The CORRESPONDING phrase can be used to minimize coding when fields with identical names are to be moved from one record to another. An example is shown in Figure A.9.

However, use of MOVE CORRESPONDING is generally discouraged within the data processing community. One reason is that if a unique prefix or suffix method of data-item naming is used, the MOVE CORRESPONDING feature becomes unusable because the data-names are not identical within two different records. Probably more important, however, changes to record definition can cause program execution effects which may not be apparent when the record-description entries are changed. Thus, use of MOVE CORRESPONDING tends to create program maintenance problems.

The ADD CORRESPONDING and SUBTRACT CORRESPONDING Statements

The CORRESPONDING option is also available for use with the ADD and SUBTRACT. Of course, only identical data-names with numeric PICTURE clauses are involved in the arithmetic. Figure A.10 shows the statement formats and provides examples. The CORRESPONDING option has limited usefulness with the ADD and SUBTRACT statements. As with the CORRESPONDING option of the MOVE statement, its use is generally discouraged.

The ON SIZE ERROR Phrase

When an arithmetic calculation generates a value that exceeds the size of the receiving field, a size error occurs. When the ON SIZE ERROR phrase is specified with an arithmetic statement, the error is detected and the statements specified following the words ON SIZE ERROR are executed. When ON SIZE ERROR is not specified for an arithmetic statement, the excess high-order positions are simply truncated; no indication of the erroneous value is provided.

The ON SIZE ERROR phrase can be used with the ADD, SUBTRACT, MULTIPLY, and DIVIDE statements. An example is shown in Figure A.11. However, when a size error occurs and the ON SIZE ERROR phrase is specified, the contents of the receiving field are

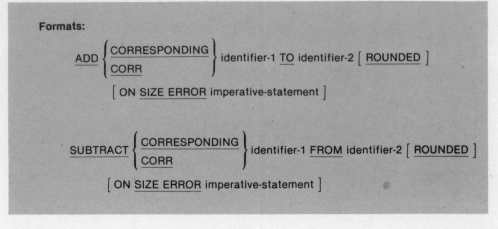

Formats:

$$\text{ADD} \left\{ \begin{array}{c} \underline{\text{CORRESPONDING}} \\ \underline{\text{CORR}} \end{array} \right\} \text{identifier-1} \ \underline{\text{TO}} \ \text{identifier-2} \ [\ \underline{\text{ROUNDED}} \ ]$$

$$[\ \text{ON} \ \underline{\text{SIZE ERROR}} \ \text{imperative-statement} \ ]$$

$$\text{SUBTRACT} \left\{ \begin{array}{c} \underline{\text{CORRESPONDING}} \\ \underline{\text{CORR}} \end{array} \right\} \text{identifier-1} \ \underline{\text{FROM}} \ \text{identifier-2} \ [\ \underline{\text{ROUNDED}} \ ]$$

$$[\ \text{ON} \ \underline{\text{SIZE ERROR}} \ \text{imperative-statement} \ ]$$

Examples:

```
ADD CORRESPONDING RECORD-A TO RECORD-B.



SUBTRACT CORRESPONDING RECORD-A FROM RECORD-B.
```

Figure A.10. ADD CORRESPONDING and SUBTRACT CORRESPONDING examples

unpredictable (that is, the receiving field usually remains unchanged rather than being filled with a truncated answer).

Use of ON SIZE ERROR is usually discouraged because it is inefficient and it is awkward under some program situations to handle exception conditions. A better technique—when a receiving field is not large enough to accommodate the results of a calculation—is to validate fields involved in calculations by a range check within a data validation program to ensure that a size error will not occur. Of course, with running total accumulations, SIZE ERROR or alternate programmer logic will be required to guard against erroneous answers.

The NOTE Statement

The NOTE statement was included in the 1968 ANS standards to allow for inclusion of comments in the PROCEDURE DIVISION. Figure A.12 shows an example. The statement was removed from the language prior to the 1974 standards. Comment lines (* in position 7) should currently be used in preference to the NOTE statement.

The PERFORM/TIMES Statement

There are a number of variations of the PERFORM statement formats. The Format-1 PERFORM statement specifying a single paragraph procedure and the Format-3 PERFORM/UNTIL statement are covered in Chapter 3. The Format-4 PERFORM/VARYING statement is covered in Chapter 12. The THRU option, that applies to all PERFORM formats, was discussed in Chapter 6. The Format-2 PERFORM/TIMES statement is probably the least used format but it does have some applications.

As shown in Figure A.13, a procedure may be performed multiple times as specified by either an integer or identifier option.

The STRING Statement

The STRING statement is a powerful character manipulation statement. It can be used to join together different fields, or parts of different fields. It is a complex statement, as it offers many options. Although it will not be covered fully here, Figure A.14 shows its format together with an example of its use in putting together a full name from three individual first, middle, and last name fields (with only one space between each name). The STRING statement is not available under the 1968 ANS standard.

Format:

arithmetic statement

[ON SIZE ERROR imperative-statement]

Example:

```
MULTIPLY FOUR-DIGIT-NBR BY THREE-DIGIT-NBR
     GIVING SIX-DIGIT-PRODUCT
          ON SIZE ERROR PERFORM 999-IDENTIFY-SIZE-ERROR.
```

Figure A.11. ON SIZE ERROR example

Format:

NOTE. comment-entry

Example:

```
NOTE.       THE NOTE STATEMENT WAS PROVIDED SO THAT EXPLANATORY
            PROGRAM DOCUMENTATION COMMENTS COULD BE PROVIDED
            IN THE PROCEDURE DIVISION.
```

1974 ANS Method:

```
*           THE NOTE STATEMENT HAS BEEN DROPPED FROM THE 1974
*           ANS COBOL STANDARDS.  COMMENT LINES
*           (* IN POSITION 7) SHOULD INSTEAD BE USED.
```

Figure A.12. NOTE statement example

Format:

PERFORM procedure-name-1 $\left\{ \begin{array}{c} \text{THROUGH} \\ \text{THRU} \end{array} \right\}$ procedure-name-2

$\left\{ \begin{array}{c} \text{identifier-1} \\ \text{integer-1} \end{array} \right\}$ TIMES

Examples:

Part A: Integer option.

```
PERFORM 999-PRINT-OUTPUT-FORM 2 TIMES.
```

Part B: Identifier option:

```
PERFORM 999-PRINT-OUTPUT-FORM WS-COPIES-REQUIRED TIMES.
```

Figure A.13. PERFORM/TIMES statement example

Format:

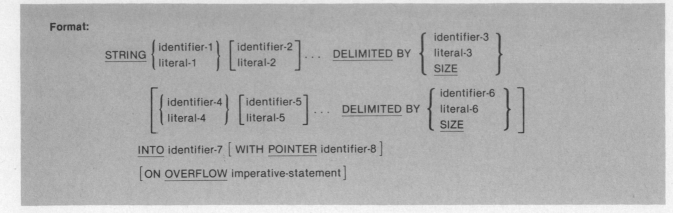

Example:

```
STRING LAST-NAME-FIELD DELIMITED BY ' '
      ' ' DELIMITED BY SIZE
      FIRST-NAME-FIELD DELIMITED BY ' '
      ' ' DELIMITED BY SIZE
      MIDDLE-NAME-FIELD DELIMITED BY ' '
INTO FULL-NAME-FIELD.
```

Figure A.14. STRING statement example

Format:

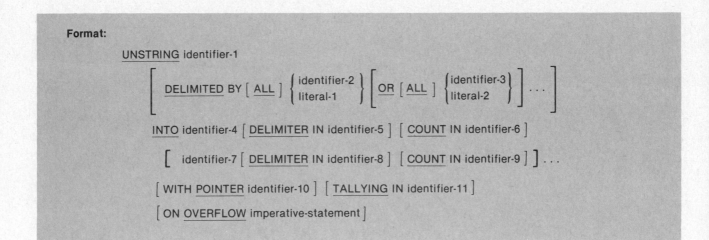

Example:

```
UNSTRING FULL-NAME-FIELD
    DELIMITED BY ' '
    INTO LAST-NAME-FIELD
        FIRST-NAME-FIELD
        MIDDLE-NAME-FIELD.
```

Figure A.15. UNSTRING statement example

The UNSTRING Statement   The UNSTRING statement is the converse of the STRING statement. It too is a complex statement, and can be used to separate one field into multiple fields. Figure A.15 shows its format with an example of a full name field separated into three individual fields for first, middle and last name. The UNSTRING statement is not available under the 1968 ANS standard.

APPENDIX B

THE COPY STATEMENT

The COPY statement is used to obtain COBOL code which has been stored in the COBOL source-statement library. When a file, record, report heading, table, procedure, or other code segment must be used by various programmers or programs, it is appropriate to place them in the source-statement library. Then, when COBOL programmers use the COPY statement to obtain the common code for their programs, four objectives are accomplished: (1) repetitious programmer coding is reduced; (2) standardization of data-names and procedures used in the installation is promoted; (3) coding errors are minimized; and (4) program revisions are simplified.

The COPY statement format together with examples is shown in Figure B.1. Notice that the statements acquired from the library are copied onto the next line following the COPY statement and usually identified by the compiler with a symbol (commonly a "C" as in the example).

As illustrated in Figure B.1, COPY statement specifications and processing vary with 1968 and 1974 ANS standards. Significant differences are as follows:

1968 ANS Standard

- The COPY statement is limited to use in certain locations of the source program. Common locations are as follows:

  FD file-name COPY library-name.
  SD file-name COPY library-name.
  01 record-name COPY library-name.
  Section-name SECTION COPY library-name.
  Paragraph-name COPY library-name.

- When the COPY statement appears as an 01-level record description, the 01-level record-name coded by the programmer replaces the 01-level record-name from the library.

1974 ANS Standard

- The COPY statement may be used practically anywhere in the source program.
- The record-name preceding the word COPY is not substituted in the copied coding.

Notice that the REPLACING phrase allows variations to be made in the copied code. However, many data processing installation standards prohibit use of the REPLACING phrase because its use is in opposition with the usually-desired standardization benefits of the COPY statement.

Methods to store, or *catalog*, source statements into the library vary with the operating system of the computer being used.

The programmer should be aware that many commercial data processing installations do not use the COBOL source statement library but instead a proprietary library program product, such as Panvalet or Librarian. The proprietary products usually offer disk storage, change control, and retention benefits. Such products require slightly different syntax.

Format:

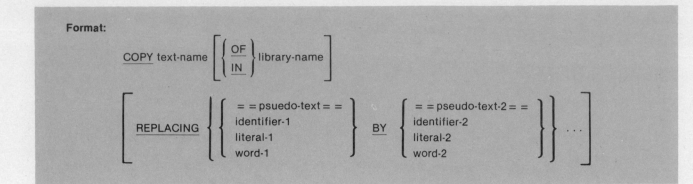

COPY text-name [{ OF / IN } library-name]

[REPLACING { ==psuedo-text== / identifier-1 / literal-1 / word-1 } BY { ==pseudo-text-2== / identifier-2 / literal-2 / word-2 }] ...

Examples:

1968 ANS Standard COPY Statement

Source statements in library entry named NARECORD:

```
01   NA-NAME-AND-ADDRESS-RECORD.
     05   NA-RECORD-CODE            PIC X(2).
     05   NA-NAME                   PIC X(20).
     05   NA-ADDRESS                PIC X(24).
     05   NA-CITY                   PIC X(13).
     05   NA-STATE                  PIC X(2).
     05   NA-ZIP-CODE               PIC X(9).
     05   NA-TELEPHONE-NUMBER       PIC X(10).
```

Programmer writes this statement on the source listing:

```
01   NA-CUSTOMER-RECORD COPY NARECORD.
```

The following code is included in the source program (note that the 01-level record-name has been replaced in the program with the name assigned by the programmer):

```
  01   NA-CUSTOMER-RECORD COPY NARECORD.
C 01   NA-CUSTOMER-RECORD.
C      05   NA-RECORD-CODE            PIC X(2).
C      05   NA-NAME                   PIC X(20).
C      05   NA-ADDRESS                PIC X(24).
C      05   NA-CITY                   PIC X(13).
C      05   NA-STATE                  PIC X(2).
C      05   NA-ZIP-CODE               PIC X(9).
C      05   NA-TELEPHONE-NUMBER       PIC X(10).
```

1974 Standard COPY Statement

Source statement in library entry named NARECORD (notice that the 01-level record-name has been specified in the library as a comment-entry):

```
*01  NA-NAME-AND-ADDRESS-RECORD.
     05   NA-RECORD-CODE            PIC X(2).
     05   NA-NAME                   PIC X(20).
     05   NA-ADDRESS                PIC X(24).
     05   NA-CITY                   PIC X(13).
     05   NA-STATE                  PIC X(2).
     05   NA-ZIP-CODE               PIC X(9).
     05   NA-TELEPHONE-NUMBER       PIC X(10).
```

Programmer writes this statement and the source listing (notice that the COPY statement is written as a separate sentence):

```
01   NA-CUSTOMER-RECORD.   COPY NARECORD.
```

The following code is included in the source program:

```
  01   NA-CUSTOMER-RECORD.   COPY NARECORD.
C *01  NA-NAME-AND-ADDRESS-RECORD.
C      05   NA-RECORD-CODE            PIC X(2).
C      05   NA-NAME                   PIC X(20).
C      05   NA-ADDRESS                PIC X(24).
C      05   NA-CITY                   PIC X(13).
C      05   NA-STATE                  PIC X(2).
C      05   NA-ZIP-CODE               PIC X(9).
C      05   NA-TELEPHONE-NUMBER       PIC X(10).
```

Figure B.1.

APPENDIX C

PROGRAM INTERRUPTIONS FOR IBM OS AND DOS SYSTEMS

With IBM medium and large-scale computer systems (and PCM's), the computer system diagnoses each machine language instruction and the results of certain arithmetic operations to ensure that incorrect processing does not occur. When an obviously incorrect instruction is provided for execution (such as one containing an invalid operation code or an address which is greater than the available storage for the computer) a program check occurs. A *program interruption* (formerly termed a *program check*) causes the system to terminate program processing and cancel the program. Programmers usually refer to this as *abnormal termination* or an "*abend*".

There are 15 types of program checks as shown in Figure C.1. Most of them are encountered only rarely with COBOL programs. A few of the ones which occur more frequently with COBOL programs are discussed below.

Operation exception (OC1)
COBOL programs which contain certain logic errors will trigger operation exceptions. Following are some typical causes.

- Attempting to READ or WRITE a file before it has been opened or after it has been closed.
- Failure to CLOSE files before the STOP RUN statement is executed.
- When the identifier field of the AFTER ADVANCING phrase of the WRITE statement contains a value outside the range of permissable values (should be 0 to 99).
- Missing JCL statement for a file.

Protection exception (OC4)
Although this error does not normally occur with COBOL programs due to boundary protection errors, it may occur due to the following programming errors:

- Subscript or index not initialized prior to use.
- Incorrect ASSIGN clause system-name.
- Assign clause system-name does not match the JCL statement system-name.
- Missing JCL statement for a file.
- Attempting to READ an unopened input file.

Addressing and specification exceptions (OC5 and OC6)
One of these exceptions may occur when one of the following programming errors is made:

- Incorrect value in a subscript or index.
- Improper exit from a performed procedure.
- Attempting to refer to a field of an input record defined within the FILE section after the AT END phrase of the READ statement has been executed.
- Attempting to refer to a field of an input record defined within the FILE section before the first READ statement has been executed.
- Attempting to refer to a field of an output record defined within the FILE section before the OPEN statement has been executed.

Data exception (OC7)
This is probably the most commonly encountered program check and one that generally haunts beginning programmers. Its cause is simple: attempting to operate numerically on non-numeric data with decimal arithmetic instructions. Fields which are being processed by decimal arithmetic instructions must contain a valid digit (0 through 9) in each

Exception	Completion code (OS)	Cause
Operation	OC1	The computer has attempted to execute an invalid operation code.
Privileged-operation	OC2	An application program has requested the computer to execute an operation code that only the operating system supervisor program is permitted to execute.
Execute	OC3	Will not normally occur with a COBOL program.
Protection	OC4	The program has attempted to access or move data to an area of storage which does not belong to the program.
Addressing	OC5	The program has attempted to reference an address beyond the limit of the computer's physical storage.
Specification	OC6	A machine language instruction address is invalid
Data	OC7	The program has requested that a decimal arithmetic operation be performed on data which is not numeric.
Fixed-point-overflow	OC8	A calculated binary value is too large to be contained within a register.
Fixed-point-divide	OC9	The program has attempted to divide a binary field by zero or the quotient exceeds the register size.
Decimal-overflow	OCA	A calculated packed decimal value is too large to be contained within the result field.
Decimal-divide	OCB	The program has attempted to divide a packed decimal field by zero or the quotient exceeds the register size.
Exponent-overflow	OCC	Will not normally occur with a COBOL program.
Exponent-underflow	OCD	Will not normally occur with a COBOL program.
Significance	OCE	Will not normally occur with a COBOL program.
Floating-point	OCF	Will not normally occur with a COBOL program.

Figure C.1 Program checks

digit position of the field and a valid sign (plus, minus, unsigned assumed positive, or unsigned) in the sign position.

There are two general situations in which a data exception will occur.

The first situation is where a WORKING-STORAGE field is not initialized before it is used in the program. When the program begins, fields that are not properly initialized by VALUE clauses or PROCEDURE DIVISION statements contain either unpredictable values or, depending upon the operating system, binary zeros. (Binary zeros do not contain a valid decimal arithmetic sign.) So, if the programmer neglects to initialize or improperly initializes a decimal arithmetic field, the field will probably contain data which is not valid for the decimal arithmetic instructions. Thus, a data exception will occur.

A second situation is where input data is read into a program which does not contain decimal numeric data in a field specified with the picture symbol 9. For example, if a quantity field is input with blank spaces, a data exception will occur if the program attempts to ADD or otherwise operate on those blank spaces numerically with decimal arithmetic instructions.

The first situation described above is generally detected early in program testing. However, the second situation—because it is usually caused by input errors rather than programming errors—can happen long after a program has been tested and put into production unless proper validation of each input field is provided at some point in the program processing. This is the reason that data validation programs, as discussed in Chapters C and 9, are so important.

It should be noted that errors in field specifications can also cause the second type of data exception. That is, if a five-digit quantity field is defined as S9(6), a data exception may well result.

The COBOL programmer should recognize that, since COBOL uses arithmetic instructions for certain other verbs, a data exception can occur with the following statements:

- Arithmetic statements (ADD, SUBTRACT, MULTIPLY, DIVIDE, and COMPUTE) which operate on DISPLAY or COMP-3 fields.
- IF statement relation and condition-name conditions where both the subject and object fields are numeric (and both are not of COMP usage).
- IF statement sign conditions where the subject field is of DISPLAY or COMP-3 usage.
- MOVE statements from a DISPLAY or COMP-3 field to a COMP-3 or COMP field.
- MOVE statements to a numeric edited field.

Following is a checklist of common data exception causes:

- A numeric field was not initialized before it was used.
- A numeric field was incorrectly initialized.
  a. Moving ZEROS to a group field will produce invalid data for COMP and COMP-3 fields within the group. (ZEROS must be moved to the elementary COMP and COMP-3 fields.)
  b. Moving SPACES to either a group or elementary numeric field will produce invalid data for numeric fields.
  c. Moving 0 (a literal of a single zero) to a group field will produce invalid data for COMP and COMP-3 fields within the group. (This causes one zero to be moved to the first position of the group field and the remainder of the positions are padded with blank spaces.)
  d. Moving LOW-VALUES or HIGH-VALUES to a DISPLAY or COMP-3 field will produce invalid numeric data.
- A subscript or index was not initialized.
- A subscript or index contains an incorrect value.
  a. zero
  b. a negative number
  c. a number greater than the number of table entry occurrences.
- Invalid data was read into a numeric field.
  a. blank spaces
  b. certain non-numeric characters
- Incorrect record-descriptions and/or data-item descriptions.
  a. wrong length specifications
  b. wrong usage specifications

Overflow exceptions (OC8 and OCA)

This exception may occur if the result of a calculation exceeds the size of a register or the result field (and the statement does not contain an ON SIZE ERROR phrase). However, COBOL will normally not cause this interruption to be triggered with DISPLAY or COMP-3 fields. Instead, a result too long to be contained in the answer field will be truncated. The overflow error will not be identified (unless the ON SIZE ERROR phrase is specified).

Divide exception (OC9 and OCB)

According to the rules of mathematics, it is impossible to divide by zero. Thus, if a divisor field contains zero and a DIVIDE operation (without an ON SIZE ERROR phrase) is executed, a divide exception occurs. Before each DIVIDE statement, it is a good practice to validate the divisor field to ensure that it does not contain a zero. If the divisor field does contain a zero, either the DIVIDE statement should not be executed or, depending upon desired handling, the divisor should be changed to a value of 1. Such processing will eliminate divide exceptions.

Other exceptions

When errors in subscript or index handling cause program data to overlay program instructions in storage, practically any program interruption can occur. In such cases the program interruption type is probably not meaningful.

APPENDIX D

COMPLETE COBOL LANGUAGE FORMATS

This appendix contains the composite language formats skeleton of the American National Standard COBOL. It is intended to completely display all COBOL language formats.

General Format for IDENTIFICATION DIVISION

```
IDENTIFICATION DIVISION.

PROGRAM-ID.  program-name.

[AUTHOR.  [comment-entry]  ... ]

[INSTALLATION.  [comment-entry]  ...]

[DATE-WRITTEN.  [comment-entry]  ...]

[DATE-COMPILED.  [comment-entry]  ...]

[SECURITY.  [comment-entry]  ...]
```

General Format for ENVIRONMENT DIVISION

```
ENVIRONMENT DIVISION.

CONFIGURATION SECTION.

SOURCE-COMPUTER.   computer-name [WITH DEBUGGING MODE] .

OBJECT-COMPUTER.   computer-name

   [, MEMORY SIZE integer  { WORDS      }  ]
                           { CHARACTERS }
                           { MODULES    }

   [, PROGRAM COLLATING SEQUENCE IS alphabet-name]

   [, SEGMENT-LIMIT IS segment-number] .

[ SPECIAL-NAMES.  [, implementor-name

   { IS mnemonic-name  [, ON STATUS IS condition-name-1  [, OFF STATUS IS condition-name-2]] }
   { IS mnemonic-name  [, OFF STATUS IS condition-name-2  [, ON STATUS IS condition-name-1]] }  ...
   { ON STATUS IS condition-name-1  [, OFF STATUS IS condition-name-2] }
   { OFF STATUS IS condition-name-2  [, ON STATUS IS condition-name-1] }

   [                  { STANDARD-1                                                  }      ]
   [                  { NATIVE                                                      }      ]
   [ , alphabet-name IS { implementor-name                                          }  ... ]
   [                  { literal-1 [ {THROUGH} literal-2                          ]  }      ]
   [                  {           {THRU   }                                      }  }      ]
   [                  {           [ ALSO literal-3 [, ALSO literal-4]...         ]  }      ]
   [                  {                                                             }      ]
   [                  {  [ literal-5 [ {THROUGH} literal-6                     ] ]  }      ]
   [                  {             [ {THRU   }                                ]  }... }   ]
   [                  {             [ ALSO literal-7 [, ALSO literal-8]...      ] ]  }      ]

   [, CURRENCY SIGN IS literal-9]

   [, DECIMAL-POINT IS COMMA ] . ]
```

```
[INPUT-OUTPUT SECTION.

 FILE-CONTROL.

    {file-control-entry} ...

[I-O-CONTROL.

   [; RERUN [ON {file-name-1        }]
                {implementor-name   }

                  { {[END OF] {REEL}}              }
         EVERY    { {         {UNIT}}  OF file-name-2 }   ...
                  { integer-1 RECORDS              }
                  { integer-2 CLOCK-UNITS          }
                  { condition-name                 }

   [; SAME [RECORD    ] AREA FOR file-name-3 {, file-name-4} ...  ] ...
           [SORT      ]
           [SORT-MERGE]

   [; MULTIPLE FILE TAPE CONTAINS file-name-5 [POSITION integer-3]

        [, file-name-6 [POSITION integer-4]] ...  ] ...   .]]
```

General Format for FILE-CONTROL Entry

```
FORMAT 1:

SELECT [OPTIONAL] file-name

   ASSIGN TO implementor-name-1 [, implementor-name-2 ] ...

   [; RESERVE integer-1 [AREA ]]
                        [AREAS]

   [; ORGANIZATION IS SEQUENTIAL]

   [; ACCESS MODE IS SEQUENTIAL]

   [; FILE STATUS IS data-name-1 ] .


FORMAT 2:

SELECT file-name

   ASSIGN TO implementor-name-1 [, implementor-name-2 ] ...

   [; RESERVE integer-1 [AREA ]]
                        [AREAS]

   ; ORGANIZATION IS RELATIVE

   [                    { SEQUENTIAL [, RELATIVE KEY IS data-name-1]}]
   [; ACCESS MODE IS    {                                          }]
   [                    {{RANDOM }                                 }]
   [                    {{DYNAMIC} , RELATIVE KEY IS data-name-1   }]

   [; FILE STATUS IS data-name-2 ] .


FORMAT 3:

SELECT file-name

   ASSIGN TO implementor-name-1 [, implementor-name-2 ] ...

   [; RESERVE integer-1 [AREA ]]
                        [AREAS]

   ; ORGANIZATION IS INDEXED

   [; ACCESS MODE IS {SEQUENTIAL}]
                     {RANDOM    }
                     {DYNAMIC   }
```

; <u>RECORD</u> KEY IS data-name-1

[; <u>ALTERNATE</u> <u>RECORD</u> KEY IS data-name-2 [WITH <u>DUPLICATES</u>]] ...

[; FILE <u>STATUS</u> IS data-name-3] .

<u>FORMAT 4</u>:

<u>SELECT</u> file-name <u>ASSIGN</u> TO implementor-name-1 [, implementor-name-2] ...

General Format for DATA DIVISION

<u>DATA DIVISION</u>.

[<u>FILE</u> SECTION.

[<u>FD</u> file-name

    [; <u>BLOCK</u> CONTAINS [integer-1 <u>TO</u>] integer-2 $\begin{Bmatrix} \underline{RECORDS} \\ \underline{CHARACTERS} \end{Bmatrix}$]

    [; <u>RECORD</u> CONTAINS [integer-3 <u>TO</u>] integer-4 CHARACTERS]

    ; <u>LABEL</u> $\begin{Bmatrix} \underline{RECORD} \text{ IS} \\ \underline{RECORDS} \text{ ARE} \end{Bmatrix}$ $\begin{Bmatrix} \underline{STANDARD} \\ \underline{OMITTED} \end{Bmatrix}$

    [; <u>VALUE</u> <u>OF</u> implementor-name-1 IS $\begin{Bmatrix} \text{data-name-1} \\ \text{literal-1} \end{Bmatrix}$

        [, implementor-name-2 IS $\begin{Bmatrix} \text{data-name-2} \\ \text{literal-2} \end{Bmatrix}$] ...]

    [; <u>DATA</u> $\begin{Bmatrix} \underline{RECORD} \text{ IS} \\ \underline{RECORDS} \text{ ARE} \end{Bmatrix}$ data-name-3 [, data-name-4] ...]

    [; <u>LINAGE</u> IS $\begin{Bmatrix} \text{data-name-5} \\ \text{integer-5} \end{Bmatrix}$ LINES [, WITH <u>FOOTING</u> AT $\begin{Bmatrix} \text{data-name-6} \\ \text{integer-6} \end{Bmatrix}$]

        [, LINES AT <u>TOP</u> $\begin{Bmatrix} \text{data-name-7} \\ \text{integer-7} \end{Bmatrix}$] [, LINES AT <u>BOTTOM</u> $\begin{Bmatrix} \text{data-name-8} \\ \text{integer-8} \end{Bmatrix}$]]

    [; <u>CODE-SET</u> IS alphabet-name]

    [; $\begin{Bmatrix} \underline{REPORT} \text{ IS} \\ \underline{REPORTS} \text{ ARE} \end{Bmatrix}$ report-name-1 [, report-name-2] ...] .

[record-description-entry] ...] ...

[<u>SD</u> file-name

    [; <u>RECORD</u> CONTAINS [integer-1 <u>TO</u>] integer-2 CHARACTERS]

    [; <u>DATA</u> $\begin{Bmatrix} \underline{RECORD} \text{ IS} \\ \underline{RECORDS} \text{ ARE} \end{Bmatrix}$ data-name-1 [, data-name-2] ...] .

{record-description-entry} ...] ...]

[<u>WORKING-STORAGE</u> SECTION.

$\begin{bmatrix} \text{77-level-description-entry} \\ \text{record-description-entry} \end{bmatrix}$ ...]

[<u>LINKAGE</u> SECTION.

$\begin{bmatrix} \text{77-level-description-entry} \\ \text{record-description-entry} \end{bmatrix}$ ...]

[<u>COMMUNICATION</u> <u>SECTION</u>.

[communication-description-entry

[record-description-entry] ...] ...]

```
[REPORT SECTION.

[RD  report-name

    [; CODE literal-1]

    [; {CONTROL IS  } {data-name-1 [, data-name-2] ...            }]
       {CONTROLS ARE} {FINAL  [, data-name-1 [, data-name-2] ...]}

    [; PAGE [LIMIT IS  ] integer-1 [LINE ]  [, HEADING integer-2]
            [LIMITS ARE]           [LINES]

        [, FIRST DETAIL integer-3]  [, LAST DETAIL integer-4]

        [, FOOTING integer-5 ] ] .

  {report-group-description-entry } ... ] ... ]
```

General Format for Data Description Entry

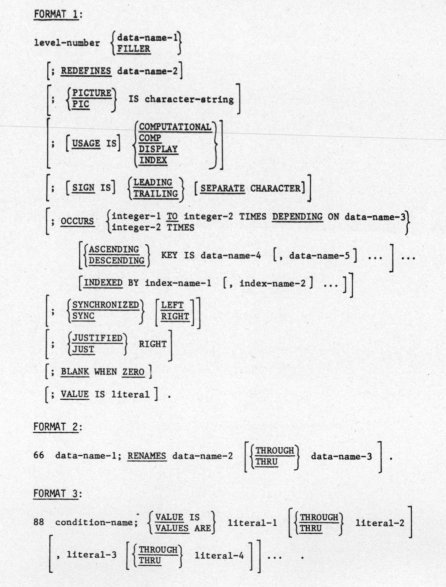

```
FORMAT 1:

level-number {data-name-1}
             {FILLER     }

    [; REDEFINES data-name-2]

    [; {PICTURE} IS character-string]
       {PIC    }

    [                        {COMPUTATIONAL} ]
    [; [USAGE IS]            {COMP         } ]
    [                        {DISPLAY      } ]
    [                        {INDEX        } ]

    [; [SIGN IS] {LEADING } [SEPARATE CHARACTER]]
                 {TRAILING}

    [; OCCURS {integer-1 TO integer-2 TIMES DEPENDING ON data-name-3}
              {integer-2 TIMES                                      }

        [{ASCENDING } KEY IS data-name-4 [, data-name-5] ... ] ...
         {DESCENDING}

        [INDEXED BY index-name-1 [, index-name-2] ... ]]

    [; {SYNCHRONIZED} [LEFT ]]
       {SYNC        } [RIGHT]

    [; {JUSTIFIED} RIGHT]
       {JUST     }

    [; BLANK WHEN ZERO]

    [; VALUE IS literal] .


FORMAT 2:

66  data-name-1; RENAMES data-name-2 [{THROUGH} data-name-3 ] .
                                      {THRU   }


FORMAT 3:

88  condition-name; {VALUE IS  } literal-1 [{THROUGH} literal-2]
                    {VALUES ARE}            {THRU   }

    [, literal-3 [{THROUGH} literal-4]] ...  .
                 {THRU   }
```

General Format for Communication Description Entry

FORMAT 1:

CD cd-name;

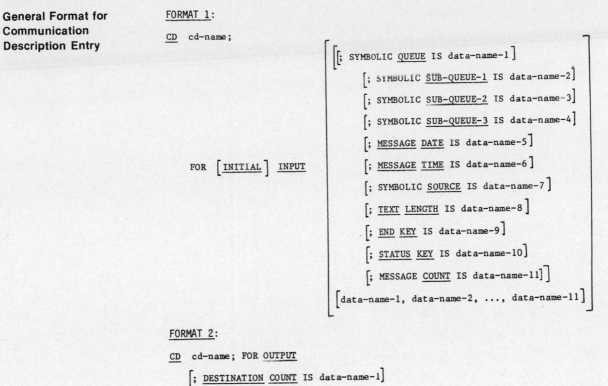

$$FOR \; [\underline{INITIAL}] \; \underline{INPUT} \left\{ \begin{array}{l} \left[\begin{array}{l} [; \underline{SYMBOLIC} \; \underline{QUEUE} \; IS \; data\text{-}name\text{-}1] \\ \quad [; \underline{SYMBOLIC} \; \underline{SUB\text{-}QUEUE\text{-}1} \; IS \; data\text{-}name\text{-}2] \\ \quad [; \underline{SYMBOLIC} \; \underline{SUB\text{-}QUEUE\text{-}2} \; IS \; data\text{-}name\text{-}3] \\ \quad [; \underline{SYMBOLIC} \; \underline{SUB\text{-}QUEUE\text{-}3} \; IS \; data\text{-}name\text{-}4] \\ \quad [; \underline{MESSAGE} \; \underline{DATE} \; IS \; data\text{-}name\text{-}5] \\ \quad [; \underline{MESSAGE} \; \underline{TIME} \; IS \; data\text{-}name\text{-}6] \\ \quad [; \underline{SYMBOLIC} \; \underline{SOURCE} \; IS \; data\text{-}name\text{-}7] \\ \quad [; \underline{TEXT} \; \underline{LENGTH} \; IS \; data\text{-}name\text{-}8] \\ \quad [; \underline{END} \; \underline{KEY} \; IS \; data\text{-}name\text{-}9] \\ \quad [; \underline{STATUS} \; \underline{KEY} \; IS \; data\text{-}name\text{-}10] \\ \quad [; \underline{MESSAGE} \; \underline{COUNT} \; IS \; data\text{-}name\text{-}11] \end{array} \right] \\ [data\text{-}name\text{-}1, \; data\text{-}name\text{-}2, \; ..., \; data\text{-}name\text{-}11] \end{array} \right\}$$

FORMAT 2:

CD cd-name; FOR <u>OUTPUT</u>

[; <u>DESTINATION</u> <u>COUNT</u> IS data-name-1]

[; <u>TEXT</u> <u>LENGTH</u> IS data-name-2]

[; <u>STATUS</u> <u>KEY</u> IS data-name-3]

[; <u>DESTINATION</u> <u>TABLE</u> <u>OCCURS</u> integer-2 TIMES

       [; <u>INDEXED</u> BY index-name-1 [, index-name-2]...]]

[; <u>ERROR</u> <u>KEY</u> IS data-name-4]

[; <u>SYMBOLIC</u> <u>DESTINATION</u> IS data-name-5] .

General Format for Report Group Description Entry

FORMAT 1:

01 [data-name-1]

$$\left[; \; \underline{LINE} \; NUMBER \; IS \; \left\{ \begin{array}{l} integer\text{-}1 \; [ON \; \underline{NEXT} \; \underline{PAGE}] \\ \underline{PLUS} \; integer\text{-}2 \end{array} \right\} \right]$$

$$\left[; \; \underline{NEXT} \; \underline{GROUP} \; IS \; \left\{ \begin{array}{l} integer\text{-}3 \\ \underline{PLUS} \; integer\text{-}4 \\ \underline{NEXT} \; \underline{PAGE} \end{array} \right\} \right]$$

$$; \; \underline{TYPE} \; IS \; \left\{ \begin{array}{l} \left\{ \begin{array}{l} \underline{REPORT} \; \underline{HEADING} \\ \underline{RH} \end{array} \right\} \\ \left\{ \begin{array}{l} \underline{PAGE} \; \underline{HEADING} \\ \underline{PH} \end{array} \right\} \\ \left\{ \begin{array}{l} \underline{CONTROL} \; \underline{HEADING} \\ \underline{CH} \end{array} \right\} \left\{ \begin{array}{l} data\text{-}name\text{-}2 \\ \underline{FINAL} \end{array} \right\} \\ \left\{ \begin{array}{l} \underline{DETAIL} \\ \underline{DE} \end{array} \right\} \\ \left\{ \begin{array}{l} \underline{CONTROL} \; \underline{FOOTING} \\ \underline{CF} \end{array} \right\} \left\{ \begin{array}{l} data\text{-}name\text{-}3 \\ \underline{FINAL} \end{array} \right\} \\ \left\{ \begin{array}{l} \underline{PAGE} \; \underline{FOOTING} \\ \underline{PF} \end{array} \right\} \\ \left\{ \begin{array}{l} \underline{REPORT} \; \underline{FOOTING} \\ \underline{RF} \end{array} \right\} \end{array} \right\}$$

[; [<u>USAGE</u> IS] <u>DISPLAY</u>] .

<u>FORMAT 2</u>:

level-number [data-name-1]

    $\left[\; ;\; \underline{\text{LINE}}\; \text{NUMBER IS}\; \left\{\begin{array}{l}\text{integer-1}\; [\text{ON}\; \underline{\text{NEXT}}\; \underline{\text{PAGE}}]\\ \underline{\text{PLUS}}\; \text{integer-2}\end{array}\right\}\right]$

    $\left[\; ;\; [\underline{\text{USAGE}}\; \text{IS}]\; \underline{\text{DISPLAY}}\right]$.

<u>FORMAT 3</u>:

level-number [data-name-1]

    $\left[\; ;\; \underline{\text{BLANK}}\; \text{WHEN}\; \underline{\text{ZERO}}\right]$

    $\left[\; ;\; \underline{\text{GROUP}}\; \text{INDICATE}\right]$

    $\left[\; ;\; \left\{\begin{array}{l}\underline{\text{JUSTIFIED}}\\ \underline{\text{JUST}}\end{array}\right\}\; \text{RIGHT}\right]$

    $\left[\; ;\; \underline{\text{LINE}}\; \text{NUMBER IS}\; \left\{\begin{array}{l}\text{integer-1}\; [\text{ON}\; \underline{\text{NEXT}}\; \underline{\text{PAGE}}]\\ \underline{\text{PLUS}}\; \text{integer-2}\end{array}\right\}\right]$

    $\left[\; ;\; \underline{\text{COLUMN}}\; \text{NUMBER IS integer-3}\right]$

    $;\; \left\{\begin{array}{l}\underline{\text{PICTURE}}\\ \underline{\text{PIC}}\end{array}\right\}\; \text{IS character-string}$

    $\left\{\begin{array}{l};\; \underline{\text{SOURCE}}\; \text{IS identifier-1}\\ ;\; \underline{\text{VALUE}}\; \text{IS literal}\\ \{;\; \underline{\text{SUM}}\; \text{identifier-2}\; [,\; \text{identifier-3}]\; ...\\ \quad\quad [\underline{\text{UPON}}\; \text{data-name-2}\; [,\; \text{data-name-3}]\; ...]\}\; ...\\ \quad\quad \left[\underline{\text{RESET}}\; \text{ON}\; \left\{\begin{array}{l}\text{data-name-4}\\ \underline{\text{FINAL}}\end{array}\right\}\right]\end{array}\right\}$

    $\left[\; ;\; [\underline{\text{USAGE}}\; \text{IS}]\; \underline{\text{DISPLAY}}\right]$.

**General Format for
PROCEDURE DIVISION**

<u>FORMAT 1</u>:

$\underline{\text{PROCEDURE}}\; \underline{\text{DIVISION}}\; \left[\underline{\text{USING}}\; \text{data-name-1}\; [,\; \text{data-name-2}]\; ...\right]$.

$\left[\underline{\text{DECLARATIVES}}\right.$.

$\{\text{section-name}\; \underline{\text{SECTION}}\; [\text{segment-number}]$. declarative-sentence

$[\text{paragraph-name}.\; [\text{sentence}]\; ...\;]\; ...\}\; ...$

$\underline{\text{END}}\; \underline{\text{DECLARATIVES}}.\left.\right]$

$\{\text{section-name}\; \underline{\text{SECTION}}\; [\text{segment-number}]$.

$[\text{paragraph-name}.\; [\text{sentence}]\; ...\;]\; ...\}\; ...$

<u>FORMAT 2</u>:

$\underline{\text{PROCEDURE}}\; \underline{\text{DIVISION}}\; \left[\underline{\text{USING}}\; \text{data-name-1}\; [,\; \text{data-name-2}]\; ...\right]$.

$\{\text{paragraph-name}.\; [\text{sentence}]\; ...\}\; ...$

General Format for Verbs

ACCEPT identifier [FROM mnemonic-name]

ACCEPT identifier FROM $\left\{ \begin{array}{l} \underline{DATE} \\ \underline{DAY} \\ \underline{TIME} \end{array} \right\}$

ACCEPT cd-name MESSAGE COUNT

ADD $\left\{ \begin{array}{l} identifier-1 \\ literal-1 \end{array} \right\}$ [, identifier-2] ... TO identifier-m [ROUNDED]

    [, identifier-n [ROUNDED]] ... [; ON SIZE ERROR imperative-statement]

ADD $\left\{ \begin{array}{l} identifier-1 \\ literal-1 \end{array} \right\}$, $\left\{ \begin{array}{l} identifier-2 \\ literal-2 \end{array} \right\}$ [, identifier-3] ...

    GIVING identifier-m [ROUNDED] [, identifier-n [ROUNDED]] ...

    [; ON SIZE ERROR imperative-statement]

ADD $\left\{ \begin{array}{l} \underline{CORRESPONDING} \\ \underline{CORR} \end{array} \right\}$ identifier-1 TO identifier-2 [ROUNDED]

    [; ON SIZE ERROR imperative-statement]

ALTER procedure-name-1 TO [PROCEED TO] procedure-name-2

    [, procedure-name-3 TO [PROCEED TO] procedure-name-4] ...

CALL $\left\{ \begin{array}{l} identifier-1 \\ literal-1 \end{array} \right\}$ [USING data-name-1 [, data-name-2] ...]

    [; ON OVERFLOW imperative-statement]

CANCEL $\left\{ \begin{array}{l} identifier-1 \\ literal-1 \end{array} \right\}$ [, identifier-2] ...

CLOSE file-name-1 $\left[\begin{array}{l} \left\{ \begin{array}{l} \underline{REEL} \\ \underline{UNIT} \end{array} \right\} \left[\begin{array}{l} WITH \ NO \ REWIND \\ FOR \ REMOVAL \end{array} \right] \\ WITH \left\{ \begin{array}{l} NO \ REWIND \\ \underline{LOCK} \end{array} \right\} \end{array} \right]$

$\left[, file-name-2 \left[\begin{array}{l} \left\{ \begin{array}{l} \underline{REEL} \\ \underline{UNIT} \end{array} \right\} \left[\begin{array}{l} WITH \ \underline{NO} \ \underline{REWIND} \\ FOR \ \underline{REMOVAL} \end{array} \right] \\ WITH \left\{ \begin{array}{l} NO \ REWIND \\ \underline{LOCK} \end{array} \right\} \end{array} \right] \right]$ ...

CLOSE file-name-1 [WITH LOCK] [, file-name-2 [WITH LOCK]] ...

COMPUTE identifier-1 [ROUNDED] [, identifier-2 [ROUNDED]] ...

    = arithmetic-expression [; ON SIZE ERROR imperative-statement]

DELETE file-name RECORD [; INVALID KEY imperative-statement]

DISABLE $\left\{ \begin{array}{l} \underline{INPUT} \ [\underline{TERMINAL}] \\ \underline{OUTPUT} \end{array} \right\}$ cd-name WITH KEY $\left\{ \begin{array}{l} identifier-1 \\ literal-1 \end{array} \right\}$

DISPLAY $\left\{ \begin{array}{l} identifier-1 \\ literal-1 \end{array} \right\}$ [, identifier-2] ... [UPON mnemonic-name]

DIVIDE $\left\{ \begin{array}{l} identifier-1 \\ literal-1 \end{array} \right\}$ INTO identifier-2 [ROUNDED]

    [, identifier-3 [ROUNDED]] ... [; ON SIZE ERROR imperative-statement]

DIVIDE $\left\{ \begin{array}{l} identifier-1 \\ literal-1 \end{array} \right\}$ INTO $\left\{ \begin{array}{l} identifier-2 \\ literal-2 \end{array} \right\}$ GIVING identifier-3 [ROUNDED]

    [, identifier-4 [ROUNDED]] ... [; ON SIZE ERROR imperative-statement]

DIVIDE $\left\{ \begin{array}{l} identifier-1 \\ literal-1 \end{array} \right\}$ BY $\left\{ \begin{array}{l} identifier-2 \\ literal-2 \end{array} \right\}$ GIVING identifier-3 [ROUNDED]

    [, identifier-4 [ROUNDED]] ... [; ON SIZE ERROR imperative-statement]

$$\text{DIVIDE} \begin{Bmatrix} \text{identifier-1} \\ \text{literal-1} \end{Bmatrix} \text{INTO} \begin{Bmatrix} \text{identifier-2} \\ \text{literal-2} \end{Bmatrix} \text{GIVING identifier-3} \; [\text{ROUNDED}]$$

REMAINDER identifier-4 [; ON SIZE ERROR imperative-statement]

$$\text{DIVIDE} \begin{Bmatrix} \text{identifier-1} \\ \text{literal-1} \end{Bmatrix} \text{BY} \begin{Bmatrix} \text{identifier-2} \\ \text{literal-2} \end{Bmatrix} \text{GIVING identifier-3} \; [\text{ROUNDED}]$$

REMAINDER identifier-4 [; ON SIZE ERROR imperative-statement]

$$\text{ENABLE} \begin{Bmatrix} \text{INPUT} \\ \text{OUTPUT} \end{Bmatrix} [\text{TERMINAL}] \text{ cd-name WITH KEY} \begin{Bmatrix} \text{identifier-1} \\ \text{literal-1} \end{Bmatrix}$$

ENTER language-name [routine-name] .

EXIT [PROGRAM] .

$$\text{GENERATE} \begin{Bmatrix} \text{data-name} \\ \text{report-name} \end{Bmatrix}$$

GO TO [procedure-name-1]

GO TO procedure-name-1 [, procedure-name-2] ... , procedure-name-n

DEPENDING ON identifier

$$\text{IF condition;} \begin{Bmatrix} \text{statement-1} \\ \text{NEXT SENTENCE} \end{Bmatrix} \begin{Bmatrix} \text{; ELSE statement-2} \\ \text{; ELSE NEXT SENTENCE} \end{Bmatrix}$$

INITIATE report-name-1 [, report-name-2] ...

INSPECT identifier-1 TALLYING

$$\left\{ \text{, identifier-2 FOR} \left\{ \left\{ \begin{matrix} \underline{\text{ALL}} \\ \underline{\text{LEADING}} \\ \text{CHARACTERS} \end{matrix} \right\} \begin{Bmatrix} \text{identifier-3} \\ \text{literal-1} \end{Bmatrix} \left[\begin{Bmatrix} \underline{\text{BEFORE}} \\ \underline{\text{AFTER}} \end{Bmatrix} \text{INITIAL} \begin{Bmatrix} \text{identifier-4} \\ \text{literal-2} \end{Bmatrix} \right] \right\} \ldots \right\} \ldots$$

INSPECT identifier-1 REPLACING

$$\left\{ \begin{matrix} \text{CHARACTERS} \underline{\text{BY}} \begin{Bmatrix} \text{identifier-6} \\ \text{literal-4} \end{Bmatrix} \left[\begin{Bmatrix} \underline{\text{BEFORE}} \\ \underline{\text{AFTER}} \end{Bmatrix} \text{INITIAL} \begin{Bmatrix} \text{identifier-7} \\ \text{literal-5} \end{Bmatrix} \right] \\ \left\{ , \begin{Bmatrix} \underline{\text{ALL}} \\ \underline{\text{LEADING}} \\ \underline{\text{FIRST}} \end{Bmatrix} \right\} \left\{ , \begin{Bmatrix} \text{identifier-5} \\ \text{literal-3} \end{Bmatrix} \underline{\text{BY}} \begin{Bmatrix} \text{identifier-6} \\ \text{literal-4} \end{Bmatrix} \left[\begin{Bmatrix} \underline{\text{BEFORE}} \\ \underline{\text{AFTER}} \end{Bmatrix} \text{INITIAL} \begin{Bmatrix} \text{identifier-7} \\ \text{literal-5} \end{Bmatrix} \right] \right\} \ldots \right\} \ldots \end{matrix} \right\}$$

INSPECT identifier-1 TALLYING

$$\left\{ \text{, identifier-2 } \underline{\text{FOR}} \left\{ , \left\{ \begin{matrix} \underline{\text{ALL}} \\ \underline{\text{LEADING}} \\ \text{CHARACTERS} \end{matrix} \right\} \begin{Bmatrix} \text{identifier-3} \\ \text{literal-1} \end{Bmatrix} \left[\begin{Bmatrix} \underline{\text{BEFORE}} \\ \underline{\text{AFTER}} \end{Bmatrix} \text{INITIAL} \begin{Bmatrix} \text{identifier-4} \\ \text{literal-2} \end{Bmatrix} \right] \right\} \ldots \right\} \ldots$$

REPLACING

$$\left\{ \begin{matrix} \text{CHARACTERS} \underline{\text{BY}} \begin{Bmatrix} \text{identifier-6} \\ \text{literal-4} \end{Bmatrix} \left[\begin{Bmatrix} \underline{\text{BEFORE}} \\ \underline{\text{AFTER}} \end{Bmatrix} \text{INITIAL} \begin{Bmatrix} \text{identifier-7} \\ \text{literal-5} \end{Bmatrix} \right] \\ \left\{ , \begin{Bmatrix} \underline{\text{ALL}} \\ \underline{\text{LEADING}} \\ \underline{\text{FIRST}} \end{Bmatrix} \right\} \left\{ , \begin{Bmatrix} \text{identifier-5} \\ \text{literal-3} \end{Bmatrix} \underline{\text{BY}} \begin{Bmatrix} \text{identifier-6} \\ \text{literal-4} \end{Bmatrix} \left[\begin{Bmatrix} \underline{\text{BEFORE}} \\ \underline{\text{AFTER}} \end{Bmatrix} \text{INITIAL} \begin{Bmatrix} \text{identifier-7} \\ \text{literal-5} \end{Bmatrix} \right] \right\} \ldots \right\} \ldots \end{matrix} \right\}$$

$$\text{MERGE file-name-1 ON} \begin{Bmatrix} \underline{\text{ASCENDING}} \\ \underline{\text{DESCENDING}} \end{Bmatrix} \text{KEY data-name-1 } [\text{, data-name-2}] \ldots$$

$$\left[\text{ON} \begin{Bmatrix} \underline{\text{ASCENDING}} \\ \underline{\text{DESCENDING}} \end{Bmatrix} \text{KEY data-name-3 } [\text{, data-name-4}] \ldots \right] \ldots$$

[COLLATING SEQUENCE IS alphabet-name]

USING file-name-2, file-name-3 [, file-name-4] ...

$$\begin{Bmatrix} \text{OUTPUT PROCEDURE IS section-name-1} \left[\begin{Bmatrix} \underline{\text{THROUGH}} \\ \underline{\text{THRU}} \end{Bmatrix} \text{section-name-2} \right] \\ \text{GIVING file-name-5} \end{Bmatrix}$$

MOVE $\left\{ \begin{array}{l} \text{identifier-1} \\ \text{literal} \end{array} \right\}$ TO identifier-2 [, identifier-3] ...

MOVE $\left\{ \begin{array}{l} \underline{\text{CORRESPONDING}} \\ \underline{\text{CORR}} \end{array} \right\}$ identifier-1 TO identifier-2

MULTIPLY $\left\{ \begin{array}{l} \text{identifier-1} \\ \text{literal-1} \end{array} \right\}$ BY identifier-2 [ROUNDED]

    [, identifier-3 [ROUNDED]] ... [; ON SIZE ERROR imperative-statement]

MULTIPLY $\left\{ \begin{array}{l} \text{identifier-1} \\ \text{literal-1} \end{array} \right\}$ BY $\left\{ \begin{array}{l} \text{identifier-2} \\ \text{literal-2} \end{array} \right\}$ GIVING identifier-3 [ROUNDED]

    [, identifier-4 [ROUNDED]] ... [; ON SIZE ERROR imperative-statement]

OPEN $\left\{ \begin{array}{l} \text{INPUT file-name-1} \left[\begin{array}{l} \text{REVERSED} \\ \text{WITH NO REWIND} \end{array} \right] \left[, \text{file-name-2} \left[\begin{array}{l} \text{REVERSED} \\ \text{WITH NO REWIND} \end{array} \right] \right] ... \\ \text{OUTPUT file-name-3 [WITH NO REWIND]} [, \text{file-name-4 [WITH NO REWIND]}] ... \\ \text{I-O file-name-5 [, file-name-6]} ... \\ \text{EXTEND file-name-7 [, file-name-8]} ... \end{array} \right\}$ ...

OPEN $\left\{ \begin{array}{l} \text{INPUT file-name-1 [, file-name-2]} ... \\ \text{OUTPUT file-name-3 [, file-name-4]} ... \\ \text{I-O file-name-5 [, file-name-6]} ... \end{array} \right\}$ ...

PERFORM procedure-name-1 $\left[\left\{ \begin{array}{l} \text{THROUGH} \\ \text{THRU} \end{array} \right\} \text{procedure-name-2} \right]$

PERFORM procedure-name-1 $\left[\left\{ \begin{array}{l} \text{THROUGH} \\ \text{THRU} \end{array} \right\} \text{procedure-name-2} \right] \left\{ \begin{array}{l} \text{identifier-1} \\ \text{integer-1} \end{array} \right\}$ TIMES

PERFORM procedure-name-1 $\left[\left\{ \begin{array}{l} \text{THROUGH} \\ \text{THRU} \end{array} \right\} \text{procedure-name-2} \right]$ UNTIL condition-1

PERFORM procedure-name-1 $\left[\left\{ \begin{array}{l} \text{THROUGH} \\ \text{THRU} \end{array} \right\} \text{procedure-name-2} \right]$

    VARYING $\left\{ \begin{array}{l} \text{identifier-2} \\ \text{index-name-1} \end{array} \right\}$ FROM $\left\{ \begin{array}{l} \text{identifier-3} \\ \text{index-name-2} \\ \text{literal-1} \end{array} \right\}$

        BY $\left\{ \begin{array}{l} \text{identifier-4} \\ \text{literal-3} \end{array} \right\}$ UNTIL condition-1

    $\left[\underline{\text{AFTER}} \left\{ \begin{array}{l} \text{identifier-5} \\ \text{index-name-3} \end{array} \right\} \text{FROM} \left\{ \begin{array}{l} \text{identifier-6} \\ \text{index-name-4} \\ \text{literal-3} \end{array} \right\} \right.$

        BY $\left\{ \begin{array}{l} \text{identifier-7} \\ \text{literal-4} \end{array} \right\}$ UNTIL condition-2

    $\left[\underline{\text{AFTER}} \left\{ \begin{array}{l} \text{identifier-8} \\ \text{index-name-5} \end{array} \right\} \text{FROM} \left\{ \begin{array}{l} \text{identifier-9} \\ \text{index-name-6} \\ \text{literal-5} \end{array} \right\} \right.$

        $\left. \left. BY \left\{ \begin{array}{l} \text{identifier-10} \\ \text{literal-6} \end{array} \right\} \text{UNTIL condition-3} \right] \right]$

READ file-name RECORD [INTO identifier] [; AT END imperative-statement]

READ file-name [NEXT] RECORD [INTO identifier]

    [; AT END imperative-statement]

READ file-name RECORD [INTO identifier] [; INVALID KEY imperative-statement]

READ file-name RECORD [INTO identifier]

    [; KEY IS data-name]

    [; INVALID KEY imperative-statement]

RECEIVE cd-name $\left\{ \begin{array}{l} \text{MESSAGE} \\ \text{SEGMENT} \end{array} \right\}$ INTO identifier-1 [; NO DATA imperative-statement]

RELEASE record-name [FROM identifier]

```
RETURN file-name RECORD [INTO identifier] ; AT END imperative-statement

REWRITE record-name [FROM identifier]

REWRITE record-name [FROM identifier] [; INVALID KEY imperative-statement]

SEARCH identifier-1 [VARYING {identifier-2  }] [; AT END imperative-statement-1]
                             {index-name-1  }

     ; WHEN condition-1 {imperative-statement-2}
                        {NEXT SENTENCE         }

     [; WHEN condition-2 {imperative-statement-3}] ...
                         {NEXT SENTENCE         }

SEARCH ALL identifier-1 [; AT END imperative-statement-1]

     ; WHEN {data-name-1 {IS EQUAL TO} {identifier-3            }}
            {            {IS =       } {literal-1               }}
            {                          {arithmetic-expression-1 }}
            {condition-name-1                                    }

          [AND {data-name-2 {IS EQUAL TO} {identifier-4            }}] ...
               {            {IS =       } {literal-2               }}
               {                          {arithmetic-expression-2 }}
               {condition-name-2                                    }

            {imperative-statement-2}
            {NEXT SENTENCE         }

SEND cd-name FROM identifier-1


SEND cd-name [FROM identifier-1] {WITH identifier-2}
                                 {WITH ESI         }
                                 {WITH EMI         }
                                 {WITH EGI         }

     [{BEFORE}           {{{identifier-3} [LINE ]}}]
     [{AFTER } ADVANCING {{{integer     } [LINES]}}]
                         {{mnemonic-name}         }
                         {{PAGE         }         }

SET {identifier-1  [, identifier-2]  ...} TO {identifier-3 }
    {index-name-1  [, index-name-2]  ...}    {index-name-3 }
                                             {integer-1    }

SET index-name-4 [, index-name-5] ... {UP BY  } {identifier-4}
                                      {DOWN BY} {integer-2   }

SORT file-name-1 ON {ASCENDING } KEY data-name-1 [, data-name-2] ...
                    {DESCENDING}

     [ON {ASCENDING } KEY data-name-3 [, data-name-4] ...] ...
         {DESCENDING}

     [COLLATING SEQUENCE IS alphabet-name]

     {INPUT PROCEDURE IS section-name-1 [{THROUGH} section-name-2]}
     {                                   {THRU   }               }
     {USING file-name-2 [, file-name-3] ...                      }

     {OUTPUT PROCEDURE IS section-name-3 [{THROUGH} section-name-4]}
     {                                    {THRU   }                }
     {GIVING file-name-4                                           }

START file-name [KEY {IS EQUAL TO     }          ]
                     {IS =            }          
                     {IS GREATER THAN } data-name
                     {IS >            }          
                     {IS NOT LESS THAN}          
                     {IS NOT <        }          

     [; INVALID KEY imperative-statement]
```

STOP $\left\{\begin{array}{l}\underline{\text{RUN}}\\\text{literal}\end{array}\right\}$

$\underline{\text{STRING}}$ $\left\{\begin{array}{l}\text{identifier-1}\\\text{literal-1}\end{array}\right\}$ $\left[\begin{array}{l},\text{ identifier-2}\\,\text{ literal-2}\end{array}\right]$ ... $\underline{\text{DELIMITED}}$ BY $\left\{\begin{array}{l}\text{identifier-3}\\\text{literal-3}\\\underline{\text{SIZE}}\end{array}\right\}$

$\left[,\left\{\begin{array}{l}\text{identifier-4}\\\text{literal-4}\end{array}\right\}\left[\begin{array}{l},\text{ identifier-5}\\,\text{ literal-5}\end{array}\right]\right.$ ... $\underline{\text{DELIMITED}}$ BY $\left.\left\{\begin{array}{l}\text{identifier-6}\\\text{literal-6}\\\underline{\text{SIZE}}\end{array}\right\}\right]$ ...

    $\underline{\text{INTO}}$ identifier-7 $\left[\text{WITH}\ \underline{\text{POINTER}}\ \text{identifier-8}\right]$

    $\left[; \text{ON}\ \underline{\text{OVERFLOW}}\ \text{imperative-statement}\right]$

$\underline{\text{SUBTRACT}}$ $\left\{\begin{array}{l}\text{identifier-1}\\\text{literal-1}\end{array}\right\}$ $\left[\begin{array}{l},\text{ identifier-2}\\,\text{ literal-2}\end{array}\right]$ ... $\underline{\text{FROM}}$ identifier-m $\left[\underline{\text{ROUNDED}}\right]$

    $\left[,\text{ identifier-n }\left[\underline{\text{ROUNDED}}\right]\right]$ ... $\left[;\text{ON}\ \underline{\text{SIZE}}\ \underline{\text{ERROR}}\ \text{imperative-statement}\right]$

$\underline{\text{SUBTRACT}}$ $\left\{\begin{array}{l}\text{identifier-1}\\\text{literal-1}\end{array}\right\}\left[\begin{array}{l},\text{ identifier-2}\\,\text{ literal-2}\end{array}\right]$ ... $\underline{\text{FROM}}$ $\left\{\begin{array}{l}\text{identifier-m}\\\text{literal-m}\end{array}\right\}$

    $\underline{\text{GIVING}}$ identifier-n $\left[\underline{\text{ROUNDED}}\right]$ $\left[,\text{ identifier-o }\left[\underline{\text{ROUNDED}}\right]\right]$ ...

    $\left[;\text{ON}\ \underline{\text{SIZE}}\ \underline{\text{ERROR}}\ \text{imperative-statement}\right]$

$\underline{\text{SUBTRACT}}$ $\left\{\begin{array}{l}\underline{\text{CORRESPONDING}}\\\underline{\text{CORR}}\end{array}\right\}$ identifier-1 $\underline{\text{FROM}}$ identifier-2 $\left[\underline{\text{ROUNDED}}\right]$

    $\left[;\text{ON}\ \underline{\text{SIZE}}\ \underline{\text{ERROR}}\ \text{imperative-statement}\right]$

$\underline{\text{SUPPRESS}}$ PRINTING

$\underline{\text{TERMINATE}}$ report-name-1 $\left[,\text{ report-name-2}\right]$ ...

$\underline{\text{UNSTRING}}$ identifier-1

    $\left[\underline{\text{DELIMITED}}\text{ BY }\left[\underline{\text{ALL}}\right]\left\{\begin{array}{l}\text{identifier-2}\\\text{literal-1}\end{array}\right\}\left[,\underline{\text{OR}}\left[\underline{\text{ALL}}\right]\left\{\begin{array}{l}\text{identifier-3}\\\text{literal-2}\end{array}\right\}\right]\right.$ ... $\Big]$

    $\underline{\text{INTO}}$ identifier-4 $\left[,\underline{\text{DELIMITER}}\text{ IN identifier-5}\right]\left[,\underline{\text{COUNT}}\text{ IN identifier-6}\right]$

        $\left[,\text{ identifier-7 }\left[,\underline{\text{DELIMITER}}\text{ IN identifier-8}\right]\left[,\underline{\text{COUNT}}\text{ IN identifier-9}\right]\right]$ ...

    $\left[\text{WITH}\ \underline{\text{POINTER}}\ \text{identifier-10}\right]\left[\underline{\text{TALLYING}}\text{ IN identifier-11}\right]$

    $\left[;\text{ON}\ \underline{\text{OVERFLOW}}\ \text{imperative-statement}\right]$

$\underline{\text{USE}}$ $\underline{\text{AFTER}}$ STANDARD $\left\{\begin{array}{l}\underline{\text{EXCEPTION}}\\\underline{\text{ERROR}}\end{array}\right\}$ PROCEDURE ON $\left\{\begin{array}{l}\text{file-name-1}\left[,\text{ file-name-2}\right]...\\\underline{\text{INPUT}}\\\underline{\text{OUTPUT}}\\\underline{\text{I-O}}\\\underline{\text{EXTEND}}\end{array}\right\}$.

$\underline{\text{USE}}$ $\underline{\text{AFTER}}$ STANDARD $\left\{\begin{array}{l}\underline{\text{EXCEPTION}}\\\underline{\text{ERROR}}\end{array}\right\}$ PROCEDURE ON $\left\{\begin{array}{l}\text{file-name-1}\left[,\text{ file-name-2}\right]...\\\underline{\text{INPUT}}\\\underline{\text{OUTPUT}}\\\underline{\text{I-O}}\end{array}\right\}$.

$\underline{\text{USE}}$ $\underline{\text{BEFORE}}$ $\underline{\text{REPORTING}}$ identifier.

$\underline{\text{USE}}$ FOR DEBUGGING ON $\left\{\begin{array}{l}\text{cd-name-1}\\\left[\underline{\text{ALL REFERENCES OF}}\right]\text{ identifier-1}\\\text{file-name-1}\\\text{procedure-name-1}\\\underline{\text{ALL}}\ \underline{\text{PROCEDURES}}\end{array}\right\}$

    $\left[,\begin{array}{l}\text{cd-name-2}\\\left[\underline{\text{ALL REFERENCES OF}}\right]\text{ identifier-2}\\\text{file-name-2}\\\text{procedure-name-2}\\\underline{\text{ALL}}\ \underline{\text{PROCEDURES}}\end{array}\right]$ ... .

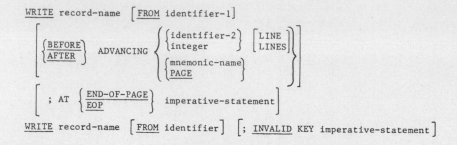

```
WRITE record-name [FROM identifier-1]

 ⎡                      ⎧⎧identifier-2⎫ ⎡LINE ⎤⎫⎤
 ⎢⎧BEFORE⎫  ADVANCING   ⎨⎩integer     ⎭ ⎣LINES⎦⎬⎥
 ⎢⎩AFTER ⎭              ⎪⎧mnemonic-name⎫        ⎪⎥
 ⎣                      ⎩⎩PAGE         ⎭        ⎭⎦

 ⎡     ⎧END-OF-PAGE⎫                      ⎤
 ⎢; AT ⎨EOP        ⎬ imperative-statement ⎥
 ⎣     ⎩           ⎭                      ⎦

WRITE record-name [FROM identifier] [; INVALID KEY imperative-statement]
```

General Format for Conditions

RELATION CONDITION:

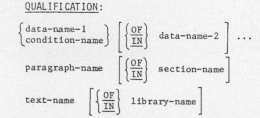

```
⎧identifier-1            ⎫ ⎧IS [NOT] GREATER THAN⎫ ⎧identifier-2           ⎫
⎨literal-1               ⎬ ⎨IS [NOT] LESS THAN   ⎬ ⎨literal-2              ⎬
⎪arithmetic-expression-1 ⎪ ⎨IS [NOT] EQUAL TO    ⎬ ⎨arithmetic-expression-2⎬
⎩index-name-1            ⎭ ⎨IS [NOT] >           ⎬ ⎩index-name-2           ⎭
                          ⎨IS [NOT] <           ⎬
                          ⎩IS [NOT] =           ⎭
```

CLASS CONDITION:

```
identifier IS [NOT] ⎧NUMERIC   ⎫
                    ⎩ALPHABETIC⎭
```

SIGN CONDITION:

```
arithmetic-expression is [NOT] ⎧POSITIVE⎫
                               ⎨NEGATIVE⎬
                               ⎩ZERO    ⎭
```

CONDITION-NAME CONDITION:

condition-name

SWITCH-STATUS CONDITION:

condition-name

NEGATED SIMPLE CONDITION:

NOT simple-condition

COMBINED CONDITION:

```
condition ⎧⎧AND⎫ condition⎫ ...
          ⎩⎩OR ⎭          ⎭
```

ABBREVIATED COMBINED RELATION CONDITION:

```
relation-condition ⎧⎧AND⎫ [NOT] [relational-operator] object⎫ ...
                   ⎩⎩OR ⎭                                    ⎭
```

Miscellaneous Formats

QUALIFICATION:

```
⎧data-name-1   ⎫ ⎡⎧OF⎫ data-name-2⎤ ...
⎩condition-name⎭ ⎣⎩IN⎭            ⎦

paragraph-name ⎡⎧OF⎫ section-name⎤
               ⎣⎩IN⎭             ⎦

text-name ⎡⎧OF⎫ library-name⎤
          ⎣⎩IN⎭             ⎦
```

SUBSCRIPTING:

$\left\{ \begin{array}{l} \text{data-name} \\ \text{condition-name} \end{array} \right\}$ (subscript-1 [, subscript-2 [, subscript-3]])

INDEXING:

$\left\{ \begin{array}{l} \text{data-name} \\ \text{condition-name} \end{array} \right\}$ ($\left\{ \begin{array}{l} \text{index-name-1} [\{\pm\} \text{ literal-2}] \\ \text{literal-1} \end{array} \right\}$

[, $\left\{ \begin{array}{l} \text{index-name-2} [\{\pm\} \text{ literal-4}] \\ \text{literal-3} \end{array} \right\}$] [, $\left\{ \begin{array}{l} \text{index-name-3} [\{\pm\} \text{ literal-6}] \\ \text{literal-5} \end{array} \right\}$]])

IDENTIFIER: FORMAT 1

data-name-1 $\left[\left\{ \begin{array}{l} \underline{OF} \\ \underline{IN} \end{array} \right\} \text{data-name-2} \right]$ ... [(subscript-1 [, subscript-2

[, subscript-3]])]

IDENTIFIER: FORMAT 2

data-name-1 $\left[\left\{ \begin{array}{l} \underline{OF} \\ \underline{IN} \end{array} \right\} \text{data-name-2} \right]$ ... [($\left\{ \begin{array}{l} \text{index-name-1} [\{\pm\} \text{ literal-2}] \\ \text{literal-1} \end{array} \right\}$

[, $\left\{ \begin{array}{l} \text{index-name-2} [\{\pm\} \text{ literal-4}] \\ \text{literal-3} \end{array} \right\}$] [, $\left\{ \begin{array}{l} \text{index-name-3} [\{\pm\} \text{ literal-6}] \\ \text{literal-5} \end{array} \right\}$]])]

General Format for COPY Statement

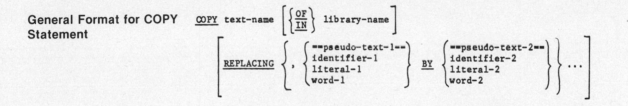

$\underline{COPY}$ text-name $\left[\left\{ \begin{array}{l} \underline{OF} \\ \underline{IN} \end{array} \right\} \text{library-name} \right]$

$\left[\underline{REPLACING} \left\{ , \left\{ \begin{array}{l} \text{==pseudo-text-1==} \\ \text{identifier-1} \\ \text{literal-1} \\ \text{word-1} \end{array} \right\} \underline{BY} \left\{ \begin{array}{l} \text{==pseudo-text-2==} \\ \text{identifier-2} \\ \text{literal-2} \\ \text{word-2} \end{array} \right\} \right\} \cdots \right]$

INDEX

COBOL reserved words

These words have preassigned meanings in COBOL and must not be used as user-defined words

ACCEPT
ACCESS
ADD
ADVANCING
AFTER
ALL
ALPHABETIC
ALSO
ALTER
ALTERNATE
AND
ARE
AREA
AREAS
ASCENDING
ASSIGN
AT
AUTHOR

BEFORE
BLANK
BLOCK
BOTTOM
BY

CALL
CANCEL
CD
CF
CH
CHARACTER
CHARACTERS
CLOCK-UNITS
CLOSE
COBOL
CODE
CODE-SET
COLLATING
COLUMN
COMMA
COMMUNICATION
COMP
COMPUTATIONAL
COMPUTE
CONFIGURATION
CONTAINS
CONTROL
CONTROLS
COPY
CORR
CORRESPONDING
COUNT
CURRENCY

DATA
DATE
DATE-COMPILED
DATE-WRITTEN
DAY
DE
DEBUG-CONTENTS
DEBUG-ITEM
DEBUG-LINE
DEBUG-NAME
DEBUG-SUB-1
DEBUG-SUB-2
DEBUG-SUB-3
DEBUGGING
DECIMAL-POINT
DECLARATIVES
DELETE
DELIMITED
DELIMITER
DEPENDING
DESCENDING
DESTINATION
DETAIL
DISABLE
DISPLAY
DIVIDE
DIVISION
DOWN
DUPLICATES
DYNAMIC

EGI
ELSE
EMI
ENABLE
END
END-OF-PAGE
ENTER
ENVIRONMENT
EOP
EQUAL
ERROR
ESI
EVERY
EXCEPTION
EXIT
EXTEND

FD
FILE
FILE-CONTROL
FILLER
FINAL
FIRST
FOOTING
FOR
FROM

GENERATE
GIVING
GO
GREATER
GROUP

HEADING
HIGH-VALUE
HIGH-VALUES

I-O
I-O-CONTROL
IDENTIFICATION
IF
IN
INDEX
INDEXED
INDICATE
INITIAL
INITIATE
INPUT
INPUT-OUTPUT
INSPECT
INSTALLATION
INTO
INVALID
IS

JUST
JUSTIFIED

KEY

LABEL
LAST
LEADING
LEFT
LENGTH
LESS
LIMIT
LIMITS
LINAGE
LINAGE-COUNTER
LINE
LINE-COUNTER
LINES
LINKAGE
LOCK
LOW-VALUE
LOW-VALUES

MEMORY
MERGE
MESSAGE
MODE
MODULES
MOVE
MULTIPLE
MULTIPLY

NATIVE
NEGATIVE
NEXT
NO
NOT
NUMBER
NUMERIC

OBJECT-COMPUTER
OCCURS
OF
OFF
OMITTED
ON
OPEN
OPTIONAL
OR
ORGANIZATION
OUTPUT
OVERFLOW

PAGE
PAGE-COUNTER
PERFORM
PF
PH
PIC
PICTURE
PLUS
POINTER
POSITION
POSITIVE
PRINTING
PROCEDURE
PROCEDURES
PROCEED
PROGRAM
PROGRAM-ID

QUEUE
QUOTE
QUOTES

RANDOM
RD
READ
RECEIVE
RECORD
RECORDS
REDEFINES
REEL
REFERENCES
RELATIVE
RELEASE
REMAINDER
REMOVAL
RENAMES
REPLACING
REPORT
REPORTING
REPORTS
RERUN
RESERVE
RESET
RETURN
REVERSED
REWIND
REWRITE
RF
RH
RIGHT
ROUNDED
RUN

SAME
SD
SEARCH
SECTION
SECURITY
SEGMENT
SEGMENT-LIMIT
SELECT
SEND
SENTENCE
SEPARATE
SEQUENCE
SEQUENTIAL
SET
SIGN
SIZE
SORT
SORT-MERGE
SOURCE
SOURCE-COMPUTER
SPACE
SPACES
SPECIAL-NAMES
STANDARD
STANDARD-1
START
STATUS
STOP
STRING
SUB-QUEUE-1
SUB-QUEUE-2
SUB-QUEUE-3
SUBTRACT
SUM
SUPPRESS
SYMBOLIC
SYNC
SYNCHRONIZED

TABLE
TALLYING
TAPE
TERMINAL
TERMINATE
TEXT
THAN
THROUGH
THRU
TIME
TIMES
TO
TOP
TRAILING
TYPE

UNIT
UNSTRING
UNTIL
UP
UPON
USAGE
USE
USING

VALUE
VALUES
VARYING

WHEN
WITH
WORDS
WORKING-STORAGE
WRITE

ZERO
ZEROES
ZEROS

+
−
*
/
**
>
<
=